DRAMAS BY
PRESENT-DAY WRITERS

EDITED BY

RAYMOND WOODBURY PENCE 1885-

PROFESSOR OF ENGLISH IN DEPAUW UNIVERSITY

CHARLES SCRIBNER'S SONS

NEW YORK   CHICAGO   BOSTON

ATLANTA   SAN FRANCISCO

TO

BENJAMIN WOODBURY

THIS VOLUME IS INSCRIBED

PREFACE

The purpose of this book has been to bring together in one convenient volume a collection of both long and short plays by present-day dramatists of England and America. They are not necessarily the "best" or "greatest" plays of to-day, but rather a group of plays that will show as large a variety of dramatic writing as possible, as many moods and as many methods. But above everything the aim has been to include plays that have been tested by actual performance on the stage and that are at the same time plays which the average reader may be expected to enjoy reading.

Among the short plays included, the range is from the little-theatre type, such as "The Slave with Two Faces," through the play in poetic form, such as "Counsel Retained" and "Cophetua" to what may be called the standard type, as seen in "Trifles," "Confessional," and "The Goal," for example. Tragedy is represented by "A Night at an Inn" and "'Ile'"; comedy by "A Marriage Has Been Arranged," "Spreading the News," and "Thursday Evening"; farce by "The Love Passage."

In the field of the long drama, that is the drama of three or four acts, the play that has on the whole something more than a temporary interest for us is usually the play with a strongly defined underlying idea, the thought-provoking play. It will be found in this collection in "Milestones" and "Loyalties." In the lighter form of drama "Monsieur Beaucaire" stands as a noteworthy example of romantic comedy and "Merton of the Movies" of farce.

"Monsieur Beaucaire," through the courtesy of Mr. Booth Tarkington, appears in print in this collection for the first time. And likewise "Merton of the Movies" appears in print for the first time in this particular form. For Mr. George Kaufman and Mr. Marc Connelly, who made the dramatic version, with the consent of Mr. Harry Leon Wilson, the author of the story on which the play is founded, have prepared for this collection a revised version.

Therefore, to Mr. Booth Tarkington, to Mr. George Kaufman, Mr. Marc Connelly, and Mr. Harry Leon Wilson I owe an unusually deep debt of gratitude for their generosity and for their very genuine interest in this undertaking. I wish to express my obligations also to the following, without whose kindness in allowing me to use valuable copyrighted material such a collection would, of course, have been impossible: Mr. John Drinkwater, Lord Dunsany, Miss Constance Mackay, Miss Susan Glaspell, Mr. Christopher Morley, Lady Gregory, Mr. Eugene O'Neill, Mr. Arthur Sutro, Mr. W. W. Jacobs, Mr. Percival Wilde, Mr. John Galsworthy, and Mr. Henry Arthur Jones; Charles Scribner's Sons, George H. Doran Company, Washington Square Book Shop, Houghton Mifflin Company, G. P. Putnam's Sons, Henry Holt and Company, Small, Maynard and Company, Doubleday, Page and Company, Samuel French, Boni and Liveright, Brentano's, and Little, Brown and Company.   R. W. P.

INTRODUCTION

Probably it is not necessary to point out that we are in the midst of a period of tremendous interest in everything connected with drama. The evidence is everywhere. More books on the theatre, the stage, on setting, on acting—in fact, on everything even remotely associated with drama— are being produced than ever before. Various types of theatrical organizations are flourishing. Even small towns have their little theatres. High schools, frequently with rather elaborate equipment, are producing meritorious results. College dramatic clubs, such as the North Carolina Folk-Players, under the direction of Professor Frederick Koch, now go on tour and give their repertory of plays throughout a territory of considerable size. Community theatre enterprises are meeting with artistic success in many places. And especially interesting is the fact that a number of little-theatre and community groups are encouraging play-writing —particularly attempts to depict the life of the people that the members of these groups know best. Certain colleges and universities, actually granting baccalaureate and advanced degrees, are developing well-equipped schools of the art of the theatre in which every branch of the subject is given adequate treatment. In fact, there has never been a time, probably, when as large a number of persons were interested in some aspect of drama as to-day.

But an even more striking manifestation of this very extensive interest is the growing popularity of printed drama. Formerly the publication of a book of plays was so precarious an undertaking financially that very few publishers would undertake it. To-day the number of volumes of plays produced each year is large. And we may reasonably expect the number to increase very materially during the next few years. Even now arrangements are frequently made between a producer and a publisher whereby a play appears in the bookstores on the same day it is given its first performance on the stage. It is evident, then, if we are to get the most from our reading of drama, that we understand all that is implied in the reason for this changed attitude; and the reason is not hard to seek.

Drama is in many ways utterly unlike every other kind of fiction; consequently, until comparatively recently the number of persons who appreciated this difference as it existed on the printed page was small. Naturally, then, the publishers could not produce much in the way of printed drama until enough readers had accustomed themselves to the reading of plays as they were already accustomed to the reading of novels and short stories. Because drama is so radically different from all other forms of fiction the reader had to build up for himself a new kind of reading technic, as it were, as applied to drama. Therefore, it is of the very greatest importance that we understand what are some of these outstanding differences if we are to derive the greatest amount of satisfaction when, instead of witnessing a play, we choose to read the printed version of it.

In the first place drama is never written to be read; it is written to be played on a stage before an audience. And the attitude of a person in an audience is something very unlike that of a reader sitting by himself reading a short story or a novel. For one thing, as a reader of a short story or a novel he is a participant in the story; he looks at the action usually over the shoulder of one of the characters. But in a play on the modern stage he is never a participant; he is rather an onlooker, a witness. And this makes a vast amount of difference. Take the matter of surprise, for instance. The spectator does not gain pleasure through being surprised himself. In fact, he is, so to speak, in on everything. Rather his pleasure comes in seeing surprise come to those on the stage, in witnessing the reaction of the characters of a play to a given situation that he already knows about. But in the short story one of the pleasures that may come to the reader is a surprise upon himself, as in De Maupassant's "The Necklace" or Aldrich's "Marjorie Daw" or Stockton's "The Lady or the Tiger." The reader of printed drama, therefore, must gradually accustom himself to this novel idea of being an onlooker of, rather than a participant in, the story if he is to make the most of his reading. As he reads he must put himself into the psychological attitude of a person in the audience at a theatrical performance.

Again, the language of drama is utterly different from that of the novel or short story. The language of the latter is what is known as written discourse; but the language of drama is spoken discourse. And spoken discourse is very different from written discourse. For one thing we have been accustomed to get written discourse through the eye and spoken discourse through the ear. But printed drama puts us into an utterly new situation; for here we have to do the unusual thing of getting spoken discourse through the eye. And as we have never been trained to do this, naturally we find it difficult at first. Learning to read spoken discourse is almost like learning a new language. The vocabulary is different, the sentence structure is different. In fact, the whole medium is different. In written discourse every shade of an idea has to be conveyed to the reader by words; but in spoken discourse pantomime, gesture, and facial expression often take the place of words. Consequently, when we read drama we must use our imaginations and supplement the actual words with the actions themselves of the characters. And it takes time for us to train ourselves to do this.

Then there is another thing. The emotional content of drama differs radically from that of prose fiction. It is an axiom of writing that the emotional capacity of an audience must equal the emotional content of a production. Now the emotional capacity of a group of people in an audience in a theatre is a very different matter from the emotional capacity of the individuals of that audience taken separately. The emotional capacity of a group is always much greater than the sum total of that of the individuals making up the group. Therefore, a dramatic production on the stage not only can have but must have a much larger emotional content than is true of the short story or of the novel. Therefore, because his audience is much more charged with emotion and is getting his lines through the ear, the dramatist must be far more obvious; he must tone up his effects, exaggerate, in fact. And above everything, he must repeat his main idea again and again if his theatre audience is to comprehend it. A great English dramatist on being asked to give his rules for writing drama replied: "There are three rules. First, tell your audience what you are going to do; then tell them what you are doing; finally, tell them what you have done. And even then they probably won't get it." It is evident, then, that when reading drama for the first time the reader will feel that things are made too obvious, that they are too bald, that there is too much repetition, that the action sometimes seems close to the melodramatic, and that the sentiment sounds like sentimentality. He will miss the pleasing subtlety of the novel and the short story. He will miss the many compliments an author pays him in merely implying or suggesting an idea without developing it fully or stating it baldly. He will miss the kind of climax he has been used to. For the story on the stage never puts off its smashing conclusion until the last line as does the short story very frequently. The dramatist must get over absolutely everything before the curtain falls. Therefore, he must allow enough time after a big emotional moment for the audience to react properly to it. For when the curtain falls the spell is broken. But in the short story, on the other hand, the spell may continue long after the last line has been read. Therefore, a De Maupassant or an O. Henry may safely leave his biggest emotional thrill to the very last line. Not so with the dramatist. He must place his at some distance before the curtain if he wishes to profit to the greatest extent with it.

To sum up then. Any one who wishes to read drama with the greatest satisfaction will need to build up a new reading technic—one that differs radically from that used in reading ordinary prose fiction. He must learn to be an onlooker to the story rather than a participant in it; he must learn to read with the eye spoken discourse that he has always been in the habit of getting through the ear only; and, finally, he must learn to key himself emotionally as if he were actually in a theatre so that his emotional capacity equals the emotional content of the play. In other words, in reading drama instead of reading a printed page one must imagine himself in a theatre with other people witnessing a performance on the stage. When he has acquired this ability he will find that the reading of drama opens up an entirely new field of pleasure and profit to him. In fact, after one has acquired this knack he can obtain from the reading of drama almost as keen a delight as from seeing the plays actually given by actors in a theatre.

Finally, it must be remembered that the lines of a drama as written by the playwright are only a part of the finished performance as given by the actors in a theatre before an audience. The person who really wishes to understand drama will inform himself about everything that goes into a dramatic performance. As has been said above, there are now available many excellent books on every aspect of the theatre—on stage-architecture, on acting, costuming, management and direction, on the history of the drama, present-day trends in drama, on the little-theatre movement, etc.—some of the most important of which have been listed in the bibliographies at the end of this volume.

CONTENTS

CONTENTS

THE SLAVE WITH TWO FACES

BY

MARY CAROLYN DAVIES

CHARACTERS

LIFE, THE SLAVE
FIRST GIRL
SECOND GIRL
A WOMAN
A MAN
A YOUNG MAN
A WORKMAN
OTHERS

Mary Carolyn Davies, a native of the State of Washington, resides in Portland, Oregon, where she is actively identified with the Women's Press Club of Oregon. A graduate of Washington High School of Portland, Oregon, she attended the University of California and later New York University. While in college she won a number of prizes in poetry. As a student at New York University she was editor of the magazine, *Judy*. She was associated with Alfred Kreymborg in founding "Others," a group of free-verse writers. She has written several volumes of child verse.

THE SLAVE WITH TWO FACES

The scene is a wood through which runs a path. Wild rose-bushes and other wood-things border it. On opposite sides of the path stand two girls waiting. They have not looked at each other. The girls wear that useful sort of gown which, with the addition of a crown, makes a queen—without, makes a peasant. The first girl wears a crown. The second carries one carelessly in her hand.

FIRST GIRL. [*Looking across at the other.*] For whom are you waiting?

SECOND GIRL. I am waiting for Life.

FIRST GIRL. I am waiting for Life also.

SECOND GIRL. They said that he would pass this way. Do you believe that he will pass this way?

FIRST GIRL. He passes all ways.

SECOND GIRL. [*Still breathing quickly.*] I ran to meet Life.

FIRST GIRL. Are you not afraid of him?

SECOND GIRL. Yes. That is why I ran to meet him.

FIRST GIRL. [*To herself.*] I, too, ran to meet him.

SECOND GIRL. Ah! he is coming!

FIRST GIRL. No. It is only the little quarrelling words of the leaves, and the winds that are always urging them to go away.

SECOND GIRL. The leaves do not go.

FIRST GIRL. Some day they will go. And that the wind knows.

FIRST GIRL. Why are you not wearing your crown?

5

SECOND GIRL. Why should we wear crowns?

[*She places the crown upon her head.*]

FIRST GIRL. Do you not know?

SECOND GIRL. No.

FIRST GIRL. That is all of wisdom—the wearing of crowns before the eyes of Life.

SECOND GIRL. I do not understand you.

FIRST GIRL. Few understand wisdom—even those who need it most——

SECOND GIRL. He is coming! I heard a sound.

FIRST GIRL. It was only the sound of a petal dreaming that it had fallen from the rose-tree.

SECOND GIRL. I have waited——

FIRST GIRL. We all long for him. We cry out to him. When he comes, he hurts us, he tortures us. He kills us. Unless we know the secret.

SECOND GIRL. What is the secret?

FIRST GIRL. That he is a slave. He pretends! He pretends! But always he knows in his heart that he is a slave. Only of those who have learned his secret is he afraid.

SECOND GIRL. Tell me more!

FIRST GIRL. Over those who are afraid of him he is a tyrant. He obeys—kings and queens!

SECOND GIRL. Then that——

FIRST GIRL. —Is why we must never let him see us without our crowns!

SECOND GIRL. How do you know these things?

FIRST GIRL. They were told me by an old wise man, who sits outside the gate of our town.

SECOND GIRL. How did he know? Because he was one of those who are kings?

FIRST GIRL. No. Because he was one of those who are afraid.

SECOND GIRL. [*Dreamily.*] I have heard that Life is very beautiful. Is he so? I have heard also that he is supremely ugly; that his mouth is wide and grinning, that his eyes slant, and his nostrils are thick. Is he so?—or is he—very beautiful?

FIRST GIRL. Perhaps you will see—for yourself— Ah!

SECOND GIRL. [*As* LIFE *saunters into view at the farthest bend of the path.*] He walks like a conqueror. But there is something ugly in his appearance. [LIFE *sees the girls just as a sudden sun-ray catches the jewels of their crowns. He cringes and walks like a hunchback slave.*] He is beautiful now.

FIRST GIRL. He has seen our crowns!

SECOND GIRL. Ah!

FIRST GIRL. Remember! You are only safe—as long as you remain his master. Never forget that he is a slave, and that you are a queen.

SECOND GIRL. [*To herself.*] I must never let him see me without my crown.

FIRST GIRL. Hush! He is coming!

SECOND GIRL. He is very beautiful——

FIRST GIRL. While he is a slave.

SECOND GIRL. [*Not hearing.*] He is—very beautiful——

FIRST GIRL. Life!

[LIFE *bows to the ground at her feet.*]

SECOND GIRL. [*In delight.*] Ah!

FIRST GIRL. Life, I would have opals on a platter.

[LIFE *bows in assent.*]

SECOND GIRL. Oh-h!

FIRST GIRL. And pearls!

[LIFE *bows.*]

SECOND GIRL. Ah!

FIRST GIRL.   And a little castle set within a hedge.

[LIFE *bows.*]

SECOND GIRL.   Yes——

FIRST GIRL.   I would have a fair prince to think tinkling words about me.   And I would have a strawberry tart, with little flutings in the crust.   Go, see that these things are made ready for me.

[LIFE *bows in assent and turns to go.*]

SECOND GIRL.   Ah!

FIRST GIRL.   See?   It is so that one must act.   It is thus one must manage him.   So and not otherwise it is done.   Now—do you try.

[*She plucks a rose from the bush beside her and twirls it in her fingers.*]

SECOND GIRL.   Life!

[LIFE *kneels.*]

I have a wish for a gown of gold.

[LIFE *bows.*]

FIRST GIRL.   Yes!

[*And over his bowed head the two laugh gaily at the ease of his subjection.*]

SECOND GIRL.   And a little garden where I may walk and think of trumpets blowing.

[LIFE *bows.*]

SECOND GIRL.   It is a good rule.

FIRST GIRL.   [*Calling slave back as he is leaving.*]   I have a wish for a gray steed.

[LIFE *bows.*]

Bring me a little page, too.   With golden hair.   And with a dimple.

[LIFE *acquiesces and starts to leave.*]

FIRST GIRL.   [*Calling him back with a gesture.*]   Life! [*An important afterthought.*]   With two dimples!

SECOND GIRL.   And an amber necklace! Bring me an amber necklace!

FIRST GIRL.   [*Tossing away the rose she has just plucked.*] And a fresh rose.

> [LIFE *bows, turns to obey. The two are convulsed with mirth at the adventure and its success.*]

FIRST GIRL.   Life!

> [LIFE *halts.*]

SECOND GIRL.   What are you going to do?

FIRST GIRL.   Come here!

> [LIFE *comes to her. With a quick movement she snatches one of the gold chains from about his neck.*]

SECOND GIRL.   [*Frightened.*] How can you dare?

FIRST GIRL.   What you see you must take.   She seizes his wrist and pulls from it a bracelet.

SECOND GIRL.   [*Frightened.*] Ah!

FIRST GIRL.   Go!

> [*Exit* LIFE.]

SECOND GIRL.   But why——

FIRST GIRL.   He does not like beggars, Life. You see, he is a slave himself.

SECOND GIRL.   He is so beautiful.

FIRST GIRL.   Do not forget that he is your slave. . . . This rose-bush [*Touches it*] is a queen who forgot.

SECOND GIRL.   Ah!

FIRST GIRL.   [*Pointing to bones that seemed part of bushes along roadside.*] Those are the bones of others who forgot.

SECOND GIRL.   But he *is* beautiful!

FIRST GIRL.   Only so long as you are his master.

SECOND GIRL.   But he is kind!

FIRST GIRL. Only so long as you are not afraid of him.

SECOND GIRL. But you snatched——

FIRST GIRL. Life is the only person to whom one should be rude.

> [*They hear sounds of moaning and cries and a harsh voice menacing some unseen crowd.*]

SECOND GIRL. What is that?

FIRST GIRL. Come! We must not be seen!

> [*Pulls her companion behind bush at side of stage.*]

SECOND GIRL. What will be done to us?

FIRST GIRL. Hush! If he should see you! He is always watching for the first sign of fear.

SECOND GIRL. What is the first sign of fear?

FIRST GIRL. It is a thought——

SECOND GIRL. But can he see one's thoughts——

FIRST GIRL. Only thoughts of fear.

SECOND GIRL. If one hides them well even from oneself?

FIRST GIRL. Even then. But words are more dangerous still. If we say we are afraid we will be more afraid, because whatever we make into words makes itself into our bodies.

VOICES OFF STAGE. Oh, master! Mercy, master!

FIRST GIRL. It spoils him, this cringing. It spoils a good servant. As long as he is kept in his place——

> [*A man enters and kneels, looking at* LIFE *off stage, in fear.*]

FIRST GIRL. [*Steals to man.*] But he is only a slave. Do you not see that he is a slave?

MAN. How can you say that? Look at his terrible face. Who that has seen his face can doubt that he is a master, and a cruel one?

FIRST GIRL. He cannot be a master unless you make him so.

MAN. What is this that you are saying? Is it true?

FIRST GIRL. Yes, it is true. Even though it can be put into words, it is true.

MAN. *Starts to rise, sinks to knee again.* Yes. I see that it is true. But go away.

FIRST GIRL. [*Crouching behind bush again.*] Ah!

> [LIFE *crosses the stage, with a whip of many thongs, driving a huddled throng of half-crouching men and women. They kneel and kiss his robe. His mouth is wide and grinning, his eyes slant, his nostrils are thick. He is hideous.*]

LIFE. You! Give me your ideals. Three ideals! Is that all you have?

YOUNG MAN. Life has robbed me of my ideals.

WORKMAN. He robbed me, too.

YOUNG MAN. But I had so few.

WORKMAN. When you have toiled to possess more, he will take those from you also.

LIFE. [*To an old man.*] For twelve hours you shall toil at what you hate. For an hour you shall work at what you love, to keep the wound fresh, to make the torture keener.

OLD MAN. Ah, pity! Do not be so cruel! Let me forget the work I love.

LIFE. Dog! Take what I give you! It is not by begging that you may win anything from me!

A VOICE. Give me a dream! A dream to strengthen my hands!

ANOTHER VOICE. A little love to make the day less terrible!

THIRD VOICE.   Only rest, a little rest! Time to think of the sea, and of grasses blowing in the wind.

A WOMAN.   Master!

> [LIFE *lashes her with his whip. The woman screams.* LIFE *draws back from them and dances a mocking dance, dancing himself into greater fury, laughing terribly, he lashes out at them. Several fall dead. He chokes a cripple with his hands. Finally he drives them off the stage before him, several furtively dragging the bodies with them.*]

SECOND GIRL.   [*As the two emerge from their hiding-place.*]   Oh! I wish never to see his face as they saw it!

FIRST GIRL.   You will not, unless you kneel—never kneel, little queen.

SECOND GIRL.   I shall never kneel to Life. I shall stand upright, as you have taught me, and I shall say: "Bring me another necklace, Life——"

FIRST GIRL.   I must go now for a little while. I shall come back. Do not forget.

> [*She goes out.*]

SECOND GIRL.   I shall say——

> [LIFE'S *voice is heard off stage.* SECOND GIRL *cowers.* LIFE *enters.*]

SECOND GIRL.   Slave! I would have the chain with the red stone! [*As* LIFE *submissively approaches, she snatches it from his neck.*] And this!

> [*Snatching at his hand and pulling the ring from a finger. The slave bows. She happens to look toward the spot where the bodies were and shivers.*]

LIFE.   [*Raising his head in time to see the look of hor-*

ror. From this moment his aspect gradually changes until from the slave he becomes a tyrant.] Are you afraid of me?

SECOND GIRL. No.

LIFE. There are many who are afraid of me.

SECOND GIRL. You are a slave.

LIFE. There are many who are afraid.

SECOND GIRL. You are only a slave.

LIFE. A slave may become a master.

SECOND GIRL. No.

LIFE. I may become——

SECOND GIRL. You are my slave.

LIFE. If I were your master——

SECOND GIRL. You are a slave.

LIFE. If I were your master, I would be kind to you. You are beautiful.

SECOND GIRL. Ah!

LIFE. You are very beautiful.

SECOND GIRL. It is my crown that makes me beautiful.

LIFE. If you should take your crown from your head, you would still be beautiful.

SECOND GIRL. That I will not do.

LIFE. You are beautiful as the slight burning of the apple-petal's cheek when the sun glances at the great flowers near it. You are beautiful as the little pool far in the forest which holds lily-buds in its hands. You are beautiful——

SECOND GIRL. [*Aside.*] I think he wants me to be afraid; so I will say it. I have heard that men are like that. I am not afraid, but I will say it to please him.

LIFE. Are you afraid of me?

SECOND GIRL. Yes.

LIFE.   Are you afraid?

SECOND GIRL.   Yes, I am afraid.

LIFE.   Ah, that pleases me.

SECOND GIRL.   [*Aside.*]   I knew that I would be able to please him!   Whatever I make into words makes itself into my body, she said, like fear—but she does not know everything!   It is impossible that she should know everything!   And it is so pleasant to please him— And so easy!   I am not afraid of him.   I have only *said* that I am afraid.

LIFE.   Will you not take your crown from your head?

SECOND GIRL.   No.

LIFE.   There is nothing so beautiful as a woman's hair flying in the wind.   I can see your hair beneath your crown.   Your hair would be beautiful flying in the wind.

SECOND GIRL.   [*Removes crown.*]   It is only for a moment.

LIFE.   Yes, you are beautiful.

SECOND GIRL.   [*To herself.*]   It may be that I was not wise——

LIFE.   You are like a new flower opening and dazzling a passing bird with sudden color.

SECOND GIRL.   She said that I must not——

LIFE.   You are like the bird that passes.   Your hair lifts like wings in the sun.

SECOND GIRL.   He has not harmed me.

LIFE.   Your crown is like jewels gathered from old galleons beneath the sea.   May I see your crown?

SECOND GIRL.   [*Holds it out cautiously toward him, then changes her mind.*]   No——

LIFE.   Let me hold it in my fingers.   I shall give it back to you.

SECOND GIRL.   No.

LIFE.   I shall give it back.

SECOND GIRL. If you will surely give it back to me——

LIFE. [*Takes crown.*] But your hair is lovelier without a crown.

       [*Flings it from him.*]

SECOND GIRL. What have you done?

LIFE. It was only in jest.

SECOND GIRL. But you promised——

LIFE. In jest.

SECOND GIRL. But——

LIFE. Ho-ho! Laugh with me. What a jest!

SECOND GIRL. [*Laughs, then shivers.*]

LIFE. [*In high good humor with himself.*] Dance for me. You are young. You are happy. Dance!

SECOND GIRL. What shall my dance say?

LIFE. That it is Spring, and that there are brooks flowing, newly awakened and mad to be with the sea. That there is a white bud widening under the moon, and in a curtained room a young girl sleeping. That the sun has wakened her——

SECOND GIRL. [*Dances these things. At first she is afraid of him, then she forgets and dances with abandon.*] And now give me back my crown.

LIFE. You do not need a crown, pretty one.

SECOND GIRL. I am afraid of you!

LIFE. Afraid of me! what have I done?

SECOND GIRL. I do not know.

LIFE. Do not be afraid.

SECOND GIRL. I am afraid.

LIFE. I shall be a kind master to you.

SECOND GIRL. Master?

LIFE. A kind master.

SECOND GIRL. You are my slave.

LIFE. I shall never be your slave again.

SECOND GIRL. And if she were right? If it is true?

LIFE. What are you saying?

SECOND GIRL. Nothing——

LIFE. You must call me master.

SECOND GIRL. No. That I will not do.

LIFE. [*Leering at her.*] Call me master. Then I shall be kind to you.

SECOND GIRL. No. I cannot.

LIFE. [*Picks up his whip from the path, toying with the whip but laughing to her.*] Then I shall be kind.

SECOND GIRL. Master——

LIFE. It has a good sound.

SECOND GIRL. You will give me——

LIFE. Greedy one! Be grateful that I do not punish you.

SECOND GIRL. But you would not strike me?

LIFE. If you do not obey——

SECOND GIRL. [*Whispering.*] You would not strike——

LIFE. You must kneel.

SECOND GIRL. [*Repeating.*] Never kneel, little queen——

LIFE. You must kneel to me.

SECOND GIRL. No.

LIFE. [*Raising the whip as if to strike.*] On your knees! Slave!

SECOND GIRL. You were kind! Life, you were kind! You said beautiful words to me.

LIFE. Kneel.

SECOND GIRL. You would be always kind, you said——

LIFE. Will you obey?

SECOND GIRL. I shall never——

[LIFE *curls his whip around her shoulders.*]

SECOND GIRL. [*Screams.*] Do not flog me. I will kneel. [*Kneels.*]

LIFE. So? In that way I can win obedience.

SECOND GIRL. Master!

LIFE. It has a good sound.

SECOND GIRL. Pity! Have pity!

LIFE. Do not whine.

[*Kicks her.*]

SECOND GIRL. [*Rises staggering.*] Spare me!

LIFE. I shall beat you, for the cries of those who fear me are sweet in my ears.

[*Beats her.*]

SECOND GIRL. Master!

LIFE. [*Flinging aside whip.*] But sweeter yet are stilled cries——

[*He seizes her; they struggle.*]

SECOND GIRL. He is too strong—I can struggle no longer!

[*They struggle.* LIFE *chokes her to death and flings her body from him. Then, laughing horribly, he goes off the stage.*]

FIRST GIRL. [*Enters, skipping merrily. Singing.*]
Heigho, in April,
Heigho, heigho,
All the town in April
Is gay, is gay!
[*She plucks a rose from the bush.*]
Heigho, in April,
In merry, merry April,
Love came a-riding,
And of a sunny day
I met him on the way!
Heigho, in April,
Heigho, heigho——

[*Suddenly seeing the body, she breaks the song and stares without moving. Then she goes very slowly toward it, smooths down the dead girl's dress, and kneels beside the body. Whispers.*]

She was young . . . he is cruel. . . . [*Touches the body.*] She also was a queen. She snatched his trinkets. See, there on her dead neck is his chain with the red fire caught in gold. And on her finger his ring. But he was too strong . . . too strong. . . . [*She stands, trembles, cowering in terror.*] Life has broken her . . . Life has broken them all. . . . Some day . . . I am afraid. . . .

[LIFE *enters, still the ugly tyrant. She remains cowering. His eyes rove slowly over the stage, but she sees him a second before he discovers her. She straightens up just in time to be her scornful self before his eyes light upon her. As she speaks* LIFE *becomes the slave again.*]

FIRST GIRL. [*Carelessly flings the rose down without seeing that it has fallen upon the body.*] Bring me a fresh rose!

[*The slave bows abjectly and goes to do her bidding.*]

CURTAIN

COPHETUA

BY

JOHN DRINKWATER

John Drinkwater, poet and dramatist, was born in England, June 1, 1882. He was a co-founder of the Pilgrim Players, now known as the Birmingham Repertory Theatre. Among his better-known works are *Poems,* 1914; *Pawns: Four Poetic Plays* (Houghton), 1920; *Abraham Lincoln,* a play (Houghton), 1918; *Mary Stuart,* a play (Houghton), 1921; *Oliver Cromwell,* a play (Houghton), 1921; *Robert E. Lee,* a play (Houghton), 1923.

THE PEOPLE OF THE PLAY

KING COPHETUA
A CAPTAIN
FIVE WISE MEN
KING'S MOTHER
THE MAID
BEGGARS

COPHETUA

*The scene is the Hall of the King's Palace. On the
left are two thrones, one above the other, with chairs
below them.*

*At the back of the stage is a tall doorway, open, showing
a path to a broad flight of steps which leads up to the
Temple. Two or three BEGGARS are sitting on the
steps.*

There is an open corridor to the right of the stage.

*The KING'S MOTHER is seated on the lower throne. On
the chairs below are five WISE MEN and a CAPTAIN.*

CAPTAIN. 'Tis noon, and with echoing wing
The days of a month have sped,
And we stay to know if the king
Will take a queen to his bed.

KING'S MOTHER. You have the oath of a king
That, be it for weal or woe,
In the space of a month he would speak of this thing,
He will come, he will come—you shall know.

FIRST WISE MAN. [*Very old.*] He will hear. Not
    in vain, not in vain
Shall his people beseech him of this,
He will hear us, nor count of the pain
Which may bloom peradventure to bliss.
I have stood at the gates of the kings,
His fathers, by year and by year,
They failed not to grant us the things
That were shaped in our prayers. He will hear.

SECOND WISE MAN.   He is haughty and fiery proud,
A spirit not easy to tame,
He will face us unbroken, unbowed,
And scorn us and put us to shame.

THIRD WISE MAN.   He is King, and howbeit he turns
To the right or the left it is well,
If he hearkens our crying or spurns,
He is King.   It is well, it is well.

FOURTH WISE MAN.   [*Blind.*]   Since the day when
    God shattered my sight
I fear whatso things may befall,
Who shall know if he answer aright?
Who shall say if of wisdom our call?

FIFTH WISE MAN.   I wait for his word unafraid.
The ways of the world are set out
By God's will; shall we tremble dismayed
However this thing come about?

CAPTAIN.   By the might of the spear, he shall speak
As we bid him to speak, or his crown
Shall be broken—what, are we so meek
That we bow if a king should but frown?

KING'S MOTHER.   I fear him.   My son, should you be
Too stubborn, how then should I set
Any peace in my heart or go free
Of a fear that I might not forget?
How then, with a sword set between
Your crown and the men of the land,
Should the pride in my heart keep clean
For a son who held hate by the hand?

> [*Enter, from the corridor,* KING COPHETUA.
> *They all rise as he goes up to his throne.   As*
> *he takes his place he motions them to sit.*]

COPHETUA.   I have come.   As a slave ye have called
    me.

As a dog to his masters I come.
With the sting of your tongues ye have galled me—
Do you bid me to speak or be dumb?
O my masters, your King is before you,
A playting, a chattel, a fool,—
Cry shame on the mothers who bore you
If you bend not his will to your rule.
Shall a king in his folly be daring
To speak as he would, to be wise
As he knows in his heart, and set flaring
His insolent flame to the skies?
Shall a king give a thought to his vision
When his masters forbid him, and frown?
Throw your dust in his teeth, and derision
Pluck out all the gems of his crown!

SECOND WISE MAN.   He is haughty and fiery proud,
A spirit not easy to tame.

FOURTH WISE MAN.   There is fear in my heart, and a
  cloud
On my soul.

FIRST WISE MAN.   O my King, when they came,
The people, to speak with the kings
Long ago they were heard.

THIRD WISE MAN.   Let him speak,
He is King, and a holiness clings
To the words of a king.

FIFTH WISE MAN.   We are weak,
We are creatures of God, and His will
Is over us all;   He alone
Is mighty to save and to spill.

KING'S MOTHER.   A sword on the steps of the throne
Is lying, and blood on the blade.

CAPTAIN.   Enough!   Shall we chaffer with speech
As men in a market dismayed,

Shall we take not the thing we may reach
With little of toil?

For a year

Has the voice of the men of the land
Cried out for a king to hear
Of his grace.   For an answer we stand.
It is little enough that we pray,
But here, in the name of the dead,
I swear you shall hearken to-day—
Will you take a queen to your bed?

COPHETUA.   It is well.   I am bidden to speak,
You are gracious to grant me this thing.
You are strong and you bear with the weak,
You will loosen the tongue of a king.

SECOND WISE MAN.   He is haughty and fiery proud.

CAPTAIN.   No more.   There are rumors that go
In the streets——

COPHETUA.   Unbroken, unbowed,
I give you your answer—I know
Of the rumors and threatening spears,
I know of the sword in the night,
But nothing of pitiful fears.
I will answer,—and hear me aright,—
I will not take a queen to my bed,
Though the world should clamor and cry,
Till my will is so shaped.   It is said.
You may go—I have spoken it, I.

[For a moment there is silence.   Then mere as-
sertion gives place to reasoning.]

FIRST WISE MAN.   Who shall be king in the end?
When you are fallen to sleep,
To whom shall our children look to keep
Peace between friend and friend?

COPHETUA.   Your children shall carve a way
To peace with the might of their hands.
Shall they bear to their doors the fruit of the lands
Because, on a far-off day,
A king of their fathers fell
And sold the gates of his soul
To the rabble ranks for a pitiful dole,
And married his love to hell?

SECOND WISE MAN.   You are haughty and fiery proud.

COPHETUA.   The meanest man of you all
May mate where he would.   Shall a king then fall
And tremble before you, cowed,
And be humbled and shorn of fame,
Be called a braggart, a knave,
That he dares no less than a thrall to save
The shrine of his heart from shame?

THIRD WISE MAN.   You are King, and I dare not
    cross
My will with a crownèd king's,
But your will so set to your people brings
Peril of branded loss.
There are kingdoms over the seas,
And kingdoms near to your gates,
Whose daughters are moulded for comely mates,
And will you not choose of these,
And gather about your throne
A safety fashioned of might?

COPHETUA.   I will break my body to dust in fight,
I am careless of blood and bone,
I will forfeit my latest breath,
I will harry the stranger lords,
I will face unfriended the outland hordes,
I will kiss the lips of death,
I will keep no secret store

Of peace in my house, I will spare
No strength in what things a man may dare
Or men have dared before;
But the doors of my love shall be
Guarded and unbetrayed,
And reckoning there shall be surely made
'Twixt none but my God and me.

FOURTH WISE MAN.   I fear the striving of men
And the challenge of boasting lips.

COPHETUA.   Old man, you are nigh to your day's
eclipse.
Would you have in your fancy, when
You pass away to the night,
The strands of a troubled tale
Of a high king setting his love for sale?

FOURTH WISE MAN.   [*Bewildered merely.*]   The Lord
hath shattered my sight.

FIFTH WISE MAN.   Be it as you have said.
God watches.

COPHETUA.   He watches well.
I have strayed too near to the gates of hell,
But He watched me, and His hand led.

CAPTAIN.   You blacken His name.   We are proud,
We people, aye, proud as a king;
You shall rue the day when you chose to fling
Your scorn as pence to the crowd.
We will that a queen should sit
On the king's right hand, and still
We stand as men for the fruits of our will,
Nor abate one word of it.

KING'S MOTHER.   My son, O my son, be not
Too stubborn—I fear the end,
I fear the day that no days may mend,

And the happening unforgot.
Is it little, my son, you lose?
There are women with faces fair,
And maddening limbs and shining hair,
And goodly women to choose;
Women whose kisses would fire
Your lips and quicken your blood,
And set a tumult, a golden flood
In your soul, and a new desire
In the season of scents and stars,
And a sweeter song in the day——

COPHETUA.   My mother, you have no word to say
Of worth.   Would you set in bars
The sacred spirit of me?
No, mother, you know I speak
As a man should speak, but your will is weak
For fear of the things to be.
You are true, my mother, you bring
A deep wise love to the child,—
Let your love be stainless, and undefiled
By craven fears for the king.

CAPTAIN.   She is wise of her fear——
COPHETUA.   Be still—
You are rude, sir, sharpen your tongue
On the steps of a throne whose king is sung
For a poor unkingly will.
I have given my answer; to each
As he spake I have answered again.
Do you hold me a gibbering clod among men,
To waver and juggle with speech?

> [*He moves from the throne to the open doorway
>   at the back.*]

For my people, I know them aright,
They will hear me, they hold not in scorn

A man whose flame without fear is borne,
With the wings of the wind in flight.
I will tell them. I wait the call
Of my soul and none else beside;
I will bring to the hall of their kings a bride
When my choice unbidden fall.

> [*During the foregoing speeches other* BEGGARS
> *have joined those sitting on the steps. Among
> them is a* MAID. *As the* KING *now goes out
> of the Hall and up the steps to the Temple, the*
> BEGGARS *hold out their hands for alms. The*
> KING *gives. The* MAID, *who is seated on an
> upper step alone, by the door of the Temple,
> asks nothing. The* KING *pauses for a mo-
> ment to look at her; she touches his cloak with
> her hand, and lifts it to her lips. He passes
> into the Temple.*]

SECOND WISE MAN. He has gone. He is fiery proud.

THIRD WISE MAN. He is King. It is well, it is well.

FOURTH WISE MAN. There is fear on my heart, and
a cloud.

KING'S MOTHER. There is building a story to tell——

FIRST WISE MAN. He leaves the clear ways that are
worn.

FIFTH WISE MAN. 'Tis the purpose of God—we must
bend.

CAPTAIN. Not in vain shall he mock us and scorn.

KING'S MOTHER. A story—who knows of the end?

SECOND WISE MAN. This day is fulfilled my foretell-
ing.

THIRD WISE MAN. The stars are in counsel with
kings.

FOURTH WISE MAN. There is gloom in the house of
our dwelling.

FIFTH WISE MAN.   To God be the shaping of things.

FIRST WISE MAN.   The thread of the years now is broken.

CAPTAIN.   To the edge of his sword be the shame.

KING'S MOTHER.   What word of this day will be spoken?

What song will be sung of our fame?

> [*The* KING *comes through the Temple doors. The* BEGGARS, *as before, hold out their hands; the* MAID *alone asks nothing.* COPHETUA *offers her a bag of gold, which she takes; she rises and stands with the* KING *at the top of the steps; she pours the gold from the bag down the steps, and the* BEGGARS *collect the scattered coins. She kisses the bag, and ties it in her girdle. The* KING *stands looking at her for a moment, then comes down to the Hall; he stands by the open doors.*]

COPHETUA.   I knelt before God's altar-rail,
And something leapt within my brain;
God's mother smiled; her beauty pale
Was over me; and then again
I heard my people crying out,
And woven in the cries of them
I heard a kiss that clung about
The colors of my raiment's hem.

My prayers went up with feathered speed,
But still I saw the face of one
Who said no word of all her need
Among the beggars in the sun,
Of one who sought no little dole
But gave great tribute to her King,

And something fiery in my soul
Stirred with the passion of the spring.

And still I heard my people cry,
"A queen! a queen! we seek a queen!"
No pride was on my lips, and I
Told God what thing I then had seen,
What rumor through my blood was sent
As I passed through His holy gate,
And surely up to God they went—
My little secret words of fate.

Out of God's house I came.   She stood
Before me.   She had naught to bring
Of land or warrant counted good
To fire the temper of a king,
Only a treasure in her eyes
Of pure and consecrated days,
And presage that her soul was wise
Of travel in the starry ways.

You counselled me.   I heard your words,
Your threats I heard, your cunning speech,
Your clamoring of sheathless swords,
But citadelled beyond the reach
Of all these things my heart was free;
Yet then a secret word was said
In the blue air.   This thing shall be—
A queen is coming to my bed.

    CAPTAIN.   The child of a beggar!
    SECOND WISE MAN.   You dare
Lift up this shame in your land?
    FIRST WISE MAN.   You speak not in wisdom—beware.

FOURTH WISE MAN.   God give me to understand.

KING'S MOTHER.   My son, O my son, but wait
A little—how should this be—
A son of proud old kings to mate
With a girl base-born?

FOURTH WISE MAN.   Ah, me!

COPHETUA.   How?   Would ye drive me to and fro
As straw beneath the goodman's flail?
God's angels laugh, I think, to know
How much a king's word may avail.
I stand, road-girt, before a sweet
New land of holy joys to-day,
And she alone has led my feet,
And she alone shall say me nay.

"Base-born," you cry—"a beggar's child."
So be it.   Yet there haply ran
Some strain of passion undefiled
When in the twilight some tall man
Bore homeward to his bridal bed
Of curling leaves beneath the sky
A clear-limbed girl whose beauty led
Love laughing in captivity.

You bid me mate.   And shall it be
To make adultery a thing
Honored from sea to shining sea
For that the sinner is a king?
My blood is kingly?   It shall take
A strain of vagrant wind and sun.
I, born a king, henceforth will make
The people and the sceptre one.

> [*He walks up the steps to the* MAID; *he stands
> speaking to her, and then leads her down into
> the Hall.*]

THE MAID. It seemed a very little thing
That you should come and lead me down
Here to your throne. You are a king,
There is a splendor on your crown,
Yet you were born of changing dust
Even as I, and when you spoke
That word to me, the great God thrust
His arm out and the barrier broke,
And I was maid and you were man,
Built of one flesh; it was as though
No word had been since time began
Of kings and beggars.

COPHETUA.   And a low
Sweet sound of music fell about
My senses, as of beating wings
Of loves that sway the world without
A thought of beggars or of kings.

THE MAID. You are king, and kings are great,
Yet, though I'd kneel before a throne,
My heart would be inviolate—
No king should claim it for his own;
I worship kingly men, I bow
Before the king's ancestral might,
Yet all these things are naught, and now
No king is standing in my sight.
I see a man who spoke to me
As a man should speak, loving well.

COPHETUA. I see a queen whose lips might be
Fashioned great histories to tell.

THE MAID. I see a man who set aflame
My womanhood and made it whole.

COPHETUA. I see a holy queen who came
As a great song into my soul.

THE MAID. I saw an eagle in the air——

COPHETUA. The eagle clove the cloudy ways——

THE MAID. Strong-winged he was, and proud and
fair——

COPHETUA. And there he met the golden rays
Hidden to earth——

THE MAID.   And far and far
He sped with swift and level flight,

COPHETUA. And wrung the glory of a star
Out of the garners of the night.

FIRST WISE MAN. Great queens might take her by the
hand,

THIRD WISE MAN. Great kings might kiss her on the
lips,

FIFTH WISE MAN. God's laughter now is on the land,

FOURTH WISE MAN. Light trembles through my day's
eclipse,

SECOND WISE MAN. The king establishes his pride.

CAPTAIN. I kneel to her, no threat is now
Upon my tongue, she is a bride
To whom a king's folk well may bow.

KING'S MOTHER. My child, what way the King may
choose
Is well; the soul of you is wise,
And a queen's crown will no way lose
Its splendor set above your eyes;
The word is spoken, and aloud
Along the day as fire it runs,
And you shall bear your King a proud
And comely line of kingly sons.

THE MAID. Not dowered as a queen might be
Who sold herself you see me here,
Yet something do I bring for fee,
Good counsel, comfortable cheer,
A body undefiled, a soul

Not alien before the Lord,
A will unbent, a purpose whole,
A passion shining as a sword.

To you in humble-wise, my King,
With naught of fear or servile greed,
My sacred love unsoiled I bring,
My service, and my woman's need.
A story of some careful days
Spent in a cloister no man knows,
Some peace of silent lilied ways,
Some beauty of the curling rose.

> [*The* KING *leads her up to the throne. They
> stand one on each side of it.*]

COPHETUA. [*To the people.*]   Am I the less a king
    that here
I choose as might a man uncrowned,
Or should you hold a queen more dear
For armèd men or tribute ground?
If so it be, the word be said,
And we will pass from out your land,
And sleep upon a stranger bed
And prosper by a stranger hand.

FIRST WISE MAN.   She too shall pass where queens
    have trod,
THIRD WISE MAN.   You, being King, have chosen
    well,
FIFTH WISE MAN.   Not niggard is the hand of God,
FOURTH WISE MAN.   No veilèd fear is now to tell,
SECOND WISE MAN.   Now beautiful is all your pride,
CAPTAIN.   My sword shall bring you peace alone,
KING'S MOTHER.   My trouble now is purified,
And love is laughing from a throne.

COPHETUA.   In the years far away, far away,
Our love shall be told as a song.

THE MAID.   Many men shall remember, and say—
They kept their love guarded from wrong.

COPHETUA.   Your beauty shall be as a tale
For the firing of hearts to the end.

THE MAID.   And never the story shall fail
Of a king who was mighty to lend
A glory to love in his land.

COPHETUA.   And the children of men unbegot
Shall listen, and understand
The tale of a love unforgot.
Our kiss shall be set on the crest
Of the travelling years, and be borne
As a torch from the east to the west,
Till the sinews of love be outworn.

CURTAIN

A NIGHT AT AN INN

BY

LORD DUNSANY

Lord Dunsany (Edward John Moreton Drax Plunkett) was born in 1878 in Ireland, where he has lived most of his life. He saw active service in the Boer War and was Captain of the Royal Inniskilling Fusiliers in the World War. He has been associated with the Irish literary renascence, in connection with which his play *The Glittering Gate* was produced at the Abbey Theatre, Dublin. Lord Dunsany's plays have been immensely popular with various little theatres in America, especially through the performances of them given by Stuart Walker and his Portmanteau Plays troupe. His best-known plays are *The Gods of the Mountain, The Golden Doom, King Argimenes and the Unknown Warrior, The Glittering Gate,* and *The Lost Silk Hat,* all to be found in the volume *Five Plays* (Little, Brown and Company, 1917), and *A Night at an Inn,* which, along with *The Tents of the Arabs, The Laughter of the Gods,* and *The Queen's Enemies,* is to be found in the volume *Plays of Gods and Men* (Putnam, 1917).

CHARACTERS

A. E. SCOTT-FORTESCUE
*(The Toff), a dilapidated
gentleman*

WILLIAM JONES *(Bill)*

ALBERT THOMAS

JACOB SMITH *(Sniggers)*

} *4
Merchant
Sailors*

FIRST PRIEST OF KLESH

SECOND PRIEST OF KLESH

THIRD PRIEST OF KLESH

} 3 Priests

1 idol

KLESH

(The curtain rises on a room in an inn.)

A NIGHT AT AN INN

The curtain rises on a room in an inn. SNIGGERS *and*
BILL *are talking,* THE TOFF *is reading a paper.*
ALBERT *sits a little apart.*

SNIGGERS. What's his idea, I wonder?

BILL. I don't know.

SNIGGERS. And how much longer will he keep us here?

BILL. We've been here three days.

SNIGGERS. And 'aven't seen a soul.

BILL. And a pretty penny it cost us when he rented the pub.

SNIGGERS. 'Ow long did 'e rent the pub for?

BILL. You never know with him.

SNIGGERS. It's lonely enough.

BILL. 'Ow long did you rent the pub for, Toffy?

[THE TOFF *continues to read a sporting paper;
he takes no notice of what is said.*]

SNIGGERS. 'E's *such* a toff.

BILL. Yet 'e's clever, no mistake.

SNIGGERS. Those clever ones are the beggars to make a muddle. Their plans are clever enough, but they don't work, and then they make a mess of things much worse than you or me.

BILL. Ah.

SNIGGERS. I don't like this place.

BILL. Why not?

SNIGGERS. I don't like the looks of it.

BILL. He's keeping us here because here those niggers

43

can't find us.   The three heathen priests what was looking
for us so.   But we want to go and sell our ruby soon.

ALBERT.   There's no sense in it.

BILL.   Why not, Albert?

ALBERT.   Because I gave those black devils the slip in
Hull.

BILL.   You give 'em the slip, Albert?

ALBERT.   The slip, all three of them.   The fellows
with the gold spots on their foreheads.   I had the ruby
then and I give them the slip in Hull.

BILL.   How did you do it, Albert?

ALBERT.   I had the ruby and they were following
me . . .

BILL.   Who told them you had the ruby?   You didn't
show it?

ALBERT.   No . . . But they kind of know.

SNIGGERS.   They kind of know, Albert?

ALBERT.   Yes, they know if you've got it.   Well, they
sort of mouched after me, and I tells a policeman, and he
says, O, they were only three poor niggers and they
wouldn't hurt me.   Ugh!   When I thought of what they
did in Malta to poor old Jim.

BILL.   Yes, and to George in Bombay before we started.

SNIGGERS.   Ugh!

BILL.   Why didn't you give 'em in charge?

ALBERT.   What about the ruby, Bill?

BILL.   Ah!

ALBERT.   Well, I did better than that.   I walks up and
down through Hull.   I walks slow enough.   And then I
turns a corner and I runs.   I never sees a corner but I
turns it.   But sometimes I let a corner pass just to fool
them.   I twists about like a hare.   Then I sits down and
waits.   No priests.

SNIGGERS.   What?

ALBERT.   No heathen black devils with gold spots on their face.   I give 'em the slip.

BILL.   Well done, Albert.

SNIGGERS.   [*After a sigh of content.*]   Why didn't you tell us?

ALBERT.   'Cause 'e won't let you speak.   'E's got 'is plans and 'e thinks we're silly folk.   Things must be done 'is way.   And all the time I've give 'em the slip.   Might 'ave 'ad one o' them crooked knives in him before now but for me who give 'em the slip in Hull.

BILL.   Well done, Albert.

SNIGGERS.   Do you hear that, Toffy?   Albert has give 'em the slip.

THE TOFF.   Yes, I hear.

SNIGGERS.   Well, what do you say to that?

THE TOFF.   O . . . Well done, Albert.

ALBERT.   And what a' you going to do?

THE TOFF.   Going to wait.

ALBERT.   Don't seem to know what 'e's waiting for.

SNIGGERS.   It's a nasty place.

ALBERT.   It's getting silly, Bill.   Our money's gone and we want to sell the ruby.   Let's get on to a town.

BILL.   But 'e won't come.

ALBERT.   Then we'll leave him.

SNIGGERS.   We'll be all right if we keep away from Hull.

ALBERT.   We'll go to London.

BILL.   But 'e must 'ave 'is share.

SNIGGERS.   All right.   Only let's go.   [*To* THE TOFF.]   We're going, do you hear?   Give us the ruby.

THE TOFF.   Certainly.

> [*He gives them a ruby from his waistcoat pocket; it is the size of a small hen's egg.   He goes on reading his paper.*]

ALBERT. Come on, Sniggers.

[*Exeunt* ALBERT *and* SNIGGERS.]

BILL. Good-by, old man. We'll give you your fair share, but there's nothing to do here, no girls, no halls, and we must sell the ruby.

THE TOFF. I'm not a fool, Bill.

BILL. No, no, of course not. Of course you ain't, and you've helped us a lot. Good-by. You'll say good-by.

THE TOFF. Oh, yes. Good-by.

[*Still reads paper. Exit* BILL.]
[THE TOFF *puts a revolver on the table beside him and goes on with his paper.*]

SNIGGERS. [*Out of breath.*] We've come back, Toffy.

THE TOFF. So you have.

ALBERT. Toffy—How did they get here?

THE TOFF. They walked of course.

ALBERT. But it's eighty miles.

SNIGGERS. Did you know they were here, Toffy?

THE TOFF. Expected them about now.

ALBERT. Eighty miles.

BILL. Toffy, old man—what are we to do?

THE TOFF. Ask Albert.

BILL. If they can do things like this there's no one can save us but you, Toffy—I always knew you were a clever one. We won't be fools any more. We'll obey you, Toffy.

THE TOFF. You're brave enough and strong enough. There isn't many that would steal a ruby eye out of an idol's head, and such an idol as that was to look at, and on such a night. You're brave enough, Bill. But you're all three of you fools. Jim would have none of my plans, and where's Jim? And George. What did they do to him?

SNIGGERS. Don't, Toffy!

THE TOFF. Well, then, your strength is no use to you. You want cleverness; or they'll have you the way that they had George and Jim.

ALL. Ugh!

THE TOFF. These black priests would follow you round the world in circles. Year after year, till they got their idol's eye. And if we died with it, they'd follow our grandchildren. That fool thinks he can escape men like that by running round three streets in the town of Hull.

ALBERT. God's truth, *you* 'aven't escaped them, because they're 'ere.

THE TOFF. So I supposed.

ALBERT. You *supposed?*

THE TOFF. Yes, I believe there's no announcement in the society papers. But I took this country-seat especially to receive them. There's plenty of room if you dig, it is pleasantly situated, and, what is most important, it is in a very quiet neighborhood. So I am at home to them this afternoon.

BILL. Well, you're a deep one.

THE TOFF. And, remember, you've only my wits between you and death, and don't put your futile plans against those of an educated gentleman.

ALBERT. If you're a gentleman, why don't you go about among gentlemen instead of the likes of us?

THE TOFF. Because I was too clever for them as I am too clever for you.

ALBERT. Too clever for them?

THE TOFF. I never lost a game of cards in my life.

BILL. You never lost a game!

THE TOFF. Not when there was money on it.

BILL. Well, well.

THE TOFF. Have a game of poker?

ALL. No thanks.

THE TOFF. Then do as you're told.

BILL. All right, Toffy.

SNIGGERS. I saw something just then. Hadn't we better draw the curtains?

THE TOFF. No.

SNIGGERS. What?

THE TOFF. Don't draw the curtains.

SNIGGERS. O, all right.

BILL. But, Toffy, they can see us. One doesn't let the enemy do that. I don't see why . . .

THE TOFF. No, of course you don't.

BILL. O, all right, Toffy.

[*All begin to pull out revolvers.*]

THE TOFF. [*Putting his own away.*] No revolvers, please.

ALBERT. Why not?

THE TOFF. Because I don't want any noise at my party. We might get guests that hadn't been invited. *Knives* are a different matter.

> [*All draw knives.* THE TOFF *signs to them not
> to draw them yet.* THE TOFF *has already
> taken back his ruby.*]

BILL. I think they're coming, Toffy.

THE TOFF. Not yet.

ALBERT. When will they come?

THE TOFF. When I am quite ready to receive them. Not before.

SNIGGERS. I should like to get this over.

THE TOFF. Should you? Then we'll have them now.

SNIGGERS. Now?

THE TOFF. Yes. Listen to me. You shall do as you see me do. You will all pretend to go out. I'll show you how. I've got the ruby. When they see me alone, they will come for their idol's eye.

BILL. How can they tell like this which of us has it?

THE TOFF. I confess I don't know, but they seem to.

SNIGGERS. What will you do when they come in?

THE TOFF. I shall do nothing.

SNIGGERS. What?

THE TOFF. They will creep up behind me. Then my friends, Sniggers and Bill and Albert, who gave them the slip, will do what they can.

BILL. All right, Toffy. Trust us.

THE TOFF. If you're a little slow, you will see enacted the cheerful spectacle that accompanied the demise of Jim.

SNIGGERS. Don't, Toffy. We'll be there all right.

THE TOFF. Very well. Now watch me.

> [*He goes past the windows to the inner door right; he opens it inward, and then under cover of the open door he slips down on his knee and closes it, remaining on the inside, appearing to have gone out. He signs to the others who understand. Then he appears to re-enter in the same manner.*]

THE TOFF. Now. I shall sit with my back to the door. You go out one by one so far as our friends can make out. Crouch very low, to be on the safe side. They mustn't see you through the window.

> [BILL *makes his sham exit.*]

THE TOFF. Remember, no revolvers. The police are, I believe, proverbially inquisitive.

> [*The other two follow* BILL. *All three are now crouching inside the door right.* THE TOFF *puts the ruby beside him on the table. He lights a cigarette.*

*The door in back opens so slowly that you can
hardly say at what moment it began.* THE
TOFF *picks up his paper.*

A NATIVE *of India wriggles along the floor
ever so slowly, seeking cover from chairs.
He moves left where* THE TOFF *is. The three
sailors are right.* SNIGGERS *and* ALBERT *lean
forward.* BILL'S *arm keeps them back. An
arm-chair had better conceal them from the
Indian. The black* PRIEST *nears* THE TOFF.

BILL *watches to see if any more are coming.
Then he leaps forward alone—he has taken his
boots off—and knifes the* PRIEST.

The PRIEST *tries to shout, but* BILL'S *left hand
is over his mouth.*

THE TOFF *continues to read his sporting paper.
He never looks round.*]

BILL. [*Sotto voce.*] There's only one, Toffy. What
shall we do?

THE TOFF. [*Without turning his head.*] Only one?

BILL. Yes.

THE TOFF. Wait a moment. Let me think. [*Still
apparently absorbed in his paper.*] Ah, yes. You go
back, Bill. We must attract another guest. Now are you
ready?

BILL. Yes.

THE TOFF. All right. You shall now see my demise
at my Yorkshire residence. You must receive guests for
me. [*He leaps up in full view of the window, flings up
both arms and falls on to the floor near the dead* PRIEST.]
Now be ready.

[*His eyes close. There is a long pause. Again
the door opens, very, very slowly. Another*
PRIEST *creeps in. He has three golden spots*

*upon his forehead. He looks round, then he
creeps up to his companion and turns him over
and looks inside each of his clinched hands.
Then he looks at the recumbent* TOFF. *Then
he creeps toward him.* BILL *slips after him
and knifes him like the other with his left hand
over his mouth.*]

BILL. [*Sotto voce.*] We've only got two, Toffy.

THE TOFF. Still another.

BILL. What'll we do?

THE TOFF. [*Sitting up.*] Hum.

BILL. This is the best way, much.

THE TOFF. Out of the question. Never play the same game twice.

BILL. Why not, Toffy?

THE TOFF. Doesn't work if you do.

BILL. Well?

THE TOFF. I have it, Albert. You will now walk into the room. I showed you how to do it.

ALBERT. Yes.

THE TOFF. Just run over here and have a fight at this window with these two men.

ALBERT. But they're——

THE TOFF. Yes, they're dead, my perspicuous Albert. But Bill and I are going to resuscitate them. Come on.

[BILL *picks up a body under the arms.*]

THE TOFF. That's right, Bill. [*Does the same.*] Come and help us, Sniggers—[SNIGGERS *comes.*] Keep low, keep low. Wave their arms about, Sniggers. Don't show yourself. Now, Albert, over you go. Our Albert is slain. Back you get, Bill. Back, Sniggers. Still, Albert. Mustn't move when he comes. Not a muscle.

[*A face appears at the window and stays for some time. Then the door opens and looking craftily round the* THIRD PRIEST *enters. He looks at his companions' bodies and turns round. He suspects something. He takes up one of the knifes and with a knife in each hand he puts his back to the wall. He looks to the left and right.*]

THE TOFF. Come on, Bill.

[*The* PRIEST *rushes to the door.* THE TOFF *knifes the last* PRIEST *from behind.*]

THE TOFF. A good day's work, my friends.

BILL. Well done, Toffy. Oh, you are a deep one.

ALBERT. A deep one if ever there was one.

SNIGGERS. There ain't any more, Bill, are there?

THE TOFF. No more in the world, my friend.

BILL. Aye, that's all there are. There were only three in the temple. Three priests and their beastly idol.

ALBERT. What is it worth, Toffy? Is it worth a thousand pounds?

THE TOFF. It's worth all they've got in the shop. Worth just whatever we like to ask for it.

ALBERT. Then we're millionaires now.

THE TOFF. Yes, and what is more important, we no longer have any heirs.

BILL. We'll have to sell it now.

ALBERT. That won't be easy. It's a pity it isn't small and we had half a dozen. Hadn't the idol any other on him?

BILL. No, he was green jade all over and only had this one eye. He had it in the middle of his forehead, and was a long sight uglier than anything else in the world.

SNIGGERS. I'm sure we ought all to be very grateful to Toffy.

BILL.   And indeed we ought.

ALBERT.   If it hadn't 'ave been for him——

BILL.   Yes, if it hadn't a been for old Toffy . . .

SNIGGERS.   He's a deep one.

THE TOFF.   Well, you see, I just have a knack of fore-seeing things.

SNIGGERS.   I should think you did.

BILL.   Why, I don't suppose anything happens that our Toff doesn't foresee.   Does it, Toffy?

THE TOFF.   Well, I don't think it does, Bill.   I don't think it often does.

BILL.   Life is no more than just a game of cards to our old Toff.

THE TOFF.   Well, we've taken these fellows' trick.

SNIGGERS.   [*Going to the window.*]   It wouldn't do for any one to see them.

THE TOFF.   O, nobody will come this way.   We're all alone on a moor.

BILL.   Where will we put them?

THE TOFF.   Bury them in the cellar, but there's no hurry.

BILL.   And what then, Toffy?

THE TOFF.   Why, then we'll go to London and upset the ruby business.   We have really come through this job very nicely.

BILL.   I think the first thing that we ought to do is to give a little supper to old Toffy.   We'll bury these fellows to-night.

ALBERT.   Yes, let's.

SNIGGERS.   The very thing.

BILL.   And we'll all drink his health.

ALBERT.   Good old Toffy.

SNIGGERS. He ought to have been a general or a premier.

[*They get bottles from cupboard, etc.*]

THE TOFF. Well, we've earned our bit of a supper.

[*They sit down.*]

BILL. [*Glass in hand.*] Here's to old Toffy who guessed everything.

ALBERT *and* SNIGGERS. Good old Toffy.

BILL. Toffy who saved our lives and made our fortunes.

ALBERT *and* SNIGGERS. Hear! Hear!

THE TOFF. And here's to Bill who saved me twice to-night.

BILL. Couldn't have done it but for your cleverness, Toffy.

SNIGGERS. Hear, hear! Hear, hear!

ALBERT. He foresees everything.

BILL. A speech, Toffy. A speech from our general.

ALL. Yes, a speech.

SNIGGERS. A speech.

THE TOFF. Well, get me some water. This whiskey's too much for my head, and I must keep it clear till our friends are safe in the cellar.

BILL. Water. Yes, of course. Get him some water, Sniggers.

SNIGGERS. We don't use water here. Where shall I get it?

BILL. Outside in the garden.

[*Exit SNIGGERS.*] (leaves)

ALBERT. Here's to fortune.

[*They all drink.*]

BILL. Here's to Albert Thomas, Esquire.

[*He drinks.*]

THE TOFF.   Albert Thomas, Esquire.

[*He drinks.*]

ALBERT.   And William Jones, Esquire.

THE TOFF.   William Jones, Esquire.

[THE TOFF *and* ALBERT *drink.* ~~returns~~

~~Re-enter~~ SNIGGERS *terrified.*]

THE TOFF.   Hullo, here's Jacob Smith, Esquire, J.P., alias Sniggers, back again.

SNIGGERS.   Toffy, I've been a-thinking about my share in that ruby.   I don't want it, Toffy, I don't want it.

THE TOFF.   Nonsense, Sniggers, nonsense.

SNIGGERS.   You shall have it, Toffy, you shall have it yourself, only say Sniggers has no share in this 'ere ruby. Say it, Toffy, say it.

BILL.   Want to turn informer, Sniggers?

SNIGGERS.   No, no.   Only I don't want the ruby, Toffy. . . .

THE TOFF.   No more nonsense, Sniggers, we're all in together in this, if one hangs we all hang; but they won't outwit me.   Besides, it's not a hanging affair, they had their knives.

SNIGGERS.   Toffy, Toffy, I always treated you fair, Toffy.   I was always one to say, give Toffy a chance. Take back my share, Toffy.

THE TOFF.   What's the matter?   What are you driving at?

SNIGGERS.   Take it back, Toffy.

THE TOFF.   Answer me, what are you up to?

SNIGGERS.   I don't want my share any more.

BILL.   Have you seen the police?

[ALBERT *pulls out his knife.*]

THE TOFF.   No, no knives, Albert.

ALBERT.   What then?

THE TOFF. The honest truth in open court, barring the ruby. We were attacked.

SNIGGERS. There's no police.

THE TOFF. Well, then, what's the matter?

BILL. Out with it.

SNIGGERS. I swear to God . . .

ALBERT. Well?

THE TOFF. Don't interrupt.

SNIGGERS. I swear I saw something *what I didn't like.*

THE TOFF. What you didn't like?

SNIGGERS. [*In tears.*] O Toffy, Toffy, take it back. Take my share. Say you take it.

THE TOFF. What has he seen?

> [*Dead silence only broken by* SNIGGERS'S *sobs. Then stony steps are heard.*
> *Enters a hideous* IDOL. *It is blind and gropes its way. It gropes its way to the ruby and picks it up and screws it into a socket in the forehead.*
> SNIGGERS *still weeps softly, the rest stare in horror. The* IDOL *steps out, not groping. Its steps move off, then stop.*]

THE TOFF. O, great heavens!

ALBERT. [*In a childish, plaintive voice.*] What is it, Toffy?

BILL. Albert, it is that obscene idol [*in a whisper*] come from India.

ALBERT. It is gone.

BILL. It has taken its eye.

SNIGGERS. We are saved.

OFF, A VOICE. [*With outlandish accent.*] Meestaire William Jones, Able Seaman.

> [THE TOFF *has never spoken, never moved. He only gazes stupidly in horror.*]

BILL.   Albert, Albert, what is this?

    [*He rises and walks out.   One moan is heard.
    SNIGGERS goes to window.   He falls back
    sickly.*]

ALBERT.   [*In a whisper.*]   What has happened?

SNIGGERS.   I have seen it.   I have seen it, O, I have
seen it.

    [*He returns to table.*]

THE TOFF.   [*Laying his hand very gently on SNIG-
GERS'S arm, speaking softly and winningly.*]   What was
it, Sniggers?

SNIGGERS.   I have seen it.

ALBERT.   What?

SNIGGERS.   O!

VOICE.   Meestaire Albert Thomas, Able Seaman.

ALBERT.   Must I go, Toffy?   Toffy, must I go?

SNIGGERS.   [*Clutching him.*]   Don't move.

ALBERT.   [*Going.*]   Toffy, Toffy.

    [*Exit.*] And he goes out.

VOICE.   Meestaire Jacob Smith, Able Seaman.

SNIGGERS.   I can't go, Toffy.   I can't go.   I can't do it.

    [*He goes.*]

VOICE.   Meestaire Arnold Everett Scott-Fortescue, late
Esquire, Able Seaman.

THE TOFF.   I did not foresee it.

    [*Exit.*]

CURTAIN

LOYALTIES

A DRAMA IN THREE ACTS

BY

JOHN GALSWORTHY

John Galsworthy was born at Coome, Surrey, England, in 1867. After graduating from New College, Oxford, with a degree in law, he practised for a time, but gave up law because, as he said, he "dislikes the profession thoroughly." He has travelled extensively all over the world. In 1899 appeared his first novel, *Jocelyn*. This was followed by such novels as *The Man of Property, The Country House, Fraternity, The Patrician,* and *The Dark Flower*. His greatest work in the field of fiction is undoubtedly *The Forsyte Saga,* which is a thorough and painstaking study of an English family. Many of his novels, and almost all of the more recent ones, deal with members of this family.

In 1906, *The Silver Box,* his first play, was produced in London. *Joy* followed in 1907, and *Strife* in 1909 (the three reprinted in one volume, Scribner). *Justice* and *The Eldest Son,* Scribner, 1913, appear in the second series of his published plays; *The Fugitive, The Pigeon,* and *The Mob,* Scribner, 1914, in the third series; *A Bit o' Love, Foundations,* and *The Skin Game,* Scribner, 1920, as the fourth series; *Loyalties, Windows,* and *A Family Man,* Scribner, 1923, as the fifth series. *Old English,* Scribner, 1926, is a recent dramatic success.

John Galsworthy has shown unusual versatility. He has achieved a place as a writer of essays and short stories; he has become one of the greatest living English novelists; and he has likewise made a name for himself as probably the most serious and thought-provoking dramatist now writing in English.

PERSONS OF THE PLAY

In the Order of Appearance

CHARLES WINSOR, *owner of Meldon Court, near New-market*

LADY ADELA, *his wife*

FERDINAND DE LEVIS, *young, rich, and new*

TREISURE, WINSOR'S *butler*

GENERAL CANYNGE, *a racing oracle*

MARGARET ORME, *a society girl*

CAPTAIN RONALD DANCY, D.S.O., *retired*

MABEL, *his wife*

INSPECTOR DEDE, *of the county constabulary*

ROBERT, WINSOR'S *footman*

A CONSTABLE, *attendant on* DEDE

AUGUSTUS BORRING, *a clubman*

LORD ST ERTH, *a peer of the realm*

A FOOTMAN, *of the club*

MAJOR COLFORD, *a brother officer of* DANCY'S

EDWARD GRAVITER, *a solicitor*

A YOUNG CLERK, *of Twisden & Graviter's*

GILMAN, *a large grocer*

JACOB TWISDEN, *senior partner of Twisden & Graviter's*

RICARDOS, *an Italian, in wine*

LOYALTIES

ACT I

SCENE I

The dressing-room of CHARLES WINSOR, *owner of
Meldon Court, near Newmarket; about eleven-thirty
at night. The room has pale gray walls, unadorned;
the curtains are drawn over a window back left
centre. A bed lies along the wall, left. An open
door, right back, leads into* LADY ADELA'S *bedroom;
a door, right forward, into a long corridor, on to
which abut rooms in a row, the whole length of the
house's left wing.* WINSOR'S *dressing-table, with a
light over it, is stage right of the curtained window.
Pyjamas are laid out on the bed, which is turned back.
Slippers are handy, and all the usual gear of a well-
appointed bed-dressing-room.* CHARLES WINSOR, *a
tall, fair, good-looking man about thirty-eight, is
taking off a smoking-jacket.*

WINSOR. Hallo! Adela!
V. OF LADY A. [*From her bedroom.*] Hallo!
WINSOR. In bed?
V. OF LADY A. No.

> [*She appears in the doorway in undergarment
> and a wrapper. She, too, is fair, about
> thirty-five, rather delicious, and suggestive of
> porcelain.*]

WINSOR. Win at Bridge?

LADY A.　No fear.

WINSOR.　Who did?

LADY A.　Lord St Erth and Ferdy De Levis.

WINSOR.　That young man has too much luck—the young bounder won two races to-day; and he's as rich as Crœsus.

LADY A.　Oh! Charlie, he did look so exactly as if he'd sold me a carpet when I was paying him.

WINSOR.　[*Changing into slippers.*]　His father did sell carpets, wholesale, in the City.

LADY A.　Really? And you say I haven't intuition! [*With a finger on her lips.*]　Morison's in there.

WINSOR.　[*Motioning toward the door, which she shuts.*]　Ronny Dancy took a tenner off him, anyway, before dinner.

LADY A.　No! How?

WINSOR.　Standing jump on to a bookcase four feet high.　De Levis had to pay up, and sneered at him for making money by parlor tricks.　That young Jew gets himself disliked.

LADY A.　Aren't you rather prejudiced?

WINSOR.　Not a bit. I like Jews.　That's not against him—rather the contrary these days.　But he pushes himself.　The General tells me he's deathly keen to get into the Jockey Club.　[*Taking off his tie.*]　It's amusing to see him trying to get round old St Erth.

LADY A.　If Lord St Erth and General Canynge backed him he'd get in if he *did* sell carpets!

WINSOR.　He's got some pretty good horses.　[*Taking off his waistcoat.*]　Ronny Dancy's on his bones again, I'm afraid.　He had a bad day.　When a chap takes to doing parlor stunts for a bet—it's a sure sign.　What made him chuck the Army?

LADY A.　He says it's too dull, now there's no fighting.

WINSOR. Well, he can't exist on backing losers.

LADY A. Isn't it just like him to get married now? He really is the most reckless person.

WINSOR. Yes. He's a queer chap. I've always liked him, but I've never quite made him out. What do you think of his wife?

LADY A. Nice child; awfully gone on him.

WINSOR. Is *he?*

LADY A. Quite indecently—both of them. [*Nodding toward the wall, left.*] They're next door.

WINSOR. Who's beyond them?

LADY A. De Levis; and Margaret Orme at the end. Charlie, do you realize that the bathroom out there has to wash those four?

WINSOR. I know.

LADY A. Your grandfather was crazy when he built this wing; six rooms in a row with balconies like an hotel, and only one bath—if we hadn't put ours in.

WINSOR. [*Looking at his watch.*] Half past eleven. [*Yawns.*] Newmarket always makes me sleepy. You're keeping Morison up.

> [LADY ADELA *goes to the door, blowing a kiss.*
> CHARLES *goes up to his dressing-table and begins to brush his hair, sprinkling on essence. There is a knock on the corridor door.*]

Come in.

> [DE LEVIS *enters, clad in pyjamas and flowered dressing-gown. He is a dark, good-looking, rather Eastern young man. His face is long and disturbed.*]

Hallo! De Levis! Anything I can do for you?

DE LEVIS. [*In a voice whose faint exoticism is broken by a vexed excitement.*] I say, I'm awfully sorry,

Winsor, but I thought I'd better tell you at once. I've just had—er—rather a lot of money stolen.

WINSOR. What! [*There is something of outrage in his tone and glance, as who should say: "In my house?"*] How do you mean *stolen?*

DE LEVIS. I put it under my pillow and went to have a bath; when I came back it was gone.

WINSOR. Good Lord! How much?

DE LEVIS. Nearly a thousand—nine hundred and seventy, I think.

WINSOR. Phew!

> [*Again the faint tone of outrage, that a man should have so much money about him.*]

DE LEVIS. I sold my Rosemary filly to-day on the course to Kentman the bookie, and he paid me in notes.

WINSOR. What? That weed Dancy gave you in the Spring?

DE LEVIS. Yes. But I tried her pretty high the other day; and she's in the Cambridgeshire. I was only out of my room a quarter of an hour, and I locked my door.

WINSOR. [*Again outraged.*] You *locked*——

DE LEVIS. [*Not seeing the fine shade.*] Yes, and had the key here. [*He taps his pocket.*] Look here! [*He holds out a pocketbook.*] It's been stuffed with my shaving papers.

WINSOR. [*Between feeling that such things don't happen, and a sense that he will have to clear it up.*] This is damned awkward, De Levis.

DE LEVIS. [*With steel in his voice.*] Yes. I should like it back.

WINSOR. Have you got the numbers of the notes?

DE LEVIS. No.

WINSOR. What were they?

De Levis. One hundred, three fifties, and the rest tens and fives.

Winsor. What d'you want me to do?

De Levis. Unless there's anybody you think——

Winsor. [*Eying him.*] Is it likely?

De Levis. Then I think the police ought to see my room. It's a lot of money.

Winsor. Good Lord! We're not in Town; there'll be nobody nearer than Newmarket at this time of night— four miles.

> [*The door from the bedroom is suddenly opened and* Lady Adela *appears. She has on a lace cap over her finished hair, and the wrapper.*]

Lady A. [*Closing the door.*] What is it? Are you ill, Mr. De Levis?

Winsor. Worse; he's had a lot of money stolen. Nearly a thousand pounds.

Lady A. Gracious! Where?

De Levis. From under my pillow, Lady Adela—my door was locked—I was in the bathroom.

Lady A. But how fearfully thrilling!

Winsor. Thrilling! What's to be done? He wants it back.

Lady A. Of course! [*With sudden realization.*] Oh! But— Oh! it's quite too unpleasant!

Winsor. Yes! What am I to do? Fetch the servants out of their rooms? Search the grounds? It'll make the devil of a scandal.

De Levis. Who's next to me?

Lady A. [*Coldly.*] Oh! Mr. De Levis!

Winsor. Next to you? The Dancys on this side, and Miss Orme on the other. What's that to do with it?

De Levis. They may have heard something.

Winsor. Let's get them. But Dancy was down-stairs

when I came up. Get Morison, Adela! No, look here! When *was* this exactly? Let's have as many alibis as we can.

De Levis. Within the last twenty minutes, certainly.

Winsor. How long has Morison been up with you?

Lady A. I came up at eleven, and rang for her at once.

Winsor. [*Looking at his watch.*] Half an hour. Then she's all right. Send her for Margaret and the Dancys—there's nobody else in this wing. No; send her to bed. We don't want gossip. D'you mind going yourself, Adela?

Lady A. Consult General Canynge, Charlie.

Winsor. Right. Could you get him too? D'you really want the police, De Levis?

De Levis. [*Stung by the faint contempt in his tone of voice.*] Yes, I do.

Winsor. Then, look here, dear! Slip into my study and telephone to the police at Newmarket. There'll be somebody there; they're sure to have drunks. I'll have Treisure up, and speak to him.

[*He rings the bell.*

Lady Adela *goes out into her room and closes the door.*]

Winsor. Look here, De Levis! This isn't an hotel. It's the sort of thing that doesn't happen in a decent house. Are you sure you're not mistaken, and didn't have them stolen on the course?

De Levis. Absolutely. I counted them just before putting them under my pillow; then I locked the door and had the key here. There's only one door, you know.

Winsor. How was your window?

De Levis. Open.

Winsor. [*Drawing back the curtains of his own*

window.] You've got a balcony like this. Any sign of a ladder or anything?

DE LEVIS. No.

WINSOR. It must have been done from the window, unless some one had a skeleton key. Who knew you'd got that money? Where did Kentman pay you?

DE LEVIS. Just round the corner in the farther paddock.

WINSOR. Anybody about?

DE LEVIS. Oh, yes!

WINSOR. Suspicious?

DE LEVIS. I didn't notice anything.

WINSOR. You must have been marked down and followed here.

DE LEVIS. How would they know my room?

WINSOR. Might have got it somehow. [*A knock from the corridor.*] Come in.

> [TREISURE, *the butler, appears, a silent, grave man of almost supernatural conformity.* DE LEVIS *gives him a quick, hard look, noted and resented by* WINSOR.]

TREISURE. [*To* WINSOR.] Yes, sir?

WINSOR. Who valets Mr. De Levis?

TREISURE. Robert, sir.

WINSOR. When was he up last?

TREISURE. In the ordinary course of things, about ten o'clock, sir.

WINSOR. When did he go to bed?

TREISURE. I dismissed at eleven.

WINSOR. But did he go?

TREISURE. To the best of my knowledge. Is there anything *I* can do, sir?

WINSOR. [*Disregarding a sign from* DE LEVIS.] Look here, Treisure, Mr. De Levis has had a large sum of money taken from his bedroom within the last half-hour.

TREISURE.   Indeed, sir!

WINSOR.   Robert's quite all right, isn't he?

TREISURE.   He is, sir.

DE LEVIS.   How do you know?

[TREISURE'S *eyes rest on* DE LEVIS.]

TREISURE.   I am a pretty good judge of character, sir, if you'll excuse me.

WINSOR.   Look here, De Levis, eighty or ninety notes must have been pretty bulky.   You didn't have them on you at dinner?

DE LEVIS.   No.

WINSOR.   Where did you put them?

DE LEVIS.   In a boot, and the boot in my suitcase, and locked it.

[TREISURE *smiles faintly.*]

WINSOR.   [*Again slightly outraged by such precautions in his house.*]   And you found it locked—and took them from there to put under your pillow?

DE LEVIS.   Yes.

WINSOR.   Run your mind over things, Treisure—has any stranger been about?

TREISURE.   No, sir.

WINSOR.   This seems to have happened between 11.15 and 11.30.   Is that right?   [DE LEVIS *nods.*]   Any noise—anything outside—anything suspicious anywhere?

TREISURE.   [*Running his mind—very still.*]   No, sir.

WINSOR.   What time did you shut up?

TREISURE.   I should say about 11.15, sir.   As soon as Major Colford and Captain Dancy had finished billiards. What was Mr. De Levis doing out of his room, if I may ask, sir?

WINSOR. Having a bath; with his room locked and the key in his pocket.

TREISURE. Thank you, sir.

DE LEVIS. [*Conscious of indefinable suspicion.*] Damn it! What do you mean? I *was*.

TREISURE. I beg your pardon, sir.

WINSOR. [*Concealing a smile.*] Look here, Treisure, it's infernally awkward for everybody.

TREISURE. It is, sir.

WINSOR. What do you suggest?

TREISURE. The proper thing, sir, I suppose, would be a cordon and a complete search—in our interests.

WINSOR. I entirely refuse to suspect anybody.

TREISURE. But if Mr. De Levis feels otherwise, sir?

DE LEVIS. [*Stammering.*] I? All I know is—the money was there, and it's gone.

WINSOR. [*Compunctious.*] Quite! It's pretty sickening for you. But so it is for anybody else. However, we must do our best to get it back for you.

[*A knock on the door.*]

WINSOR. Hallo!

[TREISURE *opens the door, and* GENERAL CANYNGE *enters.*]

Oh! It's you, General. Come in. Adela's told you?

[GENERAL CANYNGE *nods. He is a slim man of about sixty, very well preserved, intensely neat and self-contained, and still in evening dress. His eyelids droop slightly, but his eyes are keen and his expression astute.*]

WINSOR. Well, General, what's the first move?

CANYNGE. [*Lifting his eyebrows.*] Mr. De Levis presses the matter?

DE LEVIS. [*Flicked again.*] Unless you think it's too plebeian of me, General Canynge—a thousand pounds.

CANYNGE. [*Dryly.*] Just so! Then we must wait for the police, Winsor. Lady Adela has got through to them. What height are these rooms from the ground, Treisure?

TREISURE. Twenty-three feet from the terrace, sir.

CANYNGE. Any ladders near?

TREISURE. One in the stables, sir, very heavy. No others within three hundred yards.

CANYNGE. Just slip down, and see whether that's been moved.

TREISURE. Very good, General.

[*He goes out.*]

DE LEVIS. [*Uneasily.*] Of course, he—I suppose you——

WINSOR. We do.

CANYNGE. You had better leave this in our hands, De Levis.

DE LEVIS. Certainly; only, the way he——

WINSOR. [*Curtly.*] Treisure has been here since he was a boy. I should as soon suspect myself.

DE LEVIS. [*Looking from one to the other—with sudden anger.*] You seem to think—! What was I to do? Take it lying down and let whoever it is get clear off? I suppose it's natural to want my money back?

[CANYNGE *looks at his nails;* WINSOR *out of the window.*]

WINSOR. [*Turning.*] Of course, De Levis!

DE LEVIS. [*Sullenly.*] Well, I'll go to my room. When the police come, perhaps you'll let me know.

[*He goes out.*]

WINSOR. Phew! Did you ever see such a dressing-gown?

[*The door is opened.* LADY ADELA *and* MARGARET ORME *come in. The latter is a vivid*

*young lady of about twenty-five in a vivid
wrapper; she is smoking a cigarette.*]

LADY A.   I've told the Dancys—she was in bed.   And
I got through to Newmarket, Charles, and Inspector Dede
is coming like the wind on a motorcycle.

MARGARET.   Did he say "like the wind," Adela?   He
must have imagination.   Isn't this gorgeous?   Poor little
Ferdy!

WINSOR.   [*Vexed.*]   You might take it seriously,
Margaret; it's pretty beastly for us all.   What time did
you come up?

MARGARET.   I came up with Adela.   Am I suspected,
Charles?   How thrilling!

WINSOR.   Did you hear anything?

MARGARET.   Only little Ferdy splashing.

WINSOR.   And saw nothing?

MARGARET.   Not even that, alas!

LADY A.   [*With a finger held up.*]   Leste!   Un peu
leste!   Oh!   Here are the Dancys.   Come in, you two!

[MABEL *and* RONALD DANCY *enter.   She is a
pretty young woman with bobbed hair, fortu-
nately, for she has just got out of bed, and is
in her nightgown and a wrapper.   DANCY is
in his smoking-jacket.   He has a pale, determined face with high cheek-bones, small,
deep-set dark eyes, reddish crisp hair, and
looks like a horseman.*]

WINSOR.   Awfully sorry to disturb you, Mrs. Dancy;
but I suppose you and Ronny haven't heard anything.
De Levis's room is just beyond Ronny's dressing-room,
you know.

MABEL.   I've been asleep nearly half an hour, and
Ronny's only just come up.

CANYNGE. Did you happen to look out of your window, Mrs. Dancy?

MABEL. Yes. I stood there quite five minutes.

CANYNGE. When?

MABEL. Just about eleven, I should think. It was raining hard then.

CANYNGE. Yes, it's just stopped. You saw nothing?

MABEL. No.

DANCY. What time does he say the money was taken?

WINSOR. Between the quarter and half past. He'd locked his door and had the key with him.

MARGARET. How quaint! Just like an hotel. Does he put his boots out?

LADY A. Don't be so naughty, Meg.

CANYNGE. When exactly did *you* come up, Dancy?

DANCY. About ten minutes ago. I'd only just got into my dressing-room before Lady Adela came. I've been writing letters in the hall since Colford and I finished billiards.

CANYNGE. You weren't up for anything in between?

DANCY. No.

MARGARET. The mystery of the gray room.

DANCY. Oughtn't the grounds to be searched for foot-marks?

CANYNGE. That's for the police.

DANCY. The deuce! Are they coming?

CANYNGE. Directly. [*A knock.*] Yes?

[TREASURE *enters.*]

Well?

TREASURE. The ladder has not been moved, General. There isn't a sign.

WINSOR. All right. Get Robert up, but don't say anything to him. By the way, we're expecting the police.

TREISURE. I trust they will not find a mare's nest, sir, if I may say so.

[*He goes.*]

WINSOR. De Levis has got wrong with Treisure. [*Suddenly.*] But, I say, what would any of us have done if *we'd* been in his shoes?

MARGARET. A thousand pounds? I can't even conceive having it.

DANCY. We probably shouldn't have found it out.

LADY A. No—but if we had.

DANCY. Come to you—as he did.

WINSOR. Yes; but there's a way of doing things.

CANYNGE. We shouldn't have wanted the police.

MARGARET. No. That's it. The hotel touch.

LADY A. Poor young man; I think we're rather hard on him.

WINSOR. He sold that weed you gave him, Dancy, to Kentman, the bookie, and these were the proceeds.

DANCY. Oh!

WINSOR. He'd tried her high, he said.

DANCY. [*Grimly.*] He would.

MABEL. Oh! Ronny, what bad luck!

WINSOR. He must have been followed here. [*At the window.*] After rain like that, there ought to be footmarks.

[*The splutter of a motorcycle is heard.*]

MARGARET. Here's the wind!

WINSOR. What's the move now, General?

CANYNGE. You and I had better see the Inspector in De Levis's room, Winsor. [*To the others.*] If you'll all be handy, in case he wants to put questions for himself.

MARGARET. I hope he'll want me; it's just too thrilling.

DANCY. I hope he won't want me; I'm dog-tired. Come on, Mabel.

[*He puts his arm in his wife's.*]

CANYNGE. Just a minute, Charles.

[*He draws close to* WINSOR *as the others are departing to their rooms.*]

WINSOR. Yes, General?

CANYNGE. We must be careful with this Inspector fellow. If he pitches hastily on somebody in the house it'll be very disagreeable.

WINSOR. By Jove! It *will*.

CANYNGE. We don't want to rouse any ridiculous suspicion.

WINSOR. Quite. [*A knock.*] Come in!

[TREISURE *enters.*]

TREISURE. Inspector Dede, sir.

WINSOR. Show him in.

TREISURE. Robert is in readiness, sir; but I could swear he knows nothing about it.

WINSOR. All right.

[TREISURE *reopens the door, and says: "Come in, please." The* INSPECTOR *enters, blue, formal, mustachioed, with a peaked cap in his hand.*]

WINSOR. Good evening, Inspector. Sorry to have brought you out at this time of night.

INSPECTOR. Good evenin', sir. Mr. Winsor? You're the owner here, I think?

WINSOR. Yes. General Canynge.

INSPECTOR. Good evenin', General. I understand, a large sum of money?

WINSOR. Yes. Shall we go straight to the room it was taken from? One of my guests, Mr. De Levis. It's the third room on the left.

CANYNGE. We've not been in there yet, Inspector; in fact, we've done nothing, except to find out that the stable ladder has not been moved. We haven't even searched the grounds.

INSPECTOR. Right, sir; I've brought a man with me.

[*They go out.*]

CURTAIN. INTERVAL OF A MINUTE

SCENE II*

The bedroom of DE LEVIS *is the same in shape as* WINSOR'S *dressing-room, except that there is only one door—to the corridor. The furniture, however, is differently arranged; a small four-poster bedstead stands against the wall, right back, jutting into the room. A chair, on which* DE LEVIS'S *clothes are thrown, stands at its foot. There is a dressing-table against the wall to the left of the open windows, where the curtains are drawn back and a stone balcony is seen. Against the wall to the right of the window is a chest of drawers, and a wash-stand is against the wall, left. On a small table to the right of the bed an electric reading-lamp is turned up, and there is a light over the dressing-table. The* INSPECTOR *is standing plumb centre looking at the bed, and* DE LEVIS *by the back of the chair at the foot of the bed.* WINSOR *and* CANYNGE *are close to the door, right forward.*

INSPECTOR. [*Finishing a note.*] Now, sir, if this is the room as you left it for your bath, just show us exactly

*The same set is used for this scene, with the different arrangement of furniture, as specified.

what you did after takin' the pocketbook from the suit-case. Where was that, by the way?

DE LEVIS. [*Pointing.*] Where it is now—under the dressing-table.

> [*He comes forward to the front of the chair, opens the pocketbook, goes through the pretense of counting his shaving papers, closes the pocketbook, takes it to the head of the bed and slips it under the pillow. Makes the motion of taking up his pyjamas, crosses below the* INSPECTOR *to the wash-stand, takes up a bath sponge, crosses to the door, takes out the key, opens the door.*]

INSPECTOR. [*Writing.*] We now have the room as it was when the theft was committed. Reconstruct accordin' to 'uman nature, gentlemen—assumin' the thief to be in the room, what would he try first?—the clothes, the dressin'-table, the suitcase, the chest of drawers, and last the bed.

> [*He moves accordingly, examining the glass on the dressing-table, the surface of the suit-cases, and the handles of the drawers, with a spy-glass, for finger-marks.*]

CANYNGE. [*Sotto voce to* WINSOR.] The order would have been just the other way.

> [*The* INSPECTOR *goes on hands and knees and examines the carpet between the window and the bed.*]

DE LEVIS. Can I come in again?

INSPECTOR. [*Standing up.*] Did you open the window, sir, or was it open when you first came in?

DE LEVIS. I opened it.

INSPECTOR. Drawin' the curtains back first?

DE LEVIS. Yes.

INSPECTOR. [*Sharply.*] Are you sure there was nobody in the room already?

DE LEVIS. [*Taken aback.*] I don't know. I never thought. I didn't look under the bed, if you mean that.

INSPECTOR. [*Jotting.*] Did not look under bed. Did you look under it after the theft?

DE LEVIS. No. I didn't.

INSPECTOR. Ah! Now, what *did* you do after you came back from your bath? Just give us that precisely.

DE LEVIS. Locked the door and left the key in. Put back my sponge, and took off my dressing-gown and put it there. [*He points to the foot-rails of the bed.*] Then I drew the curtains, again.

INSPECTOR. Shutting the window?

DE LEVIS. No. I got into bed, felt for my watch to see the time. My hand struck the pocketbook, and somehow it felt thinner. I took it out, looked into it, and found the notes gone, and these shaving papers instead.

INSPECTOR. Let me have a look at those, sir. [*He applies the spy-glasses.*] And then?

DE LEVIS. I think I just sat on the bed.

INSPECTOR. Thinkin' and cursin' a bit, I suppose. Ye-es?

DE LEVIS. Then I put on my dressing-gown and went straight to Mr. Winsor.

INSPECTOR. Not lockin' the door?

DE LEVIS. No.

INSPECTOR. Exactly. [*With a certain finality.*] Now, sir, what time did you come up?

DE LEVIS. About eleven.

INSPECTOR. Precise, if you can give it me.

DE LEVIS. Well. I *know* it was 11.15 when I put my watch under my pillow, before I went to the bath, and I suppose I'd been about a quarter of an hour undressing. I should say after eleven, if anything.

INSPECTOR. Just undressin'? Didn't look over your bettin'-book?

DE LEVIS. No.

INSPECTOR. No prayers or anything?

DE LEVIS. No.

INSPECTOR. Pretty slippy with your undressin' as a rule?

DE LEVIS. Yes. Say five past eleven.

INSPECTOR. Mr. Winsor, what time did the gentleman come to you?

WINSOR. Half past eleven.

INSPECTOR. How do you fix that, sir?

WINSOR. I'd just looked at the time, and told my wife to send her maid off.

INSPECTOR. Then we've got it fixed between 11.15 and 11.30. [*Jots.*] Now, sir, before we go further I'd like to see your butler and the footman that valets this gentleman.

WINSOR. [*With distaste.*] Very well, Inspector; only—my butler has been with us from a boy.

INSPECTOR. Quite so. This is just clearing the ground, sir.

WINSOR. General, d'you mind touching that bell?

[CANYNGE *rings a bell by the bed.*]

INSPECTOR. Well, gentlemen, there are four possibilities. Either the thief was here all the time, waiting under the bed, and slipped out after this gentleman had gone to Mr. Winsor. Or he came in with a key that fits the lock; and I'll want to see all the keys in the house. Or he came in with a skeleton key and out by the window, probably droppin' from the balcony. Or he came in by the window with a rope or ladder and out the same way.

[*Pointing.*] There's a footmark here from a big boot which has been out-of-doors since it rained.

CANYNGE. Inspector—you er—walked up to the window when you first came into the room.

INSPECTOR. ⌈*Stiffly.*] I had not overlooked that, General.

CANYNGE. Of course.

[*A knock on the door relieves a certain tension.*]

WINSOR. Come in.

[*The footman* ROBERT, *a fresh-faced young man, enters, followed by* TREISURE.]

INSPECTOR. You valet Mr.—Mr. De Levis, I think?

ROBERT. Yes, sir.

INSPECTOR. At what time did you take his clothes and boots?

ROBERT. Ten o'clock, sir.

INSPECTOR. [*With a pounce.*] Did you happen to look under his bed?

ROBERT. No, sir.

INSPECTOR. Did you come up again, to bring the clothes back?

ROBERT. No, sir; they're still down-stairs.

INSPECTOR. Did you come up again for anything?

ROBERT. No, sir.

INSPECTOR. What time did you go to bed?

ROBERT. Just after eleven, sir.

INSPECTOR. [*Scrutinizing him.*] Now, be careful. Did you go to bed at all?

ROBERT. No, sir.

INSPECTOR. Then why did you say you did? There's been a theft here, and anything you say may be used against you.

ROBERT. Yes, sir. I meant, I went to my room.

INSPECTOR. Where is your room?

ROBERT. On the ground floor, at the other end of the right wing, sir.

WINSOR. It's the extreme end of the house from this, Inspector. He's with the other two footmen.

INSPECTOR. Were you there alone?

ROBERT. No, sir. Thomas and Frederick was there too.

TREISURE. That's right; I've seen them.

INSPECTOR. [*Holding up his hand for silence.*] Were you out of the room again after you went in?

ROBERT. No, sir.

INSPECTOR. What were you doing, if you didn't go to bed?

ROBERT. [*To* WINSOR.] Beggin' your pardon, sir, we were playin' Bridge.

INSPECTOR. Very good. You can go. I'll see *them* later on.

ROBERT. Yes, sir. They'll say the same as me.

> [*He goes out, leaving a smile on the face of all except the* INSPECTOR *and* DE LEVIS.]

INSPECTOR. [*Sharply.*] Call him back.

> [TREISURE *calls* "Robert," *and the* FOOTMAN *re-enters.*]

ROBERT. Yes, sir?

INSPECTOR. Did you notice anything particular about Mr. De Levis's clothes?

ROBERT. Only that they were very good, sir.

INSPECTOR. I mean—anything peculiar?

ROBERT. [*After reflection.*] Yes, sir.

INSPECTOR. Well?

ROBERT. A pair of his boots this evenin' was reduced to one, sir.

INSPECTOR. What did you make of that?

ROBERT. I thought he might have thrown the other at a cat or something.

INSPECTOR. Did you look for it?

ROBERT. No, sir; I meant to draw his attention to it in the morning.

INSPECTOR. Very good.

ROBERT. Yes, sir.

[*He goes again.*]

INSPECTOR. [*Looking at* DE LEVIS.] Well, sir, there's *your* story corroborated.

DE LEVIS. [*Stiffly.*] I don't know why it should need corroboration, Inspector.

INSPECTOR. In my experience, you can never have too much of that. [*To* WINSOR.] I understand there's a lady in the room on this side [*pointing left*] and a gentleman on this [*pointing right*]. Were they in their rooms?

WINSOR. Miss Orme was; Captain Dancy not.

INSPECTOR. Do they know of the affair?

WINSOR. Yes.

INSPECTOR. Well, I'd just like the keys of their doors for a minute. My man will get them.

[*He goes to the door, opens it, and speaks to a* CONSTABLE *in the corridor.*]

[*To* TREISURE.] You can go with him.

[TREISURE *goes out.*]

In the meantime I'll just examine the balcony.

[*He goes out on the balcony, followed by* DE LEVIS.]

WINSOR. [*To* CANYNGE.] Damn De Levis and his money! It's deuced invidious, all this, General.

CANYNGE. The Inspector's no earthly.

[*There is a simultaneous re-entry of the*

> INSPECTOR *from the balcony and of* TREISURE
> *and the* CONSTABLE *from the corridor.*]

CONSTABLE. [*Handing key.*] Room on the left, sir.
[*Handing key.*] Room on the right, sir.

> [*The* INSPECTOR *tries the keys in the door,
> watched with tension by the others. The keys
> fail.*]

INSPECTOR. Put them back.

> [*Hands keys to* CONSTABLE, *who goes out, fol-
> lowed by* TREISURE.]

I'll have to try every key in the house, sir.

WINSOR. Inspector, do you really think it necessary
to disturb the whole house and knock up all my guests?
It's most disagreeable, all this, you know. The loss of
the money is not such a great matter. Mr. De Levis has
a very large income.

CANYNGE. You could get the numbers of the notes
from Kentman the book-maker, Inspector; he'll probably
have the big ones, anyway.

INSPECTOR. [*Shaking his head.*] A bookie. I don't
suppose he will, sir. It's come and go with them, all the
time.

WINSOR. We don't want a Meldon Court scandal,
Inspector.

INSPECTOR. Well, Mr. Winsor, I've formed my theory.

> [*As he speaks,* DE LEVIS *comes in from the
> balcony.*]

And I don't say to try the keys is necessary to it; but
strictly, I ought to exhaust the possibilities.

WINSOR. What do you say, De Levis? D'you want
everybody in the house knocked up so that their keys can
be tried?

DE LEVIS. [*Whose face, since his return, expresses a
curious excitement.*] No, I don't.

INSPECTOR. Very well, gentlemen. In my opinion the thief walked in before the door was locked, probably during dinner; and was under the bed. He escaped by dropping from the balcony—the creeper at that corner [*he points stage left*] has been violently wrenched. I'll go down now, and examine the grounds, and I'll see you again, sir. [*He makes another entry in his note-book.*] Good night, then, gentlemen!

CANYNGE. Good night!

WINSOR. [*With relief.*] I'll come with you, Inspector.

[*He escorts him to the door, and they go out.*]

DE LEVIS. [*Suddenly.*] General, I know who took them.

CANYNGE. The deuce you do! Are you following the Inspector's theory?

DE LEVIS. [*Contemptuously.*] That ass! [*Pulling the shaving papers out of the case.*] No! The man who put those there was clever and cool enough to wrench that creeper off the balcony, as a blind. Come and look here, General. [*He goes to the window; the* GENERAL *follows.* DE LEVIS *points stage right.*] See the rail of my balcony, and the rail of the next? [*He holds up the cord of his dressing-gown, stretching his arms out.*] I've measured it with this. Just over seven feet, that's all! If a man can take a standing jump on to a narrow bookcase four feet high and balance there, he'd make nothing of that. And, look here! [*He goes out on the balcony and returns with a bit of broken creeper in his hand, and holds it out into the light.*] Some one's stood on that—the stalk's crushed—the inner corner too, where he'd naturally stand when he took his jump back.

CANYNGE. [*After examining it—stiffly.*] That other

balcony is young Dancy's, Mr. De Levis; a soldier and a gentleman. This is an extraordinary insinuation.

DE LEVIS.   Accusation.

CANYNGE.   What!

DE LEVIS.   I have intuitions, General; it's in my blood. I see the whole thing.   Dancy came up, watched me into the bathroom, tried my door, slipped back into his dressing-room, saw my window was open, took that jump, sneaked the notes, filled the case up with these, wrenched the creeper there   [*he points stage left*]   for a blind, jumped back, and slipped down-stairs again.   It didn't take him four minutes altogether.

CANYNGE.   [*Very gravely.*]   This is outrageous, De Levis.   Dancy says he was down-stairs all the time.   You must either withdraw unreservedly, or I must confront you with him.

DE LEVIS.   If he'll return the notes and apologize, I'll do nothing—except cut him in future.   He gave me that filly, you know, as a hopeless weed, and he's been pretty sick ever since, that he was such a flat as not to see how good she was.   Besides, he's hard up, I know.

CANYNGE.   [*After a vexed turn up and down the room.*]   It's mad, sir, to jump to conclusions like this.

DE LEVIS.   Not so mad as the conclusion Dancy jumped to when he lighted on my balcony.

CANYNGE.   Nobody could have taken this money who did not know you had it.

DE LEVIS.   How do you know that he didn't?

CANYNGE.   Do you know that he did?

DE LEVIS.   I haven't the least doubt of it.

CANYNGE.   Without any proof.   This is very ugly, De Levis.   I must tell Winsor.

DE LEVIS.   [*Angrily.*]   Tell the whole blooming lot. You think I've no feelers, but I've felt the atmosphere

here, I can tell you, General. If I were in Dancy's shoes and he in mine, your tone to me would be very different.

CANYNGE. [*Suavely frigid.*] I'm not aware of using any tone, as you call it. But this is a private house, Mr. De Levis, and something is due to our host and to the *esprit de corps* that exists among gentlemen.

DE LEVIS. Since when is a thief a gentleman? Thick as thieves—a good motto, isn't it?

CANYNGE. That's enough! [*He goes to the door, but stops before opening it.*] Now, look here! I have some knowledge of the world. Once an accusation like this passes beyond these walls no one can foresee the consequences. Captain Dancy is a gallant fellow, with a fine record as a soldier; and only just married. If he's as innocent as—Christ—mud will stick to him, unless the real thief is found. In the old days of swords, either you or he would not have gone out of this room alive. If you persist in this absurd accusation, you will *both* of you go out of this room dead in the eyes of Society: you for bringing it, he for being the object of it.

DE LEVIS. Society! Do you think I don't know that I'm only tolerated for my money? Society can't add injury to insult and have my money as well, that's all. If the notes are restored, I'll keep my mouth shut; if they're not, I shan't. I'm certain I'm right. I ask nothing better than to be confronted with Dancy; but, if you prefer it, deal with him in your own way—for the sake of your *esprit de corps*.

CANYNGE. 'Pon my soul, Mr. De Levis, you go too far.

DE LEVIS. Not so far as I shall go, General Canynge, if those notes aren't given back.

[WINSOR *comes in.*]

WINSOR. Well, De Levis, I'm afraid that's all we can

do for the present. So very sorry this should have happened in my house.

CANYNGE. [*After a silence.*] There's a development, Winsor. Mr. De Levis accuses one of your guests.

WINSOR. What?

CANYNGE. Of jumping from his balcony to this, taking the notes, and jumping back. I've done my best to dissuade him from indulging the fancy—without success. Dancy must be told.

DE LEVIS. You can deal with Dancy in your own way. All I want is the money back.

CANYNGE. [*Drily.*] Mr. De Levis feels that he is only valued for his money, so that it is essential for him to have it back.

WINSOR. Damn it! This is monstrous, De Levis. I've known Ronald Dancy since he was a boy.

CANYNGE. You talk about adding injury to insult, De Levis. What do you call such treatment of a man who gave you the mare out of which you made this thousand pounds?

DE LEVIS. I didn't want the mare; I took her as a favor.

CANYNGE. With an eye to possibilities, I venture to think—the principle guides a good many transactions.

DE LEVIS. [*As if flicked on a raw spot.*] In my race, do you mean?

CANYNGE. [*Coldly.*] I said nothing of the sort.

DE LEVIS. No; you don't *say* these things, any of you.

CANYNGE. Nor did I think it.

DE LEVIS. Dancy does.

WINSOR. Really, De Levis, if this is the way you repay hospitality——

DE LEVIS. Hospitality that skins my feelings and costs me a thousand pounds!

CANYNGE. Go and get Dancy, Winsor; but don't say anything to him.

[WINSOR *goes out.*]

CANYNGE. Perhaps you will kindly control yourself, and leave this to me.

[DE LEVIS *turns to the window and lights a cigarette.* WINSOR *comes back, followed by* DANCY.]

CANYNGE. For Winsor's sake, Dancy, we don't want any scandal or fuss about this affair. We've tried to make the police understand that. To my mind the whole thing turns on our finding who knew that De Levis had this money. It's about that we want to consult you.

WINSOR. Kentman paid De Levis round the corner in the farther paddock, he says.

[DE LEVIS *turns round from the window, so that he and* DANCY *are staring at each other.*]

CANYNGE. Did you hear anything that throws light, Dancy? As it was your filly originally, we thought perhaps you might.

DANCY. I? No.

CANYNGE. Didn't hear of the sale on the course at all?

DANCY. No.

CANYNGE. Then you can't suggest any one who could have known? Nothing else was taken, you see.

DANCY. De Levis is known to be rolling, as I am known to be stony.

CANYNGE. There are a good many people still rolling, besides Mr. De Levis, but not many people with so large a sum in their pocketbooks.

DANCY. He won two races.

DE LEVIS. Do you suggest that I bet in ready money?

DANCY. I don't know how you bet, and I don't care.

CANYNGE. You can't help us, then?

DANCY. No, I can't. Anything else?

[*He looks fixedly at* DE LEVIS.]

CANYNGE. [*Putting his hand on* DANCY'S *arm.*] Nothing else, thank you, Dancy.

[DANCY *goes.* CANYNGE *puts his hand up to his face. A moment's silence.*]

WINSOR. You see, De Levis? He didn't even know you'd got the money.

DE LEVIS. Very conclusive.

WINSOR. Well! You *are*——!

[*There is a knock on the door, and the* INSPECTOR *enters.*]

INSPECTOR. I'm just going, gentlemen. The grounds, I'm sorry to say, have yielded nothing. It's a bit of a puzzle.

CANYNGE. You've searched thoroughly?

INSPECTOR. We have, General. I can pick up nothing near the terrace.

WINSOR. [*After a look at* DE LEVIS, *whose face expresses too much.*] H'm! You'll take it up from the other end, then, Inspector?

INSPECTOR. Well, we'll see what we can do with the book-makers about the numbers, sir. Before I go, gentlemen—you've had time to think it over—there's no one you suspect in the house, I suppose?

[DE LEVIS'S *face is alive and uncertain.* CANYNGE *is staring at him very fixedly.*]

WINSOR. [*Emphatically.*] No.

[DE LEVIS *turns and goes out on to the balcony.*]

INSPECTOR. If you're coming in to the racing to-morrow, sir, you might give us a call. I'll have seen Kentman by then.

WINSOR. Right you are, Inspector. Good night, and many thanks.

INSPECTOR. You're welcome, sir.

[*He goes out.*]

WINSOR. Gosh! I thought that chap [*with a nod toward the balcony*] was going to—! Look here, General, we *must* stop his tongue. Imagine it going the rounds. They may never find the real thief, you know. It's the very devil for Dancy.

CANYNGE. Winsor! Dancy's sleeve was damp.

WINSOR. How d'you mean?

CANYNGE. Quite damp. It's been raining.

[*The two look at each other.*]

WINSOR. I—I don't follow——

[*His voice is hesitative and lower, showing that he does.*]

CANYNGE. It was coming down hard; a minute out in it would have been enough——

[*He motions with his chin toward the balcony.*]

WINSOR. [*Hastily.*] He must have been out on his balcony since.

CANYNGE. It stopped before I came up, half an hour ago.

WINSOR. He's been leaning on the wet stone, then.

CANYNGE. With the outside of the *upper* part of the arm?

WINSOR. Against the wall, perhaps. There may be a dozen explanations. [*Very low and with great concentration.*] I entirely and absolutely refuse to believe anything of the sort against Ronald Dancy—in my house. Dash it, General, we must do as we'd be done by. It hits us all—it hits us all. The thing's intolerable.

CANYNGE. I agree. Intolerable. [*Raising his voice.*] Mr. De Levis!

[DE LEVIS *returns into view, in the centre of the open window.*]

CANYNGE. [*With cold decision.*] Young Dancy was an officer and is a gentleman; this insinuation is pure supposition, and you must not make it. Do you understand me?

DE LEVIS. My tongue is still mine, General, if my money isn't!

CANYNGE. [*Unmoved.*] Must not. You're a member of three Clubs, you want to be member of a fourth. No one who makes such an insinuation against a fellow guest in a country house, except on absolute proof, can do so without complete ostracism. Have we your word to say nothing?

DE LEVIS. Social blackmail? H'm!

CANYNGE. Not at all—simple warning. If you consider it necessary in your interests to start this scandal —no matter how, we shall consider it necessary in ours to dissociate ourselves completely from one who so recklessly disregards the unwritten code.

DE LEVIS. Do you think your code applies to me? Do you, General?

CANYNGE. To any one who aspires to be a gentleman, sir.

DE LEVIS. Ah! But you haven't known *me* since I was a boy.

CANYNGE. Make up your mind.
        [*A pause.*]

DE LEVIS. I'm not a fool, General. I know perfectly well that you can get me outed.

CANYNGE. [*Icily.*] Well?

DE LEVIS. [*Sullenly.*] I'll say nothing about it, unless I get more proof.

CANYNGE. Good! We have implicit faith in Dancy.
        [*There is a moment's encounter of eyes; the*
        GENERAL'S *steady, shrewd, impassive;*

WINSOR'S *angry and defiant;* DE LEVIS'S *mocking, a little triumphant, malicious. Then* CANYNGE *and* WINSOR *go to the door, and pass out.*]

DE LEVIS. [*To himself.*] Rats!

CURTAIN

ACT II

SCENE I

Afternoon, three weeks later, in the card-room of a London Club. A fire is burning, left. A door, right, leads to the billiard-room. Rather left of centre, at a card-table, LORD ST ERTH, *an old John Bull, sits facing the audience; to his right is* GENERAL CANYNGE, *to his left* AUGUSTUS BORRING, *an essential Clubman, about thirty-five years old, with a very slight and rather becoming stammer or click in his speech. The fourth Bridge-player,* CHARLES WINSOR, *stands with his back to the fire.*

BORRING. And the r-rub.

WINSOR. By George! You do hold cards, Borring.

ST ERTH. [*Who has lost.*] Not a patch on the old whist—this game. Don't know why I play it—never did.

CANYNGE. St Erth, shall we raise the flag for whist again?

WINSOR. No go, General. You can't go back on pace. No getting a man to walk when he knows he can fly. The young men won't look at it.

BORRING. Better develop it so that t-two can sit out, General.

St Erth. We ought to have stuck to the old game. Wish I'd gone to Newmarket, Canynge, in spite of the weather.

Canynge. [*Looking at his watch.*] Let's hear what's won the Cambridgeshire. Ring, won't you, Winsor?

[Winsor *rings.*]

St Erth. By the way, Canynge, young De Levis was blackballed.

Canynge. What!

St Erth. I looked in on my way down.

[Canynge *sits very still, and* Winsor *utters a disturbed sound.*]

Borring. But of c-course he was, General. What did you expect?

[*A* Footman *enters.*]

Footman. Yes, my lord?

St Erth. What won the Cambridgeshire?

Footman. Rosemary, my lord. Sherbet second; Barbizon third. Nine to one the winner.

Winsor. Thank you. That's all.

[Footman *goes.*]

Borring. Rosemary! And De Levis sold her! But he got a good p-price, I suppose.

[*The other three look at him.*]

St Erth. Many a slip between price and pocket, young man.

Canynge. Cut.

[*They cut.*]

Borring. I say, is that the yarn that's going round about his having had a lot of m-money stolen in a country house? By Jove! He'll be pretty s-sick.

Winsor. You and I, Borring.

[*He sits down in* Canynge's *chair, and the* General *takes his place by the fire.*]

BORRING. Phew! Won't Dancy be mad! He gave that filly away to save her keep. He was rather pleased to find somebody who'd take her. Kentman must have won a p-pot. She was at thirty-threes a fortnight ago.

ST ERTH. All the money goes to fellows who don't know a horse from a haystack.

CANYNGE. [*Profoundly.*] And care less. Yes! We want men racing to whom a horse means something.

BORRING. I thought the horse m-meant the same to every one, General—chance to get the b-better of one's neighbor.

CANYNGE. [*With feeling.*] The horse is a noble animal, sir, as you'd know if you'd owed your life to them as often as I have.

BORRING. They always try to *take* mine, General. I shall never belong to the noble f-fellowship of the horse.

ST ERTH. [*Drily.*] Evidently. Deal!

[*As* BORRING *begins to deal the door is opened and* MAJOR COLFORD *appears—a lean and mustached cavalryman.*]

BORRING. Hallo, C-Colford.

COLFORD. General!

[*Something in the tone of his voice brings them all to a standstill.*]

COLFORD. I want your advice. Young De Levis in there [*he points to the billiard-room from which he has just come*] has started a blasphemous story——

CANYNGE. One moment. Mr. Borring, d'you mind——

COLFORD. It makes no odds, General. Four of us in there heard him. He's saying it was Ronald Dancy robbed him down at Winsor's. The fellow's mad over losing the price of that filly now she's won the Cambridge-shire.

BORRING. [*All ears.*] Dancy! Great S-Scott!

COLFORD. Dancy's in the Club. If he hadn't been I'd have taken it on myself to wring the bounder's neck.

[WINSOR *and* BORRING *have risen.* ST ERTH *alone remains seated.*]

CANYNGE. [*After consulting* ST ERTH *with a look.*] Ask De Levis to be good enough to come in here. Borring, you might see that Dancy doesn't leave the Club. We shall want him. Don't say anything to him, and use your tact to keep people off.

[BORRING *goes out, followed by* COLFORD.]

WINSOR. Result of hearing he was blackballed—pretty slippy.

CANYNGE. St Erth, I told you there was good reason when I asked you to back young De Levis. Winsor and I knew of this insinuation; I wanted to keep his tongue quiet. It's just wild assertion; to have it bandied about was unfair to Dancy. The duel used to keep people's tongues in order.

ST ERTH. H'm! It never settled anything, except who could shoot straightest.

COLFORD. [*Reappearing.*] De Levis says he's nothing to add to what he said to you before, on the subject.

CANYNGE. Kindly tell him that if he wishes to remain a member of this Club he must account to the Committee for such a charge against a fellow member. Four of us are here, and form a quorum.

[COLFORD *goes out again.*]

ST ERTH. Did Kentman ever give the police the numbers of those notes, Winsor?

WINSOR. He only had the numbers of two—the hundred, and one of the fifties.

ST ERTH. And they haven't traced 'em?

Winsor. Not yet.

> [*As he speaks,* De Levis *comes in. He is in a highly colored, not to say excited, state.* Colford *follows him.*]

De Levis. Well, General Canynge! It's a little too strong all this—a little too strong.

> [*Under emotion his voice is slightly more exotic.*]

Canynge. [*Calmly.*] It is obvious, Mr. De Levis, that you and Captain Dancy can't both remain members of this Club. We ask you for an explanation before requesting one resignation or the other.

De Levis. You've let me down.

Canynge. What!

De Levis. Well, I shall tell people that you and Lord St Erth backed me up for one Club, and asked me to resign from another.

Canynge. It's a matter of indifference to me, sir, what you tell people.

St Erth. [*Drily.*] You seem a venomous young man.

De Levis. I'll tell you what seems to me venomous, my lord—chasing a man like a pack of hounds because he isn't your breed.

Canynge. You appear to have your breed on the brain, sir. Nobody else does, so far as I know.

De Levis. Suppose I had robbed Dancy, would you chase him out for complaining of it?

Colford. My God! If you repeat that——

Canynge. Steady, Colford!

Winsor. You make this accusation that Dancy stole your money in my house on no proof—no proof; and you expect Dancy's friends to treat you as if you were a gentleman! That's too strong, if you like!

DE LEVIS. No proof? Kentman told me at New-market yesterday that Dancy *did* know of the sale. He told Goole, and Goole says that he himself spoke of it to Dancy.

WINSOR. Well—if he did?

DE LEVIS. Dancy told you he *didn't* know of it in General Canynge's presence, and mine. [*To* CANYNGE.] You can't deny that, if you want to.

CANYNGE. Choose your expressions more nicely, please!

DE LEVIS. Proof! Did they find any footmarks in the grounds below that torn creeper? Not a sign! You saw how he can jump; he won ten pounds from me that same evening betting on what he knew was a certainty. That's your Dancy—a common sharper!

CANYNGE. [*Nodding toward the billiard-room.*] Are those fellows still in there, Colford?

COLFORD. Yes.

CANYNGE. Then bring Dancy up, will you? But don't say anything to him.

COLFORD. [*To* DE LEVIS.] You may think yourself damned lucky if he doesn't break your neck.

[*He goes out. The three who are left with* DE LEVIS *avert their eyes from him.*]

DE LEVIS. [*Smouldering.*] I have a memory, and a sting too. Yes, my lord—since you are good enough to call me venomous. [*To* CANYNGE.] I quite understand —I'm marked for Coventry now, whatever happens. Well, I'll take Dancy with me.

ST ERTH. [*To himself.*] This Club has always had a decent, quiet name.

WINSOR. Are you going to retract, and apologize in front of Dancy and the members who heard you?

DE LEVIS. No fear!

St Erth. You must be a very rich man, sir. A jury is likely to take the view that money can hardly compensate for an accusation of that sort.

[De Levis *stands silent*.]

Canynge. Courts of law require proof.

St Erth. He can make it a criminal action.

Winsor. Unless you stop this at once, you may find yourself in prison. *If* you can stop it, that is.

St Erth. If I were young Dancy, nothing should induce me.

De Levis. But you didn't steal my money, Lord St Erth.

St Erth. You're deuced positive, sir. So far as I could understand it, there were a dozen ways you could have been robbed. It seems to me you value other men's reputations very lightly.

De Levis. Confront me with Dancy and give me fair play.

Winsor. [*Aside to* Canynge.] Is it fair to Dancy not to let him know?

Canynge. Our duty is to the Club now, Winsor. We must have this cleared up.

[Colford *comes in, followed by* Borring *and* Dancy.]

St Erth. Captain Dancy, a serious accusation has been made against you by this gentleman in the presence of several members of the Club.

Dancy. What is it?

St Erth. That you robbed him of that money at Winsor's.

Dancy. [*Hard and tense*.] Indeed! On what grounds is he good enough to say that?

De Levis. [*Tense too*.] You gave me that filly to save yourself her keep, and you've been mad about it ever since; you knew from Goole that I had sold her to Kent-man and been paid in cash, yet I heard you myself deny that you knew it.   You had the next room to me, and you can jump like a cat, as we saw that evening; I found some creepers crushed by a weight on my balcony on that side. When I went to the bath your door was open, and when I came back it was shut.

CANYNGE.   That's the first we have heard about the door.

DE LEVIS.   I remembered it afterward.

ST ERTH.   Well, Dancy?

DANCY.   [*With intense deliberation.*]   I'll settle this matter with any weapons, when and where he likes.

ST ERTH.   [*Drily.*]   It can't be settled that way—you know very well.   You must take it to the Courts, unless he retracts.

DANCY.   Will you retract?

DE LEVIS.   Why did you tell General Canynge you didn't know Kentman had paid me in cash?

DANCY.   Because I didn't.

DE LEVIS.   Then Kentman and Goole lied—for no reason?

DANCY.   That's nothing to do with me.

DE LEVIS.   If you were down-stairs all the time, as you say, why was your door first open and then shut?

DANCY.   Being down-stairs, how should I know?   The wind, probably.

DE LEVIS.   I should like to hear what your wife says about it.

DANCY.   Leave my wife alone, you damned Jew!

ST ERTH.   Captain Dancy!

DE LEVIS.   [*White with rage.*]   Thief!

DANCY.   Will you fight?

De Levis. You're very smart—dead men tell no tales. No! Bring your action, and we shall see.

[Dancy *takes a step toward him, but* Canynge *and* Winsor *interpose.*]

St Erth. That'll do, Mr. De Levis; we won't keep you. [*He looks round.*] Kindly consider your membership suspended till this matter has been threshed out.

De Levis. [*Tremulous with anger.*] Don't trouble yourselves about my membership. I resign it. [*To* Dancy.] You called me a damned Jew. My race was old when you were all savages. I am proud to be a Jew. *Au revoir,* in the Courts.

[*He goes out, and silence follows his departure.*]

St Erth. Well, Captain Dancy?

Dancy. If the brute won't fight, what am I to do, sir?

St Erth. We've told you—take action, to clear your name.

Dancy. Colford, you saw me in the hall writing letters after our game.

Colford. Certainly I did; you were there when I went to the smoking-room.

Canynge. How long after you left the billiard-room?

Colford. About five minutes.

Dancy. It's impossible for me to prove that I was there all the time.

Canynge. It's for De Levis to prove what he asserts. You heard what he said about Goole?

Dancy. If he told me, I didn't take it in.

St Erth. This concerns the honor of the Club. Are you going to take action?

Dancy. [*Slowly.*] That is a very expensive business, Lord St Erth, and I'm hard up. I must think it over.

[*He looks round from face to face.*]   Am I to take it that there is a doubt in your minds, gentlemen?

COLFORD.   [*Emphatically.*]   No.

CANYNGE.   That's not the question, Dancy. This accusation was overheard by various members, and we represent the Club. If you don't take action, judgment will naturally go by default.

DANCY.   I might prefer to look on the whole thing as beneath contempt.

> [*He turns and goes out.   When he is gone there is an even longer silence than after* DE LEVIS's *departure.*]

ST ERTH.   [*Abruptly.*]   I don't like it.

WINSOR.   I've known him all his life.

COLFORD.   You may have my head if he did it, Lord St Erth.   He and I have been in too many holes together. By Gad! My toe itches for that fellow's butt end.

BORRING.   I'm sorry; but has he t-taken it in quite the right way? I should have thought—hearing it s-sud-denly——

COLFORD.   Bosh!

WINSOR.   It's perfectly damnable for him.

ST ERTH.   More damnable if he did it, Winsor.

BORRING.   The Courts are b-beastly distrustful, don't you know.

COLFORD.   His word's good enough for me.

CANYNGE.   We're as anxious to believe Dancy as you, Colford, for the honor of the Army and the Club.

WINSOR.   Of course, he'll bring a case, when he's thought it over.

ST ERTH.   What are we to do in the meantime?

COLFORD.   If Dancy's asked to resign, you may take my resignation too.

Borring.   I thought his wanting to f-fight him a bit screeny.

Colford.   Wouldn't you have wanted a shot at the brute? A law-court? Pah!

Winsor.   Yes. What'll be his position even if he wins?

Borring.   Damages, and a stain on his c-character.

Winsor.   Quite so, unless they find the real thief. People always believe the worst.

Colford.   [*Glaring at* Borring.]   They do.

Canynge.   There *is* no decent way out of a thing of this sort.

St Erth.   No. [*Rising.*]   It leaves a bad taste. I'm sorry for young Mrs. Dancy—poor woman!

Borring.   Are you going to play any more?

St Erth.   [*Abruptly.*]   No, sir. Good night to you. Canynge, can I give you a lift?

[*He goes out, followed by* Canynge.]

Borring.   [*After a slight pause.*]   Well, I shall go and take the t-temperature of the Club.

[*He goes out.*]

Colford.   Damn that effeminate stammering chap! What can we do for Dancy, Winsor?

Winsor.   Colford! [*A slight pause.*]   The General felt his coat-sleeve that night, and it was wet.

Colford.   Well! What proof's that? No, by George! An old schoolfellow, a brother officer, and a pal.

Winsor.   If he did do it——

Colford.   He didn't. But if he did, I stick to him, and see him through it, if I could.

[Winsor *walks over to the fire, stares into it, turns round and stares at* Colford, *who is standing motionless.*]

Colford.   Yes, by God!

CURTAIN

SCENE II*

Morning of the following day. The DANCYS' flat. In the sitting-room of this small abode MABEL DANCY and MARGARET ORME are sitting full face to the audience, on a couch in the centre of the room, in front of the imaginary window. There is a fireplace, left, with fire burning; a door below it, left; and a door on the right, facing the audience, leads to a corridor and the outer door of the flat, which is visible. Their voices are heard in rapid exchange; then as the curtain rises, so does MABEL.

MABEL.   But it's monstrous!

MARGARET.   Of course! [*She lights a cigarette and hands the case to* MABEL, *who, however, sees nothing but her own thoughts.*]   De Levis might just as well have pitched on me, except that I can't jump more than six inches in these skirts.

MABEL.   It's wicked! Yesterday afternoon at the Club, did you say? Ronny hasn't said a word to me. Why?

MARGARET.   [*With a long puff of smoke.*]   Doesn't want you bothered.

MABEL.   But— Good heavens!— Me!

MARGARET.   Haven't you found out, Mabel, that he isn't exactly communicative? No desperate character is.

MABEL.   Ronny?

MARGARET.   Gracious! Wives *are* at a disadvantage, especially early on. You've never hunted with him, my dear. I have. He takes more sudden decisions than any man I ever knew. He's taking one now, I'll bet.

*NOTE.—This should be a small set capable of being set quickly within that of the previous scene.

MABEL. That beast, De Levis! I was in our room next door all the time.

MARGARET. Was the door into Ronny's dressing-room open?

MABEL. I don't know; I—I think it was.

MARGARET. Well, you can say so in Court anyway. Not that it matters. Wives are liars by law.

MABEL. [*Staring down at her.*] What do you mean —Court?

MARGARET. My dear, he'll have to bring an action for defamation of character, or whatever they call it.

MABEL. Were they talking of this last night at the Winsors'?

MARGARET. Well, you know a dinner-table, Mabel— Scandal is heaven-sent at this time of year.

MABEL. It's terrible, such a thing—terrible!

MARGARET. [*Gloomily.*] If only Ronny weren't known to be so broke.

MABEL. [*With her hands to her forehead.*] I can't realize—I simply can't. If there's a case would it be all right afterward?

MARGARET. Do you remember St Offert—cards? No, you wouldn't—you were in high frocks. Well, St Offert got damages, but he also got the hoof, underneath. He lives in Ireland. There isn't the slightest connection, so far as I can see, Mabel, between innocence and reputation. Look at me!

MABEL. We'll fight it tooth and nail!

MARGARET. Mabel, you're pure wool, right through; everybody's sorry for you.

MABEL. It's for *him* they ought——

MARGARET. [*Again handing the cigarette-case.*] Do smoke, old thing.

[MABEL *takes a cigarette this time, but does not
        light it.*]

It isn't altogether simple. General Canynge was there
last night. You don't mind my being beastly frank, do
you?

MABEL. No. I want it.

MARGARET. Well, he's all for *esprit de corps* and that.
But he was awfully silent.

MABEL. I hate half-hearted friends. Loyalty comes
before everything.

MARGARET. Ye-es; but loyalties cut up against each
other sometimes, you know.

MABEL. I *must* see Ronny. D'you mind if I go and
try to get him on the telephone?

MARGARET. Rather not.

[MABEL *goes out by the door left.*]

Poor kid!

[*She curls herself into a corner of the sofa, as
if trying to get away from life. The bell
rings.* MARGARET *stirs, gets up, and goes out
into the corridor, where she opens the door to*
LADY ADELA WINSOR, *whom she precedes into
the sitting-room.*]

Enter the second murderer! D'you know that child
knew nothing?

LADY A. Where is she?

MARGARET. Telephoning. Adela, if there's going to
be an action, we shall be witnesses. I shall wear black
georgette with an écru hat. Have you ever given evidence?

LADY A. Never.

MARGARET. It must be too frightfully thrilling.

LADY A. Oh! Why did I ever ask that wretch De
Levis? I used to think him pathetic. Meg—did you

know— Ronald Dancy's coat was wet? The General happened to feel it.

MARGARET. So that's why he was so silent.

LADY A. Yes; and after the scene in the Club yesterday he went to see those book-makers, and Goole—what a name!—is sure he told Dancy about the sale.

MARGARET. [Suddenly.] I don't care. He's my third cousin. Don't you feel you couldn't, Adela?

LADY A. Couldn't—what?

MARGARET. Stand for De Levis against one of ourselves?

LADY A. That's very narrow, Meg.

MARGARET. Oh! I know lots of splendid Jews, and I rather liked little Ferdy; but when it comes to the point—! They all stick together; why shouldn't we? It's in the blood. Open your jugular, and see if you haven't got it.

LADY A. My dear, my great-grandmother was a Jewess. I'm very proud of her.

MARGARET. Inoculated. [Stretching herself.] Prejudices, Adela—or are they loyalties—I don't know— criss-cross—we all cut each other's throats from the best of motives.

LADY A. Oh! I shall remember that. Delightful! [Holding up a finger.] You got it from Bergson, Meg. Isn't he wonderful?

MARGARET. Yes; have you ever read him?

LADY A. Well— No. [Looking at the bedroom door.] That poor child! I quite agree. I shall tell everybody it's ridiculous. You don't really think Ronald Dancy——?

MARGARET. I don't know, Adela. There are people who simply can't live without danger. I'm rather like that myself. They're all right when they're getting the

D.S.O. or shooting man-eaters; but if there's no excitement going, they'll make it—out of sheer craving. I've seen Ronald Dancy do the maddest things for no mortal reason except the risk. He's had a past, you know.

LADY A. Oh! Do tell!

MARGARET. He did splendidly in the war, of course, because it suited him; but—just before—don't you remember—a very queer bit of riding?

LADY A. No.

MARGARET. Most daredevil thing—but not quite. You must remember—it was awfully talked about. And then, of course, right up to his marriage——

[*She lights a cigarette.*]

LADY A. Meg, you're very tantalizing!

MARGARET. A foreign-looking girl—most plummy. Oh! Ronny's got charm—this Mabel child doesn't know in the least what she's got hold of!

LADY A. But they're so fond of each other!

MARGARET. That's the mistake. The General isn't mentioning the coat, is he?

LADY A. Oh, no! It was only to Charles.

[MABEL *returns.*]

MARGARET. Did you get him?

MABEL. No; he's not at Tattersall's, nor at the Club.

[LADY ADELA *rises and greets her with an air which suggests bereavement.*]

LADY A. Nobody's going to believe this, my dear.

MABEL. [*Looking straight at her.*] Nobody who does need come here, or trouble to speak to *us* again.

LADY A. That's what I was afraid of; you're going to be defiant. Now don't! Just be perfectly natural.

MABEL. So easy, isn't it? I could kill anybody who believes such a thing.

MARGARET. You'll want a solicitor, Mabel. Go to old Mr. Jacob Twisden.

LADY A. Yes; he's so comforting.

MARGARET. He got my pearls back once—without loss of life. A frightfully good fireside manner. Do get him here, Mabel, and have a heart-to-heart talk, all three of you!

MABEL. [*Suddenly.*] Listen! There's Ronny!

[DANCY *comes in.*]

DANCY. [*With a smile.*] Very good of you to have come.

MARGARET. Yes. We're just going. Oh! Ronny, this is quite too——

[*But his face dries her up; and sidling past, she goes.*]

LADY A. Charles sent his—love——

[*Her voice dwindles on the word, and she, too, goes.*]

DANCY. [*Crossing to his wife.*] What have they been saying?

MABEL. Ronny! Why didn't you tell me?

DANCY. I wanted to see De Levis again first.

MABEL. That wretch! How dare he? Darling! [*She suddenly clasps and kisses him. He does not return the kiss, but remains rigid in her arms, so that she draws away and looks at him.*] It's hurt you awfully, I know.

DANCY. Look here, Mabel! Apart from that muck —this is a ghastly tame-cat sort of life. Let's cut it and get out to Nairobi. I can scare up the money for that.

MABEL. [*Aghast.*] But how can we? Everybody would say——

DANCY. Let them! We shan't be here.

MABEL. I couldn't bear people to think——

DANCY. I don't care a damn what people think—

monkeys and cats. I never could stand their rotten menagerie. Besides, what does it matter how I act; if I bring an action and get damages—if I pound him to a jelly—it's all no good! I can't *prove* it. There'll be plenty of people unconvinced.

MABEL. But they'll find the real thief.

DANCY. [*With a queer little smile.*] Will staying here help them to do that?

MABEL. [*In a sort of agony.*] Oh! I couldn't—it looks like running away. We *must* stay and fight it!

DANCY. Suppose I didn't get a verdict—you never can tell.

MABEL. But you must—I was there all the time, with the door open.

DANCY. Was it?

MABEL. I'm almost sure.

DANCY. Yes. But you're my wife.

MABEL. [*Bewildered.*] Ronny, I don't understand— suppose I'd been accused of stealing pearls!

DANCY. [*Wincing.*] I can't.

MABEL. But I might—just as easily. What would you think of me if I ran away from it?

DANCY. I see. [*A pause.*] All right! You shall have a run for your money. I'll go and see old Twisden.

MABEL. Let me come! [DANCY *shakes his head.*] Why not? I can't be happy a moment unless I'm fighting this.

> [DANCY *puts out his hand suddenly and grips hers.*]

DANCY. You *are* a little brick!

MABEL. [*Pressing his hand to her breast and looking into his face.*] Do you know what Margaret called you?

DANCY. No.

MABEL. A desperate character.

DANCY. Ha! I'm not a tame cat, any more than she.
  [*The bell rings.* MABEL *goes out to the door
      and her voice is heard saying coldly.*]

MABEL. Will you wait a minute, please?
  [*Returning.*]
It's De Levis—to see you. [*In a low voice.*] Let me
see him alone first. Just for a minute! Do!

DANCY. [*After a moment's silence.*] Go ahead!
  [*He goes out into the bedroom.*]

MABEL. [*Going to the door, right.*] Come in.
  [DE LEVIS *comes in, and stands embarrassed.*]
Yes?

DE LEVIS. [*With a slight bow.*] Your husband, Mrs.
Dancy?

MABEL. He is in. Why do you want to see him?

DE LEVIS. He came round to my rooms just now,
when I was out. He threatened me yesterday. I don't
choose him to suppose I'm afraid of him.

MABEL. [*With a great and manifest effort at self-
control.*] Mr. De Levis, you are robbing my husband of
his good name.

DE LEVIS. [*Sincerely.*] I admire your trustfulness,
Mrs. Dancy.

MABEL. [*Staring at him.*] How can you do it?
What do you want? What's your motive? You can't
possibly believe that my husband is a *thief!*

DE LEVIS. Unfortunately.

MABEL. How dare you? How dare you? Don't you
know that I was in our bedroom all the time with the
door open? Do you accuse me too?

DE LEVIS. No, Mrs. Dancy.

MABEL. But you do. I must have seen, I must have
heard.

DE LEVIS. A wife's memory is not very good when her husband is in danger.

MABEL. In other words, I'm lying.

DE LEVIS. No. Your wish is mother to your thought, that's all.

MABEL. [*After staring again with a sort of horror, turns to get control of herself. Then turning back to him.*] Mr. De Levis, I appeal to you as a gentleman to behave to us as you would we should behave to you. Withdraw this wicked charge, and write an apology that Ronald can show.

DE LEVIS. Mrs. Dancy, I am not a gentleman, I am only a—damned Jew. Yesterday I might possibly have withdrawn to spare you. But when my race is insulted I have nothing to say to your husband, but as he wishes to see me, I've come. Please let him know.

MABEL. [*Regarding him again with that look of horror—slowly.*] I think what you are doing is too horrible for words.

> [DE LEVIS *gives her a slight bow, and as he does so* DANCY *comes quickly in, left. The two men stand with the length of the sofa between them.* MABEL, *behind the sofa, turns her eyes on her husband, who has a paper in his right hand.*]

DE LEVIS. You came to see me.

DANCY. Yes. I want you to sign this.

DE LEVIS. I will sign nothing.

DANCY. Let me read it: "I apologize to Captain Dancy for the reckless and monstrous charge I made against him, and I retract every word of it."

DE LEVIS. Not much!

DANCY. You will sign.

DE LEVIS. I tell you this is useless. I will sign nothing. The charge is true; you wouldn't be playing this game if it weren't. I'm going. You'll hardly try violence in the presence of your wife; and if you try it anywhere else—look out for yourself.

DANCY. Mabel, I want to speak to him alone.

MABEL. No, no!

DE LEVIS. Quite right, Mrs. Dancy. Black-and-tan swashbuckling will only make things worse for him.

DANCY. So you shelter behind a woman, do you, you skulking cur!

> [DE LEVIS *takes a step, with fists clinched and eyes blazing.* DANCY, *too, stands ready to spring—the moment is cut short by* MABEL *going quickly to her husband.*]

MABEL. Don't, Ronny. It's undignified! He isn't worth it.

> [DANCY *suddenly tears the paper in two, and flings it into the fire.*]

DANCY. Get out of here, you swine!

> [DE LEVIS *stands a moment irresolute, then, turning to the door, he opens it, stands again for a moment with a smile on his face, then goes.* MABEL *crosses swiftly to the door, and shuts it as the outer door closes. Then she stands quite still, looking at her husband—her face expressing a sort of startled suspense.*]

DANCY. [*Turning and looking at her.*] Well! Do you agree with him?

MABEL. What do you mean?

DANCY. That I wouldn't be playing this game unless——

MABEL. Don't! You hurt me!

DANCY. Yes. You don't know much of me, Mabel.

MABEL. Ronny!

DANCY.   What did you say to that swine?

MABEL.   [*Her face averted.*]   That he was robbing *us*. [*Turning to him suddenly.*]   Ronny—you—didn't?   I'd rather know.

DANCY.   Ha!   I thought that was coming.

MABEL.   [*Covering her face.*]   Oh!   How horrible of me—how horrible!

DANCY.   Not at all.   The thing looks bad.

MABEL.   [*Dropping her hands.*]   If *I* can't believe in you, who can?   [*Going to him, throwing her arms round him, and looking up into his face.*]   Ronny!   If all the world—*I'd* believe in you.   You know I would.

DANCY.   That's all right, Mabs!   That's all right! [*His face, above her head, is contorted for a moment, then hardens into a mask.*]   Well, what shall we do?

MABEL.   Oh!   Let's go to that lawyer—let's go at once!

DANCY.   All right.   Get your hat on.

> [MABEL *passes him, and goes into the bedroom, left.* DANCY, *left alone, stands quite still, staring before him.   With a sudden shrug of his shoulders he moves quickly to his hat and takes it up just as* MABEL *returns, ready to go out.   He opens the door; and crossing him, she stops in the doorway, looking up with a clear and trustful gaze as*

THE CURTAIN FALLS

ACT III

SCENE I

Three months later.   Old MR. JACOB TWISDEN'S *room, at the offices of Twisden & Graviter, in Lincoln's Inn*

Fields, is spacious, with two large windows at back,
a fine old fireplace, right, a door below it, and two
doors, left. Between the windows is a large table
sideways to the window wall, with a chair in the
middle on the right-hand side, a chair against the
wall, and a client's chair on the left-hand side.

GRAVITER, TWISDEN'S *much-younger partner, is standing*
in front of the right-hand window looking out on to
the Fields, where the lamps are being lighted, and a
taxi's engine is running down below. He turns his
sanguine, shrewd face from the window toward a
grandfather clock, between the doors, left, which is
striking "four." The door, left forward, is opened.

YOUNG CLERK. [*Entering.*] A Mr. Gilman, sir, to
see Mr. Twisden.

GRAVITER. By appointment?

YOUNG CLERK. No, sir. But important, he says.

GRAVITER. I'll see him.

> [*The* CLERK *goes.* GRAVITER *sits right of table.*
> *The* CLERK *returns, ushering in an oldish*
> *Man, who looks what he is, the proprietor of*
> *a large modern grocery-store. He wears a*
> *dark overcoat and carries a pot-hat. His*
> *gingery-gray mustache and mutton-chop*
> *whiskers give him the expression of a cat.*]

GRAVITER. [*Sizing up his social standing.*] Mr.
Gilman? Yes.

GILMAN. [*Doubtfully.*] Mr. Jacob Twisden?

GRAVITER. [*Smiling.*] His partner. Graviter my
name is.

GILMAN. Mr. Twisden's not in, then?

GRAVITER. No. He's at the Courts. They're just
up; he should be in directly. But he'll be busy.

GILMAN. Old Mr. Jacob Twisden—I've heard of him.

GRAVITER. Most people have.

[*A pause.*]

GILMAN. It's this Dancy De Levis case that's keepin' him at the Courts, I suppose?

[GRAVITER *nods.*]

Won't be finished for a day or two?

[GRAVITER *shakes his head.*]

No. Astonishin' the interest taken in it.

GRAVITER. As you say.

GILMAN. The Smart Set, eh? This Captain Dancy got the D.S.O., didn't he?

[GRAVITER *nods.*]

Sad to have a thing like that said about you. I thought he gave his evidence well; and his wife too. Looks as if this De Levis had got some private spite. *Searchy la femme,* I said to Mrs. Gilman only this morning, before I——

GRAVITER. By the way, sir, what is your business?

GILMAN. Well, my business here— No, if you'll excuse me, I'd rather wait and see old Mr. Jacob Twisden. It's delicate, and I'd like his experience.

GRAVITER. [*With a shrug.*] Very well; then, perhaps, you'll go in there

[*He moves toward the door, left back.*]

GILMAN. Thank you. [*Following.*] You see, I've never been mixed up with the law——

GRAVITER. [*Opening the door.*] No?

GILMAN. And I don't want to begin. When you do, you don't know where you'll stop, do you? You see, I've only come from a sense of duty; and—other reasons.

GRAVITER. Not uncommon.

GILMAN. [*Producing card.*] This is my card. Gilman's—several branches, but this is the 'ead.

GRAVITER. [*Scrutinizing card.*] Exactly.

GILMAN. Grocery—I dare say you know me; or your wife does. They say old Mr. Jacob Twisden refused a knighthood. If it's not a rude question, why was that?

GRAVITER. Ask him, sir; ask him.

GILMAN. I said to my wife at the time, "He's holdin' out for a baronetcy."

[GRAVITER *closes the door with an exasperated smile.*]

YOUNG CLERK. [*Opening the door, left forward.*] Mr. Winsor, sir, and Miss Orme.

[*They enter, and the* CLERK *withdraws.*]

GRAVITER. How d'you do, Miss Orme? How do you do, Winsor?

WINSOR. Twisden not back, Graviter?

GRAVITER. Not yet.

WINSOR. Well, they've got through De Levis's witnesses. Sir Frederic was at the very top of his form. It's looking quite well. But I hear they've just subpœnaed Canynge after all. His evidence is to be taken to-morrow.

GRAVITER. Oho!

WINSOR. I said Dancy ought to have called him.

GRAVITER. We considered it. Sir Frederic decided that he could use him better in cross-examination.

WINSOR. Well! I don't know that. Can I go and see him before he gives evidence to-morrow?

GRAVITER. I should like to hear Mr. Jacob on that, Winsor. He'll be in directly.

WINSOR. They had Kentman, and Goole, the Inspector, the other bobby, my footman, Dancy's banker, and his tailor.

GRAVITER. Did we shake Kentman or Goole?

WINSOR. Very little. Oh! by the way, the numbers of those two notes were given, and I see they're published in the evening papers. I suppose the police wanted that. I tell you what I find, Graviter—a general feeling that there's something behind it all that doesn't come out.

GRAVITER. The public wants its money's worth—always does in these Society cases; they brew so long beforehand, you see.

WINSOR. They're looking for something lurid.

MARGARET. When I was in the box, I thought they were looking for me. [*Taking out her cigarette-case.*] I suppose I mustn't smoke, Mr. Graviter?

GRAVITER. Do!

MARGARET. Won't Mr. Jacob have a fit?

GRAVITER. Yes, but not till you've gone.

MARGARET. Just a whiff.

[*She lights a cigarette.*]

WINSOR. [*Suddenly.*] It's becoming a sort of Dreyfus case—people taking sides quite outside the evidence.

MARGARET. There are more of the chosen in Court every day. Mr. Graviter, have you noticed the two on the jury?

GRAVITER. [*With a smile.*] No; I can't say——

MARGARET. Oh! but quite distinctly. Don't you think they ought to have been challenged?

GRAVITER. De Levis might have challenged the other ten, Miss Orme.

MARGARET. Dear me, now! I never thought of that.

[*As she speaks, the door left forward is opened and old MR. JACOB TWISDEN comes in. He is tallish and narrow, sixty-eight years old, gray, with narrow little whiskers curling round his narrow ears, and a narrow bow ribbon curling round his collar. He wears a long, narrow-tailed coat, and strapped trousers on his nar-*]

*row legs. His nose and face are narrow,
shrewd, and kindly. He has a way of narrowing his shrewd and kindly eyes. His nose
is seen to twitch and sniff.*]

TWISDEN. Ah! How are you, Charles? How do
you do, my dear?

MARGARET. Dear Mr. Jacob, I'm smoking. Isn't it
disgusting? But they don't allow it in Court, you know.
Such a pity! The Judge might have a hookah. Oh!
wouldn't he look sweet—the darling!

TWISDEN. [*With a little, old-fashioned bow.*] It does
not become everybody as it becomes you, Margaret.

MARGARET. Mr. Jacob, how charming.

[*With a slight grimace she puts out her
cigarette.*]

GRAVITER. Man called Gilman waiting in there to see
you specially.

TWISDEN. Directly. Turn up the light, would you,
Graviter?

GRAVITER. [*Turning up the light.*] Excuse me.

[*He goes.*]

WINSOR. Look here, Mr. Twisden——

TWISDEN. Sit down; sit down, my dear.

[*And he himself sits behind the table, as a cup
of tea is brought in to him by the* YOUNG
CLERK, *with two Marie biscuits in the saucer.*]

Will you have some, Margaret?

MARGARET. No, dear Mr. Jacob.

TWISDEN. Charles?

WINSOR. No, thanks.

[*The door is closed.*]

TWISDEN. [*Dipping a biscuit in the tea.*] Now, then?

WINSOR. The General knows something which on the
face of it looks rather queer. Now that he's going to be

called, oughtn't Dancy to be told of it, so that he may be ready with his explanation, in case it comes out?

TWISDEN. [*Pouring some tea into the saucer.*] Without knowing, I can't tell you.

> [WINSOR *and* MARGARET *exchange looks, and* TWISDEN *drinks from the saucer.*]

MARGARET. Tell him, Charles.

WINSOR. Well! It rained that evening at Meldon. The General happened to put his hand on Dancy's shoulder, and it was damp.

> [TWISDEN *puts the saucer down and replaces the cup in it. They both look intently at him.*]

TWISDEN. I take it that General Canynge won't say anything he's not compelled to say.

MARGARET. No, of course; but, Mr. Jacob, they might ask; they know it rained. And he is such a George Washington.

TWISDEN. [*Toying with a pair of tortoise-shell glasses.*] They didn't ask either of *you*. Still—no harm in your telling Dancy.

WINSOR. I'd rather *you* did it, Margaret.

MARGARET. I dare say.

> [*She mechanically takes out her cigarette-case, catches the lift of* TWISDEN's *eyebrows, and puts it back.*]

WINSOR. Well, we'll go together. I don't want Mrs. Dancy to hear.

MARGARET. Do tell me, Mr. Jacob; is he going to win?

TWISDEN. I think so, Margaret; I think so.

MARGARET. It'll be too frightful if he doesn't get a verdict, after all this. But I don't know what we shall do when it's over. I've been sitting in that Court all these three days, watching, and it's made me feel there's nothing we like better than seeing people skinned. Well, by-by, bless you!

[TWISDEN *rises and pats her hand.*]

WINSOR. Half a second, Margaret. Wait for me.

[*She nods and goes out.*]

Mr. Twisden, what do you really think?

TWISDEN. I am Dancy's lawyer, my dear Charles, as well as yours.

WINSOR. Well, can I go and see Canynge?

TWISDEN. Better not.

WINSOR. If they get that out of him, and recall me, am I to say he told me of it at the time?

TWISDEN. You didn't feel the coat yourself? And Dancy wasn't present? Then what Canynge told you is not evidence. *We'll* stop your being asked.

WINSOR. Thank goodness. Good-by!

[WINSOR *goes out.*]

[TWISDEN, *behind his table, motionless, taps his teeth with the eyeglasses in his narrow, well-kept hand. After a long shake of his head and a shrug of his rather high shoulders he sniffs, goes to the window and opens it. Then crossing to the door, left back, he throws it open and says:*]

TWISDEN. At your service, sir.

[GILMAN *comes forth, nursing his pot-hat.*]

Be seated.

[TWISDEN *closes the window behind him, and takes his seat.*]

GILMAN. [*Taking the client's chair, to the left of the table.*] Mr. Twisden, I believe? My name's Gilman, head of Gilman's Department Stores. You have my card.

TWISDEN. [*Looking at the card.*] Yes. What can we do for you?

GILMAN. Well, I've come to you from a sense of duty, sir, and also a feelin' of embarrassment. [*He takes from his breast-pocket an evening paper.*] You see, I've been followin' this Dancy case—it's a good deal talked of in Putney—and I read this at half past two this afternoon. To be precise, at 2.25. [*He rises and hands the paper to* TWISDEN, *and with a thick-gloved forefinger indicates a passage.*] When I read these numbers, I 'appened to remember givin' change for a fifty-pound note—don't often 'ave one in, you know—so I went to the cash-box out of curiosity, to see that I 'adn't got it. Well, I 'ad; and here it is. [*He draws out from his breast-pocket and lays before* TWISDEN *a fifty-pound bank-note.*] It was brought in to change by a customer of mine three days ago, and he got value for it. Now, that's a stolen note, it seems, and you'd like to know what I did. Mind you, that customer of mine I've known 'im—well—eight or nine years; an Italian he is—wine salesman, and so far's I know, a respectable man—foreign-lookin', but nothin' more. Now, this was at 'alf past two, and I was at my head branch at Putney, where I live. I want you to mark the time, so as you'll see I 'aven't wasted a minute. I took a cab and I drove straight to my customer's private residence in Putney, where he lives with his daughter— Ricardos his name is, Paolio Ricardos. They tell me there that he's at his business shop in the City. So off I go in the cab again, and there I find him. Well, sir, I showed this paper to him and I produced the note. "Here," I said, "you brought this to me and you got value for it." Well, that man was taken aback. If I'm a judge, Mr. Twisden, he was taken aback, not to speak in a guilty way, but he was, as you might say, flummoxed. "Now," I said to him, "where did you get it—that's the point?" He took his time to answer, and then he said: "Well, Mr. Gilman," he said, "you know me; I am an honorable man. I can't tell you offhand, but I am above the board." He's foreign, you know, in his expressions. "Yes," I said, "that's all very well," I said, "but here I've got a stolen note and you've got the value for it. Now I tell you," I said, "what I'm going to do; I'm going straight with this note to Mr. Jacob Twisden, who's got this Dancy De Levis case in 'and. He's a well-known Society lawyer," I said, "of great experience." "Oh!" he said, "that is what you do?"—funny the way he speaks! "Then I come with you!" —And I've got him in the cab below. I want to tell you everything before he comes up. On the way I tried to get something out of him, but I couldn't —I could *not*. "This is very awkward," I said at last. "It is, Mr. Gilman," was his reply; and he began to talk about his Sicilian claret—a very good wine, mind you; but under the circumstances it seemed to me uncalled for. Have I made it clear to you?

TWISDEN. [*Who has listened with extreme attention.*] Perfectly, Mr. Gilman. I'll send down for him.

[*He touches a hand-bell. The* YOUNG CLERK *appears at the door, left forward.*]

A gentleman in a taxi—waiting. Ask him to be so good as to step up. Oh! and send Mr. Graviter here again.

[*The* YOUNG CLERK *goes out.*]

GILMAN. As I told you, sir, I've been followin' this case. It's what you might call piquant. And I should be very glad if it came about that this helped Captain Dancy. I take an interest, because, to tell you the truth, [*confidentially*] I don't like—well, not to put too fine a point upon it—'Ebrews. They work harder; they're more sober; they're honest; and they're everywhere. I've nothing against them, but the fact is—they get *on* so.

TWISDEN. [*Cocking an eye.*] A thorn in the flesh, Mr. Gilman.

GILMAN. Well, I prefer my own countrymen, and that's the truth of it.

> [*As he speaks,* GRAVITER *comes in by the door left forward.*]

TWISDEN. [*Pointing to the newspaper and the note.*] Mr. Gilman has brought this, of which he is holder for value. His customer, who changed it three days ago, is coming up.

GRAVITER. The fifty-pounder. I see.

> [*His face is long and reflective.*]

YOUNG CLERK. [*Entering.*] Mr. Ricardos, sir.

> [*He goes out.* RICARDOS *is a personable, Italian-looking man in a frock coat, with a dark mustachioed face and dark hair a little grizzled. He looks anxious, and bows.*]

TWISDEN. Mr. Ricardos? My name is Jacob Twisden. My partner. [*Holding up a finger, as* RICARDOS *would speak.*] Mr. Gilman has told us about this note. You took it to him, he says, three days ago; that is, on Monday, and received cash for it?

RICARDOS. Yes, sare.

TWISDEN. You were *not* aware that it was stolen?

RICARDOS. [*With his hand to his breast.*] Oh! no, sare.

TWISDEN. You received it from——?

RICARDOS. A minute, sare; I would weesh to explain —[*with an expressive shrug*] in private.

TWISDEN. [*Nodding.*] Mr. Gilman, your conduct has been most prompt. You may safely leave the matter in our hands, now. Kindly let us retain this note; and ask for my cashier as you go out and give him [*he writes*] this. He will reimburse you. We will take any necessary steps ourselves.

GILMAN. [*In slight surprise, with modest pride.*]

Well, sir, I'm in your 'ands. I must be guided by you, with your experience. I'm glad you think I acted rightly.

TWISDEN. Very rightly, Mr. Gilman—very rightly. [*Rising.*] Good afternoon!

GILMAN. Good afternoon, sir. Good afternoon, gentlemen! [*To* TWISDEN.] I'm sure I'm very 'appy to have made your acquaintance, sir. It's a well-known name.

TWISDEN. Thank you.

> [GILMAN *retreats, glances at* RICARDOS, *and turns again.*]

GILMAN. I suppose there's nothing else I ought to do, in the interests of the law? I'm a careful man.

TWISDEN. If there is, Mr. Gilman, we will let you know. We have your address. You may make your mind easy; but don't speak of this. It might interfere with Justice.

GILMAN. Oh! I shouldn't dream of it. I've no wish to be mixed up in anything conspicuous. That's not my principle at all. Good day, gentlemen.

> [*He goes.*]

TWISDEN. [*Seating himself.*] Now, sir, will you sit down.

> [*But* RICARDOS *does not sit; he stands looking uneasily across the table at* GRAVITER.]

You may speak out.

RICARDOS. Well, Mr. Tweesden and sare, this matter is very serious for me, and very delicate—it concairns my honor. I am in a great difficulty.

TWISDEN. When in difficulty—complete frankness, sir.

RICARDOS. It is a family matter, sare, I——

TWISDEN. Let me be frank with you. [*Telling his points off on his fingers.*] We have your admission that you changed this stopped note for value. It will be our duty to inform the Bank of England that it has been traced to you. You will have to account to them for your possession of it. I suggest to you that it will be far better to account frankly to us.

RICARDOS. [*Taking out a handkerchief and quite openly wiping his hands and forehead.*] I received this note, sare, with others, from a gentleman, sare, in settlement of a debt of honor. and I know nothing of where he got them.

TWISDEN. H'm! that is very vague. If that is all you can tell us, I'm afraid——

RICARDOS. Gentlemen, this is very painful for me. It is my daughter's good name——

[*He again wipes his brow.*]

TWISDEN. Come, sir, speak out!

RICARDOS. [*Desperately.*] The notes were a settlement to her from this gentleman, of whom she was a great friend.

TWISDEN. [*Suddenly.*] I am afraid we must press you for the name of the gentleman.

RICARDOS. Sare, if I give it to you, and it does 'im 'arm, what will my daughter say? This is a bad matter for me. He behaved well to her; and she is attached to him still; sometimes she is crying yet because she lost him. And now we betray him, perhaps, who knows? This is very unpleasant for me. [*Taking up the paper.*] Here it gives the number of another note—a 'undred-pound note. I 'ave that too.

[*He takes a note from his breast-pocket.*]

GRAVITER. How much did he give you in all?

RICARDOS. For my daughter's settlement one thousand pounds. I understand he did not wish to give a check because of his marriage. So I did not think anything about it being in notes, you see.

TWISDEN.   When did he give you this money?

RICARDOS.   The middle of Octobare last.

TWISDEN.   [*Suddenly looking up.*]   Mr. Ricardos, was it Captain Dancy?

RICARDOS.   [*Again wiping his forehead.*]   Gentlemen, I am so fond of my daughter.   I have only the one, and no wife.

TWISDEN.   [*With an effort.*]   Yes, yes; but I must know.

RICARDOS.   Sare, if I tell you, will you give me your good word that my daughter shall not hear of it?

TWISDEN.   So far as we are able to prevent it—certainly.

RICARDOS.   Sare, I trust you.—It was Captain Dancy.

    [*A long pause.*]

GRAVITER.   [*Suddenly.*]   Were you blackmailing him?

TWISDEN.   [*Holding up his hand.*]   My partner means, did you press him for this settlement?

RICARDOS.   I did think it my duty to my daughter to ask that he make compensation to her.

TWISDEN.   With threats that you would tell his wife?

RICARDOS.   [*With a shrug.*]   Captain Dancy was a man of honor.   He said: "Of course I will do this."   I trusted him.   And a month later I did remind him, and he gave me this money for her.   I do not know where he got it—I do not know.   Gentlemen, I have invested it all on her—every penny—except this note, for which I had the purpose to buy her a necklace.   That is the swearéd truth.

TWISDEN.   I must keep this note.   [*He touches the hundred-pound note.*]   You will not speak of this to any one.   *I* may recognize that you were a holder for value received—others might take a different view.   Good day, sir.   Graviter, see Mr. Ricardos out, and take his address.

RICARDOS.   [*Pressing his hands over the breast of his frock coat—with a sigh.*]   Gentlemen, I beg you—remember what I said.   [*With a roll of his eyes.*]   My daughter—I am not happee.   Good day.

> [*He turns and goes out slowly, left forward, followed by* GRAVITER.]

TWISDEN.   [*To himself.*]   Young Dancy!

> [*He pins the two notes together and places them in an envelope, then stands motionless except for his eyes and hands, which restlessly express the disturbance within him.* GRAVITER *returns, carefully shuts the door, and going up to him, hands him* RICARDOS's *card.*]

[*Looking at the card.*]   Villa Benvenuto.   This will have to be verified, but I'm afraid it's true.   That man was not acting.

GRAVITER.   What's to be done about Dancy?

TWISDEN.   Can you understand a gentleman——?

GRAVITER.   I don't know, sir.   The war loosened "form" all over the place.   I saw plenty of that myself. And some men have no moral sense.   From the first I've had doubts.

TWISDEN.   We can't go on with the case.

GRAVITER.   Phew! . . .   [*A moment's silence.*]   Gosh! It's an awful thing for his wife.

TWISDEN.   Yes.

GRAVITER.   [*Touching the envelope.*]   Chance brought this here, sir.   That man won't talk—he's too scared.

TWISDEN.   Gilman.

GRAVITER.   Too respectable.   If De Levis got those notes back, and the rest of the money, anonymously?

TWISDEN.   But the case, Graviter; the case.

GRAVITER.   I don't believe this alters what I've been thinking.

TWISDEN. Thought is one thing—knowledge another. There's duty to our profession. Ours is a fine calling. On the good faith of solicitors a very great deal hangs.

> [*He crosses to the hearth as if warmth would help him.*]

GRAVITER. It'll let him in for a prosecution. He came to us in confidence.

TWISDEN. Not as against the law.

GRAVITER. No. I suppose not. [*A pause.*] By Jove, I don't like losing this case. I don't like the admission we backed such a wrong 'un.

TWISDEN. Impossible to go on. Apart from ourselves, there's Sir Frederic. We must disclose to him—can't let him go on in the dark. Complete confidence between solicitor and counsel is the essence of professional honor.

GRAVITER. What are you going to do then, sir?

TWISDEN. See Dancy at once. Get him on the 'phone.

GRAVITER. [*Taking up the telephone.*] Get me Captain Dancy's flat. . . . What? . . . [*To* TWISDEN.] Mrs. Dancy is here. That's *à propos* with a vengeance. Are you going to see her, sir?

TWISDEN. [*After a moment's painful hesitation.*] I must.

GRAVITER. [*Telephoning.*] Bring Mrs. Dancy up.

> [*He turns to the window.* MABEL DANCY *is shown in, looking very pale.* TWISDEN *advances from the fire, and takes her hand.*]

MABEL. Major Colford's taken Ronny off in his car for the night. I thought it would do him good. I said I'd come round in case there was anything you wanted to say before to-morrow.

TWISDEN. [*Taken aback.*] Where have they gone?

MABEL. I don't know, but he'll be home before ten o'clock to-morrow. Is there anything?

TWISDEN. Well, I'd like to see him before the Court sits. Send him on here as soon as he comes.

MABEL. [*With her hand to her forehead.*] Oh! Mr. Twisden, when will it be over? My head's getting awful sitting in that Court.

TWISDEN. My dear Mrs. Dancy, there's no need at all for you to come down to-morrow; take a rest and nurse your head.

MABEL. Really and truly?

TWISDEN. Yes; it's the very best thing you can do.
 [GRAVITER *turns his head, and looks at them unobserved.*]

MABEL. How do you think it's going?

TWISDEN. It went very well to-day; very well indeed.

MABEL. You must be awfully fed up with us.

TWISDEN. My dear young lady, that's our business.
 [*He takes her hand.* MABEL'S *face suddenly quivers. She draws her hand away, and covers her lips with it.*]
There, there! You want a day off badly.

MABEL. I'm so tired of—! Thank you so much for all you're doing. Good night! Good night, Mr. Graviter!

GRAVITER. Good night, Mrs. Dancy.
 [MABEL *goes.*]

GRAVITER. D'you know, I believe she knows.

TWISDEN. No, no! She believes in him implicitly. A stanch little woman. Poor thing!

GRAVITER. Hasn't that shaken you, sir? It has me.

TWISDEN. No, no! I—I can't go on with the case. It's breaking faith. Get Sir Frederic's chambers.

GRAVITER. [*Telephoning, and getting a reply, looks round at* TWISDEN.] Yes?

TWISDEN. Ask if I can come round and see him.

GRAVITER. [*Telephoning.*] Can Sir Frederic spare Mr. Twisden a few minutes now if he comes round? [*Receiving reply.*] He's gone down to Brighton for the night.

TWISDEN. H'm! What hotel?

GRAVITER. [*Telephoning.*] What's his address? What . . .? [*To* TWISDEN] The Bedford.

TWISDEN. I'll go down.

GRAVITER. [*Telephoning.*] Thank you. All right. [*He rings off.*]

TWISDEN. Just look out the trains down and up early to-morrow.

[GRAVITER *takes up an A B C, and* TWISDEN *takes up the* RICARDOS *card.*]

TWISDEN. Send to this address in Putney, verify the fact that Ricardos has a daughter, and give me a trunk call to Brighton. Better go yourself, Graviter. If you see her, don't say anything, of course—invent some excuse. [GRAVITER *nods.*] I'll be up in time to see Dancy.

GRAVITER. By George! I feel bad about this.

TWISDEN. Yes. But professional honor comes first. What time is that train?

[*He bends over the A B C.*]

CURTAIN

SCENE II

The same room on the following morning at ten-twenty-five, by the grandfather clock.

The YOUNG CLERK *is ushering in* DANCY, *whose face is*

perceptibly harder than it was three months ago, like that of a man who has lived under great restraint.

DANCY.   He wanted to see me before the Court sat.

YOUNG CLERK.   Yes, sir.   Mr. Twisden will see you in one minute.   He had to go out of town last night.

[*He prepares to open the waiting-room door.*]

DANCY.   Were *you* in the war?

YOUNG CLERK.   Yes.

DANCY.   How can you stick this?

YOUNG CLERK.   [*With a smile.*]   My trouble was to stick that, sir.

DANCY.   But you get no excitement from year's end to year's end.   It'd drive me mad.

YOUNG CLERK.   [*Shyly.*]   A case like this is pretty exciting.   I'd give a lot to see us win it.

DANCY.   [*Staring at him.*]   Why?   What is it to you?

YOUNG CLERK.   I don't know, sir.   It's—it's like football—you want your side to win.   [*He opens the waiting-room door.   Expanding.*]   You see some rum starts, too, in a lawyer's office in a quiet way.

[DANCY *enters the waiting-room, and the* YOUNG CLERK, *shutting the door, meets* TWISDEN *as he comes in, left forward, and takes from him overcoat, top-hat, and a small bag.*]

YOUNG CLERK.   Captain Dancy's waiting, sir.

[*He indicates the waiting-room.*]

TWISDEN.   [*Narrowing his lips.*]   Very well. Mr. Graviter gone to the Courts?

YOUNG CLERK.   Yes, sir.

TWISDEN.   Did he leave anything for me?

YOUNG CLERK.   On the table, sir.

TWISDEN. [*Taking up an envelope.*] Thank you.
[*The* CLERK *goes.*]

TWISDEN. [*Opening the envelope and reading.*] "All corroborates." H'm! [*He puts it in his pocket and takes out of an envelope the two notes, lays them on the table, and covers them with a sheet of blotting-paper; stands a moment preparing himself, then goes to the door of the waiting-room, opens it, and says:*] Now, Captain Dancy. Sorry to have kept you waiting.

DANCY. [*Entering.*] Winsor came to me yesterday about General Canynge's evidence. Is that what you wanted to speak to me about?

TWISDEN. No. It isn't that.

DANCY. [*Looking at his wrist-watch.*] By me it's just on the half-hour, sir.

TWISDEN. Yes. I don't want you to go to the Court.

DANCY. Not?

TWISDEN. I have very serious news for you.

DANCY. [*Wincing and collecting himself.*] Oh!

TWISDEN. These two notes. [*He uncovers the notes.*] After the Court rose yesterday we had a man called Ricardos here. [*A pause.*] Is there any need for me to say more?

DANCY. [*Unflinching.*] No. What now?

TWISDEN. Our duty was plain; we could not go on with the case. I have consulted Sir Frederic. He felt— he felt that he must throw up his brief, and he will do that the moment the Court sits. Now I want to talk to you about what you're going to do.

DANCY. That's very good of you, considering.

TWISDEN. I don't pretend to understand, but I imagine you may have done this in a moment of reckless bravado, feeling, perhaps, that as you gave the mare to De Levis, the money was by rights as much yours as his.

[*Stopping* DANCY, *who is about to speak, with a gesture.*]

To satisfy a debt of honor to this—lady; and, no doubt, to save your wife from hearing of it from the man Ricardos. Is that so?

DANCY. To the life.

TWISDEN. It was mad, Captain Dancy, mad!— But the question now is: What do you owe to your wife? She doesn't dream—I suppose?

DANCY. [*With a twitching face.*] No.

TWISDEN. We can't tell what the result of this collapse will be. The police have the theft in hand. They may issue a warrant. The money could be refunded, and the costs paid—somehow that can all be managed. But it may not help. In any case, what end is served by your staying in the country? You can't save your honor— that's gone. You can't save your wife's peace of mind. If she sticks to you—do you think she will?

DANCY. Not if she's wise.

TWISDEN. Better go! There's a war in Morocco.

DANCY. [*With a bitter smile.*] Good old Morocco!

TWISDEN. Will you go, then, at once, and leave me to break it to your wife?

DANCY. I don't know yet.

TWISDEN. You must decide quickly, to catch a boat train. Many a man has made good. You're a fine soldier.

DANCY. There are alternatives.

TWISDEN. Now, go straight from this office. You've a passport, I suppose; you won't need a *visa* for France, and from there you can find means to slip over. Have you got money on you? [DANCY *nods.*] We will see what we can do to stop or delay proceedings.

DANCY. It's all damned kind of you. [*With diffi-*

culty.] But I must think of my wife. Give me a few minutes.

TWISDEN. Yes, yes; go in there and think it out.

> [*He goes to the door, right, and opens it. DANCY passes him and goes out. TWISDEN rings a bell and stands waiting.*]

CLERK. [*Entering.*] Yes, sir?

TWISDEN. Tell them to call a taxi.

CLERK. [*Who has a startled look.*] Yes, sir. Mr. Graviter has come in, sir, with General Canynge. Are you disengaged?

TWISDEN. Yes.

> [*The CLERK goes out, and almost immediately GRAVITER and CANYNGE enter.*]

Good morning, General. [*To GRAVITER.*] Well?

GRAVITER. Sir Frederic got up at once and said that since the publication of the numbers of those notes, information had reached him which forced him to withdraw from the case. Great sensation, of course. I left Bromley in charge. There'll be a formal verdict for the defendant, with costs. Have you told Dancy?

TWISDEN. Yes. He's in there deciding what he'll do.

CANYNGE. [*Grave and vexed.*] This is a dreadful thing, Twisden. I've been afraid of it all along. A soldier! A gallant fellow, too. What on earth got into him?

TWISDEN. There's no end to human nature, General.

GRAVITER. You can see queerer things in the papers, any day.

CANYNGE. That poor young wife of his! Winsor gave me a message for you, Twisden. If money's wanted quickly to save proceedings, draw on him. Is there anything *I* can do?

Twisden. I've advised him to go straight off to Morocco.

Canynge. I don't know that an asylum isn't the place for him. He must be off his head at moments. That jump—crazy! He'd have got a verdict on that alone— if they'd seen those balconies. I was looking at them when I was down there last Sunday. Daring thing, Twisden. Very few men, on a dark night— He risked his life twice. That's a shrewd fellow—young De Levis. He spotted Dancy's nature.

[*The* Young Clerk *enters.*]

Clerk. The taxi's here, sir. Will you see Major Colford and Miss Orme?

Twisden. Graviter— No; show them in.

[*The* Young Clerk *goes.*]

Canynge. Colford's badly cut up.

[Margaret Orme *and* Colford *enter.*]

Colford. [*Striding forward.*] There must be some mistake about this, Mr. Twisden.

Twisden. Hssh! Dancy's in there. He's admitted it.

[*Voices are subdued at once.*]

Colford. What? [*With emotion.*] If it were my own brother, I couldn't feel it more. But—damn it! What right had that fellow to chuck up the case—without letting him know, too. I came down with Dancy this morning, and he knew nothing about it.

Twisden. [*Coldly.*] That was unfortunately unavoidable.

Colford. Guilty or not, you ought to have stuck to him—it's not playing the game, Mr. Twisden.

Twisden. You must allow me to judge where my duty lay, in a very hard case.

Colford. I thought a man was safe with his solicitor.

CANYNGE. Colford, you don't understand professional etiquette.

COLFORD. No, thank God!

TWISDEN. When you have been as long in your profession as I have been in mine, Major Colford, you will know that duty to your calling outweighs duty to friend or client.

COLFORD. But I serve the Country.

TWISDEN. And I serve the Law, sir.

CANYNGE. Graviter, give me a sheet of paper. I'll write a letter for him.

MARGARET. [*Going up to* TWISDEN.] Dear Mr. Jacob—pay De Levis. You know my pearls—put them up the spout again. Don't let Ronny be——

TWISDEN. Money isn't the point, Margaret.

MARGARET. It's ghastly! It really is.

COLFORD. I'm going in to shake hands with him.

[*He starts to cross the room.*]

TWISDEN. Wait! We want him to go straight off to Morocco. Don't upset him. [*To* COLFORD *and* MARGARET.] I think you had better go. If, a little later, Margaret, you could go round to Mrs. Dancy——

COLFORD. Poor little Mabel Dancy! It's perfect hell for her.

[*They have not seen that* DANCY *has opened the door behind them.*]

DANCY. It is!

[*They all turn round in consternation.*]

COLFORD. [*With a convulsive movement.*] Old boy!

DANCY. No good, Colford. [*Gazing round at them.*] Oh! clear out. I can't stand commiseration—and let me have some air.

[TWISDEN *motions to* COLFORD *and* MARGARET *to go; and as he turns to* DANCY, *they go out.*]

> GRAVITER *also moves toward the door. The*
> GENERAL *sits motionless.* GRAVITER *goes*
> *out.*]

TWISDEN. Well?

DANCY. I'm going home, to clear up things with my wife. General Canynge, I don't quite know why I did the damned thing. But I did, and there's an end of it.

CANYNGE. Dancy, for the honor of the Army, avoid further scandal if you can. I've written a letter to a friend of mine in the Spanish War Office. It will get you a job in their war.

> [CANYNGE *closes the envelope.*]

DANCY. Very good of you. I don't know if I can make use of it.

> [CANYNGE *stretches out the letter, which*
> TWISDEN *hands to* DANCY, *who takes it.*
> GRAVITER *reopens the door.*]

TWISDEN. What is it?

GRAVITER. De Levis is here.

TWISDEN. De Levis? Can't see him.

DANCY. Let him in!

> [*After a moment's hesitation* TWISDEN *nods,*
> *and* GRAVITER *goes out. The three wait in*
> *silence with their eyes fixed on the door, the*
> GENERAL *sitting at the table,* TWISDEN *by his*
> *chair,* DANCY *between him and the door right.*
> DE LEVIS *comes in and shuts the door. He is*
> *advancing toward* TWISDEN *when his eyes*
> *fall on* DANCY, *and he stops.*]

TWISDEN. You wanted to see me?

DE LEVIS. [*Moistening his lips.*] Yes. I came to say that—that I overheard—I am afraid a warrant is to be issued. I wanted you to realize—it's not *my* doing. I'll give it no support. I'm content. I don't want my money.   I don't even want costs.   Dancy, do you understand?

> [DANCY *does not answer, but looks at him with nothing alive in his face but his eyes.*]

TWISDEN.   We are obliged to you, sir.   It was good of you to come.

DE LEVIS.   [*With a sort of darting pride.*]   Don't mistake me.   I didn't come because I feel Christian; I am a Jew.   I will take no money—not even that which was stolen.   Give it to a charity.   I'm proved right. And now I'm done with the damned thing.   Good morning!

> [*He makes a little bow to* CANYNGE *and* TWISDEN, *and turns to face* DANCY, *who has never moved.   The two stand motionless, looking at each other, then* DE LEVIS *shrugs his shoulders and walks out.   When he is gone there is a silence.*]

CANYNGE.   [*Suddenly.*]   You heard what he said, Dancy.   You have no time to lose.

> [*But* DANCY *does not stir.*]

TWISDEN.   Captain Dancy?

> [*Slowly, without turning his head, rather like a man in a dream,* DANCY *walks across the room, and goes out.*]

CURTAIN

SCENE III

The DANCYS' *sitting-room, a few minutes later.*

MABEL DANCY *is sitting alone on the sofa with a newspaper on her lap; she is only just up, and has a bottle of smelling-salts in her hand.   Two or three*

other newspapers are dumped on the arm of the sofa.
She topples the one off her lap and takes up another
as if she couldn't keep away from them; drops it in
turn, and sits staring before her, sniffing at the salts.
The door, right, is opened and DANCY *comes in.*

MABEL. [*Utterly surprised.*] Ronny! Do they want me in Court?

DANCY. No.

MABEL. What is it, then? Why are you back?

DANCY. Spun.

MABEL. [*Blank.*] Spun? What do you mean? What's spun?

DANCY. The case. They've found out through those notes.

MABEL. Oh! [*Staring at his face.*] Who?

DANCY. Me!

MABEL. [*After a moment of horrified stillness.*] Don't, Ronny! Oh! No! Don't!

> [*She buries her face in the pillows of the sofa.*
> DANCY *stands looking down at her.*]

DANCY. Pity you wouldn't come to Africa three months ago.

MABEL. Why didn't you tell me then? I would have gone.

DANCY. You wanted this case. Well, it's fallen down.

MABEL. Oh! Why didn't I face it? But I couldn't —I *had* to believe.

DANCY. And now you can't. It's the end, Mabel.

MABEL. [*Looking up at him.*] No.

> [DANCY *goes suddenly on his knees and seizes*
> *her hand.*]

DANCY. Forgive me!

MABEL. [*Putting her hand on his head.*] Yes; oh,

yes! I think I've known a long time, really. Only—
why? What made you?

DANCY. [*Getting up and speaking in jerks.*] It was
a crazy thing to do; but, damn it, I was only looting a
looter. The money was as much mine as his. A decent
chap would have offered me half. You didn't see the
brute look at me that night at dinner as much as to say:
"You blasted fool!" It made me mad. That wasn't a
bad jump—twice over. Nothing in the war took quite
such nerve. [*Grimly.*] I rather enjoyed that evening.

MABEL. But—money! To keep it!

DANCY. [*Sullenly.*] Yes, but I had a debt to pay.

MABEL. To a woman?

DANCY. A debt of honor—it wouldn't wait.

MABEL. It was—it was to a woman. Ronny, don't
lie any more.

DANCY. [*Grimly.*] Well! I wanted to save your
knowing. I'd promised a thousand. I had a letter from
her father that morning, threatening to tell you. All the
same, if that tyke hadn't jeered at me for parlor tricks!—
But what's the good of all this now? [*Sullenly.*] Well
—it may cure you of loving me. Get over that, Mab; I
never was worth it—and I'm done for!

MABEL. The woman—have you—since——?

DANCY. [*Energetically.*] No! You supplanted her.
But if you'd known I was leaving a woman for you,
you'd never have married me.

> [*He walks over to the hearth.* MABEL *too gets
> up. She presses her hands to her forehead,
> then walks blindly round to behind the sofa
> and stands looking straight in front of her.*]

MABEL. [*Coldly.*] What has happened, exactly?

DANCY. Sir Frederic chucked up the case. I've seen
Twisden; they want me to run for it to Morocco.

MABEL.   To the war there?

DANCY.   Yes.   There's to be a warrant out.

MABEL.   A prosecution? Prison? Oh, go! Don't wait a minute! Go!

DANCY.   Blast them!

MABEL.   Oh, Ronny! Please! Please! Think what you'll want. I'll pack. Quick! No! Don't wait to take things.   Have you got money?

DANCY.   [*Nodding.*] This'll be good-by, then!

MABEL.   [*After a moment's struggle.*] Oh! No! No, no!   I'll follow—I'll come out to you there.

DANCY.   D'you mean you'll stick to me?

MABEL.   Of course I'll stick to you.

> [DANCY *seizes her hand and puts it to his lips.* *The bell rings.*]

MABEL.   [*In terror.*] Who's that?

> [*The bell rings again.* DANCY *moves toward* *the door.*]

No! Let *me!*

> [*She passes him and steals out to the outer door* *of the flat, where she stands listening.   The* *bell rings again.   She looks through the slit* *of the letter-box.   While she is gone* DANCY *stands quite still, till she comes back.*]

MABEL.   Through the letter-box—I can see— It's— it's police. Oh! God! . . . Ronny! I can't bear it.

DANCY.   Heads up, Mab! Don't show the brutes!

MABEL.   Whatever happens, I'll go on loving you. If it's prison—*I'll wait.* Do you understand? I don't care what you did—I don't *care!* I'm just the same.   I will be just the same when you come back to me.

DANCY.   [*Slowly.*] That's not in human nature.

MABEL.   It is.   It's in *me.*

DANCY. I've crocked up your life.

MABEL. No, no! Kiss me!

> [*A long kiss, till the bell again startles them apart, and there is a loud knock.*]

DANCY. They'll break the door in. It's no good—we must open. Hold them in check a little. I want a minute or two.

MABEL. [*Clasping him.*] Ronny! Oh, Ronny! It won't be for long—I'll be waiting! I'll be waiting—I swear it.

DANCY. Steady, Mab! [*Putting her back from him.*] Now!

> [*He opens the bedroom door, left, and stands waiting for her to go. Summoning up her courage, she goes to open the outer door. A sudden change comes over* DANCY'S *face; from being stony it grows almost maniacal.*]

DANCY. [*Under his breath.*] No! No! By God! No!

> [*He goes out into the bedroom, closing the door behind him.* MABEL *has now opened the outer door, and disclosed* INSPECTOR DEDE *and the* YOUNG CONSTABLE *who were summoned to Meldon Court on the night of the theft, and have been witnesses in the case. Their voices are heard.*]

MABEL. Yes?

INSPECTOR. Captain Dancy in, madam?

MABEL. I am not quite sure—I don't think so.

INSPECTOR. I wish to speak to him a minute. Stay here, Grover. Now, madam!

MABEL. Will you come in while I see?

> [*She comes in, followed by the* INSPECTOR.]

INSPECTOR. I should think you must be sure, madam. This is not a big place.

MABEL. He was changing his clothes to go out. I think he has gone.

INSPECTOR. What's that door?

MABEL. To our bedroom.

INSPECTOR. [*Moving toward it.*] He'll be in there, then.

MABEL. What do you want, Inspector?

INSPECTOR. [*Melting.*] Well, madam, it's no use disguising it. I'm exceedingly sorry, but I've a warrant for his arrest.

MABEL. Inspector!

INSPECTOR. I'm sure I've every sympathy for you, madam; but I must carry out my instructions.

MABEL. And break my heart?

INSPECTOR. Well, madam, we're—we're not allowed to take that into consideration. The Law's the Law.

MABEL. Are you married?

INSPECTOR. I am.

MABEL. If you—your wife——

[*The* INSPECTOR *raises his hand, deprecating.*] [*Speaking low.*] Just half an hour! Couldn't you? It's two lives—two whole lives! We've only been married four months. Come back in half an hour. It's such a little thing—nobody will know. Nobody. Won't you?

INSPECTOR. Now, madam—you must know my duty.

MABEL. Inspector, I beseech you—just half an hour.

INSPECTOR. No, no—don't you try to undermine me —I'm sorry for you; but don't you try it!

[*He tries the handle, then knocks at the door.*]

DANCY'S VOICE. One minute!

INSPECTOR. It's locked. [*Sharply.*] Is there another door to that room? Come, now!

[*The bell rings.*

Moving toward the door, left; to the CONSTA-
BLE.]

that out there?

NSTABLE.   A lady and gentleman, sir.

PECTOR.   What lady and——   Stand by, Grover!

NCY'S VOICE.   All right!   You can come in *now*.

[*There is the noise of a lock being turned. And
almost immediately the sound of a pistol-shot
in the bedroom.* MABEL *rushes to the door,
tears it open, and disappears within, followed
by the* INSPECTOR, *just as* MARGARET ORME
and COLFORD *come in from the passage,
pursued by the* CONSTABLE. *They, too, all
hurry to the bedroom door and disappear for
a moment; then* COLFORD *and* MARGARET *re-
appear, supporting* MABEL, *who faints as they
lay her on the sofa.* COLFORD *takes from her
hand an envelope, and tears it open.*]

COLFORD.   It's addressed to *me*.

[*He reads it aloud to* MARGARET *in a low voice.*]

"DEAR COLFORD,—This is the only decent thing I can
do.   It's too damned unfair to her.   It's only another
jump.   A pistol keeps faith.   Look after her.   Colford
—my love to her, and you."

[MARGARET *gives a sort of choking sob, then,
seeing the smelling-bottle, she snatches it up,
and turns to revive* MABEL.]

COLFORD.   Leave her!   The longer she's unconscious,
the better.

INSPECTOR.   [*Re-entering.*]   This is a very serious
business, sir.

COLFORD.   [*Sternly.*]   Yes, Inspector; you've done for
my best friend.

Inspector. I, sir? He shot himself.

Colford. Hari-kari.

Inspector. Beg pardon?

Colford. [*He points with the letter to* Mabel
her sake, and his own.

Inspector. [*Putting out his hand.*] I'll want
sir.

Colford. [*Grimly.*] You shall have it read at
inquest. Till then—it's addressed to me, and I s
to it.

Inspector. Very well, sir. Do you want to have a
look at him?

> [Colford *passes quickly into the bedroom,
> followed by the* Inspector. Margaret re-
> mains kneeling beside* Mabel.
>
> Colford *comes quickly back.* Margaret
> looks up at him. He stands very still.*]

Colford. Neatly—through the heart.

Margaret. [*Wildly.*] Keeps faith! We've all done
that. It's not enough.

Colford. [*Looking down at* Mabel.] All right, old
boy!

THE CURTAIN FALLS

TRIFLES

A PLAY IN ONE ACT

BY

SUSAN GLASPELL

Susan Glaspell (Mrs. George Cram Cook) was born in Davenport, Iowa, July 1, 1882. She took her baccalaureate degree at Drake University and pursued graduate work in the University of Chicago. After several years' experience in newspaper work she became identified with the Little Theatre Movement through the Provincetown Players. Here she met and married George Cram Cook, with whom she collaborated in writing the famous one-act play *Suppressed Desires*. Her one-act plays were collected in one volume, *Plays* (Small, Maynard), in 1920.

CHARACTERS

GEORGE HENDERSON, *county attorney*
HENRY PETERS, *sheriff*
LEWIS HALE, *a neighboring farmer*
MRS. PETERS
MRS. HALE

TRIFLES

SCENE: *The kitchen in the now abandoned farmhouse of* JOHN WRIGHT, *a gloomy kitchen, and left without having been put in order—unwashed pans under the sink, a loaf of bread outside the bread-box, a dish-towel on the table—other signs of incompleted work. At the rear the outer door opens and the* SHERIFF *comes in followed by the* COUNTY ATTORNEY *and* HALE. *The* SHERIFF *and* HALE *are men in middle life, the* COUNTY ATTORNEY *is a young man; all are much bundled up and go at once to the stove. They are followed by the two women—the* SHERIFF'S *wife first; she is a slight wiry woman, a thin nervous face.* MRS. HALE *is larger and would ordinarily be called more comfortable-looking, but she is disturbed now and looks fearfully about as she enters. The women have come in slowly, and stand close together near the door.*

COUNTY ATTORNEY. [*Rubbing his hands.*] This feels good. Come up to the fire, ladies.

MRS. PETERS. [*After taking a step forward.*] I'm not—cold.

SHERIFF. [*Unbuttoning his overcoat and stepping away from the stove as if to mark the beginning of official business.*] Now, Mr. Hale, before we move things about, you explain to Mr. Henderson just what you saw when you came here yesterday morning.

COUNTY ATTORNEY. By the way, has anything been moved? Are things just as you left them yesterday?

SHERIFF. [*Looking about.*] It's just the same. When it dropped below zero last night I thought I'd better send Frank out this morning to make a fire for us—no use getting pneumonia with a big case on, but I told him not to touch anything except the stove—and you know Frank.

COUNTY ATTORNEY. Somebody should have been left here yesterday.

SHERIFF. Oh—yesterday. When I had to send Frank to Morris Center for that man who went crazy—I want you to know I had my hands full yesterday. I knew you could get back from Omaha by to-day and as long as I went over everything here myself——

COUNTY ATTORNEY. Well, Mr. Hale, tell just what happened when you came here yesterday morning.

HALE. Harry and I had started to town with a load of potatoes. We came along the road from my place and as I got here I said, "I'm going to see if I can't get John Wright to go in with me on a party telephone." I spoke to Wright about it once before and he put me off, saying folks talked too much anyway, and all he asked was peace and quiet—I guess you know about how much he talked himself; but I thought maybe if I went to the house and talked about it before his wife, though I said to Harry that I didn't know as what his wife wanted made much difference to John——

COUNTY ATTORNEY. Let's talk about that later, Mr. Hale. I do want to talk about that, but tell now just what happened when you got to the house.

HALE. I didn't hear or see anything; I knocked at the door, and still it was all quiet inside. I knew they must be up, it was past eight o'clock. So I knocked again, and I thought I heard somebody say, "Come in." I wasn't sure, I'm not sure yet, but I opened the door—this door [*indicating the door by which the two women are still standing*] and there in that rocker—[*pointing to it*] sat Mrs. Wright.

[*They all look at the rocker.*]

COUNTY ATTORNEY. What—was she doing?

HALE. She was rockin' back and forth. She had her apron in her hand and was kind of—pleating it.

COUNTY ATTORNEY. And how did she—look?

HALE. Well, she looked queer.

COUNTY ATTORNEY. How do you mean—queer?

HALE. Well, as if she didn't know what she was going to do next. And kind of done up.

COUNTY ATTORNEY. How did she seem to feel about your coming?

HALE. Why, I don't think she minded—one way or other. She didn't pay much attention. I said, "How do, Mrs. Wright, it's cold, ain't it?" And she said, "Is it?" —and went on kind of pleating at her apron. Well, I was surprised; she didn't ask me to come up to the stove, or to set down, but just sat there, not even looking at me, so I said, "I want to see John." And then she—laughed. I guess you would call it a laugh. I thought of Harry and the team outside, so I said a little sharp: "Can't I see John?" "No," she says, kind o' dull like. "Ain't he home?" says I. "Yes," says she, "he's home." "Then why can't I see him?" I asked her, out of patience. "'Cause he's dead," says she. *"Dead?"* says I. She just nodded her head, not getting a bit excited, but rockin' back and forth. "Why—where is he?" says I, not knowing what to say. She just pointed up-stairs—like that [*himself pointing to the room above*]. I got up, with the idea of going up there. I walked from there to here—

then I says, "Why, what did he die of?" "He died of a
rope round his neck," says she, and just went on pleatin'
at her apron. Well, I went out and called Harry. I
thought I might—need help. We went up-stairs and there
he was lyin'——

COUNTY ATTORNEY. I think I'd rather have you go
into that up-stairs, where you can point it all out. Just go
on now with the rest of the story.

HALE. Well, my first thought was to get that rope off.
It looked . . . [*stops, his face twitches*] but Harry,
he went up to him, and he said, "No, he's dead all right,
and we'd better not touch anything." So we went back
down-stairs. She was still sitting that same way. "Has
anybody been notified?" I asked. "No," says she, un-
concerned. "Who did this, Mrs. Wright?" said Harry.
He said it businesslike—and she stopped pleatin' of her
apron. "I don't know," she says. "You don't *know?*"
says Harry. "No," says she. "Weren't you sleepin' in
the bed with him?" says Harry. "Yes," says she, "but
I was on the inside." "Somebody slipped a rope round
his neck and strangled him and you didn't wake up?"
says Harry. "I didn't wake up," she said after him. We
must 'a looked as if we didn't see how that could be, for
after a minute she said, "I sleep sound." Harry was
going to ask her more questions but I said maybe we ought
to let her tell her story first to the coroner, or the sheriff,
so Harry went fast as he could to Rivers's place, where
there's a telephone.

COUNTY ATTORNEY. And what did Mrs. Wright do
when she knew that you had gone for the coroner?

HALE. She moved from that chair to this one over
here [*pointing to a small chair in the corner*] and just sat
there with her hands held together and looking down.
I got a feeling that I ought to make some conversation,

so I said I had come in to see if John wanted to put in a telephone, and at that she started to laugh, and then she stopped and looked at me—scared. [*The* COUNTY ATTORNEY, *who has had his note-book out, makes a note.*] I dunno, maybe it wasn't scared. I wouldn't like to say it was. Soon Harry got back, and then Dr. Lloyd came, and you, Mr. Peters, and so I guess that's all I know that you don't.

COUNTY ATTORNEY. [*Looking around.*] I guess we'll go up-stairs first—and then out to the barn and around there. [*To the* SHERIFF.] You're convinced that there was nothing important here—nothing that would point to any motive.

SHERIFF. Nothing here but kitchen things.

> [*The* COUNTY ATTORNEY, *after again looking around the kitchen, opens the door of a cupboard closet. He gets up on a chair and looks on a shelf. Pulls his hand away, sticky.*]

COUNTY ATTORNEY. Here's a nice mess.

> [*The women draw nearer.*]

MRS. PETERS. [*To the other woman.*] Oh, her fruit; it did freeze. [*To the* LAWYER.] She worried about that when it turned so cold. She said the fire'd go out and her jars would break.

SHERIFF. Well, can you beat the women! Held for murder and worryin' about her preserves.

COUNTY ATTORNEY. I guess before we're through she may have something more serious than preserves to worry about.

HALE. Well, women are used to worrying over trifles.

> [*The two women move a little closer together.*]

COUNTY ATTORNEY. [*With the gallantry of a young politician.*] And yet, for all their worries, what would we do without the ladies? [*The women do not unbend. He goes to the sink, takes a dipperful of water from the pail and pouring it into a basin, washes his hands. Starts to wipe them on the roller-towel, turns it for a cleaner place.*] Dirty towels! [*Kicks his foot against the pans under the sink.*] Not much of a housekeeper, would you say, ladies?

MRS. HALE. [*Stiffly.*] There's a great deal of work to be done on a farm.

COUNTY ATTORNEY. To be sure. And yet [*with a little bow to her*] I know there are some Dickson County farmhouses which do not have such roller-towels.

> [*He gives it a pull to expose its full length again.*]

MRS. HALE. Those towels get dirty awful quick. Men's hands aren't always as clean as they might be.

COUNTY ATTORNEY. Ah, loyal to your sex, I see. But you and Mrs. Wright were neighbors. I suppose you were friends, too.

MRS. HALE. [*Shaking her head.*] I've not seen much of her of late years. I've not been in this house—it's more than a year.

COUNTY ATTORNEY. And why was that? You didn't like her?

MRS. HALE. I liked her all well enough. Farmers' wives have their hands full, Mr. Henderson. And then——

COUNTY ATTORNEY. Yes——?

MRS. HALE. [*Looking about.*] It never seemed a very cheerful place.

COUNTY ATTORNEY. No—it's not cheerful. I shouldn't say she had the home-making instinct.

MRS. HALE. Well, I don't know as Wright had, either.

COUNTY ATTORNEY. You mean that they didn't get on very well?

MRS. HALE. No, I don't mean anything. But I don't think a place'd be any cheerfuller for John Wright's being in it.

COUNTY ATTORNEY. I'd like to talk more of that a little later. I want to get the lay of things up-stairs now.

[*He goes to the left, where three steps lead to a stair door.*]

SHERIFF. I suppose anything Mrs. Peters does'll be all right. She was to take in some clothes for her, you know, and a few little things. We left in such a hurry yesterday.

COUNTY ATTORNEY. Yes, but I would like to see what you take, Mrs. Peters, and keep an eye out for anything that might be of use to us.

MRS. PETERS. Yes, Mr. Henderson.

[*The women listen to the men's steps on the stairs, then look about the kitchen.*]

MRS. HALE. I'd hate to have men coming into my kitchen, snooping around and criticising.

[*She arranges the pans under sink which the* LAWYER *had shoved out of place.*]

MRS. PETERS. Of course it's no more than their duty.

MRS. HALE. Duty's all right, but I guess that deputy sheriff that came out to make the fire might have got a little of this on. [*Gives the roller-towel a pull.*] Wish I'd thought of that sooner. Seems mean to talk about her for not having things slicked up when she had to come away in such a hurry.

MRS. PETERS. [*Who has gone to a small table in the left rear corner of the room, and lifted one end of a towel that covers a pan.*] She had bread set.

[*Stands still.*]

Mrs. Hale. [*Eyes fixed on a loaf of bread beside the bread-box, which is on a low shelf at the other side of the room. Moves slowly toward it.*] She was going to put this in there. [*Picks up loaf, then abruptly drops it. In a manner of returning to familiar things.*] It's a shame about her fruit. I wonder if it's all gone. [*Gets up on the chair and looks.*] I think there's some here that's all right, Mrs. Peters. Yes—here; [*holding it toward the window*] this is cherries, too. [*Looking again.*] I declare I believe that's the only one. [*Gets down, bottle in her hand. Goes to the sink and wipes if off on the outside.*] She'll feel awful bad after all her hard work in the hot weather. I remember the afternoon I put up my cherries last summer.

> [*She puts the bottle on the big kitchen table, centre of the room. With a sigh, is about to sit down in the rocking-chair. Before she is seated realizes what chair it is; with a slow look at it, steps back. The chair which she has touched rocks back and forth.*]

Mrs. Peters. Well, I must get those things from the front-room closet. [*She goes to the door at the right, but after looking into the other room, steps back.*] You coming with me, Mrs. Hale? You could help me carry them.

> [*They go into the other room; reappear, Mrs. Peters carrying a dress and skirt, Mrs. Hale following with a pair of shoes.*]

Mrs. Peters. My, it's cold in there.

> [*She puts the clothes on the big table, and hurries to the stove.*]

Mrs. Hale. [*Examining the skirt.*] Wright was close. I think maybe that's why she kept so much to herself. She didn't even belong to the Ladies' Aid. I suppose she felt she couldn't do her part, and then you don't enjoy things when you feel shabby. She used to wear pretty clothes and be lively, when she was Minnie Foster, one of the town girls singing in the choir. But that—oh, that was thirty years ago. This all you was to take in?

MRS. PETERS. She said she wanted an apron. Funny thing to want, for there isn't much to get you dirty in jail, goodness knows. But I suppose just to make her feel more natural. She said they was in the top drawer in this cupboard. Yes, here. And then her little shawl that always hung behind the door. [*Opens stair door and looks.*] Yes, here it is.

[*Quickly shuts door leading up-stairs.*]

MRS. HALE. [*Abruptly moving toward her.*] Mrs. Peters?

MRS. PETERS. Yes, Mrs. Hale?

MRS. HALE. Do you think she did it?

MRS. PETERS. [*In a frightened voice.*] Oh, I don't know.

MRS. HALE. Well, I don't think she did. Asking for an apron and her little shawl. Worrying about her fruit.

MRS. PETERS. [*Starts to speak, glances up, where footsteps are heard in the room above. In a low voice.*] Mr. Peters says it looks bad for her. Mr. Henderson is awful sarcastic in a speech and he'll make fun of her sayin' she didn't wake up.

MRS. HALE. Well, I guess John Wright didn't wake when they was slipping that rope under his neck.

MRS. PETERS. No, it's strange. It must have been done awful crafty and still. They say it was such a— funny way to kill a man, rigging it all up like that.

MRS. HALE. That's just what Mr. Hale said. There was a gun in the house. He says that's what he can't understand.

MRS. PETERS. Mr. Henderson said coming out that

what was needed for the case was a motive; something to show anger, or—sudden feeling.

MRS. HALE. [*Who is standing by the table.*] Well, I don't see any signs of anger around here. [*She puts her hand on the dish-towel which lies on the table, stands looking down at table, one half of which is clean, the other half messy.*] It's wiped to here. [*Makes a move as if to finish work, then turns and looks at loaf of bread outside the bread-box. Drops towel. In that voice of coming back to familiar things.*] Wonder how they are finding things up-stairs. I hope she had it a little more red-up up there. You know, it seems kind of *sneaking*. Locking her up in town and then coming out here and trying to get her own house to turn against her!

MRS. PETERS. But Mrs. Hale, the law is the law.

MRS. HALE. I s'pose 'tis. [*Unbuttoning her coat.*] Better loosen up your things, Mrs. Peters. You won't feel them when you go out.

[MRS. PETERS *takes off her fur tippet, goes to hang it on hook at back of room, stands looking at the under part of the small corner table.*]

MRS. PETERS. She was piecing a quilt.

[*She brings the large sewing-basket and they look at the bright pieces.*]

MRS. HALE. It's log-cabin pattern. Pretty, isn't it? I wonder if she was goin' to quilt it or just knot it?

[*Footsteps have been heard coming down the stairs. The* SHERIFF *enters followed by* HALE *and the* COUNTY ATTORNEY.]

SHERIFF. They wonder if she was going to quilt it or just knot it!

[*The men laugh, the women look abashed.*]

COUNTY ATTORNEY. [*Rubbing his hands over the*

stove.]   Frank's fire didn't do much up there, did it?
Well, let's go out to the barn and get that cleared up.

[*The men go outside.*]

MRS. HALE.   [*Resentfully.*]   I don't know as there's
anything so strange, our takin' up our time with little
things while we're waiting for them to get the evidence.
[*She sits down at the big table smoothing out a block with
decision.*]   I don't see as it's anything to laugh about.

MRS. PETERS.   [*Apologetically.*]   Of course they've
got awful important things on their minds.

[*Pulls up a chair and joins* MRS. HALE *at the
table.*]

MRS. HALE.   [*Examining another block.*]   Mrs.
Peters, look at this one.   Here, this is the one she was
working on, and look at the sewing!   All the rest of it has
been so nice and even.   And look at this!   It's all over
the place!   Why, it looks as if she didn't know what she
was about!

[*After she has said this they look at each other,
then start to glance back at the door.   After
an instant* MRS. HALE *has pulled at a knot and
ripped the sewing.*]

MRS. PETERS.   Oh, what are you doing, Mrs. Hale?

MRS. HALE.   [*Mildly.*]   Just pulling out a stitch or
two that's not sewed very good.   [*Threading a needle.*]
Bad sewing always made me fidgety.

MRS. PETERS.   [*Nervously.*]   I don't think we ought
to touch things.

MRS. HALE.   I'll just finish up this end.   [*Suddenly
stopping and leaning forward.*]   Mrs. Peters?

MRS. PETERS.   Yes, Mrs. Hale?

MRS. HALE.   What do you suppose she was so nervous
about?

MRS. PETERS.   Oh—I don't know.   I don't know as

she was nervous. I sometimes sew awful queer when I'm just tired. [MRS. HALE *starts to say something, looks at* MRS. PETERS, *then goes on sewing*.] Well, I must get these things wrapped up. They may be through sooner than we think. [*Putting apron and other things together*.] I wonder where I can find a piece of paper, and string.

MRS. HALE. In that cupboard, maybe.

MRS. PETERS. [*Looking in cupboard*.] Why, here's a bird-cage. [*Holds it up*.] Did she have a bird, Mrs. Hale?

MRS. HALE. Why, I don't know whether she did or not—I've not been here for so long. There was a man around last year selling canaries cheap, but I don't know as she took one; maybe she did. She used to sing real pretty herself.

MRS. PETERS. [*Glancing around*.] Seems funny to think of a bird here. But she must have had one, or why would she have a cage? I wonder what happened to it.

MRS. HALE. I s'pose maybe the cat got it.

MRS. PETERS. No, she didn't have a cat. She's got that feeling some people have about cats—being afraid of them. My cat got in her room and she was real upset and asked me to take it out.

MRS. HALE. My sister Bessie was like that. Queer, ain't it?

MRS. PETERS. [*Examining the cage*.] Why, look at this door. It's broke. One hinge is pulled apart.

MRS. HALE. [*Looking too*.] Looks as if some one must have been rough with it.

MRS. PETERS. Why, yes.

> [*She brings the cage forward and puts it on the table*.]

Mrs. Hale. I wish if they're going to find any evidence they'd be about it. I don't like this place.

Mrs. Peters. But I'm awful glad you came with me, Mrs. Hale. It would be lonesome for me sitting here alone.

Mrs. Hale. It would, wouldn't it? [*Dropping her sewing.*] But I tell you what I do wish, Mrs. Peters. I wish I had come over sometimes when *she* was here. I— [*looking around the room*] wish I had.

Mrs. Peters. But of course you were awful busy, Mrs. Hale—your house and your children.

Mrs. Hale. I could've come. I stayed away because it weren't cheerful—and that's why I ought to have come. I—I've never liked this place. Maybe because it's down in a hollow and you don't see the road. I dunno what it is, but it's a lonesome place and always was. I wish I had come over to see Minnie Foster sometimes. I can see now——

[*Shakes her head.*]

Mrs. Peters. Well, you mustn't reproach yourself, Mrs. Hale. Somehow we just don't see how it is with other folks until—something comes up.

Mrs. Hale. Not having children makes less work— but it makes a quiet house, and Wright out to work all day, and no company when he did come in. Did you know John Wright, Mrs. Peters?

Mrs. Peters. Not to know him; I've seen him in town. They say he was a good man.

Mrs. Hale. Yes—good; he didn't drink, and kept his word as well as most, I guess, and paid his debts. But he was a hard man, Mrs. Peters. Just to pass the time of day with him— [*Shivers.*] Like a raw wind that gets to the bone. [*Pauses, her eye falling on the cage.*] I should think she would 'a wanted a bird. But what do you suppose went with it?

MRS. PETERS. I don't know, unless it got sick and died.

[*She reaches over and swings the broken door, swings it again, both women watch it.*]

MRS. HALE. You weren't raised round here, were you? [MRS. PETERS *shakes her head.*] You didn't know—her?

MRS. PETERS. Not till they brought her yesterday.

MRS. HALE. She—come to think of it, she was kind of like a bird herself—real sweet and pretty, but kind of timid and—fluttery. How—she—did—change. [*Silence; then as if struck by a happy thought and relieved to get back to every-day things.*] Tell you what, Mrs. Peters, why don't you take the quilt in with you? It might take up her mind.

MRS. PETERS. Why, I think that's a real nice idea, Mrs. Hale. There couldn't possibly be any objection to it, could there? Now, just what would I take? I wonder if her patches are in here—and her things.

[*They look in the sewing-basket.*]

MRS. HALE. Here's some red. I expect this has got sewing things in it. [*Brings out a fancy box.*] What a pretty box. Looks like something somebody would give you. Maybe her scissors are in here. [*Opens box. Suddenly puts her hand to her nose.*] Why— [MRS. PETERS *bends nearer, then turns her face away.*] There's something wrapped up in this piece of silk.

MRS. PETERS. Why, this isn't her scissors.

MRS. HALE. [*Lifting the silk.*] Oh, Mrs. Peters— it's——

[MRS. PETERS *bends closer.*]

MRS. PETERS. It's the bird.

MRS. HALE. [*Jumping up.*] But, Mrs. Peters—look

at it! Its neck! Look at its neck! It's all—other side *to*.

MRS. PETERS. Somebody—wrung—its—neck.

> [*Their eyes meet. A look of growing compre-*
> *hension, of horror. Steps are heard outside.*
> MRS. HALE *slips box under quilt pieces, and*
> *sinks into her chair. Enter* SHERIFF *and*
> COUNTY ATTORNEY. MRS. PETERS *rises.*]

COUNTY ATTORNEY. [*As one turning from serious things to little pleasantries.*] Well, ladies, have you decided whether she was going to quilt it or knot it?

MRS. PETERS. We think she was going to—knot it.

COUNTY ATTORNEY. Well, that's interesting, I'm sure. [*Seeing the bird-cage.*] Has the bird flown?

MRS. HALE. [*Putting more quilt pieces over the box.*] We think the—cat got it.

COUNTY ATTORNEY. [*Preoccupied.*] Is there a cat?

> [MRS. HALE *glances in a quick covert way at*
> MRS. PETERS.]

MRS. PETERS. Well, not *now*. They're superstitious, you know. They leave.

COUNTY ATTORNEY. [*To* SHERIFF PETERS, *continuing an interrupted conversation.*] No sign at all of any one having come from the outside. Their own rope. Now let's go up again and go over it piece by piece. [*They start up-stairs.*] It would have to have been some one who knew just the——

> [MRS. PETERS *sits down. The two women sit*
> *there not looking at one another, but as if peer-*
> *ing into something and at the same time hold-*
> *ing back. When they talk now it is in the*
> *manner of feeling their way over strange*
> *ground, as if afraid of what they are saying,*
> *but as if they cannot help saying it.*]

Mrs. Hale.   She liked the bird.   She was going to bury it in that pretty box.

Mrs. Peters.   [*In a whisper.*]   When I was a girl— my kitten—there was a boy took a hatchet, and before my eyes—and before I could get there—   [*Covers her face an instant.*]   If they hadn't held me back I would have— [*Catches herself, looks up-stairs where steps are heard, falters weakly*] hurt him.

Mrs. Hale.   [*With a slow look around her.*]   I wonder how it would seem never to have had any children around.   [*Pause.*]   No, Wright wouldn't like the bird— a thing that sang.   She used to sing.   He killed that, too.

Mrs. Peters.   [*Moving uneasily.*]   We don't know who killed the bird.

Mrs. Hale.   I knew John Wright.

Mrs. Peters.   It was an awful thing was done in this house that night, Mrs. Hale.   Killing a man while he slept, slipping a rope around his neck that choked the life out of him.

Mrs. Hale.   His neck.   Choked the life out of him.

       [*Her hand goes out and rests on the bird-cage.*]

Mrs. Peters.   [*With rising voice.*]   We don't know who killed him.   We don't *know*.

Mrs. Hale.   [*Her own feeling not interrupted.*]   If there'd been years and years of nothing, then a bird to sing to you, it would be awful—still, after the bird was still.

Mrs. Peters.   [*Something within her speaking.*]   I know what stillness is.   When we homesteaded in Dakota, and my first baby died—after he was two years old, and me with no other then——

Mrs. Hale.   [*Moving.*]   How soon do you suppose they'll be through, looking for the evidence?

Mrs. Peters.   I know what stillness is.   [*Pulling her-*

self back.] The law has got to punish crime, Mrs. Hale.

MRS. HALE. [*Not as if answering that*.] I wish you'd seen Minnie Foster when she wore a white dress with blue ribbons and stood up there in the choir and sang. [*A look around the room*.] Oh, I *wish* I'd come over here once in a while! That was a crime! That was a crime! Who's going to punish that?

MRS. PETERS. [*Looking up-stairs*.] We mustn't—take on.

MRS. HALE. I might have known she needed help! I know how things can be—for women. I tell you, it's queer, Mrs. Peters. We live close together and we live far apart. We all go through the same things—it's all just a different kind of the same thing. [*Brushes her eyes, noticing the bottle of fruit, reaches out for it*.] If I was you I wouldn't tell her her fruit was gone. Tell her it *ain't*. Tell her it's all right. Take this in to prove it to her. She—she may never know whether it was broke or not.

MRS. PETERS. [*Takes the bottle, looks about for something to wrap it in; takes petticoat from the clothes brought from the other room, very nervously begins winding this around the bottle. In a false voice*.] My, it's a good thing the men couldn't hear us. Wouldn't they just laugh! Getting all stirred up over a little thing like a—dead canary. As if that could have anything to do with —with—wouldn't they *laugh*!

[*The men are heard coming down-stairs*.]

MRS. HALE. [*Under her breath*.] Maybe they would —maybe they wouldn't.

COUNTY ATTORNEY. No, Peters, it's all perfectly clear except a reason for doing it. But you know juries when it comes to women. If there was some definite thing. Something to show—something to make a story about—a

thing that would connect up with this strange way of doing
it——

> [*The women's eyes meet for an instant.   Enter*
> HALE *from outer door.*]

HALE.   Well, I've got the team around.   Pretty cold
out there.

COUNTY ATTORNEY.   I'm going to stay here a while by
myself.   [*To the* SHERIFF.]   You can send Frank out
for me, can't you?   I want to go over everything.   I'm
not satisfied that we can't do better.

SHERIFF.   Do you want to see what Mrs. Peters is going to take in?

> [*The* LAWYER *goes to the table, picks up the
> apron, laughs.*]

COUNTY ATTORNEY.   Oh, I guess they're not very
dangerous things the ladies have picked out.   [*Moves a
few things about, disturbing the quilt pieces which cover
the box.   Steps back.*]   No, Mrs. Peters doesn't need
supervising.   For that matter, a sheriff's wife is married to
the law.   Ever think of it that way, Mrs. Peters?

MRS. PETERS.   Not—just that way.

SHERIFF.   [*Chuckling.*]   Married to the law.   [*Moves
toward the other room.*]   I just want you to come in here
a minute, George.   We ought to take a look at these
windows.

COUNTY ATTORNEY.   [*Scoffingly.*]   Oh, windows!

SHERIFF.   We'll be right out, Mr. Hale.

> [HALE *goes outside.   The* SHERIFF *follows the*
> COUNTY ATTORNEY *into the other room.
> Then* MRS. HALE *rises, hands tight together,
> looking intensely at* MRS. PETERS, *whose eyes
> make a slow turn, finally meeting* MRS.
> HALE'S.   *A moment* MRS. HALE *holds her,
> then her own eyes point the way to where the*

box is concealed. Suddenly Mrs. Peters *throws back quilt pieces and tries to put the box in the bag she is wearing. It is too big. She opens box, starts to take bird out, cannot touch it, goes to pieces, stands there helpless. Sound of a knob turning in the other room.* Mrs. Hale *snatches the box and puts it in the pocket of her big coat. Enter* County Attorney *and* Sheriff.]

County Attorney. [*Facetiously.*] Well, Henry, at least we found out that she was not going to quilt it. She was going to—what is it you call it, ladies?

Mrs. Hale. [*Her hand against her pocket.*] We call it—knot it, Mr. Henderson.

CURTAIN

SPREADING THE NEWS

BY

LADY GREGORY

Lady Augusta Gregory was born in 1859 in Ireland, where she has lived all her life. She has interested herself in the development of Irish literature and has done much work in translating early Irish legends and tales. She was one of the founders thirty years ago of the Irish Literary Theatre, which later became the famous Abbey Theatre, in connection with which most of her plays had their first performances. Among her most popular plays are *Spreading the News, Hyacinth Halvey, The Gaol Gate, The Jackdaw, The Rising of the Moon,* and *The Workhouse Ward,* all of which may be found in the volume *Seven Short Plays* (Putnam, 1911). *New Comedies* (Putnam) is a second volume of short plays of Lady Gregory that is available.

CHARACTERS

Bartley Fallon

Mrs. Fallon

Jack Smith

Shawn Early

Tim Casey

James Ryan

Mrs. Tarpey

Mrs. Tully

A Removable Magistrate

Jo Muldoon, *a policeman*

SPREADING THE NEWS

SCENE: *The outskirts of a fair. An apple-stall.* MRS. TARPEY *sitting at it.* MAGISTRATE *and* POLICEMAN *enter.*

MAGISTRATE. So that is the fair green. Cattle and sheep and mud. No system. What a repulsive sight!

POLICEMAN. That is so, indeed.

MAGISTRATE. I suppose there is a good deal of disorder in this place?

POLICEMAN. There is.

MAGISTRATE. Common assault?

POLICEMAN. It's common enough.

MAGISTRATE. Agrarian crime, no doubt?

POLICEMAN. That is so.

MAGISTRATE. Boycotting? Maiming of cattle? Firing into houses?

POLICEMAN. There was one time, and there might be again.

MAGISTRATE. That is bad. Does it go any further than that?

POLICEMAN. Far enough, indeed.

MAGISTRATE. Homicide, then! This district has been shamefully neglected! I will change all that. When I was in the Andaman Islands, my system never failed. Yes, yes, I will change all that. What has that woman on her stall?

POLICEMAN. Apples mostly—and sweets.

MAGISTRATE. Just see if there are any unlicensed goods underneath—spirits or the like. We had evasions of the salt tax in the Andaman Islands.

POLICEMAN. [*Sniffing cautiously and upsetting a heap of apples.*] I see no spirits here—or salt.

MAGISTRATE. [*To* MRS. TARPEY.] Do you know this town well, my good woman?

MRS. TARPEY. [*Holding out some apples.*] A penny the half-dozen, your honor.

POLICEMAN. [*Shouting.*] The gentleman is asking do you know the town! He's the new magistrate!

MRS. TARPEY. [*Rising and ducking.*] Do I know the town? I do, to be sure.

MAGISTRATE. [*Shouting.*] What is its chief business?

MRS. TARPEY. Business, is it? What business would the people here have but to be minding one another's business?

MAGISTRATE. I mean what trade have they?

MRS. TARPEY. Not a trade. No trade at all but to be talking.

MAGISTRATE. I shall learn nothing here.

[JAMES RYAN *comes in, pipe in mouth. Seeing* MAGISTRATE *he retreats quickly, taking pipe from mouth.*]

MAGISTRATE. The smoke from that man's pipe had a greenish look; he may be growing unlicensed tobacco at home. I wish I had brought my telescope to this district. Come to the post-office, I will telegraph for it. I found it very useful in the Andaman Islands.

[MAGISTRATE *and* POLICEMAN *go out left.*]

MRS. TARPEY. Bad luck to Jo Muldoon, knocking my apples this way and that way. [*Begins arranging them.*] Showing off he was to the new magistrate.

[*Enter* BARTLEY FALLON *and* MRS. FALLON.]

BARTLEY. Indeed it's a poor country and a scarce country to be living in. But I'm thinking if I went to

America it's long ago the day I'd be dead!

MRS. FALLON. So you might, indeed.

> [*She puts her basket on a barrel and begins putting parcels in it, taking them from under her cloak.*]

BARTLEY. And it's a great expense for a poor man to be buried in America.

MRS. FALLON. Never fear, Bartley Fallon, but I'll give you a good burying the day you'll die.

BARTLEY. Maybe it's yourself will be buried in the graveyard of Cloonmara before me, Mary Fallon, and I myself that will be dying unbeknownst some night, and no one a-near me. And the cat itself may be gone straying through the country, and the mice squealing over the quilt.

MRS. FALLON. Leave off talking of dying. It might be twenty years you'll be living yet.

BARTLEY. [*With a deep sigh.*] I'm thinking if I'll be living at the end of twenty years, it's a very old man I'll be then!

MRS. TARPEY. [*Turns and sees them.*] Good morrow, Bartley Fallon; good morrow, Mrs. Fallon. Well, Bartley, you'll find no cause for complaining to-day; they are all saying it was a good fair.

BARTLEY. [*Raising his voice.*] It was not a good fair, Mrs. Tarpey. It was a scattered sort of a fair. If we didn't expect more, we got less. That's the way with me always; whatever I have to sell goes down and whatever I have to buy goes up. If there's ever any misfortune coming to this world, it's on myself it pitches, like a flock of crows on seed potatoes.

MRS. FALLON. Leave off talking of misfortunes, and listen to Jack Smith that is coming the way, and he singing.

[*Voice of* JACK SMITH *heard singing.*]

I thought, my first love,
  There'd be but one house between you and me,
And I thought I would find
  Yourself coaxing my child on your knee.

Over the tide
  I would leap with the leap of a swan,
Till I came to the side
  Of the wife of the Red-haired man!

> [JACK SMITH *comes in; he is a red-haired man,*
>   *and is carrying a hay-fork.*]

MRS. TARPEY. That should be a good song if I had my hearing.

MRS. FALLON. [*Shouting.*] It's *The Red-haired Man's Wife.*

MRS. TARPEY. I know it well. That's the song that has a skin on it!

> [*She turns her back to them and goes on ar-*
>   *ranging her apples.*]

MRS. FALLON. Where's herself, Jack Smith?

JACK SMITH. She was delayed with her washing; bleaching the clothes on the hedge she is, and she daren't leave them, with all the tinkers that do be passing to the fair. It isn't to the fair I came myself, but up to the Five Acre Meadow I'm going, where I have a contract for the hay. We'll get a share of it into tramps to-day.

> [*He lays down hay-fork and lights his pipe.*]

BARTLEY. You will not get it into tramps to-day. The rain will be down on it by evening, and on myself too. It's seldom I ever started on a journey but the rain would come down on me before I'd find any place of shelter.

JACK SMITH. If it didn't itself, Bartley, it is my belief you would carry a leaky pail on your head in place of a hat, the way you'd not be without some cause of complaining.

[*A voice heard, "Go on, now, go on out o' that. Go on, I say."*]

JACK SMITH. Look at that young mare of Pat Ryan's that is backing into Shaughnessy's bullocks with the dint of the crowd! Don't be daunted, Pat, I'll give you a hand with her.

[*He goes out, leaving hay-fork.*]

MRS. FALLON. It's time for ourselves to be going home. I have all I bought put in the basket. Look at there, Jack Smith's hay-fork he left after him! He'll be wanting it. [*Calls.*] Jack Smith! Jack Smith!—He's gone through the crowd—hurry after him, Bartley, he'll be wanting it.

BARTLEY. I'll do that. This is no safe place to be leaving it. [*He takes up fork awkwardly and upsets the basket.*] Look at that now! If there is any basket in the fair upset, it must be our own basket!

[*He goes out to right.*]

MRS. FALLON. Get out of that! It is your own fault, it is. Talk of misfortunes and misfortunes will come. Glory be! Look at my new egg-cups rolling in every part —and my two pound of sugar with the paper broke——

MRS. TARPEY. [*Turning from stall.*] God help us, Mrs. Fallon, what happened your basket?

MRS. FALLON. It's himself that knocked it down, bad manners to him. [*Putting things up.*] My grand sugar that's destroyed, and he'll not drink his tea without it. I had best go back to the shop for more, much good may it do him!

[*Enter TIM CASEY.*]

TIM CASEY. Where is Bartley Fallon, Mrs. Fallon? I want a word with him before he'll leave the fair. I was afraid he might have gone home by this, for he's a temperate man.

MRS. FALLON. I wish he did go home! It'd be best for me if he went home straight from the fair green, or if he never came with me at all! Where is he, is it? He's gone up the road [*jerks elbow*] following Jack Smith with a hay-fork.

[*She goes out to left.*]

TIM CASEY. Following Jack Smith with a hay-fork! Did ever any one hear the like of that. [*Shouts.*] Did you hear that news, Mrs. Tarpey?

MRS. TARPEY. I heard no news at all.

TIM CASEY. Some dispute I suppose it was that rose between Jack Smith and Bartley Fallon, and it seems Jack made off, and Bartley is following him with a hay-fork!

MRS. TARPEY. Is he now? Well, that was quick work! It's not ten minutes since the two of them were here, Bartley going home and Jack going to the Five Acre Meadow; and I had my apples to settle up, that Jo Muldoon of the police had scattered, and when I looked round again Jack Smith was gone, and Bartley Fallon was gone, and Mrs. Fallon's basket upset, and all in it strewed upon the ground—the tea here—the two pound of sugar there—the egg-cups there— Look, now, what a great hardship the deafness puts upon me, that I didn't hear the commincement of the fight! Wait till I tell James Ryan that I see below; he is a neighbor of Bartley's, it would be a pity if he wouldn't hear the news!

[*She goes out. Enter* SHAWN EARLY *and* MRS. TULLY.]

TIM CASEY. Listen, Shawn Early! Listen, Mrs. Tully, to the news! Jack Smith and Bartley Fallon had a falling out, and Jack knocked Mrs. Fallon's basket into the road, and Bartley made an attack on him with a hay-fork, and away with Jack, and Bartley after him. Look at the sugar here yet on the road!

SHAWN EARLY. Do you tell me so? Well, that's a queer thing, and Bartley Fallon so quiet a man!

MRS. TULLY. I wouldn't wonder at all. I would never think well of a man that would have that sort of a mouldering look. It's likely he has overtaken Jack by this.

[*Enter* JAMES RYAN *and* MRS. TARPEY.]

JAMES RYAN. That is great news Mrs. Tarpey was telling me! I suppose that's what brought the police and the magistrate up this way. I was wondering to see them in it a while ago.

SHAWN EARLY. The police after them? Bartley Fallon must have injured Jack so. They wouldn't meddle in a fight that was only for show!

MRS. TULLY. Why wouldn't he injure him? There was many a man killed with no more of a weapon than a hay-fork.

JAMES RYAN. Wait till I run north as far as Kelly's bar to spread the news!

[*He goes out.*]

TIM CASEY. I'll go tell Jack Smith's first cousin that is standing there south of the church after selling his lambs.

[*Goes out.*]

MRS. TULLY. I'll go telling a few of the neighbors I see beyond to the west.

[*Goes out.*]

SHAWN EARLY. I'll give word of it beyond at the east of the green.

[*Is going out when* MRS. TARPEY *seizes hold of him.*]

MRS. TARPEY. Stop a minute, Shawn Early, and tell

me did you see Red Jack Smith's wife, Kitty Keary, in any place?

SHAWN EARLY. I did. At her own house she was, drying clothes on the hedge as I passed.

MRS. TARPEY. What did you say she was doing?

SHAWN EARLY. [*Breaking away.*] Laying out a sheet on the hedge.

[*He goes.*]

MRS. TARPEY. Laying out a sheet for the dead! The Lord have mercy on us! Jack Smith dead, and his wife laying out a sheet for his burying! [*Calls out.*] Why didn't you tell me that before, Shawn Early? Isn't the deafness the great hardship? Half the world might be dead without me knowing of it or getting word of it at all! [*She sits down and rocks herself.*] O my poor Jack Smith! To be going to his work so nice and so hearty, and to be left stretched on the ground in the full light of the day!

[*Enter* TIM CASEY.]

TIM CASEY. What is it, Mrs. Tarpey? What happened since?

MRS. TARPEY. O my poor Jack Smith!

TIM CASEY. Did Bartley overtake him?

MRS. TARPEY. O the poor man!

TIM CASEY. Is it killed he is?

MRS. TARPEY. Stretched in the Five Acre Meadow!

TIM CASEY. The Lord have mercy on us! Is that a fact?

MRS. TARPEY. Without the rites of the church or a ha'porth!

TIM CASEY. Who was telling you?

MRS. TARPEY. And the wife laying out a sheet for his corpse. [*Sits up and wipes her eyes.*] I suppose they'll wake him the same as another?

[*Enter* MRS. TULLY, SHAWN EARLY, *and*
JAMES RYAN.]

MRS. TULLY.   There is great talk about this work in
every quarter of the fair.

MRS. TARPEY.   Ochone! cold and dead.   And myself
maybe the last he was speaking to!

JAMES RYAN.   The Lord save us!   Is it dead he is?

TIM CASEY.   Dead surely, and the wife getting pro-
vision for the wake.

SHAWN EARLY.   Well, now, hadn't Bartley Fallon
great venom in him?

MRS. TULLY.   You may be sure he had some cause.
Why would he have made an end of him if he had not?
[*To* MRS. TARPEY, *raising her voice.*]   What was it rose
the dispute at all, Mrs. Tarpey?

MRS. TARPEY.   Not a one of me knows.   The last I
saw of them, Jack Smith was standing there, and Bartley
Fallon was standing there, quiet and easy, and he listening
to *The Red-haired Man's Wife*.

MRS. TULLY.   Do you hear that, Tim Casey?   Do you
hear that, Shawn Early and James Ryan?   Bartley Fallon was here this morning listening to Red Jack Smith's
wife, Kitty Keary that was!   Listening to her and whispering with her!   It was she started the fight so!

SHAWN EARLY.   She must have followed him from her
own house.   It is likely some person roused him.

TIM CASEY.   I never knew, before, Bartley Fallon was
great with Jack Smith's wife.

MRS. TULLY.   How would you know it?   Sure it's not
in the streets they would be calling it.   If Mrs. Fallon
didn't know of it, and if I that have the next house to them
didn't know of it, and if Jack Smith himself didn't know
of it, it is not likely you would know of it, Tim Casey.

SHAWN EARLY.   Let Bartley Fallon take charge of her

from this out so, and let him provide for her. It is little pity she will get from any person in this parish.

TIM CASEY. How can he take charge of her? Sure he has a wife of his own. Sure you don't think he'd turn souper and marry her in a Protestant church?

JAMES RYAN. It would be easy for him to marry her if he brought her to America.

SHAWN EARLY. With or without Kitty Keary, believe me it is for America he's making at this minute. I saw the new magistrate and Jo Muldoon of the police going into the post-office as I came up—there was hurry on them—you may be sure it was to telegraph they went, the way he'll be stopped in the docks at Queenstown!

MRS. TULLY. It's likely Kitty Keary is gone with him, and not minding a sheet or a wake at all. The poor man, to be deserted by his own wife, and the breath hardly gone out yet from his body that is lying bloody in the field!

[*Enter* MRS. FALLON.]

MRS. FALLON. What is it the whole of the town is talking about? And what is it you yourselves are talking about? Is it about my man Bartley Fallon you are talking? Is it lies about him you are telling, saying that he went killing Jack Smith? My grief that ever he came into this place at all!

JAMES RYAN. Be easy now, Mrs. Fallon. Sure there is no one at all in the whole fair but is sorry for you!

MRS. FALLON. Sorry for me, is it? Why would any one be sorry for me? Let you be sorry for yourselves, and that there may be shame on you forever and at the day of judgment, for the words you are saying and the lies you are telling to take away the character of my poor man, and to take the good name off of him, and to drive him to destruction! That is what you are doing!

SHAWN EARLY. Take comfort now, Mrs. Fallon.

The police are not so smart as they think.   Sure he might give them the slip yet, the same as Lynchehaun.

MRS. TULLY.   If they do get him, and if they do put a rope around his neck, there is no one can say he does not deserve it!

MRS. FALLON.   Is that what you are saying, Bridget Tully, and is that what you think?   I tell you it's too much talk you have, making yourself out to be such a great one, and to be running down every respectable person!   A rope, is it?   It isn't much of a rope was needed to tie up your own furniture the day you came into Martin Tully's house, and you never bringing as much as a blanket, or a penny, or a suit of clothes with you and I myself bringing seventy pounds and two feather beds.   And now you are stiffer than a woman would have a hundred pounds!   It is too much talk the whole of you have.   A rope is it?   I tell you the whole of this town is full of liars and schemers that would hang you up for half a glass of whiskey. [*Turning to go.*]   People they are you wouldn't believe as much as daylight from without you'd get up to have a look at it yourself.   Killing Jack Smith indeed!   Where are you at all, Bartley, till I bring you out of this?   My nice quiet little man!   My decent comrade!   He that is as kind and as harmless as an innocent beast of the field! He'll be doing no harm at all if he'll shed the blood of some of you after this day's work!   That much would be no harm at all.   [*Calls out.*]   Bartley!   Bartley Fallon! Where are you?   [*Going out.*]   Did any one see Bartley Fallon?

[*All turn to look after her.*]

JAMES RYAN.   It is hard for her to believe any such a thing, God help her!

[*Enter* BARTLEY FALLON *from right, carrying hay-fork.*]

BARTLEY.   It is what I often said to myself, if there is
ever any misfortune coming to this world it is on myself
it is sure to come!

[*All turn round and face him.*]

BARTLEY.   To be going about with this fork and to find
no one to take it, and no place to leave it down, and I
wanting to be gone out of this— Is that you, Shawn
Early? [*Holds out fork.*] It's well I met you. You
have no call to be leaving the fair for a while the way I
have, and how can I go till I'm rid of this fork? Will you
take it and keep it until such time as Jack Smith——

SHAWN EARLY.   [*Backing.*] I will not take it, Bartley Fallon, I'm very thankful to you!

BARTLEY.   [*Turning to apple-stall.*] Look at it now,
Mrs. Tarpey, it was here I got it; let me thrust it in under
the stall. It will lie there safe enough, and no one will
take notice of it until such time as Jack Smith——

MRS. TARPEY.   Take your fork out of that! Is it to
put trouble on me and to destroy me you want? putting
it there for the police to be rooting it out maybe.

[*Thrusts him back.*]

BARTLEY.   That is a very unneighborly thing for you
to do, Mrs. Tarpey. Hadn't I enough care on me with
that fork before this, running up and down with it like
the swinging of a clock, and afeard to lay it down in any
place! I wish I never touched it or meddled with it at all!

JAMES RYAN.   It is a pity, indeed, you ever did.

BARTLEY.   Will you yourself take it, James Ryan?
You were always a neighborly man.

JAMES RYAN.   [*Backing.*] There is many a thing I
would do for you, Bartley Fallon, but I won't do that!

SHAWN EARLY.   I tell you there is no man will give
you any help or any encouragement for this day's work.
If it was something agrarian now——

BARTLEY. If no one at all will take it, maybe it's best to give it up to the police.

TIM CASEY. There'd be a welcome for it with them surely!

[*Laughter.*]

MRS. TULLY. And it is to the police Kitty Keary herself will be brought.

MRS. TARPEY. [*Rocking to and fro.*] I wonder now who will take the expense of the wake for poor Jack Smith?

BARTLEY. The wake for Jack Smith!

TIM CASEY. Why wouldn't he get a wake as well as another? Would you begrudge him that much?

BARTLEY. Red Jack Smith dead! Who was telling you?

SHAWN EARLY. The whole town knows of it by this.

BARTLEY. Do they say what way did he die?

JAMES RYAN. You don't know that yourself, I suppose, Bartley Fallon? You don't know he was followed and that he was laid dead with the stab of a hay-fork?

BARTLEY. The stab of a hay-fork!

SHAWN EARLY. You don't know, I suppose, that the body was found in the Five Acre Meadow?

BARTLEY. The Five Acre Meadow!

TIM CASEY. It is likely you don't know that the police are after the man that did it?

BARTLEY. The man that did it!

MRS. TULLY. You don't know, maybe, that he was made away with for the sake of Kitty Keary, his wife?

BARTLEY. Kitty Keary, his wife!

[*Sits down bewildered.*]

MRS. TULLY. And what have you to say now, Bartley Fallon?

BARTLEY. [*Crossing himself.*] I to bring that fork

here, and to find that news before me! It is much if I can ever stir from this place at all, or reach as far as the road!

TIM CASEY. Look, boys, at the new magistrate, and Jo Muldoon along with him! It's best for us to quit this.

SHAWN EARLY. That is so. It is best not to be mixed in this business at all.

JAMES RYAN. Bad as he is, I wouldn't like to be an informer against any man.

> [*All hurry away except* MRS. TARPEY, *who remains behind her stall. Enter* MAGISTRATE *and* POLICEMAN.]

MAGISTRATE. I knew the district was in a bad state, but I did not expect to be confronted with a murder at the first fair I came to.

POLICEMAN. I am sure you did not, indeed.

MAGISTRATE. It was well I had not gone home. I caught a few words here and there that roused my suspicions.

POLICEMAN. So they would, too.

MAGISTRATE. You heard the same story from every one you asked?

POLICEMAN. The same story—or if it was not altogether the same, anyway it was no less than the first story.

MAGISTRATE. What is that man doing? He is sitting alone with a hay-fork. He has a guilty look. The murder was done with a hay-fork!

POLICEMAN. [*In a whisper.*] That's the very man they say did the act; Bartley Fallon himself!

MAGISTRATE. He must have found escape difficult— he is trying to brazen it out. A convict in the Andaman Islands tried the same game, but he could not escape my system! Stand aside— Don't go far—have the handcuffs ready. [*He walks up to* BARTLEY, *folds his arms, and stands before him.*] Here, my man, do you know anything of John Smith?

BARTLEY. Of John Smith! Who is he, now?

POLICEMAN. Jack Smith, sir—Red Jack Smith!

MAGISTRATE. [*Coming a step nearer and tapping him on the shoulder.*] Where is Jack Smith?

BARTLEY. [*With a deep sigh, and shaking his head slowly.*] Where is he, indeed?

MAGISTRATE. What have you to tell?

BARTLEY. It is where he was this morning, standing in this spot, singing his share of songs—no, but lighting his pipe—scraping a match on the sole of his shoe——

MAGISTRATE. I ask you, for the third time, where is he?

BARTLEY. I wouldn't like to say that. It is a great mystery, and it is hard to say of any man, did he earn hatred or love.

MAGISTRATE. Tell me all you know.

BARTLEY. All that I know—— Well, there are the three estates; there is Limbo, and there is Purgatory, and there is——

MAGISTRATE. Nonsense! This is trifling! Get to the point.

BARTLEY. Maybe you don't hold with the clergy so? That is the teaching of the clergy. Maybe you hold with the old people. It is what they do be saying, that the shadow goes wandering, and the soul is tired, and the body is taking a rest—— The shadow! [*Starts up.*] I was nearly sure I saw Jack Smith not ten minutes ago at the corner of the forge, and I lost him again—— Was it his ghost I saw, do you think?

MAGISTRATE. [*To* POLICEMAN.] Conscience-struck! He will confess all now!

BARTLEY. His ghost to come before me! It is likely it

was on account of the fork! I to have it and he to have
no way to defend himself the time he met with his death!

MAGISTRATE. [*To* POLICEMAN.] I must note down
his words. [*Takes out note-book.*] [*To* BARTLEY.] I
warn you that your words are being noted.

BARTLEY. If I had ha' run faster in the beginning,
this terror would not be on me at the latter end! Maybe
he will cast it up against me at the day of judgment— I
wouldn't wonder at all at that.

MAGISTRATE. [*Writing.*] At the day of judgment——

BARTLEY. It was soon for his ghost to appear to me—
is it coming after me always by day it will be, and strip-
ping the clothes off in the night-time?— I wouldn't
wonder at all at that, being as I am an unfortunate man!

MAGISTRATE. [*Sternly.*] Tell me this truly. What
was the motive of this crime?

BARTLEY. The motive, is it?

MAGISTRATE. Yes; the motive; the cause.

BARTLEY. I'd sooner not say that.

MAGISTRATE. You had better tell me truly. Was it
money?

BARTLEY. Not at all! What did poor Jack Smith ever
have in his pockets unless it might be his hands that would
be in them?

MAGISTRATE. Any dispute about land?

BARTLEY. [*Indignantly.*] Not at all! He never was
a grabber or grabbed from any one!

MAGISTRATE. You will find it better for you if you tell
me at once.

BARTLEY. I tell you I wouldn't for the whole world
wish to say what it was—it is a thing I would not like to
be talking about.

MAGISTRATE. There is no use in hiding it. It will be discovered in the end.

BARTLEY. Well, I suppose it will, seeing that mostly everybody knows it before. Whisper here now. I will tell no lie; where would be the use? [*Puts his hand to his mouth, and* MAGISTRATE *stoops.*] Don't be putting the blame on the parish, for such a thing was never done in the parish before—it was done for the sake of Kitty Keary, Jack Smith's wife.

MAGISTRATE. [*To* POLICEMAN.] Put on the handcuffs. We have been saved some trouble. I knew he would confess if taken in the right way.

[POLICEMAN *puts on handcuffs.*]

BARTLEY. Handcuffs now! Glory be! I always said, if there was ever any misfortune coming to this place it was on myself it would fall. I to be in handcuffs! There's no wonder at all in that.

[*Enter* MRS. FALLON, *followed by the rest. She is looking back at them as she speaks.*]

MRS. FALLON. Telling lies the whole of the people of this town are; telling lies, telling lies as fast as a dog will trot! Speaking against my poor respectable man! Saying he made an end of Jack Smith! My decent comrade! There is no better man and no kinder man in the whole of the five parishes! It's little annoyance he ever gave to any one! [*Turns and sees him.*] What in the earthly world do I see before me? Bartley Fallon in charge of the police! Handcuffs on him! O Bartley, what did you do at all at all?

BARTLEY. O Mary, there has a great misfortune come upon me! It is what I always said, that if there is ever any misfortune——

MRS. FALLON. What did he do at all, or is it bewitched I am?

MAGISTRATE. This man has been arrested on a charge of murder.

MRS. FALLON. Whose charge is that? Don't believe them! They are all liars in this place. Give me back my man!

MAGISTRATE. It is natural you should take his part, but you have no cause of complaint against your neighbors. He has been arrested for the murder of John Smith, on his own confession.

MRS. FALLON. The saints of heaven protect us! And what did he want killing Jack Smith?

MAGISTRATE. It is best you should know all. He did it on account of a love-affair with the murdered man's wife.

MRS. FALLON. [*Sitting down.*] With Jack Smith's wife! With Kitty Keary!— Ochone, the traitor!

THE CROWD. A great shame, indeed. He is a traitor, indeed.

MRS. TULLY. To America he was bringing her, Mrs. Fallon.

BARTLEY. What are you saying, Mary? I tell you——

MRS. FALLON. Don't say a word! I won't listen to any word you'll say! [*Stops her ears.*] O, isn't he the treacherous villain? Ochone go deo!

BARTLEY. Be quiet till I speak! Listen to what I say!

MRS. FALLON. Sitting beside me on the ass car coming to the town, so quiet and so respectable, and treachery like that in his heart!

BARTLEY. Is it your wits you have lost or is it I myself that have lost my wits?

MRS. FALLON. And it's hard I earned you, slaving, slaving—and you grumbling, and sighing, and coughing, and discontented, and the priest wore out anointing you, with all the times you threatened to die!

BARTLEY. Let you be quiet till I tell you!

MRS. FALLON. You to bring such a disgrace into the parish. A thing that was never heard of before!

BARTLEY. Will you shut your mouth and hear me speaking?

MRS. FALLON. And if it was for any sort of a fine handsome woman, but for a little fistful of a woman like Kitty Keary, that's not four feet high hardly, and not three teeth in her head unless she got new ones! May God reward you, Bartley Fallon, for the black treachery in your heart and the wickedness in your mind, and the red blood of poor Jack Smith that is wet upon your hand!

[*Voice of* JACK SMITH *heard singing.*]

"The sea shall be dry,

The earth under mourning and ban!

Then loud shall he cry

For the wife of the red-haired man!"

BARTLEY. It's Jack Smith's voice—I never knew a ghost to sing before— It is after myself and the fork he is coming! [*Goes back. Enter* JACK SMITH.] Let one of you give him the fork and I will be clear of him now and for eternity!

MRS. TARPEY. The Lord have mercy on us! Red Jack Smith! The man that was going to be waked!

JAMES RYAN. Is it back from the grave you are come?

SHAWN EARLY. Is it alive you are, or is it dead you are?

TIM CASEY. Is it yourself at all that's in it?

MRS. TULLY. Is it letting on you were to be dead?

MRS. FALLON. Dead or alive, let you stop Kitty Keary, your wife, from bringing my man away with her to America!

JACK SMITH. It is what I think, the wits are gone astray on the whole of you. What would my wife want bringing Bartley Fallon to America?

MRS. FALLON. To leave yourself, and to get quit of you she wants, Jack Smith, and to bring him away from myself. That's what the two of them had settled together.

JACK SMITH. I'll break the head of any man that says that! Who is it says it? [*To* TIM CASEY.] Was it you said it? [*To* SHAWN EARLY.] Was it you?

ALL TOGETHER. [*Backing and shaking their heads.*] It wasn't I said it!

JACK SMITH. Tell me the name of any man that said it!

ALL TOGETHER. [*Pointing to* BARTLEY.] It was *him* that said it!

JACK SMITH. Let me at him till I break his head!

> [BARTLEY *backs in terror. Neighbors hold* JACK SMITH *back.*]

JACK SMITH. [*Trying to free himself.*] Let me at him! Isn't he the pleasant sort of a scarecrow for any woman to be crossing the ocean with! It's back from the docks of New York he'd be turned [*trying to rush at him again*] with a lie in his mouth and treachery in his heart, and another man's wife by his side, and he passing her off as his own! Let me at him, can't you.

> [*Makes another rush, but is held back.*]

MAGISTRATE. [*Pointing to* JACK SMITH.] Policeman, put the handcuffs on this man. I see it all now. A case of false impersonation, a conspiracy to defeat the ends of justice. There was a case in the Andaman Islands, a murderer of the Mopsa tribe, a religious enthusiast——

POLICEMAN. So he might be, too.

MAGISTRATE. We must take both these men to the scene of the murder. We must confront them with the body of the real Jack Smith.

JACK SMITH. I'll break the head of any man that will find my dead body!

MAGISTRATE. I'll call more help from the barracks.
[*Blows* POLICEMAN'S *whistle.*]

BARTLEY. It is what I am thinking, if myself and Jack Smith are put together in the one cell for the night, the handcuffs will be taken off him, and his hands will be free, and murder will be done that time surely!

MAGISTRATE. Come on!
[*They turn to the right.*]

CURTAIN

A LOVE PASSAGE

BY

W. W. JACOBS

IN COLLABORATION WITH

PHILIP E. HUBBARD

William Wymath Jacobs was born in London in 1863. He has devoted most of his life to writing—chiefly short stories of sailor folk. His most noteworthy characteristic is humor; in fact, he is generally recognized as one of the greatest writers of humor of the present day. Like our own Irvin Cobb, he has cultivated another field in short fiction, the story of fantasy and tragedy. A number of his short stories he has dramatized into one-act plays—notably, *The Monkey's Paw* and *Beauty and the Barge*, in collaboration with Louis N. Parker; *The Boatswain's Mate* and *The Changeling*, with Herbert Sargent; *The Ghost of Jerry Bundler* and *The Gray Parrot*, with Charles Rock; *Admiral Peters*, with Horace Mills; and *A Love Passage*, with Philip E. Hubbard.

CHARACTERS

JACK HALL, *first officer of the S. S. "Jessica"*

SAM BROSS, *Captain Alsen's steward*

CAPTAIN ALSEN, *of the S. S. "Jessica"*

HETTY ALSEN, *his daughter*

SCENE: *The saloon of the S. S. "Jessica" (moored in the Pool).*

A LOVE PASSAGE

*The scene is the saloon of the tramp steamer "Jessica,"
and shows a view of the saloon looking along the
length of the ship from aft. The ceiling and borders
show the deck-beams and stringers. The back flat
has a centre opening with double door and coaming.
Behind this through the open doors can be seen the
companion-ladder with an alleyway on each side
of it. Right and left are staterooms which at a length
of eight feet end off to give place to the side of the
ship with two practical scuttles on each side. Under
the scuttles each side is a plush-covered settee. In
the space between stateroom door and end of room
on starboard side is a stove and a mantel-shelf.
Centre is a saloon table and left, right, and above it
are swivel chairs.*

As the curtain rises JACK HALL *enters smartly down
the companion-ladder, goes left to settee—sits and
fills pipe.* SAM BROSS *enters from alleyway carrying tea-tray. He puts it on table—puts cruet off
tray on to table, and starts laying places.*

BROSS.   Will you 'ave yer tea now, sir?
HALL.   No, thank 'ee, Sam, I'll wait for the Skipper.
    [*Lights pipe.*]
BROSS.   There's a boat just put off from the wharf,
sir.   P'raps that is Cap'n Alsen, sir?
HALL.   [*Rises. Looks out of port-hole.*]   I don't
think it is.   There's a girl in the boat.   He didn't say
anything about a passenger.

BROSS. Cap'n Alsen said 'e'd be aboard before six bells, sir.

HALL. Well, it's gone that already. By Jove! it is the Cap'n. I wonder who the girl is? Wonder whether——

BROSS. [*Leaving table and putting head out of next port.*] Nice little piece, ain't she, sir?

HALL. You fetch your ugly head in. D'you want to frighten the girl? Go and get the tea; they'll be alongside in half a tick.

BROSS. Yes, sir.

HALL. [*Left.*] Why, it *is* the old man's daughter!
[*He skips.* BROSS *stares at him.*]

BROSS. Young lady w'at we 'ad with us last trip but one, sir? Verry nice young lady, too—I remember.

HALL. [*Stopping dance suddenly, looking rather foolish.*] You go and get that tea. [*Calls through port.*] Good afternoon, Cap'n.
[*Exit* BROSS.]

ALSEN. [*Off.*] Make fast that line there. Going to be all night about it?

VOICE. [*Off.*] Aye, aye, sir.

HALL. Good afternoon, Miss Hetty—pleasant surprise.

HETTY. [*Off.*] Good afternoon, Mr. Hall; do come and get me out of this horrid little boat.

HALL. Aye, aye, Miss Hetty.
[*Dashes for centre opening.*]

ALSEN. [*Off.*] Catch hold of that bandbox there.
[BROSS *enters with butter on a plate. He collides with* HALL. *The butter rolls off plate on to deck.*]

HALL. Silly fool! Out of my way.
[*Exit up ladder.*]

BROSS *picks up butter, looks round cautiously,* *then blows on it; absently wipes it on his coat-* *sleeve and puts it on table.*]

ALSEN. [*Entering down ladder.*] Now then, my girl, mind you don't fall. [*He puts bag on settee and goes to stove.*] Sam, lend a hand with that gear up there, an' get the tea, an' look sharp!

BROSS. Just coming, sir.

[*Exit. He goes to ladder, waits till* HETTY *is down, then goes up and fetches box.*

HALL *and* HETTY *enter by ladder,* HALL *carry-* *ing box.*]

HALL. Let me give you a hand, Miss Hetty.

[*Hands her down.*]

HETTY. [*As she enters.*] What a stuffy little cabin it is. I'd forgotten it was so small.

[*She sits. Removes gloves.*]

ALSEN. Now then, my girl, don't you get finding fault. What's good enough for your betters is good enough for you.

HETTY. I dare say, but this wouldn't be good enough for my betters.

[BROSS *enters with trunk, down ladder, and exit by alleyway.*]

ALSEN. Well, Jack, you didn't expect a passenger this trip, did you?

HALL. No, but I'm jolly glad to see Miss Alsen's com-ing with us again.

ALSEN. You might tell Sam to make her bed up in that spare bunk, Jack.

[*Turns away and opens bag.*]

HALL. Aye, aye, sir.

[*Goes to bunk and opens door.*]

HETTY. [*Rising indignantly, going up toward head of*

table.] Thank you, I'll do that myself; no man's going to make up my bed.

HALL. [*Moving out sacks, etc.*] There's a few things'll want moving.

ALSEN. Yes; I don't know where Sam's to keep· the onions now.

HALL. We'll find a place for 'em somewhere.

[*Deposits sack outside centre door to right.*]

HETTY. [*Goes to door of cabin, looking into bunk.*] I'm not going to sleep in there. Ugh! There's a beetle.

[*She runs above table.*]

HALL. [*Going to cabin door and peering in.*] It's only a *dead* one.

HETTY. I'm not going to sleep with a *beetle, dead* or *alive*. I want to go home.

ALSEN. [*Going up toward stove.*] Steady, my girl, steady!

HETTY. [*Turning to* ALSEN.] You've no business to make me come when I don't want to.

ALSEN. [*At stove.*] You should behave yourself then.

HALL. [*Above table.*] Why not let her have your *stateroom,* Cap'n?

ALSEN. 'Cos I want it myself.

HETTY. Selfish! I'm going up on deck. I shall be ill if I stay here.

[*She goes toward companion-ladder.*]

HALL. [*Following her as* HETTY *goes to ladder.*] Let me give you a hand, Miss Hetty.

HETTY. [*Turning on him.*] Thank you, I can manage.

ALSEN. [*Picking up bandbox.*] All right, Jack. Let her go by herself. You give me a hand with these boxes. Tea'll be ready directly, Hetty.

HETTY. [*Coming down two steps.*] Yes, with a beetle in it, I shouldn't wonder!

[*Exit by ladder.*]

HALL. [*Takes box from* ALSEN, *puts it into cabin.
Then takes trunk and puts into cabin.*] She made up
her mind to come with us rather sudden, didn't she?

[ALSEN *puts his bag in stateroom, goes to settee.
Sits. Takes out pipe.*]

ALSEN. She didn't make up her mind at all; we did
it for 'er—me an' the missus. It's a plan on our part.

[*Lays finger on nose.* HALL *sits on corner of
table, facing* ALSEN.]

HALL. Wants sea-air?

ALSEN. What she *wants* is a rope's end. That might
bring 'er to 'er senses.

HALL. What's the trouble?

ALSEN. 'Eadstrong young minx—that's w'at she is.
The fact is, Jack, there's a friend of mine—a provision-
dealer in a large way o' business—wants to marry my
girl, an' me an' the missus wants 'er to marry 'im—so o'
course, *she* wants to marry somebody else.

HALL. [*In dismay.*] M—m—marry!

[*Turns away.*]

ALSEN. Yes. Why not?

HALL. Who does she fancy?

ALSEN. A young sprig of a clurk; so me an' 'er
mother, we put our 'eads together and decided for 'er to
come this trip with me.

HALL. What for?

ALSEN. [*Rising, going mysteriously to* HALL.] To
keep 'er out of 'is way. When she's at 'ome, instead of
waiting in to see Mr. Towson—that's my friend—the
moment 'er mother's back's turned, she's out with the
clurk.

HALL. [*Gloomily.*] He's a nice-looking young feller, I suppose?

ALSEN. Nice-looking! Not a bit of it—ugly swab. Now my friend Towson, 'e *is* all right!

HALL. What's Towson look like?

ALSEN. Well, he's a man of about my own figger.

[*Throws out his stomach and stands up.*]

HALL. She'll marry the clerk.

ALSEN. What d'you mean? I'll bet you she don't. I'm an artful man, Jack, and, generally speaking, I gets me own way. [*Whispering.*] I've got a plan, I have.

HALL. Plan?

ALSEN. [*Takes photo from pocket. Very mysterious in manner.*] Yes, and a jolly good one. I've got this cabinet fortygraff of Towson for the mantelpiece here— 'e give it me a' purpose. She'll see this when she won't see the clurk, an' by an' by she'll come round. [*In sudden rage.*] Anyway, she's going to stay aboard here till she does!

HALL. [*With false admiration.*] You know your way about, Cap'n.

ALSEN. Ah! there's very few can teach me anything, Jack. I'm a born manager. [HALL *laughs and turns it to a cough.*] I couldn't live peaceable with my missus if I wasn't. She's a jealous woman, an' Hetty takes after her, Jack. A jealous woman takes a lot o' handling.

HALL. [*Rising from table, goes a step toward* ALSEN. *In squeaky surprise.*] Jealous? What of?

ALSEN. [*Stiffly.*] Why, me!

HALL. Oh, how absurd!

ALSEN. Absurd? What d'you mean?

HALL. I mean with a man of your appear— [*coughs*] principles.

ALSEN. [*Sulkily and not convinced.*] Humph!

Well, it's a good idea I've got, and I want you to give me a hand, Jack.

HALL. Of course I will.

ALSEN. I want you to talk to Hetty as much as ever you can.

HALL. [*Seizing* ALSEN'S *hand.*] I'll do it, Cap'n.

ALSEN. Admire this fortygraff, an' say what a good-lookin' chap he is.

HALL. I will. [ALSEN *turns away.*] I don't think——

ALSEN. [*Turning on him suddenly.*] What?

HALL. I don't think I'd better say anything about the clerk.

ALSEN. O' course not. Tell 'er about a lot o' young girls you know as married young middle-aged men, an' loved 'em more an' more every day o' their lives.

HALL. Not another word. I know just what you want. She shan't marry the clerk if I can help it!

[*Claps* ALSEN *on shoulder.*]

ALSEN. [*Hands on* HALL'S *shoulders.*] If ever you're a father, Jack, I hope as how somebody'll stand by you, as you're standing by me.

HALL. That's all right, Cap'n. You leave it to me.

ALSEN. [*Crossing to stove.*] Now, I'll stick this fortygraff up here—there! Fine-lookin' man I call 'im.

HALL. I've seen worse. What's that lump on his nose?

ALSEN. Lump! Lump be damned! That's the bridge of it. Roman, it is. Look 'ee here, it's time we got off—tide's just on the turn.

[*Crosses below table and turns up in time to see* HALL *move.*]

HALL. Aye, aye, sir.

[*Moves toward ladder.*]

ALSEN.   No, no, you stay and have your tea.   Morgan and me'll take her out.   I'll send Hetty down for her tea, and I'll have mine later on, when we get·down river a bit. [*Going to ladder.*]   Now, don't forget.   You praise that fortygraff all you know how.

[*Exit.*   BROSS *enters with teapot.*]

HALL.   Sure to do that!   Ugly blighter.   [*To* BROSS.] Sam, what d'you think of that photo?

BROSS.   [*Puts teapot on tray, crosses to photo.*]   'Oo is it?   Friend o' yours, sir?

HALL.   No, he's no friend of mine.

BROSS.   Well, if anybody was to arst me, sir, I should say 'ee was a silly fool to 'ave 'is likeness took.

HALL.   Sam, you've got more sense than anybody'd think to look at you.

BROSS.   Thank 'ee, sir.

[*Touches forelock and smiles.*   HETTY *appears at top of ladder.*]

HALL.   Here's a drink for you next time you go ashore. [*Gives money.*]

BROSS.   Thank 'ee, sir.   [*Grinning confidently.*] 'Ere's the young lady a-comin' down, sir.

HALL.   That'll do, Sam.   [BROSS *starts arranging tea-things.*]   You—can—go!

[*Enter* HETTY *down ladder.* BROSS *goes to stateroom; ostentatiously starts unpacking bag.   Shout off,* "Let go that warp there," "Aye, aye, sir!" *Engine-room telegraph clangs.   Whistle sounds.   Splash of water. Telegraph clangs again.   Whistle sounds.*]

HALL.   [*Helping* HETTY *down last steps with arm round her.*]   Well! we're off!

HETTY.   Yes, worse luck!

[HALL *hands her to chair above table, still hold-*

ing her by waist. She frees herself and sits in chair.]

HETTY.   Thank you, Mr. Hall, I can sit down by myself!

HALL.   [*Nervously.*]   Yes, Miss Hetty, I was only afraid you might slip—not being used to ships.

HETTY.   [*Snappily.*]   I hate ships!

HALL.   [*Abashed.*]   Yes.   May I cut you some bread and butter?

HETTY.   Yes, please.   D'you take sugar?

HALL.   Two lumps, please.   Will you pass me the butter?

HETTY.   [*Picking up butter-dish.*]   Yes.   Here!   I say!   What is the matter with the butter?

HALL.   [*Looking at it.*]   It's got whiskers all over it! Sam!

BROSS.   [*Entering from stateroom.*]   Sir?

HALL.   What's the matter with the butter?

BROSS.   Don't know, sir.   What's wrong with it, sir?

HALL.   [*Sternly.*]   What's all this?

          [*Pointing to butter.*]

BROSS.   [*Looking nervously at butter.*]   Them, sir? Oh, those ain't nothing, sir—just a few hairs, sir—they gets into it orf the cow, sir.

HETTY.   First time I ever heard of a blue-serge cow!

HALL.   Take it away and wash it.

BROSS.   Yes, sir.

          [*Takes butter and goes toward door.*]

HETTY.   You'd better comb it too, and after that you can throw it overboard!

          [*Exit BROSS.*]

HALL.   [*Genially.*]   It's quite like old times to see you aboard again, Miss Hetty.   How d'you like the idea of going to sea again?

HETTY. [*Sulkily.*] I've got to like it. I'm sure I didn't want to come. Father made me.

HALL. [*With an air of great wisdom.*] Ah, your father told me something about that.

HETTY. [*Angrily.*] Didn't he tell the cook and the cabin-boy too? What did he tell you?

HALL. Told me about a man called Towson—that chap in the photo up there.

[*Points to photo.*]

HETTY. [*Swinging round in chair.*] Who put that thing up there?

HALL. Your father.

HETTY. What for?

[*Rises, goes to photo and looks at it.*]

HALL. I don't know. I suppose he wanted to make you feel homesick!

HETTY. Seasick, more likely! [*Turns away from photo.*] The cabin's ugly enough without that thing. Well! What's father been saying?

HALL. He told me about Mr. Towson—and another chap.

HETTY. Oh, him! [*Laughing.*] I took a little notice of him just to annoy old Towson.

HALL. [*Eagerly, leaning toward her, knife in one hand, bread in the other.*] You don't like him then?

HETTY. [*Head in air.*] Of course not! I don't like any men.

HALL. I'm sorry to hear you say that. I thought you were beginning to like me!

HETTY. You did, did you? Well!

HALL. [*Lovingly.*] Yes, that last time you went a trip with us.

HETTY. I don't mind you so much. [*Hands him tea-cup. Pause.*] You don't count.

HALL. [*Taking cup away, dismally.*] Oh! What about this clerk chap, though?

HETTY. Well, what about him? I tell you I only noticed him to annoy Towson and father.

HALL. [*Jealously, turning away from* HETTY *toward audience.*] And yet they've sent you to sea to be out of his way!

HETTY. Yes. I wish they'd sent *him* to sea, instead.

HALL. [*Nervously.*] Well, d'you know the best thing you can do?

HETTY. No. What?

HALL. [*Awkwardly.*] It's this way. Cap'n Alsen's brought you to sea to get you away from this chap—so if you fall in love with somebody on the ship he'll send you home again.

HETTY. So he will! So he will! I'll pretend to fall in love with that nice-looking sailor that helped us on board, the one you called Harry. What a lark!

[*Clapping her hands together.*]

HALL. [*Shaking his head.*] I shouldn't do that.

HETTY. Why not?

HALL. 'Tisn't discipline—'twouldn't do at all.

HETTY. Why not?

HALL. Why, he's only a deck-hand.

HETTY. [*Mockingly.*] Oh! I see!

[*Sits back in chair and looks mischievously at* HALL.]

HALL. [*Nervously.*] Now—now—if you were to—to fall in love with me——

HETTY. That would be all right, I suppose?

[*Laughing at him.*]

HALL. Er—yes.

[*Looking away from* HETTY.]

HETTY. *Of course!* Well? How are we to fall in love?

HALL. I don't know much about these things, but we'll have to look at each other a lot.

[*Looks adoringly at* HETTY.]

HETTY. That wouldn't help *me* much. [HALL *turns away.*] Well, go on—look away!

HALL. [*Facing her.*] And then we might hold one another's hands [*hesitates; finally plucks up courage*] like this.

[*Holds her hand across table.*]

HETTY. [*Freeing herself.*] Or we might slap one another's face like that.

[*Does so.*]

HALL. [*Humbly.*] I—I beg your pardon. [*Rubbing his face.*] I thought we'd better get accustomed to it.

HETTY. Well, *you* can get accustomed to *that* to go on with. We'll start by looking at each other—*if*—*you*—*please.* I don't mind that.

HALL. Then we'll get on by degrees. I expect we shall both find it come easier after a time.

HETTY. Anything to get home again!

[BROSS *enters with fresh butter on plate. He puts it on table by* HETTY, *who inspects it.* BROSS *waits.*]

HETTY. Thank you. That looks more tempting.

BROSS. Anything else, sir?

HALL. No, thank 'ee, Sam.

BROSS. Thank 'ee, sir.

[*Exit, looking round and grinning.*]

HETTY. [*After short pause.*] How long shall we be before we get home again, Mr. Hall?

HALL. About ten days.

HETTY. TEN DAYS!

HALL. Yes, time enough to make a good sailor of you.

HETTY. You couldn't. There isn't such a thing as a *good* sailor. They're all *bad*. And they're mostly such scrubby little men.

> [*She looks at* HALL *with a twinkle in her eye.*]

HALL. [*In a pained voice.*] Scrubby!

HETTY. Yes, I'd sooner be a soldier. Soldiers are so brave. Oh, I do wish there was a soldier here now.

> [*With rapture.*]

HALL. [*Sulkily.*] What d'you want a soldier here for?

HETTY. I'd dare him to *do* something for me!

HALL. [*Casually.*] Do what?

HETTY. Oh, it's no use telling *you!*

HALL. [*Firmly.*] Do *what?*

HETTY. [*Insinuatingly.*] Put some mustard on old Towson's nose.

HALL. But Towson isn't here!

HETTY. [*Leaning toward him.*] No, but his photograph is!

> [*Points to it.*]

HALL. What's the good of putting mustard on a photograph?

HETTY. Just to show father I'm not going to look at old Towson.

HALL. But the Cap'n'd be in a terrible way if you did that!

HETTY. *I'm* not going to—I'm not brave enough; but if there was a soldier here, *he'd* do it. I suppose you daren't?

HALL. [*Quickly.*] Oh, yes, I *do* dare!

HETTY. You daren't—cowardy, cowardy custard!

> [*Pointing at him.*]

HALL. [*Rising, firmly.*] Where's your father's mustard?

HETTY. There you are—in the cruet. I don't believe you dare do it—I'm sure you daren't!

HALL. [*Takes mustard spoon, hesitates a moment, goes to photo, and then wipes spoon across photo.*] There!

> [ALSEN *enters down ladder.* HETTY *rises and stands behind* HALL *while he does it.*]

HETTY. Ooh, hoo! You'll catch it when father sees it! Oh [*hears* ALSEN *descending ladder*] Christmas! Here he is. [*Runs across above table to cabin.*] You'll catch it.

> [*Exit* HETTY *to cabin.* HALL *replaces mustard spoon. Enter* ALSEN, *goes to table and sits head of it.* HALL *stands with back to photo, keeping himself between it and* ALSEN, *and trying to look unconscious.*]

ALSEN. Any tea left, Jack?

HALL. Tea? Oh, yes—yes, plenty, Cap'n.

> [ALSEN *pours out cup and starts to drink it.*]

ALSEN. Thank 'ee. Looks like holding fine to-night. Let's have that light on, Jack. [HALL *switches on light. The switch is outside centre door.* HALL *hesitates. Then crosses to door at rear, switches on light over door, tries to get back to hide photo, but only gets above* ALSEN, *when the latter sees photo.*] Did you talk to Hetty about that forty— [*Sees photo.*] Who the—what the—who the devil's done that? [*Rises, goes to photo and picks it up.*] Who did it?

> [HETTY *looks out of cabin, catches* HALL's *eye.*]

HALL. [*Doggedly.*] I did.

ALSEN. *You* did! What for?

HALL. I don't know. Something seemed to come over me—sudden like, and I felt as though I must do it.

> [*Crosses above table.* HETTY *withdraws her head.*]

ALSEN. But what *for?* Where's the *sense* of it?

HALL. I don't know.

ALSEN. But what d'you want to do such a silly monkey trick *for?*

HALL. I don't know, I keep telling you. It's done, ain't it? You don't make it any better talking about it.

ALSEN. You'd better see a doctor when we get to port, Jack. You go an' show that 'ead of yours to a doctor. A doctor what knows.

HALL. It's all right, Cap'n.

> [*Turns away as if to go to ladder, gets to table.*]

ALSEN. [*Taking out handkerchief, wiping photograph.*] But it isn't all right! Now look here, I've wiped this fortygraff as clean as I can get it, an' it's going up on that shelf again, and, mind you, if it only so much as smells mustard [*enters* HETTY] there'll be such a row aboard this ship as you never 'eard.

> [*He replaces photo.*]

HETTY. What's the matter, father?

ALSEN. Matter? He's been putting mustard on Towson's fortygraff—all over his face it was!

HETTY. What for?

HALL. Well—I'm damned!

HETTY. Oh!

ALSEN. Jack! I'm surprised at you! Before my daughter, too. You get off up on deck an' go your rounds an' cool that 'ead of yours. [HALL *goes to ladder.*] And mind me—no more mustard!

HALL. [*Dismally.*] Aye, aye, sir.

> [*Exit by ladder.* HETTY *sits head of table.*]

ALSEN. Did you know anything about this, miss?

HETTY. Oh, no, father dear! How could I? I was in that little cubby-hole there.

ALSEN. What d'you mean, cubby-hole? That's a cabin.

HETTY. What d'you call it a cabin for?

ALSEN. Well, you'll 'ave to put up with it till you make up your mind to marry Towson.

[*Turns impatiently away toward stove.*]

HETTY. I shall be very old before that happens!

ALSEN. There's no satisfying you. What's the matter with him?

HETTY. I don't know. I've often wondered what *is* the matter with him. I think it must be his face.

[ALSEN *turns away.*]

ALSEN. He's a very fine-looking man, miss.

HETTY. Is he?

ALSEN. Yes, he is, miss; and what's more, he's well-to-do. He's got a good business. I knows that, cos we carry a lot of the stuff he buys. [*Impressively.*] Why last trip he had over five hundred hams out of Esjberg!

HETTY. [*Suddenly.*] That's what it is!

ALSEN. W'at is?

HETTY. Why, he's lived among hams till he's got to look like one. [ALSEN *turns away in disgust.*] I thought the mustard seemed to suit his face!

[ALSEN *turns suddenly on her, pointing an accusing finger.*]

ALSEN. Then you *did* know about the mustard, miss!

HETTY. You've just been telling me, father dear!

ALSEN. [*Turns away to stateroom door.*] H'm. Well, don't you let me hear you talk like that about a respectable provision-dealer again, see?

HETTY. But, father dear, you wouldn't like me to sit opposite a man like that every day?

[*Swinging round on chair toward* ALSEN.]

ALSEN. Why not? You've got to sit opposite somebody, haven't you? Your mother has to sit opposite me, don't she? Very well, then!

[*Moves toward ladder.*]

HETTY. Where are you going? Shall I come?

[*Rises to follow.*]

ALSEN. [*Turning at foot of ladder.*] No, I'm only going up topsides for a minute. Get the cards out, an' we'll have a hand when I come down.

[*Exit by ladder.*]

HETTY. [*Crossing to photo, shakes fist at it.*] I hate you. [HALL *enters by alley-way, looks round door.*] I hate you! I wouldn't marry you if you were the last chance I had. [*She sticks out her tongue at the photograph.*] Ugh!

HALL. Yes, he is a terror, isn't he?

HETTY. [*Coldly.*] I've seen worse. [*Coaxingly.*] He looked much better with the mustard on him, didn't he?

HALL. You'll find the mustard pot in the cruet.

HETTY. [*Taking mustard spoon and doing a back-and-forth war-dance.*] I'm going to give him another dose— I'm going to give him another dose——

HALL. Don't you do it!

[*Planting himself firmly in front of photo.*]

HETTY. Shall!

[*Makes for photo. He heads her off. Crossing below table.*]

HALL. Don't do it, I say.

HETTY. Why not?

HALL. He'll think it's me.

HETTY. Of course he will. [*She dances round, and tries to reach photo.*] You don't suppose I want him to think I did it, do you?

HALL. [*Heading her off.*] You put that spoon down!

HETTY. Shan't!

[*She runs round table.*]

HALL. [*Heading her off.*] You put that spoon down!

HETTY. Shan't!

[HALL *catches her and kisses her.*]

HETTY. Oh!

[*She draws back indignantly, about a yard.*]

HALL. Will you give it me now?

HETTY. Take it!

[*Wipes the mustard across his face.*

Enter ALSEN *by ladder.* HALL *turns up to see who it is.*]

ALSEN. Sakes alive! If he ain't a-mustarding his *own* face now! 'E's mad—that's what it is, 'e's *mad!* Don't you go near him, Hetty. Jack!

HALL. Well?

[*Wiping mustard off his face.*]

ALSEN. You've never been took this way afore, have you?

HALL. O' course not!

ALSEN. Don't you say o' course not to me, after behaving like this. A straight weskit's w'at you want. I shall go an' see Sam about it. He's got a uncle in an asylum. You go up on deck, my girl. You can't stop here with a loonatic!

[*He pushes* HETTY *toward ladder, then goes out by alley-way.* HETTY *watches him off.*]

HETTY. Ja— Mr. Hall!

[*He smiles, but does not answer, and keeps turned away from her.*]

HETTY. I'm so sorry—does it smart?

[*Coming slowly toward him.*]

HALL. A little. Don't you trouble about me.

HETTY. You see what you get for behaving badly!

HALL. It's worth it!

HETTY. I'm afraid it'll blister. [*Moving toward him and looking closely at his face.*] Three marks!

HALL. I only had one.

HETTY. One what?

HALL. Those!

[*Kisses her. She does not resist. He takes her in his arms. She kisses him. As she does so ALSEN and BROSS appear at centre door, peering round. ALSEN starts. BROSS laughs. ALSEN pushes BROSS back, the latter resisting. HALL and HETTY separate and sit at table, HALL left of table, HETTY right of table, with back to others. Re-enter BROSS.*]

BROSS. Can I clear, sir?

[*Coughs.*]

HALL. Yes.

[*ALSEN re-enters, comes to head of table and stands eying them foxily.*]

ALSEN. Now then, Sam, look sharp with that truck.

BROSS. Aye, aye, sir.

[*Takes tray and exits.*]

ALSEN. Feelin' better, Jack?

[*Sits head of table, still deep in thought and glancing at them carefully.*]

HALL. I'm all right.

ALSEN. Well, mind you stay all right! Now, what do you say to a hand at cards? Where are they, Hetty?

[*HETTY and HALL smile at each other.*]

HETTY.   I couldn't find them.

[*Rather confused.*]

HALL.   [*Hastily.*]   They're in my bunk, I think. [*Rises.*]   I'll go and get them.

[*Exit by alley-way.*]

ALSEN.   [*Looking suspiciously after him.*]   I can't think what's come to Jack, playin' about with the mustard like that.   He must be mad.

HETTY.   I think he's rather sensible!

ALSEN.   [*Angrily.*]   Now, look here, my girl, you stop that!   Don't you start flirtin' with a loonatic.   *Towson's* what you've got to keep *your* eye on.

HETTY.   I won't—he's so ugly.

ALSEN.   Well, well, we shall see!   Anyway, you stay aboard here till you change your mind; but if you like to be sensible, I'll send you back by train from Fairhaven.

HETTY.   Thanks!   I'll tell you which way I'm going back when we get there.

ALSEN.   [*Looks suspiciously at* HETTY.]   Where the dooce has Jack got to with them cards?   I hope he ain't putting mustard on *them!*

HETTY.   [*Looking toward photo.*]   He really isn't so bad-looking.

ALSEN.   [*Smiling.*]   I always told you Towson was a fine-looking man.

HETTY.   Oh, I wasn't thinking of old Towson.   I meant Mr. Hall.

ALSEN.   [*Banging table in a rage.*]   Now, look here, my girl—once and for all—   [*Enter* HALL.]   Ah [*subsiding*] yes—there you are then, Jack, come along—what shall it be?   Nap or three-handed crib?

[HETTY *and* HALL *smile at each other.*]

HETTY.   Oh, nap—cribbage is so dull.

[*They all sit.* ALSEN *deals.* HETTY *and* HALL

smile at each other. ALSEN, *grinning, watches them. They look at their cards.* HALL *and* HETTY *look at each other over theirs. There is a slight pause.*]

HALL. [*Hastily.*] Pass!

HETTY. Pass!

ALSEN. Four!

[*They play.* ALSEN *loses and pays each.*]

HALL. Twopence to the good!

ALSEN. Save it up for the home! [*Puts money on table. Speaks slowly.*] By the way, how is she, Jack?

HALL. She? Who?

ALSEN. [*Mock surprise.*] Who? Why, Kitty!

HALL. [*Conscious of* HETTY'*s glance.*] Kitty! Kitty who?

ALSEN. [*More surprised.*] Why, Kitty Loney!

HALL. And who's she, when she's at home?

ALSEN. Why, the little girl you're going to marry.

HETTY. [*Sitting up in sudden surprise.*] What!

HALL. Who are you getting at?

ALSEN. [*Injured.*] I'm not getting at anybody. I'm aloodin' to Kitty Loney—the little girl in the red hat and white feathers, you introduced me to as your future.

HALL. What the blazes d'you mean?

[*Throws down the cards.*]

ALSEN. You don't mean to say you've chucked her?

HALL. Chucked who? There never was anybody to chuck!

ALSEN. Jack! I'm surprised at you! After getting an advance from me to buy the ring, too! Didn't you spend the money on a ring?

HALL. No—I—no! Of course not! What on earth are you talking about?

ALSEN. I'm sorry, Jack, if I've said anything to annoy you, or anyways hurt your feelings. It's your business, of course, not mine. P'raps you'll say you never heard of Kitty Loney?

> [*Looks very cunningly at* HALL.]

HALL.   I do say so, I do say so!

> [*Enter* BROSS.]

BROSS.   [*To* ALSEN.]   If you please, sir, the second officer would like you to step up on the bridge a moment, sir.

ALSEN.   All right.   What is it?

BROSS.   I don't know, sir.   The message just comed down, sir.

ALSEN.   All right, Sam.   [*Exit* BROSS.   ALSEN *rises*.] Come, Jack!   Don't be ashamed of your girl before Hetty!   [*Going to ladder*.]   She's a nice little girl, that Kitty Loney, and you're a lucky feller!

> [*Exit by ladder. He turns before he goes and gives a complacent nod and wink at* HALL, *who is staring at* HETTY.]

HALL.   I don't know what you must think of me? I don't know what your father was talking about.

HETTY.   [*Looking away from him*.]   I don't think anything.   Shall we go on playing?

HALL.   I suppose it's a joke of his?

HETTY.   Shall I deal?

HALL.   [*Piteously, leaning across table*.]   But you don't believe it?

HETTY.   Oh, don't be silly!   What does it matter whether I believe it or not?

HALL.   It matters a great deal to me!

HETTY.   Oh, nonsense!   She won't know about your foolishness.   I won't tell her.

HALL.   I tell you it's all a lie.   I know what it is! Your father must have seen us just now, and he's made

up this fairy-tale to make you jealous. He told me just
now you took after your mother! I tell you there never
was a Kitty Loney! What d'you think of that?

HETTY. I think you're very mean. Don't talk to me
any more, please.

[*Turns away.*]

HALL. All right. I won't talk to you! I'll talk to
your father when he comes back. *I'll* give him Kitty
Loney! *I'll* Kitty Loney him! You wait! Two can
play at that game.

[*Picks up cards and shuffles.*

Enter ALSEN. *He looks at* HETTY, *then at*
HALL, *and smiles complacently.*]

HALL. Anything wrong, Cap'n?

ALSEN. No. Morgan thought he saw a capsized boat.
I couldn't see anything.

HALL. Morgan's always seeing things—got a gift of
imagination, he has [*meaningly*] like some other people!

[ALSEN *sits at table.*]

HETTY. When do we get to Fairhaven, father?

[*Still turned away.*]

ALSEN. To-morrow afternoon.

HETTY. I think I'll go back by train—I've had enough
of this.

ALSEN. [*Laughing to himself.*] Ah, I thought you'd
be a sensible girl!

HETTY. Yes. I shall have ham for breakfast every
morning of my life.

[*She wipes her eyes.*]

ALSEN. Come on! Let's finish the game. There's
just time before you take over, Jack. [*In an excess of
triumph.*] You'll have to give up playing cards and all
that sort of thing when you're married, Jack!

HALL. Aye, aye, Kitty don't like cards.

HETTY. [*Turning round and staring at* HALL, *coldly.*]
I thought there was no Kitty!

HALL. [*Calmly but decidedly.*] Kitty don't like
cards, I tell you. Lord! what a spree we had, Cap'n,
when we went to the Crystal Palace with her that night!

ALSEN. [*Startled but assenting.*] Aye, that we did.

HALL. Remember the roundabouts?

ALSEN. [*Forcing a laugh.*] I'll never forget 'em!

HALL. And the swings? Ha, ha!

ALSEN. My word, it was a go! Ha, ha!

HALL. [*Getting more and more jovial.*] You and
that friend of hers, Bessie Watson. [ALSEN's *face loses
its smile.*] Lord! How you did go on!

[HETTY *catches* HALL's *eye and laughs.*]

ALSEN. [*Stiffening in his chair.*] What?

HALL. Bessie Watson! Kitty Loney's friend.

ALSEN. What on earth are you talking about?

HALL. Bessie Watson! Little girl with a blue hat
and white feathers and a blue frock, that came with us—
leastways she was with *you* most of the time!

ALSEN. [*Hissing.*] You're drunk!

HALL. Don't you *remember* when you two got lost, an'
me an' Kitty were looking for you all over the place?
Found you in that arbor at last—all in the dark!

[*He digs* ALSEN *in the ribs.*]

ALSEN. [*Springing up and throwing down cards.*]
You've been drinking! How dare you say such things
before my daughter?

HETTY. [*Spitefully, but laughing.*] It's only right I
should know! I wonder what mother will say?

ALSEN. You say anything to your mother if you dare,
miss! [*Appealingly.*] You know how jealous she is.
It's all the mate's nonsense!

HALL. I'm very sorry, Cap'n, if I've said anything to

annoy you or anyway hurt your feelings—of course it's your business. [*Rises. Throws down cards.*] P'raps you'll say you never heard of Bessie Watson?

HETTY.   Mother shall hear of her!

> [ALSEN *makes an inarticulate noise of rage.* HETTY *rises and runs to* HALL.]

HETTY.   And I expect you'll never hear the last of her!

ALSEN.   [*Comes round table, choking with rage.*] P'raps you'll tell us who this Bessie Watson is, and where she lives?

HALL.   [*Simply.*]   She lives with Kitty Loney!

> [HETTY *kisses* HALL. ALSEN *collapses into chair.*]

CURTAIN

THE GOAL

A DRAMATIC FRAGMENT

BY

HENRY ARTHUR JONES

Henry Arthur Jones was born in England, September 20, 1851. He holds an honorary degree from Harvard University. Among his more important dramas are *The Dancing Girl,* 1891; *Mrs. Dane's Defense,* 1900; *The Hypocrites,* 1906; *Mary Goes First,* 1913; all of which may now be found in his *Representative Plays,* Four volumes (Little, 1925); and *The Theatre of Ideas,* 1915, a collection of one-act plays.

PERSONS REPRESENTED

Sir Stephen Famariss, *the great Engineer*
Daniel Famariss, *his son, Engineer*
Sir Lydden Crane, *M.D.*
Adams, *Sir Stephen's butler*
Peggie Lovel
Nurse Clandon

SCENE: Sir Stephen's bedroom in Belgravia.
TIME: 1897.

THE GOAL

SCENE: The dressing-room of SIR STEPHEN FAMARISS,
*Belgrave Square. A very richly furnished apart-
ment, with every evidence of wealth and luxury. Up
stage right an archway, set diagonally, shows a bedroom beyond with foot of brass bedstead placed sideways to audience. The bedroom is dimly lighted. A
large bow-window, rather deeply recessed, runs along
the left at back, and looks across a courtyard to,
another house, whose windows are brilliantly lighted.
Figures dancing are seen moving across the windows
in accordance with indications given through the play.
Between archway and window a large handsome
bureau. A door left down stage. Down stage right,
fireplace with fire burning. A mirror over fireplace.
A large comfortable sofa down stage right. A table
left of sofa near centre of stage, with bottle of champagne and glasses on it. Another table up stage left
above door. Upon it medicine bottles, spirit lamp,
and other paraphernalia of a sick-room. A large pier
looking-glass up stage above sofa. Other furniture
as required, all indicating great wealth and comfort.
Time, about ten on an April evening. Discover on
sofa, asleep,* SIR STEPHEN FAMARISS. *A rug is
thrown over him, and his head is buried in a pillow, so
that nothing is seen of him but a figure under the
rug.* NURSE CLANDON, *in nurse's costume, about
thirty, is seated in chair at table, reading. The door,
left, is very softly opened, and* SIR LYDDEN CRANE
enters, a little, dry, shrewd, wizened old man about

seventy, with manners of a London physician.
NURSE *rises and puts down her book.*

CRANE. Well? How has he been all the afternoon?

NURSE. Just as usual. He won't keep quiet. About an hour ago he fell asleep.

[*Pointing to* SIR STEPHEN.]

CRANE. Mr. Daniel Famariss has not arrived?

NURSE. No. He sent another telegram for him this evening. And he keeps on asking for the evening papers.

CRANE. Well?

NURSE. I've kept them from him. They all have long accounts of his illness. [*Taking an evening paper from under the table cover, giving it to* CRANE.] Look!

CRANE. *Taking paper, reading.*] *"Sir Stephen Famariss, the great engineer, is dying—"* Hum!

[*A very gentle knock is heard at door left.*
NURSE *goes to it, opens it.* ADAMS *comes in a step.*]

ADAMS. I beg pardon. Mrs. Lovel has sent in to ask how Sir Stephen is; and to say that she's very sorry the ballroom is so near his bedroom; and if the noise of the ball will upset Sir Stephen, she'll be very pleased to put it off, and send her guests away?

NURSE. What do you think, Sir Lydden?

CRANE. All excitement is very dangerous for Sir Stephen. The next attack may be fatal. Will you give my compliments to Mrs. Lovel, and say that since she is so kind I will beg her to postpone the ball?

[SIR STEPHEN *stirs, throws off the quilt. He is in a rich dressing-gown. A wiry, handsome, very intellectual-looking man about seventy-five; well-seasoned, vigorous frame; pale, sharp, strong features, showing signs of great recent pain.*]

SIR STEPHEN. Will you give my compliments to Mrs. Lovel, and say that since she is so kind I will beg her to do nothing of the kind. What rubbish, Crane! Because I happen to be dying, to stop the innocent pleasure of a couple of hundred young people! Thank Mrs. Lovel very much, Adams, for sending in, and say that I'm not at all sure that I shall die to-night; but that if I do, her dancing won't in the least interfere with my dying, and I hope she won't allow my dying to interfere with her dancing. I very much wish the ball to take place. [*Very imperiously.*] It's not to be put off! You understand?

ADAMS. Yes, Sir Stephen.

[*Going.*] ... .

SIR STEPHEN. And, Adams, give my compliments to Mrs. Lovel, and say that if she doesn't mind, I should like to see Miss Lovel in her ball-dress for a moment before the ball. Say that I'm quite presentable, and I won't frighten Miss Lovel.

[*Exit* ADAMS.]

SIR STEPHEN. Well, Crane, am I going off this time?

CRANE. This last attack coming so quickly after the other is very alarming and—very dangerous.

SIR STEPHEN. Yes, but am I going to pull through again, or must I put up the shutters?

CRANE. Well—well——

SIR STEPHEN. [*Seeing paper on table where* CRANE *has put it.*] Is that to-night's paper? [*No reply.*] Give it to me.

CRANE. [*Deprecatingly.*] Famariss——

SIR STEPHEN. Give it to me.

[CRANE *gives it to him reluctantly.*]

SIR STEPHEN. [*Reading from paper.*] "Alarming illness of Sir Stephen Famariss. Angina Pectoris. Fatal symptoms. Sir Stephen Famariss, the great engineer, is dying—" There's nothing like making sure of your facts.

CRANE. Too sure!

SIR STEPHEN. [*Dryly.*] So I think. What do you say? How long am I going to live?

CRANE. Well——

SIR STEPHEN. Come out with it, old friend. I'm not afraid to hear.

CRANE. With the greatest care, I see no reason why you shouldn't live some weeks—or months.

SIR STEPHEN. Shall I live long enough to carry out my Milford Haven scheme? Tell me the truth.

CRANE. No. You certainly won't.

SIR STEPHEN. [*Shows intense disappointment.*] You're sure?

CRANE. I'm sure.

SIR STEPHEN. But I shall live long enough to start it, to put it into other hands, into my son's hands—if the rebellious fool will only learn wisdom and make it up with me before I die. I shall live long enough for that?

CRANE. No. I fear not.

SIR STEPHEN. [*Going to bureau.*] But I've got a third of it on paper. [*Taking out plans.*] I've kept it here. I've worked at it when I couldn't sleep. If I can last out another six months, I can do it. Come, Crane, don't be stingy. Give me another six months! Eh?

CRANE. Famariss, you won't last six months even with the greatest care. You may not last six weeks——

SIR STEPHEN. Nor six days?

CRANE. Nor six days.

SIR STEPHEN. Nor six hours?

CRANE. Oh——!

SIR STEPHEN. Nor six hours. Thank you. I'm prepared.

CRANE. Your son hasn't come yet?

SIR STEPHEN. No. I've telegraphed him twice—and my terms.

CRANE. Is it worth while—of course, you know best —is it worth while to stick out for terms when——?

SIR STEPHEN. When one is in face of death. Yes— on a matter of principle. If Dan comes here, he comes on my terms. I'll keep my word; I won't set eyes on him —he shan't pass that door until he owns he was wrong.

CRANE. But——

SIR STEPHEN. [*Getting excited.*] But he was wrong. He was wrong, and no power on earth shall make me——

CRANE. [*Soothing him.*] Hush! If he does come, you must avoid all excitement in meeting him. Your only chance of prolonging your life is to keep absolutely quiet. You must lay up all day——

SIR STEPHEN. Lay up all day! Don't talk nonsense!

CRANE. If you don't——

SIR STEPHEN. If I don't——

CRANE. You may die at any moment.

SIR STEPHEN. But if I do, I'm dead already. No, Crane, I'll live to my last moment, whenever it comes. When I do take to my bed, I'll take to it once for all, in the churchyard, beside my Peggie! [*Very softly, very tenderly, half to himself.*] My Peggie! My Peggie! If I do go off, I shall see her again, I suppose—if it isn't all moonshine! Open the window, Nurse! It's getting hot here! [*The* NURSE *opens window.*] Open that champagne, Crane, and pour yourself out a glass, and pour me out a glass. My Peggie! My Peggie! I wonder if it is all moonshine!

[*The musicians in tne ball-room opposite begin to tune up their fiddles.* NURSE *comes down.*]

SIR STEPHEN. That's right! Tune up! Tune up!

And Peggie Lovel promised me the first dance! Tune
up!

NURSE. You must keep quiet——

SIR STEPHEN. [*Pettishly.*] Run away! Run away!
  [CRANE *makes* NURSE *a sign, and she goes off
   into bedroom.* CRANE *has opened the champagne and poured out two glasses. He brings
   one to* SIR STEPHEN.]

SIR STEPHEN. It's the eighty-four Saint Marceaux.
I've left you half what's left of this, Crane, and I've left
my mule of a boy the other half. He's my heir. I won't
see him; no, not if I——

CRANE. Hush! Hush!

SIR STEPHEN. I won't see him unless he submits.
But I've left him every penny, except what goes to
charities and churches. It's very puzzling to know what
to do with one's money, Crane. I've left a heap to
charities, and I've squared all the churches. I hope it
won't do much harm. [*A little chuckle.*] There's one
thing I regret in dying, Crane: I shan't be able to hear
my funeral sermons. But you will——

CRANE. Don't make too sure. I may go off first; but
if I am doomed, I hope the oratory will be of as good
a vintage as this.

SIR STEPHEN. It ought to be, considering what I've
left them all. Give them a hint, Crane, not to whitewash
my sepulchre with any lying cant. Don't let them make
a plaster-of-Paris saint of me! I won't have it! I won't
have it! I've been a man, and never less than a man.
I've never refused to do the work that came in my way,
and, thank God, I've never refused to taste a pleasure.
And I've had a rare good time in this rare good world.
I wish I'd got to live it all over again!

CRANE. You do?

Sir Stephen. Yes; every moment of it, good and evil, pleasure and pain, love and work, success and failure, youth and age, I'd fill the cup again, and I'd drain it to the dregs if I could. You wouldn't?

Crane. No. Once is enough for me.

Sir Stephen. You see, Crane, before starting in life, I took the one great step to secure success and happiness.

Crane. What's that?

Sir Stephen. I made an excellent choice of my father and mother. Not rich. Not aristocratic. But a good, sound, healthy stock on both sides. What's the cause of all the weak, snivelling pessimism we hear? What's the cause of nine-tenths of the misery around us—ruined lives; shattered health; physical, moral, intellectual beggary? What's the cause of doctors' bills?

Crane. Well, what is?

Sir Stephen. Men and women exercise no care in choosing their fathers and mothers. You doctors know it! You doctors know it! Once choose your father and mother wisely, and you can play all sorts of tricks with your constitution. You can drink your half-bottle of champagne at seventy-five and enjoy it! Another glass!

Crane. No, I must be going! [*Rising.*] And [*tapping bottle*] you mustn't take any more.

Sir Stephen. Don't talk nonsense! Sit down! Sit down! Another glass! Hobnob, man; hobnob! Life's but a span! Why, this may be the last time, eh?

Crane. Any time may be the last time. Any moment may be the last moment.

Sir Stephen. Well, then, let's enjoy the last moment! I tell you, Crane, I'm ready. All my affairs are in perfect order. I should have liked to finish that Milford Haven scheme; but if it isn't to be—[*deep sigh*]— Hobnob, man; hobnob!

CRANE. What a lovely wine!

SIR STEPHEN. Isn't it? I remember Goethe says that the man who drinks wine is damned, but the man who drinks bad wine is doubly damned. Pray God you and I may be only damned once, Crane.

CRANE. Oh, that's past praying for—in my case!

SIR STEPHEN. Eighty-four! I was boring a hole through the Rockies that summer—ah, Crane, what glorious summers I've had!—seventy-five glorious golden summers—and now— Hobnob, man; hobnob! You've had a good innings, too, Crane.

CRANE. Hum! Pretty fair. I eat well, drink well, sleep well, get my early morning jog in the Park and enjoy it, get my two months on the moors, and enjoy them. I feel as fit to-day as I did thirty years ago. There's only one pleasure that fails me—[*with a grimace at* SIR STEPHEN]—Gone! Gone! Gone!

SIR STEPHEN. Don't fret about that! We thought it a pleasure, old crony, while it lasted. Now it's gone, let's call it a plague and a sin, and thank God for giving us a little peace in our old age. Ah, dear, dear, what a havoc women have made of the best half of my life; but— [*brightening*]—I've left some good work behind me, in spite of the hussies! And, thank Heaven, my *throat* has held out to the last.

[*Drinking.*]

CRANE. [*Drinking.*] And mine!

SIR STEPHEN. Crane, what was that joke that came up at poor Farley's funeral?

CRANE. Joke?

SIR STEPHEN. Don't you remember while we were waiting for them to bring dear old Farley down-stairs, Maidment began telling that story about the geese and the Scotch boy——

CRANE. Yes, yes; to be sure!

[*Beginning to laugh.*]

SIR STEPHEN. And just as we were enjoying the joke, we suddenly remembered where we were, and you pulled us up, and spoiled the joke!

CRANE. Yes, yes, I remember.

SIR STEPHEN. Crane, if Maidment tells that story at my funeral, don't pull him up——

CRANE. Eh?

SIR STEPHEN. It's a good joke, man! Don't waste it! Have your laugh out, and say from me that, other conditions being favorable, I'm enjoying it as heartily as any of you! You will, eh? You will?

CRANE. Yes, I will! I will!

[*They both laugh a little.* ADAMS *opens door left, and comes in a step.*]

ADAMS. Miss Lovel has come, Sir Stephen.

SIR STEPHEN. Show her in, Adams.

[*Exit* ADAMS.]

CRANE. I must be going.

[*Re-enter* ADAMS, *showing in* PEGGIE LOVEL, *a débutante of eighteen, in her first ball-dress; radiant, excited, beautifully dressed, a vision of girlish loveliness. She is frivolous and self-conscious, and full of little airs and graces, constantly glancing at herself in the two mirrors.*]

ADAMS. [*Announcing.*] Miss Lovel.

[*Exit* ADAMS.]

SIR STEPHEN. Come in, Peggie. I mustn't call you Peggie any more. Come in, Miss Lovel.

PEGGIE. Mamma said you would like to see me for a minute before the ball!

SIR STEPHEN. If you don't mind.

PEGGIE.   How d'ye do, Sir Lydden?

    [*Shaking hands.*]

CRANE.   How d'ye do, Miss Lovel?   Good night, Sir Stephen.

    [*Holding out hand.*]

SIR STEPHEN.   Don't go, old chum.

    [*Taking his hand, retaining it, keeping* CRANE.]

CRANE.   I must.   [*Taking out watch.*]   I have a consultation at eleven.

SIR STEPHEN.   [*Piteously.*]   Don't go, old chum.

CRANE.   It's really pressing.   It's Lord Albert Swale. He won't last till the morning.

SIR STEPHEN.   Don't go.   I may be meeting him soon, and I'll make your apologies.   [*Very piteously.*]   Don't go, old chum!

CRANE.   I must.   [NURSE *enters from bedroom.*] Nurse, I want a word with you down-stairs.   [NURSE *crosses to left, and exit.*]   [*To* SIR STEPHEN.]   I'll look in, the first thing in the morning.

SIR STEPHEN.   Do.   You'll find me—at home.

CRANE.   Good night.   Good night, Miss Lovel.

PEGGIE.   Good night, Sir Lydden.

CRANE.   [*In a low tone to* PEGGIE.]   You mustn't stay long, and you mustn't let Sir Stephen excite himself. [*To* SIR STEPHEN.]   I'd rather see you in bed——

SIR STEPHEN.   [*Very impatiently.*]   Tut! Tut! Tut! I won't be buried before I'm dead.   [*Rather curtly.*] Good night.

    [CRANE *waits.*]

SIR STEPHEN.   [*Imperiously.*]   Good night!   [CRANE *is going.*]   And, Crane, remember—no whitewash on my sepulchre!

      [*Exit* CRANE, *left.* PEGGIE *meantime has taken off her cloak. All through she is eager and excited, glances at herself in the glasses very often.*]

PEGGIE. I'm so sorry you're ill, Sir Stephen.

SIR STEPHEN. I'm not ill, my dear. The old machine seems just as strong and tough as ever, only—it's gone *crack* in a weak place. Well, I've knocked it about all over the world for seventy-five years, and if it hadn't gone crack in one place, I suppose it would in another. Never mind me. Let's talk about you. Go and stand there, and let me look at you.

PEGGIE. [*Displaying her dress.*] Do you like me? Do you like my dress?

SIR STEPHEN. It's a triumph!

PEGGIE. [*Chattering on.*] You can't imagine what trouble mama and I have taken over it. Long sleeves are coming in for evening wear. So I had long sleeves at first. I was all sleeves. So I had them taken out and short sleeves put in. The dressmaker made a horrible muddle of them. So we tried long sleeves again. I looked a perfect fright!

SIR STEPHEN. I won't believe it.

PEGGIE. Yes, I did, I assure you. So at the last moment I had the long sleeves taken out and the short sleeves dodged up with lace. Which do you like best? Long sleeves or short sleeves?

SIR STEPHEN. Long sleeves for ugly arms—short sleeves for beautiful arms!

PEGGIE. [*Frowning at him and shaking her head.*] Ah! What do you think of the bodice?

SIR STEPHEN. Enchanting!

PEGGIE. It is rather neat, isn't it?

SIR STEPHEN. Neat? I should call it gorgeous!

PEGGIE. Oh, you must see the one I've got for the Lardner's dance next Monday. Would you like to see it?

SIR STEPHEN. Very much—on Monday.

PEGGIE. I'll run in for a moment before I go.

SIR STEPHEN. Do.

PEGGIE. That's a square-cut bodice. This is a round-cut bodice. Which do you like best? Round-cut bodices, or square-cut bodices?

SIR STEPHEN. To-night I like round-cut bodices. On Monday I think I shall prefer square-cut bodices.

PEGGIE. I think I prefer a square-cut bodice. I had a square-cut bodice to this at first. I looked a perfect monster, so I had it taken out and this round-cut bodice put. I'm not sure that it's quite right now, and I've tried it on fifty times—I'm worrying you to death.

SIR STEPHEN. No! no!

PEGGIE. Yes, I am, and I can't stay five minutes. Are you sure you wouldn't rather have the ball put off? We will put if off even now, if you wish.

SIR STEPHEN. Not for the world! not for the world!

PEGGIE. That's so good of you! But I really think you'll be better to-morrow. I'm sure you will. You aren't really very ill, are you? Do you like this embroidery?

[*Pointing to trimming on her skirt.*]

SIR STEPHEN. It's beautiful! Isn't it Indian work?

PEGGIE. Yes; hand-made. It took a man twelve or fifteen years to make this one strip.

SIR STEPHEN. A quarter of a lifetime to decorate you for a few hours. It was time well spent. Ah, Peggie, that's the sum and meaning of all our toil and money-grubbing!

PEGGIE. What is?

SIR STEPHEN. To make our women-folk beautiful. It all comes to that in the end. Let Nature and Art knock their heads together till doomsday, they'll never teach one another any finer trick than to show a beautiful maiden to a handsome young fellow, or a handsome young fellow to a beautiful maiden.

> [PEGGIE *has got behind him and is admiring herself in the glass.*]

PEGGIE. Really! Really! Yes, I suppose you're right. You're sure I'm not worrying you——

SIR STEPHEN. No, no. Don't go. I'm quite at leisure now to the end of my life.

PEGGIE. Oh, you mustn't talk like that! So I may tell mama that you like my dress? What do you think of the skirt?

SIR STEPHEN. Isn't there too much trimming on it?

PEGGIE. Oh, no! Oh, no!

SIR STEPHEN. Yes, there's too much trimming.

PEGGIE. Oh, no! Oh, no! The dressmaker said there wasn't enough.

SIR STEPHEN. Stupid hussies, dressmakers! They're like other folks! They're always the last to know anything about their own business. Tell your dressmaker that simplicity is the key-note of a great style in dressmaking, and engineering—subtle simplicity. The next time she is going to make you a dress, tell her to take a walk through our National Gallery——

PEGGIE. Oh, Sir Stephen, you surely wouldn't dress me like those old guys in the National Gallery! What would my partners say?

SIR STEPHEN. Your partners! Ah, you pretty tyrant, you'll turn a great many heads, and set a great many hearts beating to-night.

PEGGIE. Shall I? Shall I?

SIR STEPHEN. Why, you've set my old worn-out heart fluttering, and, goodness knows, it ought to have done beating for pretty girls at seventy-five—it ought to know

better at seventy-five! But it doesn't, and—[*rising with
great determination*]—I've a great mind——

PEGGIE. [*A little alarmed.*] Sir Stephen, what are
you going to do?

SIR STEPHEN. Don't you remember your promise?

PEGGIE. My promise?

SIR STEPHEN. Your birthday party six years ago!
You danced with me, and you promised that I should be
your first partner at your first ball after you came out!

PEGGIE. Of course—I'd forgotten!

SIR STEPHEN. But I hadn't! Will you keep your
promise, Peggie? Will you keep your promise?

PEGGIE. Wouldn't it be dangerous, and—you don't
really wish it?

SIR STEPHEN. [*Sinking down.*] You're right, my
dear. I'm foolish with old age. Forgive me!

PEGGIE. I'm sorry to disappoint you. But you'll be
able to see us dancing across the garden. You can stand
at that window and look on.

SIR STEPHEN. Look on! That's all I'm fit for now—
to look on at life!

　　　　[*Turning away his head.*]

PEGGIE. Sir Stephen, what's the matter?

SIR STEPHEN. I've always been in the thick of the
fight, Peggie. And I feel to-night as strong as ever I did,
and they tell me I must lay up and look on—[*rising with
great energy and determination*]—I won't! I won't!

PEGGIE. Sir Stephen.

SIR STEPHEN. I can't bear it, Peggie. I've enjoyed
my life, and I don't want to leave it. I want to live, and
live, and live—and I will! Ah, what a selfish old coward
I am! I'm like a man who has sat down to a good table
d'hôte, and eaten and drunk his fill, and now the host tells
me my place is wanted for another guest, I cry out and

want to have my dinner over again! Don't take any notice of me, dear. Tell me about your partners. Who's going to dance with you to-night?

PEGGIE. Oh, I suppose Mr. Lascelles, Freddie Lister, Lord Doverbury, Johnny Butler, Sir Egerton Wendover, Dick French—amongst others.

SIR STEPHEN. Peggie——

PEGGIE. Yes——

SIR STEPHEN. You won't misunderstand me, dear. I'm old enough to be your grandfather. [*Takes her hand very tenderly.*] You won't misunderstand me. [*Very seriously.*] Take care how you choose your partner for life. You'll have a wide choice, and all your future happiness, and the happiness perhaps of many generations to come, will depend on the one moment when you say "Yes" to one of the scores of young fellows who'll ask you to be his wife. Take care, dear! Take care! Look him thoroughly up and down! Be sure that he has a good full open eye that can look you straight in the face; and be sure that the whites of his eyes are clear. Take care he hasn't got a queer-shaped head, or a low forehead. A good round head, and a good full high forehead, do you hear? Notice the grip of his hand when he shakes hands with you! Take care it's strong and firm, and not cold and dry. No young man should have a cold dry hand. Don't say "Yes" till you've seen him out of trousers, in riding dress, or court dress. Look at the shape of his legs—a good, well-shaped leg, eh, Peggie? And take care it is his leg! See that he's well-knit and a little lean, not flabby; doesn't squint; doesn't stammer; hasn't got any nervous tricks or twitchings. Don't marry a bald man! They say we shall all be bald in ten generations. Wait ten generations, Peggie, and then don't marry a bald man! Can you remember all this, dear? Watch his walk! See that he has a good springy step, and feet made of elastic —can do his four or five miles an hour without turning a hair. Don't have him if he has a cough in the winter or the spring. Young men ought never to have a cough. And be sure he can laugh well and heartily—not a snigger, or a wheeze, or a cackle, but a good, deep, hearty laugh right down from the bottom of his chest. And if he has a little money, or even a good bit, so much the better! There now! You choose a man like that, Peggie, and I won't promise you that you'll be happy, but if you're not, it won't be your fault, and it won't be his, and it won't be mine!

PEGGIE. Very well, Sir Stephen, I'll try and remember.

SIR STEPHEN. Do, my dear, do! It's a good legacy, my dear. I've left you another. You won't be disappointed when my will's read——

PEGGIE. Oh, Sir Stephen!

SIR STEPHEN. No, you won't; but remember my advice to-night. That's the best wedding-present for any girl.

PEGGIE. Very well, Sir Stephen! I must be going. Good-by.

[*Giving her hand.*]

SIR STEPHEN. Yes, I suppose you mustn't stay. [*Taking her hand, keeping it as he had kept* CRANE'S, *as if he couldn't bear to let her go.*] Good-by.

[*Looking longingly at her with a mute entreaty to stay.* PEGGIE *draws her hand away, puts on cloak, and goes to door, left. He watches her all the while.*]

PEGGIE. [*At door, runs back to him.*] Sir Stephen, I'll keep my promise. You shall be my first partner. [*Offering her card.*] Write your name down for my first dance.

Sir Stephen. But I shan't be there.

Peggie. I'll sit out, and keep it for you.

Sir Stephen. No, no——

Peggie. Yes, yes! I insist. Put your name down!

[*He writes on her card. Enter* Nurse, *left.*]

Peggie. Good-by, Sir Stephen.

Sir Stephen. Good-by, Peggie! [*Softly.*] Peggie! Her name was Peggie! My wife's name was Peggie!

[*She bends and kisses his forehead; then goes to door, turns and looks at him.*]

Peggie. Au 'voir.

[*Blows him a kiss and exit, left.* Sir Stephen *looks longingly after her, walks a little up and down the room.*]

Nurse. [*Anxiously.*] Sir Stephen, don't you think you might lie down now?

Sir Stephen. Run away! Run away!

Nurse. Won't you rest a little on the sofa?

Sir Stephen. Run away! Run away!

Nurse. Can I get you anything?

Sir Stephen. Run away! Run away! [*Pacing up and down.*] Mr. Daniel Famariss hasn't come yet?

Nurse. No. You know they said that he was away surveying in an out-of-the-way country, where no message could reach him.

Sir Stephen. If he should come too late, tell him— tell him—I've gone surveying in an out-of-the-way country—where no message can reach me! [*Changing tone.*] Dear me, Nurse, I'm afraid this dying is going to be a very tiresome business for both of us!

Nurse. Oh, Sir Stephen, I'm sure I don't mind!

Sir Stephen. You don't mind? That's very good of you. You're in no hurry? Well, neither am I.

Nurse. Sir Stephen, don't you think——

SIR STEPHEN. What?

NURSE. Last night you said you'd send for a clergy-man.

SIR STEPHEN. Did I? That was at two o'clock in the morning. How horribly demoralized a man gets at two o'clock in the morning!

NURSE. But, Sir Stephen——

SIR STEPHEN. Well?

NURSE. Don't you think you ought to begin to think of better things?

SIR STEPHEN. Well. I'm seventy-five. Perhaps it is nearly time. What better things?

NURSE. Death and—judgment.

SIR STEPHEN. Don't talk nonsense. I don't call death and judgment better things.

NURSE. But, Sir Stephen—you will be judged.

SIR STEPHEN. Judged? Yes. But I shan't be judged by the prayers I've said, and the psalms I've sung. I shan't be judged by the lies I've told, and the deceits I've practised, and the passions I've given way to. I shan't be judged by the evil and rottenness in me. No; I shall be judged by the railways I've made, and the canals I've scooped, and the bridges I've built—and let me tell you, my dear creature, my accounts are in good order, and ready for inspection at any moment, and I believe there's a good balance on my side. [*Guests have been assembling in the ballroom. Dance music bursts out. Dancing begins.*] Ah! What tune is that?

> [*Goes up to window, begins dancing a few steps, swaying with the music.*]

NURSE. [*Frightened.*] Sir Stephen! Sir Stephen!

SIR STEPHEN. Run away! Run away!

NURSE. Sir Stephen, you wouldn't be found dancing at the end?

SIR STEPHEN. Why not? I've done my work! Why shouldn't I play for a little while? [*A bell is heard.*] Hark! The front-door bell——

NURSE. Yes.

> [*Goes to door, left.*]

SIR STEPHEN. Go down-stairs and see if that's my son. If it is, tell him——

> [*Gentle knock at door, left. ADAMS enters a step. The dancing and music are continued in the ballroom.*]

ADAMS. I beg pardon, Sir Stephen. Mr. Daniel Famariss has arrived——

SIR STEPHEN. Ah!

> [*Getting excited.*]

ADAMS. And would like to see you.

SIR STEPHEN. Tell him he knows the conditions.

NURSE. But, Sir Stephen——

SIR STEPHEN. Run away, my good soul! Run away. [*To Adams.*] He knows the conditions. If he accepts them, I shall be pleased to see him.

DAN. [*Voice outside door.*] Father!

SIR STEPHEN. Shut that door!

> [ADAMS *nearly closes door, which is kept open a few inches from the other side.*]

DAN. [*Outside.*] Father! You won't shut the door in my face?

SIR STEPHEN. Keep on that side of it, then. Adams, you can go. Leave the door ajar.

> [*Exit* ADAMS, *left.* SIR STEPHEN, *with an imperious gesture, points* NURSE *to archway right. Exit* NURSE, *into bedroom, with an appealing gesture to* SIR STEPHEN.]

SIR STEPHEN. [*Goes to door, left; it is still open a few inches.*] Are you there, Dan?

DAN. [*Outside.*] Yes, father.

SIR STEPHEN. I vowed I'd never set eyes on you again, till you owned you were wrong about those girders. You were wrong? [*No reply.*] You were wrong? [*No reply.*] Do you hear? Confound you, you know you were wrong! [*No reply.*] Do you hear, Dan? Why won't you say you were wrong? You won't! [*Slams door, goes right, has an outburst of anger, recovers, listens, goes back to door, opens it a little.*] Are you there, Dan?

DAN. [*Outside.*] Yes, father.

SIR STEPHEN. You were wrong, Dan. [*No reply.*] I haven't got long to live, Dan. It's angina pectoris, and the next attack will kill me. It may come at any moment. [*Very piteously.*] Dan, you were wrong? Why won't you say so? Even if you tell a lie about it?

DAN. [*Outside.*] I was wrong.

SIR STEPHEN. Ah! [*Flings open the door,* DAN *runs in.* SIR STEPHEN *meets him, embraces him affectionately, with a half sob.*] Why didn't you say it before? You knew how much I loved you. Why did you keep apart from me all these years?

DAN. I'm sorry, sir. But perhaps it was for the best. I've done very well.

SIR STEPHEN. Of course you have. You're my son. But how much better you'd have done if you had stuck to me! How much better we both should have done! I'm sorry, too, Dan. I was wrong, too—not about the girders. You *were* wrong about them, Dan. But I was wrong to be angry and to swear I wouldn't see you. Ah, what could I have done with you at my side! I could have carried out my Milford Haven scheme. Perhaps it isn't too late! [*Going to bureau, getting more and more excited.*] I've got all the plans here——

[*Taking out a heap of plans.*]

DAN. Not now, father; not now!

SIR STEPHEN. Yes, now, my boy! To-morrow may be too late! [*Going to table.*] Come here, my lad! Oh, Dan, what years we've wasted! Come here! I want you to carry this out. You'll have immense opposition. Beat it down! You'll have to buy Shadwell and his lot. They're a dirty gang. But you'll have to do it. I hate bribery, Dan; but when you've got to do it, do it thoroughly! Then there's Mincham. Buy him over, if you can, at a small figure—say a thousand pounds—he's a mean little cur; but offer him that, and if he won't take it, snap your fingers at him, and swamp him! Remember the trick, the scoundrel's trick, he served me over the granite for the viaduct. Remember it, Dan, and don't spare him! Swamp him! Swamp him!*

[*With great energy of hate.*]

DAN. Father——

SIR STEPHEN. Bring your chair up. I must go on now —while it's all before me! I want you to carry this Milford Haven scheme out! I want it to be said that what old Stephen Famariss couldn't do, young Dan Famariss could! The father was a great man, the son shall be a greater, eh? Look here, you must start on this side. I've had all the soundings made——

DAN. To-morrow, father; to-morrow!

SIR STEPHEN. No, now! There's no such thing as to-morrow! We'll go through it now—in case—— There's a great world-tussle coming, Dan—I shan't live to see it— but it's coming, and the engineer that ties England and America will do a good turn to both countries. England to America in four days! I want that crown to rest on your head! Look! You must begin here! Look! Just there! You must throw a bridge over——

[*Stops suddenly, puts his hand to his heart;*

* 1 Kings, chap. ii., verses 8, 9.

his face indicates intense agony. NURSE
enters from bedroom.]

DAN.   Father——

SIR STEPHEN.   [*Persisting, with a wild aimless gesture.*]   Throw a bridge from here—to the other side, and then——

DAN.   Father, what is it?

SIR STEPHEN.   The end, Dan.   [*His face shows that he is suffering great pain.   A great burst of dance music. They offer to support him.   He waves them off.*]   No, thank you.   I'll die standing.   England to America in four days.   [*Long pause.   He stands bolt upright with great determination.*]   You were wrong about those girders, Dan——   My Peggie—I wonder if it's all moonshine—Peggie——   My Peggie——

[*Dies, tumbles over table.   Music and dancing in ballroom louder than ever.*]

CURTAIN

COUNSEL RETAINED

BY

CONSTANCE D'ARCY MACKAY

Constance D'Arcy Mackay (Mrs. Roland Holt) was born in St. Paul, Minnesota. Educated in public and private schools, she spent one year at Boston University. In connection with her writing she has directed a number of famous historical pageants. Besides writing a number of volumes of plays and pageants for children she has written several books on the producing of plays. Her *Little Theatre in the United States* (Holt, 1917) was the first serious study of this new movement in this country. *The Beau of Bath and Other One-Act Plays* (Holt, 1915) has justly become immensely popular. Other volumes are *Plays of the Pioneers: A Book of Historical Pageants* (Harper, 1915); *The Forest Princess and other Masques* (Holt, 1916); and *Patriotic Plays and Pageants for Young People* (Holt, 1922).

CHARACTERS

PEG WOFFINGTON
RICHARD GREVILLE
EDMUND BURKE
SOME UNSEEN GALLANTS, ADMIRERS
OF PEG WOFFINGTON

PLACE: *London*
TIME: 1750. *A cold spring night*
SCENE: *The apartment of* EDMUND BURKE

COUNSEL RETAINED

*A room that gives evidence of extreme poverty. It is on
the ground floor of what was once a fine mansion,
but is now a lodging-house dreary and down-at-heel.
At background, left, a French window with rusty lock
and broken panes, one of which is stuffed with an old
hat. At right background a couch with a faded and
tattered damask cover.*

*At left centre a hearth with a low fire. Andirons. A
battered iron kettle on a hob. A dilapidated hearth-
broom. Drawn near the hearth and facing audience
a highbacked chair with arms, the remains of what
was once a fine carved piece of furniture. Tossed
over the back of it a lawyer's black gown, very frayed.*

*At right, near background, a door opening into the hall of
the house. Near foreground a cupboard with a few
dishes, etc.*

*In the centre of the room a black table with an iron strong
box, a pile of battered law books, briefs, portfolios,
papers. A chair drawn up to the right of this.*

*On the table and mantelshelf are stubs of candles, two in
battered pewter candlesticks, and one in the neck of a
bottle.*

*At the rise of the curtain the room is in absolute darkness,
save for the red spark of the fire burning jewel-like in
the gloom. A moment afterward a hand from without tries the lock of the French window, and wrenches
the window open. A woman in a dark cloak enters
quickly, and lets in a flood of Spring moonlight that*

*falls in a broad shaft across the floor. She has no
time to close the window, but steps quickly into the
shadows by the fire, and stands silent and motionless,
her face hidden by the hood of her cloak. From
outside comes an excited tumult of men's voices.*

FIRST VOICE.   Peg! Mistress Woffington!

       *[RICHARD GREVILLE steps through the window,
       a fine-looking young dandy in king's blue
       velvet, with white wig, small sword, flashing
       shoe-buckles. He gives a quick look about
       him, does not perceive the hooded figure and
       speaks back through the window.]*

GREVILLE.   She isn't here.

       [With another quick glance at the room.]

Some pettifogger's lodgings. Gad! It's clear
That she won't let us chair her through the town.

VOICES.   *[Without.]*   Huzzah for Woffington!
FIRST VOICE.   Come on!
SECOND VOICE.   We'll drown

Our ardor at the *Crown* or *Serpentine.*

       *[This is hailed with a cheer that instantly grows
       fainter as its givers move rapidly away.]*

WOFFINGTON.   *[With involuntary indignation.]*

What! Will they drown my memory in wine!

GREVILLE.   *[Surprised and entranced.]*

Peg!

WOFFINGTON.   *[Sharply.]*

       S-sh, I tell you! I will not be found.
Wait till they leave. I'm weary of this round
Of cheering and of torchlight. Let me be.

       *[As she sinks into the chair near hearth the
       moonlight shows her wonderful mobile face.
       The sparkle of excitement and the immortal*

*youth of the artist make her look younger than
she really is. She gives the effect of being
not more than two and twenty. Her thin
black silk hooded cloak lined in flame-scarlet
satin falls back and reveals that over a black
taffeta petticoat she wears an over-dress of
black gauze on which are thickly embroidered
broad love-knots of silver. She has a black
lace scarf caught with a huge scarlet rose.
Above the darkness of her dress her neck
rises superbly white. She wears no jewels.
Her dark hair is unpowdered. Her little slippers are of the finest make, and rest lightly on
the ground like two black butterflies. They
are without buckles.]*

GREVILLE. [*Bending over her.*]

Why, Peg! Sweet Woffington!

WOFFINGTON.

  [*Closing her eyes for a moment and leaning back
   wearily in the chair.*]

         Ah, can't you see

An actress may grow tired? I'm fagged to death!

  [*Sudden impish humor lights her face. She
   opens her eyes.*]

Besides, you know, I wish to save my breath.

I want a *little* left with which to speak.

My case against Miss Spleen comes off next week.

GREVILLE.

Gad! So it does. I'm stupid to forget.

Have you engaged your counsel?

WOFFINGTON.   Nay, not yet.

Sure, Mr. Greville, I have had no time.

   [*Sagely.*]

But I'll be ready when the hour shall chime.

GREVILLE.
Who will you take?

WOFFINGTON.   [*With a gleam.*]
                    'Faith, set your mind at rest.
I'll choose the one who can defend me best!
Be sure of that.

  GREVILLE.   How did you *come* here?

  WOFFINGTON.   I
Stepped in to let the crowd go sweeping by,
And did what women can do when they will.

  GREVILLE.   And what was that?

  WOFFINGTON.   [*With a deliberate brogue.*]
                    I managed to keep still!

  GREVILLE.   [*Glancing scornfully about the room.*]
Who do you think can own this—caravan?

  WOFFINGTON.
Sure, I don't know.   It must be some poor man
Who's having a hard time to make things meet.
Well, may kind fortune set him on his feet!
I was poor once.
    [*Pensively.*]

  VOICES.   [*In distance, without.*]   Huzzah!

  WOFFINGTON.   I must stay here
Until the streets without begin to clear.
Fetch me a chair.   Come back in half an hour.
Meanwhile I'll rest.

  GREVILLE.   I will obey.

  WOFFINGTON.   [*Slight brogue.*]   More power
To you, Dick Greville.

     [GREVILLE *smiles delightedly, kisses her hand,*
     and exits through French window, which he
     half closes, so that WOFFINGTON *is left partly*
     in light, partly in shadow. The moment he
     is gone a key turns in the lock of the door,

right. WOFFINGTON *starts, looks toward door, and draws her cloak about her prepared for flight if flight prove necessary.* EDMUND BURKE *enters, young, shabby, careworn, wearing a black suit and a black cloak seen sharply for a moment as he takes a flint from his pocket and tries to strike a light. He has not seen* WOFFINGTON, *who instantly draws his old gown about her, and slips her arm into its sleeves. She stoops forward, rubs her handkerchief in the ash that has sifted out beyond the hearth, puts a smirch of it on her hands, tucks her feet under her, and huddling deep in the chair assumes a forlorn look, closing her eyes. She has slyly managed to pick up the hearth-broom, and it lies against her knee. She might, seen in the shadow, be a crossing sweeper, instead of an actress. Meanwhile* BURKE *has lighted the stump of candle standing in the neck of a bottle. As soon as it is lit he looks about and sees* WOFFINGTON.]

BURKE.   [*Astonished.*]   What is this?
WOFFINGTON.

[*With the effect of astonishment, bewilderment, the "Where am I" look of a person just wakened.*]

Why, oh!——

[*She looks at him in consternation, pretends to gather her wits together. Speaks coaxingly, as one afraid of a reprimand.*]

There was a crowd outside, and so—and so——
I stepped in here a moment, and 'twas warm,
And I dozed off——

BURKE. I'm sure you meant no harm.

> [*He crosses, closes the window, but does not try to lock it. Then goes to hearth and lights the stumps of candles on the hearth-shelf.*]

WOFFINGTON. [*Very Irish throughout.*]
None in the least, sir.

BURKE. And your name is——

WOFFINGTON. Meg
Some people call me, and the others Peg.
I like Meg best.

> [*She looks at him with the engagingness of a gamin.*]

BURKE. [*Kindly.*] Well, Meg, I greatly fear
That I can only offer you small cheer.

WOFFINGTON. I don't mind that.

BURKE. Stale bread, stale cheese, scant light.

> [*He has crossed to cupboard, right, and while he goes on talking to her sets between them on the table cracked plates, a loaf of bread, and some cheese.*]

What do you do?

WOFFINGTON. [*With an inspiration.*]
I—sweep the boards at night!

BURKE. A crossing sweeper?

WOFFINGTON. [*Looking down on his cloak.*]
'Faith, I know 'twas bold
To take this cloak: but I was tired and cold,
And I——

BURKE. [*With a whimsical glance at his supper table.*]
Ah, the poor know the poor. Sit still.

WOFFINGTON. You're very kind.

BURKE. I know how night can chill
The very marrow.

WOFFINGTON. Are you Irish, too?

BURKE.   Yes.

WOFFINGTON.   [*Slowly.*]
          If it's not—asking too much of you
What is your name, sir?

BURKE.   Burke.   Unknown to fame.
Just Edmund Burke.

WOFFINGTON.   [*Sagely.*]   That's a good Irish name.
And it will bring you luck.   Now, tell me true,
What do you need most?

BURKE.   Clients.   One or two
Friends in the great world.

WOFFINGTON.   Have you none?

BURKE.   Nay, none.

WOFFINGTON.   [*Encouragingly.*]
Keep up your heart.   Perhaps you'll meet with one.

BURKE.   [*Kindly.*]   Why, thank you, Meg.

WOFFINGTON.   You're welcome.

BURKE.   [*Bowing.*]   Will you share
My bread and cheese?
          [*They begin to eat.*]

WOFFINGTON.   You offer me your fare
As if I were a lady!

BURKE.   Aren't you?
Isn't a lady one whose words ring true
From a kind heart?

WOFFINGTON.   There's Mistress Woffington—
She's kind, they say, and yet she isn't one.

BURKE.   [*Indulgently.*]   Isn't a lady?

WOFFINGTON.   You have seen her?

BURKE.   Yes.
As Harry Wildair, wearing a boy's dress
With youthful swagger!   Lovely!   Debonair!
The darling of the wits!

WOFFINGTON.   [*Dryly: with malice.*]
                              Then I dare swear
You've never seen her in her right clothes?
    BURKE.   No.
Not yet.
    WOFFINGTON.   But, sir——
    BURKE.   The times are hard, and so——
            [*He looks down regretfully at his shabby clothes,
                and makes a rueful gesture.*]
When I've more silver I shall go each night.
    WOFFINGTON.   [*With deep conviction.*]
You'd spend your good coin on a worthless sight.
She's just an actress.
            [*She manages to keep her hands in the shadow.*]
    BURKE.   [*Quietly.*]   Tell me what you mean.
    WOFFINGTON.
            [*With the proper amount of hesitation.*]
Well, on the stage, sir, she may be a queen,
But off the stage——!   A zany, underbred,
Without a scrap of learning in her head.
    BURKE.   [*Indignantly.*]
And I suppose her beauty's false as well?
    WOFFINGTON.
Sure, they do say (though you can never tell!)
That underneath the powder and the paint
You'll find a—*something that is not a saint.*
    BURKE.   [*Furious.*]   Be silent!
            [*He rises, pale with anger.*]
    WOFFINGTON.   Oh, is Woffington your friend?
Sure, sir, I had no meaning to offend.
    BURKE.   [*More quietly.*]
Peg Woffington is not a friend of mine.
I saw her once upon the stage.   So fine,

So true an artist that the gossips slur
Her name through arrant jealousy of her
      [With growing power.]
Who is as far above them as the light
Of the first stars. Her genius burns as bright
As does Orion. Can you look at her——

  WOFFINGTON. *[To herself.]* (I often do!)

  BURKE. *[Sweeping on, unheeding.]*

              —without a great heart-stir
Of Irish pride, to think what high renown
Is worn by lovely Peg of Dublin town?
      [All the fire that will one day be his flames
        through his words.]
From Ireland, land of all that's brave and sweet . . .

  WOFFINGTON. *[Provocatively.]*

Famed for its lawyers, actresses, and—peat!
      [He turns from her indignantly.]
Sure, don't be angry. I am Irish, too.

  BURKE. *[Turning on her.]*

Take shame, then, to yourself, to think that you
Speak lightly of Peg Woffington——

  WOFFINGTON.

      [Suddenly standing up, returning to her natural
      voice and manner, and tossing off his cloak so
      that the black and silver and scarlet of her
      costume shows up wondrously in the candle-
      light.]

                    Nay, hold!
I think I know all that I need be told!
I'll choose the one who can defend me best!

  BURKE. *[With icy pride.]*

Madam, I'm glad that we have proved a jest
To pass your time, my poverty and I.

WOFFINGTON.   [*With a cry.*]
How can you think that!

BURKE.   [*Bowing sardonically.*]   And the moments fly
When one is well amused.   I trust that you
Have spent your evening profitably.   Do
Remember me at court.

        [*He bows again.*]

WOFFINGTON.   I shall, sir!

        [*They have been too engrossed with their own
          emotions to notice* GREVILLE, *who has opened
          the window and stepped in.*]

    GREVILLE.   Peg,
I've brought your chair.

    BURKE.   [*Suddenly looking at her indignantly.*]
                    You said your name was Meg.

    WOFFINGTON.   [*With a return of her gamin accent.*]
Well, Meg or Peg, 'tis very much the same:
And even Shakespeare says: "What's in a name?"

        [*Again the fine lady.*]
Mr. Burke, Mr. Greville.

        [*Stiff bows.* WOFFINGTON *indicates* BURKE.]
                          He's the one
Who's to be lawyer for Peg Woffington.

        [*Indicates herself.*]

    BURKE.   [*Staring at her, fascinated.*]
Peg Woffington—you don't mean——

    WOFFINGTON.   [*Laughing.*]   Man, you're blind!
I'm Peg!

        [*She sweeps him a curtsey.*]

    BURKE.   And I, who said you were unkind
To mock me——

    WOFFINGTON.   Find a client here instead!
The suit's against Miss Spleen.   Say what you said

To Meg, the crossing sweeper, and all will be well.
Good night.

> [GREVILLE *pauses, waiting for her at the*
> *window.*]

BURKE.   [*Gazing at her.*]

Good night.   Your beauty's like a spell
That holds thanks tongue-tied.

WOFFINGTON.   [*Drolly.*]   Wouldn't you have known
We both kissed Ireland's gem—the Blarney Stone.

> [*Curtseys.*]

Good night, then.

> [*The men bow to each other, and* WOFFINGTON
> *starts to join* GREVILLE.   *Then turns impetu-*
> *ously, runs back to the table, tears the crim-*
> *son rose from her dress, kisses it lightly and*
> *tosses it to the table with a charming gesture.*]

Here's success!   And great renown!

> [*She runs back, and exits hastily by way of the*
> *window,* GREVILLE *following.*   BURKE *stands*
> *for an instant looking after her.   Then he*
> *lifts the rose to his lips.*]

BURKE.   Peg Woffington!   The rose of Dublin Town.

> [*He stands, smiling dreamily at the rose as the*
> *curtain falls.*]

THURSDAY EVENING

A COMEDY IN ONE ACT

BY

CHRISTOPHER MORLEY

Christopher Morley was born in Haverford, Pennsylvania, May 5, 1890. After taking his A.B. degree from Haverford College he became a Rhodes scholar at Oxford. He has acted in an editorial capacity for a number of the more prominent New York papers and publishers. At present he conducts the "Bowling Green" column in *The Saturday Review of Literature*. His writings have been decidedly varied—he has written novels like *Parnassus on Wheels* (Doubleday, 1917), *Kathleen* (Doubleday, 1920), *Where the Blue Begins* (Doubleday, 1922), and *Thunder on the Left* (Doubleday, 1925); volumes of poems like *Songs for a Little House* (Doran, 1917), *The Rocking Horse* (Doran, 1919), *Hide and Seek* (Doran, 1920), and *Chimneysmoke* (Doran, 1921); and volumes of essays like *Shandygaff* (Doubleday, 1918), *Mince Pie* (Doran, 1919), *Pipefuls* (Doubleday, 1920), *Plum Pudding* (Doubleday, 1921), and *The Powder of Sympathy* (Doubleday, 1923). His one collection of one-act plays, *One-Act Plays,* was published in 1924 (Doubleday).

CHARACTERS

GORDON JOHNS, *a young business man*

LAURA, *Mrs. Gordon Johns*

MRS. SHEFFIELD, *Laura's mother*

MRS. JOHNS, *Gordon's mother*

THURSDAY EVENING

SCENE: *A small suburban kitchen in the modest home
of Mr. and Mrs. Gordon Johns. A meal has recently been cooked, as is shown by a general confusion of pots and pans and dish-cloths. At the rear,
an ice-box standing in the corner. Rear, centre, two
shelved cabinets, one containing groceries and household sundries, the other dishes and glassware. Rear,
left, an oil range. Some baby linen and very small
shirts (such as would be suitable for a child of about
ten months) are hanging on a clothes-horse near the
stove. Door right leads out to back porch; there are
two windows in right wall, one each side of door.
Door left to dining-room. At the corner in the rear,
left, door opening on back stairs, which ascend to
upper parts of the house. Down stage, left, against
side wall, a sink and oil-cloth covered drain-board or
shelf beside it. In the centre of stage a small table
covered with oil-cloth. A kitchen chair in corner,
down right.*

When the scene opens, GORDON *and* LAURA *are carrying in
soiled dishes through door, left. They come in and
out several times, making methodical arrangements
for cleaning up. They pile the dishes on the shelf
by the sink.* GORDON *takes dishpan from a hook
under the sink, and fills it with hot water from the
kettle on the stove.* LAURA, *who is an attractive little
person, aged about twenty-three, is in that slightly
tense condition of a young hostess who has had a
long and trying day with house and baby, and has also
cooked and served a dinner for four.*

GORDON. All right, Creature, just wait till I light my pipe and we'll polish this up.

[*Lights pipe and rolls up shirt-sleeves.*]

LAURA. [*Taking an apron from chair in corner.*] Put this on first. That's the only decent pair of trousers you've got.

[*Enter* MRS. SHEFFIELD, *carrying dishes.*]

MRS. SHEFF. Now you children run along and take it easy. I'll do all this.

LAURA. No, no, Mother. You go and talk to Mrs. Johns. [*Pointedly.*] Don't let her come in here.

MRS. SHEFF. [*Ultramaternally.*] Poor baby, she's tired. You've been on your feet all day, now let Mother wash up for you. That was a big dinner to cook.

LAURA. No tireder than you are, Mother darling. You cooked lunch.

GORDON. Both of you clear out; I can get this done in no time.

MRS. SHEFF. [*Patting* LAURA's *cheek.*] Busy with the baby all afternoon, and then cooking such a delicious dinner— Dearie, won't you let Mother do this for you?

LAURA. There isn't room in this kitchen for everybody——

[*Enter* MRS. JOHNS, *carrying dishes.*]

MRS. JOHNS. Gordon, you and Laura go and rest. Let the two grandmothers——

GORDON. Now listen, little people, this is my job. I always wash up on Thursday evenings——

MRS. JOHNS. You go and read your newspaper. I can see you're all fagged out after that long day in the office——

MRS. SHEFF. [*To* LAURA.] *Please* go and lie down, Baby. You're *so* tired.

LAURA. [*With waning patience.*] You two go and amuse yourselves; Gordon and I'll attend to this.

[*They gently eject the two mothers-in-law.*]

GORDON. Come on, now, the good old system!

[*He takes the small table from centre of stage, and puts it carefully midway between sink and dish-cabinet. Takes chair from corner, down right, and sets it beside table. LAURA sits down on chair and wipes silverware and dishes as he hands them to her after washing.*]

LAURA. The silver first, while the water's clean.

GORDON. Right. We make a pretty good team at this, don't we?

LAURA. [*Holds up a small silver jug.*] That darling old cream jug. Mother used that when she was a little girl.

GORDON. I love our little Thursday evening suppers. I think they're more fun than any other night

LAURA. I'm glad, Gordie.

GORDON. We get better grub on Thursdays, when Ethel goes out, than we ever do when she's in.

LAURA. I tried to have everything specially nice to-night. Some visitors are very critical.

GORDON. It was lovely. I'm afraid it was hard for you, Creature, to have Mother come just now. [*A short pause.*] Especially when *your* mother was here.

LAURA. Didn't she know Mother was here?

GORDON. No. I hadn't told her. You see your mother is here so much more often. I didn't know your mother would still be here. I was afraid Mother might be a little hurt——

LAURA. Mother helps me a great deal. I think it's a queer thing if a wife can't have her mother stay with her once in a while——

GORDON. [*Aware of danger, changes the subject.*] Ye Gods, Ethel has cracked the Copenhagen platter. [LAURA *is silent.*] That's one of the set Mother gave us when we were married.

LAURA. It's a stock pattern. You can get another at any department store.

GORDON. I'll bet that coon didn't empty the ice-box pan before she went. I never saw a cook yet who could remember to do that——

LAURA. If you had to go out and hunt for them you wouldn't be so particular. She's better than no one.

GORDON. [*Goes to ice-box and removes a large, brimming pan from under it.*] What did I tell you!

[*The water slops over from pan as he carries it gingerly to sink and empties it. He replaces the pan under ice-box.*]

LAURA. You'd better heat some more water. You've poured that ice-water into the dish-pan.

GORDON. [*Getting a little peevish; refills kettle and puts it on stove.*] It's perfectly absurd not having any pantry to keep the ice-box in. In here, the heat of the stove melts the ice right away. [*Goes back to ice-box and slams its doors shut.*] Of course, she never keeps the doors properly closed. [*He returns to sink and resumes dish-washing.*] It's a funny thing.

LAURA. What is?

GORDON. Why, that a presumably intelligent coon can't understand the doors of an ice-box are meant to be kept tight shut, to save ice. What does she suppose those little clamps are for? [LAURA *is silent. There is a pause, while* GORDON *scrapes portions of food off the soiled plates. He examines some of these plates rather carefully, and picks out several large pieces of meat, lettuce, butter, etc., which he puts on one plate at one side. Then*

he seems to resume his good humor and relights his pipe.]
Well, it's jolly to have both the grandmothers here together, isn't it?

LAURA. Gordon, dear, put the silver away in the sideboard before it gets wet again.

> [*He gathers up silver from the table in front of
> her and exit left.* LAURA *steps outside door
> right, and returns, bringing garbage-can,
> which she puts down by the sink. She begins
> to wash dishes, and sees the plate of odds and
> ends which* GORDON *has carefully put to one
> side. She scrapes its contents into the gar-
> bage-pail. While she is washing,* GORDON
> enters, left.*]

GORDON. Now, Creature, let me do that. You don't
want to spoil those pretty hands.

> [*Takes them, with an attempt to be affectionate.*]

LAURA. I guess it isn't any worse for them than washing the baby's things.

GORDON. Come on, old man, let me. [*Gently removes
her from sink, and pushes her to the chair by the table.
She sits down and wipes dishes as he hands them to her.*]
It doesn't take long when there are two of us.

LAURA. Gordie, these dishes aren't properly clean.
You can't get that grease off without hot water.

GORDON. I guess that kettle's hot by now. [*To stove,
feels water in kettle.*] Give it a minute longer. [*Stands
by stove and puffs at his pipe. In a moment of false se-
curity, he foolishly reopens a dangerous topic.*] You
know, I'm a little worried about Mother.

LAURA. [*Putting away dishes.*] Why?

GORDON. I don't think she's as well as usual. She
hardly ate any of her salad.

LAURA. [*Turns as though about to say something,*

but checks herself and pauses a moment. This time it is she who tries honorably to avert the gathering storm.] Oh, Gordie, I forgot to tell you! Junior drank out of a cup to-day—the first time!

GORDON. He did! The little rascal!

LAURA. Look, here's the cup.

[*Shows a small silver cup.*]

GORDON. [*Affectionately, putting his arm around her.*] Well, well. [*Looks at cup.*] What cup is that? I don't seem to remember it——

LAURA. Why—Mother brought it with her. She used it when she was a baby.

GORDON. Where's that nice old christening-mug of mine? I think Junior would like to use that once in a while, too.

LAURA. I put it away, dear. I was afraid Ethel might dent it.

GORDON. [*Takes kettle from stove, goes back to sink.*] I hope Mother isn't feeling poorly. I noticed at supper——

LAURA. When hot meat is served, refined people usually call it *dinner*——

GORDON. [*Looks at her cautiously, and suddenly seems to realize that they are on the edge of an abyss.*] Now, honey, you're tired. You go and rest, I'll finish up here.

LAURA. No, thank you. I like to see that everything gets cleaned up properly. Some one might come snooping out here, and then there'd be hints about my housekeeping. Of course, I'll admit I wasn't brought up to be a cook——

GORDON. [*Seeks inspiration by relighting his pipe, and takes up a handsome silver coffee-pot.*] One thing I never can make out is, how to prevent coffee-grounds from going down the sink. [*He talks desperately, trying to tide over the mutually realized danger-point.*] Perhaps if I could invent some kind of a little coffee-ground strainer I'd make our fortune. That coffee was delicious, Creature.

LAURA. Take care of that urn, it's one of the few handsome things we have.

GORDON. It *is* a beauty.

LAURA. Jack Davis gave it to me——

GORDON. [*Puts it down with distaste.*] I guess I'd better attend to the garbage.

LAURA. [*Nervously.*] It's all fixed.

GORDON. I always like Thursdays because that's the one evening Ethel doesn't get a chance to throw away about five dollars worth of good food.

LAURA. I fixed the garbage. You can put the pail outside.

GORDON. [*Hunting among plates on the shelf beside sink.*] Where's that plate I put here? There was a lot of perfectly good stuff I saved——

LAURA. [*Blows up at last.*] Well, if you think I'm going to keep a lot of half-eaten salad your mother picked over——

GORDON. [*Seizes garbage-pail, lifts it up to the sink and begins to explore its contents. His fuse also is rapidly shortening.*] My Lord, it's no wonder we never have any money to spend if we chuck half of it away in waste. [*Picking out various selections.*] Waste! Look at that piece of cheese, and those potatoes. You could take those things, and some of this meat, and make a nice economical hash for lunch——

LAURA. It's a wonder you wouldn't get a job as a scavenger. I never *heard* of a husband like you, rummaging through the garbage-pail.

GORDON. [*Blows up.*] Do you know what the one

unforgivable sin is? The sin against the Holy Ghost? It's *Waste!* It makes me wild to think of working and working like a dog, and half of what I earn just thrown away by an ignorant coon. Look at this, just look at it! [*Displays a grisly object.*] There's enough meat on that bone to make soup. And ye gods, here's that jar of anchovy paste! [*Holds it up.*] I thought you got that for me as a little treat. I wondered where it had gone to. Why, I hadn't eaten more than just the top of it.

LAURA.   Well, you left it, and left it, and it got mildewed.

GORDON.   Scrape it off. A little mildew won't hurt anybody. There'll be mildew on my bank-account if this kind of thing goes on. [*Still examining garbage-pail.*] Look here, about half a dozen slices of bread. What's the matter with *them,* I'd like to know.

LAURA.   I think it's the most disgusting thing I ever heard of. To go picking over the garbage-pail like that. You attend to your affairs and I'll attend to mine.

GORDON.   I guess throwing away good, hard-earned money is my affair, isn't it?

LAURA.   You're always quick enough to find fault. I know Ethel's careless, but she's the best I can get out here in this God-forsaken suburb. Maybe you'll be good enough to find me a better servant. A well-trained girl wouldn't work in this old dump, where there isn't even gas. You don't seem to know when you're lucky. You come back at night and find your home well cared for and me slaving over a hot dinner, and do you ever say a word of thanks? No, all you can think of is finding fault. I can't imagine how you were brought up. Your mother——

GORDON.   Just leave my mother out of it. I guess she didn't spoil me the way yours did you. Of course, I wasn't an only daughter——

LAURA. I wish you had been. Then I wouldn't have married you.

GORDON. I suppose you think that if you'd married Jack Davis or some other of those profiteers you'd never have had to see the inside of a kitchen——

LAURA. If Junior grows up with your disposition, all I can say is, I hope he'll never get married.

GORDON. If he gets married, I hope it'll be to some girl who understands something about economy——

LAURA. If he gets married, I hope he'll be man enough not to be always finding fault——

GORDON. Well, he *won't* get married! I'll put him wise to what marriage means, fussing like this all the time——

LAURA. Yes, he *will* get married. He *shall* get married!

GORDON. Oh, this is too absurd——

LAURA. He *shall* get married, just to be a humiliating example to his father. I'll bring him up the way a husband *ought* to be.

GORDON. In handcuffs, I suppose——

LAURA. And his wife won't have to sit and listen to perpetual criticism from his mother——

GORDON. If you're so down on mothers-in-law, it's queer you're anxious to be one yourself. The expectant mother-in-law!

LAURA. All right, be vulgar. I dare say you can't help it.

GORDON. Great Scott, what did you think marriage was like, anyway? Did you expect to go through life having everything done for you, without a little hard work to make it interesting?

LAURA. Is it necessary to shout?

GORDON. Now let me tell you something. Let's see if

you can ratify it from your extensive observation of life. Is there anything in the world so cruel as bringing up a girl in absolute ignorance of housework, believing that all her days she's going to be waited on hand and foot, and that marriage is one long swoon of endearments——

LAURA. There's not much swooning while you're around.

GORDON. Why, I believe you actually think your life is wrecked if you aren't being petted and praised every minute. You pretend to think marriage is so sacred and yet you're buffaloed by a few greasy dishes. I like my kind of sacredness better than yours, and that's the sacredness of common sense. Marriage ought not to be performed before an altar, but before a kitchen sink.

LAURA. [*Furiously.*] I ought to have known that oil and water won't mix. I ought to have known that a vulgar, selfish, conceited man couldn't make a girl happy who was brought up in a refined family. I was a Sheffield, and why I ever became a Johns is more than I can imagine. Johns—I suppose that's camouflage for Jones. You're too common, too ordinary, to know when you're lucky. You get a charming aristocratic wife and expect her to grub along like a washerwoman. You try to crush all the life and spirit out of her. You ought to have married an ice-box—that's the only thing in this house you're really attentive to.

GORDON. Now listen——

LAURA. [*Will not be checked.*] Talk about being spoiled—why, your mother babies you so, you think you're the only man on earth. [*Sarcastically.*] Her poor, over-worked boy, who tries so hard and gets all fagged out in the office and struggles so nobly to support his family! I wonder how you'd like to run this house and bear a child and take care of it and shuffle along with an ignorant coon

for a maid and then cook a big dinner and be sneered at
and never a word of praise.   All you can think of is picking over the garbage-pail and finding fault——

GORDON.   [*Like a fool.*]   I didn't find fault.   I found
some good food being wasted.

LAURA.   All right, if you love the garbage-pail better
than you do your wife, you can live with it.

> [*Flings her dish-towel on the floor and exit, left.*
> GORDON *stands irresolutely at the sink, and
> makes a few gloomy motions among the un-
> finished dishes. He glares at the garbage-
> can. Then he carefully gathers those portions
> of food that he had chosen as being still usable,
> contemplates them grimly, then puts them on a
> plate and, after some hesitation, puts the plate
> in the ice-box. He takes the garbage-can and
> puts it outside door, right. He returns into
> the kitchen, but then a sudden fit of anger
> seizes him.*]

GORDON.   It's always the way!

> [*Tears off apron, throws it on the floor, and exit
> right, slamming door.*
> *After a brief pause, the door at the rear, open-
> ing onto the back stairs, is cautiously opened,
> and* MRS. SHEFFIELD *enters quietly. She
> takes one swift look around the disordered
> kitchen, picks up dish-towel and apron from
> the floor, and sets to work rapidly to clean up.
> Then the back-stairs door is again opened in
> the same stealthy way, and* MRS. JOHNS *enters.
> The two ladies seem to take each other's
> measure with instinctive shrewdness, and fall
> into a silent, businesslike team-play in put-
> ting things to rights.* MRS. JOHNS *takes*

charge at the sink, and the remaining dishes spin under her capable hands. MRS. SHEF-FIELD *takes them from her, rapidly polishes them, and puts them away on the shelves. There is unconscious comedy in the trained precision and labor-saving method of their actions, which are synchronized so that every time* MRS. JOHNS *holds out a washed dish,* MRS. SHEFFIELD *is moving back from the cabinet, ready to receive it. They work like automatons; for perhaps two minutes not a word is said, and the two seem, by searching sideglances, to be probing each other's mood.*]

MRS. JOHNS. If it wasn't so tragic I'd laugh.

[*A pause, during which they work busily.*]

MRS. SHEFFIELD. If it wasn't so comic I'd cry. [*Another pause.*] I guess it's my fault. Poor Laura, I'm afraid I *have* spoiled her.

MRS. JOHNS. *My* fault, I think. Two mothers-in-law at once is too much for any young couple. I didn't know you were here, or I wouldn't have come.

MRS. SHEFF. Laura is so dreadfully sensitive, poor child——

MRS. JOHNS. Gordon works so hard at the office. You know he's trying to get promoted to the sales department, and I suppose it tells on his nerves——

MRS. SHEFF. If Laura could afford to have a nurse to help her with the baby she wouldn't get so exhausted——

MRS. JOHNS. Gordon says he wants to take out some more insurance, that's why he worries so about economy. It isn't for himself, he's really very unselfish——

MRS. SHEFF. [*A little tartly.*] Still, I do think that sometimes— [*They pause and look at each other quick-*

ly.] My gracious, we'll be at it ourselves if we don't look out!

> [*She goes to the clothes-horse and rearranges the garments on it. She holds up a lilliputian shirt, and they both smile.*]

MRS. JOHNS. That darling baby! I hope he won't have poor Gordon's quick temper. It runs in the Johns family, I'm afraid. I was an Armstrong before I married Gordon's father—I didn't know what temper was until I married—either my own or his.

MRS. SHEFF. I was a Thomson—Thomson without the P, you know, from Rhode Island. All families are hot-tempered. All husbands' families, anyway.

MRS. JOHNS. Gordon's father used to say that Adam and Eve didn't know when they were well off. He said that was why they called it the Garden of Eden.

MRS. SHEFF. Why?

MRS. JOHNS. Because there was no mother-in-law there.

MRS. SHEFF. Poor children, they have such a lot to learn! I really feel ashamed, Mrs. Johns, because Laura is an undisciplined little thing, and I'm afraid I've always petted her too much. She had such a lot of attention before she met Gordon, and was made so much of, it gave her wrong ideas.

MRS. JOHNS. I wish Gordon was a little younger, I'd like to turn him up and spank him. He's dreadfully stubborn and tactless——

MRS. SHEFF. But I'm afraid I *did* make a mistake. Laura was having such a good time as a girl, I was always afraid she'd have a hard awakening when she married. But Mr. Sheffield had a good deal of money at that time, and he used to say, "She's only young once, let her enjoy herself."

MRS. JOHNS. My husband was short-sighted, too. He had had to skimp so, that he brought up Gordon to have a terror of wasting a nickel.

MRS. SHEFF. Very sensible. I wish Mr. Sheffield had had a little more of that terror. I shall have to tell him what his policy has resulted in. But really, you know, when I heard them at it, I could hardly help admiring them. [*With a sigh.*] It brings back old times!

MRS. JOHNS. So it does! [*A pause.*] But we can't let them go on like this. A little vigorous quarrelling is good for everybody. It's a kind of spiritual laxative. But they carry it too far.

MRS. SHEFF. They're awfully ingenious. They were even bickering about Junior's future mother-in-law. I suppose she's still in school, whoever she may be!

MRS. JOHNS. Being a mother-in-law is almost as painful as being a mother.

MRS. SHEFF. I think every marriage ought to be preceded by a treaty of peace between the two mothers. If they understand each other, everything will work out all right.

MRS. JOHNS. You're right. When each one takes sides with her own child, it's fatal.

MRS. SHEFF. [*Lowering her voice.*] Look here, I think I know how we can make them ashamed of themselves. Where are they now?

MRS. JOHNS. [*Goes cautiously to door left, and peeps through.*] Laura is lying on the couch in the living-room. I think she's crying—her face is buried in the cushions.

MRS. SHEFF. Splendid. That means she's listening with all her ears—[*Tiptoes to window, right.*] I can't see Gordon, but I think he's walking round the garden——

MRS. JOHNS. [*Quietly.*] If we were to talk a little louder he'd sit on the back steps to hear it——

MRS. SHEFF. Exactly. Now listen!

> [*They put their heads together and whisper; the audience does not hear what is said.*]

MRS. JOHNS. Fine! Oh, that's fine! [MRS. SHEFFIELD *whispers again, inaudible to the spectators.*] But wait a moment. Don't you think it would be better if *I* praise Laura and *you* praise Gordon? They won't expect that, and it might shame them——

MRS. SHEFF. No, no! Don't you see——

> [*Whispers again, inaudibly.*]

MRS. JOHNS. You're right. Cunning as serpents and harmless as doves——

> [*They carefully set both doors, left and right, ajar.*]

MRS. SHEFF. I only hope we won't wake the baby——

> [*They return to the task of cleaning up, and talk very loud, in pretended quarrel.*]

MRS. JOHNS. Where do these dessert plates go?

MRS. SHEFF. On this shelf.

MRS. JOHNS. You're here so much more often than I, naturally you know Laura's arrangements better.

MRS. SHEFF. It's a lucky thing I *am* here. I don't know what poor Laura would do without me at such a dreadful time——

MRS. JOHNS. Poor Laura! I should say she's very fortunate, such a good husband——

MRS. SHEFF. I think it's rather sad for a girl who has had as much as she has, to come down to this——

MRS. JOHNS. It's perfectly wonderful how Gordon has got on in business——

MRS. SHEFF. He ought to, with such a lovely home, run like a clock——

MRS. JOHNS. Yes. An alarm-clock.

Mrs. Sheff.   Well, I'm not going to see my daughter's happiness ruined——

Mrs. Johns.   I always knew he'd make some girl a fine husband——

Mrs. Sheff.   Perhaps. But he seems to have picked the wrong girl. Laura has too much spirit to be bullied——

Mrs. Johns.   Well, perhaps it was all a mistake. Poor Gordon, he works so hard. I believe his hair is going white over his ears already.

Mrs. Sheff.   Stuff! That's lather from where he shaved this morning. He's too slovenly to wash it off.

Mrs. Johns.   It isn't right that a young man should have to slave the way he does——

Mrs. Sheff.   [*Apparently in a passion.*] Do you think that business slavery can compare to household slavery? I think it's heart-rending to see an attractive girl like Laura shut up in a poky little house doing drudgery and tending a baby. Think of it, having to take care of her own baby! Why, it's an outrage. If Gordon was half a man, he'd get her a trained baby nurse so she wouldn't have to *look* at the poor little thing——

Mrs. Johns.   [*Scathing.*] Yes, how sad that Gordon should have to intrust his son to amateur care when it needs scientific attention.

Mrs. Sheff.   Poor darling Laura—she never ought to have had a baby.

Mrs. Johns.   Gordon is too intellectual to be bothered with these domestic details. He ought to be able to concentrate on his work.

Mrs. Sheff.   [*Coming close to* Mrs. Johns, *feigning great rage, but grimacing to show it is merely acting.*] Well, if you don't think my daughter is good enough for your son, I can always take her home with *me*. I guess

I can find room for her, and we can put the child in an institution.

[*Both nearly laugh, but recover themselves.*]

MRS. JOHNS. Don't worry. I'll take the child. He's a Johns anyway, not a Sheffield. And you just watch Gordon, when he's relieved of all this family worry and quarrelling. He'll make his mark in the world. He's too fine to be tied down by a wife that doesn't understand him.

MRS. SHEFF. Oh, how happy Laura will be to hear this! My sweet, clever, attractive, economical, sensible little girl, free at last. Her married life has been a nightmare. That great, hulking, selfish man has tried to trample all the joy out of her. He shan't do it.

MRS. JOHNS. I never heard of a young husband as self-sacrificing as Gordon. I don't belive he *ever* goes out for an evening with other men, and he *never* spends anything on himself——

MRS. SHEFF. I think the way Laura runs her little home is just wonderful. See how she struggles to keep her kitchen in order—this miserable, inconvenient little kitchen, no gas, no pantry, no decent help. I think it's *terrible* she has had to put up with so much——

[*They pause, and listen at the door, left. The kitchen is now spick and span. MRS. JOHNS makes a gesture to indicate that Laura is taking it all in, offstage.*]

MRS. JOHNS. Well, then, it's all settled.

MRS. SHEFF. Yes. As Laura's mother, I can't let her go on like this. A husband, a home, and a baby—it's enough to ruin any woman.

MRS. JOHNS. It's only fair to both sides to end it all. I never heard of such brutal hardships. Gordon can't fight against these things any longer. Throwing away a soupbone and three slices of bread! I wonder he doesn't go mad.

MRS. SHEFF. We've saved them just in time.

[*They look at each other knowingly, with the air of those who have done a sound bit of work. Then they stealthily open the door at the rear, and exeunt up the back stairs.*

There is a brief pause; then the door left opens like an explosion, and LAURA *bursts in. She stands for a moment, wild-eyed, stamps her foot in a passion. Then she seizes one of the baby shirts from the rack, and drops into the chair by the table, crying. She buries her head in her arms, concealing the shirt. Enter* GORDON, *right. He stands uncertainly, evidently feeling like a fool.*]

GORDON. I'm sorry, I—I left my pipe in here.

[*Finds it by the sink.*]

LAURA. [*Her face still hidden.*] Oh, Gordie, *was* it all a mistake?

GORDON. [*Troubled, pats her shoulder tentatively.*] Now listen, Creature, don't. You'll make yourself sick.

LAURA. I never thought I'd hear such things—from my own mother.

GORDON. I never heard such rot. They must be mad, both of them.

LAURA. Then you were listening, too——

GORDON. Yes. Why, they're deliberately trying to set us against each other.

LAURA. They wouldn't have *dared* speak like that if they had known we could hear. Gordon, I don't think it's *legal*——

GORDON. I'm afraid the law doesn't give one much protection against one's mothers.

LAURA. [*Miserably.*] I guess she's right. I *am* spoiled, and I *am* silly, and I *am* extravagant——

GORDON. Don't be silly, darling. That's crazy stuff. I'm *not* overworked, and even if I were I'd love it, for *you*——

LAURA. I don't *want* a nurse for Junior. I wouldn't have one in the house. [*Sits up, dishevelled, and displays the small shirt she has been clutching.*] Gordon, I'm *not* an amateur! I love that baby and I *am* scientific. I keep a chart of his weight every week.

GORDON. Yes, I know, ducky, Gordon understands. Soon we'll be able to buy that scales you want, and we won't have to weigh him on the meat-balance.

LAURA. *Nobody* can take away my darling baby——

GORDON. It was my fault, dear. I *am* obstinate and disagreeable——

LAURA. I'll speak to Ethel about the garbage——

GORDON. Ethel's all right. We're lucky to have her.

LAURA. Gordon, you mustn't work too hard. You know you're all I have [*a sob*]—since Mother's gone back on me.

GORDON. [*Patting her.*] I think it's frightful, the things they said. What are they trying to do, break up a happy home?

LAURA. We *are* happy, aren't we?

GORDON. Well, I should say so. Did you ever hear me complain?

[*Takes her in his arms.*]

LAURA. No, Gordie. It was cruel of them to try to make trouble between us—but, perhaps, some of the things they said——

GORDON. Were true?——

LAURA. Well, not exactly true, dear, but—interesting! —your mother is right, you *do* have a hard time, and I'll try——

GORDON. [*Stops her.*] No, *your* mother is right. I've been a brute——

LAURA. I'm lucky to have such a husband——

[*They are silent a moment.*]

GORDON. I suppose you'll think it an awful anti-climax——

LAURA. What, dear?

GORDON. Suppose we have something to eat?

LAURA. [*Happily.*] Good idea. Quarrelling always makes me hungry. [*They go to the ice-box.*] I didn't really get any supper to speak of; I was worrying about everything so——

GORDON. [*Opening ice-box.*] You mean *dinner,* honey —among refined people!

LAURA. Don't be a tease. Come on, we'll have a snack——

[*She discovers Gordon's plate of left-overs.*]

GORDON. Throw out that junk—I was idiotic to save it.

LAURA. No, Gordie, you were quite right. We must save everything we can. Four or five heads of lettuce would make a new shirt for Junior.

GORDON. [*Bewildered.*] Lettuce?

LAURA. I mean, if we saved that much, it would make enough money to buy him a new little vest. He's getting so *enormous*——

[*She puts plate of left-overs on the table, with some other cold food.*]

GORDON. There, now, this is better.

[*They sit down at table.*]

LAURA. [*Thoughtfully.*] You know, Gordie, we mustn't let them know we heard them.

GORDON. No, I suppose not. But it's hard to for-give that sort of talk.

LAURA.   Even if they did say atrocious things, I think they really love us——

GORDON.   We'll be a bit cold and stand-offish until things blow over.

LAURA.   [*Complacently.*] If I'm ever a mother-in-law, I shall try to be *very* understanding——

GORDON.   Yes, Creature.   Do you remember why I call you Creature?

LAURA.   Do I not?

GORDON.   There was an adjective omitted, you remember.

LAURA.   Oh, Gordie, that's one of the troubles of married life.   So many of the nice adjectives seem to get omitted.

GORDON.   Motto for married men: Don't run short of adjectives!—— You remember what the adjective was?

LAURA.   Tell me.

GORDON.   *Adorable.*   It was an abbreviation for Adorable Creature— [*Holds her. They are both perfectly happy.*]   I love our little Thursday evenings.

LAURA.   [*Partly breaks from his embrace.*]   Sssh! [*Listens.*]   Was that the baby?

CURTAIN

ILE

A PLAY IN ONE ACT

BY

EUGENE O'NEILL

Eugene O'Neill was born in New York City, October 16, 1888. He spent a year at Princeton and later a year at Harvard. After engaging in business for a number of years in this country, South America, and Africa, spending two years at sea, and some experience on the stage in a vaudeville version of *The Count of Monte Cristo*, a play made famous by his father, he turned his attention seriously to dramatic writing. His *Moon of the Caribbees* (Liveright, 1919) definitely placed him as a master of drama in one-act. *Beyond the Horizon* (Liveright, 1919) was his first success in the full-length play. Among his other successes are *The Emperor Jones* (Liveright, 1921), *Diff'rent* (Liveright, 1921), *Anna Christie* (Liveright, 1922), *The Hairy Ape* (Liveright, 1922), *All God's Chillun Got Wings* (Liveright, 1923), and *Desire under the Elms* (Liveright, 1924). His plays have been rearranged by his publishers in six volumes, which include those named above and such later plays as *The Great God Brown, Gold, The Dreamy Kid, Welded,* and his very latest, *Marco Millions.*

CHARACTERS

Ben, *the cabin boy*

The Steward

Captain Keeney

Slocum, *second mate*

Mrs. Keeney

Joe, *a harpooner*

Members of the crew of the steam whaler *Atlantic Queen*

ILE

SCENE—Captain Keeney's *cabin on board the steam whaling-ship* Atlantic Queen—*a small, square compartment about eight feet high with a skylight in the centre looking out on the poop-deck. On the left [the stern of the ship] a long bench with rough cushions is built in against the wall. In front of the bench, a table. Over the bench, several curtained port-holes.*

In the rear, left, a door leading to the captain's sleeping-quarters. To the right of the door a small organ, looking as if it were brand-new, is placed against the wall.

On the right, to the rear, a marble-topped sideboard. On the sideboard, a woman's sewing-basket. Farther forward, a doorway leading to the companionway, and past the officer's quarters to the main deck.

In the centre of the room, a stove. From the middle of the ceiling a hanging lamp is suspended. The walls of the cabin are painted white.

There is no rolling of the ship, and the light which comes through the skylight is sickly and faint, indicating one of those gray days of calm when ocean and sky are alike dead. The silence is unbroken except for the measured tread of some one walking up and down on the poop-deck overhead.

It is nearing two bells—one o'clock—in the afternoon of a day in the year 1895.

At the rise of the curtain there is a moment of intense silence. Then The Steward *enters and commences*

*to clear the table of the few dishes which still remain
on it after the* CAPTAIN'S *dinner. He is an old, griz-
zled man dressed in dungaree pants, a sweater, and a
woolen cap with ear-flaps. His manner is sullen and
angry. He stops stacking up the plates and casts a
quick glance upward at the skylight, then tiptoes
over to the closed door in rear and listens with his ear
pressed to the crack. What he hears makes his face
darken and he mutters a furious curse. There is a
noise from the doorway on the right and he darts back
to the table.*

BEN *enters. He is an overgrown, gawky boy with a
long, pinched face. He is dressed in sweater, fur cap,
etc. His teeth are chattering with the cold and he
hurries to the stove, where he stands for a moment
shivering, blowing on his hands, slapping them against
his sides, on the verge of crying.*

THE STEWARD. [*In relieved tones—seeing who it is.*]
Oh, 'tis you, is it? What're ye shiverin' 'bout? Stay by
the stove where ye belong and ye'll find no need of chat-
terin'.

BEN. It's c-c-cold. [*Trying to control his chattering
teeth—derisively.*] Who d'ye think it were—the Old
Man?

THE STEWARD. [*Makes a threatening move—*BEN
shrinks away.] None o' your lip, young un, or I'll learn
ye. [*More kindly.*] Where was it ye've been all o' the
time—the fo'c'stle?

BEN. Yes.

THE STEWARD. Let the Old Man see ye up for'ard
monkeyshinin' with the hands and ye'll get a hidin' ye'll
not forget in a hurry.

BEN. Aw, he don't see nothin'. [*A trace of awe in his*

tones—he glances upward.]   He just walks up and down like he didn't notice nobody—and stares at the ice to the no'th'ard.

THE STEWARD.   [*The same tone of awe creeping into his voice.*]   He's always starin' at the ice.   [*In a sudden rage, shaking his fist at the skylight.*]   Ice, ice, ice! Damn him and damn the ice!   Holdin' us in for nigh on a year—nothin' to see but ice—stuck in it like a fly in molasses!

BEN.   [*Apprehensively.*]   Ssshh!   He'll hear ye.

THE STEWARD.   [*Raging.*]   Aye, damn him, and damn the Arctic seas, and damn this stinkin' whalin' ship of his, and damn me for a fool to ever ship on it!   [*Subsiding as if realizing the uselessness of this outburst—shaking his head—slowly, with deep conviction.*]   He's a hard man— as hard a man as ever sailed the seas.

BEN.   [*Solemnly.*]   Aye.

THE STEWARD.   The two years we all signed up for are done this day.   Blessed Christ!   Two years o' this dog's life, and no luck in the fishin', and the hands half starved with the food runnin' low, rotten as it is; and not a sign of him turnin' back for home!   [*Bitterly.*]   Home!   I begin to doubt if ever I'll set foot on land again.   [*Excitedly.*]   What is it he thinks he' goin' to do?   Keep us all up here after our time is worked out till the last man of us is starved to death or frozen?   We've grub enough hardly to last out the voyage back if we started now.   What are the men goin' to do 'bout it?   Did ye hear any talk in the fo'c'stle?

BEN.   [*Going over to him—in a half-whisper.*]   They said if he don't put back south for home to-day they're goin' to mutiny.

THE STEWARD.   [*With grim satisfaction.*]   Mutiny? Aye, 'tis the only thing they can do; and serve him right after the manner he's treated them—'s if they weren't no better nor dogs.

BEN. The ice is all broke up to s'uth'ard. They's clear water 's far 's you can see. He ain't got no excuse for not turnin' back for home, the men says.

THE STEWARD. [*Bitterly.*] He won't look nowheres but no'th'ard where they's only the ice to see. He don't want to see no clear water. All he thinks on is gittin' the ile—'s if it was our fault he ain't had good luck with the whales. [*Shaking his head.*] I think the man's mighty nigh losin' his senses.

BEN. [*Awed.*] D'you really think he's crazy?

THE STEWARD. Aye, it's the punishment o' God on him. Did ye ever hear of a man who wasn't crazy do the things he does? [*Pointing to the door in rear.*] Who but a man that's mad would take his woman—and as sweet a woman as ever was—on a stinkin' whalin' ship to the Arctic seas to be locked in by the rotten ice for nigh on a year, and maybe lose her senses forever—for it's sure she'll never be the same again.

BEN. [*Sadly.*] She useter be awful nice to me before [*his eyes grow wide and frightened*]—she got—like she is.

THE STEWARD. Aye, she was good to all of us. 'Twould have been hell on board without her; for he's a hard man—a hard, hard man—a driver if there ever was one. [*With a grim laugh.*] I hope he's satisfied now—drivin' her on till she's near lost her mind. And who could blame her? 'Tis a God's wonder we're not a ship full of crazed people—with the damned ice all the time, and the quiet so thick you're afraid to hear your own voice.

BEN. [*With a frightened glance toward the door on right.*] She don't never speak to me no more—jest looks at me 's if she didn't know me.

THE STEWARD. She don't know no one—but him. She talks to him—when she does talk—right enough.

BEN. She does nothin' all day long now but sit and sew —and then she cries to herself without makin' no noise. I've seen her.

THE STEWARD. Aye, I could hear her through the door a while back.

BEN. [*Tiptoes over to the door and listens.*] She's cryin' now.

THE STEWARD. [*Furiously—shaking his fist.*] God send his soul to hell for the devil he is!

> [*There is the noise of some one coming slowly down the companionway stairs.* THE STEW-ARD *hurries to his stacked-up dishes. He is so nervous from fright that he knocks off the top one, which falls and breaks on the floor. He stands aghast, trembling with dread.* BEN *is violently rubbing off the organ with a piece of cloth which he has snatched from his pocket.* CAPTAIN KEENEY *appears in the doorway on right and comes into the cabin, removing his fur cap as he does so. He is a man of about forty, around five-ten in height but looking much shorter on account of the enormous pro-portions of his shoulders and chest. His face is massive and deeply lined, with gray-blue eyes of a bleak hardness, and a tightly clenched, thin-lipped mouth. His thick hair is long and gray. He is dressed in a heavy blue jacket and blue pants stuffed into his sea-boots.*
>
> *He is followed into the cabin by* THE SECOND MATE, *a rangy six-footer with a lean weather-beaten face. The* MATE *is dressed about the*

> *same as the captain. He is a man of thirty or so.*]

KEENEY. [*Comes toward* THE STEWARD—*with a stern look on his face.* THE STEWARD *is visibly frightened and the stack of dishes rattles in his trembling hands.* KEENEY *draws back his fist and* THE STEWARD *shrinks away. The fist is gradually lowered and* KEENEY *speaks slowly.*] 'Twould be like hitting a worm. It is nigh on two bells, Mr. Steward, and this truck not cleared yet.

THE STEWARD. [*Stammering.*] Y-y-yes, sir.

KEENEY. Instead of doin' your rightful work ye've been below here gossipin' old woman's talk with that boy. [*To* BEN, *fiercely.*] Get out o' this, you! Clean up the chart-room. [BEN *darts past the* MATE *to the open door-way.*] Pick up that dish, Mr. Steward!

THE STEWARD. [*Doing so with difficulty.*] Yes, sir.

KEENEY. The next dish you break, Mr. Steward, you take a bath in the Bering Sea at the end of a rope.

THE STEWARD. [*Tremblingly.*] Yes, sir.

> [*He hurries out. The* SECOND MATE *walks slowly over to the* CAPTAIN.]

MATE. I warn't 'specially anxious the man at the wheel should catch what I wanted to say to you, sir. That's why I asked you to come below.

KEENEY. [*Impatiently.*] Speak your say, Mr. Slocum.

MATE. [*Unconsciously lowering his voice.*] I'm afeard there'll be trouble with the hands by the look o' things. They'll likely turn ugly, every blessed one o' them, if you don't put back. The two years they signed up for is up to-day.

KEENEY. And d'you think you're tellin' me somethin' new, Mr. Slocum? I've felt it in the air this long time past. D'you think I've not seen their ugly looks and the grudgin' way they worked?

> [*The door in rear is opened and* MRS. KEENEY
> *stands in the doorway. She is a slight, sweet-
> faced little woman primly dressed in black.
> Her eyes are red from weeping and her face
> drawn and pale. She takes in the cabin with
> a frightened glance and stands as if fixed to
> the spot by some nameless dread, clasping and
> unclasping her hands nervously. The two
> men turn and look at her.*]

KEENEY. [*With rough tenderness.*] Well, Annie?

MRS. KEENEY. [*As if awakening from a dream.*] David, I——

> [*She is silent. The* MATE *starts for the door-
> way.*]

KEENEY. [*Turning to him—sharply.*] Wait!

MATE. Yes, sir.

KEENEY. D'you want anything, Annie?

MRS. KEENEY. [*After a pause, during which she seems to be endeavoring to collect her thoughts.*] I thought maybe—I'd go up on deck, David, to get a breath of fresh air.

> [*She stands humbly awaiting his permission.
> He and the* MATE *exchange a significant
> glance.*]

KEENEY. It's too cold, Annie. You'd best stay below to-day. There's nothing to look at on deck—but ice.

MRS. KEENEY. [*Monotonously.*] I know—ice, ice, ice! But there's nothing to see down here but these walls.

> [*She makes a gesture of loathing.*]

KEENEY. You can play the organ, Annie.

MRS. KEENEY. [*Dully.*] I hate the organ. It puts me in mind of home.

KEENEY. [*A touch of resentment in his voice.*] I got it jest for you.

MRS. KEENEY. [*Dully.*] I know. [*She turns away from them and walks slowly to the bench on left. She lifts up one of the curtains and looks through a port-hole; then utters an exclamation of joy.*] Ah, water! Clear water! As far as I can see! How good it looks after all these months of ice! [*She turns round to them, her face transfigured with joy.*] Ah, now I must go up on deck and look at it, David.

KEENEY. [*Frowning.*] Best not to-day, Annie. Best wait for a day when the sun shines.

MRS. KEENEY. [*Desperately.*] But the sun never shines in this terrible place.

KEENEY. [*A tone of command in his voice.*] Best not to-day, Annie.

MRS. KEENEY. [*Crumbling before this command—abjectly.*] Very well, David.

> [*She stands there staring straight before her as if in a daze. The two men look at her uneasily.*]

KEENEY. [*Sharply.*] Annie!

MRS. KEENEY. [*Dully.*] Yes, David.

KEENEY. Me and Mr. Slocum has business to talk about—ship's business.

MRS. KEENEY. Very well, David.

> [*She goes slowly out, rear, and leaves the door three-quarters shut behind her.*]

KEENEY. Best not have her on deck if they's goin' to be any trouble.

MATE. Yes, sir.

KEENEY. And trouble they's goin' to be. I feel it in

my bones. [*Takes a revolver from the pocket of his coat and examines it.*] Got your'n?

MATE. Yes, sir.

KEENEY. Not that we'll have to use 'em—not if I know their breed of dog—jest to frighten 'em up a bit. [*Grimly.*] I ain't never been forced to use one yit; and trouble I've had by land and by sea 's long as I kin remember, and will have till my dyin' day, I reckon.

MATE. [*Hesitatingly.*] Then you ain't goin'—to turn back?

KEENEY. Turn back! Mr. Slocum, did you ever hear 'o me pointin' s'uth for home with only a measly four hundred barrel of ile in the hold?

MATE. [*Hastily.*] No, sir—but the grub's gittin' low.

KEENEY. They's enough to last a long time yit, if they're careful with it; and they's plenty o' water.

MATE. They say it's not fit to eat—what's left; and the two years they signed on fur is up to-day. They might make trouble for you in the courts when we git home.

KEENEY. To hell with 'em! Let them make what law trouble they kin. I don't give a damn 'bout the money. I've got to git the ile! [*Glancing sharply at the* MATE.] You ain't turnin' no damned sea lawyer, be you, Mr. Slocum?

MATE. [*Flushing.*] Not by a hell of a sight, sir.

KEENEY. What do the fools want to go home fur now? Their share o' the four hundred barrel wouldn't keep 'em in chewin' terbacco.

MATE. [*Slowly.*] They wants to git back to their folks an' things, I s'pose.

KEENEY. [*Looking at him searchingly.*] 'N you want to turn back, too. [*The* MATE *looks down confusedly before his sharp gaze.*] Don't lie, Mr. Slocum. It's writ down plain in your eyes. [*With grim sarcasm.*] I hope, Mr. Slocum, you ain't agoin' to jine the men agin me.

MATE. [*Indignantly.*] That ain't fair, sir, to say sich things.

KEENEY. [*With satisfaction.*] I warn't much afeard o' that, Tom. You been with me nigh on ten year and I've learned ye whalin'. No man kin say I ain't a good master, if I be a hard one.

MATE. I warn't thinkin' of myself, sir—'bout turnin' home, I mean. [*Desperately.*] But Mrs. Keeney, sir— seems like she ain't jest satisfied up here, ailin' like—what with the cold an' bad luck an' the ice an' all.

KEENEY. [*His face clouding—rebukingly but not severely.*] That's my business, Mr. Slocum. I'll thank you to steer a clear course o' that. [*A pause.*] The ice'll break up soon to no'th'ard. I could see it startin' to-day. And when it goes and we git some sun Annie'll perk up. [*Another pause—then he bursts forth:*] It ain't the damned money what's keepin' me up in the Northern seas, Tom. But I can't go back to Homeport with a measly four hundred barrel of ile. I'd die fust. I ain't never come back home in all my days without a full ship. Ain't that truth?

MATE. Yes, sir; but this voyage you been icebound, an'——

KEENEY. [*Scornfully.*] And d'you s'pose any of 'em would believe that—any o' them skippers I've beaten voyage after voyage? Can't you hear 'em laughin' and sneerin'—Tibbots 'n' Harris 'n' Simms and the rest—and all o' Homeport makin' fun o' me? "Dave Keeney what boasts he's the best whalin' skipper out o' Homeport comin' back with a measly four hundred barrel of ile?" [*The thought of this drives him into a frenzy, and he smashes his fist down on the marble top of the sideboard.*]

Hell! I got to git the ile, I tell you. How could I figger on this ice? It's never been so bad before in the thirty year I been acomin' here. And now it's breakin' up. In a couple o' days it'll be all gone. And they's whale here, plenty of 'em. I know they is and I ain't never gone wrong yit. I got to git the ile! I got to git it in spite of all hell, and by God, I ain't agoin' home till I do git it!

> [*There is the sound of subdued sobbing from the door in rear. The two men stand silent for a moment, listening. Then* KEENEY *goes over to the door and looks in. He hesitates for a moment as if he were going to enter— then closes the door softly.* JOE, *the har- pooner, an enormous six-footer with a bat- tered, ugly face, enters from right and stands waiting for the captain to notice him.*]

KEENEY. [*Turning and seeing him.*] Don't be standin' there like a gawk, Harpooner. Speak up!

JOE. [*Confusedly.*] We want—the men, sir—they wants to send a depitation aft to have a word with you.

KEENEY. [*Furiously.*] Tell 'em to go to— [*Checks himself and continues grimly.*] Tell 'em to come. I'll see 'em.

JOE. Aye, aye, sir.

> [*He goes out.*]

KEENEY. [*With a grim smile.*] Here it comes, the trouble you spoke of, Mr. Slocum, and we'll make short shift of it. It's better to crush such things at the start than let them make headway.

MATE. [*Worriedly.*] Shall I wake up the First and Fourth, sir? We might need their help.

KEENEY. No, let them sleep. I'm well able to handle this alone, Mr. Slocum.

> [*There is the shuffling of footsteps from out-*

*side and five of the crew crowd into the cabin,
led by* JOE. *All are dressed alike—sweaters,
seaboots, etc. They glance uneasily at the*
CAPTAIN, *twirling their fur caps in their
hands.*]

KEENEY. [*After a pause.*] Well? Who's to speak
fur ye?

JOE. [*Stepping forward with an air of bravado.*] I
be.

KEENEY. [*Eying him up and down coldly.*] So you
be. Then speak your say and be quick about it.

JOE. [*Trying not to wilt before the* CAPTAIN'S *glance
and avoiding his eyes.*] The time we signed up for is
done to-day.

KEENEY. [*Icily.*] You're tellin' me nothin' I don't
know.

JOE. You ain't pintin' fur home yit, far's we kin see.

KEENEY. No, and I ain't agoin' to till this ship is full
of ile.

JOE. You can't go no further no'th with the ice afore
ye.

KEENEY. The ice is breaking up.

JOE. [*After a slight pause during which the others
mumble angrily to one another.*] The grub we're gittin'
now is rotten.

KEENEY. It's good enough fur ye. Better men than
ye are have eaten worse.

[*There is a chorus of angry exclamations from
the crowd.*]

JOE. [*Encouraged by this support.*] We ain't agoin'
to work no more less you puts back for home.

KEENEY. [*Fiercely.*] You ain't, ain't you?

JOE. No; and the law courts'll say we was right.

KEENEY.   To hell with your law courts!   We're at sea now and I'm the law on this ship.   [*Edging up toward the harpooner.*]   And every mother's son of you what don't obey orders goes in irons.

> [*There are more angry exclamations from the crew.   MRS. KEENEY appears in the doorway in rear and looks on with startled eyes.   None of the men notice her.*]

JOE.   [*With bravado.*]   Then we're agoin' to mutiny and take the old hooker home ourselves.   Ain't we, boys?

> [*As he turns his head to look at the others, KEENEY'S fist shoots out to the side of his jaw. JOE goes down in a heap and lies there.   MRS. KEENEY gives a shriek and hides her face in her hands.   The men pull out their sheath knives and start a rush, but stop when they find themselves confronted by the revolvers of KEENEY and the MATE.*]

KEENEY.   [*His eyes and voice snapping.*]   Hold still! [*The men stand huddled together in a sullen silence. KEENEY'S voice is full of mockery.*]   You've found out it ain't safe to mutiny on this ship, ain't you?   And now git for'ard where ye belong, and— [*He gives JOE's body a contemptuous kick.*]   Drag him with you.   And remember the first man of ye I see shirkin' I'll shoot dead as sure as there's a sea under us, and you can tell the rest the same.   Git for'ard now!   Quick!   [*The men leave in cowed silence, carrying JOE with them.   KEENEY turns to the MATE with a short laugh and puts his revolver back in his pocket.*]   Best get up on deck, Mr. Slocum, and see to it they don't try none of their skulkin' tricks.   We'll have to keep an eye peeled from now on.   I know 'em.

MATE.   Yes, sir.

> [*He goes out, right.   KEENEY hears his wife's*

hysterical weeping and turns around in surprise—then walks slowly to her side.]

KEENEY. [*Putting an arm around her shoulder—with gruff tenderness.*] There, there, Annie. Don't be afeard. It's all past and gone.

MRS. KEENEY. [*Shrinking away from him.*] Oh, I can't bear it! I can't bear it any longer!

KEENEY. [*Gently.*] Can't bear what, Annie?

MRS. KEENEY. [*Hysterically.*] . All this horrible brutality, and these brutes of men, and this terrible ship, and this prison-cell of a room, and the ice all around, and the silence.

[*After this outburst she calms down and wipes her eyes with her handkerchief.*]

KEENEY. [*After a pause during which he looks down at her with a puzzled frown.*] Remember, I warn't hankerin' to have you come on this voyage, Annie.

MRS. KEENEY. I wanted to be with you, David, don't you see? I didn't want to wait back there in the house all alone as I've been doing these last six years since we were married—waiting, and watching, and fearing—with nothing to keep my mind occupied—not able to go back teaching school on account of being Dave Keeney's wife. I used to dream of sailing on the great, wide, glorious ocean. I wanted to be by your side in the danger and vigorous life of it all. I wanted to see you the hero they make you out to be in Homeport. And instead— [*Her voice grows tremulous.*] All I find is ice and cold—and brutality!

[*Her voice breaks.*]

KEENEY. I warned you what it'd be, Annie. "Whalin' ain't no ladies' tea-party," I says to you, and "you better stay to home where you've got all your woman's comforts." [*Shaking his head.*] But you was so set on it.

MRS. KEENEY. [*Wearily.*] Oh, I know it isn't your

fault, David. You see, I didn't believe you. I guess I was dreaming about the old Vikings in the story-books and I thought you were one of them.

KEENEY. [*Protestingly.*] I done my best to make it as cosey and comfortable as could be. [MRS. KEENEY *looks around her in wild scorn.*] I even sent to the city for that organ for ye, thinkin' it might be soothin' to ye to be playin' it times when they was calms and things was dull like.

MRS. KEENEY. [*Wearily.*] Yes, you were very kind, David. I know that. [*She goes to left and lifts the curtains from the port-hole and looks out—then suddenly bursts forth:*] I won't stand it—I can't stand it—pent up by these walls like a prisoner. [*She runs over to him and throws her arms around him, weeping. He puts his arm protectingly over her shoulders.*] Take me away from here, David! If I don't get away from here, out of this terrible ship, I'll go mad! Take me home, David! I can't think any more. I feel as if the cold and the silence were crushing down on my brain. I'm afraid. Take me home!

. KEENEY. [*Holds her at arm's length and looks at her face anxiously.*] Best go to bed, Annie. You ain't yourself. You got fever. Your eyes look so strange like. I ain't never seen you look this way before.

MRS. KEENEY. [*Laughing hysterically.*] It's the ice and the cold and the silence—they'd make any one look strange.

KEENEY. [*Soothingly.*] In a month or two, with good luck, three at the most, I'll have her filled with ile and then we'll give her everything she'll stand and pint for home.

MRS. KEENEY. But we can't wait for that—I can't wait. I want to get home. And the men won't wait.

They want to get home. It's cruel, it's brutal for you to keep them. You must sail back. You've got no excuse. There's clear water to the south now. If you've a heart at all you've got to turn back.

KEENEY. [*Harshly.*] I can't, Annie.

MRS. KEENEY. Why can't you?

KEENEY. A woman couldn't rightly understand my reason.

MRS. KEENEY. [*Wildly.*] Because it's a stupid, stubborn reason. Oh, I heard you talking with the second mate. You're afraid the other captains will sneer at you because you didn't come back with a full ship. You want to live up to your silly reputation even if you do have to beat and starve men and drive me mad to do it.

KEENEY. [*His jaw set stubbornly.*] It ain't that, Annie. Them skippers would never dare sneer to my face. It ain't so much what any one'd say—but— [*He hesitates, struggling to express his meaning.*] You see— I've always done it—since my first voyage as skipper. I always come back—with a full ship—and--it don't seem right not to—somehow. I been always first whalin' skipper out o' Homeport, and— Don't you see my meanin', Annie? [*He glances at her. She is not looking at him but staring dully in front of her, not hearing a word he is saying.*] Annie! [*She comes to herself with a start.*] Best turn in, Annie, there's a good woman. You ain't well.

MRS. KEENEY. [*Resisting his attempts to guide her to the door in rear.*] David! Won't you please turn back?

KEENEY. [*Gently.*] I can't, Annie—not yet awhile. You don't see my meanin'. I got to git the ile.

MRS. KEENEY. It'd be different if you needed the money, but you don't. You've got more than plenty.

KEENEY. [*Impatiently.*] It ain't the money I'm thinkin' of. D'you think I'm as mean as that?

MRS. KEENEY. [*Dully.*] No—I don't know—I can't understand— [*Intensely.*] Oh, I want to be home in the old house once more and see my own kitchen again, and hear a woman's voice talking to me and be able to talk to her. Two years! It seems so long ago—as if I'd been dead and could never go back.

KEENEY. [*Worried by her strange tone and the faraway look in her eyes.*] Best go to bed, Annie. You ain't well.

MRS. KEENEY. [*Not appearing to hear him.*] I used to be lonely when you were away. I used to think Homeport was a stupid, monotonous place. Then I used to go down on the beach, especially when it was windy and the breakers were rolling in, and I'd dream of the fine free life you must be leading. [*She gives a laugh which is half a sob.*] I used to love the sea then. [*She pauses; then continues with slow intensity:*] But now—I don't ever want to see the sea again.

KEENEY. [*Thinking to humor her.*] 'Tis no fit place for a woman, that's sure. I was a fool to bring ye.

MRS. KEENEY. [*After a pause—passing her hand over her eyes with a gesture of pathetic weariness.*] How long would it take us to reach home—if we started now?

KEENEY. [*Frowning.*] 'Bout two months, I reckon, Annie, with fair luck.

MRS. KEENEY. [*Counts on her fingers—then murmurs with a rapt smile.*] That would be August, the latter part of August, wouldn't it? It was on the twenty-fifth of August we were married, David, wasn't it?

KEENEY. [*Trying to conceal the fact that her memories have moved him—gruffly.*] Don't *you* remember?

MRS. KEENEY. [*Vaguely—again passes her hand over*

her eyes.]   My memory is leaving me—up here in the ice.
It was so long ago.   [*A pause—then she smiles dreamily.*]
It's June now.   The lilacs will be all in bloom in the front
yard—and the climbing roses on the trellis to the side of
the house—they're budding.

>   [*She suddenly covers her face with her hands
>   and commences to sob.*]

KEENEY.   [*Disturbed.*]   Go   in   and   rest,   Annie.
You're all wore out cryin' over what can't be helped.

MRS. KEENEY.   [*Suddenly throwing her arms around
his neck and clinging to him.*]   You love me, don't you,
David?

KEENEY.   [*In amazed embarrassment at this outburst.*]
Love you?   Why d'you ask me such a question, Annie?

MRS. KEENEY.   [*Shaking him—fiercely.*]   But you do,
don't you, David?   Tell me!

KEENEY.   I'm your husband, Annie, and you're my
wife.   Could there be aught but love between us after all
these years?

MRS.   KEENEY.   [*Shaking   him   again—still   more
fiercely.*]   Then you do love me.   Say it!

KEENEY.   [*Simply.*]   I do, Annie.

MRS. KEENEY.   [*Gives a sigh of relief—her hands drop
to her sides.   KEENEY regards her anxiously.   She passes
her hand across her eyes and murmurs half to herself:*]
I sometimes think if we could only have had a child.
[KEENEY *turns away from her, deeply moved.   She grabs
his arm and turns him around to face her—intensely.*]
And I've always been a good wife to you, haven't I,
David?

KEENEY.   [*His voice betraying his emotion.*]   No man
has ever had a better, Annie.

MRS. KEENEY.   And I've never asked for much from
you, have I, David?   Have I?

KEENEY. You know you could have all I got the power to give ye, Annie.

MRS. KEENEY. [*Wildly.*] Then do this this once for my sake, for God's sake—take me home! It's killing me, this life—the brutality and cold and horror of it. I'm going mad. I can feel the threat in the air. I can hear the silence threatening me—day after gray day and every day the same. I can't bear it. [*Sobbing.*] I'll go mad, I know I will. Take me home, David, if you love me as you say. I'm afraid. For the love of God, take me home!

> [*She throws her arms around him, weeping against his shoulder. His face betrays the tremendous struggle going on within him. He holds her out at arm's length, his expression softening. For a moment his shoulders sag, he becomes old, his iron spirit weakens as he looks at her tear-stained face.*]

KEENEY. [*Dragging out the words with an effort.*] I'll do it, Annie—for your sake—if you say it's needful for ye.

MRS. KEENEY. [*With wild joy—kissing him.*] God bless you for that, David!

> [*He turns away from her silently and walks toward the companionway. Just at that moment there is a clatter of footsteps on the stairs and the SECOND MATE enters the cabin.*]

MATE. [*Excitedly.*] The ice is breakin' up to no'th'ard, sir. There's a clear passage through the floe, and clear water beyond, the lookout says.

> [*KEENEY straightens himself like a man coming out of a trance. MRS. KEENEY looks at the MATE with terrified eyes.*]

KEENEY. [*Dazedly—trying to collect his thoughts.*] A clear passage? To no'th'ard?

MATE. Yes, sir.

KEENEY. [*His voice suddenly grim with determination.*] Then get her ready and we'll drive her through.

MATE. Aye, aye, sir.

MRS. KEENEY. [*Appealingly.*] David!

KEENEY. [*Not heeding her.*] Will the men turn to willin' or must we drag 'em out?

MATE. They'll turn to willin' enough. You put the fear o' God into 'em, sir. They're meek as lambs.

KEENEY. Then drive 'em—both watches. [*With grim determination.*] They's whale t'other side o' this floe and we're going to git 'em.

MATE. Aye, aye, sir.

> [*He goes out hurriedly. A moment later there is the sound of scuffling feet from the deck outside and the* MATE'S *voice shouting orders.*]

KEENEY. [*Speaking aloud to himself—derisively.*] And I was agoin' home like a yaller dog!

MRS. KEENEY. [*Imploringly.*] David!

KEENEY. [*Sternly.*] Woman, you ain't adoin' right when you meddle in men's business and weaken 'em. You can't know my feelin's. I got to prove a man to be a good husband for ye to take pride in. I got to git the ile, I tell ye.

MRS. KEENEY. [*Supplicatingly.*] David! Aren't you going home?

KEENEY. [*Ignoring this question—commandingly.*] You ain't well. Go and lay down a mite. [*He starts for the door.*] I got to git on deck. [*He goes out. She cries after him in anguish:*] David!

> [*A pause. She passes her hand across her eyes —then commences to laugh hysterically and*

goes to the organ. She sits down and starts to play wildly an old hymn. KEENEY *reenters from the doorway to the deck and stands looking at her angrily. He comes over and grabs her roughly by the shoulder.*]

KEENEY. Woman, what foolish mockin' is this? [*She laughs wildly and he starts back from her in alarm.*] Annie! What is it? [*She doesn't answer him.* KEENEY'S *voice trembles.*] Don't you know me, Annie? [*He puts both hands on her shoulders and turns her around so that he can look into her eyes. She stares up at him with a stupid expression, a vague smile on her lips. He stumbles away from her, and she commences softly to play the organ again.*]

KEENEY. [*Swallowing hard—in a hoarse whisper, as if he had difficulty in speaking.*] You said—you was a-goin mad—God! [*A long wail is heard from the deck above.*] Ah bl-o-o-o-ow!

[*A moment later the* MATE'S *face appears through the skylight. He cannot see* MRS. KEENEY.]

MATE. [*In great excitement.*] Whales, sir—a whole school of 'em—off star'b'd quarter 'bout five mile away—big ones!

KEENEY. [*Galvanized into action.*] Are you lowerin' the boats?

MATE. Yes, sir.

KEENEY. [*With grim decision.*] I'm a-comin' with ye.

MATE. Aye, aye, sir. [*Jubilantly.*] You'll git the ile now right enough, sir.

[*His head is withdrawn and he can be heard shouting orders.*]

KEENEY. [*Turning to his wife.*] Annie! Did you hear him? I'll git the ile. [*She doesn't answer or seem to know he is there. He gives a hard laugh, which is almost a groan.*] I know you're foolin' me. Annie. You ain't out of your mind— [*Anxiously.*] Be you? I'll git the ile now right enough—jest a little while longer, Annie—then we'll turn hom'ard. I can't turn back now, you see that, don't ye? I've got to git the ile. [*In sudden terror.*] Answer me! You ain't mad, be you?

> [*She keeps on playing the organ, but makes no reply. The* MATE'S *face appears again through the skylight.*]

MATE. All ready, sir.

> [KEENEY *turns his back on his wife and strides to the doorway, where he stands for a moment and looks back at her in anguish, fighting to control his feelings.*]

MATE. Comin', sir?

KEENEY. [*His face suddenly grown hard with determination.*] Aye.

> [*He turns abruptly and goes out.* MRS. KEENEY *does not appear to notice his departure. Her whole attention seems centred in the organ. She sits with half-closed eyes, her body swaying a little from side to side to the rhythm of the hymn. Her fingers move faster and faster and she is playing wildly and discordantly as the curtain falls.*]

A MARRIAGE HAS BEEN ARRANGED . . .

BY
ALFRED SUTRO

Alfred Sutro was born in England, August 7, 1863, and was educated in London and Brussels. His lifework has been that of a playwright. The best of his short plays, including *A Marriage Has Been Arranged,* have been collected in the volume, *Five Little Plays* (Brentano, 1912). The most popular of his long plays are *The Walls of Jericho,* (French, 1906); *The Perfect Lover,* 1905; *John Glayde's Honor,* (French, 1907); *The Builder of Bridges,* 1908; *Far Above Rubies,* 1924; and *A Man with a Heart,* 1925.

THE PERSONS OF THE PLAY

Mr. Harrison Crockstead
Lady Aline de Vaux

A MARRIAGE HAS BEEN ARRANGED . . .

SCENE: The conservatory of No. 300 Grosvenor Square. Hour, close on midnight. A ball is in progress, and dreamy waltz music is heard in the distance.

LADY ALINE DE VAUX *enters, leaning on the arm of* MR. HARRISON CROCKSTEAD.

LADY ALINE *is a tall, exquisitely gowned girl, of the conventional and much-admired type of beauty. Put her in any drawing-room in the world, and she would at once be recognized as a highborn Englishwoman. She has in her, in embryo, all those excellent qualities that go to make a great lady: the icy stare, the haughty movement of the shoulder, the disdainful arch of the lip; she has also, but only an experienced observer would notice it, something of wistfulness, something that speaks of a sore and wounded heart—though it is sufficiently evident that this organ is kept under admirable control. A girl who has been placed in a position of life where artificiality rules, who has been taught to be artificial and has thoroughly learned her lesson; yet one who would unhesitatingly know the proper thing to do did a camel bolt with her in the desert, or an eastern potentate invite her to become his two hundred and fifty-seventh wife. In a word, a lady of complete self-possession and magnificent control.* MR. CROCKSTEAD *is a big, burly man of forty or so, and of the kind to whom the ordinary West End butler would consider himself perfectly justified in declaring that her ladyship was not at home. And yet his evening clothes sit well on him;*

327

*and there is a certain air of command about the man
that would have made the butler uncomfortable.
That functionary would have excused himself by declaring that* MR. CROCKSTEAD *didn't look a gentleman.
And perhaps he doesn't. His walk is rather a slouch;
he has a way of keeping his hands in his pockets, and
of jerking out his sentences; a way, above all, of
seeming perfectly indifferent to the comfort of the
people he happens to be addressing. The impression
he gives is one of power, not of refinement; and the
massive face, with its heavy lines, and eyes that are
usually veiled, seems to give no clew whatever to the
character of the man within.*

The couple break apart when they enter the room; LADY
ALINE *is the least bit nervous, though she shows no
trace of it;* MR. CROCKSTEAD *absolutely imperturbable
and undisturbed.*

CROCKSTEAD. [*Looking around.*] Ah—this is the
place—very quiet, retired, romantic—et cetera. Music in
the distance—all very appropriate and sentimental. [*She
leaves him, and sits, quietly fanning herself; he stands,
looking at her.*] You seem perfectly calm, Lady Aline?

ALINE. [*Sitting.*] Conservatories are not unusual
appendages to a ballroom, Mr. Crockstead; nor is this
conservatory unlike other conservatories.

CROCKSTEAD. [*Turning to her.*] I wonder why
women are always so evasive?

ALINE. With your permission we will not discuss the
sex. You and I are too old to be cynical, and too young
to be appreciative. And besides, it is a rule of mine,
whenever I sit out a dance, that my partner shall avoid the
subjects of women—and golf.

CROCKSTEAD. You limit the area of conversation. But

then, in this particular instance, I take it, we have not come here to talk?

ALINE. [*Coldly.*] I beg your pardon!

CROCKSTEAD. [*Sitting beside her.*] Lady Aline, they are dancing a cotillon in there, so we have half an hour before us. We shall not be disturbed, for the Duchess, your aunt, has considerately stationed her aged companion in the corridor, with instructions to ward off intruders.

ALINE. [*Very surprised.*] Mr. Crockstead!

CROCKSTEAD. [*Looking hard at her.*] Didn't you know? [ALINE *turns aside, embarrassed.*] That's right —of course you did. Don't you know why I have brought you here? That's right; of course you do. The Duchess, your aunt, and the Marchioness, your mother—observe how fondly my tongue trips out the titles—smiled sweetly on us as we left the ballroom. There will be a notice in the *Morning Post* to-morrow: "A Marriage Has Been Arranged Between——"

ALINE. [*Bewildered and offended.*] Mr. Crockstead! This—this is——

CROCKSTEAD. [*Always in the same quiet tone.*] Because I have not yet proposed, you mean? Of course I intend to, Lady Aline. Only as I know that you will accept me——

ALINE. [*In icy tones, as she rises.*] Let us go back to the ballroom.

CROCKSTEAD. [*Quite undisturbed.*] Oh, please! That won't help us, you know. Do sit down. I assure you I have never proposed before, so that naturally I am a trifle nervous. Of course I know that we are only supers really, without much of a speaking part; but the spirit moves me to gag, in the absence of the stage-manager, who is, let us say, the Duchess——

ALINE. I have heard of the New Humor, Mr. Crock-

stead, though I confess I have never understood it.   This
may be an exquisite example——

CROCKSTEAD.   By no means.   I am merely trying to do
the right thing, though perhaps not the conventional one.
Before making you the formal offer of my hand and fortune, which amounts to a little over three millions——

ALINE.   [*Fanning herself.*]   How people exaggerate!
Between six and seven, *I* heard.

CROCKSTEAD.   Only three at present, but we must be
patient.   Before throwing myself at your feet, metaphor-
ically, I am anxious that you should know something of
the man whom you are about to marry.

ALINE.   That is really most considerate!

CROCKSTEAD.   I have the advantage of you, you see,
inasmuch as you have many dear friends, who have told
me all about you.

ALINE.   [*With growing exasperation, but keeping very
cool.*]   Indeed?

CROCKSTEAD.   I am aware, for instance, that this is
your ninth season——

ALINE.   [*Snapping her fan.*]   You are remarkably
well-informed.

CROCKSTEAD.   I have been told that again to-night,
three times, by charming young women who vowed that
they loved you.   Now, as I have no dearest friends, it is
unlikely that you will have heard anything equally definite
concerning myself.   I propose to enlighten you.

ALINE.   [*Satirically.*]   The story of your life—how
thrilling!

CROCKSTEAD.   I trust you may find it so.   [*He sits,
and pauses for a moment, then begins, very quietly.*]
Lady Aline, I am a self-made man, as the foolish phrase
has it—a man whose early years were spent in savage and
desolate places, where the devil had much to say; a man

in whom whatever there once had been of natural kindness was very soon kicked out. I was poor, and lonely, for thirty-two years: I have been rich, and lonely, for ten. My millions have been made honestly enough; but poverty and wretchedness had left their mark on me, and you will find very few men with a good word to say for Harrison Crockstead. I have no polish, or culture, or tastes. Art wearies me, literature sends me to sleep——

ALINE. When you come to the chapter of your personal deficiencies, Mr. Crockstead, please remember that they are sufficiently evident for me to have already observed them.

CROCKSTEAD. [*Without a trace of annoyance.*] That is true. I will pass, then, to more intimate matters. In a little township in Australia—a horrible place where there was gold—I met a woman whom I loved. She was what is technically known as a bad woman. She ran away with another man. I tracked them to Texas, and in a mining camp there I shot the man. I wanted to take the woman back, but she refused. That has been my solitary love affair; and I shall never love any woman again as I loved her. I think that is all that I have to tell you. And now—will you marry me, Lady Aline?

ALINE. [*Very steadily, facing him.*] Not if you were the last man in this world, Mr. Crockstead.

CROCKSTEAD. [*With a pleasant smile.*] At least that is emphatic.

ALINE. See, I will give you confidence for confidence. This is, as you suggest, my ninth season. Living in an absurd milieu where marriage with a wealthy man is regarded as the one aim in life, I have, during the past few weeks, done all that lay in my power to wring a proposal from you.

CROCKSTEAD. I appreciate your sincerity.

ALINE. Perhaps the knowledge that other women were doing the same lent a little zest to the pursuit, which otherwise would have been very dreary; for I confess that your personality did not—especially appeal to me.

CROCKSTEAD. [*Cheerfully.*] Thank you very much.

ALINE. Not at all. Indeed, this room being the Palace of Truth, I will admit that it was only by thinking hard of your three millions that I have been able to conceal the weariness I have felt in your society. And now will you marry me, Mr. Crockstead?

CROCKSTEAD. [*Serenely.*] I fancy that's what we're here for, isn't it?

ALINE. [*Stamping her foot.*] I have, of course, been debarred from the disreputable amours on which you linger so fondly; but I loved a soldier cousin of mine, and would have run away with him had my mother not packed me off in time. He went to India, and I stayed here; but he is the only man I have loved or ever shall love Further, let me tell you I am twenty-eight; I have always been poor—I hate poverty, and it has soured me no less than you. Dress is the thing in life I care for most, vulgarity my chief abomination. And to be frank, I consider you the most vulgar person I have ever met. Will you still marry me, Mr. Crockstead?

CROCKSTEAD. [*With undiminished cheerfulness.*] Why not?

ALINE. This is an outrage. Am I a horse, do you think, or a ballet-dancer? Do you imagine I will sell myself to you for your three millions?

CROCKSTEAD. Logic, my dear Lady Aline, is evidently not one of your more special possessions. For, had it not been for my—somewhat eccentric preliminaries—you *would* have accepted me, would you not?

ALINE. [*Embarrassed.*] I—I——

CROCKSTEAD. If I had said to you, timidly: "Lady Aline, I love you: I am a simple, unsophisticated person; will you marry me?" You would have answered, "Yes, Harrison, I will."

ALINE. It is a mercy to have escaped marrying a man with such a Christian name as Harrison.

CROCKSTEAD. It has been in the family for generations, you know; but it is a strange thing that I am always called Harrison, and that no one ever adopts the diminutive.

ALINE. That does not surprise me: we have no pet name for the East wind.

CROCKSTEAD. The possession of millions, you see, Lady Aline, puts you into eternal quarantine. It is a kind of yellow fever, with the difference that people are perpetually anxious to catch your complaint. But we digress. To return to the question of our marriage——

ALINE. I beg your pardon.

CROCKSTEAD. I presume that it is—arranged?

ALINE. [*Haughtily.*] Mr. Crockstead, let me remind you that frankness has its limits: exceeding these, it is apt to degenerate into impertinence. Be good enough to conduct me to the ballroom.

[*She moves to the door.*]

CROCKSTEAD. You have five sisters, I believe, Lady Aline? [ALINE *stops short.*] All younger than yourself, all marriageable, and all unmarried?

[ALINE *hangs her head and is silent.*]

CROCKSTEAD. Your father——

ALINE. [*Fiercely.*] Not a word of my father!

CROCKSTEAD. Your father is a gentleman. The breed is rare, and very fine when you get it. But he is exceedingly poor. People marry for money nowadays; and your mother will be very unhappy if this marriage of ours falls through.

ALINE. [*Moving a step towards him.*] Is it to oblige my mother, then, that you desire to marry me?

CROCKSTEAD. Well, no. But you see I must marry some one, in mere self-defense; and honestly, I think you will do at least as well as any one else. [ALINE *bursts out laughing.*] That strikes you as funny?

ALINE. If you had the least grain of chivalrous feeling, you would realize that the man who could speak to a woman as you have spoken to me——

[*She pauses.*]

CROCKSTEAD. Yes?

ALINE. I leave you to finish the sentence.

CROCKSTEAD. Thank you. I will finish it my own way. I will say that when a woman deliberately tries to wring an offer of marriage from a man whom she does not love, she deserves to be spoken to as I have spoken to you, Lady Aline.

ALINE. [*Scornfully.*] Love! What has love to do with marriage?

CROCKSTEAD. That remark rings hollow. You have been good enough to tell me of your cousin, whom you did love——

ALINE. Well?

CROCKSTEAD. And with whom you would have eloped, had your mother not prevented you.

ALINE. I most certainly should.

CROCKSTEAD. So you see that at one period of your life you thought differently. You were very fond of him?

ALINE. I have told you.

CROCKSTEAD. [*Meditatively.*] If I had been he, mother or no mother, money or no money, I would have carried you off. I fancy it must be pleasant to be loved by you, Lady Aline.

ALINE. [*Dropping a mock courtesy, as she sits on the sofa.*] You do me too much honor.

CROCKSTEAD. [*Still thoughtful, moving about the room.*] Next to being king, it is good to be maker of kings. Where is this cousin now?

ALINE. In America. But might I suggest that we have exhausted the subject?

CROCKSTEAD. Do you remember your "Arabian Nights," Lady Aline?

ALINE. Vaguely.

CROCKSTEAD. You have at least not forgotten that sublime Caliph, Haroun Al-Raschid?

ALINE. Oh, no—but why?

CROCKSTEAD. We millionaires are the Caliphs to-day; and we command more faithful than ever bowed to them. And, like that old scoundrel Haroun, we may at times permit ourselves a respectable impulse. What is your cousin's address?

ALINE. Again I ask—why?

CROCKSTEAD. I will put him in a position to marry you.

ALINE. [*In extreme surprise.*] What!

  [*She rises.*]

CROCKSTEAD. Oh, don't be alarmed, I'll manage it pleasantly. I'll give him tips, shares, speculate for him, make him a director of one or two of my companies. He shall have an income of four thousand a year. You can live on that.

ALINE. You are not serious?

CROCKSTEAD. Oh, yes; and though men may not like me, they always trust my word. You may.

ALINE. And why will you do this thing?

CROCKSTEAD. Call it caprice—call it a mere vulgar desire to let my magnificence dazzle you—call it the less vulgar desire to know that my money has made you happy with the man you love.

ALINE. That is generous.

CROCKSTEAD. I remember an old poem I learned at school—which told how Frederick the Great coveted a mill that adjoined a favorite estate of his; but the miller refused to sell. Frederick could have turned him out, of course—there was not very much public opinion in those days—but he respected the miller's firmness, and left him in solid possession. And mark that, at that very same time, he annexed—in other words stole—the province of Silesia.

ALINE. Ah——

CROCKSTEAD. [*Moving to the fireplace.*]

"Ce sont là jeux de Princes :
Ils respectent un meunier,
Ils volent une province."

[*The music stops.*]

ALINE. You speak French?

CROCKSTEAD. I am fond of it. It is the true and native language of insincerity.

ALINE. And yet you seem sincere.

CROCKSTEAD. I am permitting myself that luxury to-night. I am uncorking, let us say, the one bottle of '47 port left in my cellar.

ALINE. You are not quite fair to yourself, perhaps.

CROCKSTEAD. Do not let this action of mine cause you too suddenly to alter your opinion. The verdict you pronounced before was, on the whole, just.

ALINE. What verdict?

CROCKSTEAD. I was the most unpleasant person you ever had met.

ALINE. That was an exaggeration.

CROCKSTEAD.   The most repulsive——

ALINE.   [*Quickly.*]   I did not say that.

CROCKSTEAD.   And who prided himself on his repulsiveness.   ~~Very true, in the main, and~~ yet consider!   My wealth dates back ten years; till then I had known hunger, and every kind of sorrow and despair.   ~~I had stretched~~ out longing arms to the world, but not a heart opened to me.   And suddenly, when the taste of men's cruelty was bitter in my mouth, capricious fortune snatched me from abject poverty and gave me delirious wealth.   I was ploughing a barren field, and flung up a nugget.   From that moment gold dogged my footsteps.   I enriched the few friends I had—they turned howlingly from me because I did not give them more.   I showered money on whoever sought it of me—they cursed me because it was mine to give.   In my poverty there had been the bond of common sorrow between me and my fellows: in my wealth I stand alone, a modern Ishmael, with every man's hand against me.

ALINE.   [*Gently.*]   Why do you tell me this?

CROCKSTEAD.   Because I am no longer asking you to marry me.   Because you are the first person in all these years who has been truthful and frank with me.   And because, perhaps, in the happiness that will, I trust, be yours, I want you to think kindly of me.   [*She puts out her hand, he takes it.*]   And now, shall we return to the ballroom?   The music has stopped; they must be going to supper.

ALINE.   What shall I say to the Marchioness, my mother, and the Duchess, my aunt?

CROCKSTEAD.   You will acquaint those noble ladies with the fact of your having refused me.

> [*They have both risen, and move up the room together.*]

ALINE. I shall be a nine days' wonder. And how do you propose to carry out your little scheme?

CROCKSTEAD. I will take Saturday's boat—you will give me a line to your cousin. I had better state the case plainly to him, perhaps?

ALINE. That demands consideration.

CROCKSTEAD. And I will tell you what you shall do for me in return. Find me a wife!

ALINE. I?

CROCKSTEAD. You. I beg it on my knees. I give you carte blanche. I undertake to propose, with my eyes shut, to the woman you shall select.

ALINE. And will you treat her to the—little preliminaries—with which you have favored me?

CROCKSTEAD. No. I said those things to you because I liked you.

ALINE. And you don't intend to like the other one?

CROCKSTEAD. I will marry her. I can trust you to find me a loyal and intelligent woman.

ALINE. In Society?

CROCKSTEAD. For preference. She will be better versed in spending money than a governess, or country parson's daughter.

ALINE. But why this voracity for marriage?

CROCKSTEAD. Lady Aline, I am hunted, pestered, worried, persecuted. I have settled two breach-of-promise actions already, though Heaven knows I did no more than remark it was a fine day, or inquire after the lady's health. If you do not help me, some energetic woman will capture me—I feel it— and bully me for the rest of my days. I raise a despairing cry to you—Find me a wife!

ALINE. Do you desire the lady to have any—special qualifications?

CROCKSTEAD. No—the home-grown article will do. One thing, though—I should like her to be—merciful.

ALINE. I don't understand.

CROCKSTEAD. I have a vague desire to do something with my money: my wife might help me. I should like her to have pity.

ALINE. Pity?

CROCKSTEAD. In the midst of her wealth I should wish her to be sorry for those who are poor.

ALINE. Yes. And, as regards the rest——

CROCKSTEAD. The rest I leave to you, with absolute confidence. You will help me?

ALINE. I will try. My choice is to be final?

CROCKSTEAD. Absolutely.

ALINE. I have an intimate friend—I wonder whether she would do?

CROCKSTEAD. Tell me about her.

ALINE. She and I made our début the same season. Like myself she has hitherto been her mother's despair.

CROCKSTEAD. Because she has not yet——

ALINE. Married—yes. Oh, if men knew how hard the lot is of the portionless girl, who has to sit, and smile, and wait, with a very desolate heart—they would think less unkindly of her, perhaps— [*She smiles.*] But I am digressing, too.

CROCKSTEAD. Tell me more of your friend.

ALINE. She is outwardly hard, and a trifle bitter, but I fancy sunshine would thaw her. There has not been much happiness in her life.

CROCKSTEAD. Would she marry a man she did not love?

ALINE. If she did you would not respect her?

CROCKSTEAD. I don't say that. She will be your choice; and therefore deserving of confidence. Is she handsome?

ALINE. Well—no.

CROCKSTEAD. [*With a quick glance at her.*] That's a pity. But we can't have everything.

ALINE. No. There is one episode in her life that I feel she would like you to know——

CROCKSTEAD. If you are not betraying a confidence——

ALINE. [*Looking down.*] No. She loved a man, years ago, very dearly. They were too poor to marry, but they vowed to wait. Within six months she learned that he was engaged.

CROCKSTEAD. Ah!

ALINE. To a fat and wealthy widow——

CROCKSTEAD. The old story.

ALINE. Who was touring through India, and had been made love to by every unmarried officer in the regiment. She chose him.

CROCKSTEAD. India?

[*He moves toward her.*]

ALINE. Yes.

CROCKSTEAD. I have an idea that I shall like your friend.

[*He takes her hand in his.*]

ALINE. I shall be careful to tell her all that you said to me—at the beginning——

CROCKSTEAD. It is quite possible that my remarks may not apply after all.

ALINE. But I believe myself from what I know of you both that—if she marries you—it will not be—altogether —for your money.

CROCKSTEAD.   Listen—they're playing "God Save the King."   Will you be my wife, Aline?

ALINE.   Yes—Harry.

[*He takes her in his arms and kisses her.*]

CURTAIN

CONFESSIONAL

A PLAY IN ONE ACT

BY

PERCIVAL WILDE

Percival Wilde was born in New York City, March 1, 1887, and was educated at Columbia University, where he took a B.S. degree in 1906. For a time after his graduation he was connected with the banking business. Then he turned to writing, first as a reviewer on the *New York Times* and later in the field of creative writing. Most of his work has been in the drama, and especially in the one-act play. In fact, it is sometimes said that he has had more plays produced by little-theatre societies than any other one writer in America. *Dawn and Other One-Act Plays* (Little, 1915), *A Question of Morality and Other One-Act Plays* (Little, 1916); *The Unseen Host and Other War Plays* (Little, 1917), and *Eight Comedies for Little Theatres* (Little, 1922) are volumes that include his best work in the short form. In *The Craftsmanship of the One-Act Play* (Little, 1923) he has produced the standard volume on the one-act play.

CHARACTERS

ROBERT BALDWIN
MARTHA, *his wife*
JOHN, *his son*
EVIE, *his daughter*
MARSHALL
A MAID

CONFESSIONAL

It is a rather hot and sultry Sunday afternoon, and the
sun overhead and the baked clay underfoot are merci-
less.   In the distance, lowering clouds give promise
of coming relief.   And at the parlor window of a
trim little cottage the Baldwin family is anxiously
awaiting the return of its head.

JOHN, *the son, an average young man of twenty-seven, is*
smoking a pipe as philosophically as if this day were
in no whit more momentous than any other.   But his
mother, trying to compose herself with her knitting,
has made little progress in the last half-hour; and
EVIE, *his sister, takes no pains to conceal her nervous-*
ness.

There is a tense pause.   It seems as if none of them likes
to break the silence.   For the tenth time in ten
minutes, EVIE *goes to the window and looks out along*
the sultry road.

MARTHA.   It's time he was home.

EVIE.   Yes, mother.

MARTHA.   I do hope he hasn't forgotten his umbrella:
he has such a habit of leaving it behind him——

EVIE.   Yes, mother.

MARTHA.   It might rain.   Don't you think so, Evie?
[*Without waiting for an answer she goes to the window*
and looks out anxiously.]   The sky is so dark.   [*She*
starts.]   There was a flash of lightning!   [JOHN *rises*
slowly, moves to a centre-table, and knocks the ashes out
of his pipe.   His mother turns to him.]   John, run into
your father's room and see that the windows are closed.
There's a good boy.

JOHN. Right-o.

[*He goes.*]

EVIE. [*After a pause.*] Mother. [*There is no answer.*] Mother! [MRS. BALDWIN *turns slowly.*] What does Mr. Gresham want with him? Has he done anything wrong?

MARTHA. [*Proudly.*] Your father? No, Evie.

EVIE. Then why did Mr. Gresham send for him?

MARTHA. He wanted to talk to him.

EVIE. What about? Mr. Gresham has been arrested: they're going to try him to-morrow. What can he want with father?

MARTHA. Your father will have to testify.

EVIE. But he's going to testify *against* Mr. Gresham. Why should Mr. Gresham want to see him?

MARTHA. I don't know, Evie. You know, your father doesn't say much about his business affairs. [*She pauses.*] *I* didn't know there was anything wrong with the bank until I saw it in the papers. Your father wouldn't tell me to draw my money out—he thought it wasn't loyal to Mr. Gresham. [EVIE *nods.*] I did it of my own accord—against his wishes—when I suspected——

EVIE. [*After a pause.*] Do you think that father had anything to do with—with——

[*She does not like to say it.*]

MARTHA. With the wrecking of the bank? You know him better than that, Evie.

EVIE. But did he know what was going on? You know what the papers are saying——

MARTHA. They haven't been fair to him, Evie.

EVIE. Perhaps not. But they said he must have been a fool not to know. They said that only he could have known—he and Mr. Gresham. Why didn't he stop it?

MARTHA. He was acting under Mr. Gresham's orders.

EVIE. [*Contemptuously.*] Mr. Gresham's orders! Did he have to follow them?

MARTHA. [*After a pause.*] Evie, I don't believe your father ever did a wrong thing in his life—not if he knew it was wrong. He found out by accident—found out what Mr. Gresham was doing.

EVIE. How do you know that?

MARTHA. I don't know it: I suspect it—something he said. [*Eagerly.*] You see, Evie, he *can't* have done anything wrong. They haven't indicted him.

EVIE. [*Slowly.*] No. They didn't indict him—because they want him to testify against Mr. Gresham. That's little consolation, mother.

[JOHN *re-enters.*]

MARTHA. [*Seizing the relief.*] Were the windows open, John?

JOHN. [*Shortly.*] I've closed them. [*He crosses to the table, takes up his pipe, and refills it.*] Look here, mater: what does Gresham want with the governor?

EVIE. [*Nodding.*] I've just been asking that.

MARTHA. I don't know, John.

JOHN. Didn't you ask him? [*As she does not answer.*] Well?

MARTHA. Yes, I asked him. He didn't say, John. [*Anxiously.*] I don't think he knew himself.

JOHN. [*After an instant's thought.*] I was talking to the assistant cashier yesterday.

EVIE. Donovan?

JOHN. Yes, Donovan. I saw him up at the Athletic Club. He said that nobody had any idea that there was anything wrong until the crash came. Donovan had been there eight years. He thought he was taken care of for the rest of his life. He had gotten married on the strength of it. And then, one morning, there was a sign up on the door. It was like a bolt out of a clear sky.

EVIE. And father?

JOHN. He says the governor must have known. He'll swear nobody else did. You see, father was closer to Gresham than any one else. That puts him in a nice position, doesn't it?

MARTHA. What do you mean, John?

JOHN. The governor the only witness against John Gresham—and me named after him! John Gresham Baldwin, at your service!

MARTHA. Your father will do his duty, John, no matter what comes of it.

JOHN. [*Shortly.*] I know it. And I'm not sure but what it's right. [*They look at him inquiringly.*] There's John Gresham, grown rich in twenty years, and the governor pegging along as his secretary at sixty dollars a week!

MARTHA. Your father never complained.

JOHN. No; that's just the pity of it. He didn't complain. Well, he'll have his chance to-morrow. He'll go on the stand, and when he's through, they'll put John Gresham where he won't be able to hurt anybody for a while. Wasn't satisfied with underpaying his employees: had to rob his depositors! Serves him jolly well right!

MARTHA. [*Rather timidly.*] I don't think your father would like you to talk that way, John.

JOHN. [*Shrugs his shoulders with a contemptuous:*] "Humph!"

MARTHA. Your father has nothing against Mr. Gresham. He will tell the truth—nothing but the truth.

JOHN. Did you think I expected him to lie? Not father! He'll tell the truth: just the truth. It'll be plenty!

EVIE. [*At the window.*] There's father now!
[*There is the click of a latch-key outside.* EVIE
makes for the door.]

MARTHA. Evie! You stay here: let me talk to him
first.

[MARTHA *hurries out.* JOHN *and* EVIE *look at
each other.*]

JOHN. Wonder what Gresham had to say to him?
[EVIE *shrugs her shoulders. He turns away to the window.*] It's started to rain.

EVIE. Yes.

[*There is a pause. Suddenly* JOHN *crosses to
the door, and flings it open.*]

JOHN. Hullo, dad!

BALDWIN. [*Coming in, followed by* MARTHA.] How
are you, my boy? [*He shakes hands with* JOHN.] Evie!
[*He kisses her.*]

MARTHA. You are sure your shoes aren't wet, Robert?

BALDWIN. [*Shaking his head.*] I took the car. Not
a drop on me. See?

[*He passes his hands over his sleeves. He goes
to a chair: sits. There is an awkward pause.*]

JOHN. Well, dad? Don't you think it's about time
you told us something?

BALDWIN. Told you something? I don't understand,
John.

JOHN. People have been talking about you—saying
things——

BALDWIN. What kind of things, John?

JOHN. You can imagine: rotten things. And I
couldn't contradict them.

BALDWIN. Why not, John?

JOHN. Because I didn't know.

BALDWIN. Did you *have* to know? Wasn't it enough that you knew your father?

JOHN. [*After a pause.*] I beg your pardon, sir.

BALDWIN. It was two days before the smash-up that I found out what Gresham was doing. [*He pauses. They are listening intently.*] I told him he would have to make good. He said he couldn't——

EVIE. [*As he does not continue.*] And what happened?

BALDWIN. I told him he would have to do the best he could—and the first step would be to close the bank. He didn't want to do that.

MARTHA. But he did it.

BALDWIN. I made him do it. He was angry—very angry, but I had the whip hand.

EVIE. The papers didn't mention that.

BALDWIN. I didn't think it was necessary to tell them.

MARTHA. But you let your name rest under a cloud meanwhile.

BALDWIN. It will be cleared to-morrow, won't it? [*He pauses.*] To-day Gresham sent for me. The trial begins in twenty-four hours. I'm the only witness against him. He asked—you can guess what——

JOHN. [*Indignantly.*] He wanted you to lie to save his skin, eh? Wanted you to perjure yourself?

BALDWIN. That wouldn't be necessary, John. He just wanted me to have an attack of poor memory. If I tell all I know, John Gresham will go to jail—no power on earth can save him from it. But he wants me to forget a little—just the essential things. When they question me I can answer "I don't remember." They can't prove I *do* remember. And there you are.

JOHN. It would be a lie, dad!

BALDWIN. [*Smiling.*] Of course. But it's done

every day. And they couldn't touch *me*—any more than they could convict him.

MARTHA. [*Quivering with indignation.*] How dared he—how dared he ask such a thing——!

EVIE. What did you say, father?

BALDWIN. [*Smiling, and raising his eyes to* JOHN'S.] Well, son, what would *you* have said?

JOHN. I'd have told him to go to the devil!

BALDWIN. [*Nodding.*] I did.

JOHN. Bully for you, governor!

MARTHA. [*Half to herself.*] I knew! I knew!

BALDWIN. I didn't use your words, John. He's too old a friend of mine for that. But I didn't mince matters any. He understood what I meant.

EVIE. And what did he say then?

BALDWIN. There wasn't much to say. You see, he wasn't surprised. He's known me for thirty-five years, and, well, [*with simple pride*] anybody who's known me for thirty-five years doesn't expect me to haggle with my conscience. If it had been anybody else than John Gresham I would have struck him across the face. But John Gresham and I were boys together. We worked side by side. And I've been in his employ ever since he started in for himself. He is desperate—he doesn't know what he is doing—or he wouldn't have offered me money.

JOHN. [*Furious.*] Offered you money, dad?

BALDWIN. He'd put it aside, ready for the emergency. If they don't convict him, he'll hand it over to me. The law can't stop him. But if I live until to-morrow night, they will convict him! [*He sighs.*] God knows I want no share in bringing about his punishment— [*He breaks off.* EVIE *pats his hand silently.*] Young man and old man, I've worked with him or for him the best part of my life. I'm loyal to him—I've always been loyal to him—

but when John Gresham ceases to be an honest man, John Gresham and I part company!

MARTHA. [*Weeping softly.*] Robert! Robert!

BALDWIN. I've got only a few years to live, but I'll live those as I've lived the rest of my life. I'll go to my grave clean! [*He rises presently, goes to the window, and looks out.*] The rain's stopped, hasn't it?

EVIE. [*Following him and taking his hand.*] Yes, father.

BALDWIN. It'll be a fine day to-morrow.

[*There is a pause.*]

JOHN. Dad.

BALDWIN. Yes?

JOHN. What did Gresham offer you?

BALDWIN. [*Simply.*] A hundred thousand dollars.

EVIE. What?

MARTHA. Robert!

BALDWIN. He put it aside for me without anybody knowing it. It's out of his private fortune, he says. It's not the depositors' money—as if that made any difference.

EVIE. [*As if hypnotized.*] He offered you a hundred thousand dollars?

BALDWIN. [*Smiling at her amazement.*] I could have had it for the one word "Yes"—or even for nodding my head—or a look of the eyes.

JOHN. How—how do you know he meant it?

BALDWIN. His word is good.

JOHN. Even now?

BALDWIN. He never lied to me, John. [*He pauses.*] I suppose my eyes must have shown something I didn't feel. He noticed it. He unlocked a drawer and *showed* me the hundred thousand.

JOHN. In cash?

BALDWIN. In thousand-dollar bills. They were genuine: I examined them.

EVIE. [*Slowly.*] And for that he wants you to say "I don't remember."

BALDWIN. [*Smiling.*] Just that: three words only.

JOHN. But you won't?

BALDWIN. [*Shaking his head.*] Those three words would choke me if I tried to speak them. For some other man, perhaps, it would be easy. But for me? All of my past would rise up and strike me in the face. It would mean to the world that for years I had been living a lie: that I was not the honorable man I thought I was. When John Gresham offered me money, I was angry. But when I rejected it, and he showed no surprise, then I was pleased. It was a compliment, don't you think so?

JOHN. [*Slowly.*] Rather an expensive compliment.

BALDWIN. Eh?

JOHN. A compliment which cost you a hundred thousand dollars.

BALDWIN. A compliment which was *worth* a hundred thousand dollars. I've never had that much money to spend in my life, John, but if I had I couldn't imagine a finer way to spend it.

JOHN. [*Slowly.*] Yes. I suppose so.

MARTHA. [*After a pause.*] Will the depositors lose much, Robert?

BALDWIN. [*Emphatically.*] The depositors will not lose a cent.

EVIE. [*Surprised.*] But the papers said——

BALDWIN. [*Interrupting.*] They had to print something: they guessed. *I* know. *I* tell you.

MARTHA. But you never said so before.

BALDWIN. I left that for Gresham. It will come out to-morrow.

JOHN. Why to-morrow? Why didn't you say so before? The papers asked you often enough.

BALDWIN. Nothing forced me to answer, John.

JOHN. That wasn't your real reason, was it, dad? You knew the papers would keep right on calling you names. [BALDWIN *does not answer.* JOHN'S *face lights up with sudden understanding.*] You wanted to let Gresham announce it himself: because it will be something in his favor! Eh?

BALDWIN. Yes. . . . We were able to save something from the wreck, Gresham and I. It was more than I had expected—almost twice as much—and with what Gresham has it will be enough.

EVIE. Even without the hundred thousand?

[BALDWIN *does not answer.*]

JOHN. [*Insistently.*] Without the money that Gresham had put away for you?

BALDWIN. Yes. I didn't know there *was* the hundred thousand until to-day. Gresham didn't tell me. We reckoned without it.

EVIE. Oh!

JOHN. And you made both ends meet?

BALDWIN. Quite easily. [*He smiles.*] Marshall is running the re-organization; Marshall, of the Third National. He hasn't the least idea that it's going to turn out so well.

[*There is a pause.*]

JOHN. They're going to punish Gresham, aren't they?

BALDWIN. I'm afraid so.

JOHN. What for?

BALDWIN. Misappropriating the funds of the——

JOHN. [*Interrupting.*] Oh, I know that. But what *crime* has he committed?

BALDWIN. That's a crime, John.

EVIE. But if nobody loses anything by it?

BALDWIN. It's a crime nevertheless.

JOHN. And they're going to *punish* him for it!

BALDWIN. They can't let him go, John. He's too conspicuous.

JOHN. Do you think that's right, governor?

BALDWIN. *My* opinion doesn't matter, John.

JOHN. But what do you think?

BALDWIN. I think—I think that I'm sorry for John Gresham—terribly sorry.

JOHN. [*Slowly.*] It's nothing but a technicality, dad. Nobody loses a cent. It's rather hard on Gresham, I say.

BALDWIN. [*After a pause.*] Yes, John.

EVIE. [*Timidly.*] Would it be such an awful thing, father, if you let him off?

BALDWIN. [*Smiling.*] I wish I could, Evie. But I'm not the judge.

EVIE. No, but——

BALDWIN. But what?

EVIE. You're the only witness against him.

BALDWIN. [*Nonplussed.*] Evie!

JOHN. She's right, governor.

BALDWIN. You too, John?

JOHN. It's going to be a nasty mess if they put John Gresham in jail—with your own son named after him! It's going to be pleasant for *me!* John Gresham Baldwin!

MARTHA. [*After a pause.*] Robert, I'm not sure I understood what you said before. What did Mr. Gresham want you to do for him?

BALDWIN. Get him off to-morrow.

MARTHA. You could do that?

BALDWIN. Yes.

MARTHA. How?

BALDWIN. By answering "I don't remember" when they ask me dangerous questions.

MARTHA. Oh! And you *do* remember?

BALDWIN. Yes. Nearly everything.

JOHN. No matter what they ask you?

BALDWIN. I can always refresh my memory. You see, I have notes.

JOHN. But without those notes you wouldn't remember?

BALDWIN. What do you mean, John?

JOHN. [*Without answering.*] As a matter of fact, you will have to rely on your notes nearly altogether, won't you?

BALDWIN. Everybody else does the same thing.

JOHN. Then it won't be far from the truth if you say "I don't remember"?

MARTHA. I don't see that Mr. Gresham is asking so much of you.

BALDWIN. Martha!

MARTHA. Robert, I'm as honorable as you are——

BALDWIN. That goes without saying, Martha.

MARTHA. It doesn't seem right to me to send an old friend to jail. [*As he speaks she holds up her hand.*] Now don't interrupt me! I've been thinking. The day John was baptized: when Mr. Gresham stood sponsor for him: how proud we were! And when we came home from the church you said—do you remember what you said, Robert?

BALDWIN. No. What was it?

MARTHA. You said, "Martha, may our son always live up to the name which we have given him!" Do you remember that?

BALDWIN. Yes—dimly.

JOHN. Ha! Only *dimly,* governor?

BALDWIN. What do you mean, John?

MARTHA. [*Giving* JOHN *no opportunity to answer.*] It would be sad—very sad—if the name of John Gresham, our son's name, should come to grief through you, Robert.

BALDWIN. [*After a pause.*] Martha, are you telling me to accept the bribe money that John Gresham offered me?

EVIE. Why do you call it bribe money, father?

BALDWIN. [*Bitterly.*] Why indeed? Gresham had a prettier name for it. He said that he had underpaid me all these years. You know, I was getting only sixty dollars a week when the crash came——

JOHN. [*Impatiently.*] Yes, yes?

BALDWIN. He said a hundred thousand represented the difference between what he had paid me and what I had actually been worth to him.

MARTHA. That's no less than true, Robert. You've worked for him very faithfully.

BALDWIN. He said that if he had paid me what he should have, I would have put by more than a hundred thousand by now.

JOHN. That's so, isn't it, dad?

BALDWIN. Who knows? I never asked him to raise my salary. When he raised it, it was of his own accord. [*There is a pause. He looks around.*] Well, what do you think of it, Evie?

EVIE. [*Hesitantly.*] If you go on the stand to-morrow——

BALDWIN. Yes?

EVIE. And they put John Gresham in jail, what will people say?

BALDWIN. They will say I have done my duty, Evie; no more and no less.

EVIE. *Will* they?

BALDWIN. Why, what should they say?

EVIE. *I* don't think so, of course, but other people might say that you had turned traitor to your best friend.

BALDWIN. You don't mean that, Evie?

EVIE. When they find out that they haven't lost any money—when John Gresham tells them that he will pay back every cent—then they won't *want* him to go to jail. They'll feel sorry for him.

BALDWIN. Yes, I believe that. I hope so.

JOHN. And they won't feel too kindly disposed toward the man who helps put him in jail.

MARTHA. They'll say you went back on an old friend, Robert.

JOHN. When you pull out your notes in court, to be *sure* of sending him to jail—— !

[*He breaks off with a snort.*]

EVIE. And Mr. Gresham hasn't done anything really wrong.

JOHN. It's a technicality, that's what it is. Nobody loses a cent. Nobody wants to see him punished.

EVIE. Except you, father.

JOHN. Yes. And you're willing to jail the man after whom you named your son!

MARTHA. [*After a pause.*] I believe in being merciful, Robert.

BALDWIN. Merciful?

MARTHA. Mr. Gresham has always been very good to you.

[*There is another pause. Curiously enough, they do not seem to be able to meet each other's eyes.*]

MARTHA. Ah, well! What are you going to do now, Robert?

BALDWIN. What do you mean?

MARTHA. You have been out of work since the bank closed.

BALDWIN. [*Shrugging his shoulders.*] Oh, I'll find a position.

MARTHA. [*Shaking her head.*] At your age——?

BALDWIN. It's the *man* that counts.

MARTHA. Yes. You said that a month ago.

JOHN. I heard from Donovan——

BALDWIN. [*Quickly.*] What did you hear?

JOHN. He's gone with the Third National, you know.

BALDWIN. Yes; he's helping with the reorganization.

JOHN. They wouldn't take you on there——

BALDWIN. Their staff was full. They couldn't very well offer me a position as a clerk.

JOHN. That was what they told *you.*

BALDWIN. Wasn't it true?

JOHN. [*Shakes his head.*] Marshall said he wouldn't employ a man who was just as guilty as John Gresham.

BALDWIN. But I'm not!

JOHN. Who knows it?

BALDWIN. Everybody will to-morrow!

JOHN. Will they believe you? Or will they think you're trying to save your *own* skin?

BALDWIN. I found out only a day before the smash.

JOHN. Who will believe that?

BALDWIN. They will *have* to!

JOHN. How will you make them? I'm afraid you'll find that against you wherever you go, governor. Your testifying against John Gresham won't make things any better. If you ever get another job, it will be with *him!* [*This is a startling idea to* BALDWIN, *who shows his surprise.*] If Gresham doesn't go to jail, he'll start in business again, won't he? And he can't offer you anything less than a partnership.

BALDWIN.   A partnership?

JOHN.   [*With meaning.*]   With the hundred thousand
capital you could put in the business, dad.

BALDWIN.   John!

JOHN.   Of course, the capital doesn't matter.   He'll
owe you quite a debt of gratitude besides.

[*There is a pause.*]

MARTHA.   A hundred thousand would mean a great
deal to us, Robert.   If you don't find a position soon
John will have to support us.

JOHN.   On thirty dollars a week, dad.

EVIE.   That won't go very far.

MARTHA.   It's not fair to John.

JOHN.   [*Angrily.*]   Oh, don't bother about *me*.

[EVIE *begins to weep.*]

JOHN.   Look here, governor, you've said nothing to the
papers.   If you say nothing more to-morrow what does
it amount to but sticking to your friend?   It's the square
thing to do—he'd do as much for you.

BALDWIN.   [*Looks appealingly from one face to another.   They are averted.   Then:*]   You—you want me
to take this money?   [*There is no answer.*]   Say "Yes,"
one of you.   [*Still no answer.*]   Or "No."   [*A long
pause.   Finally:*]   I couldn't go into partnership with
Gresham.

MARTHA.   [*Promptly.*]   Why not?

BALDWIN.   People wouldn't trust him.

JOHN.   Then you could go into business with some
one else, dad.   A hundred thousand is a lot of money.

BALDWIN.   [*Walks to the window.   Looks out.*]   God
knows I never thought this day would come!   I know
—I know no matter how you try to excuse it—I know that
if I take this money I do a dishonorable thing.   And you

know it! You, and you, and you! All of you! Come, admit it!

JOHN. [*Resolutely.*] Nobody'll ever hear of it.

BALDWIN. But amongst ourselves, John! Whatever we are to the world, let us be honest with each other, the four of us! Well? [*His glance travels from* JOHN *to* EVIE, *whose head is bowed; from her to his wife, who is apparently busied with her knitting. He raises* MARTHA's *head: looks into the eyes. He shudders.*] Shams! Liars! Hypocrites! Thieves! And I no better than any of you! We have seen our souls naked, and they stink to Almighty Heaven! Well, why don't you answer me?

MARTHA. [*Feebly.*] It's not wrong, Robert.

BALDWIN. It's not right.

JOHN. [*Facing him steadily.*] A hundred thousand is a lot of money, dad.

BALDWIN. [*Nodding slowly.*] You can look into my eyes *now,* my son, can't you?

JOHN. [*Without moving.*] Dad: why did you refuse? Wasn't it because you were afraid of what *we'd* say?

BALDWIN. [*After a long pause.*] Yes, John.

JOHN. Well, nobody will ever know it.

BALDWIN. Except the four of us.

JOHN. Yes—father.

> [*Abruptly they separate.* EVIE *weeps in silence.* MARTHA, *being less emotional, blows her nose noisily, and fumbles with her knitting.* JOHN, *having nothing better to do, scowls out of the window, and* BALDWIN, *near the fireplace, clenches and unclenches his hands.*]

JOHN. Some one's coming.

MARTHA. [*Raising her head.*] Who is it?

JOHN. I can't see. [*With sudden apprehension.*] It looks like Marshall.

BALDWIN. Marshall?

> [*The door-bell rings. They are motionless as a* MAID *enters at one side and goes out the other. The* MAID *re-enters.*]

THE MAID. A gentleman to see you, sir.

BALDWIN. [*Pulling himself together.*] Who, me?

THE MAID. Yes, sir.

> [*She hands him a card on a salver.*]

BALDWIN. It is Marshall.

MARTHA. The President of the Third National?

BALDWIN. Yes. What does he want here?

THE MAID. Shall I show him in, sir?

BALDWIN. Yes. Yes. By all means.

> [*The* MAID *goes out.*]

MARTHA. [*Crossing to him quickly.*] Robert! Be careful of what you say: you're to go on the stand to-morrow.

BALDWIN. [*Nervously.*] Yes, yes. I'll look out.

> [*The* MAID *re-enters, opening the door for* MAR-SHALL.]

MARSHALL. [*Coming into the room very buoyantly.*] Well, well, spending the afternoon indoors? How are you, Mrs. Baldwin? [*He shakes hands cordially.*] And you, Baldwin?

MARTHA. We were just going out. Come, Evie.

MARSHALL. Oh, you needn't go on my account. You can hear what I have to say. [*He turns to the head of the family.*] Baldwin, if you feel like coming around to the Third National some time this week, you'll find a position waiting for you.

BALDWIN. [*Thunderstruck.*] Do you mean that, Mr. Marshall?

MARSHALL. [*Smiling.*] I wouldn't say it if I didn't. [*He continues more seriously.*] I was in to see Gresham this afternoon. He told me about the offer he had made you. But he knew that no amount of money would make you do something you thought wrong. Baldwin, he paid you the supreme compliment: rather than go to trial with you to testify against him, he confessed.

BALDWIN. [*Sinking into a chair.*] Confessed!

MARSHALL. Told the whole story. [*He turns to* MARTHA.] I can only say to you what every man will be saying to-morrow: how highly I honor and respect your husband! How sincerely——

MARTHA. [*Seizing his hand piteously.*] Please! Please! Can't you see he's crying?

THE CURTAIN FALLS SLOWLY

MILESTONES

A PLAY IN THREE ACTS

BY

ARNOLD BENNETT

AND

EDWARD KNOBLOCK

Enoch Arnold Bennett was born in England, May 27, 1867. He abandoned law in 1893 to become editor of *Woman,* a position he resigned in 1900 in order to devote all his time to literature. Among his better-known novels are *Old Wives' Tale* (Doran, 1908); *Clayhanger* (Doran, 1910); *The Pretty Lady* (Doran, 1918); and *Mr. Prohack* (Doran, 1922). His most successful dramatic productions have been *Milestones,* with Edward Knoblock (Doran, 1912); *The Great Adventure* (Doran, 1913); *The Love Match* (Doran, 1922).

Edward Knoblock was born in England, April 7, 1874. His life has been devoted almost exclusively to dramatic writing. Among his better-known dramas are *Kismet* (Doran, 1912); *Milestones,* with Arnold Bennett (Doran, 1912); *My Ladies' Dress* (Doubleday, 1915); and *Lullaby and Other Plays*—including *Lullaby, Marie Odille,* and *Tiger, Tiger* (Putnam, 1924).

CHARACTERS IN THE PLAY

JOHN RHEAD

GERTRUDE RHEAD

MRS. RHEAD

SAMUEL SIBLEY

ROSE SIBLEY

NED PYM

EMILY RHEAD

ARTHUR PREECE

NANCY SIBLEY

LORD MONKHURST

THE HONORABLE MURIEL PYM

RICHARD SIBLEY

THOMPSON

WEBSTER

FOOTMAN

The scene is laid throughout in the drawing-room of a house in Kensington Gore.

The First Act is in 1860.
The Second Act is in 1885.
The Third Act is in 1912.

MILESTONES

ACT I

1860

[NOTE.—Right and left are from the point of view of the actor.]

The scene represents the drawing-room of a house in Kensington Gore. The house is quite new at the time: all the decorations, pictures, and furniture are of the mid-Victorian period. On the left three long windows look out on Kensington Gardens. On the right a large double door leads into the back drawing-room. A single door on the same side of the room leads to the hall and stairs. In the centre at back a large fireplace with a fire burning in it. The blinds and curtains are drawn; the lamps are lighted.

It is about half past nine at night of the 29th of December, 1860.

[MRS. RHEAD, *a woman of nearly sixty, is sitting on the sofa, crocheting some lace, which is evidently destined to trim petticoats. Her hair is dressed in the style of* 1840, *though her dress is of the* 1860 *period. Near her, in an armchair, sits* ROSE SIBLEY, *a gentle, romantic-looking girl of twenty-one, who is dressed in the height of fashion of the period. She is at work on a canvas wool-work pattern. Cups of after-dinner coffee stand near both ladies.*

MRS. R.   Do permit me to look at your work one moment, my dear Rose.

Rose. With pleasure, Mrs. Rhead.

Mrs. R. Very pretty indeed. Nothing could be in better taste than these Berlin wool patterns.

Rose. I got the design from the *Englishwoman's Domestic Magazine*. It's to be one of three cushions for father's study.

Mrs. R. I had an idea of doing the same sort of thing for my husband, after we moved into the new house here, three years ago. But then, when he died, I hadn't the heart to go on. So I'm crocheting lace now instead for Gertrude's trousseau. Will you have some more coffee?

Rose. No, thank you.

Mrs. R. Just a drop. Gertrude, pour out— [*She looks about.*] Now where has Gertrude disappeared to?

Rose. She left the room some moments ago.

Mrs. R. Even between dinner and coffee she must be off.

Rose. But why?

Mrs. R. Do I know, my dear? Just managing the house, and managing it, and managing it. Upon my word, Gertrude performs the duties of the place as if it were the foundry and she were John. My son and daughter are so alike.

Rose. [*Interjecting enthusiastically.*] One's as splendid as the other.

Mrs. R. She keeps account-books now.

Rose. [*Rather startled.*] Of the house?

Mrs. R. [*Nods.*] And she says she shall show John a balance-sheet at quarter-day. Did you ever hear of such behavior?

Rose. She always was very active, wasn't she? It's in the blood.

Mrs. R. It is not in mine, and I am her mother. No! It is all due to these modern ways; that is what it is.

ROSE. I suppose John's rather pleased.

MRS. R. Yes, John! But what about *your* brother? Will he be pleased? Is Gertrude going to make him the wife his position demands?

ROSE. I'm sure he'll be delighted to have his house managed as this one's managed.

MRS. R. But will it stop at that? Once one begins these modern ways, one never knows where they will end.

ROSE. I must say I was surprised she ever accepted Sam.

MRS. R. [*Deprecatingly.*] Surprised? But why?

ROSE. We Sibleys are such an extremely old-fashioned family. Look at father! And I do believe Sam's worse. Yes, I do believe Sam's worse than father. Thank goodness they have your son for a partner—two such slow-coaches, as they are.

MRS. R. Slow-coaches! My dear, remember the respect due to your father.

ROSE. [*Eagerly.*] Oh, I adore father, and Sam, too! I wouldn't have either of them altered for the world. But I do think Sam's very fortunate in getting Gertrude.

MRS. R. She also is very fortunate, very fortunate indeed. I have the highest respect for Sam's character, and my hope and prayer is that he and Gertrude will influence each other for nothing but good. But, between you and me, my dear, the first six months will be—well— lively, to say the least.

> [GERTRUDE RHEAD *enters by the door from the hall, carrying in her hand a cloak of the latest pattern of the period. She is twenty-one, high-spirited, independent, afraid of no one.*]

ROSE. What on earth's that, Gertrude?

GERT. I've just been up-stairs to get it. Help me, will you? I wanted to show it you. [ROSE *helps* GER-

TRUDE *with the cloak*.] I only bought it to-day, with the money John gave me for Christmas. Thank you— Well?

ROSE. Very daring, isn't it? I suppose it's quite the latest?

GERT. Next year's. Mother says it's "fast."

MRS. R. I hope you'll put it away before the men come up.

GERT. [*With assumed innocence*.] Why?

MRS. R. Because Samuel will surely not approve of it.

GERT. I bet you he will.

MRS. R. Gertrude!

GERT. The truth is, Rose, mother's only taken a prejudice against it because I brought it home myself this afternoon in a hansom cab.

ROSE. [*Staggered*.] Alone? In a hansom cab?

MRS. R. You may well be shocked, dear. My lady refuses the carriage, because of keeping the horses standing in this terrible frost. And then she actually hails a hansom-cabriolet! What Samuel would say if he knew I dare not imagine.

GERT. Well, what harm is there in it, mama darling? [*Caresses her*.] I do wish you'd remember we're in the year 1860—and very near '61. You really must try to keep up with the times. Why, girls will be riding on the tops of omnibuses some day.

ROSE. [*Protesting*.] Gertrude!

MRS. R. I hope I shan't live to see it.

[*Enter* THOMPSON, *a young butler, from the hall. He collects the coffee-cups, putting them all on a tray.*]

GERT. Is the hot-water apparatus working properly, Thompson?

THOMPSON. Moderate, miss.

GERT. [*Rather annoyed.*] It ought to work perfectly.

ROSE. What's the hot-water apparatus?

GERT. It's for the bathroom, you know.

ROSE. Yes. I know you'd got a bathroom.

GERT. It's just the latest device. John had it put in the week mother was down at Brighton. It was his Christmas surprise for her.

ROSE. Yes, but I don't understand.

GERT. It's quite simple. We have a boiler behind the kitchen range, and pipes carry the hot water up to the bath. There's one tap for hot and another for cold.

ROSE. How wonderful!

GERT. So when you want a hot bath all you have to do——

MRS. R. [*Dryly.*] All we have to do is to tell cook to put down a shoulder of mutton to roast. Very modern!

GERT. [*Caressing her mother again.*] Horrid old dear! Thompson, why is it working only moderately?

THOMPSON. [*By the door.*] No doubt because cook had orders that the beef was to be slightly underdone, miss.

[*Exit quickly with tray.*]

GERT. [*To* ROSE.] That was to please your carnivorous daddy, Rose, and he never came.

MRS. R. I do hope there's been no trouble down at the foundry between him and my son.

ROSE. So do I.

GERT. Why are you both pretending? You know perfectly well there has been trouble between them. You must have noticed the chilliness when our respective brothers met to-night.

Rose. I assure you, Gertrude, I know *nothing*. Sam said not a single word in the carriage.

Gert. Well, wasn't that enough? Or does he never speak in the carriage?

Rose. [*To* Mrs. Rhead.] Has John said anything?

Mrs. R. I understood you to say that the reason your father didn't come to dinner was that he had an urgent appointment, quite unexpectedly, at the last moment.

Rose. Yes, he asked me to tell you and make his excuses.

Gert. Urgent appointment at his club—most likely!

Mrs. R. I wonder what the trouble can have been.

Gert. You don't, mother. You know! It's the old story—Sam and his father with their set ideas, pulling one way; and John with his go-ahead schemes, pulling the other—with the result——

Mrs. R. The result is that we've had one of the most mournful dinners to-night that I have ever had the pleasure of giving.

Gert. I know! What a good thing we asked Ned Pym. If he hadn't come to the rescue with his usual facetious, senseless chatter, I do believe Sam and John——

Mrs. R. [*Quickly, stopping her.*] Here are the gentlemen! Gertrude, take that cloak off.

> [*Enter from the hall* Samuel Sibley, Ned Pym, *and* John Rhead. Samuel Sibley *is twenty-eight, heavy, with a serious face, a trifle pompous, but with distinct dignity.* Ned Pym, *who is a little over twenty, is the young dandy of the day; handsome, tall, with excellent manners, which allow him to carry off his facetious attitude rather successfully.* John Rhead *comes last. He is twenty-five,*

*full of determination and purpose.   He knows
what he wants and is going to get it.*]

MRS. R.   [*In a smooth tone to* ROSE.]   Have you
seen the new number of *Great Expectations,* dear?

NED.   What's this, Gertrude?   Charades?

GERT.   [*Flouncing her cloak half defiantly at* SAM.]
Paris!

NED.   [*Coming between* SAM *and* GERTRUDE.]   Evidently it has lost nothing on the journey over.

GERT.   Ned, would you mind . . . I'm showing it to
Sam.   [*To* SAM.]   Don't you like it?

SAM.   [*Forcing himself.*]   On my betrothed, yes.

NED.   [*Facetiously.*]   By the exercise of extreme self-
control the lover conceals his enthusiasm for the cloak
of his mistress.

GERT.   [*Appealing to* SAM.]   But you do like it—
don't you?

SAM.   [*Evasively.*]   Isn't it rather original?

GERT.   Of course it is.   That's just the point.

SAM.   [*Surprised.*]   Just the point?

GERT.   [*Taking the cloak off and flinging it half pettishly on a chair.*]   Oh!

JOHN.   It's original, and therefore it has committed a
crime.   [*Looking at* SAM.]   Isn't that it, Sam?

SAM.   [*Gives* JOHN *a look and turns to* MRS. RHEAD
with an obvious intention of changing the conversation.]
What were you saying about *Great Expectations,* Mrs.
Rhead?

MRS. R.   [*At a loss.*]   What *were* we saying about
Great Expectations?

NED.   Well, I can tell you one thing about it; it's made
my expectations from my uncle smaller than ever.

[*He sits by* MRS. RHEAD.]

MRS. R.   Oh, how is dear Lord Monkhurst?

NED. He's very well and quarrelsome, thank you. And his two sons, my delightful cousins, are also in excellent health. Well, as I was going to tell you; you know how my uncle has turned against Dickens since *Little Dorrit*. I happened to say something about *Great Expectations* being pretty fairish, and he up and rode over me like a troop of cavalry.

MRS. R. [*Puzzled.*]   A troop of cavalry?

NED. It was at his Christmas party, too, worse luck. He as good as told me I disagreed with him on purpose to annoy him. Now I cannot agree with him solely and simply because he allows me seven hundred a year, can I?

ROSE. Is he so difficult to get on with?

NED. Difficult? He's nothing but a faddist! An absolute old faddist! What can you do with a man that's convinced that spirits'll turn his dining-table, and that Bacon wrote Shakespeare; and that the Benecia Boy's a better man than Tom Sayers?

MRS. R. It seems a great pity you cannot do something to please your uncle.

NED. Would you believe it? He even wanted me to join the Rifle Volunteers. Now, I ask you, can you see me in the Rifle Volunteers, me among a lot of stockbrokers and chimney-sweeps?

GERT. We cannot, Ned.

NED. And in order to raise my patriotism last night— [*Slapping his knee violently.*] By Jove! [*He jumps up.*] By Heavens! Jiggered! Jiggered!

GERT and ROSE. Ned!

NED. I am a ruined man! You see before you, kind friends, a man ruined and without hope! Last night my uncle sent me a ticket for the launching of the *Warrior*.

SAM. [*With a sneer.*] The *Warrior!* You didn't miss much!

NED. But my beloved aunt was commanded to be in attendance on Her Royal Highness at the said function. . . . Well, I forgot all about it. I repeat I forgot all about it. My uncle will certainly call this the last straw. There will be no quarterly check for me on New Year's Day.

ROSE. What *is* the *Warrior?*

JOHN. [*Bursting out.*] The *Warrior* is a steam-frigate—first vessel of the British Navy to be built entirely of iron. She's over six thousand tons burden, and she represents the beginning of a new era in iron.

ROSE. [*Adoringly.*] How splendid!

JOHN. [*Responding quickly to her mood.*] Ah, you agree with me!

ROSE. [*Enthusiastically.*] Of course! [*She breaks off self-consciously.*] Of course I agree with you.

JOHN. [*After a slight pause—quickly.*] This 29th of December marks a great day in the history of the British Navy.

SAM. [*With a slight superior smile, trying to be gay.*] Nonsense. All this day marks is the folly of the Admiralty. You may take it as an absolute rule that whatever the Admiralty does is wrong. Always has been, always will be. The *Great Eastern* was the champion White Elephant of the age. And now the *Warrior* has gone her one better.

JOHN. Sam, you don't know what you're saying. How can you talk about the *Warrior* when you've never even so much as laid eyes on the ship?

SAM. Well, have *you?*

JOHN. Yes—I went to the launch to-day.

SAM. You?

MRS. R. Why did you go, John? You never said a word to me.

JOHN. I went on business.

SAM. You told me you had an appointment with the bank.

JOHN. I only said that because I couldn't stop to argue just then.

SAM. So you said what wasn't so.

JOHN. I said what was necessary at the moment. I wasn't going to leave you in the dark; never fear.

SAM. [*Curtly controlling himself.*] I see. [*A slight pause, then* SAM *turns abruptly to* GERTRUDE *and says gently.*] Come and sing, dear. I haven't heard you sing for over a fortnight.

GERT. [*Moved by the quarrel—after a pause, in a low voice.*] What shall I sing?

SAM. Sing "Nita, Juanita."

GERT. No! I heard Madame Sainton Dolby sing it last week.

SAM. Do!—to please me.

> [GERTRUDE *turns toward the double doors and goes off in silence with* SAM. NED *is about to follow instantly, but* MRS. RHEAD *stops him.*]

MRS. R. [*Whispering.*] Give them just one instant alone.

NED. I beg pardon. My innocence at fault. [*The song is heard. A pause.*] Is that long enough?

> [MRS. RHEAD *taps him, then she goes off after the others, followed by* NED. *A slight pause.*]

ROSE. [*Moving toward the doors.*] What a lovely voice she has!

JOHN. [*Abruptly, closing the doors.*] I want to talk to you.

ROSE. [*Nervous and self-conscious.*] To me?

JOHN. I wish I'd asked you to come to that launch.

ROSE. Where was it?

JOHN. At Greenhithe; only two stations beyond the foundry. Would you have come?

ROSE. I should have loved to . . . if Gertrude had come too.

JOHN. [*Musing.*] You should have seen her go into the water—the wave she made! All that iron—and rivets! Iron, mind you. . . . And then float like a cork. I never was at a launch before, and it gave me a thrill, I can tell you. And I'm not easily thrilled.

ROSE. [*Adoringly, but restraining herself.*] I'm sure you're not. I do wish I'd seen it. It must have been almost sublime.

JOHN. You'd have understood. You'd have felt like I did. Do you know how I know that?

ROSE. [*Shaking her head.*] No——

JOHN. By the way you said "how splendid" when I was telling the others just now.

ROSE. Really!

JOHN. Fact! That gave me more encouragement in my schemes than any words I ever heard.

ROSE. Please don't say that. Gertrude is always on your side. She's so like you in every way.

JOHN. Yes, Gertrude's all right. But she's got no poetry in her, Gertrude hasn't. That's the difference between you and her. She's very go-ahead; but she doesn't feel. You feel.

ROSE. [*Breathless.*] Do I, John?
[*She looks down.*]

JOHN. I'll tell you something—tears came into my eyes when that frigate took the water. Couldn't help it! [ROSE *raises her eyes to his.*] In thirty years every big ship in the world will be built of iron. Very few people to-day believe in iron for ship-building, and I know there's a lot of silly, easy sarcasm about it—especially in the papers. But it's coming! It's coming!

ROSE. [*Religiously.*] I'm sure you're right.

JOHN. If only your father and your brother thought as you do!

ROSE. [*Faintly.*] Yes.

JOHN. I'm in the minority, you see; two partners against one. If my father had lived, I know which side *he'd* have been on! I shouldn't have been in the minority then.

ROSE. You'd have been equal.

JOHN. [*Enthusiastically.*] No! We should certainly have rolled your excellent father and brother straight into the Thames!

ROSE. [*Amiably protesting.*] Please——

JOHN. [*Smiling.*] Forgive me—you know what I mean, don't you?

ROSE. I love to see you when you are enthusiastic!

JOHN. It's so plain. We've got probably the largest iron foundry on Thames-side. But our business isn't increasing as quickly as it used to do. It can't. We've come to about the limit of expansion on present lines. Ship-building is simply waiting for us. There it is—asking to be picked up! We're *in* iron. We know all about iron. The ships of the future will be built of nothing but iron. And we're right in the middle of the largest port in the world. What more can any one want? But no! They won't see it! They—will—not—see—it!

ROSE. I wonder why they won't!

JOHN. Simply because they can't.

ROSE. Then one oughtn't to blame them.

JOHN. Blame them! Good Heavens, no! I don't blame them. I'm fond of them, and I rather feel for them. But that's just why I want to smash them to smithereens! They've got to yield. The people who live in the past *must* yield to the people who live in the future. Otherwise, the earth would begin to turn the other way round, and we should be back again in the eighteenth century before we knew where we were, making for the Middle Ages.

ROSE. Then you think a conflict is unavoidable?

JOHN. Absolutely unavoidable! That's the point. It's getting nearer every hour. . . . Why is your father not here to-night?

ROSE. I don't know, but I was afraid——

JOHN. *I* know and *Sam* knows. It must be because he has heard somehow of an enterprise I am planning, and the news has upset him. He's vexed.

ROSE. Poor dear old thing! Then you've started a scheme already?

JOHN. [*Nods.*] I have. But I can't carry it out alone.

ROSE. If there is one man in the world who could stand alone, I should have said you were that man.

JOHN. I know. That's the impression I give. And yet nobody ever needed help more than I do. I'm not all on the surface, you know.

ROSE. What sort of help?

JOHN. Sympathy—understanding.

ROSE. [*Low.*] I see.

JOHN. Of course you see! And that's why I suddenly decided I must have a bit of a chat with you—this very night. It's forced on me. And I feel I'm rather forcing it on you. But I can't help it—honestly I can't. Rose, you're on my side, aren't you?

ROSE. I believe you're in the right.

JOHN. Would you like to see me win—[*silence*] or lose?

Rose. I don't think I could bear to see you beaten.

John. Well, then, help me! When you look at me with that trustful look of yours, I can do anything—anything. No other woman's eyes ever had the same effect on me. It's only because you believe in me. No, that isn't the only reason; it isn't the chief reason. The chief reason is that I'm in love with you—there you have it!

Rose. [*Sinking her head.*] Oh!——

John. [*Coming to her.*] Curious! I've known you all my life. But I wasn't aware of all that you meant to me, until these difficulties began. You're essential to me. You can't imagine how much depends on just you!

Rose. Really?

John. You're too modest, too womanly to realize it. Why, sometimes a tone of yours, a mere inflection, almost knocks me over— You aren't crying, surely? What are you crying for?

Rose. It's too much for me, coming like this, with no warning.

John. Rose, be mine! I'll work for you, I'll succeed for you. No woman in this country shall have a finer position than yours.

Rose. I don't want a fine position—except for you.

John. I'm not hard, really.

Rose. But I like you to be hard. It's when you're inflexible and brutal that I like you the most.

John. Then you do like me a little—sometimes?
[*Kisses her hands.*]

Rose. I can't help telling you. I didn't hope for this. Yes, I did. But the hope seemed absurd. Is this real —now?

John. My love!

Rose. John, you say I don't realize how much I mean to you. Perhaps I do though. But it's impossible for *you* to realize how I want to give my life to you, to serve you. No *man* could realize that. A woman could. I shall be your slave. [JOHN *looks at her with a little start.*] Yes, I know it sounds queer for me to be talking like this. But I must. It thrills me to tell you. . . . I shall be your slave.

JOHN. Don't make me afraid, my darling!

ROSE. Afraid?

JOHN. Afraid of being unworthy.

ROSE. Please. . . . [*A slight pause.*] Has the singing stopped?

JOHN. A long time ago.

ROSE. They'll be coming in, perhaps.

JOHN. [*Vaguely without conviction.*] No.

ROSE. What will your mother and Gertrude say?

JOHN. You know as well as I do, they'll be absolutely delighted.

ROSE. And father?

JOHN. [*Alertly.*] Rose, you're mine, whatever happens?

ROSE. Oh, nothing must happen now! Nothing shall happen!

JOHN. But suppose I couldn't carry out my scheme without quarrelling with your father? And he refused his consent to our being married?

ROSE. My heart would be yours for ever and ever. But I couldn't marry without father's consent.

JOHN. But——

ROSE. I couldn't——

JOHN. Why not?

ROSE. It would not be right.

JOHN. But you love me?

ROSE. Yes, but I love father, too. And he's getting very old. And he's very dependent on me. In any case to give me up would be a great sacrifice for him. To lose me against his will—well, I don't know what would happen!

JOHN. As things are just now—he's bound to refuse.

ROSE. But are you so sure he won't have anything to do with your scheme?

JOHN. You heard Sam!

ROSE. Yes; but you haven't discussed your plans very thoroughly with Sam. He seemed quite surprised.

JOHN. Suppose I speak to Sam to-night; tell him everything. At any rate, I shall know then where I stand.

ROSE. To-night?

JOHN. Now! I *might* win him over. Anyhow, he'll do what he can to make things smooth for us with your father—surely! After all, he's engaged to Gertrude!

ROSE. Just as you think best. . . . And Sam's very fond of me, though he never shows it.

JOHN. Let me get it over now, instantly. Will you go in to the others?

> [ROSE *looks at him in silence, then rises and goes to the double doors.* JOHN *stops her and solemnly and passionately kisses her, then opens the doors and she passes through.*]

JOHN. [*Calling into the other room.*] I say, Sam! Mother, I want a word with Sam alone.

> [SAMUEL *enters by the double doors.* JOHN *closes them behind him.*]

SAM. [*Suspicious, and not overfriendly.*] What is it? Not business, I hope?

JOHN. [*With a successful effort to be cordial.*] No, no!

SAM. [*Following* JOHN'S *lead, and to make conversa-*

tion.] I was wondering what you and Rosie were pa-
lavering about.

JOHN. Samuel, you've gone right into the bull's-eye
at the first shot—Sam. I've just been through a very
awkward moment.

SAM. Oh, I see! That's it, is it?

JOHN. I've made a proposal of marriage to my partner's sister. Startling, ain't it?

SAM. No! If you care to know, I was talking to your
mother about it last week.

JOHN. About what?

SAM. About the betting odds—whether it was more
likely to come off this year or next. Your mother was
right, and I was wrong—by a couple of days.

JOHN. [*Startled.*] But you'd none of you the slightest ground. I've never shown— Certainly Rose has
never shown——

SAM. [*Teasingly.*] No, of course not. But you
know how people *will* gossip, and jump to conclusions,
don't you? I know, I went through it myself, not very
long ago either. I remember the clever way in which you
all knew about it before I'd got half-way to the end of my
first sentence.

JOHN. Sam, you're devilish funny.

SAM. Even the dullest old Tory is funny once in his
life. Am I right in assuming that Rose did not uncon-
ditionally refuse your offer?

JOHN. She did me the honor to accept it.

SAM. I must confess I'm not entirely surprised that
she didn't spurn you.

JOHN. All right, old cock. Keep it up. I don't mind.
But when you're quite done, you might congratulate me.

SAM. [*Not effusively.*] I do, of course.

JOHN. I suppose you'll admit, even as a brother, that

I'd have to go rather far before I met a woman with half Rose's qualities.

SAM. Yes, Rosie's all right. Of course she's cold; she hasn't got what I call poetry in her. That's the difference between her and Gertrude.

JOHN. [*Facing him.*] Do you honestly think Rose has no poetry in her? Rose?

SAM. Easy does it, my tulip! Have it your own way!

JOHN. [*Good-humoredly.*] I suppose where sisters are concerned, all brothers are alike.

SAM. Well, I'm looking at one. We're a pair.

JOHN. Shake! [*They shake hands,* SAM *rather perfunctorily.*] Now, Sam, I'm going to rely on you.

SAM. What for?

JOHN. I don't think you had any fault to find with my attitude toward your engagement, had you? I welcomed it with both arms. Well, I want you to do the same with me.

SAM. But, my dear fellow, I'm nobody in the affair. You're the head of a family; I'm not.

JOHN. But you have enormous influence with the head of a family, my boy.

SAM. [*Rather falsely.*] Why! Are you anticipating trouble with the governor?

JOHN. I'm not anticipating it—but you know as well as I do—probably much better—that he ain't very friendly disposed this last day or two. The plain truth is—he's sulking. Now why? Nothing whatever has passed between us except just every-day business.

SAM. Well, the fact is, he suspects you're keeping something nasty up your sleeve for him.

JOHN. Has he told you?

SAM. [*Somewhat pugnaciously.*] Yes, he has.

JOHN. And what is it I'm supposed to have up my sleeve?

SAM. Look here, Jack. I'm not here to be cross-examined. If there's anything up your sleeve, you're the person to know what it is. It's not my sleeve we're talking about. Why don't you play with the cards on the table?

JOHN. I'm only too anxious to play with the cards on the table.

SAM. Then it is business you really wanted to talk about after all!

JOHN. [*Movement of irritation concealed.*] I expect your father's heard about me and Macleans, though how it's got abroad I can't imagine.

SAM. Macleans? Macleans of Greenhithe?

JOHN. Yes. That's what's worrying the old man, isn't it?

SAM. I don't know.

JOHN. He hasn't mentioned Macleans to you?

SAM. He has not. He isn't a great talker, you know. He merely said to me he suspected you were up to something.

JOHN. And what did you say?

SAM. Briefly, I said I thought you *were*. [*Disgustedly.*] But, by gad! I never dreamed you were hob-nobbing with the Maclean gang.

JOHN. Macleans are one of the oldest ship-building firms in the South of England. I went to the launch to-day with Andrew Maclean.

SAM. What's ship-building got to do with us?

JOHN. It's got nearly everything to do with us. Or it will have. Now listen, Sammy. I've arranged a provisional agreement for partnership between Macleans and ourselves.

SAM. You've——

JOHN. Half a minute. Macleans are rather flattered at the idea of a connection with the august firm of Sibley, Rhead, and Sibley.

SAM. By God! I should think they were.

[*Walks away.*]

JOHN. They've had an output of over 25,000 tons this year. All wood. Naturally they want to go in for iron. They'll pay handsomely for our help and experience. In fact, I've got a draft agreement, my boy, that is simply all in our favor.

SAM. Did you seriously suppose——

JOHN. Let me finish. It's a brilliant agreement. In three years it'll mean the doubling of our business. And we shall have the satisfaction of being well established in the great industry of the future. Your father's old. I don't expect him to be very enthusiastic about a new scheme. But you're young, and you can influence him. He'll be retiring soon, and you and I will be together— just the two of us. We're marrying each other's sisters. And we shall divide an enormous fortune, my boy.

SAM. And have you had the impudence to try to make an agreement behind our backs?

JOHN. [*Controlling himself.*] I've made no agreement. I've only got the offer. It's open to you to refuse or accept. I only held my tongue about it so as to keep the job as easy as possible.

SAM. You had no right to approach any one without consulting us.

JOHN. I was going to tell you to-morrow. But I guessed from your father's attitude these last two days that something had leaked out. That's why I'm telling you first, Sam—to-night. Come now, look at the thing calmly—reasonably. Don't condemn it offhand. A very great deal depends on your decision—more than you think.

SAM. I don't see that anything particular depends on my decision. If we refuse, we refuse. And we shall most decidedly refuse.

JOHN. But it's impossible you should be so blind to the future! Impossible!

SAM. See here, John! Don't you make the mistake of assuming that any man who doesn't happen to agree with you is a blind fool. To begin with, it isn't polite. I know you *do* think we're blind, old-fashioned, brainless dolts, father and I. We've both felt that for some time.

JOHN. I think you're blind to the future of iron ships, that's all.

SAM. Well, shall I tell you what we think of *you?* We think you've got a bee in your bonnet. That's all. We think you're a faddist in the style of Ned Pym's noble uncle!

JOHN. [*His lips curling.*] Me like Lord Monkhurst! Ha!

SAM. Precisely. Don't you go and imagine that all the arguments are on one side. They aren't. Five-sixths of the experts in England have no belief whatever in the future of iron ships. You know that! Iron ships indeed! And what about British oak? Would you build ships of the self-same material as bridges? Why not stone ships, then? Oh, yes, I know there's a number of faddists up and down the land—anything in the nature of a novelty is always bound to attract a certain type of brain. Unfortunately we happen to have that type of brain just now in the Cabinet. I quite agree with my father that the country is going to the dogs. Another Reform Bill this year! And actually an attempt to repeal the paper duty. But, of course, people who believe in iron ships would naturally want to unsettle the industrial classes by a poisonous flood of cheap newspapers! However, we've had enough common sense left to knock both those schemes on the head. And I've no doubt the sagacity of the country will soon also put an end to this fantastic notion of iron ships.

JOHN. [*Quietly.*] I see.

SAM. Oh, don't think I'm not fond of iron! Iron means as much to me as it does to you. But I flatter myself I can keep my balance. [*More quietly.*] We didn't expect this of you, John, with your intellect.

JOHN. [*As before.*] Very well.

SAM. I've made it clear, haven't I?

JOHN. Quite.

SAM. That's all right.

JOHN. [*Still quietly.*] Only I shall dissolve partnership.

SAM. Dissolve partnership? What for?

JOHN. I shall go on with Macleans alone.

SAM. You don't mean it.

JOHN. I mean every single word of it!

[*He rises. They look at each other.*]

SAM. Then I can tell you one thing. You won't marry Rosie.

JOHN. Why shan't I marry Rosie?

SAM. After such treachery.

JOHN. [*Raising his voice.*] Treachery! I merely keep my own opinion—I leave you to yours.

SAM. Do you think father will let you drag Rose into this fatuous scheme of yours? Do you think he'll give his daughter to a traitor?

JOHN. [*Sarcastic and cold.*] Don't get on stilts. [*Then suddenly bursting out.*] And what has my marriage got to do with you? When I want your father's opinion, I'll go to your father for it.

SAM. Don't try to browbeat me, John. I know my father's mind, and what's more, you know I know it. And I repeat, my father will never let his daughter marry a——

JOHN. [*Shouting.*] Silence!

[*Enter* MRS. RHEAD *by the double doors, followed by* NED PYM, GERTRUDE, *and* ROSE. *The women remain silent.*]

NED. [*Facetiously coming forward.*] Why silence? Go on. We've only come in because we thought it might interest us. What's it all about? A hint will suffice.

JOHN. Ned, you're a blundering donkey, and you will be a blundering donkey to the end of your life.

NED. My one desire is to please.

GERT. [*Coming to* SAM, *in a quiet, firm tone.*] Sam, what's the matter?

SAM. Nothing! We must go! Rosie, get ready. [*Very respectfully to* MRS. RHEAD.] I'm sorry to break up the evening.

GERT. But you can't go like this.

SAM. [*With deference.*] My dear Gertrude, please leave matters to your brother and me. You're a woman, and there are things——

GERT. [*Stopping him.*] It is possible I am a woman, but I'm a reasonable creature, and I intend to be treated as such.

MRS. R. [*Very upset.*] My dear child, remember you are speaking to your future husband.

GERT. That's just why I'm speaking as I am. I ask Sam what's the matter—[*scornfully*] and he says "Nothing." Am I a child? Are we all children?

SAM. [*Curtly.*] Come, now, Rose.

GERT. And why must Rose go off like this? She's engaged to John.

SAM. Who told you?

GERT. Her eyes told me when she came out of this room.

MRS. R. We all knew it, and no word said. We've been expecting it for weeks.

[MRS. RHEAD *and* ROSE *embrace*.]

SAM. You are mistaken, Gertrude. Rose is not engaged to John, and she is not likely to be.

GERT. You object?

SAM. I do, and I know my father will.

GERT. You object to John for a brother-in-law? John! Why?— You might at least condescend to tell Rosie, if not me. It's an affair that rather interests her, you see.

SAM. If you must know, John is going to leave our firm.

MRS. R. John?

SAM. He thinks my father and I are old-fashioned, and so he's leaving us.

MRS. R. John! Leave the firm? Surely you're not thinking of breaking up Rhead and Sibley?

SAM. Sibley, Rhead—and Sibley.

MRS. R. It was Rhead and Sibley in my young days, when your father and John's were founding it. John, you cannot mean it!

SAM. [*Sarcastically*.] He's going to build iron ships.

GERT. And is that any reason why you should make poor Rosie unhappy and spoil her life?

SAM. I do not propose to argue.

GERT. The man who does not propose to argue with me is not going to be my husband.

MRS. R. Gertrude!

GERT. [*Looking at* SAM.] I mean it.

[SAM *bows*.]

MRS. R. Please don't listen to her, Sam.

SAM. All my apologies, Mrs. Rhead.

GERT. And you, Rosie, what do you say to all this?

ROSE. [*Humbly and tearfully.*] I—I hardly understand. Sam, what is the matter?

JOHN. [*Coming to* ROSE.] It's quite simple. I believe in the future of iron ships and I have the courage of my convictions. Therefore you are not to be allowed to marry me. You see the connection is perfectly clear. But you shall marry me, all the same!

SAM. [*Confidently.*] You don't know my sister.

NED. [*To* SAM, *facetiously.*] And you don't know John.

SAM. [*Turning to* NED, *firmly.*] Ned, go and order my carriage, there's a good fellow.

NED. [*Going off by the door into the hall.*] Oh, very well.

[*He closes the door behind him.*]

MRS. R. John, John, why are you so set in your own ideas? Everything was going perfectly smoothly. We were all so happy. And now you must needs fall out with your partners over iron ships. Do you prefer your iron ships to Rose's happiness and your own? *Is everything* to be sacrificed to iron ships?

JOHN. There need be no question of sacrifice, if——

SAM. If you can have it your own way. Of course. Mrs. Rhead, your son wants to risk the ruin of all of us. Now, so far as we Sibleys are concerned, we won't allow him to do so. If he still persists in his purpose, very well, that's *his* lookout. Only—he can hardly be surprised if Rose's family object—and very strongly—to letting him make her his wife. One does not intrust one's daughter or one's sister to a traitor.

GERT. Sam, don't be childish!

SAM. [*Drawing himself up.*] I beg your pardon.

MRS. R. John, I'm your mother. Listen to me. Give up this idea of yours. For my sake—for the sake of all of us.

JOHN. I cannot.

MRS. R. But if it means so much unhappiness.

JOHN. I should be ashamed of myself if I gave it up. I believe in it. It's my religion.

MRS. R. John, I beg you not to be profane.

JOHN. [*A little quieter.*] I cannot give up my idea, mother. I should be a coward to give it up. I should be miserable for the rest of my days. I could never look any one in the face, not even my wife.

[*Enter* NED *from the hall.*]

NED. [*To* SAM *in a flunky's voice.*] Carriage is waiting, my lord.

SAM. Now, Rose! Good evening, Mrs. Rhead.

GERT. Just a moment. [*Drawing a ring off her finger.*] Ned! Hand this ring to Mr. Sibley with my compliments.

NED. Must I?

GERT. Yes.

NED. [*Taking the ring.*] The donkey becomes a beast of burden. [*Handing ring to* SAM.] Sam, you get this, but you lose something that's worth a lot more.

SAM. [*Taking the ring.*] Of course I have no alternative.

ROSE. Good-by, John.

MRS. R. John, she's going. Will you let her?

JOHN. [*Rigidly.*] I cannot give up my idea.

SAM. [*Going into the hall as* ROSE *stands hesitating.*] Come along, child. I'm waiting.

ROSE. [*Moving a step toward* JOHN.] Stick to your idea! Let me go! I love you all the more for it!

JOHN. Don't worry, Rose. The future is on our side.

ROSE. [*Looking straight at him.*] I——

[*Her emotion gets the better of her; she turns quickly and hurries from the room.*]

GERT. [*Blankly, in spite of herself.*] The future!

[*She sinks down on a sofa and bursts into sobs. JOHN stands, looking after ROSE.*]

CURTAIN

ACT II
1885

The scene represents the same drawing-room as in Act I. But twenty-five years have passed. We are now in the year 1885. Consequently great changes have occurred. The furniture has been rearranged and added to. The flowered carpet of the first act has given place to an Indian carpet. There are new ornaments amongst some of the old ones. The room is overcrowded with furniture in the taste of the period.

It is about four o'clock of an afternoon in June. The curtains are drawn back and the sun is shining brightly outside.

ROSE SIBLEY, *now* MRS. JOHN RHEAD, *forty-six years of age and dressed in the fashion of 1885, her hair slightly gray at the temples, is seated writing some notes at a desk near the windows.* NED PYM *enters from the hall, followed by* JOHN RHEAD. *The former has developed into a well-preserved, florid, slightly self-sufficient man of forty-six. The latter, now fifty, has not changed so much physically except that his hair is gray and his features have become much firmer. But his manner has grown even more self-*

*assured than it was in the first act. He is in fact a
person of authority; the successful man whose word
is law.*

JOHN.   Oh, you *are* there, Rosie.   I've brought a person of importance to see you.

ROSE.   [*Rising.*]   Ned——

        [*They shake hands.*]

NED.   Now please don't say what you were going to
say.

ROSE.   And what was I going to say?

NED.   That I'm quite a stranger since I came into the
title.

ROSE.   [*Courtesying and teasing.*]   Lord Monkhurst,
we are only too flattered—I was merely going to say that
you look younger than ever.

NED.   [*Seriously.*]   Don't I?   That's what every one
says.   Time leaves me quite unchanged, don't you know.

JOHN.   In every way.   How old *are* you, Ned?

NED.   [*With a sigh.*]   Well, I shall never see thirty
again.

JOHN.   What about forty?

NED.   Or forty either.   But my proud boast is I'm
nearer forty than fifty.

JOHN.   Well, it can only be by a couple of months.

NED.   Sh!—It's a lot more than you say, Jack.

JOHN.   I was fifty in April.   There's just five years'
difference between us.

ROSE.   [*To* NED.]   You look more like John's son.

NED.   Say nephew; don't be too hard on him.

ROSE.   But I do wish you would go out of mourning.
It doesn't suit you.

NED.   Not these beautiful continuations?

ROSE.   No!

NED. Well, I'm awfully sorry. But I can't oblige you yet. Please remember I've got three sudden deaths to work off. I think that when a man loses a harsh but beloved uncle in a carriage accident, and two amiable cousins through a misunderstanding about toadstools, all in twelve months, why [*gesture*] the least he can do is to put himself unreservedly into the hands of his tailor.

ROSE. I——

JOHN. [*Stopping her, kindly but rather tyrannically.*] Now enough of this graceful badinage. Ned and I are here on business. What are you up to, there, Rose?

ROSE. [*With eager submissiveness.*] I was doing the invitations for the dinner, or rather for the reception.

JOHN. Good. I've got some more names in my study. You'd better come in there with me.

ROSE. Yes, love.

NED. Am I invited to this dinner? I generally get very hungry about eight o'clock at nights.

ROSE. [*Teasing.*] Yes, I *think* I put you down. It's our wedding-day.

NED. Don't tell me how long you've been married. It would age me!

ROSE. Considering that we have a daughter who is turned twenty-two.

JOHN. Yes, Ned, you must face the facts bravely. Old Mr. Sibley died in January, 1860——

ROSE. Sixty-one, love.

JOHN. [*After a frown at being corrected.*] Sixty-one. And we were married in June of the following year. Surely you recall the face Sam pulled when he gave my little Rosie away.

ROSE. But, love, it was a great concession for him to give me away at all, wasn't it?

JOHN. Oh, yes!

Rose. By the by, he's coming up to town this afternoon.

John. What, here?

Ned. Oh! But I ought to see old Sam.

Rose. Stay for tea, and you'll see *him* and his wife, too.

Ned. His wife? His what did you say?

Rose. Now, Ned, it's no use pretending you don't know all about it.

Ned. I remember hearing a couple of years ago, before I went to India, that Sam had staggered his counting-house by buying one of these new typewriting-machines, and getting a young woman to work it for him.

Rose. That's the person. Her name is Nancy.

Ned. Is it? Only fancy; Nancy, Nancy, in the counting-*house*! I say—are these girl-clerks or clerk-girls going to be a regular thing? What's coming over the world?

John. [*Shakes his head.*] Passing craze! Goes with all this Votes-for-Women agitation and so on. You'll see, it won't last a year—not a year! Of course, Sam—susceptible bachelor of fifty and over—just the man to fall a victim. Inevitable!

Rose. She's a very well-meaning, honest creature.

Ned. You intimate with her, Rose?

Rose. I went to see her several times after she had her baby. They're living at Brockley.

Ned. Baby! Brockley! No more typewriting then. The typewriter has served its turn—eh? Of course it was a great catch for her.

John. Yes, but it wouldn't have been if Samuel hadn't sold out.

Ned. How much did he retire with about?

John. Well, you see he was losing three thousand a year. He got twenty thousand pounds net cash.

Ned. I'm not a financier, but twenty thousand pounds cash in exchange for a loss of three thousand pounds a year doesn't seem so bad! Think of the money he'd have made though, if he'd taken up with your ideas!

John. [*Ironically.*] You recollect the folly of iron ships? And the bee in my bonnet? [*Laughs.*] There were only four wooden steamships built in this country last year. The rest were iron; and I was responsible for half a dozen of 'em.

Ned. What's all this talk about steel for ships?

John. [*Disdainfully.*] Just talk.

Ned. Well, of course, if you're building at the rate of six steamers a year, I can understand your generosity in the matter of subscriptions.

Rose. He *is* generous, isn't he?

Ned. Told your wife about your latest contribution?

John. No, I was just going to.

Rose. [*Proudly.*] John tells me everything.

John. And Rosie always approves, don't you, Rosie? Ah! The new generation can't show such wives.

Rose. [*Eagerly.*] Well?

John. I've decided to give ten thousand pounds to the party funds—politics, you know.

Ned. You see, it's to save the country. That's what it amounts to practically, in these days. *I* know, since I've gone into politics.

Rose. How noble! I'm so glad, John.

Ned. And the great secret—shall I tell her, or will you, Jack?

John. Go on.

Ned. How should you like your husband to be a baronet, Rose?

Rose. A baronet?

Ned. Sir John Rhead, Bart., and Lady Rhead!

Rose. [*Ecstatic.*] Is he going to be?

Ned. As soon as our side comes into power—and we shall be in power in a month. John'll be on the next Honor' List.

Rose. In a month!

Ned. The Budget's bound to be thrown out. They're trying to increase the taxes on beer and spirits—I've studied the question deeply. I know what will happen.

Rose. How magnificent!

John. Then you approve? [Rose *kisses* John *fondly.*] That's all we've called in for, just to make sure.

Rose. [*Weeping.*] I——

John. What's the matter?

Rose. I'm only sorry we haven't had a son.

Ned. There, there! I'm sure you did your best, Rose.

Rose. [*To* John.] Are they making you a baronet because you're giving ten thousand to the party funds?

Ned. My dear woman! Of course not! That's pure coincidence.

Rose. [*Convinced.*] Oh!

Ned. Your beloved John will be made a baronet solely on account of his splendid services to commerce. Doesn't he deserve it?

Rose. No one better. Do you know, I can scarcely believe it. Who—? Tell me all about it.

John. Well, it's thanks to Ned in the first place.

Rose. To Ned?

Ned. [*Pretending to be hurt.*] You needn't be so surprised, Rose. You seem to be unaware that I've gone into politics. Don't you read the newspapers?

Rose. No, I leave the newspapers to my daughter.

NED. If you did, you'd know that I made a sensation in the Indian Debate, in the House of Lords. All that Afghanistan business, don't you know.

ROSE. Really!

NED. Oh, I became quite a Nob, at once. Bit of luck me having gone to India, wasn't it? I'd spent the best part of a month in India; so, of course, I knew all about it.

ROSE. [*Solemnly.*] Of course.

NED. The leader of the Opposition said I had a great future!

JOHN. No doubt.

NED. [*Simply.*] I shall specialize in India and the Navy. You see my father being a rear-admiral, I ought to be familiar with the subject. If fellows like me don't begin to take an interest in our neglected Navy, England 'll be playing second fiddle to Russia in five years' time. Mark my word, in 1890. In 1890.

ROSE. Perhaps you'll be in the Government some day?

NED. There's no "perhaps" about it. I shall! There's only one difficulty.

ROSE. What's that?

NED. [*Mysterious and important.*] I'm told I ought to marry.

JOHN. [*Rather self-consciously.*] Nothing simpler.

NED. I know! I've had seventeen indirect offers this last six months, and that's a fact.

ROSE. None suitable?

NED. I'm afraid of 'em. It's no joke going and marrying a perfect stranger. I want somebody I know— somebody I've known all my life, or at least all hers.

ROSE. And can't you find her?

NED. I can. I *have* done.

ROSE. Who is it, may one ask?

NED. Jack knows.

JOHN. [*Turning to* ROSE *and clearing his throat.*]
Ned would like to marry into *our* family, Rose.

NED. [*Eagerly.*] You know I've been dead sweet on
Emily for a couple of years at least.

ROSE. [*After a pause.*] I know you're very fond of
her, and she of you.

NED. [*As above.*] You think she is, really?

ROSE. But it seems so queer.

JOHN. [*Peremptorily.*] How queer? We're respectable enough for the young rascal, aren't we?

ROSE. Of course. It would be ideal—ideal! My
poor little Emily!

NED. Well, I've got that off my chest. I'll be moving. I must be at the Carlton at three-thirty to settle up
John's business with the panjandrum.

ROSE. You'll come back for tea. *She* 'll be here.

> [*Enter from the hall* EMILY *and* GERTRUDE.
> *Both are dressed to go out.* EMILY *is a hand-
> some girl of twenty-two. She has fine quali-
> ties, combining her father's pluck with her
> mother's loving nature. But she has been
> rather spoilt by her parents.* GERTRUDE *fol-
> lows. She has grown into a faded, acidy
> spinster with protective impulses for her niece,*
> EMILY, *on whom she spends all her suppressed
> maternal feelings.*]

EMILY. [*Slightly disconcerted.*] Why, father! How
is it you aren't at the works this afternoon earning our
bread-and-butter?

JOHN. [*Delighted.*] Such impertinence!

ROSE. Emily, I really wonder at you! What your
grandmother Rhead would have said to such manners if

she'd been alive, I daren't think. And Lord Monkhurst here, too!

EMILY. Well, mama, you see, grandmother isn't alive! [*To* NED, *who, after shaking hands with* GERTRUDE, *advances toward her.*] And as for dear old Uncle Ned— [NED, JOHN, *and* ROSE *are all somewhat put about by this greeting.* NED *hesitates, his hand half out.*] Aren't you going to shake hands, then?

NED. [*Shaking hands.*] Why "uncle?" You've never called me uncle before?

EMILY. Haven't I? It seems to suit you.

NED. I'm severely wounded. And I shall retire into my wigwam until you make it up to me.

ROSE. You really are very pert, Emily.

EMILY. [*Affectionately.*] I should have thought you would adore being my uncle. I'm sure I like you lots more than I like Uncle Sam, for instance.

NED. That's better. I'm peeping out of my wigwam now. Only I won't be your uncle. I won't be anybody's uncle. I don't mind being your cousin, if that's any use to you.

GERT. [*Sharply.*] He's afraid of being taken for the same age as your auntie, darling.

NED. [*To* GERTRUDE.] Half a moment, Gertrude, and I'll try to think of a compliment that will turn your flank.

GERT. My flank, Ned?

NED. I mean——

EMILY. [*To her parents and* NED.] Where were you all off to?

ROSE. Your father and I are going to the study.

NED. And I'm going on an errand, but I shan't be long.

JOHN. And may we ask where you and Auntie Gertrude are "off to," Miss Inquisitive?

GERT. Oh, Mr. Preece is calling for us to take us to the Royal Academy.

EMILY. And then we shall have tea at the new Hotel Métropole, in Northumberland Avenue. It's the very latest thing.

JOHN. [*In a different tone.*] Preece? But he was here last Sunday.

EMILY. Yes, it was then we arranged it.

JOHN. I don't like the idea of your seeing so much of Preece. And your mother doesn't like it, either.

ROSE. No, indeed!

GERT. But why not? He's the cleverest man in your works. You've often said so.

JOHN. He may be the cleverest man in my works; but he isn't going to be the cleverest man in my house. Who gave him leave to take half a day off, I should like to know?

GERT. He said he had business in the West End.

EMILY. [*To* NED.] Now if you want to make yourself useful as a cousin, please explain to these called-so parents that they oughtn't to spoil me one day, and rule me with a rod of iron the next. It's not fair. It's very bad for my disposition.

NED. [*To* JOHN.] Is this man-about-town the same Preece you were telling me of?

EMILY. There you are, you see! He tells every one about Mr. Preece. He's as proud as Punch of Mr. Preece.

JOHN. [*More kindly.*] Arthur Preece is a youth that I discovered in my drawing office. Last year I took out a patent for him for bending metal plates at a low temperature; and it's attracted some attention. But our relations are purely business.

GERT. Still, it was you who first asked him to the house.

JOHN. [*Drily.*] It was. And Rose kept him for tea. It's all our fault as usual. However—[*rising*]—you'll kindly tell Master Preece that you can't give yourselves the pleasure of his society this afternoon.

EMILY. But why?

JOHN. [*Continuing.*] And if he's obstreperous, inform him that *I* am in my study, and rather anxious to know exactly what his business in the West End is.

EMILY. [*Insisting.*] But why, father?

JOHN. [*Firmly.*] Simply because your mother and I wish you to be in this afternoon. Uncle Sam and Aunt Nancy are coming, for one thing.

EMILY. [*Disdainfully.*] Uncle Sam! Aunt Nancy!

ROSE. Emily! I won't have you bandying words with your father; you seem to have lost all sense of respect.

EMILY. [*To* NED *angrily.*] Aren't they tyrants!
　　　[*She goes to a little table and takes off her bonnet, in a quick annoyed way.*]

ROSE. [*Very politely and nicely to* GERTRUDE.] Gertrude, if *you* aren't going out, could you come into the study about those addresses?

GERT. [*Somewhat snappishly, taking* EMILY's *bonnet.*] Of course!
　　　[*She goes out quickly.*]

JOHN. [*To* NED.] Well, you've got to be off then, for the moment.
　　　[*All are near the door now, except* EMILY, *who is drawing off her gloves savagely.*]

ROSE. [*In a low voice to* NED.] Till tea, then.

[*She goes out, nodding her head significantly.*]

NED. [*Hesitating.*] Yes. [*To* JOHN.] But I must just kiss the hand of this new cousin of mine first.

JOHN. [*In a peculiar tone.*] Oh! All Right!

[*He follows* ROSE.]

NED. [*Going up to* EMILY, *whose face is turned away ingratiatingly.*] Now, I'm not included in this frown, am I?

EMILY. [*Facing him and bursting out.*] But don't you think it's a shame, seriously?

NED. Of course if you've *promised* Mr. Preece, and don't want to disappoint him——

EMILY. [*With false lightness.*] Oh, Mr. Preece is nothing to me! Only I *do* want to know where I am. The fact is they let me do as I like in little things, and they're frightfully severe in big things. Not really big things, but—you know——

NED. Middling big things.

EMILY. After all I'm twenty-two.

NED. A mature age.

EMILY. [*Huffily.*] Oh! Naturally you take their side!

NED. Honor bright, I don't! I tell you I feel far more like your age than theirs. I'm much younger than your father—much! That's why I don't like being called uncle.

EMILY. Really?

NED. Really.

EMILY. [*Confidentially.*] And there's another thing. They oughtn't to treat Auntie Gertrude like that, ought they? She's got more brains than anybody else here.

NED. Than your father?

EMILY. No, not than father. I meant mother, and Uncle Sam, and me—and you——

NED. I see.

EMILY. Who is it runs the house? You don't suppose it's mother, do you? Mother is absorbed in father, quite absorbed in him. No! It's auntie does everything. And yet she's nobody, simply nobody. She arranges to take me out, and they stop it without so much as apologizing to her.

NED. Well, you see, she's an old maid.

EMILY. I don't care whether she's an old maid or not. She's the only friend I have. Father and mother are most awfully fond of me and all that, and mother *is* sweet, isn't she? But still that makes no difference. There are two camps in this house; they're in one, and auntie and I are in the other. And I tell you we have to be regular conspirators, in self-defence. Of course I'm trusting you.

NED. [*Who has been playing with a book he has picked up from a table.*] You may.

EMILY. For instance, they won't let me read Ouida. They don't even like auntie to read Ouida.

NED. This isn't Ouida.

EMILY. I know it isn't. That's William Black. They're always throwing William Black at me, and I hate him. I want to read Ouida.

NED. You must wait till you're married.

EMILY. I won't. And I do so want to go to the Hotel Métropole.

NED. I thought it was the Royal Academy.

EMILY. The Academy too.

NED. Look here, Emily. Suppose I arrange a little theatre party?

EMILY. Not with father and mother. They'll want to go to something silly.

NED. No. Just your auntie and me—and you, of course.

EMILY. Will you?

NED. Rather!

EMILY. You're quite coming out. But will they allow it?

NED. You bet they will.

EMILY. Where?

NED. Anywhere you like.

EMILY. Do you know "The Mikado's" been running three months, and I haven't seen it yet?

NED. "Here's a 'How d'you do!'" The Savoy then.

EMILY. Oh! Hurrah! Hurrah! Thanks; you are a dear.

NED. [*Pleased.*] Am I? That's all right then. Au revoir.

[*Turns to the door.*]

EMILY. [*Calling him back.*] Cousin! [*She beckons him to come to her.*] What's this secret between you and father and mother?

NED. What secret?

EMILY. [*Crossly.*] Now you needn't pretend. I could see it as plain as anything when I came in. And when they went out too, for that matter.

NED. I can't stand being bullied.

EMILY. Tell me, and I won't bully you.

NED. [*Solemnly.*] You're going to be related to a baronet.

EMILY. [*Disturbed.*] They don't want me to marry a baronet, do they?

NED. Foolish creature! No. It's the opposite camp that's about to receive a title.

EMILY. [*Delighted.*] Father—a baronet!

NED. I'm just off to make the final arrangements now.

EMILY. Truly?

NED. Don't be misled by my modest exterior. I'm a terrific nob—really.

[*He turns to go.*]

EMILY. [*As he is going.*] Didn't you say something about kissing my hand? One of your jokes, I suppose.

[NED *comes and kisses it, then hurries to the door. As he opens it he looks back and says "The Mikado," and hurries out.* EMILY *stands a moment lost in thought, a smile on her lips. Then she hums, quite unconsciously, "For he's going to marry Yum-Yum, Yum-Yum!" Goes back to the table on which the William Black is lying, picks it up—opens it, reading a bit, then flings the book aside, muttering in disgust, "Black!"* THOMPSON *enters. He has grown old in the service of the Rheads.*]

THOMPSON. [*Announcing.*] Mr. Preece.

[*He withdraws.* ARTHUR PREECE *enters. His age is twenty-five; he is a man of the clerk class, whose talent and energy have made him what he is. He is full of enthusiasm, earnest, but with a rough sense of humor. Rather short and stocky in figure, but important. His clothes are neat and useful—but very simple.*]

PREECE. [*Excited.*] Good afternoon, Miss Rhead. I'm afraid I'm a little early.

EMILY. [*Putting on the manner of a woman of the world.*] Not at all, Mr. Preece. I'm sure Auntie Gertrude will be delighted.

PREECE. [*Vaguely.*] She's not here now, your aunt?

EMILY. [*Looking around.*] No.

PREECE. [*Eagerly.*] I wonder if I should have time to tell you something before she comes in. It isn't that

it's a secret.   But nobody knows yet, and I should like you
to be the first.

EMILY.   How very kind of you, Mr. Preece!

PREECE.   I've only just known it myself.

EMILY.   It seems to be very thrilling.

PREECE.   It is, rather.   It's just this.   I've succeeded
in making mild steel nearly five per cent lighter than it's
ever been made before.   Nearly five per cent lighter, and
no extra cost.

EMILY.   Really!   How much is five per cent?

PREECE.   It's one-twentieth part.   You know, it's
enormous.

EMILY.   I suppose it is.

PREECE.   I dare say you don't quite realize what it
means—this enormous change in the specific gravity.   But
it *is* enormous.

EMILY.   What is specific gravity?   In a word?

PREECE.   It's—well—Now supposing—Do you mind if
I explain that to you some other time?   I'd like to,
awfully!

EMILY.   Oh!   Any time!

PREECE.   It's quite O.K., you know.   And the thing
comes to this.   Assume the steel for a biggish ship cost
£20,000.   Under my new process you'd get the same result with steel that weighed about a twentieth less and cost,
roughly, £19,000.   Net saving of nearly one thousand
pounds!

EMILY.   [*Impressed.*]   And did you——

PREECE.   [*Continuing.*]   And not only that.   As the
hull weighs so much less, you can carry a proportionately
heavier cargo in the same bottom.

EMILY.   Well, I never heard of such a thing!   And am
I really the first to know?

PREECE.   You are.

EMILY. And you found out this all alone?

PREECE. Oh, yes! Except the manager, nobody has any idea of what I've been experimenting on.

EMILY. Not even father?

PREECE. No.

EMILY. I suppose he knows you *are* experimenting.

PREECE. Of course. That's my job. That's what he took me out of the drawing office for. I'm always experimenting on something.

EMILY. I expect you're what they call an inventor.

PREECE. [*Humorously.*] I expect I am. [*Eagerly.*] I'd practically finished this experiment a week ago. But I had to make sure whether there was any manganese left in the steel. I've been getting a friend at the City and Guilds of London Institute to analyse it for me—you know, the big, red building in Exhibition Road. I've just come from there.

EMILY. So *that* was your business in the West End? [*Preece nods.*] I'm sure auntie and I hadn't an idea it was anything half so romantic.

PREECE. It *is* romantic, isn't it?

EMILY. No wonder you're so excited.

PREECE. Am I? Well, I don't care! It's all right. That's all I care about. Here's a bit of the steel now.

[*He offers her a small sample.*]

EMILY. Is it for me? May I keep it?

PREECE. I want you to.

EMILY. Rather a strange thing for a girl to keep, isn't it?

PREECE. You don't mind——

EMILY. I'd part with all my jewelry before I parted with this. D'you know, it makes me feel very proud. And when I think of poor old father not knowing *any-thing* about it——

PREECE. I shall tell him to-morrow if he can spare time to see me.

EMILY. Spare time to see *you*—why?

PREECE. Oh! you don't know, but Mr. Rhead's a sort of crowned head on the works. You can't walk into his office as if it was a public-house, I can tell you.

EMILY. But it's so important for him.

PREECE. Rather! Much more important for him than for me.

EMILY. Why?

PREECE. Under our agreement! Our agreement has five years to run yet, and during that time everything I do belongs to the firm. I only get a percentage on whatever my inventions bring in.

EMILY. What percentage?

PREECE. Ten. For every hundred pounds profit I get ten pounds and the firm gets ninety.

EMILY. But what a frightful shame! It ought to be the other way about—you ninety pounds and the firm ten.

PREECE. Oh, no! It's fair enough—really! They pay me a very good salary. And you must remember if Mr. Rhead hadn't taken me out of the drawing office, I should be there now getting two pounds a week!

EMILY. I don't care! I think it's a frightful shame. I shall tell father.

PREECE. [*Half playfully.*] Please don't, unless you want to ruin me with him. I owe just about everything to your father.

EMILY. But it's so horridly unfair.

PREECE. Oh, no! I assure you. I shall have all the money I want, and more. And it will always be *my* invention. That's the point.

EMILY. Then you don't care for money?

PREECE. Yes, I do. I want enough. In fact, I want

a good deal. But what's interesting is to *do* things, and to do 'em better and quicker, and less clumsily than ever they were done before. If I can make nineteen tons of steel do the work of twenty— Well, I reckon I've accomplished something for the world.

EMILY. I like that. It's very original.

PREECE. Not my notion, you know. I'm a disciple of William Morris.

EMILY. Oh! He's a poet, isn't he?

PREECE. You should read "The Earthly Paradise."

EMILY. I should love to.

PREECE. If people would read a bit more William Morris, and less of these silly gim-crack novels about lords and actresses—Ouida and so on— What's the matter?

EMILY. Nothing. [*With a certain self-satisfaction.*] William Black's silly too, isn't he?

PREECE. Of course.

EMILY. [*Firmly.*] I'm going to read "The Earthly Paradise."

PREECE. Let me lend it you. I've got a signed copy, from the author.

EMILY. You know an author!

PREECE. I know William Morris. I was up at his stable last night.

EMILY. His stable?

PREECE. He gives lectures in a stable behind his house at Hammersmith. I wish you'd heard him pitching into the House of Lords. "A squad of dukes."

EMILY. But why?

PREECE. Oh, because they aren't interested in the right thing.

EMILY. What is the right thing?

PREECE.   The right thing is to make the world fit to live in.

EMILY.   But isn't it?

PREECE.   Have you ever been to the East End?

EMILY.   I did some slumming once, just to see.   But I was so ashamed to go into their awful houses, that I never tried again.

PREECE.   [*Getting up, excited.*]   That's grand! That's grand!   That's just how I feel.   Every one feels like that that's got any imagination and any sense of justice.   We *ought* to be ashamed of the East End.   At least the governing classes ought.   Not for the poor, but for themselves.   They ought to go and get buried if they can't govern better than that.

EMILY.   [*After a pause, rising as in thought; moved.*] But how are you going to change it?

PREECE.   Not by slumming, that's a certainty.   You can only change it by getting some decent laws passed, and by playing fair, and doing your job, and thinking a great deal less about eating and drinking, and fine clothes, and being in the swim and all that sort of nonsense.   Do you know what I am going to do as soon as I can afford?   I'm going to be a Member of Parliament.

EMILY.   [*Low.*]   Why did you offer to take us to the Hotel Métropole?

PREECE.   [*Confused.*]   I thought you'd like it.   I— I——

EMILY.   You despise it yourself.

PREECE.   I'm human.

EMILY.   But——

[*She draws close to him.*]

PREECE.   I'm very ambitious.   I want a whole lot of things.   But if I thought I could find some one—find a woman who—who feels as I feel; who'd like before everything to help to make the world decent—I'd——

EMILY. I——

[*Profoundly stirred, she falls into his arms.*]

PREECE. Emily!

[*He kisses her long, holding her close.*]

EMILY. [*Gently releases herself and walks away. With effort.*] I haven't told you. I forgot. Father doesn't wish me to go out with you this afternoon. He's here now, in the study.

[GERTRUDE *enters from the hall, without her bonnet this time.*]

GERT. Good afternoon, Mr. Preece. [*They shake hands. To* EMILY.] I suppose you—er—told Mr. Preece that the excursion is countermanded?

[*She goes to the fireplace.*]

EMILY. Yes, Mr. Preece was just going. [*Gently.*] Good afternoon. [*She holds out her hand to Preece, who hesitates.* EMILY *repeats in firmer tone.*] Good afternoon. [*In a tender voice.*] Please! [*With a smile.*] Another time!

[PREECE *shakes hands and, bowing to* GERTRUDE, *retires. As he departs* GERTRUDE *rings the bell by the fireplace.*]

GERT. Well, I've been catching it, I can tell you!

EMILY. [*Shaken.*] What about?

GERT. About you. They simply asked me to go into the study so that I could be talked to—for your good, my girl.

EMILY. They weren't rude, were they?

GERT. You know your mother's always most considerate. She's an angel. But your father rubbed it in finely. How many times had you seen the young man? — If ever alone?— What on earth was I thinking of?

— What on earth was your mother doing to have noticed nothing? (As if your mother ever noticed anything!) And so on! Of course, I told them pretty straight that they were making a most ridiculous fuss about nothing.

EMILY. Well, anyhow, I've let him kiss me.

GERT. You've let him kiss you? When?

EMILY. Just now. Here.

GERT. But what——

EMILY. Don't ask me. I don't know, I really don't. But I've felt it coming for some time.

GERT. Do you mean to say he walked in here and proposed to you straight off, and you accepted him?

EMILY. I didn't accept him, because he didn't propose. He was talking about his ideas.

GERT. What ideas?

EMILY. [*With a vague gesture.*] Oh, about the world in general, and all that he means to do. He's made another marvellous invention, only no one knows except me. It was the excited way he talked—somehow—I couldn't help it—before I knew what we were doing, he'd got his arms round me.

GERT. [*Rather sternly, in spite of her tender feeling.*] Well, Emily, I must say I'm very surprised.

EMILY. So am I.

GERT. Of course you're engaged to him?

EMILY. Am I?

GERT. And it'll be all my fault. However, it's got to be seen through to the end now.

EMILY. He has very strange ideas. They sound splendid when he's explaining them. But d'you know, he thinks Ouida's silly.

GERT. Does he?

EMILY. And he really doesn't care about money and

fashion and all that sort of thing. He despises going to the Hotel Métropole. He only offered to go there because he thought it would please our horrid little minds— I was so ashamed.

GERT. But surely you knew all this before—at least you guessed it?

EMILY. I didn't, auntie. I never thought about his ideas, never! I just——

GERT. You just simply fell into his arms as soon as you heard them, that's all. Well, surely in that case, you must admire these ideas of his tremendously.

[*She sits in an armchair.*]

EMILY. I don't know. Yes. I *admire* them, but——

GERT. Listen, young woman! Are you in love with him, or aren't you?

EMILY. I—I— How can you tell whether you're in love with a man or not?

GERT. Supposing you were alone with him here, now —would you let him kiss you again?

[*Pause.*]

EMILY. I——

GERT. Now, out with it!

EMILY. I shouldn't be able to stop him, should I?

GERT. That's enough.

EMILY. Yes. But then what about father? He would be frightfully angry, I can see that. Oh, I do hate unpleasantness, auntie. And Mr. Preece's ideas are really very peculiar.

GERT. [*After a look at* EMILY.] Listen, Emily! I was once engaged to be married.

EMILY. Oh, auntie! I always knew you must have been. Do tell me. Who was it?

GERT. Your Uncle Sam.

EMILY. [*Staggered.*] Not Uncle Sam?

GERT. You're surprised, naturally. But you mustn't be too hard. Remember it was twenty-five years ago, Uncle Sam was a splendid fellow then. He's old now. We're all old, except you—and Mr. Preece. You've got the only thing worth having, you two.

EMILY. [*Sitting at* GERTRUDE'S *feet.*] What's that?

GERT. Youth. Your Uncle Sam lived the miserable life of a bachelor till he was fifty. He'd have been a very different man if I'd married him. And I should have been a very different woman.

EMILY. Why did you break it off?

GERT. I broke it off because there were difficulties; and because I thought his ideas were peculiar; and because I hated unpleasantness! And now look at me! Couldn't I have ruled a house and a family? Couldn't I have played the hostess? [*In another tone.*] To-day the one poor little joy I have in life is to pretend I'm your mother. Look at my position here. I'm only——

EMILY. [*Passionately.*] Oh, auntie, don't! I can't bear to hear you say it. I know!

GERT. We were opposite in every way, your uncle and I, but I—I loved him.

EMILY. [*Softly.*] Do you still love him, auntie?

GERT. [*In a flat tone of despair.*] No! Love dies out.

EMILY. [*After a moment.*] Why didn't you marry somebody else?

GERT. There *was* nobody else. There never is anybody else when you've made the mistake I made. Marry! I could have chosen among a dozen men! But they were all the wrong men. Emily! Fancy pouring out tea every day of your life for the wrong man. Every breakfast time—every afternoon! And there he sits, and nothing will move him. Think of that, Emily—think of that.

[*A pause.*]

EMILY. [*Embracing her again.*] Oh, auntie! *I* love you awfully!

GERT. You must show some courage, my girl. Don't be afraid of anything—and especially not of arguments and threats. What does unpleasantness matter, after all? It's over in a month; but a mistake lasts forever.

EMILY. You'll help me?

GERT. That's all I live for. [*She kisses* EMILY *tenderly.*] Is that Sam's voice?

[THOMPSON *enters.*]

THOMPSON. [*Announcing.*] Mr. and Mrs. Sibley.

> [*He retires.* SAMUEL SIBLEY *and his wife*
> NANCY *enter.* SAMUEL, *who is now fifty-*
> *three, has grown into a rather flabby nonentity,*
> *gray-haired with longish side whiskers and*
> *glasses. His manner is important and fussy.*
> NANCY *is a buxom, Yorkshire woman of*
> *thirty-two, round-faced, good-natured, full of*
> *energy. She wears the fashionable jersey of*
> *1885 and a very definite "bustle."*]

SAM. Well, Gertrude? Well, my little Emmie!

> [*He kisses* EMILY, *who gives her cheek unwill-*
> *ingly; then shakes hands with* GERTRUDE.]

GERT. How are you, Sam; and you, Mrs. Sam?

NANCY. Nicely, thank you! [*Shaking hands vigor-ously with* GERTRUDE *and* EMILY.] Everybody well, here?

EMILY. Yes, thank you.

NANCY. That's fine! Then your mother got Sam's letter saying we were coming?

EMILY. [*Drily.*] Oh, yes!

NANCY. I said to Sam it would happen be best to write and tell you. So he wrote—[*with a look at* SAM]—finally.

SAM. [*With a serious tone.*]   We nearly didn't come.

GERT.   Anything wrong?

SAM.   Infant's temperature up at a hundred last night. However, it was normal this morning.

NANCY.   You know he takes the baby's temperature every night.

EMILY.   Oh, do you, uncle?   How funny!

SAM.   I don't see anything funny about it, niece. Good thing if some parents took their responsibilities a bit more seriously.

NANCY.   I must say Sam makes a very good father.

GERT.   Let me see—how old is Dickie now?

SAM.   We never call him Dickie—Richard, better; less nonsensical.

[*He settles down solemnly in a chair.*]

NANCY.   You've no idea what I call him when you're not there, Sam! [*To* GERTRUDE.]   He was two on the second of the month.   He talks like anything!   You ought to see him and his father together.   It's killing! The little thing's so *exactly* like Sam.

EMILY.   [*Examining* SAM.]   Is he?   We must go down to Brockley, mustn't we, auntie?

NANCY.   [*Drily.*]   I've been expecting you for the better part of some time. [*Then cordially.*]   I should love you to come as soon as I've got a new cook. [*With emphasis.*]   Oh, my!

GERT.   Are you having trouble?

NANCY.   Trouble's not the word.   And as for the nurse-maid!   If it wasn't for Sam being free——

GERT.   D'you take your share, Sam?

NANCY.   By the hour he wheels that child up and down.

EMILY.   Not in the street?

SAM. Why not, niece? Anything to be ashamed of in being a father?

NANCY. That's what we came up for to-day, to buy a new perambulator. He did try to repair the other in the little workshop he's made himself at the end of the garden—and most useful he is for odd jobs. Upon my word, he's busy from morning to night! But we thought it better to buy a new pram altogether.

SAM. [*Discontented.*] Nancy would insist on having one of those new things with indiarubber tires, as they call them.

NANCY. [*Very definitely.*] Now, Sam. I thought we'd done with that question.

SAM. Yes; but rubber tires on gravel paths! It's obvious they'll not last a——

NANCY. I told you Mrs. Caton across the road told me——

SAM. Oh, very well! Very well! Only it's very light and flimsy.

EMILY. [*Restless.*] I think I'll go and tell father and mother you're here.

[*Going toward the door.*]

NANCY. [*Rising, very convinced.*] Come and see for yourself what you think of the pram and the rubber tires.

EMILY. [*Rising.*] Is it here?

NANCY. Yes, in the hall.

SAM. I deemed it imprudent to let them send it down by train. So we brought it away on the roof of a four-wheeler.

EMILY. [*Patronizingly.*] Well, let's go and inspect it, Aunt Nancy.

[EMILY *and* NANCY *go off.*]

GERT. [*Waiting till the door is closed; in low, quiet tones.*] Sam, I'm so glad you've come. There's going to be another tragedy in this house, if some of us don't do something.

SAM. *Another* tragedy? What do you mean?

GERT. I just mean a tragedy. That child's head over heels in love with young Arthur Preece, at the works, and John simply won't hear of it.

SAM. Why?

GERT. [*Shrugs her shoulders.*] Why, indeed? Sam, if there's any discussion while you're here I want you to help me all you can.

SAM. But really, Gertrude, how can I meddle in an affair like that? I have my own responsibilities.

GERT. Sam, it's many years since I asked the slightest favor of you.

SAM. [*Moved, friendly.*] Come, come. Don't go so far back as all that. We're all very comfortable as we are, I think.

[*The door opens.*]

GERT. [*Quick and low.*] But will you? You've got more influence than I have.

SAM. [*Low.*] All right. [*Pats her arm.*] All right.

[*Enter* ROSE *and* JOHN.]

JOHN. [*Coming up to* SAM *a little patronizingly.*] Sam, glad to see you! How's the precious family getting on? Any new trouble lately?

SAM. [*A little sharply.*] Oh, no! And what about yours? [*In a significant, bantering tone.*] Any new trouble lately?

JOHN. Mine? Trouble? No!

ROSE. [*Kissing* SAM *fondly.*] Your wife's here?

SAM. She's downstairs somewhere——

JOHN. [*Interrupting sharply.*] Where's Emily?

GERT. She's just gone with Mrs. Sam to look at a new——

JOHN. [*Interrupting again.*] Preece hasn't been, has he?

GERT. He's been and gone.

JOHN. Were you here?

GERT. I was here part of the time.

JOHN. You ought to have been here all of the time. What did you tell him?

GERT. Emily told him you wished us to stay at home this afternoon.

JOHN. [*Nodding curtly.*] So much for that.

SAM. So even you are not quite without 'em, Jack?

JOHN. Not quite without what?

SAM. Family troubles.

JOHN. What in heaven's name are you driving at?

SAM. Nothing. I only gathered from your tone that Preece was considered—er—dangerous.

JOHN. [*Hedging.*] Oh, no! I'm merely taking precautions. Preece is an excellent fellow in his way—brilliant even.

SAM. But you wouldn't care for him as a son-in-law.

JOHN. [*Positively.*] I should not.

ROSE. [*Shaking her head.*] No!

SAM. I've always understood he had a great career before him.

JOHN. So he has, undoubtedly. You should see what he's got me to do at the works. Made me install the telephone. And his latest is that he wants me to put down an electric light plant. What do you think of that?

SAM. He must be very enthusiastic.

GERT. I should think he just is!

JOHN. Why, the boy's invention mad. He thinks of nothing else.

SAM. Well, if you ask me I'd sooner have that kind of madness than most kinds I meet with. Seems to me people have gone mad on bicycles or banjo-playing or this lawn-tennis, as it's called. It was different in our day, Jack, when young men took an interest in volunteering and the defence of their country. I've quite decided when our boy grows up——

GERT. [*Putting a hand on* SAM's *arm.*] Sam!—Emily may be back any moment. We were talking about Arthur Preece.

SAM. So we were. [*Turns again to* JOHN.] Well, Jack——

JOHN. [*Annoyed.*] Look here, Sam— I don't mind being frank with you. Her mother and I have somebody else in view for Emily.

SAM. Oh!

GERT. [*Bitterly.*] I thought as much.
[*A slight pause.*]

JOHN. [*Carelessly to* SAM.] Have you heard I'm going to have a title?

SAM. No! What title?

JOHN. Baronet.

GERT. [*Quickly.*] You never told me.

ROSE. [*Soothingly.*] It only came out this afternoon, Gertrude dear.

SAM. Oh—ho.

JOHN. [*Still with an affectation of carelessness.*] And what's more, Emily can marry—under the very happiest auspices—into the peerage. That's why we don't want her to see too much of young Preece.

SAM. And may one ask who is the Peer?

JOHN. Monkhurst, of course.

SAM. Ned!

GERT. Ned?

ROSE. Wouldn't it be ideal, Sam!

SAM. He's keen—Ned?

JOHN. Very! Put that in your pipe and smoke it, my boy.

[EMILY *and* NANCY *re-enter rather suddenly. All the others have a self-conscious air.*]

JOHN. [*Rather negligently.*] Well, Nancy. How are you? It seems the infant's grown out of his pram. [*Shakes hands.*]

NANCY. [*Rather proud of being able to call the great man "John" and yet trying not to be proud.*] Glad to see you, John.

[ROSE *and* NANCY *embrace. An awkward pause.*]

EMILY. [*With suspicion.*] What's the matter here? More secrets?

GERT. [*In an outburst.*] It's being arranged that you are to marry Lord Monkhurst.

JOHN. [*Nonplussed, coldly angry.*] Gertrude, are you stark staring mad—blurting things out like that?

ROSE. [*Shocked.*] Gertrude, dear—really!

GERT. [*Firmly.*] She'd better know, hadn't she?

JOHN. You——

NANCY. [*Blandly.*] Well, anyhow, the fat's in the fire now, isn't it, John?

JOHN. [*Turning to* NANCY.] Sorry you've been let in for a bit of a scene, Nancy.

NANCY. [*Cheerfully.*] Oh! Don't mind me. I know what family life is—my word! I'm from York-shire! Best to have it out fair and square—that's my experience.

SAM. That's what she always says when the infant's obstreperous. Why, the night before last, just as we were getting off to sleep——

JOHN. There's nothing to have out!

GERT. Oh, yes, there is. Emily's in love with Arthur Preece.

JOHN. What's this?

EMILY. [*Very nervous; to* GERTRUDE.] What do you mean—it's being arranged for me to marry Lord Monkhurst? Me—marry old Ned!

JOHN. He's not old.

EMILY. Isn't he old enough to be my father?

JOHN. Certainly not.

SAM. [*Mischievously.*] I doubt it.

JOHN. [*Turning on him.*] You're the last man to talk about difference of age between husband and wife.

ROSE. [*Smoothing over the awkwardness.*] But you're very happy, aren't you, dear?

SAM. Naturally.

NANCY. I don't see that age matters—so long as people really fancy each other. I'm sure Sam gets younger every day.

JOHN. Of course! [*Turning to* EMILY *angrily.*] What's this tale about you being in love with Preece?

EMILY. I——

JOHN. Has he been proposing to you?

EMILY. No.

JOHN. [*Disdainfully.*] Then how can you be in love with him?

EMILY. [*Resenting his tone.*] Well, I *am* in love with him, if you want to know, father.

JOHN. You have the audacity——

NANCY. Come, John, it's not a crime.

JOHN. Preece is not of our class at all. It's a gross mistake to marry out of your class.

NANCY. [*Bantering.*] Now, John, that's not very tactful, seeing that Sam married out of *his* class.

SAM. Don't be foolish, Nan! I married a lady. Even a marquis couldn't do more.

JOHN. My dear Nancy, you belong to the family—that's enough! Preece is quite a different affair. Just a common clerk until I——

EMILY. I can't see what more you want. He has the most beautiful manners, and, as for money, he'll make lots.

JOHN. How will he make lots?

EMILY. With his inventions. You haven't heard about his latest. But I have. He's told me. Here it is.

[*Hands piece of steel to her father.*]

JOHN. [*Taking it.*] And what's this?

EMILY. I don't know exactly. But it's very wonderful. It's steel, I think—a new kind.

JOHN. [*Drily.*] Yes. I see it's steel.

EMILY. And I think it's a great shame for you to take nine-tenths of all the money from his inventions, and for him to only have one-tenth.

JOHN. [*Flashing up.*] What? Has he been whining to you in that style?

EMILY. [*Passionately.*] No, he hasn't been whining to me in that style. He hasn't been whining at all. He thought it was quite fair. It only came out by pure accident, and I promised I'd never breathe a word. You must forget what I've said.

JOHN. I'll teach him——

EMILY. [*More passionately.*] If you ever say a single thing, father, I'll run away and never come back.

ROSE. Child! Please!

[*She tries to soothe her.*]

SAM. [*To calm the stress.*] Hand over, Jack. [*Takes the piece of steel and looks at it.*] I fully admit I was wrong about iron. But even *you* won't prophesy that steel's going to take the place of iron for ships!

JOHN. [*Shortly.*] I don't think it is in *my* works. But, as for prophesying—I don't prophesy. Heaven knows no one can accuse me of being conservative in my ideas. But I must say the new generation seems to be going clean off its head. If one of these up-to-date inventors came along and told me he'd made a flying-machine, I should keep my nerve. I shouldn't blench.

SAM. Good! Good!

GERT. Now you're at flying-machines! What have flying-machines got to do with Emily's happiness? If she wants to marry young Preece——

EMILY. Yes, if I want to marry him, why shouldn't I?

ROSE. Because your father objects.

EMILY. Oh, mother. Didn't you marry father, in spite of every one?

JOHN. Who's told you that?

EMILY. I know.

[*General glances at* GERTRUDE.]

ROSE. [*Indignant.*] Do you mean to compare young Preece with your father?

EMILY. Why not? You loved father, and I——

JOHN. I'll tell you why not. I was independent. I was my own master. Young Mr. Preece isn't. That's why.

GERT. [*Sarcastically.*] Surely it's a free country—for men!

JOHN. It's not a country where honest men break their contracts. Young Preece can't patent an invention without me. Can't do anything without me. If I like, I can force him to mark time for five years, five solid years.

EMILY. Does that mean that if I married him in spite of you——

ROSE. [*Horrified.*] Child! Well may you say we've spoilt you!

JOHN. [*Calmly.*] It means that if he had the impudence to marry you, I'd scotch him—*that* I would.

EMILY. But why? Who's going to suffer? How can my marriage affect anybody but me?

JOHN. Don't talk like a little fool. Your marriage is the most important thing in the whole world to your mother and me. And if you persist in doing something against our will, I shall retaliate—that's all.

EMILY. [*With a despairing gesture.*] I can't make out your objections to Mr. Preece. Why, he's a genius; every one *knows* he's a genius.

JOHN. And what if he is? Are geniuses to be the kings of the earth? Not quite! Geniuses have to be kept in order like criminals. If there's one thing above all to be said in favor of the English character, it is that we've known the proper way to treat geniuses.

SAM. I'm inclined to agree with you there.

JOHN. [*To* EMILY.] Oh, it isn't Preece's class I object to. He's presentable enough. The whole truth is he's a highly dangerous sort of young man we're breeding in these days. He—he makes you feel—uncomfortable. On the works, under discipline, admirable. Outside the works—no, no! And no! I've been following Master Preece's activities far more closely than he thinks. He little guesses I know he's a Socialist!

SAM. A Socialist! Good God! Gertrude, you never told me that. A Socialist!

GERT. Why are men always so frightened by names?

JOHN. A Socialist. [*To* EMILY, *an ultimatum.*] And I don't intend you to marry him. If you do, you ruin him. That's the long and short of it. Now, Emily, have we heard the last of Preece—or not?

ROSE. [*To* EMILY.] Darling!

GERT. I really think you ought——

JOHN. [*Curtly.*] Pardon me, Gertrude. This isn't your affair. It's my daughter's.

GERT. [*To* EMILY.] Your father is right. It's your affair. It depends solely on you.

EMILY. [*Weeping imploringly.*] What am I to do, auntie?

> [GERTRUDE *turns away with a movement of pain and disgust.*]

EMILY. I don't want to make everybody miserable.

GERT. [*Reproachfully.*] Oh, Emily!

EMILY. I couldn't stand—in Mr. Preece's light! I couldn't.

JOHN. There! There! Of course you couldn't.

ROSE. [*Comforting her.*] My poor lamb!

JOHN. And don't go and suppose I want to compel you to marry Monkhurst—or anybody. You're absolutely free.

GERT. [*Sniffs audibly.*] H'm!

JOHN. [*Glaring at* GERTRUDE, *to* EMILY.] Only, as your aunt *has* dragged in his name, I don't see any harm in telling you this much. He adores you. We all like him. His wife will have a position second to none in London Society. But don't let that influence you. Take him or refuse him as you please; your mother and I won't complain.

ROSE. Indeed we shan't, my love.

JOHN. Still a marriage like this is not to be sneezed at. Is it, Emily? [*Pause.*] I say, *is* it?

EMILY. [*Trying to smile; weakly.*] No.

JOHN. [*Continuing.*] Not that I think it wouldn't be a big slice of luck for Monkhurst, too! There's only one Emily! [*He pats her.*] And then my title——

NANCY. Your title, John?

JOHN. [*Carelessly.*] Haven't you heard?

NANCY. No!

JOHN. [*As above.*] Baronetcy!

NANCY. [*Staggered.*] Wonders'll never cease. [*To* ROSE.] What a pity you've got no son, dear!

ROSE. [*With a trace of bitterness.*] Don't crow over us, dear!

[*She clasps* EMILY *to her.*]

SAM. [*With a sigh of regret for himself.*] Well, well! And I've retired into private life!

JOHN. [*Surveying him patronizingly.*] And you've retired into private life. You're safe at Brockley. But then you see you hadn't got a bee in your bonnet.

SAM. [*Accepting the sarcasm with a foolish smile.*] Well, well!

NANCY. [*Sharply.*] I don't see that there's any need for so much well-welling.

JOHN. Come and give your father a kiss, Em.

[EMILY *obeys.*]

GERT. [*Rising as she does so, full of emotion.*] I——
[THOMPSON *enters followed by a* FOOTMAN. *They bring in tea.* GERTRUDE *pulls herself together. There is a slight pause while the* SERVANTS *arrange the tea-things. They leave the room.*]

ROSE. Emily, dear, will you pour out?

EMILY. [*Demurely.*] Yes, mother.

ROSE. I hope Ned won't be late.

NANCY. Is Lord Monkhurst coming for tea?

ROSE. He promised to.

NANCY. Oh, dear! If I'd known I was going to meet him— [*She rises and arranges her bustle and the draperies of her skirt.*] I do hope he won't notice that pram. A pram in a hall looks so common.

[*She reseats herself.* THOMPSON *enters.*]

THOMPSON. [*Announcing.*] Lord Monkhurst!

[*He retires.*]

GERT. [*Passionately.*] Here's your lord!

[NED *enters rapidly.*]

NED. Well, kind friends. Hullo, Sam!

SAM. Hullo, Ned! [*They shake hands.*] By the way, my wife—Nancy, Lord Monkhurst.

[NANCY, *flustered, bows.*]

NED. [*Going toward* EMILY.] Delighted! Any of that tea for me?

GERT. [*With great feeling.*] And there's your tea— your daily tea, for the rest of your life.

JOHN. [*Angrily.*] Gertrude!

GERT. No, I will speak! Ned, what would *you* do, if I told you that——

EMILY. [*Pleading.*] Aunt Gertrude, please——

GERT. Emily?

EMILY. [*Weakly.*] It's all right, auntie.

GERT. All right? Oh, very well! [*Desperately.*] What's the use!

[*She turns and walks quickly out of the room.*]

NED. [*Surprised at* GERTRUDE'S *tone.*] What's the matter with dear Gertrude?

JOHN. Nothing. One of her moods. [*Drawing up a chair, with authority.*] Now then, Emily,—tea!

CURTAIN

ACT III

1912

*The same drawing-room, but now in 1912, it has under-
gone an entire change. All of the old mid-Victorian
furniture has been crowded out by furniture of later
style. Changes of ornaments, etc. The lights are
electric; so is the bell by the fireplace.*

*It is a June evening, about half-past ten at night. Signs
of festivity—flowers, presents [in gold] are standing
about. It is the evening of the Golden Wedding of
JOHN and ROSE. [WEBSTER, a smart, military-look-
ing butler of forty, is arranging a tray of whiskey and
soda. The door to the hall opens, and a FOOTMAN
enters.]*

FOOTMAN. [*Announcing.*] Lord Monkhurst.
      [*He withdraws.* LORD MONKHURST *enters.
      He is a young man about town of twenty-two,
      tall, hollow-chested, careless in his manners,
      very self-assured and properly bored.*]

MONK. I say, Webster.

WEBSTER. Good evening, my lord.

MONK. [*Cheerfully.*] I suppose dinner's over?

WEBSTER. [*Looking at his watch.*] It's half-past ten,
my lord.

MONK. Of course, they'll all say I'm late for dinner.

WEBSTER. Oh, no, my lord. Shall I order some
dinner for your lordship?

MONK. No. Who's here now?

WEBSTER. Lady Monkhurst and Miss Muriel; Miss
Rhead, Mrs. Samuel Sibley, and Mr. Richard Sibley.

MONK. Yes. I know *he's* here. Many people at the reception this afternoon?

WEBSTER. Droves, my lord.

MONK. I suppose these ghastly things are the presents?

WEBSTER. As your lordship says.

MONK. Dashed if I can understand why my grandfather should make such a fuss about his golden wedding. [*Very cheerfully.*] Was he very angry at me not turning up?

WEBSTER. Considering his age, no, my lord. I took the liberty of suggesting to him that this might be one of your busy weeks, my lord, and that your lordship could never tell beforehand——

MONK. You're a clever chap, Webster. Why the devil did you leave the army?

WEBSTER. Probably because, as your lordship says, I'm clever. There's more brains outside the army than in it, my lord. And like turns to like.

MONK. [*Laughing in a superior way.*] Ha! ha! Really!

WEBSTER. Fact is, I enlisted under a misapprehension, when I was in a temper. I have to thank your lordship's late father for helping me to re-enter my old profession, and under the most auspicious circumstances.

MONK. Well, we could do with more fellahs like you. I've not yet found any sergeant to draw my sketch maps for me half as well as you used to.

[*He is looking over the tray with drinks.*]

WEBSTER. Ah, my lord! Those half-guineas came in very handy, very handy. Glorious times, no doubt. But I wouldn't go back.

MONK. Bring me a benedictine, will you?

[EMILY, *now* LADY MONKHURST, *forty-eight*,

*enters by the double doors. She has devel-
oped into a handsome, well-preserved woman
of the world. She wears an evening dress of
rich brocade, and magnificent pearls.*]

Monk. Well, mater, I don't see much sign of the fatted calf.

Emily. [*Annoyed.*] Gerald, your poor father was witty; you are merely facetious. I wish you could cure yourself.

Monk. Now, what's the matter now?

Emily. What's the matter? You must needs choose your grandparents' golden wedding to go to Sandown. You promised me you'd be back early, at any rate in time for the tail end of the reception; and you don't even appear for dinner. Your grandfather is very displeased.

Monk. If a fellow keeps a stable, he keeps a stable. Somebody's got to look after the gees in these days. And then——

[*Hesitates.*]

Emily. Please don't tell me your car broke down. I've heard that too often.

Monk. It didn't—this time.

Emily. Have you dined?

Monk. I have.

Emily. Whom with? [*Silence.*] One of your numerous "lady friends," I presume. Gerald, I'm ashamed of you.

Monk. You've no right to be ashamed of me. If you want to know, I dined at the House of Lords.

Emily. At the House of Lords?

Monk. At the House of Lords. They telephoned to me at Sandown to come up for an important division, and I was kept hanging about there till after ten o'clock. Jolly amusing place, the House of Lords.

EMILY. [*Rather taken aback.*] Why didn't you tell me at first?

MONK. Because I just wanted to teach you a lesson, mater. You're always ragging me about something or other.

EMILY. You might at least have telephoned.

MONK. When a chap's doing his duty to his country, he can't always think about telephoning.

EMILY. My dear Gerald, if you mean to follow in your father's footsteps, nobody will be more delighted than your mother. There'd be nothing to prevent you from being Master of the Horse, if you chose. Only, my chick——

MONK. Only your what?

EMILY. You must alter your manner of living.

MONK. My manner of living, my dear mater, is my own affair. [*With meaning.*] If you'd leave me alone, and look after your other "chick" a little bit more——

EMILY. What do you mean? Muriel?

MONK. Precisely. The Honorable Muriel.

EMILY. Why?

MONK. Oh! I know Muriel can do no wrong. Still I spotted her at the top of the stairs just now practically in the arms of the good Richard.

EMILY. Richard!

MONK. [*Intoning.*] And Samuel took to wife Nancy, and begat Richard. And Samuel passed away in the fulness of years and his son Richard reigned in his stead. And Richard looked upon Muriel, and lo! she was beautiful in the eyes of Richard——

EMILY. Hush, Gerald! Aren't you mistaken? I've never seen the slightest thing——

MONK. That shows how blind you are, then! Of course I'm not mistaken.

EMILY. Are you sure?

MONK. Do you take me for a fool, mater?

EMILY. [*Positively.*] Richard, indeed! I shall put a stop to it.

MONK. [*Almost savagely.*] I should jolly well think you would.

> [*Enter* WEBSTER *from the hall with a liqueur on a salver.* MONKHURST *takes it and drinks it slowly.*]

EMILY. Webster, will you kindly ask Miss Muriel to come here?

WEBSTER. Very good, my lady.

> [*He goes out.* MONKHURST *nods knowingly to his mother as if to say, "Now you'll see!"* NANCY *enters by the double doors. She has grown into a rather red-faced, plump, old woman of fifty-eight. She is good-natured, but is quick to retort. Her laugh is rather loud, her manner more definite than ever.*]

NANCY. Good evening, young man.

MONK. Good evening.

NANCY. So you've come at——

EMILY. [*Interrupting her.*] Aunt Nancy, I've just had to send for Muriel to come here.

NANCY. What's amiss?

EMILY. I—well—I hardly like——

MONK. Your excellent son Richard has been seen trying to kiss my sister.

NANCY. What was *she* doing?

EMILY. Well, that's not the point.

NANCY. And supposing he *was* trying to kiss Muriel?

EMILY. I must say, Aunt Nancy, you don't seem very surprised.

NANCY. Who *would* be? You invite young people to a golden wedding, and then you're startled when you catch 'em kissing. What else do you expect?

EMILY. I expect a good deal else.

NANCY. Then you're likely to be disappointed. As a matter of fact, I knew Richard was going to kiss Muriel to-night.

EMILY. Who told you?

NANCY. *He* did, of course. At least, he let out to me he was going to propose to her. He usually gets what he wants, you know.

EMILY. [*Angrily surprised.*] H'm!

MONK. [*Very definitely.*] He won't get what he wants this time.

NANCY. Oh?

MONK. You must see that my sister can't marry an engineer.

NANCY. Well—why not an engineer? What are *you?* I can tell you what you might have been, if you hadn't been born in the right bedroom: you might have been a billiard-marker. What have you done? Tell me a single thing you've done?

MONK. I've—oh! What tripe!

EMILY. Really, Aunt Nancy——

NANCY. Yes, my son *is* an engineer. And if you want to know what sort of an engineer he is, go to Mr. Arthur Preece.

MONK. [*Disdainfully.*] Who's Preece?

NANCY. [*Imitating his tone.*] Ask your mother who *Preece* is.

EMILY. [*Self-consciously.*] Aunt Nancy!

NANCY. [*Continuing.*] You aren't old enough to remember Mr. Preece as an engineer, but, at any rate, you know he's in the House of Commons, whereas you're only in the House of Lords. And I'd like you to tell me where your grandfather'd have been last week with all his workmen on strike—but for Mr. Preece!

MONK. Oh, *that* Preece!

NANCY. Exactly. And it's that Preece that thinks the world of my son. My son's been out to Canada, and look how he got on in Winnipeg! And now he's going out again, whose capital is he taking but your grandfather's? I should like to see your grandfather trust *you* with thirty thousand pounds and a ticket to Canada.

MONK. I'm in no need of capital, thank ye.

NANCY. Lucky for you you aren't! My husband left me very badly off, poor man, but I could count on Richard. A pretty look-out for your mother if she'd had to count on you!

EMILY. [*Impatient.*] Really, Aunt Nancy——

NANCY. [*Nettled.*] Well, you leave my son alone.

> [*Enter from the hall* MURIEL *and* RICHARD. MURIEL *is a handsome girl of twenty-four, rather thin and eager with a high forehead, and with much distinction. She has herself under absolute control.* RICHARD *is a tall, broad, darkish fellow of twenty-seven, with a clean-shaven heavy face and rough hair. He is very taciturn.*]

EMILY. Muriel, it was you that I asked for.

MURIEL. [*Quite calmly.*] We were both just coming to tell you.

EMILY. Tell me what?

MURIEL. We're engaged.

EMILY. Does Richard leave you to say this to me?

MURIEL. Well, you know he was never a great talker.

RICHARD. There it is—we're engaged.

NANCY. [*To* MURIEL.] How matter-of-fact you are, you girls, nowdays.

> [*She caresses* RICHARD.]

MURIEL. Well nobody seems strikingly enthusiastic here.

EMILY. I should think not. I don't like these underhand ways.

MURIEL. What underhand ways? Surely you didn't expect Richard to announce in advance the exact place and hour he was going to propose to me.

EMILY. Please don't try to imitate your dear father. You're worse than Gerald sometimes.

MURIEL. Oh, very well, mama! What else?

EMILY. Do you mean to tell me you're seriously thinking of going out to Canada—to Winnipeg—for the rest of your days?

MURIEL. Of course, mama! I'm sure I shall be happier there than here.

EMILY. You'll leave England?

MURIEL. Certainly. Politics are much more satisfactory over there, except for woman's suffrage. All the questions that all the silly statesmen are still wrangling about here have been settled over there ages ago.

EMILY. My poor girl!

MURIEL. Mama, I wish you wouldn't say "my poor girl."

EMILY. What have politics to do with happiness?

MURIEL. They have a great deal to do with mine. But, of course, what most attracts me is all those thousands of square miles of wheat fields, and Richard making reaping-machines for them. The day I first see one of Richard's new machines at work on a Canadian wheat-farm will be the happiest day of my life—except to-day.

NANCY. [*Amazed at these sentiments.*] Well, you're a caution.

MONK. [*With disgust.*] Why not marry an agricultural implement while you're about it?

RICHARD. [*Threateningly.*] You shut up!

MURIEL. But aren't you glad, mama?

EMILY. I can't discuss the matter now.

MURIEL. But what is there to discuss?

EMILY. [*After a pause.*] Muriel, I tell you at once, both of you, I shan't allow this marriage.

MURIEL. Not allow it? My poor mama!

MONK. Certainly not.

RICHARD. I've told you to shut up once.

EMILY. And your grandfather won't allow it, either.

MURIEL. Of course, mama, you and I have always been devoted to each other. You've made allowances for me, and I've made allowances for you. But you must please remember that we're in the year 1912. I've promised to marry Richard, and I shall marry him. There's no question of being "allowed." And if it comes to that, why shouldn't I marry him, indeed?

EMILY. You—your father's daughter, to think of going out to Winnipeg as the wife of a—your place is in London.

RICHARD. [*Stiffening at the sight of trouble.*] But I say, Cousin Emily——

MURIEL. [*Gently, but firmly.*] Richard,—please. [*Turning to her mother.*] Mama, you really do shock me. Just because I'm the Honorable Muriel Pym! [*Laughs.*] I won't say you're a snob, because everybody's a snob, in some way or other. But you don't understand the new spirit, not in the least—and I'm so sorry. Why! Hasn't it occurred to you even yet that the aristocracy racket's played out?

> [ROSE *and* JOHN *enter by the double doors.*
> *They have both grown very old,* ROSE *being*
> *seventy-three and* JOHN *seventy-seven.* ROSE

has become short-sighted, white-haired, and stoutish. JOHN *has grown a little deaf; his hair is thin, his eyes sunken, his complexion of wax, his features sharply defined.* GERTRUDE *follows them, now seventy-three. She has grown into a thin shrivelled old woman, erect, hard with a high, shrill voice, and keen, clear eyes.*]

ROSE. Oh! It's here they seem to be collected. [*To* MONKHURST.] Is that you, Gerald? Wherever has the poor lamb been?

[*She kisses him.*]

MONK. Grandma, congratulations. [*To* JOHN.] Congratulations, sir.

JOHN. [*Sternly.*] Is this what you call good manners, boy?

MONK. Sorry, sir. I was kept.

JOHN. [*Sarcastically.*] Kept?

MONK. At the House of Lords. A division.

MURIEL. Good Heavens! Break it to us gently. Has his grandma's lamb gone into politics?

MONK. [*Haughtily, ignoring his sister.*] They telephoned me from headquarters. I thought you would prefer me——

JOHN. Certainly, my boy. [*Shakes his hand.*] You couldn't have celebrated our golden wedding in a fashion more agreeable to us than by recording your first vote in the House of Lords. Could he, granny?

ROSE. [*Feebly.*] Bless us! Bless us!

JOHN. What was the division?

MONK. [*Mumbling.*] Er—the Trades Union Bill, sir. Third reading.

JOHN. [*Not hearing.*] What did you say?

MONK. [*Louder.*] Trades Union Bill, sir.

MURIEL. Oh, my poor lamb! The Trades Union Bill division isn't to be taken till to-morrow!

MONK. [*Hastily.*] What am I thinking of? It must have been the Extended Franchise Bill, then. . . . Anyhow, I voted.

JOHN. [*Coughing.*] H'm! H'm!

GERT. [*Drawing a shawl round her shoulders, fretfully.*] Couldn't we have that window closed?

ROSE. Auntie Gertrude, how brave you are! I daren't have asked. I declare I'm a martyr to this ventilation in my old age.

GERT. I daresay I'm very old-fashioned, but when I was young we didn't try to turn a drawing-room into a park.

ROSE. [*To* RICHARD, *as he closes the window.*] Thank you, Richard.

JOHN. [*Pettishly.*] Put a match to the fire, boy, and have done with it.

> [RICHARD *goes to the fireplace, kneels down, and lights the fire.*]

GERT. What's the matter, Emily?

EMILY. [*Who has begun to weep.*] Oh, Auntie Gertrude!

NANCY. [*Soothingly.*] Come, come, Emily.

JOHN. What's that? What's that?

ROSE. [*Peering at* EMILY.] What is it, John?

JOHN. Monkhurst, have you been upsetting your mother again?

MURIEL. I think it's *us,* grandpapa.

JOHN. What does she say?

MURIEL. I'm afraid it's us—Richard and me. We're engaged to be married.

[MURIEL *points to* RICHARD, *who is still on his knees busy with the fire.*]

ROSE. Oh, my dear—how sudden! What a shock! What a shock! I can understand your mother crying. I must cry myself. Come and kiss me! It's astonishing how quietly you young people manage these things nowadays.

[*Embraces* MURIEL.]

JOHN. Who's engaged to be married? Who's engaged to be married?

RICHARD. [*Loudly, rising and dusting his hands.*] Muriel and I, sir.

JOHN. Mu—Mu—! What the devil do you mean, sir? Emily, what in God's name are you thinking of?

EMILY. [*Whimpering.*] It's just as much of a surprise to me as to anybody. I don't approve of it.

MONK. I've told them already you would never approve, sir.

NANCY. You haven't, young man. It was your mother who told us that.

JOHN. [*To* NANCY.] I asked you to my golden wedding, Nancy——

NANCY. You did, Sir John. I shouldn't have come without.

JOHN. Do you countenance this—affair?

NANCY. What's wrong with it?

ROSE. [*Timidly.*] Yes, John. What's wrong with it? Why shouldn't my Muriel marry her Richard?

JOHN. What's wrong with it, d'you say? What——!

EMILY. [*Passionately.*] I won't agree with it.

JOHN. [*To* NANCY.] Nothing wrong with it, from your point of view. Nothing! [*Laughing.*] Only I shan't have it. I won't have it.

ROSE. Grandpa, why do you always try to cross me?

JOHN. I? You?

ROSE. I've been yielding to you in everything for fifty years. I think I'm old enough to have my own way now—just once.

JOHN. [*Startled.*] What's come over you?

ROSE. Nothing's come over me. But I really——

JOHN. [*Subduing her.*] Be silent, granny!

NANCY. We thought you thought very highly of Richard.

JOHN. So I do. But what's that got to do with it? It's nothing but this genius business over again.

NANCY. Genius business?

JOHN. Yes. I shall be told Richard's a genius, therefore he must be allowed to marry Muriel. Nonsense! I had just the same difficulty with her mother twenty-six years ago. You ought to remember; you were there! Hadn't I, Emily?

EMILY, [*Faintly.*] Yes.

JOHN. [*Not hearing.*] What's that?

EMILY. Yes, father. Yes.

JOHN. Of course I had. I wouldn't have it then, and I won't have it now. What? Here's a young fellow, a very smart engineer. Insists on going to Canada. Wants capital! Well, I give it him! I tell him he may go. Everything's settled. And then, if you please, he calmly announces his intention of carrying off my granddaughter —him!

ROSE. If she's your granddaughter, he's my nephew.

JOHN. [*Glaring at her.*] Sh!

ROSE. No! I wo——

JOHN. [*Continuing, staring at* ROSE.] My granddaughter has got to marry something very different from an engineer.

NANCY. If she did she might marry something that'll turn her hair gray a good deal sooner.

JOHN. I have my plans for Muriel.

EMILY. Imagine Muriel in Winnipeg!

MURIEL. What plans, granddad? You've never told me about any plans.

JOHN. Not told you! At your age, your mother had a conspicuous place in London society. And it's your duty to carry on the family tradition. Your mother didn't marry into the peerage so that you could gallivant up and down Winnipeg as the wife of a manufacturing engineer. You have some notion of politics, though it's a mighty queer one——

MURIEL. I hardly think my politics would further your plan, granddad. I should have supposed the whole of my career would have made it plain that I have the greatest contempt for official politics.

JOHN. Your "career"! Your "contempt"! [*Laughs good-humoredly, then more softly.*] My child——

MURIEL. [*Nettled.*] I'm not a child.

JOHN. [*Angrily.*] Enough! Don't make yourself ridiculous. [*More quietly.*] Your mother and your brother think as I do. Let that suffice.

RICHARD. Pardon me, sir, but suppose it won't suffice?

JOHN. [*Furious.*] I—I——

MURIEL. [*Violently.*] Granddad, do please keep calm.

JOHN. [*As above.*] I'm perfectly calm, I believe.

NANCY. [*To* GERTRUDE.] Then he'd believe anything!

MURIEL. You don't seem to have understood that we're engaged to be married.

GERT. I must say——

JOHN. And what must *you* say? You'll side with my wife against me, and the girl's own mother, I suppose?

GERT. I fail to see any objection whatever.

JOHN. Do you, indeed! Well, objection or no objection, I mean it to be stopped—now, at once.

MURIEL. But how shall you stop it, granddad?

JOHN. If I hear one more word of this, one more word—there'll be no thirty thousand pounds for Richard. Not from me, at any rate. And I don't imagine that your mother will help him, or Monkhurst either. Where is he?

MONK. Not much.

MURIEL. But that won't stop it, granddad!

ROSE. [*Rising, and going to the hall door.*] John, you're a hard, hard old man. The one thing I ask of you, and on our golden wedding day, too, and you won't even listen. You shut me up as though I were a—a— I do think it's a shame. The poor things.

[*She goes out in tears.*]

NANCY. [*Hurrying out after her.*] Rose! Rose! Don't!

JOHN. Here I arrange a nice little family dinner to celebrate the occasion. I invite no outsiders, so that we shall be nice and homely and comfortable. And this is how you treat me. You induce your grandmother to defy me—the first time in her life. You bring your mother to tears, and you——

EMILY. There's nothing to be said in favor of it—nothing. The very thought of it——

RICHARD. I'm awfully sorry.

JOHN. No, you aren't, sir. So don't be impudent.

[WEBSTER *enters.*]

WEBSTER. Mr. Arthur Preece, Sir John. I've shown him into the study.

JOHN. Very good.

[WEBSTER *goes out.*]

GERT. Why can't Mr. Preece come up here?

JOHN. Because he's come to see me on private business, madam. Private, do I say? It's public enough. Everybody knows that I can't keep my own workmen in order without the help of a Labor M.P. The country's going to the dogs! My own father used to say so, and I never believed him. But it's true.

[*He goes to the door.*]

MONK. May I come with you, sir? [*With a superior glance at* MURIEL.] These family ructions——

JOHN. Come!

[JOHN *goes off, followed by* MONKHURST.]

GERT. [*Meaningly.*] Richard, go and see where your mother is, will you?

[RICHARD *follows the others. A slight pause.*]

EMILY. [*Still weakly and tearfully.*] How your poor grandmother is upset!

MURIEL. Yes, I'm very sorry.

EMILY. That's something.

MURIEL. It's such a humiliating sight. No real arguments. No attempt to understand *my* point of view! Nothing but blustering and bullying and stamping up and down. He wants to make out that I'm still a child with no will of my own. But it's he who's the child.

GERT. Come, come, Muriel.

MURIEL. Yes, it is. A spoilt child! When anything happens that doesn't just please him, there's a fine exhibition of temper. Don't we all know it. And this is the great Sir John Rhead! Bah!

EMILY. [*Amazed.*] Muriel!

MURIEL. Oh, of course it isn't his fault! Every one's always given him his own way—especially grandma. It's positively pathetic; grandma trying to turn against him now. Poor old thing! As if she could! Now!

EMILY. Muriel, your cold-bloodedness absolutely frightens me.

MURIEL. But, mother, I'm not cold-blooded. It's only common-sense.

GERT. [*Clumsily caressing* EMILY.] Darling!

EMILY. Common-sense will be the finish of me; I've no one left in the world now.

GERT. [*Hurt.*] Then I suppose I'm too old to count. And yet for nearly fifty years I've lived for nobody but you. Many and many a time I should have been ready to die—yes, glad to—only you were there.

EMILY. [*Affectionately.*] And yet you're against me now.

GERT. I only want you not to have any regrets.

EMILY. Any regrets! My life has been all regrets. Look at me.

GERT. Not all your life, dear—your marriage.

[MURIEL *looks up.*]

EMILY. [*Firmly, and yet frightened, with a look at* MURIEL.] Hush, auntie!

GERT. Why? Why should I hush? You say your life's been all regrets. If you care about being honest with Muriel, you ought to tell her now that you did not marry the man you were in love with.

EMILY. [*In an outburst.*] Don't believe it, Muriel. No one could have been a kinder husband than your father was, and I always loved him.

MURIEL. [*Intimidated by these revelations of feelings.*] Mother!

GERT. Then what do you regret? You had an affection for Ned, but if you had loved him as you loved—the other one—what is there to regret? And now you seem

to be doing your best to make regrets for Muriel—and—
and—oh, Emily, why do you do it?

MURIEL. [*Moved, but controlling herself.*] Yes,
mama! Why? I'm sure I'm open to hear reason on any
subject—even marriage.

EMILY. [*Blackly.*] Reason! Reason! There you
are again! My child, you're my oldest, and I've loved
you beyond everybody. You've never been attached to
me. It isn't your fault, and I don't blame you. Things
happen to be like that, that's all. You don't know how
hard you are. If you did, you'd be ready to bite your
tongue off. Here I am, with you and Gerald. Gerald
is not bad at heart, but he's selfish and he's a fool. I
could never talk freely to him, as I do to you. One day
he'll be asking me to leave Berkeley Square, and I shall
go and finish my days in the country. And here you
calmly announce you're off to Canada, and you want my
reasons for objecting! There's only one reason—all the
others are nothing—mere excuses—and you couldn't
guess that one reason. You have to be told. If you cared
for me, you wouldn't force me to the shame of telling you.

MURIEL. [*Whispering.*] Shame?

EMILY. Isn't it humiliating for a mother to have to
tell her daughter, who never's even thought of it, that
she cannot bear to lose her,—cannot bear?—Canada!

MURIEL. [*Throwing herself at her mother's knees.*]
Mother, I'll never leave you!

[*She sobs, burying her face in her mother's lap.*]

GERT. [*Softly.*] All this self-sacrifice is a sad mistake. [*To* MURIEL.] None of us can live for ever.
When your mother is gone—what will you do then?

MURIEL. [*Climbing up and kissing her mother.*] I'll
never leave you!

EMILY. My child!

GERT. [*Gently.*] It's wrong of you Emily! All wrong!

> [ARTHUR PREECE *enters from the hall. His hair and moustache have grown gray. His expression and manner slightly disillusioned and cynical. In figure he is the same.*]

PREECE. Good evening.

MURIEL. [*On seeing him, rises quickly rather like a school-girl.*] Good evening.

> [*She goes out rapidly.* PREECE *looks after her a little surprised.*]

EMILY. [*At once the woman of the world.*] Good evening. You've soon finished your business with father.

PREECE. [*Puzzled by the appearance of things.*] Good evening. [*He shakes hands with* EMILY.] What is the matter? The old gentleman really wasn't equal to seeing me. I just told him what I had to tell him about the strikers, and then he said I'd perhaps better come up here. I think he wanted to be alone.

EMILY. Poor dear!

PREECE. Nothing serious, I hope?

GERT. [*Briskly, shaking* PREECE *by the hand.*] The usual thing, Mr. Preece, the usual thing! A new generation has got to the marrying age. You know what it is. I know what it is. Now, Emily, don't begin to cry again. People who behave as selfishly as you're doing have no right to weep—except for their sins.

EMILY. [*Protesting.*] Auntie, this can't possibly interest Mr. Preece.

GERT. [*Still more briskly.*] Don't talk that kind of conventional nonsense, Emily! You know quite well it *will* interest Mr. Preece extremely. [*Rising.*] Now just tell him all about it and see what he says. [*With a peculiar tone.*] I suppose you'll admit he ought to be a good judge of such matters?

[*She moves to the door.*]

EMILY. Where are you going?

GERT. [*Imitating* EMILY *slightly.*] That can't possibly interest you. [*Wearily.*] I'm out of patience.

[*She goes out of the room.*]

EMILY. [*Trying to force a light tone.*] I hope you had some good news about the workmen for my poor old father. What a finish for his golden wedding day!

PREECE. [*Following her lead.*] Yes, I think his little affair's pretty well fixed up—anyhow for the present. He's shown himself pretty reasonable. If he'd continued to be as obstinate as he was at the start, the thing would have run him into a lot of money.

EMILY. I wonder he doesn't retire.

PREECE. He's going to. There's to be a Limited Company.

EMILY. Father—a Limited Company! He told you?

PREECE. Yes.

EMILY. Then he must have been feeling it's getting too much for him.

PREECE. Well, considering his years—seventy-seven, isn't it? Some of us will be beaten long before that age.

[*He sighs.*]

EMILY. Why that sigh? You aren't getting ready to give up, are you?

PREECE. No, I expect I shall go on till I drop.

EMILY. I should have thought you had every reason to be satisfied with what you have done.

PREECE. Why?

EMILY. Unless you regret giving up steel for politics.

PREECE. No. I don't regret that. I'd done all I really wanted to do there. I'd forced your father to take

up steel on a big scale. I'd made more than all the money
I needed. And other processes were coming along, better
than mine.

EMILY. I wonder how many men there are who've
succeeded as you have done, both in politics and out of
politics.

PREECE. Do you think I've succeeded in politics?

EMILY. You haven't held office, but I've always
understood it was because you preferred to be independent.

PREECE. It was. I could have sold my soul over and
over again for a seat at an Under-Secretary's desk. I
wouldn't even lead the Labor Party.

EMILY. But every one knows you're the strongest
man in the Labor Party.

PREECE. Well, if I am—the strongest man in the
Labor Party is rather depressed.

EMILY. Why?

PREECE. Difficult to say. Twenty years ago, I thought
the millennium would be just about established n 1912.
Instead of that, it's as far off as ever. It's even further
off.

EMILY. Further off?

PREECE. Yes. And yet a lot of us have worked. By
God, we have! But there's a different spirit now. The
men are bitter. They can't lead themselves and they won't
be led. And nobody knows what's going to happen next.
Except that trouble's going to happen. I often wonder
why I was cursed with the reforming spirit. How much
happier I should have been if I'd cared for nothing in this
world but my own work—like young Richard Sibley, for
instance.

EMILY. Isn't he interested in reform?

PREECE. Not he! He's an engineer, only an engineer.

He minds his own business. I suppose he's here to-night.

EMILY. Yes.

PREECE. [*In an ordinary tone.*] Why won't you let him marry Miss Muriel?

EMILY. [*Startled.*] Then father's told you?

PREECE. Not a word. But Richard and I are great pals. He's told me his plans. Why shouldn't they marry?

EMILY. [*Weakly.*] Muriel won't go to Canada.

PREECE. Won't go to Canada? But I understand she had a tremendous notion of Canada.

EMILY. She's promised me she won't go.

PREECE. But why should she do that?

EMILY. [*Half breaking down.*] Oh, I know I'm selfish. But—but—I should be quite alone, if she went. And then, it's not what we'd anticipated for her. We naturally hoped——

PREECE. Oh! Of course, if you're in the marriage market——

EMILY. No. Really it's not that—at least as far as I'm concerned. I should be so utterly alone. And she's promised me. If she deserted me——

PREECE. Deserted—rather a strong word——

EMILY. Please don't be hard! You don't know how unhappy I am. You admit you're discouraged.

PREECE. I said "depressed."

EMILY. Well, depressed, then. Can't you feel for others?

PREECE. [*Rather roughly.*] And who made me admit it? Who kept questioning me and worming it out of me? You wouldn't leave it alone. You're like all the other women—and I've had to do with a few.

EMILY. [*Affronted.*] Please——

PREECE. It isn't sufficient for you to make a man unhappy. You aren't satisfied till he admits you've made him unhappy.

EMILY. [*Protesting.*] Oh!

PREECE. How many times have I seen you since this cursed strike brought me among the family again? Half-a-dozen, perhaps. And every single time I've noticed you feeling your way toward it. And to-night you've just got there.

EMILY. Arthur, you must forgive me. It's quite true. We can't help it.

PREECE. What should I care about lost millenniums and labor troubles ahead, if I'd any genuine personal interest in my own? Not a jot. Not a tinker's curse! Do you remember you let me kiss you—once?

EMILY. Forgive me! I know I oughtn't to be forgiven. But life's so difficult. Ever since I've been seeing you again I've realized how miserable I am—it's such a long time since. It seems as it was some other girl and not me—twenty-six years ago—here! And yet it's like yesterday.

> [*She sobs.* PREECE *embraces her first roughly and then very tenderly.*]

PREECE. My child!

EMILY. I'm an old woman.

PREECE. You said it was like yesterday—when you were twenty-three—so it is.

> [*They kiss again.*]

EMILY. [*With a little laugh.*] This will kill father.

PREECE. Not it. Your father has a remarkable constitution. It's much more likely to kill the Labor Party.

> [JOHN *enters, agitated and weary.*]

JOHN. [*Brusquely.*] Where's your mother? She's

not in the other room. I thought she was in here. I want to see her.

EMILY. She's probably gone to her own room—poor dear!

JOHN. Can't you go and find her?
[*He sits down, discouraged.*]

EMILY. [*Coming over to him.*] Father, I've been thinking it over, and I'm afraid we shall have to agree to Muriel's marriage.

JOHN. We shall have to agree to it? I shan't agree to it.

EMILY. As Mr. Preece says——

JOHN. Mr. Preece?

EMILY. You know how friendly he is to Richard—as Mr. Preece says, why shouldn't they marry?

PREECE. I merely ventured to put the question, Sir John.

JOHN. Why shouldn't they? Because they shouldn't. Isn't that enough? [*To* EMILY.] A quarter of an hour ago you yourself agreed in the most positive way that there was nothing whatever to be said in favor of such a match.

EMILY. I was rather overlooking the fact that they're in love with each other [*Glancing at* PREECE] a quarter of an hour ago.

JOHN. Are all you women gone mad to-night? Preece, do you reckon *you* understand women?

PREECE. Now and then one gets a glimpse, sir.

JOHN. [*Realizing state of affairs between* PREECE *and* EMILY.] H'm!

EMILY. [*Noticing her father watch her, rather self-consciously.*] After all, what difference can it make to us? We shan't be here as long as they will.

JOHN. What? What?

EMILY. [*Louder.*] We shan't be here as long as they will, I say.

JOHN. That's it! Tell me I'm an old man! Of course, it can't make any difference to us. I was looking at the matter solely from their point of view. How can it affect me—*whom* Muriel marries?

EMILY. Well, then! Let them judge for themselves. You agree? [JOHN *stares before him obstinately.*] Father— [JOHN *shakes his head impatiently.*] Dad!

JOHN. [*Looking up like a sulky child.*] Oh, have it your own way. I'm not the girl's mother. If you've made up your mind, there's nothing more to be said.

EMILY. And Richard's capital?

JOHN. Oh, it's all lying ready. [*Shrugs his shoulders.*] May as well have it, I suppose.

EMILY. You're a dear!

JOHN. I'm not a dear, and I hate to be called a dear.

EMILY. What a shocking untruth! I shall go and tell them, I think.

[*She goes to the door.*]

JOHN. [*Calling her back.*] Emily!

EMILY. Yes.

JOHN. Don't let them come in here. I couldn't bear it.

EMILY. Oh, but——

JOHN. I couldn't stand the strain of another scene. It's late now—I'm an old man, and people have no right to upset me in this way.

EMILY. Couldn't they just say good-night?

JOHN. Very well. They must say good-night and go at once. Another day——

EMILY. [*Very soothingly.*] I'll tell them you're very tired.

[*She nods smilingly at her father and leaves the room. A slight pause.*]

PREECE. A difficult job, being the head of a family.

JOHN. I've done with it, Preece. I've decided that to-night—that's what a golden wedding comes to in these days. Things aren't what they were. In my time a man was at any rate master in his own house and on his own works. Seemed natural enough! But you've changed all that.

PREECE. I've changed it?

JOHN. [*Continuing confidentially.*] Why, even my own wife's gone against me to-night. My own wife! [*Troubled.*] Did you ever hear of such a thing?

PREECE. I *have* heard of it, Sir John.

JOHN. [*Grimly.*] You laugh. Wait till you're married.

PREECE. I may have to wait a long time.

JOHN. Eh, what? A long time? Don't try to hoodwink me, Preece. I know what you all say when I'm not there. "Old Rhead." "Be breaking up soon, the old man!" But I'm not yet quite doddering. [*Pointedly.*] You'll be married inside six months—and every newspaper in London will be full of it. Yes, answer that. My workmen go out on strike, and you poke your nose in and arrange it for me. Then my family go out on strike, and upon my soul, you poke your damned nose in there, too, and arrange that for me—on your own terms. Tut—tut! Shake hands, man! You and your like are running the world to the devil, and I'm too old to step in and knock you down. But—but—I wish you luck, my lad. You're a good sort.

[*They shake hands.* EMILY, NANCY, MURIEL, RICHARD, *and* GERTRUDE *all enter from the hall.*]

PREECE. Well, good-night, Sir John.

EMILY. [*Cheerfully.*] We're just coming to say good-night, grandpapa. I'm sure you must be very tired. We've said good-night to granny.

JOHN. [*Feebly.*] Where is she? Where is granny?

NANCY. [*Heartily shaking hands.*] Good-night, John, and thank you for a very pleasant time.

> [*She goes to* GERTRUDE, *who now stands near the door, and kisses her good-night.*]

RICHARD. [*Heartily shaking hands.*] Thank you, sir.

> [NANCY *passes out by the door.* GERTRUDE *now shakes hands with* RICHARD, *who follows his mother.*]

EMILY. [*Kisses* JOHN.] Good-night, dear.

> [JOHN, *turning from* EMILY, *moves with a generous gesture to* MURIEL, *who, however, keeps a very stiff demeanor and shakes hands in cold silence.* EMILY *has reached* GERTRUDE. *They both watch* MURIEL.]

EMILY. [*With a shade of disappointment turns to* GERTRUDE.] Good-night, auntie.

> [GERTRUDE *and* EMILY *embrace, then* EMILY *passes quickly out of the door.*]

JOHN. [*Stiffly, looking about.*] Where's Monkhurst?

GERT. Oh, he is gone! He said he had an appointment at the Club.

JOHN. What Club? The Carlton?

MURIEL. [*Shaking hands with* GERTRUDE.] The Automobile, you may depend.

> [*She goes off by the door quickly.*]

GERT. Well, this day is over.

> [WEBSTER *enters from the hall.*]

WEBSTER. Any orders, Sir John?

JOHN. None.

GERT.   Can't we have some of the blaze of electricity turned off?

JOHN.   As you like.

> [WEBSTER *extinguishes several clusters with the switches at the door, then goes out. The room is left in a discreet light.*]

JOHN.   [*Almost plaintively.*]   Where's Rose?

> [ROSE *enters timidly from the hall.*]

GERT.   Here she is.

ROSE.   [*Going up to* JOHN.]   John, forgive me for having dared to differ from my dear husband.

JOHN.   [*Taking her hand softly.*]   Old girl—[*then half humorously shaking his head*]—you'll be the death of me, if you do it again.

GERT.   I think I'm going to bed.

JOHN.   No, not yet.

ROSE.   Gertrude, will you do me a favor, on my golden wedding-day?

GERT.   What is it?

ROSE.   Sing for us.

GERT.   Oh! My singing days are over long ago.

JOHN.   [*Persuasively.*]   Go on—go on.   There's nobody but us to hear.

GERT.   Really it is—   [*Stops.*]   Very well.

> [GERTRUDE *goes through the double doors.* ROSE *draws her lace shawl round her.*]

JOHN.   Let's sit by the fire if you're cold.

> [*He moves a chair in place for her gallantly.* ROSE *sits to the left of the fire.* JOHN *takes a seat to the right of the fire. The song "Juanita" is heard in a cracked and ancient voice, very gently and faintly.*]

ROSE.   [*Softly, by the fire.*]   When I think of all this room has seen——

JOHN. [*Looking into the fire.*] Ah!

ROSE. I'm sure it's very pleasant to remember.

JOHN. Ah! That's because you're pleasant. I've said it before, and I say it again. The women of to-day aren't what women used to be. They're hard. They've none of the old charms. Unsexed—that's what they are —unsexed.

> [MURIEL *enters quickly from the hall in a rich white cloak. She pauses smiling, then hurries delicately across to her grandfather and embraces him; releases him, shyly takes a flower from her bosom, drops it into his hand, turns and gives her grandmother a smile, whispering "Good-night. They're waiting for me," and hurries out again.*]

JOHN. [*Looking at the flower.*] We live and learn.

ROSE. [*Nodding her head.*] Yes, John.

> [*The song continues.*]

CURTAIN

MERTON OF THE MOVIES

IN FOUR ACTS

A DRAMATIZATION OF HARRY LEON WILSON'S STORY OF THE SAME NAME

BY

GEORGE S. KAUFMAN

AND

MARC CONNELLY

CAUTION

George S. Kaufman was born in Pittsburgh, Pa., November 16, 1889. Most of his life has been spent in newspaper work. At the present time he is on the staff of the *New York Times* in the dramatic department. In collaboration with Mr. Marc Connelly he produced the play *Dulcy* (Putnam, 1921), which has proved immensely popular. *The Deep Tangled Wildwood, To the Ladies* (French, 1923), and two musical productions—*Helen, of Troy, N. Y.,* and *Be Yourself*—were likewise produced in collaboration. *Merton of the Movies,* dramatized by Mr. Kaufman and Mr. Connelly from Harry Leon Wilson's popular novel, appeared on the stage in 1922 with Glenn Hunter, the accomplished actor, in the title rôle. In 1924, they produced the very remarkable play *Beggar on Horseback* (Liveright, 1924). Mr. Kaufman collaborated with Edna Ferber in 1924 in making a stage version of her short story, "Old Man Minick," under the title of *Minick*. A popular play of his, produced alone, has been *The Butter and Egg Man*. He has also written the musical piece, *The Cocoanuts,* to tunes by Irving Berlin.

Marc Connelly, the other member of this talented team, was born in McKeesport, Pa., December 13, 1890. Like Mr. Kaufman he has spent most of his life in newspaper work, first in Pittsburgh and later in New York City. *The Wisdom Tooth,* a popular success, is his first independent play.

PRODUCED AT THE CORT THEATRE, NEW
YORK, NOVEMBER 13, 1922

BY GEORGE C. TYLER AND HUGH FORD, WITH THE FOL-
LOWING CAST:

MERTON GILL.............. GLENN HUNTER
AMOS G. GASHWILER......... EDWARD M. FAVOR
ELMER HUFF................ BERT MELVILLE
TESSIE KEARNS............. ESTHER PINCH
THE CASTING DIRECTOR...... LUCILLE WEBSTER
J. LESTER MONTAGUE......... J. K. MURRAY
SIGMUND ROSENBLATT........ EDWIN MAXWELL
WELLER.................... TOM HADAWAY
J. SLOANE HENSHAW......... ROMAINE CALLENDAR
HIS CAMERAMAN............ ALBERT COWLES
THE MONTAGUE GIRL........ FLORENCE NASH
HAROLD PARMALEE........... ALEXANDER CLARK, JR.
BEULAH BAXTER............. GLADYS FELDMAN
MURIEL MERCER............. MARY FORBES
A VIOLINIST................ MAX SAUL
JEFF BAIRD................. JOHN WEBSTER
JIMMY .... BILLY JANNEY
THE CROSS-EYED MAN........ BERT MELVILLE
MRS. PATTERSON............ CLARA SIDNEY
MR. PATTERSON............. ALBERT COWLES
MR. WALBERG............... EDWIN MAXWELL
A MYSTERIOUS VISITOR....... LYNN PRATT
CAMERAMEN, FOOTMEN, EXTRAS, MUSICIANS, COWBOYS,
SHEIKS, MAIDS, *and the various hangers-on of the
Movies.*

SYNOPSIS OF SCENES

Act I: Gashwiler's General Store, Simsbury, Illinois.   A Saturday Night.

Act II: Outside the Holden Lot, Hollywood. A month later.

Act III: On the Lot.
 Scene I: Stage No. 6.   The following day.
 Scene II: Elsewhere on the lot.   A week later.

Act IV:
 Scene I: Jeff Baird's Office.   A few weeks later.
 Scene II: Merton's Rooming House.   Three months later.

MERTON OF THE MOVIES

ACT I

*The scene is Gashwiler's general store in Simsbury,
Illinois—ten o'clock on a Saturday night. At one
side is the outside door, with a reverse glimpse of the
plate-glass window and its usual display; somewhere at the rear, behind the counter, is a door that
evidently leads to living quarters on the floors above.
There is still another door leading to the back rooms
of the store. Presumably a country store calls for
no description—you have but to imagine the usual
counter, and above and below and upon it the endless rows of all kinds of vendible products, as well
as the inevitable advertising-signs calling attention
to the merit of this particular brand of ham, of that
especial variety of soap.*

When the curtain rises GASHWILER *himself is back of the
counter. Through the street door comes* ELMER
HUFF, *a youth of the village.*

GASHWILER. [*None too pleased to see him.*] How
are you, Elmer?

ELMER. [*Not meeting* GASHWILER's *eye.*] I'm—all
right, I guess. [*A pause.*] How are you, Mr. Gashwiler?

GASHWILER. I don't change much.

ELMER. [*Agreeing with him a little too enthusiastically.*] That's right. [*An awkward pause.*] It's getting—late, isn't it?

GASHWILER.   M'm.

ELMER.   Guess you'll be closing up pretty soon.

GASHWILER.   M'm.   [*Puts the ledger away—a pause.*]
There's still time, though, Elmer, if you want to buy
something.

ELMER.   Huh? Oh, no, thanks. I wasn't thinking of
that.   [*Another awkward pause.*] Is—ah—is Mrs.
Gashwiler all right?

   [*Takes hat off.*]

GASHWILER.   I suppose you want to see Merton?

ELMER.   Well, as long as I'm here, I did think I'd
drop in on him.

GASHWILER.   [*Comes from back of counter to* ELMER
—seriously.]   Elmer?

ELMER.   Yes, sir.

GASHWILER.   I—I don't want you to get Merton in no
bad habits.

ELMER.   Me?

GASHWILER.   Now hold on. I don't mean this personal—exactly—but Merton's different from most of you
boys. He's—funny, sort of. But he's got the makings
of a fine boy, and I don't want to see him get started
wrong.

ELMER.   I'm not going to do anything to him.

GASHWILER.   You see, it ain't as though he had any
parents—I been sort of looking after him ever since he
came to work here.   [*A look off, presumably in the general direction of* MERTON.] Besides, if he goes out
nights, he ain't no good in the store mornings.

ELMER.   But honest, Mr. Gashwiler, I'm only going
to talk to him.

GASHWILER.   I wish I knew what you and him talk
about all the time. Merton's been awful dreamy lately—
can't keep his mind on things a bit.

ELMER. It ain't me, Mr. Gashwiler. I can't get him to come out with us or nothing.

GASHWILER. Oh, then you do try?

ELMER. [*Trapped.*] Well—well, anyhow, he won't.

GASHWILER. You're telling me the truth, Elmer?

ELMER. [*Turns to* GASHWILER.] Yes, sir. Why, he hasn't even played poker with us for months. He doesn't go anywhere— [*He remembers that this is not strictly true.*] —except——

[*He stops, rather abruptly.*]

GASHWILER. [*Slowly.*] Yes. I know what you're going to say. [*He looks off, then turns back again.*] Moving-pictures.

ELMER. Yes, sir. That's all he'll talk about to anybody.

GASHWILER. I hope they ain't going to his head. Merton's an awful sensitive boy.

ELMER. Just the same, he goes to them all the time, Mr. Gashwiler, and I think you ought to know it. Why, he—he imitates the people in 'em, too.

GASHWILER. I don't know what he's coming to. [*He looks around to see if* MERTON *is coming; then brings up a magazine from under the counter.*] I—I found this underneath the counter a while ago. Know what it is?

ELMER. [*Reading the title.*] *Cameraland.* It's a moving-picture magazine.

GASHWILER. Yes, I know it is. [*He turns a few pages, idly.*] Even got magazines about 'em. Got a lot of pictures in it of bungalows and—Japanese hired help. I hope Merton don't get all worked up by it.

[*Puts it away.*]

ELMER. Charley Harper seen him down in Ford's meadow at five o'clock yesterday morning. He had your horse there.

GASHWILER. My Dexter?

ELMER. Yes, sir.

GASHWILER. Are you sure?

ELMER. Pretty sure. Lem Hardy was there with his picture camera, and Merton had his arm around the horse's neck one time, and was talking to it.

GASHWILER. Did Charley hear what he said?

ELMER. He wasn't close enough. At first he didn't know what to make of it, and then he remembered there'd been a William S. Hart picture at the Bijou Palace the night before.

GASHWILER. You mean—Merton was imitating him?

ELMER. That's what.

GASHWILER. You think—he might want to be a picture actor?

ELMER. It certainly looks like it.

> [GASHWILER *hesitates a second and then goes determinedly to the rear entrance.*]

GASHWILER. Merton! [*Pause.*] Merton!

MERTON. [*Off.*] Yes, sir.

GASHWILER. Leave off whatever you're doing and look here a minute.

MERTON. [*Off.*] Yes, sir. [*He enters—a diffident youth of about twenty.*] Oh, hello, Elmer.

ELMER. [*Uneasily.*] 'Lo, Merton.

MERTON. [*To* GASHWILER.] It's—ten o'clock.

GASHWILER. You can close up in a minute. First I want to ask you a question.

MERTON. Yes, sir.

GASHWILER. Was it you down in the meadow—yesterday morning?

MERTON. [*With a quick glance at* ELMER.] Yes, sir.

GASHWILER. With—the horse, again?

MERTON. Yes, sir.

GASHWILER. You couldn't have been hitching him up
—before six—could you?

MERTON. No, sir. I just—wanted to see if he was all
right.

GASHWILER. I don't know as I understand you lately,
Merton.

MERTON. I'm—just the same.

GASHWILER. No, you ain't—you're different. [*A
pause.*] And I know what it is.

MERTON. It's not anything.

GASHWILER. Yes, it is. It's moving-pictures. You
just keep on working steady and you'll get there much
faster than if you was always running out to picture
shows.

MERTON. Yes, sir.

GASHWILER. Here! Here's your money.

[*Handing him three five-dollar bills.*]

MERTON. Thank you.

GASHWILER. Hope you're saving it.

MERTON. Well, I can't save the whole fifteen, each
week.

GASHWILER. If you wasn't so flighty, I'd say you had
the makin's of a wealthy man.

MERTON. I don't think I'm flighty.

GASHWILER. Well, you seem to moon around a lot.
You're not going out, are you?

MERTON. No, sir.

GASHWILER. That's good. [*There is a knock on the
ceiling.*] There's mother tapping for me. Oh—when
you lock up, don't forget to bring them new dummies
back here. I don't want no sunlight to get on them and
ruin 'em to-morrow.

MERTON. Yes, sir.

GASHWILER. Well, I'm going to bed. Good night.

MERTON. Good night!

GASHWILER. [*Looks up at a small window high at one side.*] Don't forget to lock that window.

MERTON. No, sir.

GASHWILER. And don't waste them lamps.

MERTON. [*After a look that should wither.*] No, sir.

[GASHWILER *goes.* MERTON *turns to* ELMER.] Where were you—at the pictures?

ELMER. Me? No. [MERTON *turns away.*] How soon'll you be through?

MERTON. I'm through now except for putting things away.

[*Starts to cover the counters.*]

ELMER. How about a little session with My Lady Luck?

MERTON. No. I can't.

ELMER. Oh, why can't you? Gee whiz, that's the third time this month you've stayed away. [*Pauses.*] What's the matter, Merton? Are you sore at anybody?

MERTON. No!

ELMER. [*Laughs.*] I thought maybe it was because Dan Turner kidded you about buying that cowboy outfit.

MERTON. Nobody got me sore about anything. [*He looks at* ELMER.] That's right, Elmer. I'm not sore.

ELMER. Then what's the reason you don't meet up with the crowd any more? I'd think you'd want some relaxation.

MERTON. Well, I'll put it frankly to you, Elmer. I can't afford to run around with the crowd. I've got other interests.

ELMER. What other interests?

MERTON. Well, I have them . . . that's all.

ELMER. [*Nearer to* MERTON.] You're not in love with some girl?

MERTON. [*With a bit of disgust.*]   Is that what they think?

ELMER.   No, but—[*Confidentially.*]   Is that it, Merton?   Are you in love with some girl?

MERTON.   Why, how rid— [*He is about to say "ridiculous" when a realization of the truth makes him change his statement.*]   Well, maybe I am, in a way.

ELMER.   Who is she?

MERTON. [*Dramatizing it.*]   I don't think you have the honor of her acquaintance, Elmer.

ELMER. [*Concerned only in the news.*]   Where does she live?

MERTON.   In a place far away.

ELMER. [*Laughs.*]   Where did you ever meet anybody in a place far away?   You've never been anywheres —except like when you went to Peoria last month.

[MERTON *gives him a quick look.*]

MERTON.   She could be a visitor here in Simsbury, couldn't she?

ELMER. [*Giving it quite a lot of thought.*]   No, she couldn't!   I've seen everybody that ever visited here. [*Suddenly.*]   It ain't that girl that come over from Masonville to help at the restaurant?   She's terrible. Why, she's——

MERTON. [*Stopping him with a gesture.*]   That isn't the person.   Really, you don't know her.   And as for this lady being a mere restaurant girl—why, she's on a mountain peak!

ELMER. [*Affected by MERTON's air.*]   Oh, boy!

MERTON. [*Reprovingly.*]   This thing's all pretty sacred to me, Elmer.

ELMER.   Well, it's your funeral.   But I certainly think a man ought to have a little amusement.   Here——

[*He extends cigarettes.*]

MERTON. No, thanks, Elmer.

ELMER. Don't you even smoke any more?

MERTON. No. [*He turns away from adjusting the last cover.*] I guess you think I must be nutty, don't you, Elmer?

ELMER. No, I don't, no matter what people say.

MERTON. How do you mean—what they say?

ELMER. Oh, about—things you do. You can trust me, Merton—tell me, *were* you in the pasture this morning, talking to the horse?

MERTON. What horse?

ELMER. Gashwiler's horse. Charlie Harper said he saw you with your arm around his neck.

MERTON. What would I be talking to a horse for?

ELMER. Of course, I can understand—I mean, if you were—lonesome.

MERTON. It isn't—that—I never said I was— [*There is a knock on the outside door.*] It's Tessie Kearns. [*He opens up.*] Hello!

[TESSIE KEARNS *enters—a prim little old maid.*]

MISS KEARNS. Hello, Merton. I thought I'd come and tell you about the picture.

MERTON. Thanks.

MISS KEARNS. Good evening, Elmer.

ELMER. [*Without much cordiality.*] H'llo, Miss Kearns. [*To* MERTON.] Well, I guess I'll meander.

MISS KEARNS. I hope I'm not interrupting you gentlemen.

MERTON. [*Quickly.*] Oh, no!

ELMER. [*In the same breath.*] We were just talking. I gotta get down to a meeting, anyway. Sorry you can't come, Mert. G'night, Miss Kearns. G'night, Mert.

[ELMER *goes as* MERTON *murmurs a goodnight.*]

Miss Kearns. Are you sure I didn't interrupt?

Merton. No, I was glad you came. I want to hear about the picture. He only wanted me to go to a poker game.

Miss Kearns. [*Politely.*] Maybe you wanted to go.

Merton. No! You see, with me it's either idle pleasure or a career, and I'm going to have the career. Was the picture good to-night?

Miss Kearns. It was great! Oh, here are some prints Mr. Hardy asked me to give you. I nearly forgot.

Merton. Thanks. [*Takes them consciously.*] You know what they are?

Miss Kearns. You, ain't they?

Merton. [*Trying to pass it off lightly.*] They're— stills of me—in different characters.

Miss Kearns. Oh, Merton! Can I see them?

Merton. Would you really like to?

Miss Kearns. I'd be delighted. [Merton *starts to open the envelope.*] And oh, yes! Mr. Hardy said to tell you he'd meet you at two-thirty to-morrow, just as you said.

Merton. [*Casually.*] On the lot.

Miss Kearns. [*Awed by this technical knowledge.*] Uh-huh.

Merton. He's— [*Handing her a photograph.*] a great help to a man like me who is studying.

Miss Kearns. [*Inspecting the photograph.*] Oh, this is fine. You look wonderful in evening dress. Merton, why, you just seem to be an actor already.

Merton. [*Abandoning the consideration of the photograph in his hand to go over and examine the one he has given* Miss Kearns.] That's a society-man type. [*He draws back a pace and looks at it from a distance.*]   No-tice anything particular about it?

MISS KEARNS.   [*After a moment.*]   Well, you look very refined and dignified.

MERTON.   No, I mean the face.

MISS KEARNS.   [*Doing her best to find something.*] Why, ah——

MERTON.   Wait!   [*He crosses to a counter at the side and throws back a curtain that has masked a cot, a small trunk, and two or three boxes.   From one of the boxes he takes out a photograph and carries it to* MISS KEARNS.] Know who that is?

MISS KEARNS.   Harold Parmalee!   A wonderful artist.

MERTON.   Perhaps the greatest star in a certain type of part the screen will ever see.   [*He holds it beside the photograph of himself.*]   Now do you notice anything?

MISS KEARNS.   [*Looks at him.*]   Yes, sir!   You do! You do!   With that suit and everything——   It's really remarkable.   I don't know that your shoulders are quite——

[*This hurts.   He almost grabs the picture.*]

MERTON.   No, I know they're not.   Of course, I don't intend to imitate him, anyway.   When I begin acting professionally, I intend creating my own particular types.

MISS KEARNS.   Have you made up your mind yet when you're going?

MERTON.   Pretty soon now.   I've got two hundred and seventy dollars.   I figure in another month or so I'll have a clear three hundred.

MISS KEARNS.   And then you'll go out to California?

MERTON.   The minute I get three hundred.   I've got about all the clothes I need now.   They can't say I haven't the equipment. I've got Western suits, automobile clothes, a suit for polo, everything!

Miss KEARNS. [*Depressed.*] I'll be sorry to see you go—in a way, Merton. But I know you're going to be a big success as an actor.

MERTON. Well, I've been working hard at it. But I guess I'm still pretty far from perfect.

Miss KEARNS. Nonsense! You took all that correspondence course, didn't you?

MERTON. [*Laughs.*] It was funny, my thinking I knew everything before I took that course. Did I show you their certificate?

[*Brings it out of his pocket.*]

Miss KEARNS. Um! All engraved.

MERTON. You bet.

Miss KEARNS. "Film Incorporation Bureau, Station N, Stebbinsville, Kansas." It's a wonderful name you took, Merton. [*Reads from the certificate.*] "Clifford Armytage."

MERTON. I picked it myself.

Miss KEARNS. It sounds so real. You're an actor now, all right. [*A pause.*] Only I had no idea you might be going so soon.

MERTON. Just the minute I get three hundred.

Miss KEARNS. It'll be pretty quiet here.

MERTON. You ought to come out, too, Tessie. That's the place for a scenario writer.

Miss KEARNS. Not on what the millinery business is paying.

MERTON. You know a photo playwright ought to be right on the ground just as much as an actor. All the world-famous authors go out there. Rex Beach, Elinor Glyn, Maeterlinck, Rupert Hughes——

Miss Kearns.   But I'm nowhere near world famous.
I haven't sold even one story yet.

Merton.   You mark my words, you'll sell *Passion's
Perils*.   I'll bet you the Touchstone people take it.

Miss Kearns.   No, they won't.   I got it back this
evening.

Merton.   Well, they make me sick!   But we've both
got to be patient.   We can't succeed all at once—remember that.

Miss Kearns.   Oh, I'm patient—but I guess we'd both
get discouraged sometimes if it wasn't for our sense of
humor.

Merton.   I know I would.   If it wasn't for fine artists
like Beulah Baxter—   [*He recalls that he has not yet
heard about the film.*]   You said it was a good instalment
to-night, huh?

Miss Kearns.   [*Enthusiastic.*]   M'm!   The best yet.

Merton.   Just my luck it would come on a Saturday.
What happened?

Miss Kearns.   Well, this episode's still up in Alaska.

Merton.   I'll bet she was wonderful.   What was the
menace?

Miss Kearns.   They got the cabin surrounded by
wolves and then set fire to it.   It was harrowing.   I don't
blame you for admiring her.   She's certainly fearless.

Merton.   The wonder woman of the silver screen, I
call her.

Miss Kearns.   One time to-night she fought a wolf,
hand to hand.

Merton.   Gee!

Miss Kearns.   I thought for a minute it was a double
—it was so—daring.

Merton.   Well, you can get that idea out of your
head.   I told you what she said at that personal appear-

ance in Peoria. She said if she ever used a double in *Hazards of Hortense,* why, she'd feel she wasn't keeping faith with her public.

MISS KEARNS. It must have been wonderful, being virtually face to face with her.

MERTON. It certainly was, and very inspiring. Why, she just swayed that audience.

MISS KEARNS. Mr. Gashwiler never found out why you went up to Peoria, did he?

MERTON. No, but if he did I wouldn't hesitate to admit it. Miss Baxter is a great influence in my life. That Elmer Huff got me a little sore just now.

MISS KEARNS. Why, what did he do?

MERTON. Nothing, really. But Miss Baxter's name almost came up in the course of conversation. If he'd have spoken lightly of her I'd have lost control of myself. [*A pause.*] Say, Tessie, wouldn't it be wonderful if— when I went out there—I got a chance to work with her in a picture?

MISS KEARNS. I hope you do, Merton.

MERTON. Gee!

MISS KEARNS. Well, I'll be getting along. [*Starts; then remembers something.*] You know, Merton, in a way I'm just as glad you didn't see the show to-night. They had another of those comedies.

MERTON. Jeff Baird's? She'd be revolted if she knew her work was on the same bill. Here's a wonderful artist, on one hand, trying to do better and finer things all the time, like *Hazards of Hortense,* and alongside of her they put a cheap thing like one of those Jeff Baird comedies. Was the cross-eyed man in it again?

MISS KEARNS. Yes, he was.

MERTON. It's enough to discourage a real artist.

MISS KEARNS.   Still, there were times when I could hardly keep from laughing.

MERTON.   They oughtn't to allow them to be made.

MISS KEARNS.   No, I suppose not. [*A pause.*] Well, good night.

> [*Gathering up her belongings.*]

MERTON.   What's that? *Silver Screenings?*

MISS KEARNS.   Yes, I've finished with it—if you want it.

MERTON.   [*Taking it.*] Thanks. [*A look at the cover.*] Corliss Palmer is beautiful, isn't she? [*He starts looking through it.*] Here's an interview with Harold Parmalee! I've got a cap something like that.

MISS KEARNS.   It's an awful good piece about him. I liked it where he says— [*She looks at the story to refresh her memory.*] Ah——

MERTON.   [*Reading.*] "Hard work and the constant striving toward an ideal . . ."

MISS KEARNS.   [*Turns a page.*] No—here at the end.

MERTON.   Oh! About his wife! [*Reads.*] "She is not only my best pal, but my severest critic."

MISS KEARNS.   It's a lovely tribute.

MERTON.   And to a splendid woman.

MISS KEARNS.   [*A pause.*] Well, I got to be going.

MERTON.   [*Following her.*] Good night. Did Mr. Samuels tell you what he was going to show week after next?

MISS KEARNS.   He wasn't sure yet. [*Turns.*] Probably a return engagement of "A Fool's Paradise." Good night.

MERTON.   Good night, Tessie. [*She goes. He closes the door, pulls the shades on windows and doors. Then notices the two dummies and remembers that they are to be*

*moved to the back of the store,   The female figure wears
a checked gingham dress, with the card: "Our Latest for
Milady: Only $6.98."   The male dummy wears a rain-
coat, and a card reading: "Rainproof or You Get Your
Money Back."   The male dummy has a small, tip-curled
black moustache.*   MERTON *places the dummies near the
counter.   He sneers at the male dummy.*]   You cur!

> [*His mind still on the dummies, he crosses to the
> open trunk and takes out his wallet.   As he
> puts his money in it, he notices his sombrero
> near by.   He puts it on, with another glance
> at the dummies; crosses to the string regulat-
> ing the ceiling lamp and pulls it, dramatically,
> throwing the room into virtual darkness, save
> for the spot about the small lamp on the coun-
> ter and the moonlight pouring in through the
> window.*]

MERTON.   [*He is now ready to play the drama.   To
male dummy—as the Man.*]   One-a-little kiss, Señorita
[*As the woman.*]   Ah, God in heaven, is there no help at
hand!   [MERTON *himself speaks.*]   Just a minute, my
friend.   [*To the female dummy, as* BUCK BENSON.]   I
trust I am not too late, Miss St. Clair?   Yes, it's me,
Buck Benson—at your service, ma'am.   I suppose this
—this gentleman has been annoying you.   Oh, he has, has
he?   [*Turns to the villain.*]   Now, curse you, you shall
fight me in American fashion, man to man!   Viper
though you are, I hesitate to put a bullet through your
craven heart!   [*He screams—turns to female dummy.*]
Don't be afraid, Miss St. Clair!   [*To the villain.*]   Now,
you dog!   [*Strips off his coat.*]   We shall learn whose
body goes over yonder cliff.

> [*He seizes the dummy and backs him well over
> the counter.   The door opens and* GASH-

WILER *enters.* MERTON *lifts the dummy over
his head and is apparently about to throw him
over the counter when* GASHWILER'S *voice
stops him.*]

GASHWILER.   Merton Gill, put down that dummy!

MERTON.   [*Doing so.*]   Yes, sir!

GASHWILER.   What do you think you're doin', anyway?
Sounded up-stairs like riotin'. Suppose you think I got
them things down from Chicago just for you to play
horse with. Where do you think you are? Actin' in
grand op'ry?

> [*He is examining the male figure for possible
> damage.*]

MERTON.   I didn't do it any harm.

GASHWILER.   Maybe you didn't and maybe you did.
How'd you like me to lift you up and throw you over
that counter?

MERTON.   I'm sorry.

GASHWILER.   I declare, Merton, I don't know what to
make of you. If you had a father or mother you'd certainly be a trial. What are you wearin' that big hat for?

MERTON.   It's part of a costume.

> [*Takes it off.*]

GASHWILER.   You look like a cowboy. You ain't try-
in' to be a cowboy?

MERTON.   I might.

GASHWILER.   Well, you can't be one around here. I
swear I think you go to them movies too much. They're
not the right thing for a feller that's got your nature.
You're too hysterical.

MERTON.   I go to them to study, Mr. Gashwiler, and
I certainly don't intend to stop.

GASHWILER.   Just what do you mean—study?

MERTON. Well, I may as well tell you. I'm studying the movies, with the idea of going into them.

GASHWILER. Actin'?

MERTON. Yes, sir.

GASHWILER. [*Astounded.*] My God, you are crazy! Well, let me tell you this, young man! I don't want any more studyin' while you're workin' for me.

MERTON. You don't mean that, do you, Mr. Gashwiler?

GASHWILER. I certainly do. There's a limit, Merton. I can't afford havin' anybody around whose spare time ain't spent in something worth while.

MERTON. And you don't think motion pictures—are worth while?

GASHWILER. I certainly do not.

MERTON. Well, then, I'll leave, Mr. Gashwiler, right now.

GASHWILER. You'll what?

MERTON. I'll leave. I'm going out to California and —enter the films. I was going anyhow—in a month— but I'll go right away.

GASHWILER. To—to California?

MERTON. Yes, sir.

GASHWILER. To be an actor?

MERTON. Yes, sir, and I'll succeed, too.

GASHWILER. [*Thinks this over.*] 'Tain't likely—a boy from Simsbury.

MERTON. Lincoln walked four miles for a book.

GASHWILER. Yes, but you ain't studying for President. You're trying to get into something that nobody I ever heard of succeeded in.

MERTON. Well, just the same, Mr. Gashwiler, I'm going to follow my star.

GASHWILER. All right, Merton, if that's what you

want to do. [*A pause.*] Then I'm to go right ahead
—and—get somebody else?

MERTON. Yes, sir.

GASHWILER. [*Considers.*] You got much money?

MERTON. Two hundred and seventy dollars.

GASHWILER. [*Almost takes money out of his pocket.*]
Well, I . . . I hope you make a big success of it, Merton.
Good night!

MERTON. Good night, Mr. Gashwiler, and I'm sorry
about the dummies.

GASHWILER. That's all right. You didn't hurt them
none. [*Looks at* MERTON.] I can't quite make you out,
Merton. You're a nice boy, one of the nicest I ever knew,
but I guess you're just crazy.

> [*He goes.* MERTON *looks after him for a sec-
> ond, then settles to the final work of the night.
> He starts the phonograph. It is a Walter
> Camp Daily Dozen record. He follows the
> instructions of the voice from the phonograph:
> "Hands on hips, bend trunk forward to angle
> of forty-five degrees; now back; forward;
> back," etc. Then gradually he stops exercis-
> ing, and talks through the phonograph to the
> male dummy.*]

MERTON. Some day we shall meet again. [*Phono-
graph.*] This time your life has been spared. [*Another
pause;* MERTON *changes his tactics and begins to address
an imaginary interviewer.*] You ask me to tell the readers of your magazine to what I owe my success? Hard
work, young lady. Hard work and the constant striving
toward an ideal: to give the best that is in me to my
public. Perhaps I owe most, however, to Mrs. Armytage,
my wife. She is more than a wife. She is my best pal,
and, I may say, my severest critic. [*He stops the ma-*

chine and blows out the lamp lights. He pulls the cot from under the counter into the moonlight. He kneels beside it.] Oh, God, make me a good movie actor! Make me one of the best. For Jesus' sake, amen!

CURTAIN

ACT II

The time is about three weeks later—the scene is the waiting-room outside the Holden Lot. It is nearly rectangular, and quite bare. There are two doors—one at the left that leads to and from the outside world, and one at the right that leads on into the mysteries of the lot. On this latter door is a sign: "No Admittance Except on Order." The rectangle of the room is broken only by a small window in the upper right corner—and over it the words, "Casting Director." On a ledge just inside this window is a telephone, and through the window can also be seen a sparsely furnished office. As for the reception-room itself, its floor is bare, and its walls, of some dull-toned and uninspiring stuff, are almost so. A bare bench runs the length of the rear wall. There is a sign on the wall:

ATTENTION, ARTISTES!

Costumes Should Be Returned Promptly to the Wardrobe Room.

Not Responsible for Damage to Wardrobe Furnished by Artistes.

Talent Checks Should Be Cashed Promptly.

Report Changes of Address or Telephone Numbers.

HOLDEN MASTER PICTURES CORP.

At the rise of the curtain four or five hopeful extras are sitting on the bare benches—sitting there with a certain desperateness that hints at endless hours so spent. Within the railing that marks the CASTING DIRECTOR'S *office is that lady herself—a genial-looking woman of middle age or less, who takes the job ever so casually. In her day she has said "Nothing doing" to actors by the thousands; it is no treat to her.*

The casting director's 'phone rings. Instantly the line-up of extras leans forwardly expectantly—it may be a director calling for anything from Apaches to society people. The CASTING DIRECTOR *takes up the phone.*

CASTING DIRECTOR. Hello. . . . No—nothing to-day. [*Her voice has a mechanical ring.*] . . . I know, but I can't write a part in for you.

> [*As she hangs up a group of cowboys hurry across the stage.*]

A COWBOY. Come on, boys—snap it up!

> [*They hurry out at the other side; again the 'phone rings; the waiting line of hopefuls leans forward once more, only to sink back again when the Casting Director's answer plainly reveals that it is just another job-seeker.*]

CASTING DIRECTOR. Sorry—nothing to-day. [*She hangs up. A few extras leave; others arrive to take their places. A man hurriedly crosses with a camera and a roll of film. He greets the Casting Director as he goes by, addressing her familiarly as "Countess." She tosses a greeting back at him. The 'phone rings again.*] Hello. . . . Wait a minute. [*She consults a record.*] They're

doing the Nile scenes in *The Tiger Woman.* . . . Yeh
—desert stuff. Won't be back for a week. [*She hangs
up. An old man with a long beard shuffles on; presents
himself at her counter. She throws him hardly a glance.*]
No.   No hermit parts to-day.

> [PA MONTAGUE *enters from outside. A man
> slightly over middle age, somewhat seedy, but
> possessed of a good deal of dignity.*]

MONTAGUE. Good morning. Is it within the possibilities that you could furnish employment for an actor?

CASTING DIRECTOR. Sorry, Mr. Montague. Nothing
to-day.

MONTAGUE. You understand that I am not applying
for extra work.

CASTING DIRECTOR. Well, I'll tell you, Mr. Montague
—things are pretty dull just now.

MONTAGUE. However, I might be willing to masquer-
ade as an extra for the time being.

> [SIGMUND ROSENBLATT, *a director, enters
> from the lot. A Semitic-appearing young
> man, rather crude.*]

ROSENBLATT. [*Pausing in the doorway to call back to
an unseen figure.*] All right, Ralph! Don't keep me
waitin'!

VOICE. [*Heard off.*] Right away!

> [*The owner of the voice enters. He is a Camera-
> man.*]

MONTAGUE. [*Advancing somewhat timidly.*] Mr.
Rosenblatt——

ROSENBLATT. [*To the Cameraman, not noticing
MONTAGUE.*] That's where we lose the time. And then
they blame we directors.

MONTAGUE. If I might—make so bold——

ROSENBLATT. [*Examining a bit of film.*]   Got to be a retake on them Chinatown scenes—the fan-tan game.

CAMERAMAN.   Yes, sir.

MONTAGUE.   Mr. Rosenblatt——

ROSENBLATT.   You take all that China stuff—   [*He notices* MONTAGUE.]   What is it?

MONTAGUE.   If by any chance the scenario calls for a real actor——

ROSENBLATT.   All full up!

MONTAGUE.   You may recall that I played a desperado when you were taking——

ROSENBLATT.   Oh, yes—what's the name?

MONTAGUE.   Montague.   Lester Montague.

ROSENBLATT.   Haven't got a thing.
　　　　[*Still studying his film.*]

MONTAGUE.   I was with you in "The Little Shepherd of the Bar Z."   That was the working-title.   I believe it was released as "I Want More Children."

ROSENBLATT.   Well, water stuff next week.   Can you swim?

　　　　[ROSENBLATT'S *assistant enters from the lot.*
　　　　For the sake of argument, call him JOE.]

MONTAGUE.   [*Proudly.*]   Of course.   I am an actor.

ROSENBLATT.   [*Calls.*]   Phil!   Phil!   God, he's a snail!

JOE.   Say, Commander, I got an idea you and Baxter'll go nuts about!

ROSENBLATT.   Well?

JOE.   The place to leave Baxter for the next episode!

ROSENBLATT.   What's that?

JOE.   Dangling from the end of the human ladder, two hundred feet up!

ROSENBLATT.   [*Judicially.*]   H'm!   Well—maybe.

JOE.   Surest thing you know! And the Chinks shooting at her from the roof!

ROSENBLATT.   Not so bad—not so bad!

[*His other Cameraman enters.*]

CAMERAMAN.   All ready, Chief?

ROSENBLATT.   Come on, now—make it snappy! I just got a big idea for the end of this instalment! Came to me like that!

[MERTON *enters—from the outside, of course. It is his first visit to this room, although he has spent several weeks waiting outside the lot. Naturally he is all eyes.*]

ROSENBLATT.   Listen! The human ladder swings Hortense clear from the window ledge when the fire starts, see—just as we had it.

CAMERAMAN.   I got you!

[MERTON *is gaping at them, and is about to be walked into at any second.*]

ROSENBLATT.   Now! Instead of the reporter rescuing her in this instalment—see?—we leave her hanging there, four hundred feet up!

JOE.   Aw, say, Chief—that's my idea!

ROSENBLATT.   Just at the finish another Chink shoots the poisoned bullet from the roof.

[*Still talking, he goes at left wth his Cameramen and the assistant.* MERTON, *rather dazed, stands looking after them.* MONTAGUE, *left alone, also looks after them, but with more resignation in his glance. Slowly* MERTON *shifts his gaze to the rest of the room, then to* MONTAGUE.]

MONTAGUE.   [*Tragically—partly to* MERTON *and partly to the whole room.*]   Swim!

[*He takes a seat on the bench.* MERTON, *nerv-*

> *ing himself for the ordeal, advances to the
> little window and presents himself. It is the
> closest that he has yet come to the inside of the
> game, and his attitude reflects his eager excite-
> ment.*]

MERTON.   Is—is this where the actors are—selected?

CASTING DIRECTOR.   What's that?

MERTON.   I say, do you—that is, are the actors—is
there likely to be——

CASTING DIRECTOR.   [*Comprehending.*]   Oh!   [*Back
to the every-day tone again.*]   Nothing to-day.   Sorry.

> [BERT CHESTER, *the cross-eyed man, comes on
> from the lot.   He is accompanied by another
> actor dressed as a sheik, and is laughing in
> evident appreciation of something as he walks
> on.*]

BERT.   If that scene don't make them howl and fall
off their seats——   [*Stops at the Director's window.*]   Oh,
say!   Countess!

CASTING DIRECTOR.   Yes, Bert?

BERT.   Oh, Countess—Jeff says he wants a big bow-
legged man for the pig to slip through in that new one.

CASTING DIRECTOR.   How big is the pig?

BERT.   Oh, it's a hog!

CASTING DIRECTOR.   All right—I know just the fellow.

BERT.   O. K.!   Come on, Spike!

> [*He goes out with the Sheik.*]

MERTON.   [*Looking after him.*]   Why, that was the
cross-eyed man, wasn't it?

CASTING DIRECTOR.   Sure!   Bert Chester.   And he's
a nice fellow, too.

MERTON.   He must be.   Acting with a hog!

> [*She turns away, and* MERTON *must perforce
> do likewise.   With nothing else to do, he*

[*starts looking the place over. He reads the
signs on the wall; peeps through the mysterious door that leads onto the lot. If he had
the nerve, you gather, he would walk right
through. Finally, however, he does get up
courage enough to approach the Countess on
the subject. He presents himself at her window; waits patiently until she gives her attention to him.*]

CASTING DIRECTOR. Well?

MERTON. I—I don't suppose it would be possible—for anybody to—to go inside—would it? I mean just—look around.

CASTING DIRECTOR. [*Giving him a quick look.*] Working here?

MERTON. Not yet.

CASTING DIRECTOR. Sorry!

[MERTON *turns away again; seems about to give
up. But he goes back to the window a third
time.*]

MERTON. [*Trying to attract her attention.*] Excuse me——

CASTING DIRECTOR. My Lord, you again!

MERTON. I just wanted to ask you——

CASTING DIRECTOR. [*Not unkindly.*] There's nothing doing, and you can't go in.

MERTON. I know, but—if there were—something doing—you'd know about it first, wouldn't you?

CASTING DIRECTOR. Yes. Next to Will Hays.

MERTON. Well, then, you wouldn't mind if I waited here a while, would you, just in case—there was something?

CASTING DIRECTOR. Help yourself, but there's only two companies shooting on the lot.

[*The* Montague Girl *enters.   She is winded,
and fanning herself.*]

Girl.   Sixth and last lap! Hello, Pa!

Montague.   How are you, my dear?

Girl.   All jake, but it's certainly tough on us extras.
I've been in every studio in Hollywood in the last hour
and a half.   Covered 'em so fast they thought I was a
tourist!

Montague.   Conditions *are* discouraging.

Girl.   [*Powders her nose.*]   Tell me they're going to
shoot some Arab stuff up at the Consolidated to-morrow,
but I says, no thanks—I've been bit by my last camel.

Montague.   [*Wavering.*]   Still,   any   employment
would be grateful in times like these.

Girl.   [*Sighs.*]   Well, you can go to it if you want to.
Besides, I'm getting too beautiful for the films.   Baxter's
jealous of me already.

Montague.   You said the Consolidated, I believe?

Girl.   [*Observing* Merton, *and answering with di-
vided attention.*]   Huh? Oh—the desert stuff? Yah,
but look out for those camels.   They sink a pretty tooth.

Montague.   [*About to go.*]   Oh, I know a remedy
for camel bites.

[*He goes.*]

Girl.   [*Rises.*]   Hello, Newcomer!

[*This to* Merton.]

Merton.   [*Caught by her mention of* Baxter, *but
feeling a vague animosity toward the* Montague *girl.*]
Oh—excuse me, but——

Girl.   Sure!

Merton.   Did you—you didn't mean Beulah Baxter,
did you, that was jealous, I mean?

Girl.   Jealous?   Say!   Last time I starred with her
she said she'd quit cold if I kept on arriving in a dif-

ferent automobile every day. Had to sell my third assistant Pierce Arrow.

MERTON. But nobody ever stars with Beulah Baxter.

GIRL. Well, I wasn't really starred. My parents wouldn't let me.

MERTON. They wouldn't?

GIRL. Nope. Too young.

MERTON. Oh!

GIRL. New on the lot, ain't you?

MERTON. No, not exactly.

GIRL. Didn't remember seeing you before. Still, they come and go.

MERTON. [*Quick to agree.*] Yes.

CASTING DIRECTOR. [*Calling to the Girl*] Hello! [*At the telephone, as usual.*] No, nothing to-day.

[*Hangs up.*]

GIRL. Hello, Countess! [*To* MERTON.] Excuse me —my public's calling. [*At the window.*] Can't you give the camera a little peek at me or at Pa? No, nothing to-day, dearie!

[*Imitating her voice.*]

CASTING DIRECTOR. Pretty dull here. How is it around?

GIRL. Could have gone on in a harem tank scene at the Bigart, but they wanted me to dress like a fish.

CASTING DIRECTOR. You're not so good at that.

GIRL. No. Built more like home folks. But, honest, Countess, can't you give my old dad a little job? He's been stickin' home lately making old Kentucky bourbon in thirty minutes. If he don't quit he's going to see some moving-pictures that nobody else can.

CASTING DIRECTOR. Sorry—nothing doing.

GIRL. Oh, well. . . . . Say, you haven't seen Jeff Baird around?

CASTING DIRECTOR. He's on the lot some place.

GIRL. I got a date to give him some ideas. Bet he's sitting around not doing a thing—just waiting for me. [*She is starting off, but stops as she observes the highly disgusted* MERTON.] What's the matter, Trouper?

MERTON. Do you—do you have anything to do with those Jeff Baird things? Those—those comedies?

GIRL. Do I? Countess, tell him who I am! [*Hastily.*] No, don't—let him find out for himself. [J. SLOANE HENSHAW, *another director, enters. Puttees and all.*] Well, if he's on the lot——

[*Stops as she observes* HENSHAW.]

HENSHAW. [*Personifying the very important man— pays no attention to the Girl, but crosses quickly to the window—*MERTON *scrambles out of the way.*] Mr. Parmalee been in?

[*At the mention of Parmalee,* MERTON *becomes very conscious.*]

CASTING DIRECTOR. I don't believe so, Mr. Henshaw.

HENSHAW. Telephone No. 21, and get one of my assistants. [*Snaps fingers.*] I forget his name. Have him tell Parmalee that the commander is waiting. And hurry—my time's valuable.

CASTING DIRECTOR. Yes, sir.

[*The Girl regards* HENSHAW *with a good deal of amusement in her eyes.*]

GIRL. Oh, Commander!

HENSHAW. Yes . . . yes?

GIRL. Could you—could you give me just a minute, please?

HENSHAW. Well, I'm very busy, very busy, but——

GIRL. Well, you see, it's this way, Commander. I got a great idea for a story, see, and I was thinking who to take it to, and I thought of a lot of them, and I asked my friends, and they all said, "Oh, take it to Mr. Henshaw, because he's the one director on the lot that can get every ounce of value out of it." So I thought—but of course if you're busy——

HENSHAW. Well, I *am* busy, but then I'm always busy. They run me to death here. Still, it was very kind of your friends, and of course . . .

GIRL. Thank you a thousand times, Mr. Henshaw. [*She assumes a worshipping pose.*] It starts off kind of like this. You see, I'm a Hawaiian princess——

HENSHAW. [*Correcting her.*] The *character's* an Hawaiian princess.

GIRL. Oh, excuse me. Well, anyway, I'm this Hawaiian princess, and my father, Old King Muana Loa, dies, and leaves me two thousand volcanoes and a billiard-cue. Now——

HENSHAW. Ah—just a minute A billiard-cue?

GIRL. Yes, sir. And every morning I have to go out and ram it down the volcanoes to see if they're all right. Now, then——

HENSHAW. What are you *talking* about?

GIRL. Now, the villain is very wealthy. He owns one of the largest ukulele plantations on the island. . . .

HENSHAW. Tush, tush! Absurd, absurd! [*He turns to the Casting Director.*] Any word yet?

GIRL. Oh, dear! Well, of course, I knew it was crude—but no one ever listens to you until you break into the magazines. Really, really, said Miss Montague, termed by many the most beautiful woman in the world, I am at a loss to understand why the public should be so interested in me. What can I say to your readers? Oh, please, please go away and leave me to my books and my art!

[*She walks off.*]

MERTON. [*To* HENSHAW.] I—I knew in a minute her scenario wasn't any good.

HENSHAW. [*Regarding him.*] How's that?

MERTON. [*Fussed.*] Yes, sir.

HENSHAW. What?

MERTON. I say, the minute she said all those volcanoes.

HENSHAW. [*Yelling.*] What, what, what!

MERTON. I say, I knew right away it wouldn't be practical——

[HENSHAW's *assistant enters. Also in puttees, and answering to the name of* WELLER.]

HENSHAW. Oh, hello, Weller! Thank God! Parmalee coming?

WELLER. He's on the way—I just talked to one of his valets.

[HENSHAW *grunts.*]

MERTON. [*Awed.*] Is—is Harold Parmalee coming here?

WELLER. [*Regarding him.*] Where'd you come from?

MERTON. [*Nervously.*] Sir?

WELLER. Not that it matters.

HENSHAW. You know, if this stuff looks all right to-day, we can get back on Crusoe in the morning.

WELLER. That's fine.

HENSHAW. I'm anxious to get that under way.

WELLER. Great idea of yours—*Robinson Crusoe.*

HENSHAW. And it'll be a great picture, the way I treat it. Can't you imagine— [*Starts pacing; nearly runs into* MERTON.] Good heavens, who is this boy, anyhow? Go away—go away—sit down some place! [MERTON *backs off.*] Now, what was I talking about?

WELLER. *Robinson Crusoe.*

HENSHAW. Oh, yes! Well, I've got it all doped out. What happens is this——

> [HAROLD PARMALEE, *a film star who looks the part, joins the merry group.* MERTON *is so excited at his appearance that he can hardly move.*]

PARMALEE. Good morning.

WELLER. Good morning, Mr. Parmalee.

HENSHAW. Oh, hello, Harold. I was just telling Weller about the Crusoe stuff. The way we work it is this. Friday—Friday has a sister, see—only she can't be his real sister because she's white—get what I mean?

PARMALEE. Yes, I thought of that.

HENSHAW. Well, we'll work it out later. She's the daughter of an English Earl that was wrecked near the Island, and Friday's mother brought her up as her own child. She's saved the papers that came ashore and she has the Earl's coat-of-arms tattooed on her shoulder blade. Get this finish, Weller! Finally, after Robinson Crusoe has fallen in love with her, along comes the old Earl, her father, in a ship and rescues them all. What do you think? Great, isn't it?

WELLER. Great!

HENSHAW. Now come on and let's look at this stuff. You see, in that way we get the sex into it.

> [HENSHAW *and* WELLER *go.* PARMALEE *is about to follow when* MERTON *halts him.*]

MERTON. [*To* PARMALEE, *his heart in his mouth.*] Mr. . . . Mr. Parmalee, Mr. Parmalee——

PARMALEE. [*Condescendingly.*] Yes, old chap?

MERTON. I have long been one of your admirers, and appreciate the fine things that you are trying to do in screen art.

[PARMALEE *looks at him, then reaches into*
pocket and takes out an elaborate watch.]

PARMALEE. [*Good-naturedly.*] I suppose you want
to see the watch.

MERTON. [*Eagerly taking it in his hand.*] Oh, is that
the one they gave you?

PARMALEE. [*Bored to death.*] Five thousand exhibitors, representing forty-two States.

MERTON. A wonderful trophy. [*He continues,*
hastily.] But—what I was going to say was—I want to
do something artistic myself. I read—in your last interview—that you always encouraged beginners, and——

PARMALEE. [*Trying to escape.*] Oh, yes, yes!

MERTON. And I—I'm really coming to what I was
going to say now—because I thought maybe you might be
especially interested in me because—because— [*He is*
trying his best to look like Parmalee at this instant.]
Well, do you notice—anything?

PARMALEE. Do I what?

MERTON. [*Posing himself.*] Do you—notice anything?

PARMALEE. [*Sniffing.*] I don't think so.

MERTON. No—no—I mean—now, you see, you're
standing that way, and I'm standing just the same way—
see? I mean, in the way *you* look and the way *I* look—do
you notice anything?

PARMALEE. Really, I don't know what you're talking
about.

MERTON. Well, I mean—don't you think we—that is,
that I look——

PARMALEE. What? This is all very silly . . . very
silly indeed!

[*A dismissing wave of the hand. He strides off.*
MERTON—*a pretty crushed* MERTON—*is left*

> *alone as he watches* PARMALEE *depart.   Then
> he walks over to the bench; sits.   Waits there
> a moment, then again approaches the* CASTING
> DIRECTOR.]

MERTON.   [*Peering within.*]   Say!

CASTING DIRECTOR.   [*Suddenly appearing, and observing that it is* MERTON *again.*]   For God's sake!

MERTON.   Well, I thought——

CASTING DIRECTOR.   There's nothing doing and you can't go in!

> [MERTON *takes his seat again; thinks things
> over, then gets to thinking of* PARMALEE *and
> his final words—gets up and poses himself as*
> PARMALEE, *wave of the hand and all.*]

MERTON.   [*In imitation.*]   It's all very silly, very silly indeed!

CASTING DIRECTOR.   [*Who has been watching him.*] Well!

MERTON.   [*Turns quickly and takes off his hat; grins sheepishly.*]   Ma'am?

CASTING DIRECTOR.   I suppose your trunks are coming?

MERTON.   You mean my—costumes?

CASTING DIRECTOR.   You're new, aren't you?

MERTON.   [*Reluctantly.*]   Well, I am now, but I won't be!

CASTING DIRECTOR.   Have you registered?

MERTON.   Ma'am?

CASTING DIRECTOR.   Have I got your name and address?

MERTON.   Oh—no.

CASTING DIRECTOR.   You are new.   [*She has picked up a pencil.*]   Come on·

MERTON.   Ma'am?

CASTING DIRECTOR. What's your name? [*He hesitates.*] You've got a name, haven't you?

MERTON. [*Almost afraid to utter it.*] Clifford Armytage.

CASTING DIRECTOR. [*The pencil poised.*] Come again!

MERTON. [*Louder this time.*] Clifford Armytage.

CASTING DIRECTOR. Clifford Armytage? [*She thinks it over before writing.*] Well, why not? [*She writes.*] Address?

MERTON. Two thousand four hundred and sixty, Oakdale Avenue.

CASTING DIRECTOR. Line of parts?

MERTON. Huh?

CASTING DIRECTOR. What's your line?

MERTON. Oh! Well, that's what I was going to show you. [*He draws out the art photographs.*] You see, those'll give you a pretty good idea. I mean, that's——

CASTING DIRECTOR. [*Inspecting them.*] Oh, my goodness! You don't mean these are all the same person?

MERTON. [*Proudly.*] They are, though.

CASTING DIRECTOR. Oh, what do you think of that? Cowboy, and—society man, and—now don't tell me that's you with the horse!

MERTON. Yes, it is. I just wanted you to see what I could do. Of course, I wouldn't expect big parts to begin with. I'm willing to work hard and sacrifice in the beginning.

CASTING DIRECTOR. [*Looking at the photographs.*] You'll sacrifice, all right.

MERTON. Because it's only out of hard work and sacrifice that the finer things come. You take Beulah Baxter or Harold Parmalee, or any of them, and they all started that way.

CASTING DIRECTOR. [*Regarding him.*]   Say, you're a regular bug, aren't you?

MERTON. [*Looking around.*]   Say—say—does Beulah Baxter—does she ever come in this way?

CASTING DIRECTOR.   Sure—mostly.

MERTON.   Right along here?

CASTING DIRECTOR.   Just like a mortal.

MERTON. [*Turns and surveys the room, worshippingly, then turns back to the window.*]   Is—is Beulah Baxter married?

CASTING DIRECTOR.   Let me see.   I never can remember.

MERTON.   She's the little wonder woman, all right. I'll bet you she sacrificed before she got up to where she is.

CASTING DIRECTOR. [*A wicked gleam in her eye.*] *I'll* say she did! [*The 'phone rings.*]   Yes, yes, I understand—stage eight, all right.

[*Hangs up.*]

MERTON.   I don't suppose you could fix it so that I could work in a picture with her—some time?

CASTING DIRECTOR.   Now, listen, son.   I might not be able to get you *anything* for a long, long time.

MERTON.   Oh, I don't mind—struggling.   The only thing is—I want to do something really significant, and not just—comedies.

CASTING DIRECTOR.   Well, I'll remember you.   And I can always reach you at two thousand four hundred and so forth?

MERTON.   Yes, only—during the day I'll be right here.

CASTING DIRECTOR. [*Gives him a look.*]   All day?

MERTON.   Yeh!

CASTING DIRECTOR.   Aren't you ever going to try the other studios?

MERTON. Oh, no!

CASTING DIRECTOR. Well, I ought to enjoy that.

> [*The* MONTAGUE GIRL *returns, accompanied by*
> JEFF BAIRD, *the Buckeye Comedy King. He
> is rather a bluff soul with a prominent mus-
> tache. The* GIRL *is talking gaily as she enters.*
> MERTON, *his distaste evident, is already back-
> ing away.*]

GIRL. That's the stuff, Jeff! Then when he tries to get up, the chandelier drops right on him. But the gag is, instead of breaking, it's a rubber chandelier and it bounces —see?

BAIRD. Great! I'll get you a little check for that.

GIRL. It's all right, Jeff—I like you and that makes it all jake with me. [*To* MERTON.] Hello, Trouper! Still hanging on?

MERTON. [*Forced to reply.*] I—guess so.

GIRL. Well, you stick to it—that's the way I got my success. Jeff, meet my friend the trouper. Trouper, Mr. Jeff Baird, the Buckeye Comedy King!

BAIRD. [*Putting out his hand.*] How are you, kid? What's your line—comedy?

MERTON. [*Shaking hands with great dignity.*] No, sir. It is my wish to do something of a finer nature than mere comedies. And I would not even entertain an offer to associate myself with them. [*He turns and walks away.*]

BAIRD. [*To the* GIRL—*after a moment.*] Is that final?

GIRL. So help me God!

BAIRD. [*Looks after Merton.*] It certainly messes up my plans. [*Laughs.*] Come on! Let's go over and see those rushes.

GIRL. [*Absorbed in thought of Merton.*] You get 'em ready. I'll come right over!

BAIRD. [*With an understanding look from the girl to* MERTON.] Want to take soundings, eh?

GIRL. Uh, huh!

BAIRD. All right—I'll look for you in ten minutes. [*He goes.*]

> [MERTON *is wrapped in disdainful dignity. She pauses squarely in front of him.*]

GIRL. Hello, kid!

MERTON. [*Compelled to reply, but keeping his dignity.*] Good morning.

GIRL. How about a little dialogue? Name your own weapons.

MERTON. I—haven't anything to say.

GIRL. Sure you have—you're just modest. Come on over here and talk it over. [MERTON *goes, unwillingly.*] That's the stuff—be sociable. Now, tell me. What have you got against poor Jeff Baird?

MERTON. [*Compelled to defend himself.*] I don't like his comedies. They degrade a—an art.

GIRL. Well, now we're getting some place. [*She turns to him and whispers.*] What art?

MERTON. [*With dignity.*] The art of the motion-picture.

GIRL. [*Changing her key.*] You haven't been around here long? [MERTON *is silent.*] Huh?

MERTON. I—I don't care to discuss my—private affairs.

GIRL. All right, kid. Only take an old trouper's word for it—it's a tough game. Work is few and far between, and when it does come it's generally pretty cheesy. You take even an old-timer like Pa. Last month he got a job in a moonshining play.

MERTON. You mean where the revenue officer falls in love with the moonshiner's daughter?

GIRL. That's it. Well, anyhow, Pa gets this job and they won't stand for the crape hair, so he has to go and raise a garden. Gives a month to raising it—all his spare time—and what happens?

MERTON. I'm sure I don't know.

GIRL. After four days' work they go and have him killed off. Pa goes around for a week and tries to rent the garden, but by that time nobody's doing anything but Chinese pictures. That's what you're up against in this game, kid.

MERTON. But I couldn't raise a beard anyhow.

GIRL. [*A pause.*] You win. [MERTON *starts to turn away.*] Say!

MERTON. Well?

GIRL. You understand I'm not inquisitive or anything, but—don't you think I've been doing a lot of the talking?

MERTON. Oh, I don't know.

GIRL. How long you been around here?

MERTON. About—three weeks.

GIRL. Funny I didn't see you before.

MERTON. I wasn't—I didn't know about this place.

GIRL. Where were you?

MERTON. Out there.

GIRL. On the street? For three weeks?

MERTON. [*Melting a little.*] Oh, I didn't mind it.

GIRL. You're hell-bent on being an actor, ain't you?

MERTON. I expected I'd have to struggle.

GIRL. Well, don't say I didn't warn you.

MERTON. Thanks.

[*He is about to turn away.*]

GIRL. Hold on—don't go. [*She sits.*] That's right.

Come on over here and sit down. [*He does so.*] Where'd you come from—before you came here?

MERTON. I—came from a little town.

GIRL. Still afraid of me, ain't you?

MERTON. Oh, no, I'm not.

GIRL. Well, don't you be. I'm just a poor mug, the same as you, only I've been at it a little longer, that's all— [*A pause.*] I like you.

MERTON. [*Very fussed.*] Well, it isn't—I don't want you to think I don't appreciate——

GIRL. That's all right. You're a nice kid, only you're awful green. Don't think I talk to all of them like this, but somehow there's something about you that made me do it. If you want somebody to pilot you around, maybe introduce you at the other studios——

MERTON. Oh, no—thanks. I—I'm going to work just at this studio, if you don't mind.

GIRL. What's the big notion?

MERTON. Well, you see—what I want— [*He is quite fussed.*] —I mean, this is the company where Beulah Baxter is, and I figured——

GIRL. [*Rises—regarding him closely.*] Say, kid, look at me. [*He does so.*] You haven't gone and fallen in love with a picture, have you?

MERTON. [*Gulping.*] I—I didn't say that.

GIRL. I know you didn't, but I'm awful quick.

MERTON. It is merely that I am a great admirer of Miss Baxter's art, and regard her as the wonder woman of the silver screen.

GIRL. Honest?

MERTON. You—of course you were only joking about starring with her, weren't you? Because she doesn't ever have anybody. She doesn't even have anybody ever

double for her, the way some of them do when it's dangerous.

GIRL. Oh!

MERTON. So I thought if I could only get with her
company, I mean no matter how small a part it was, why,
I thought I'd rather do that than go to one of the other
studios and maybe work with somebody who—whose ideals
weren't as fine as hers.

GIRL. I see.

MERTON. You—you don't know of anybody whose
ideals are as fine as hers—do you?

GIRL. No. She's got the finest set of ideals on the
lot. [*The phone rings.* CASTING DIRECTOR *answers—
her voice is unheard in the beginning.*] She's certainly
the—— What was it you called her?

MERTON. The wonder woman of the silver screen.

GIRL. That was it.

MERTON. That was the appellation *Photoland* gave her
when——

CASTING DIRECTOR. [*Into 'phone.*] All right, Mr.
Henshaw! A dozen of them!

GIRL. My God, it's work!

> [*She grabs* MERTON *by the arm and pulls him to-
> ward the window. A group of extras, sensi-
> tive to anything that means work, have heard
> the call and troop in for their tickets. They
> press close around the Countess's desk.*]

CASTING DIRECTOR. Evening clothes! Stage No. Six
at eight-thirty in the morning! Society stuff with Harold
Parmalee in *Robinson Crusoe.* Don't forget—evening
things, jewelry, and all you've got!

MERTON. [*Bobbing around.*] Will you please let
me——

CASTING DIRECTOR. Eight-thirty to-morrow morning

on Stage No. Six! Here's your ticket—full evening dress! Have you got evening dress?

MERTON. [*Excited.*] Yes!

CASTING DIRECTOR. Atta baby!

MERTON. And I want to thank you——

CASTING DIRECTOR. Harold Parmalee in *Robinson Crusoe.* Evening dress!

> [PA MONTAGUE *rushes on, making for the window.*]

MONTAGUE. I understand—that is, I was just informed——

CASTING DIRECTOR. Sorry, Mr. Montague—all full up.

MONTAGUE. But I was informed only three seconds ago——

CASTING DIRECTOR. Sorry—only wanted a dozen.

MONTAGUE. [*As he turns away.*] A dozen. [*He notices his daughter.*] And I left here for your camels.

GIRL. What's the matter—were they full up?

MONTAGUE. They were not. It wasn't camels. It was wild cats.

> [*He goes. There is a moment's pause. Then the* GIRL *turns back to* MERTON.]

GIRL. Well, kid, you're going to be an actor now, all right. You know, Countess, there's only one thing gets me.

CASTING DIRECTOR. What's that?

GIRL. Who the devil wears evening clothes in *Robinson Crusoe?*

MERTON. [*To* CASTING DIRECTOR.] Say, should— should I have my breakfast before I come in the morning?

CASTING DIRECTOR. It might not be a bad idea.

MERTON. [*To the* MONTAGUE GIRL.] We're to have breakfast first, before we get here.

GIRL. Those who can eat.

MERTON. [*Stands in sheer excitement—for a moment, his eyes sparkling—finally looks at his watch.*]   It's about two o'clock now.   That's—not so long, is it?

GIRL.   No time at all.

MERTON.   I mean, if I go to bed early, why, that'll make the time pass so much more quickly.

GIRL.   [*To the* CASTING DIRECTOR.]   I didn't think it was possible.

MERTON.   What?

GIRL.   Nothing.

MERTON.   [*His face alight with a new idea—rushes to the window.*]   I—I'm working here now!

CASTING DIRECTOR.   So?

MERTON.   You remember before I asked if I could go in, and you asked if I was working here?   Well, now I am!   [*He waits in suspense for the decision.*]

> [*The* CASTING DIRECTOR *looks up at the* MONTAGUE GIRL, *who nods.*]

CASTING DIRECTOR.   Why, sure.   Go right in.

MERTON.   [*In a trance.*]   Thanks.

> [*He starts to walk toward the door leading to the lot, when he is conscious of a slight commotion at the other side of the room. A* FOOTMAN *enters—stiff, eyes straight ahead. He walks across the stage and disappears into the lot.* MERTON *looks after him—all eyes. In that moment another* FOOTMAN *comes on, this one with an automobile rug folded over his arm. He too crosses and goes out—all dignity. You get the feeling that he is preceding no one less than the Queen of England.*]

MERTON.   [*To the* GIRL, *in an awed whisper.*]   Who is it?

GIRL.   I think it's a friend of yours.

MERTON. You don't mean— [*He can hardly utter
the name.*] —Beulah Baxter?

> [*The* GIRL *nods. A second's impressive pause—
> and then* BEULAH BAXTER *herself enters. A
> gorgeous, gorgeous creature—particularly in
> the eyes of* MERTON. *Behind her comes a
> French maid, carrying a fluffy dog.* BEULAH
> *walks majestically across the stage, throws a
> condescending look back at her Maid, goes
> with dignity onto the lot.* MERTON, *trans-
> ported to a seventh heaven, stumbles blindly
> after her.*]

CURTAIN

ACT III

SCENE I

*The scene is Stage No. 6 on the Holden Lot—the time
about two-thirty on the following afternoon. It is a
typical motion-picture studio stage, inclosed in glass.
It is cluttered with all of the lighting paraphernalia
that the movies find so helpful—endless quantities of
it, great ropes of cable that cross and recross each
other on the floor, lights that beat down from overhead, lights from the side, lights from everywhere.
In the centre of the studio are set two walls of a lux-
urious room—a room filled with rich carpets, and
tapestries, and paintings, and fine furniture. In the
centre of this room is a platform, and on it a young
woman in evening dress, seated in a chair. She is
crying madly, and two motion-picture cameras are
grinding away at her.* HENSHAW *is there, directing
the scene, tearing his hair. A violinist is playing.*

Merton and the Montague Girl are standing around—so are numerous other extras, all in evening clothes. So is Harold Parmalee. A scene of enormous color, and life, and incident and excitement.

Henshaw. [*Directing the crying girl as the curtain rises.*] That's it! That's it! Hold it! Getting it, Phil? That's the stuff! Your heart's breaking, you're absolutely miserable! Give me tears!—give me tears! Everything is terrible—things couldn't be worse! There's been a big earthquake; the ship's gone down! I'm sick! I'm dying! Don't cover your face with your handkerchief—we're taking your face, not the hair on your head! I'm getting worse! You can't have that car! More tears! Damn it—more tears! Oh, my God, but you're miserable! [*His tone suddenly becomes matter-of-fact.*] All right —save it!

Weller. Save it! [*He blows a whistle—the more fierce of the lights are turned off.*]

Henshaw. That's the flask-back, Harold—when you sit there thinking. We'll take some more of it to-morow. Shift, Weller!

Weller. Shift! [*The whistle again—the centre platform is removed.*]

Henshaw. [*To the crying one.*] Muriel.

Muriel. Yeh?

Henshaw. We'll take some more of that to-morrow. So be here promptly.

Muriel. [*Carelessly.*] All right, sweetheart.

Henshaw. [*Warningly.*] Not here, not here! [*Turns to Parmalee.*] Now, Harold, ready for you! We're back in your rooms. Now everybody get this. You, Harold, are— [*He stops short as a mysterious and important-looking stranger enters briskly, followed by two other men. Every one in the studio stops work immediately; is extremely respectful. The stranger looks the place over; whispers to the men who are with him.* HENSHAW *greets him with affability; the stranger tosses a* "How are you?" *to him and goes on his way.* HENSHAW *then resumes his instructions.*] Now, Harold! You're Schuyler Van Rensselaer, a New York society man. We'll use those shots of you on a polo pony. But he's sick of the whole game. Now for this new scene! In the midst of a party, when he has a whole lot of guests, he goes to— [*He sits on a chair specially reserved for him, only to find* MERTON *sitting there already. He gets up and bows to* MERTON *with elaborate sarcasm.*] I beg your pardon!

MERTON. [*Scrambling out of the way.*] Ex—excuse me!

HENSHAW. Good Lord! Now where was I? [*He is screaming.*] Where was I? Where was I?

WELLER. [*Prompting him.*] He has a whole lot of guests.

HENSHAW. Yes—he has a whole lot of guests. [*Turns to* MERTON.] Idiot! [*To* HAROLD.] Society people. And he turns on them and bawls them out—there's a big kick for you, Harold—and says he's going to go some place and live alone. The simple life—see? And somebody says, "Oh, like Robinson Crusoe?" Only we introduce it natural, with the book on the table. [*Indicates the book.*] And he says, "Yes—that's just what he's going to do—live on an island like Robinson Crusoe." Then he drives them all out, and settles down in a chair to think. He takes up the book, begins to look through it, and here's the big kick! [*He pauses for effect.*] He dreams he's Robinson Crusoe. [WELLER *indulges in a long, low whistle, implying that the majesty of the idea is too much for words to express.* HENSHAW *turns to him.*] Like it?

WELLER. Big stuff, Chief.

PARMALEE. Ah—how about the scene—you know, the scene in the book about—fifteen men on a dead man's chest? Do you show that later?

HENSHAW. [*Puzzled.*] I don't just remember that. As a matter of fact, I just skimmed that passage.

PARMALEE. Well, I thought that would be rather a good scene, you know. The—the dead man, and all that.

HENSHAW. Oh, yes. [*Vaguely.*] I thought that was in *Monte Cristo.*

WELLER. I don't think it's in *Crusoe.*

PARMALEE. Well, I remember as a child——

GIRL. [*meekly.*] Excuse me, Mr. Rosenblatt.

HENSHAW. Yes—what is it?

GIRL. I think that's from *Romeo and Juliet.*

HENSHAW. Oh, yes—the court-room scene. [*A pause.*] Well, now we'll start presently. I've got to think a minute—I want to get just the right atmosphere. How'll we begin? How'll we begin?

WELLER. Can I help you, Commander?

HENSHAW. [*Pacing.*] No, no, I must work these things out myself. Now, let's see—which is the best method to reach the big moment—the——

WELLER. [*Calling.*] Max! Max! Here with your fiddle!

[*The* VIOLINIST *enters.*]

HENSHAW. Haven't you a harp?

WELLER. Got a harp?

MAX. No, sir.

HENSHAW. H'm. Well, go ahead.

[MAX *begins to play.*]

HENSHAW. No, no, no! Give me a Venetian motif!

[MAX *resumes playing.* HENSHAW *paces;* MAX *walks after him, playing. They pace up and down, followed by* MERTON, *intent on seeing how it is done.* HENSHAW, VIOLINIST, *and* MERTON *walk off.*]

GIRL. The guy they need for this picture is Fritz Kreisler.

[HENSHAW *re-enters, followed by* MAX, *still playing.*]

HENSHAW. [*Clapping his hands.*] Come, come!

WELLER. [*Rings bell.*] Come, now—Mr. Henshaw's ready. Did you get it, Chief?

HENSHAW. [*Nods.*] I'm just in the mood. Now, then, Harold, this retake! Prominent young clubman, lavish home—lots of class—and just a little bit bored. You remember.

PARMALEE. Oh, by the way. [*Produces a rich dressing-gown.*] Suppose I have this on, and then take it off and put on my dinner coat. It's rather a good bit. They *do* it.

HENSHAW. All right! You remember: you're thinking, "Oh, if I could get away from it all!" See?

PARMALEE. [*Slightly bored.*] I can do it.

HENSHAW. I'm sure you can. Give him some music, there! Society stuff!

WELLER. [*Calling.*] Society music!

[MAX *begins to play.*]

HENSHAW. Now, then, everybody ready! Lights!

WELLER. Kick it!

[*Whistles—lights go on.*]

HENSHAW. Ready, Phil?

WELLER. Just a minute, Commander. [*He goes up to a door.*] This door has to be closed. [*Speaks to spotlight man.*] And you up there—be sure and keep those

spots directly on him!   [*To* HENSHAW.]   Take a look at
the set, Commander.

[*Walks back to his camera.*]

HENSHAW.   [*Looking through a blue glass.*]   Just
right, Weller!   Now, Harold!   More poise, more poise!
How about you, Weller?

WELLER.   All right, Commander.

HENSHAW.   Camera!   That's it—take your time—
you're thinking, "Oh, if I could get away from it all!"

PARMALEE.   Just a minute.   [*He stops the scene; beck-
ons to his Jap valet, who comes forward with a mirror.
PARMALEE takes a look at himself; is apparently satisfied.*]
Go ahead!

HENSHAW.   Camera!   That's the stuff—you're dead
tired—you've been dancing till six o'clock—you're sick of
the whole game—nothing means a thing to you—you're all
in—you're tired—save it!

WELLER.   Save it!

[*The lights go off with a clank; the music stops.
WELLER rushes in front of the camera, holding
up a numbered slate.   PARMALEE relaxes,
rises.*]

HENSHAW.   All right—all right!   Let's get some of
this dance stuff.

WELLER.   Dance stuff!

PARMALEE.   Ah—the scene with the dressing-gown.

HENSHAW.   Oh,   all   right, all   right.   Camera!
[*Cameras turn and PARMALEE removes his coat and gets
into his dressing-gown.*]   Come on, Harold, not too much
footage—it's just a five-reeler.   Save it!

WELLER.   Save it!

HENSHAW.   Now we'll take the dance stuff.

WELLER.   Dance stuff!

HENSHAW.   [*To the Extras.*]   You people get around

to this side for the dance stuff and make it snappy! Shake a leg! [*He picks up the copy of "Robinson Crusoe."*] Wait a minute! I'll do the book scene first. [*Opens the book; looks at title-page.*] H'm. It's an old story, isn't it? [*A pause.*] Now I want somebody to come down and discover this book on the table. Who can do that?

MERTON. [*As the extras press forward.*] I can, sir.

HENSHAW. All right—you'll do. You find the book on the table, see? It's *Robinson Crusoe,* and you're a little surprised. It isn't the book you'd expect to find on a gentleman's table. Then you say: "Ah!"—let's hear that sub-title, Weller.

WELLER. [*Reading it.*] "I see you are a book-worm."

HENSHAW. Splendid! Then, Harold, *you* say—what is it?

[*Snaps fingers.*]

WELLER. [*Reading again.*] "Yes, that is *Robinson Crusoe,* a fascinating romance, and one of the greatest stories ever written. There are times when I envy him."

HENSHAW. Exactly! Now run through that. There's the book—see? You come down casually and discover it —I'll just move this table down and get a better perspective. Now run through that. [HENSHAW *sits and* MERTON *goes up, smiling at the* GIRL *as he does so. Then he walks down to the table, but does not exactly make a success of it.*] No! No! Not as if you *knew* you were going to find it—accidental! Try it again! [MERTON *tries it again, but does not do it much better.* HENSHAW *turns with disgust.*] All right—you discover the book—pick it up. [MERTON *gives a sharp reaction of surprise upon discovering the book; starts back as though struck.* HENSHAW *throws his MSS. on the floor and paces.*] No—no —nothing like it! [*Goes up to* MERTON; *holds the book in front of his nose.*] It's a book, not a rattlesnake!

[*Slams it down.*]   Didn't you ever see a book before?

MERTON.   Yes, sir.

HENSHAW.   I don't believe it!

GIRL.   Mr. Henshaw!

HENSHAW.   Yes, yes?

GIRL.   I think if you give him another chance he could do it.

HENSHAW.   All right—try it again.   [*Sits.* MERTON *falls back, and approaches this time with elaborate carelessness. He finds the book with extreme languor.* HENSHAW *sits with head in hands.*]   No—no—that won't do at all!   No—no!   [*To* MERTON.]   We've got to get—oh Lord!   It certainly takes it out of a man mentally.

MERTON.   I think I understand now, if you'll let me try again.

HENSHAW.   No, no, my nerves are going.   I must do something new.

WELLER.   You ought to take a rest, Commander.

HENSHAW.   Oh, I don't mind it when I get something in return, but these extras they give me—bah!

WELLER.   I'd knock off, Commander—you're all in! It's been a long day.

HENSHAW.   I *am* wearied.   My brain——

WELLER.   Call 'em again to-morrow.

HENSHAW.   [*Considering it.*]   Perhaps you're right. I must feel fresh.

WELLER.   Shall I tell them?

HENSHAW.   I will.   [*He raises his voice.*]   That's all to-day.   Everybody again at eight-thirty to-morrow morning; same clothes and make-up.

WELLER.   Eight-thirty to-morrow morning.

MERTON.   Mr. Henshaw.

HENSHAW.   Oh, yes, *you*.   You needn't bother to report to-morrow morning.

MERTON. Sir?

HENSHAW. Mr. Weller will give you your pay order.

MERTON. You mean—I wasn't any good?

HENSHAW. I—I need a different type for this sort of thing, that's all. [*He calls.*] Tim!

[*He starts to move off.*]

VOICE. [*Somewhere in the distance.*] Yes, sir?

HENSHAW. Just leave this whole set where it is. I'm going to use it again in the morning.

VOICE. Yes, sir.

WELLER. All right, boys, you're through for the day.

MERTON. But, Mr. Henshaw——

HENSHAW. [*Calling to* TIM *again.*] Oh! You're not to touch a thing, understand?

VOICE. [*Off.*] Yes, sir.

MERTON. Mr. Henshaw, can't I——

HENSHAW. And Weller!

WELLER. Yes, sir.

HENSHAW. Now I want——

MERTON. [*Follows* HENSHAW.] All I ask is to speak to you just for——

HENSHAW. What? What is it? What do you want?

MERTON. If you could only give me one more chance——

HENSHAW. Good heavens—I can't use you! Isn't that enough? Coming, Weller?

WELLER. Yes—yes. Here's your pay check.

[*Hands it to* MERTON.]

HENSHAW. [*To* VIOLINIST.] Oh, Max!

MAX. Yes, sir?

HENSHAW. I'm going to dope out a new scene in my office. I want you and your fiddle.

MAX. All right, sir.

HENSHAW. Now don't go away.

MAX. No, sir.

HENSHAW. Now, Weller, this island stuff that we're going to take——

> [HENSHAW, WELLER, and MAX *depart.* MERTON *and the* GIRL *are left alone.*]

GIRL. It's—it's all right, kid. That doesn't mean anything. You'll get lots of bumps like that.

MERTON. No, I—I——

GIRL. The big bum's crazy, that's all. [*She forces herself back to the optimistic mood.*] But don't let it do anything to you. They—they can't put you down, can they?

MERTON. I'm not—down.

GIRL. Of course you're not.

MERTON. I didn't know what he meant—when——

GIRL. Who does?

MERTON. When a person's making their first appearance and all—why——

GIRL. Sure. I know. Why, the first time they aimed a camera at me I thought there was bullets in it.

MERTON. But still, it *was* my chance, and I had to go and—fail.

GIRL. Fail? Just because of a little thing like that? Why, you're going to succeed big. All you need is—confidence in yourself.

MERTON. Is it?

GIRL. That's all most of them have.

MERTON. I wish he'd given me another chance. I could have done it the next time.

GIRL. I know! Don't you worry about *him.* Why, he even fired Parmalee once.

MERTON. He did? [*Thinks it over.*] I could act the way Parmalee does if I—practised enough.

GIRL. Of course you could. The only thing is——
[*She stops.*]

MERTON. What?

GIRL. Well—sometimes it takes a long while before
you really—that is, before they give you a chance.

MERTON. Oh, I *want* to struggle.

GIRL. [*Quickly.*] Yah, but—if it *should* take a while
—I mean before you—well—are you fixed all right for
it? Money, I mean?

MERTON. [*Turning away.*] Oh—yes.

GIRL. [*Watching him narrowly.*] That's good. Say,
maybe I can get you something over at the Bigart next
week.

MERTON. Oh, no, thanks. You remember—I want to
work only at this studio.

GIRL. Still sticking to that idea, eh?

MERTON. Oh, yes. Yes, indeed. Do you think—do
you think there'd be any chance of my getting into her
company—Miss Baxter's, I mean?

GIRL. Well, I wouldn't work with her just yet, if I
were you.

MERTON. You wouldn't? Why not?

GIRL. Oh, I don't know. I just wouldn't.

MERTON. Oh, but I want to. That's one of the things
I came out for.

GIRL. Well, if that's what you insist on doing——

MERTON. I bet if I got with her I could learn how to
act. And then if I practised at the same time——

GIRL. And you're—you're sure you've got plenty of
money?

MERTON. Oh, I don't care about that. I mean, what
does money matter when—when—you just watch me.
I'll practise, and some time when I'm acting with Miss
Baxter, why, Mr. Henshaw'll come along, and——

GIRL.   Well, there's nobody can say you're not trying.
[*Pause.*]   Coming?

MERTON.   Oh, no.   I don't want to go off the lot—
just yet.   I mean——

    [*He looks involuntarily at the table and book.*]

GIRL.   Suit yourself.   Sure you're not coming?

MERTON.   Not—just yet.

GIRL.   Well, will I find you around—some time?

MERTON.   Oh, yes.   I'll be on the lot.

GIRL.   That's good.   So will I—if—if the time ever
comes when you need me.   So-long!

MERTON.   So-long!

    [*She goes.   MERTON, left alone, quickly re-ar-
    ranges the book on the table.   He plays the
    book scene over again, with pathetic eagerness.
    He walks down-stage, as before, picks up the
    book, then he pauses, and brushes away a tear.
    You hear MAX's violin in the distance.   He
    keeps at it—goes up again.   He comes down
    perfectly, times all gestures perfectly, picks
    up book with a slow, graceful motion, and a
    boyish grin of pleasure comes over his face at
    knowing he has done it all correctly.   The
    music reaches a crescendo off-stage.*]

CURTAIN

SCENE II

*The scene is elsewhere on the lot—the time is a week later,
at night.   Shafts of light reveal the fact that it is a
water scene.   There is a huge boat rocking on the
water; if it were not for the lights that play on it you
might imagine that it was all real.*

You hear ROSENBLATT's voice before the curtain rises.

ROSENBLATT. Now, Harry, you understand this is your camera line—catching this point of the boat—you'll get your flashes through the lightning— [*The curtain rises.*] And Harry—try to cut under the bowsprit! All right, boys! Now stand ready on those lights and don't let them wabble—I don't want a retake on this and I don't want to stay here all night. Now watch them——

[BEULAH BAXTER *enters.*]

BEULAH. [*Indicating sailor suit.*] How's this?

ROSENBLATT. All right!

[*He goes.* BEULAH'S *Maid enters.*]

MAID. The—the young man is hanging around again.

BEULAH. What young man? Not that—same one?

MAID. Yes, ma'am.

BEULAH. He's going to drive me crazy—I've been telling them for a week to get rid of him. Why, it's been over a week.

MAID. [*Nods.*] Since the picture began.

BEULAH. He's beginning to get on my nerves. Following me every place.

MAID. Perhaps if you would speak to him once—tell him to go away——

BEULAH. [*Sits on a rough bench.*] I certainly will. Ah—where is he?

MAID. Why—there he is.

BEULAH. Oh, young man! Come here.

[MERTON *enters—a* MERTON *worn, bedraggled, and unshaven.*]

MERTON. [*Eagerly.*] Yes, Miss Baxter?

BEULAH. You've been following me around for a week, and now it must stop.

MERTON. But I—I haven't. All I wanted was——

BEULAH. What *do* you want? That's just what I'd like to know.

MERTON. Oh, I—I only thought if you'd just let me be around——

BEULAH. Oh!

MERTON. [*Noticing the boat.*]   Are you going to do the scene on the ship to-night?

BEULAH. I suppose so. But tell me—you've seen me in my pictures, is that it?

MERTON. Oh, yes. And I've admired you, Miss Baxter—I think you're wonderful.

BEULAH. [*Pleased.*]   You don't say so.

MERTON. You're—you're my ideal—practically.

BEULAH. Really? Won't you sit down?

MERTON. [*Sits.*]   Do you remember—when you made that personal appearance—in Peoria? I don't suppose you saw me—I was right in the front row, though—and I was the one that—opened the door of your automobile, afterward.

BEULAH. [*Amused but pleased.*]   You did?

MERTON. Yes. Of course I wouldn't expect you to remember—me. It was May 19th.

BEULAH. And you . . . you've been following me because you——

MERTON. Because I just wanted to see you—actually taking a picture—   [*He rises; looks again at the boat.*] And especially here on the ship—and I thought, maybe, if there was ever——

[ROSENBLATT *returns.*]

ROSENBLATT. All right—come on! Let's get at this! And, Beulah, you get out—you only interrupt me!

BEULAH. Is that so?

ROSENBLATT. Yes, it is! I'd have been finished long ago if you hadn't bothered me all the time.

BEULAH. It isn't my fault if you always do things wrong.

ROSENBLATT. Now, what do you mean by that?

BEULAH. Exactly what I say. There hasn't been a thing all week——

ROSENBLATT. Oh, for God's sake, shut up!

MERTON. [*Unable to stand it any longer.*] I beg your pardon, but you're forgetting yourself.

ROSENBLATT. What—what's that?

MERTON. You forget that there are ladies present. I must insist that you apologize.

[BEULAH *breaks into laughter.*]

ROSENBLATT. Apologize? [*To* MERTON.] For God's sake, get away from here! Get out! I've got enough trouble without you! Get out!

MERTON. All right, but be careful how you treat this lady—because I won't be very far away.

[*He makes a dignified exit.*]

ROSENBLATT. Well, well, I'll be—well— [BEULAH *laughs again.*] Come on, we'll take this ship scene and then we're through for the night. Where's that girl? Come on, you people—come on! [*The* GIRL *and* MON-TAGUE *enter—the former in a replica of* BEULAH's *sailor suit, the latter dressed as a seaman.*] Well, hurry up. Now we're going to shoot this jump, and——

BEULAH. Please make it clear to her that it must be a very high dive. My reputation is at stake.

ROSENBLATT. All right, all right!

BEULAH. She'll have to do better than she did in the tenement jump. Why, I'd have been ashamed to do a jump like that.

GIRL. Oh, everybody knows you'd be ashamed to do any kind of a jump, Miss Baxter.

BEULAH. [*Wheeling.*] What's that?

ROSENBLATT. Now, now! Come back here and sit down! [*The* GIRL *is mounting the boat, and presently appears high on its deck.*]   Now, what we've got to get here is action.   [*To* MONTAGUE.]   When you come out there with the gun I want you to pretty near fall off the boat a couple of times.

MONTAGUE.   [*With dignity.*]   Mr. Rosenblatt, since giving my services to the motion pictures I have been killed in a great many ways, and generally very early in the story, but——

ROSENBLATT.   All right, all right!   Now we'll shoot this one scene and then we're through for the night.

BEULAH.   Well, I for one shall not remain.   You will have to get on as well as you can without me.   I never could stand night work.

[*She goes.*]

ROSENBLATT.   Oh, you make me sick!   Now come on, people—let's get at this.   And put some guts into it! And for God's sake, Harry, watch your camera line!

[*He takes up a position just off-stage.*]

MONTAGUE.   *Guts!*   And to think that the Montagues were actors when the Rosenblatts were just Rosenblatts.

[*He goes up onto the boat.*]

ROSENBLATT.   Now make it snappy!

GIRL.   [*On the boat.*]   All right, Commander, but it's certainly not what I'd call a quiet evening with my books.

[JEFF BAIRD *strolls in.*]

BAIRD.   Hello, kid!

GIRL.   Hello, Jeff!   Still waiting?

BAIRD.   [*To* ROSENBLATT, *who has entered.*]   Hello, Rosie.

ROSENBLATT.   How are you, Baird?   [*To the* GIRL.] Now I'm going to catch this from over here—and we're going to see if we can't get it right.   Remember Miss Baxter.

GIRL.   I'll never forget her.   Will you?

ROSENBLATT. Well, let's all try!

[*Takes up his off-stage position.*]

BAIRD. Still at it, eh?

GIRL. Sure—you know Rosie. But don't go far—I'll only be ten minutes—then I'll belong to the ages. Oh, Jimmy!

[*A boy dashes on; she tosses him a blanket that she has been carrying.*]

ROSENBLATT. All right, Montague!

GIRL. All right! [*Turns to* JEFF.] It's a nice little game, Jeff, and what makes it especially good are the lovely people *in* it.

[*She disappears into the boat's cabin.*]

ROSENBLATT. [*As* BAIRD *stands looking after the girl.*] And make it snappy!

[*The lights change.* BAIRD, *whistling idly, starts to stroll off. He encounters* JIMMY; *peers at him in the semi-darkness.*]

BAIRD. Hello, Jimmy!

JIMMY. Hello, Mr. Baird.

BAIRD. Tough night, eh?

JIMMY. Certainly is.

[BAIRD *resumes his whistling and goes off.*]

ROSENBLATT. [*Off.*] Now! Let's get it right this time! Ready, back there?

MONTAGUE. [*From rear.*] Ready!

ROSENBLATT. All right! Lights! Let's have the rain—come on with the rain! [*Rain pours down; the boat rocks; the lightning flashes.*] Good! Action! Camera!

[*The* MONTAGUE GIRL *steals fearsomely out of the cabin. Just as she appears,* MERTON *strolls onto the scene. "Strolls" is not quite the word, for there is nothing debonair about*

*him just at present.   He has been sleeping on
the lot for a week, most of the time in his
clothes.   He has not shaved for four days, nor
eaten for two.   The result of his starvation is
that his thoughts are jumbled and confused,
and likely to pour forth irrelevantly.*]

MERTON.   [*To* JIMMY, *after watching for a second.*]
Gee, she's doing the ship scene, isn't she?

JIMMY.   Huh?

MERTON.   I just want to feast my eyes on her—the
wonder woman of the silver screen.

ROSENBLATT.   Come on—come on—along that rail—
keep in the camera—I want your face—come on, Montague—keep in the lightning flashes—action; action; now
you see her, Montague—get ready to jump——

[*As the* GIRL *swings to the rope and jumps,*
MONTAGUE *fires.*]

MERTON.   [*Just before she jumps.*]   She's going to
jump.

MONTAGUE.   [*After he has fired.*]   Ha, ha, ha——

MERTON.   Gosh!

ROSENBLATT.   All right, let it go at that; throw on
the guide lights, Tom—knock off till morning——

[*Effects are thrown off and the rain stops.*]

MERTON.   Gee! she's coming up right here.

JIMMY.   Sure she is.

MERTON.   Gosh!

[MERTON *falls back a few steps, awe-stricken.
There is a pause, then the* MONTAGUE GIRL
climbs up out of the water. JIMMY *throws
the blanket over her.*]

GIRL.   [*Not seeing* MERTON *at first.*]   Yes, sir!   The
bird that said they heated the water was just an ordinary
liar!

MERTON. [*Swept off his feet.*] Wh-wh-what?

GIRL. [*Peering at him.*] Hello, trouper. [*There is both surprise and concern in her voice.*] Haven't seen you for a long time. How's everything—all jake?

MERTON. Why—why— [*He looks into the water.*] —how do you come to—isn't Beulah Baxter——

JIMMY. Miss Montague's *doubling* for her. I've been trying to tell you.

GIRL. [*Regretfully.*] Jimmy!

JIMMY. [*Dully.*] Huh?

MERTON. Why—why—no—no! She doesn't ever have anybody—I heard her say so her own self.

[*JIMMY, with a shrug, walks out of the circle of light, but does not leave the stage.*]

GIRL. I'm sorry, kid, but it had to come out sooner or later. I don't like to bust up any dreams, but I've been doubling for her all along.

[*She is wringing out her skirt.*]

MERTON. [*Nearly hysterical.*] No—she wouldn't do it! I don't believe it! Why, she's the most wonderful— [*He grows incoherent.*] I don't think—Gashwiler——

GIRL. Hey! Take it easy, trouper. And—ah—let me take a look at you. You know, I haven't seen you for a week. [*MERTON makes no move to come closer. She peers at him.*] Sure everything's jake? [*MERTON nods, unable to answer.*] Had any work since that one we did together? [*No answer.*] Come on, kid—let's hear.

MERTON. [*With difficulty.*] I—I've been all right. [*Desperately.*] I've really got to get back—on—location.

[*He starts to go.*]

GIRL. Hold on! Don't hurry. If you go, I'll be all alone. [*He pauses—the GIRL turns to JIMMY.*] Oh, Jimmy!

JIMMY. [*From the darkness.*] Yes, Miss Montague.

GIRL. Run over and get two cups of coffee and about four of those sandwiches.

JIMMY. Right!

[*He disappears.*]

MERTON. Not—anything for me, thank you.

GIRL. Oh, I know—that's for Jimmy and me.

MERTON. So then if you don't mind I'll be getting back.

GIRL. Don't run away! Come on over here where I can see you. [*He comes, reluctantly.*] That's the stuff. Take a seat. [*He sits on an upturned box. She looks at him closely.*] What makes you look like that?

MERTON. I—we were taking miner stuff, and——

GIRL. Miner stuff?

MERTON. [*Suddenly conscious of his appearance.*] That's the reason I— [*His hand goes to his chin.*] —raised a garden. [*The word comes strangely from him. He is imitating her, of course.*] I've got to get back.

[*He rises—the note of hysteria is again in his voice.*]

GIRL. [*In cool tones of command.*] You're not going yet, trouper. [*A pause.*] You know you've got to learn to face the music.

MERTON. [*His resistance wearing down.*] Yes?

GIRL. You've had a little dream go back on you to-night, and you're sort of broken up. But as long as things have gone that far you might as well hear the rest of it.

MERTON. [*Irrelevantly.*] She said she was keeping faith with her public.

GIRL. They all say it. In the first place, Rosenblatt—[MERTON *looks up. The* GIRL *proceeds gently.*] Well, he's her husband.

MERTON. That—director?

GIRL. And that ain't all. He's her fourth—since she began counting.

MERTON. [*Dully.*] He's her—husband? Beulah Baxter is—Mrs. Rosenblatt?

GIRL. [*Sympathetically.*] That's right.

MERTON. And you've been—doubling for her?

GIRL. That's right.

MERTON. But—where she rode across the canyon in a bucket— [*The* GIRL *nods.*] —and drove her automobile off the bridge— [*Another nod.*] —and crept along the side of that building——

GIRL. [*Nods.*] All Little Eva.

MERTON. [*Completely crushed.*] Oh, my God!

> [JIMMY *appears with the coffee and sandwiches.*]

GIRL. Here we are! Have a sandwich, trouper?

MERTON. [*Scoring the dramatic triumph of his life.*] No, thanks. I couldn't eat a mouthful.

GIRL. [*With determination this time.*] Sit down! [*He does so.*] It was a grand performance, kid, but it didn't fool mother for a minute. [MERTON *averts his gaze.*] Have a sandwich. [*This time* MERTON *takes the sandwich. He eats it voraciously—in about three bites. No word is spoken—but when the sandwich is finished the* GIRL *simply hands him another.*] Hey! Slow up for the curves. [*It goes like the first—still without a word. He seems to expect a third.*] You've got to start in easy. Have some coffee? [*He takes it. He calms down a little.*] When did you eat last?

MERTON. [*In a whisper.*] I can't remember.

GIRL. [*Looking at his clothes.*] You haven't been home?

MERTON. [*Beginning to find himself.*] I—I didn't have any money—except what I got that one day.

GIRL. With *Crusoe?*

MERTON. [*Nods.*] It lasted till—a couple of days ago.

GIRL. [*Puzzled.*] But if you didn't go home——

MERTON. I—I been right on the lot.

GIRL. For a week?

MERTON. [*Another nod.*] I was afraid if I went out —I couldn't get back on again. So I—I found a cabin they'd put up, and—there was a bed in it, and then when they tore that down, after the fight, why, there was a picture where a girl was told to come home, her mother was dying, and I waited, and pretty soon they showed the mother and she was in bed. That night, after they'd all gone, I—slept there.

GIRL. [*Shaking her head.*] Well, you're certainly made out of the stuff that gets there. Where'd you come from?

MERTON. Simsbury, Illinois. I worked in a store there.

GIRL. I see.

MERTON. But I always wanted to be a picture actor. I used to go to see— [*His voice changes.*] —Beulah— Baxter—whenever they showed one of her pictures—and —Harold Parmalee, and all of them. And I read where they were trying to do something bigger and finer, and I thought if *I* came out here—well, it's worth sacrificing to do something worth while—don't you think?

GIRL. Go on! Don't ask *me* anything.

MERTON. So I saved up two hundred and seventy dollars, and while I was doing it I practised acting all I could.

GIRL. How did you practise?

MERTON. [*Digging a document from his pocket.*]

Well, well, you see, this is it! It's the Film Incorporation Bureau's course—see, it certifies, right there——

GIRL. [*Examining it.*] A course in acting?

MERTON. Yes.

GIRL. [*Still looking at it.*] Stebbensville, Kansas.

MERTON. That's where their main school is, but then they can tell if you're talented, because they send you a list of questions, and if you don't answer them right, why, they won't accept you, but if you do, then they let you have the course.

GIRL. And you answered them all right?

MERTON. They—they said my answers showed unusual talents. Then besides, I—I sent them my art studies— [*He delves into his pocket.*] —you see, showing me as different characters——

[*Hands pictures to* GIRL.]

GIRL. [*Half to herself, as she takes them.*] For God's sake!

MERTON. [*Looking at them with her.*] You see, That's—that's me as Two-Gun Benson.

GIRL. [*Her eyes beginning to light up.*] Saying good-by to the horse!

MERTON. Yes—you know that scene——

GIRL. Do I? I've raised horses for it.

MERTON. And then here I am for society dramas. I mean where the girl's father is a power in Wall Street— like that one where——

GIRL. [*Rises, still more excited as she inspects this photograph.*] What a minute! Kid, this one is great— positively great!

MERTON. [*Pleased.*] Do you think so?

GIRL. [*Reading the inscription.*] "Yours truly, Clifford Armytage."

GIRL. [*She looks from* MERTON *to the photograph.*]

There's—there's something here I can't put my finger on —it reminds me of somebody. [MERTON, *pleased, waits for her to guess.*]   Somebody I've seen lately—somebody that—I've got it! Harold Parmalee!

MERTON.   I hoped you'd notice it!   That's what I want to do—like he does—really serious things that—that will help to uplift screen art—I mean big things in a really big way, and——

GIRL.   [*Looking at him as though transfixed.*]   Kid!

MERTON.   Yes?

GIRL.   Turn your face that way! [*He does so.*] Now toward me again! [MERTON *does so.*]   It's great —positively great—even with the lace you can't miss it!

MERTON.   Huh!

GIRL.   [*She whisks out some bills.*]   I want you to take this and go home and get all cleaned up and some food inside of you and come back and meet me here at eight o'clock in the morning!   Got that straight?

MERTON.   Oh, I couldn't accept——

GIRL.   I'm only lending it to you, and you're going to pay me back.   You're going to be a big success—I got something all planned out!   God help me!

[*This last is in lowered voice.*]

BAIRD.   [*From off.*]   How are you coming kid?

GIRL.   Don't go away, Jeff—just the guy I want! Jimmy! Oh, Jimmy!

[JIMMY *appears.*]

JIMMY.   Yes, Miss Montague?

GIRL.   Jimmy, I want you to go with the trouper here — [*She turns to* MERTON.]   What's your name?

MERTON.   [*A second's hesitation.*]   Clifford Armytage.

GIRL.   Your name, not your residence.

MERTON. [*Glad to get it out.*] Merton Gill.

GIRL. That's better. [*Back to* JIMMY.] I want you to travel along with Merton here while he goes home and gets cleaned up. [*To* MERTON.] Do you remember where you live?

MERTON. Yes, but I——

GIRL. That's enough! [*Back to* JIMMY.] Then take him to a restaurant and feed him till he cries for help! Get that?

JIMMY. [*Catching her excitement.*] Yes!

GIRL. After that, go back home with him and don't leave him! Get this straight—sit up with him all night if necessary and see that he's on this spot at nine o'clock to-morrow morning!

MERTON. [*As* JIMMY *starts to take him away.*] But —I—I—don't want to——

GIRL. And if you don't go right away I'll come along myself. [JIMMY *and* MERTON *disappear;* JEFF BAIRD *returns.*] Jeff, I've found a million dollars for you!

BAIRD. [*With a half-turn away.*] It's yours.

GIRL. [*Grabbing him.*] No, get this! He's a galoot that came here from Cranberry or some place to be an actor! He took an acting course by correspondence and got a lot of photographs taken! Here they are! [*She passes them over.*] Who's he look like?

BAIRD. Good Lord!

GIRL. A dead ringer!

BAIRD. But what are you going to do about it?

GIRL. Don't you see? He looks like Parmalee and he wants to do Parmalee stuff! All right, put him in a Buckeye comedy, and let him kid the life out of Parmalee! Only don't tell him he's supposed to be funny.

BAIRD. [*Letting it dawn on him slowly, looks at the*

photograph again.]   It looks wonderful, but can we put it over?

GIRL.   Yes, but not if he knows it's a comedy.   He hates comedies.

BAIRD.   It's taking an awful chance.

GIRL.   We can fix it easy.

BAIRD.   But it's a bear of an idea.   You're sure he doesn't know he's funny?

GIRL.   He doesn't know anything's funny.   You've got to put him absolutely serious in one of those screams of yours, with Bert Chester's cross-eyes, and he'll be immense!

BAIRD.   But suppose he finds out?

GIRL.   That's the only thing I'm afraid of.   We've got to keep it from him for a while, that's all.   He's got a trusting way of looking at you that's sort of got me, and if he ever finds out I did it, I couldn't stand it.   He's a nice kid, but he certainly looks like the second plume on a hearse.

BAIRD.   [*Noticing* MERTON, *who has returned with* JIMMY.]   Psst!

GIRL.   [*In a quick, tense undertone.*]   Do you think he heard?

BAIRD.   [*In the same tone.*]   I'm not sure.

MERTON.   I—I didn't remember if I'd—that is—I came back to thank you for——

GIRL.   Oh, that's all right.   You remember Mr. Baird, don't you—Jeff Baird?

BAIRD.   How are you, kid?

MERTON.   Oh, yes.

BAIRD.   Well, you're going to work for me, now.

MERTON.   What?

GIRL.   Surest thing you know.

BAIRD. I'm going to give you a *real* chance and in *real* pictures.

MERTON. But he—he only makes—comedies.

GIRL. Comedies? I should say not! Why, he's——

BAIRD. Well, I used to make comedies, but I'm through with them. From now on I'm going to make serious pictures.

MERTON. Serious pictures? [*To the* GIRL.] Is he— honestly?

GIRL. Why—yes.

BAIRD. Of course I may make a comedy once in a while, but I'm anxious to enter a bigger field.

MERTON. Oh, I'm awfully glad. You're sure you mean—regular serious ones?

BAIRD. Yes, indeed!

MERTON. Significant—I mean?

BAIRD. That's the word, exactly.

MERTON. And—and you want me to—come with you?

BAIRD. You bet I do! You've had a wonderful recommendation.

[*He glances at the photos.*]

MERTON. [*To the* GIRL.] You did it! You did it all! It's everything I ever hoped for! It's my great opportunity! I've always dreamed about it! And now you've made it possible! You've opened the door for me!

GIRL. [*More than willing not to be thanked.*] That's all right.

MERTON. [*Back to* BAIRD.] And—and Mr. Baird, too! You're going to make serious pictures at last! I— I'm awfully glad to hear that. I'll give you my best, my very best. [*He shakes* BAIRD's *hand.*] And oh! I certainly congratulate you, Mr. Baird—I certainly congratulate you!

CURTAIN

ACT IV

SCENE I

The scene is JEFF BAIRD'S *office—the time a few months later. The walls are adorned with advertisements of the various Buckeye films of the past—illustrated with cross-eyed men caught in embarrassing positions, and carrying such titles as "How's Grandpa?" and "Should an Uncle Tell?" For furniture there is chiefly* JEFF BAIRD'S *desk. At one side, however, is a cutting-table, and a youth named* EDDIE *is busily cutting and pasting film as the curtain rises.*

Instantly BERT CHESTER, *the cross-eyed man, enters. He is doubling up with laughter.*

BERT.   Oh, gosh!

EDDIE.   [*Turning.*]   What's the matter?

BERT.   Just took a retake on the kid's picture. You know—young Armytage.

EDDIE.   Yah?   How was it?

BERT.   Swell, but he don't know it. If I'd stayed there another second I'd have given the whole game away. Bust right out laughing.

EDDIE.   Haven't they told him yet?

BERT.   Not a word.   And when he finds out——

EDDIE.   Well, he hasn't got long to wait.

BERT.   What do you mean?

EDDIE.   I just got orders to rush it through for a public showing.   It goes on at the Fresco to-morrow night.

BERT.   To-morrow night?   Does he know it?

EDDIE.   I suppose so.

BERT.   And he'll *be* there?

EDDIE.   Don't know why not.

BERT. [*A long, low whistle; speaks softly, half to himself.*] To-morrow night, eh?

EDDIE. [*Turning to his work again.*] That's right.

    [JEFF BAIRD *enters—evidently with something on his mind.*]

BAIRD. [*Sternly, to* BERT.] Oh, there you are!

BERT. Who? Me?

BAIRD. Yes, you! You pretty near queered the whole picture by laughing in the middle of that scene. And the kid saw you, too.

BERT. I don't know what you're talking about.

BAIRD. Oh, yes, you do! I'm talking about the way you laughed while Armytage was acting just now.

BERT. Well, I can't help it if it's comic.

BAIRD. But he doesn't know it's comic. Can't you understand that?

BERT. Anyhow, Eddie says you're going to show the picture to-morrow night. He'll be there, won't he?

BAIRD. To-morrow night is different. The point is, I don't want him to find out while I'm around.

EDDIE. [*A piece of film in his hand.*] Here's the other half of the fight.

BAIRD. [*To* EDDIE.] All right. [*To* BERT *again.*] Don't you see, Bert? We've got to break it to him just so, or he won't make any more for us. Now, to-morrow we're finished and we're all right.

BERT. Yah—we're fine. [*He is standing at the door.*] If he doesn't shoot us.

    [*He goes.*]

BAIRD. [*To* EDDIE.] Find it?

EDDIE. Yah. Here's where he knocks the screen off the free lunch.

BAIRD. [*Inspecting it.*] Mm. [*Hands it back.*]

Leave it just like that and then put in that piece where the cheese jumps up and bites the bartender.

EDDIE. I'm on. Say, that'll give him a jolt, won't it?

[*The* MONTAGUE GIRL *enters—a bit uncertainly, and lacking her old spring.*]

GIRL. Hello, Jeff.

BAIRD. Hello.

GIRL. Jeff, could I see you alone for a minute?

BAIRD. Sure. Eddie, take that new No. 6 title over to Jackson.

EDDIE. Yes, sir.

[*He goes, carrying a printed title with him.*]

BAIRD. [*As he sits.*] Now then, kid. What's the matter?

GIRL. He's outside there, waiting to see you.

BAIRD. [*Gets up at once.*] Yah? Well, we'll soon——

GIRL. [*Stopping.*] No! No—wait, Jeff.

BAIRD. Sounds serious. [*He sits again.*] All right.

GIRL. Is—is it true you're going to show the picture to-morrow night?

BAIRD. That's what.

GIRL. Isn't that awful quick?

BAIRD. Well, maybe, but it's a new stunt and they want to get a line on it. The order came from up above.

GIRL. Oh, gee! That means—he's going to find out at last.

BAIRD. [*Compelled to admit it.*] Well—yes.

GIRL. I'm scared, Jeff. Scared of what he's going to do.

BAIRD. Nonsense. Why, he'll take it all right.

GIRL. I'm sorry we ever did it, Jeff. It was a mean trick.

BAIRD. He'll behave all right.

GIRL. I just watched him out there, waiting. I never felt so guilty in my life. He was so trustful, Jeff. He really believes in his heart he's doing a big, vital drama.

BAIRD. He's getting good money and you've saved his life.

GIRL. I'm wondering whether anybody could have forced him to take that money if he'd known what he was doing. When I think of him coming all the way out here to Hollywood, so innocent he didn't know a close-up from a censor; and of our making a Buckeye comedy out of him without him knowing it——

BAIRD. Say, you're not getting emotional, are you?

GIRL. What?

BAIRD. I say, you're not falling for this kid?

GIRL. I don't know. What do you think?

BAIRD. I don't know—yet.

GIRL. If you find out, I wish you'd tell me. I never felt this way before. You know, he came out here with a lot of ideals and he's lost one or two of them already. And when I think of that look in his eyes——

BAIRD. Still, he's got to find out some day—hasn't he?

GIRL. I suppose so.

BAIRD. Well, then, let nature take its course.

GIRL. I wonder just what that'll be, Jeff. Is it going to knock him out, or will he bounce? And I was also kind of wondering whether he'd ever speak to me again. [*Pause, then brightly.*] Oh, well! You're ready for the kid now, huh?

BAIRD. Sure. Let him come in.

GIRL. [*Opening the door.*] All right, Merton. Merton!

> [*She goes. MERTON enters, wearing chaps, sombrero, and spurs.*]

BAIRD. Well?

MERTON. Mr. Baird, there's something I want to talk to you about.

BAIRD. Sure.

MERTON. I—I don't like to say anything about anybody that isn't fair, Mr. Baird, but——

BAIRD. I want to hear any complaints, Merton.

MERTON. Well, it's—Mr. Bert Chester.

BAIRD. Yes?

MERTON. Yes. I think he's taking his work pretty lightly, Mr. Baird.

BAIRD. How do you mean, Merton?

MERTON. Well, inasmuch as you let him keep on acting in spite of his cross-eyes—I mean, because of his sick mother, and all that—I don't think he ought to laugh when people are doing serious work.

BAIRD. Oh, you mean this morning? For a minute *I* thought he was laughing, too. Then I saw it was just an old lip trouble he's had for years. It's a sort of nervous tickling he gets. He apologized to me and asked me to apologize to you. I guess he was afraid you'd laugh at him—he *is* kind of ridiculous, with all his ailments.

MERTON. I wouldn't have laughed.

BAIRD. No. I know you wouldn't. But he's just terribly sensitive. However, if you want me to——

MERTON. Oh, no. I wouldn't hurt his feelings—for worlds.

BAIRD. Don't let it worry you any more, then.

MERTON. But while we're on the subject, Mr Baird——

BAIRD. Yes?

MERTON. I think I ought to have a little better support in my—next picture.

BAIRD. Oh, better support, eh?

MERTON. Yes. And—ah—I think it's time for me to do something different from Harold Parmalee. I wouldn't want the public to—ah—that is, to think——

BAIRD. Oh, sure, you're right.

MERTON. Besides, I was watching one of Parmalee's pictures the other day, and—I don't think he's quite as good as he used to be, Mr. Baird.

BAIRD. That so?

MERTON. Yes. Of course it may just be that my view-point is changing, but I think he's falling off a little. Mind you, I think he's still good, but——

[HENSHAW *strides on.*]

HENSHAW. Excuse me.

[*He pushes past* MERTON.]

MERTON. Excuse *me,* Mr. Henshaw.

HENSHAW. Yes, yes. [*To* BAIRD.] Kerrigan says you want that other projection-room at nine o'clock, Baird. Do you think that's fair?

BAIRD. It's fair if I send in my notice first.

HENSHAW. You ought to know *I'm* cutting *Mother of the World* right now. You ought to know as a gentleman that I need that room every spare minute——

BAIRD. Well, calm down and I'll tell you something. I'll be through with it at nine-fifteen.

HENSHAW. Oh, why didn't they say so? They told me you wanted it till midnight.

BAIRD. Well, I don't.

HENSHAW. Well, thanks very much, old man. I had no idea——

[*Suddenly he is face to face with* MERTON.]

MERTON. Hello, Mr. Henshaw.

HENSHAW. [*Vaguely.*] Oh, how are you?

MERTON. I guess you don't remember me, do you?

HENSHAW. No, I don't believe I do.

MERTON. Merton Gill. Ah—Clifford Armytage.

HENSHAW. Gill—Armytage. H'm. Why, no, I can't say that I do remember just—ah——

MERTON. A couple of months ago, when you were starting on *Robinson Crusoe?* [*A pause.*] Remember—you fired me from the scene in the library?

HENSHAW. [*Still vaguely.*] Oh, yes, I think I do recall——

MERTON. Gee, I've often thought of that, Mr. Henshaw. That was one of my earlier struggles, all right. You must have thought I was pretty green that day, when I didn't know how to walk down to the camera or anything. I guess I *was* pretty green.

HENSHAW. [*More definitely.*] Yes, yes—I remember. What are you doing now?

BAIRD. [*Quickly.*] He's with me now.

HENSHAW. Oh!

BAIRD. I'm going to feature him.

> [*Motions to* HENSHAW *not to give the joke away.*]

HENSHAW. [*To* MERTON.] Oh, yes. I've heard about you.

BAIRD. [*Nervously.*] Well—let's get after that retake.

MERTON. Just a minute. [*With a light laugh.*] Those were great times you and I had together, Mr. Henshaw. I guess you'll never forget how terrible I was.

HENSHAW. [*Who has forgotten long ago.*] Oh, I don't know.

BAIRD. [*Anxious to get rid of him.*] Waiting for you, kid.

> [*Opens door.*]

MERTON. Yes, sir. [*Turns to* HENSHAW, *a hand on his shoulder. He gives a long, retrospective sigh.*] Some day—some day you and I will have many a good laugh over those days, Mr. Henshaw. Very glad you dropped in. So long.

> [*He goes out, with such dignity as the spurs permit.* BAIRD *and* HENSHAW *exchange looks.*]

CURTAIN

SCENE II

*The scene is the living-room in the home of the Patter-sons—*MERTON'S *boarding-house. It is the morning after the showing of* MERTON'S *first picture.*

MR. PATTERSON, *an elderly gentleman in carpet slippers, is coming down the stairs as the curtain rises. He opens a door and calls off.*

PATTERSON. You needn't cook his breakfast, ma.

MRS. PATTERSON. [*Heard in the distance.*] What?

PATTERSON. I say you needn't cook his breakfast. [MRS. PATTERSON *enters. A lady of the ample type.*] He's not in his room. I knocked three times, and then went in.

MRS. PATTERSON. You mean he's gone out already?

PATTERSON. I tell you he ain't been in at all. His bed ain't been slept in.

MRS. PATTERSON. Well, what do you think of that?

PATTERSON. What?

MRS. PATTERSON. I bet they went and give him a big party, celebrating the success of the picture.

PATTERSON. Yes, sir, ma—that's just what.

MRS. PATTERSON. Now I'm sorry about that. I hope he don't go and dissipate just because he made such a big hit last night.

PATTERSON. Oh, I don't think he'd do that.

MRS. PATTERSON. [*Laughing.*] My, but he was funny though. Them spurs!

PATTERSON. And that hat!

[*They both laugh at this recollection. The telephone rings.*]

MRS. PATTERSON. I'll go. [*She takes up the receiver.*] Hello. . . . Oh, hello, Miss Montague . . . Why, no, he ain't here. I thought maybe you knew. . . . Huh? . . . No, I mean he wasn't here all night. Ain't that funny, after his picture making such a big hit? . . . Oh, I should say we was there. And funny! I don't remember when we've laughed so much. Didn't *you* think it was funny? . . . Hello. . . . Hello. . . . [*She turns to* PATTERSON.] She's gone. Sounded right worried, too. Oh, dear! I hope nothing's happened to Mr. Armytage.

PATTERSON. Oh, no, ma. You'll see—just out with the boys, hitting it up.

MRS. PATTERSON. Well, he certainly is entitled to it if anybody ever was. Did you see the write-ups the papers gave him?

PATTERSON. Yes, indeed!

MRS. PATTERSON. He certainly made an awful big success. [*She suddenly remembers something.*] Oh, my!

PATTERSON. What's the matter?

MRS. PATTERSON. Mrs. Gimbel'll be awful interested about his not coming home all night. I think I'll run over and tell her.

PATTERSON. Well, all right.

MRS. PATTERSON. You come and help me fix them rooms. [*She starts up the stairs.*] Out all night! It just shows how success goes to a person's head.

PATTERSON. [*Following her.*] I sort of had an idea I'd see the picture again this afternoon.

> [*The* PATTERSONS *are gone. There is an instant's wait—then* JIMMY *enters uncertainly from the outside door. He turns back to look at some one behind him.*]

JIMMY. [*With definite weariness.*] Come on. You've come this far. [MERTON *enters—a* MERTON *dispirited and worn.*] Now, will you stay here till I get Miss Montague?

MERTON. I suppose so.

> [*Sits.*]

JIMMY. You ought to eat some breakfast.

MERTON. Food!

JIMMY. Or go to bed or something.

MERTON. Bed!

JIMMY. Well, anyhow, I got you home.

MERTON. [*Dully.*] Ya. [*Pause.*] Thanks, Jimmy. Thanks for—walking around all night, and—sitting in the park and everything.

JIMMY. Oh, that's all right. [*He turns to go.*] Good night.

MERTON. [*Breaking out again—rises.*] The shame of it! The shame of it all!

JIMMY. Haven't I been telling you there ain't any shame in it?

MERTON. They shamed me! Shamed me in front of all those people!

JIMMY. Good morning— [*Yawns.*] —Mr. Gill. And for the thousandth time, nobody shamed you. You made the biggest hit in the world, and they simply laughed their heads off.

MERTON. Yes! You give them the best and finest

that's in you, and they laugh! That's a *hit*! Jeff Baird
meant it to be funny! So did she!

JIMMY. Well, it *was* funny.

MERTON. I'll never trust a woman again.

JIMMY. Good morning.

[*He goes wearily out.*]

MERTON. [*Stares into space—sees paper—reads.*]
"The funniest newcomer in the realm of comedy."

[MERTON *tosses the paper aside.* MRS. PAT-
TERSON *returns.*]

MRS. PATTERSON. *Well!* Good morning!

MERTON. Good morning.

MRS. PATTERSON. I'm certainly awfully glad you got
home. We were worried about you.

MERTON. I'm—all right.

MRS. PATTERSON. [*Fulsomely.*] Congratulations!

MERTON. What?

MRS. PATTERSON. Congratulations on your success!

MERTON. Oh!

MRS. PATTERSON. [*Laughs.*] My, my! I don't think
we ever laughed so much in our lives as we did last night.
And I just want to tell you how proud we are of you.
[MERTON *starts for the stairs.*] Now, can I get you some
breakfast?

MERTON. No, thanks. I'm not a bit hungry.

[*He goes up-stairs.*]

MRS. PATTERSON. [*Calling after him.*] If you want
any later, I'll be back. I'm just going over to Mrs.
Gimbel's.

[*There is a knock on the door;* MRS. PATTERSON
*opens it. The gentleman who comes in is
named* WALBERG. *He speaks with the merest
touch of Jewish accent.*]

WALBERG. Morning. Mr. Armytage live here?

Mrs. Patterson. [*Genially.*] Mr. Clifford Armytage, I suppose you mean?

Walberg. Yes, ma'am.

Mrs. Patterson. Won't you come in? [*She closes
the door.*] Who shall I say's calling, please?

Walberg. Just tell him there's a gentleman wants to
see him on business.

Mrs. Patterson. [*As engagingly as possible.*] You
a movie man?

Walberg. Yes.

Mrs. Patterson. We saw Mr. Armytage's picture at
the opening last night. We're all very proud about it.
My, the way that audience laughed!

Walberg. Are you *Mrs.* Armytage?

Mrs. Patterson. Oh, no. Mr. Armytage is a single
gentleman. I'm Mrs. J. Emery Patterson. [Walberg
*loses interest in her. There is a pause until his detach-
ment sinks in. She goes to the stairs.*] Well, I'll tell
him you're here. [*She apparently is about to call up-
stairs, but changes her mind.*] Just wait!

> [*She goes up.* Walberg *waits patiently. He
> inspects a picture with the air of a connois-
> seur; otherwise occupies himself. In a few
> moments* Merton *appears. He wears a dress-
> ing-gown. He is very dejected.*]

Merton. Did you want to see me?

Walberg. [*Attempting ingratiation.*] Good morning, Mr. Armytage! I suppose you feel pretty good to-
day!

Merton. [*After looking him over carefully.*] Not so
very.

Walberg. [*Trying to appraise him.*] You certainly
were a scream last night.

[MERTON *gives him a long look, feeling a martyr.*]

MERTON.   I suppose Mr. Baird sent you.

WALBERG.   He did not.   My name's Walberg, Mr. Armytage, and I'm with the Bigart.   I got your address from the Holden office because I thought we ought to have a little talk.

MERTON.   I don't want to talk.

WALBERG.   Now, wait!   Suppose you let me talk, then. I've got something that's going to interest you.   I saw your picture last night, Mr. Armytage.   [MERTON *gives a sigh that is half sob.*]   Is it definitely certain you're going to stick with Baird?

MERTON.   No!

WALBERG.   That's fine.   [MERTON *gives him a puzzled look.*]   You're new to pictures, I understand?

MERTON.   Yes.

WALBERG.   Well, don't do like a lot of other comics and try to do straight stuff.   You know how far you'd get.

MERTON.   I know how far I *got*.

WALBERG.   You stick to comedy, because you've got everything.   Why, you've got the best low-comedy face I've seen in ages.   It's got genuine pathos, more pathos than Parmalee, the guy you were kidding.   And you've got the gift of the world in knowing just how to kid bad acting.   Frankly, I don't believe you could ever make the grade in a serious picture.   I candidly don't believe you could register if you imitated a *good* actor.   But you've got pathos—pathos and acting plus.   I don't have to tell you that.   You and Baird have found out your limits and have started off on what God meant you for.

MERTON.   [*Hardly able to stand it.*]   Mr. Walberg, I——

WALBERG. Now, hold on! Now, there's only one thing the matter with you—you're too good. Parmalee makes hokum and the public wants hokum. You make satire, which is over the heads of most of the public. Take a beautiful Moron like Beulah Baxter. She can't act. She probably wouldn't know two and two made four if she didn't get it by gossip. You're different— you've got intelligence. Now, how about doing some stuff for us?

MERTON. You mean—you mean—comedies?

WALBERG. Certainly.

MERTON. I wouldn't think of it!

WALBERG. You mean you wouldn't come with Bigart at all—on any proposition?

MERTON. That's what I mean.

WALBERG. Wouldn't three hundred a week interest you?

MERTON. [*After gulping.*] No.

WALBERG. Three fifty?

MERTON. No.

WALBERG. [*Rises; thinks.*] Four hundred!

MERTON. No.

> [WALBERG *takes his hat, looks at* MERTON, *then crosses to the street door.*]

WALBERG. Well, you're a tough egg, Mr. Armytage. But we'll have you with Bigart yet. Yes, sir, even if Mr. Strausheimer has to come here himself. Good day.

> [*He goes.*]

MERTON. [*As* WALBERG *exits.*] Good morning.

> [*He crosses to the fireplace, terribly disturbed.* MRS. PATTERSON *comes down-stairs.*]

MRS. PATTERSON. I'm sorry, Mr. Armytage, but I overheard a little of that gentleman's talk. I must say he seems to feel about you just the same as we feel.

MERTON. [*Rises.*] You mean my low-comedy face?

MRS. PATTERSON. [*Laughs.*] Yes, indeed. Why, you were funnier than that cross-eyed man ever was.

MERTON. Thank you.

MRS. PATTERSON. Now I wish you'd let me get you some breakfast.

MERTON. I don't want any.

MRS. PATTERSON. It's all ready. [*The telephone-bell rings.*] Won't take a second. [*At 'phone.*] Hello. . . . Yes. . . . Yes, ma'am, he's here now. If you'll hold the —What? . . . Oh! Why, he seems to be all right. [*She looks at* MERTON.] It's Miss Montague, but she doesn't want to talk to you. [*Into 'phone.*] What? . . . Yes, he's terribly happy over it, I guess, though he don't say much. . . . All right, I'll tell him. . . . Yes, m'm. Good-by. [*Hangs up.*] Miss Montague says she'll be over in a few minutes. [MERTON *stands helpless, then starts for the stairs.*] Now, about that breakfast, Mr. Armytage.

MERTON. No! No! And if Miss Montague comes, why—I had to keep an engagement somewhere.

[*He stumbles blindly up the stairs.*]

MRS. PATTERSON. H'm! [*She starts for the street door just as the bell rings. Of all people, it is* MR. GASHWILER *who enters.*] Yes, sir?

GASHWILER. Good morning. Is there a Mr. Armytage stopping here?

[*He uses a hard "g" and a long "a" in* ARMYTAGE.]

MRS. PATTERSON. I suppose you mean Mr. Clifford Armytage.

GASHWILER. Yes, ma'am. Is he home?

MRS. PATTERSON. Yes, sir. What is the name, please?

GASHWILER. Gashwiler.

MRS. PATTERSON. Mr. Gashwiler?

GASHWILER. Yes, ma'am. He used to work for me.

MRS. PATTERSON. He did?

GASHWILER. In Illinois.

MRS. PATTERSON. And you don't even know his name!

GASHWILER. Well, this Armytage is a kind of a stage name. He was Merton Gill when he worked for me.

MRS. PATTERSON. Oh, I see. If you'll excuse me, I'll see if he's in. [*She goes to the stairs*—MERTON *is coming down, with hat and coat.*] Oh, I was just going to your room. This gentleman——

MERTON. Mr. Gashwiler!

GASHWILER. Hello, Merton. Well, well, well!

MERTON. Well, you look fine, Mr. Gashwiler! Oh, I'm terribly glad to see you, Mr. Gashwiler.

GASHWILER. I'm mighty glad to see you, too, Merton.

MRS. PATTERSON. [*With a self-conscious smile.*] Well, excuse me——

[*She departs.*]

MERTON. What are you doing out here?

GASHWILER. Oh, just tourin'. Mrs. Gashwiler and I thought we'd take in the Golden West, and here we are. Here for four days, then we go on to San Francisco.

MERTON. I wish I were going with you, Mr. Gashwiler.

GASHWILER. Well, we'd feel pretty honored if you could come, Merton—a great big man like you. Just by a miracle, last night, we seen you in the new picture.

MERTON. Did you see it, too?

GASHWILER. I guess I laughed about as much as any one. Merton, I never knowed what I was talkin' about when I said you hadn't ought ever try to get into the movies. Why, you're funnier than anybody I ever seen.

Wait'll we get back to Simsbury. That place is going to have a plate.

MERTON.   A what?

GASHWILER.   A plate. Yessir. "Here worked Merton Gill." If I have any influence, that town's goin' to honor her illustrious son the way he ought to be honored. I'm goin' to have a brass plate made for the front of the store.

MERTON.   No!

GASHWILER.   Yes, sir.

MERTON.   Oh, my! [*A pause. He is definitely pleased.*]   How's Mrs. Gashwiler?

GASHWILER.   Fine! Wants to see you. I was lucky to get your address. Miss Kearns happened to come in the store the day we left and said she had it, so she gave it to me.

MERTON.   [*Now a great artist.*]   Dear old Tessie! How's she getting along?

GASHWILER.   Oh, fine, fine! Says she's thinking of comin' out here herself.

MERTON.   Yes, she wrote me about that. But I don't think she ought to, Mr. Gashwiler.

GASHWILER.   No?

MERTON.   No. It's a pretty stiff game, the movies. You've got to have a certain amount of what they call hokum to get your scenarios over. Tessie's an awfully nice girl and all that, but I don't think she could get away with it. It might break her heart.

[*There is a knock on the outer door.*]

GASHWILER.   [*Having listened to the oracle.*]   Well, I'll tell her that.

MERTON.   I hope she doesn't try it.

GASHWILER.   And now, how about comin' down to the

hotel with me and seein' Mrs. Gashwiler? I'll treat you to lunch.

[*Again the knock.*]

MERTON. [*Feels sure that it is the* MONTAGUE GIRL *at the door; nerves himself to admit her. He mumbles an excuse as he crosses to the door.*] Excuse me, I——

[*He opens the door. It is the* GIRL. *She stands looking at him a second;* MERTON *returns her gaze. Then she enters—scared stiff, eyes straight ahead. She ventures a stiff greeting.*]

GIRL. Hello.

MERTON. [*Not looking at her.*] Good morning. [*A pause; he embarks on a formal introduction.*] This is—Miss Montague.

GASHWILER. How do you do—I'm sure.

GIRL. [*Conscious of the tenseness of the situation.*] How are—you?

GASHWILER. You in the movies, too?

GIRL. I'm not quite sure just where I am.

GASHWILER. Huh?

GIRL. I was joking. [*A pause.*] Do you—live here?

GASHWILER. No, I'm from Illinois. Merton used to work for me.

GIRL. You're not Mr. Gooseberry, or whatever it is?

GASHWILER. No. Gashwiler's my name.

GIRL. That's it. I remember—Gooseberry's the name of the town.

GASHWILER. No, the town's name is Simsbury.

GIRL. I guess my memory's just gone dead.

GASHWILER. Merton a good friend of yours?

GIRL. [*Uncertainly.*] We've *seen* a lot of each other.

GASHWILER. [*Decides to make a break.*] Well—I hope I see you again.

GIRL. Yes.

GASHWILER. See you later, Merton. Telephone me at the Hollywood.

MERTON. [*Forcing himself to speak.*] Yes—I will.

[GASHWILER *goes.*]

GIRL. [*Eyes still straight ahead; does not even know that* GASHWILER *is already out the door.*] By-By.

[*Still conscious of the charged atmosphere, she steals a look at* MERTON. *That youth nerving himself up for the great moment of his life—certainly for his greatest piece of acting. As a forerunner he strikes what is intended to be an easy pose, and somehow conjures up a smile. Then with a gaiety that is close to heart-breaking, he breaks out.*]

MERTON. Well?

GIRL. [*Astonished at the cheery tone, but decides that she must have heard wrong.*] Well? You've seen the picture. Shoot!

MERTON. [*The grin broader than ever.*] All right. I certainly kidded the life out of all of you, didn't I?

GIRL. [*Now convinced that she did hear it.*] What?

MERTON. [*The words tumbling over each other in his nervousness.*] I've certainly kidded the whole crowd of you. You thought all along that I thought it was a serious picture, didn't you? You and Baird thought you had me kidded all along, didn't you? Ho, ho! A serious picture, with a cross-eyed man doing comedy stuff all around me every minute. I thought it was serious, did I? Yes, I did! Like fun!

GIRL. [*Not quite able to realize it.*] Just say some of that again!

MERTON. [*Choking back the tears.*] Didn't you people know what I could do and what I couldn't do? Didn't you suppose I knew as well as anybody that I've got a low-comedy face and that I couldn't make the grade in a serious picture? Of course I've got real pathos, but any one can see I couldn't imitate a good actor. Didn't you and Baird ever suppose I found out my limits and decided to be what God intended me to be? Straight satire—that's what I'm doing—and it's over the heads of most of the public. Why, they tell me that I was funnier than that cross-eyed man ever was in his life. And what happens this morning?

GIRL. What happens?

MERTON. Nothing except that people are coming around to sign me up for four hundred dollars a week. Why, this Bamberger from the Bigart company comes in before I'm really up this morning, asking me if I won't go with his company, and . . . why . . .

[He breaks off as he notices her steady gaze.]

GIRL. So you know everything, do you? You know you look just enough like Parmalee so that you're funny? [MERTON *is hit.*] I mean, you look the way Parmalee would if he had brains.

MERTON. *[Still bluffing it out.]* Certainly! Parmalee? Why, Parmalee's got nothing but hokum in his pictures, anyway. Why, anyway, satire——

[Breaks down and turns.]

GIRL. Merton! [MERTON *crosses to her and falls into her arms, sobbing. The jig is up.*] There, don't you worry! Mother's got you now and she's never going to let you go.

MERTON. *[Sobbing.]* It's like that night on the lot when I found out about you and Beulah Baxter, and you were so——

GIRL. There, there! Don't you worry. Did he have his poor old mother going for a minute? Yes, he did! He had her going for a minute, all right. But he didn't

fool her very long, not very long, because he can't ever
fool her very long. And he can bet a lot of money on
that.

MERTON. I feel a little better.

GIRL. Of course you do.

MERTON. I didn't see at first how I ever could live
down what I saw last night. I guess I didn't understand,
some way.

[*He shows he doesn't yet, for that matter.*]

GIRL. Don't worry, honey. Mother knows what's
what, and she'll tell you all about it in good time.

MERTON. You think I ought to—keep on—making
comedies?

GIRL. You will as long as I last. [*There is a whistle,
three sharp blasts, outside.*] That's a friend of ours.
He said he wanted to see you, if you were—feeling well.

MERTON. [*Gaily.*] There's nothing the matter with
me.

[*The* GIRL *goes to the street door and opens it.*
BAIRD'S *head appears.*]

BAIRD. Is he gunless?

GIRL. I've a pleasant surprise for you.

[BAIRD *enters.*]

BAIRD. Good morning, kid!

MERTON. [*Smiling.*] Well, I guess we did it.

BAIRD. [*Smiles and shakes hands.*] I'll say we did.
[*Quickly to* GIRL.] How did *you* do it?

GIRL. Oh, I've got ways.

BAIRD. I got a piece of news at the office that made me
come over. You know your picture's a knockout, I suppose?

MERTON. So they tell me.

BAIRD. Yes, and the groundhogs are at work. A

mysterious voice called up and got your address this morning. Has anybody been here?

MERTON. Yes, a gentleman from the Bigart dropped in. He wanted to give me a very fine contract. A very fine contract indeed.

[*In an instant he is a movie star.*]

BAIRD. Well, don't let those babies tempt you. Remember, you and I have a nice little contract, too, for three years.

MERTON. Oh, I turned him down. I know my place is with you, Mr. Baird. And I want to put everything I can into comedies. I want to give the best that's in me, because I realize that that's where you and God intended me to be.

BAIRD. That's the talk. In three years we'll be giving you a salary that'll knock the eye off the ones Parmalee and them other Swift Premiers get.

MERTON. Still, the public wants that hokum. Why, you take Beulah Baxter, for instance. She's nothing but a high-grade Mormon. Why, she wouldn't know two and two was four if she didn't hear people talking.

[GIRL *peers at him to see if it can really be* MERTON—*then she gives it up.*]

BAIRD. [*An eloquent look at the* GIRL.] Well, I'm off. By the way, we'll start another one next week, and I don't mind telling you that it'll be good. [*A second's pause.*] Good-by.

GIRL. Good-by, Jeff.

BAIRD. [*To the* GIRL; *standing a bit apart from* MERTON.] He's a nice kid.

GIRL. He's a wonderful kid.

[BAIRD *throws open the door; then halts as he sees some one coming. The* GIRL, *too, sights*

[*the impending figure; she and* BAIRD *stand motionless as he enters. The visitor is the mysterious stranger whose sudden appearance in the studio had caused such a respectful halt a few weeks before. His name, it develops, is* WHEATON.]

BAIRD. [*Impressed.*] Why, how do you do?

WHEATON. [*Rather loftily.*] How do you do? Is—ah—is Mr. Armytage— [*He is looking about; sees* MERTON.] Hello, Armytage! I couldn't resist dropping in to congratulate you.

MERTON. Oh, thank you.

GIRL. [*With a flourish.*] Kid, meet Mr. John Wheaton, former Secretary of Agriculture, now head of the motion-picture industry!

MERTON. [*Gaping.*] How do you do? Won't—won't you sit down?

WHEATON. No, thanks. I've only got a minute.

MERTON. I—I'm certainly glad to know you. I've seen you around.

WHEATON. And I'm proud to know you. It's men like you that the motion-pictures need, Mr. Armytage.

MERTON. Well, it's awfully good of you to say so.

WHEATON. Yes, indeed! You're going to help us a lot. [*He gives* MERTON *an encouraging pat on the shoulder.*] This is not a one-man fight, Mr. Armytage—I must have the help of all of you if the motion-pictures are to be put on a higher plane.

MERTON. [*Right at home when it comes to this sort of thing.*] Yes, sir. That's what I want to do if I can—put them up higher, and higher, until——

WHEATON. [*Has found his equal at last.*] My idea,

exactly. We must strive ever upward, or there is no progress.

MERTON. [*With emphasis.*] Yes, sir!

WHEATON. Some time I'd like to get together with you for a serious talk.

MERTON. I'd be delighted.

WHEATON. I'd like to hear your ideas. [*He consults his watch.*] And now I'm sure you'll pardon me—I have to address some exhibitors.

MERTON. Yes, sir.

WHEATON. Good day.

MERTON. Good day!

GIRL. [*As she hands* WHEATON *his hat and stick.*] Good day.

WHEATON. [*Taking them.*] Thank you. [*He turns.*] And again—my congratulations. This would be a sad world indeed, Mr. Armytage, if it were not for the leavening force of humor. Good day.

> [*An imposing and probably calculated departure. The others look after him. Then the* GIRL *turns to* MERTON.]

GIRL. Well! What do you think of that?

MERTON. A great man.

GIRL. Ah—yes.

MERTON. Say! I haven't had any breakfast yet. Did you eat?

GIRL. I should say not.

MERTON. [*Calling.*] Mrs. Patterson! Mrs. Patterson!

BAIRD. Well, I guess you can get along without me. So long.

MERTON. So long, Mr. Baird.

GIRL.   Good-by, Jeff.

[BAIRD *goes;* MRS. PATTERSON *enters.*]

MRS. PATTERSON.   Yes, Mr. Armytage.

MERTON.   I was wondering if there's enough breakfast for two.

MRS. PATTERSON.   Indeed there is.   [*She turns to the* GIRL.]   I've kept some things on the stove in case Mr. Armytage changed his mind.   He's got to eat a lot to keep himself in condition.   [*Suddenly remembers something.*] Oh!   Mrs. Gimbel wanted to know, and I do, too, whether you'd mind giving us a picture of yourself, autographed.   I'd feel very honored.   [*The telephone bell rings.* MRS. PATTERSON *answers it.*]   Yes, he's here. Just a minute, please.

GIRL.   [*Halting* MERTON *on his way to the 'phone.*] Who is it?

MRS. PATTERSON.   [*Into 'phone.*]   Who is it, please? . . . Oh! . . . Just a minute.   [*To the* GIRL.]   It's the *Silver Screenings Magazine.*   For Mr. Armytage.

MERTON.   [MERTON, *with terrific manner, takes up the telephone.* MRS. PATTERSON *departs.*]   Hello! . . . Yes, this is Mr. Armytage.

GIRL.   By the way, your name's going to be Merton Gill from now on.

MERTON.   [*To her.*]   Is it?   [*She nods.*]   Hello. . . . Yes, this is Mr. Armytage.   That isn't my regular name, though. . . . What? . . . Gill—G-i-l-l. . . . Yes. Merton. . . . That's right. . . . What? . . . Any time you say.   If there's anything I can tell the public I'd be very glad to.   I don't know what your readers would want to know about me, however. . . . What? . . . I say I don't know what your readers would want to know about me, however.   [*He throws a peculiar stress on the "however."*]   . . . Oh, just hard work, I guess.   I've struggled and sacrificed to give the public—What? . . . No, I'm not yet, but I think I'm going to be. [*Looks to the* GIRL.] Miss Montague. . . . Yes, that's the lady. . . . Oh, I should say so. More like a pal. And, I might also add, my severest critic.

> [*She leans a little closer to him as the curtain falls.*]

MONSIEUR BEAUCAIRE

BY

BOOTH TARKINGTON

Newton Booth Tarkington was born in Indianapolis in 1869. After a year at Purdue University he went to Princeton, where he took his A.B. and A.M. degrees. *Monsieur Beaucaire* and *Cherry,* two of his most delightful—and justly most famous fictions—were actually begun while he was an undergraduate at Princeton, although not actually published until later. In 1920 Mr. Tarkington won the Pulitzer Prize for the best novel of the year with *The Magnificent Ambersons* (Doubleday, 1920) and two years later was again awarded the prize for *Alice Adams* (Doubleday, 1922). A recent book, *Women* (Doubleday, 1925), really a collection of short stories, is certainly one of his most delightful works if not his best. His latest novel is *The Plutocrat* (Doubleday, 1927). His most successful dramas have been *Clarence* (French, 1921), *The Intimate Strangers* (French, 1924), *Penrod* (French, 1921), and *Seventeen* (French, 1925). He collaborated with Harry Leon Wilson in 1908 in producing the well-known play, *The Man from Home* (Harper, 1908). The dramatization which was made of his world-famous story of Monsieur Beaucaire, although immensely popular on the stage (in fact, being made into a very successful light opera on the basis of its stage success) has never before appeared in print.

CHARACTERS IN THE PLAY

Monsieur Beaucaire
Richard (Beau) Nash
Mr. Bantison
Mr. Raikell
Lord Townbrake
Molyneaux
Duke of Winterset
Marquis de Mirepoix
Captain Badger
Mr. Bicksit
Lady Mary Carlisle
Lucy Rellerton
Miss Presbrey
Miss Paitelot
Mrs. Mabsley
Lady Rellerton
Jolliffe
François
Servants

SCENES OF THE PLAY

Act I. The Assembly Room of Beau Nash's.

Act II. A room at Beaucaire's lodgings. A month later.

Act III. The ballroom at Lady Rellerton's. The next day.

Act IV. Living-room of Mr. Bantison's. A few days later.

Act V. An ante-room of the Assembly. A week later.

PLACE. Bath, England.

TIME. Early part of the eighteenth century.

ACT I

The room is done in the Georgian style. Deep semi-circular recess down half-way on the right. In the recess at the back is a niche in which stands the life-size picture of RICHARD NASH; *upon each side of the statue a small bust, one of Dryden, the other of Pope. A little in front of the statue and below is the Tempion clock, in front of which is a large open vase from which the water flows into a marble basin. A bar runs across the semicircular recess and upon the bar are rows of cups.*

Two attendants in the livery of MR. NASH *stand within the bar. Corinthian columns are placed at regular intervals around the room. There are an open double door at the back and a single door at the left. Down stage on the right is a heavy handsome table, at which three gentlemen are seated, throwing dice out of a small gold pocket cup. No stakes are visible.*

One, MR. BANTISON, *is about 45, and very stout, his purple neck bulging out of the tight white stock and throat laces fluffing around his double chin. He is in brown and leather, with a white waistcoat worn very long as the fashion is. Leather leggins come over the knees.* MR. RAIKELL, *opposite him, lounges upon the table with one leg swinging over a corner of it. He has a look of dissipation and humor; is about 28 and somewhat carelessly dressed. His coat is green cloth trimmed with gold; his waistcoat is scarlet. He also wears leather leggins and spurs, and he flicks his calves with a light riding whip, which hangs at his wrist. He is standing behind the table, leaning*

*upon it to watch the dice. At the bar on the right
stands* LORD TOWNBRAKE, *a pale young man, drinking water from the cup which the attendant hands
him. He wears a light gray coat, excessively crin-
olined so as to expand the whole full skirts below
the waist, a great deal of lace, and a yellow waistcoat. His breeches and stockings, which pass over
the knees, and shoes are light gray. He wears silver
buckles, and his coat, waistcoat, and hat, which rests
upon a chair near by, are trimmed with silver. He is
about 24, fair-haired, and his manner bespeaks a
solemn fastidiousness, his gesture being dainty and
well considered.*

MR. RAIKELL *wears his hat.* MR. BANTISON'S *reposes
beside his riding-whip on the floor. None of the
gentlemen are in powder and no swords are worn.*
RAIKELL *and* BANTISON *are at the table,* TOWN-
BRAKE *at the spring.*

BANTISON. [*Examining a throw of the dice.*] No
man's income can stand this.

[*The three men make notes in their tablets.*]

RAIKELL. [*Throwing.*] Yours, will— [*Turning to
look at* LORD TOWNBRAKE.] Townie, Beau Nash will fine
you if you drink that spring dry.

BANTISON. [*Picking up the words.*] Nash! Nash!
Nash! Everywhere Blood! I tire of that name of his!

TOWNBRAKE. And I of his b'ged portrait. Glances at
the picture.

RAIKELL. And I of his rules. Does he think *I* come
here to drink the waters?

[*A gentleman has appeared outside the door at
the left in the street. He is a handsome,
brown-cheeked man of forty and wears the
uniform of a major of the Grenadiers. He*

*reaches the threshold just in time to overhear
the last remark.   He speaks sharply.*]

MOLYNEAUX.   Waters?   You?   Having the honor of
your acquaintance, Raikell, I dare swear he does not.

ALL.   Ah!   Philip!

[TOWNBRAKE *goes forward and greets* MOLY-
NEAUX.   *Those at the table rise and greet the
newcomer.*   BANTISON *sits as before.*]

RAIKELL.   We were abusing Richard Nash—Beau
Nash!

[*Sits.*]

TOWNBRAKE.   Begad!   King of Bath.

BANTISON.   The Master of Ceremonies.

MOLYNEAUX.   My old friend, Dick Nash of the Temple!   What's his offense against your laws, gentlemen?

[*A servant takes* MOLYNEAUX' *cloak.*]

TOWNBRAKE.   He goes too b'ged far for *us.*

RAIKELL.   He does.   He makes a little ladies' dancing room of Bath.   No one is allowed to wear boots—a
sword—or to curse, except Beau Nash.

BANTISON.   There's a duke he'd not curse for doing
anything he chose.

TOWNBRAKE.   There's few would care to curse His
Grace of Winterset.

MOLYNEAUX.   Or to play cards with him.

TOWNBRAKE.   Poor Charlie Tappingford!

BANTISON.   He couldn't prove his Grace cheated——

[*The men cry "Sh" and look about—A pause.*]

RAIKELL.   Tappingford had to swallow his bolus.
Nobody actually saw—and he daren't bring charges.

MOLYNEAUX.   Would you play His Grace of Winterset, Townbrake?

TOWNBRAKE.   [*Casting the dice.*]   Among gentlemen

and not too loud— [*In a whisper.*] Not without a confederate of my own, I'm d—d if I would!

[*All laugh.*]

RAIKELL. There's one that will.

BANTISON. Who, begad?

RAIKELL. Monsieur Beaucaire.

MOLYNEAUX. Beaucaire? I don't know him.

RAIKELL. [*Ruefully.*] You're damned lucky.

MOLYNEAUX. I am new in Bath this morning. He's a gambler, is he? A capable hand with those?

[*Points to the dice cup.*]

TOWNBRAKE. Capable b'ged hand! He's robbed us all!

MOLYNEAUX. Robbed you?

RAIKELL. Oh, aye, but fairly. I'll say he's the finest gambler alive. I'm not through with him, be Heaven!

TOWNBRAKE. [*To* MOLYNEAUX.] Nor His Grace b'ged of Winterset. He took all the Duke's ready money —nigh ruined him and now lets him play for paper. [*Turns to others. All the gentlemen laugh.*] The Duke's b'ged paper. It's worth— [RAIKELL *snaps his fingers.*] Oh, Beaucaire plays like a b'ged gentleman!

MOLYNEAUX. Who is he?

RAIKELL. He came here without introduction, presented himself in the pump room, and fell into our Grace's company. I've heard he came over in the same ship with the Marquis de Mirepoix, the French Ambassador.

TOWNBRAKE. Yes, that is all that is known of him.

[*Takes a glass of water from a servant.*]

MOLYNEAUX. Ah, what is his appearance?

RAIKELL. He will be here presently for a morning cup. You can see for yourself. He's delighted with the water and drinks almost as much as Townbrake, only Beaucaire drinks water for its own sake!

[*All laugh.*]

TOWNBRAKE. [*Returns cup.*] I drink to wash my b'ged sins away.

RAIKELL. No wonder you're thirsty!

[*Laughs.*]

BANTISON. Lord! Bath is not the ocean.

TOWNBRAKE. You'll find Bath much the same, Major. Nash is King, monarch of all.

RAIKELL. Lady Mary, the Queen, beauty and toast!

BANTISON. All the world resorts hither, the same customs prevail.

TOWNBRAKE. Three glasses of a morning suffice for the regular.

RAIKELL. The ladies and more sober kind of men will presently appear for their first glass. After that, the fair will loll in their coffee house across the way for a time and then return for their second glass.

TOWNBRAKE. Next they will stroll on the parade.

BANTISON. [*Interrupting.*] Lord, it's an interesting recital!

[*All laugh.*]

RAIKELL. But what are you doing here, Philip? Have you left the Ambassador? 'Tis not more than three weeks since you were sent to join him at Versailles.

MOLYNEAUX. Versailles is bad for the liver, Harry. The Ambassador granted me a month to repair mine at Bath.

[*The gentlemen laugh.*]

RAIKELL. The fellow is a poorish liar, friends. Why not own up that you were love sick? The bells rang last night for Lady Mary Carlisle, who brings her cousin, Mistress Lucy Rellerton, to Bath. Your presence is thus easily explained as that of those two. *You* follow Miss

Lucy, your betrothed, just as they follow Lady Mary, who refuses to be betrothed to either of them.

MOLYNEAUX. Aye, you're very knowing—and is this all the news?

RAIKELL. Faith, no. [*Rises.*] Have any of you seen Nash this morning?

BANTISON. [*Rises and gets cup of water.*] Aye, on the Parade, very grumpy, and did not bow to me. He was with Winterset and Captain Badger, who came last night.

TOWNBRAKE. Aye, Badger came over on the same ship as the Marquis de Mirepoix. I heard him say so.

MOLYNEAUX. Ah, then he may know your Monsieur Beaucaire.

TOWNBRAKE. Possibly! But what is wrong with Nash?

RAIKELL. Oh, Faugh! I overheard him talking with Winterset. "I'll expel him," he cried. "I'll do it publicly to-morrow! Aye, when the room's most crowded. By the Lord, I'll have him lashed!"

[*An attendant brings water to all.*]

ALL. What! What! Who?

RAIKELL. I lost that. They turned away, but we mustn't miss it.

BANTISON. No, begad!

RAIKELL. I think it's Townie for drinking all the water.

MOLYNEAUX. [*Takes drink from the attendant. Standing to left of* RAIKELL, *speaks to him, indicating the other gentlemen.*] They are as completely Lady Mary's slaves as before?

RAIKELL. [*Takes drink from the attendant, laughing.*] Oh, aye, many seasons of refusal only whet them.

MOLYNEAUX. [*His cup in his hand.*]   Here's your health, gentlemen!

> [*The attendant has brought down glasses for all the gentlemen on a tray. Each has accepted a glass.*]

BANTISON. [*To* MOLYNEAUX *hastily.*]   No.

TOWNBRAKE. [*Quickly.*]   No.

RAIKELL. [*Laughing.*]   No?

MOLYNEAUX. [*Surprised.*]   No?

BANTISON.   No.   No, damme, etiquette is etiquette. There's but one first toast to be drunk in Bath, gentlemen —I give you Lady Mary Carlisle!

TOWNBRAKE.   The begad beauty of Bath!

ALL.   The Beauty of Bath!

RAIKELL.   Faith! We've drunk it in water. [*Sound of laughter and voices is heard without in the street and a crowd of ladies appears at doors.*]   Now what's to do?

> [MRS. MABSLEY, *a mature, rather stout woman in lavender, steps just within the threshold, laughing and excited.*]

MRS. MABSLEY.   Lord, gentlemen! Come, quick. Here's old Mr. Bicksit has got a new scandal and refuses to tell.   Come, fetch him in for us and make him out with it.

BANTISON.   Yoicks, Yoicks! Haloo! Man, we're in for you!

ALL GENTLEMEN.   Aye, we're in for you! Show us the old fox. Yoicks, Yoicks!

> [RAIKELL *exits. All except* MOLYNEAUX *rush for the door, laughing and crying, "Faith, where is he?" "Show us the old fox!" "Yoicks, Yoicks, haloo!"* LUCY RELLERTON, *a very pretty girl of 18, in lilac, enters, laughing, passing the gentlemen as they go out.*

MOLYNEAUX *meets her and takes both her hands.*]

MOLYNEAUX.   [*Happily.*]   Sweetheart!   Where   is Lady Mary?

[*Kissing her hand.*]

LUCY.   Coming, with Mr. Nash and Captain Badger. Philip, Mr. Nash is in a temper.

MOLYNEAUX.   We do not care for Mr. Nash's temper, do we?

LUCY.   [*Earnestly; back of table.*]   I want you to be careful not to offend Lady Mary. You know that I think you're the greatest man in the world, but she is so lofty—   [*Sighs.*]   She is not over-pleased with the match—she thinks every man should be an Earl.

MOLYNEAUX.   Faith, Sweet, I'll be her slave as well as yours.   Oh!   I'll be very careful to please her.

[*Sounds of great laughter heard without the doors at centre in the street. Three ladies enter rapidly and gaily just ahead of the gentlemen. MISS PRESBREY and MISS PAITELOT, two girls of nineteen, in pink and white. MRS. MABS- LEY comes first laughing very heartily.*]

MRS. MABSLEY.   [*Calling to LUCY as she enters.*] The rogues are fetching old Mr. Bicksit.

[*Beyond the doors RAIKELL, BANTISON, and TOWNBRAKE appear, surrounding an old gen- tleman in white tie wig. He is in white striped brocade, is stout, with purple face, and wears ordinarily a look of solemn cunning and mystery. At present he is laughing and strik- ing in mock anger at the young men with his cane, who are bringing him forward with a sort of dancing step, forming a circle about him. All are noisily laughing and talking—*]

> *reaching the threshold first, crying out, "New*
> *gossip! New gossip!"*]

TOWNBRAKE. [*Bowing.*] Ladies, I have the honor.

RAIKELL. [*Thrusting* BICKSIT *forward.*] Out with the story, old tattler!

BICKSIT. [*Panting.*] Before the Lord, you'll kill me! [*Protesting.*] My dear ladies— [*To the men again.*] Now gentlemen!

> [*All but* LUCY *and* MOLYNEAUX *throng about him.*]

TOWNBRAKE. Out with it!

> [RAIKELL *tickles* BICKSIT.]

BICKSIT. [*Shouts.*] Don't tickle me! I dislike telling my bits of scandal twice.

RAIKELL. [*To* MISS PRESBREY.] I hear he has told it four times already this morning.

> [*All laugh.*]

MRS. MABSLEY. Now, what is it, Mr. Bicksit?

BICKSIT. [*With solemn and unctious mystery.*] A most intricate piece of scandal of the French court direct from Versailles.

ALL. Out with it.

> [*Tickle* BICKSIT.]

BICKSIT. You will have it.

ALL. ·Yes, yes. Surely, at once.

BICKSIT. [*Undecided, appearing as if to go.*] 'Tis not really so agitating after all.

ALL. Oh!

BICKSIT. But I say 'tis in the very highest quarters, though foreign.

MISS PRESBREY. Do let there be a Prince in it, Mr. Bicksit.

MISS PAITELOT. Oh, I hope there's a Prince.

BICKSIT. There is, and—a Princess. Very well!

You must know, ladies, then, that the French King is indolent, does nothing but hunt and watch the performances of comedy which the nobles of his Court give at Versailles —but hath a high temper. You have heard that he fixed a marriage between his young cousin, the Duke of Orleans, and the Princess Henrietta de Bourbon Centi, cousin to them both—'twas given out two months ago in our own Court Journal.

ALL. Well!

BICKSIT. [*Chuckles madly.*] Now this is the pith of the story! Ah, ah, ah, ah! The lady, it seems, was willing but the young Duke of Orleans refused the match.

MRS. MABSLEY. Refused it?

MISS PRESBREY. Why?

BICKSIT. Because he said he had seen the lady but twice in his life, ah, ah, ah, ah! as any one of any consequence knows. The Princess Henrietta, though pretty, is a termagant and also a little—a little inclined——

MRS. MABSLEY. A little inclined?

RAIKELL. A little inclined?

[*All laugh.*]

BICKSIT. Just a little—but these were not the Duke's reasons for refusing.

ALL. Ah! No?

BICKSIT. He declared he would make no marriage without love on either side and that he would wed to suit himself, whom, when, and how he begad pleased.

TOWNBRAKE. What did His B'ged Majesty do?

BICKSIT. Clapped him into prison at Vincennes.

ALL. Good gracious!

MRS. MABSLEY. Heavens! In prison?

BICKSIT. [*Chuckling.*] Aye! 'Tis supposed to be a secret, and they think in France that the Duke has retired to one of his chateaux. But he's locked up in Vincennes tight enough! Ha, ha, because he won't marry. He'll get over that!

[*All laugh.*]

BANTISON. Young, is he not?

BICKSIT. [*Importantly.*] Precisely thirty-three.

ALL. Thirty-three?

MISS PAITELOT. Is he handsome?

MRS. MABSLEY. Yes, is he handsome?

BICKSIT. Ha! Um! I have not seen the Duke for several years, though on the occasion of my last visit to Paris he entertained me lavishly.

BANTISON. The last time you were in Paris? Faith, that was thirty years ago! Consequently, when the Duke of Orleans entertained you so lavishly——

[*Laughing.*]

RAIKELL. He was precisely three years of age!

BANTISON. I suppose the Duke passed you his nursing bottle.

[*All laugh.*]

BICKSIT. [*Stolidly.*] What of that, sir? What of that?

[*Goes to the fountain.*]

ALL. Ha, ha, ha!

MISS PAITELOT. I am determined to know if Mr. Bicksit's Hero is handsome!

MISS PRESBREY. Does *no* one know his appearance?

MRS. MABSLEY. Major Molyneaux is just from Versailles.

ALL LADIES. [*Pleadingly.*] Oh, Major Molyneaux!

[*They gather around him.*]

MOLYNEAUX. I have never seen him.

ALL. Well, well.

MOLYNEAUX. He is the French King's and the Court's and the new favorite's best actor in the little theatre at

Versailles. He speaks English well. He's mad for the cards and dice, and fortune favors him with both. He exercises two hours a day with the best master of arms in Europe, and is the finest swordsman of the Court. He is gay, debonnaire, and that's all I know.

MISS PRESBREY. But his features—his voice?

MRS. MABSLEY. Oh, and his smile!

BANTISON. Ask some Frenchman!

RAIKELL. Ask Monsieur Beaucaire.

MISS PAITELOT. [To RAIKELL.] Monsieur Beaucaire! Do you mean the Frenchman? Where is he?

RAIKELL. He is just beyond the door!

ALL LADIES. He will tell us!

RAIKELL. [Announcing.] Monsieur Beaucaire! I introduce him, ladies!

> [BEAUCAIRE appears in the doorway and stands
> for an instant upon the threshold. He wears
> a heavy curled black periwig, which falls for-
> ward down to his cheeks; very large black
> patches; a coach and four, a crescent and a
> star are pasted on his cheek, brow, and chin.
> He has a small black mustache. His clothes
> are entirely of black silk, except the white lace
> and gold buckles. The shoe buckles and those
> at the throat and knees are set with diamonds.
> At RAIKELL's introduction he removes his hat
> with a sweeping bow.]

ALL LADIES. [Making courtesy on BEAUCAIRE's entrance and starting forward eagerly.] Have you ever seen the Duke of Orleans?

BEAUCAIRE. [Starts and claps his hand to his heart.] Mort Dieu! [He looks at the ladies strangely and draws a deep breath.] What is it you say?

MISS PAITELOT. He is but thirty-three!

Miss Presbrey and Miss Paitelot. [*At the same time.*] We are sure that he is beautiful!

Mrs. Mabsley. [*Repeating the question.*] Have you ever seen the Duke of Orleans?

Beaucaire. [*Recovers himself, speaks with an accent but that of a man of education.*] I beg you—forgive me. [*Turns to* Mrs. Mabsley.] That gentleman you speak of, M. le Duc D'Orleans, he has made me such a great trouble all my life.

Mrs. Mabsley. Is it possible? Your enemy? How romantic!

Beaucaire. [*Smiling.*] Madam, my worst one, and much trouble to all my family. I can tell you they have had the bad time with him, and me. I ask your pardon, but if you please, I prefer not to speak of that person. You forgive me! [*He laughs lightly an interrogative laugh with a rising inflection.*] Ha, ha, if you please?

Miss Paitelot. [*Stepping toward him.*] Only tell me, is he beautiful?

Beaucaire. [*Coming toward* Miss Paitelot.] I hear he behafe very ogly.

Miss Presbrey. Oh, but do tell us that much!

Beaucaire. Let us speak of something better than that wicked fellow.

Bicksit. Better than a Duke?

Mrs. Mabsley. Better than a prince of the blood?

Beaucaire. [*Lifting his eyes to the ceiling.*] Even better than the Prince of the blood. They're not all jus' angels, Madame.

Mrs. Mabsley. [*To* Baniston.] Well, for my part, I find little favor in Frenchmen, Dukes or Varlets.

Beaucaire. Madame, you must be more lenient. Remember, all our wives cannot be English women.

[Mrs. Mabsley *courtesies; he bows.*]

BICKSIT. Pretty wit.

MISS PAITELOT. [*Crying out.*] Oh, are you married?

BEAUCAIRE. Non, mademoiselle. I had a prejudice against it until this moment.

> [*Bowing to her.*]

BANTISON. [*In a burly voice and with a glance of little kindness to* BEAUCAIRE.] Well, I thank God I'm not a Frenchman!

BEAUCAIRE. [*With a brief upward turn of the eye.*] I send my thanks to Him with yours!

> [*All laugh.*]

BICKSIT. Neatly parried.

> [*All laugh.* BANTISON *bows profoundly.* BEAUCAIRE *returns the bow.* RAIKELL *laughs behind* TOWNBRAKE.]

MISS PAITELOT. But he doesn't tell us about the Duke of Orleans!

TOWNBRAKE. [*To* MISS PAITELOT *aside.*] Try to find out who this man is. Every one is dying to know.

MISS PAITELOT. [*Going to* BEAUCAIRE.] Why do *you* come to Bath, Monsieur?

BEAUCAIRE. Mademoiselle, do we not all come to Bath to drink the waters?

> [*Takes glass from an attendant.*]

MRS. MABSLEY. Nay! We are all persuaded there is a mystery about you!

BEAUCAIRE. [*Smiling.*] Madame, the waters!

> [*He sips.*]

MISS PAITELOT. He won't tell—how provoking!

BEAUCAIRE. [*Grandly.*] I am M. le Duc D'Orleans!

> [*All laugh heartily.*]

MISS PRESBREY. [*During the laugh.*] Why he's safe locked up in the Prison of Vincennes.

BEAUCAIRE. Then you mus' believe in the waters!

[*He drinks and returns the cup.*]

BICKSIT. As if I shouldn't have recognized him.

MRS. MABSLEY. La, aren't we to have our walk, our chat in our coffee house, before the second cup?

> [*She gives* BEAUCAIRE *her hand and makes a courtesy. She exits with* TOWNBRAKE.]

ALL. Yes, yes! Let's go! Ah, ah.

BICKSIT. Come, gentlemen.

> [*All except* MOLYNEAUX, *talking and laughing, exeunt.*]

MOLYNEAUX. [*To* BEAUCAIRE *as the latter starts to go.*] Can you spare a moment for me?

> [*He speaks quickly in a grave, businesslike tone.*]

BEAUCAIRE. [*Turning, not stopping, and answering in the same tone.*] At once, Monsieur.

MOLYNEAUX. Jolliffe!

> [*He motions to an attendant slightly. Exit Jolliffe.*]

BEAUCAIRE. Monsieur! You have something to say to me?

MOLYNEAUX. I throw myself on your mercy, M. Beaucaire. I beg your help in a matter of great importance.

BEAUCAIRE. Oh, Monsieur, how can I serve you?

MOLYNEAUX. Perhaps you know that I am just from the Court of France?

BEAUCAIRE. Ah!

MOLYNEAUX. I take you as a man of honor and I shall trust you to regard what I say as a confidence. [BEAUCAIRE *nods slightly.*] Besides, I believe you know it already and are a party to the secret.

BEAUCAIRE. I know secrets?

MOLYNEAUX. I think so.

BEAUCAIRE. [*Laughing.*]   My good friend!

MOLYNEAUX. Listen, M. Beaucaire, I am not idling in England. I shall be utterly frank with you. I went to Versailles one month ago to attend the English Ambassador. He has just sent me home on a mission. It is this —we have private information that the Duke of Orleans——

BEAUCAIRE. Oh, this eternal Orleans! He must be a bad boy! A very bad boy.

MOLYNEAUX. That the Duke of Orleans has escaped from Paris on the eve of his arrest. He is not in the prison at Vincennes.

BEAUCAIRE. No! Ah, the rascal! Why did he run away? I hear they have very good things to eat at Vincennes! Such a cook!

MOLYNEAUX. The Marquis de Mirepoix, France's Ambassador to our Court, was leaving for England. He is a dear friend of the Duke's, and the young man persuaded the Marquis to take him in his suite and bring him to London as his hairdresser.

BEAUCAIRE. As his hairdresser! Monseigneur le Duc D'Orleans, ha, ha, ha! A barber! Je lui fais mes compliments! [*Seriously.*] How many know this?

MOLYNEAUX. In France—the King, the Governor of Vincennes, and the English Ambassador. In England— M. de Mirepoix, you, and I.

BEAUCAIRE. [*Turns slightly toward* MOLYNEAUX.] And you want to arrest him, eh? For the King of France?

MOLYNEAUX. No, M. Beaucaire, I wish to find him.

BEAUCAIRE. Eh? What then?

MOLYNEAUX. He has left M. de Mirepoix, but the Marquis knows where he has gone. My business is to obey the instructions of the English Ambassador and watch over the wild young Duke and see he comes to no harm, or war between England and France might be the result.

BEAUCAIRE. He seems very important—this young man?

MOLYNEAUX. The Duke himself will preserve his incognito to the last drop of his blood, knowing that if the matter of his escape came out his friend, M. de Mirepoix, would be sacrificed. I appeal to you in despair. I have never seen him.

BEAUCAIRE. Monsieur, Monsieur, why do you ask me these things?

MOLYNEAUX. Because I think you can help me to find him.

BEAUCAIRE. I?

MOLYNEAUX. Be frank with me, M. Beaucaire, what harm can come of it? It is known that you crossed the channel in the same ship. You told Raikell so the other day, and, besides, Captain Badger knows it. You will tell me what you know? It is in a good cause.

BEAUCAIRE. I can tell you nothing. It is time for my second glass.
    [Rises.]

MOLYNEAUX. You mean I have failed to convince you.
    [Rises.]

BEAUCAIRE. [Heartily.] No, Monsieur, I mean I do not meddle with dangerous secrets.

MOLYNEAUX. Your caution is commendable. There is nothing more dangerous to possess than a secret.

BEAUCAIRE. Oh, yes, there is. There is one thing much more dangerous to possess than a secret.

MOLYNEAUX. A woman, you mean! Aye, they go together.

BEAUCAIRE. No, they do not. You cannot have both at the same time.

MOLYNEAUX. Some women.

BEAUCAIRE. Some women! Ah, Monsieur, there is but one woman in the world.

MOLYNEAUX. You mean your ideal——

BEAUCAIRE. No, Monsieur, I mean the lady for whom the bells rang last night.

MOLYNEAUX. You saw her?

BEAUCAIRE. This morning.

MOLYNEAUX. She is very beautiful?

BEAUCAIRE. Beautiful? That is the least of it.

MOLYNEAUX. The bells rang last night, M. Beaucaire, for Lady Mary Carlisle. A very great personage, M. Beaucaire!

BEAUCAIRE. Yes. Even a King would have seen that.

MOLYNEAUX. [*Continuing quietly in a kindly tone.*] Royal blood runs in her veins, Monsieur.

BEAUCAIRE. Monsieur, that is the best thing that ever I heard about royal blood.

MOLYNEAUX. But unless one is of that blood or near it one would do well to forget her.

BEAUCAIRE. Monsieur, you have honored me with your confidence. I will give you mine.

[MOLYNEAUX *crosses and sits at the table.*]

BEAUCAIRE. I shall throw myself on your mercy. I tell you, my friend, I have seen my heart! My heart— in a woman's eyes! A lady with roses—with the happiest roses, the most beautiful red roses, in all the world. And the hand of that lady let fall a rose—a red rose, and I gave my heart with her rose upon my knees. I shall ask the great favor of you to present me to the lady.

MOLYNEAUX. For myself I would undertake it gladly.

I promise to ask her permission, but I must tell you I
doubt if she will grant it.

BEAUCAIRE. [*Sitting at the table.*] Why should she
refuse, Monsieur?

MOLYNEAUX. Because she is a great lady who knows
well that she is one.

BEAUCAIRE. Then that comes because she knows she
has a great heart!

MOLYNEAUX. Why, sir, she is the haughtiest woman in
England. She is followed by a crowd of suitors. Squire
Bantison, the richest man in Bath——

BEAUCAIRE. [*Compassionately.*] That poor old fat
man with the red nose? Money is enough for him to
think about.

MOLYNEAUX. My Lord Townbrake! Of the oldest
family of the kingdom!

BEAUCAIRE. Ah! The oldest family in the kingdom!
Well, 'tis time they were all dead.

MOLYNEAUX. [*Leaning forward eagerly.*] My Lord
of Winterset, M. Beaucaire. 'Tis said he wears a rose of
hers in his breast every day.

BEAUCAIRE. [*Striking the floor lightly with his cane
and rising.*] Then I shall release you from your promise,
Monsieur! Monseigneur le Duc de Winterset, *he* shall
present me to Lady Carlisle! He is the highest here. I
shall be introduced by no other.

MOLYNEAUX. My dear sir, do not ask him! Even if
you could force the Duke to do it, she would not ac-
knowledge the presentation. You will relieve me of the
intention to offend? But you are, I believe, heretofore
unknown to Bath, coming without letters or vouchers——

BEAUCAIRE. [*Speaking decisively.*] Monsieur le Duc
de Winterset shall present me to Lady Mary Carlisle.

[*Sounds of many voices and laughter without.*]

MOLYNEAUX. I am sorry for you, sir. [*He goes to the door at centre. A crowd is seen in the gardens. He then turns to* BEAUCAIRE.] Here's the Duke himself with Richard Nash.

BEAUCAIRE. Ah!

MOLYNEAUX. For the last time, M. Beaucaire. The Duke will refuse you; that will mean a quarrel. He will not meet you himself and instead you will find yourself involved with an unsavory henchman, a hired follower of his, one Captain Badger, a very marvellous fellow with the rapier, the best sword in England. A dog, but 'tis a pleasure to see him fight.

BEAUCAIRE. I suppose people have died of that pleasure?

MOLYNEAUX. Six, I think.

> [RAIKELL *walks in from the door at centre with a careless yet rapid stride. His voice is loud, careless, not unkindly.*]

RAIKELL. Molyneaux!

MOLYNEAUX. Well?

RAIKELL. I have heard who it is Nash intends to expel from the rooms this morning. It is you, Monsieur Beaucaire.

> [*Turns to* BEAUCAIRE.]

BEAUCAIRE. What is it you say?

MOLYNEAUX. Expel him? Why?

BEAUCAIRE. Expel me?

RAIKELL. As I told Molyneaux before, earlier this morning, I overheard Nash raving about some scoundrel, as he called him, who had forced his way into Bath society under false pretenses, and Nash, who is a stickler for etiquette, swore that as soon as the facts were proved he would expel the intruder publicly. I have since heard

it was you, M. Beaucaire, whom they mean to expel, and I
thought you might like to leave before it happened.

BEAUCAIRE. Me? Mon Dieu! What have I done?

[*Enter* FRANÇOIS, *going to* BEAUCAIRE.]

RAIKELL. I don't know.

FRANÇOIS. Monseigneur——

BEAUCAIRE. What is it, François?

MOLYNEAUX. Who is that?

BEAUCAIRE. My servant.

FRANÇOIS. [*Aside to him.*] Monseigneur! Je
vous supplie c'est M. Beau Nash qui vient. It is Monsieur
Beau Bath who comes to expel you.

BEAUCAIRE. Laissez moi! Expel me! It is impossible. I shall stay here.

MOLYNEAUX. [*Going to the centre doors and looking
out.*] Lady Mary's chair— [*Turns.*] In the garden.
Do you wish to be insulted in her presence?

> [*An increasing noise of voices and laughter is
> heard without. Enter* TOWNBRAKE *and* MRS.
> MABSLEY. *They go over toward the bar.*
> BICKSIT, MISS PAITELOT, *and* MISS PRESBREY
> *enter talking.* BANTISON *and other ladies
> enter.*]

FRANÇOIS. Monseigneur, pardon. Je vous implore—It
will be the ruin of the French Ambassador.

BEAUCAIRE. [*Quickly.*] Bien, mon fils. I will go.

> [*He turns and goes rapidly four or five steps
> toward the door at the centre.*]

MOLYNEAUX. [*As* BEAUCAIRE *turns.*] Believe me, you
are wiser.

JOLLIFFE. [*At the door centre announcing.*] His
Grace the Duke of Winterset!

MOLYNEAUX. It is too late!

BEAUCAIRE. [*Pausing as* MOLYNEAUX *addresses him.*]

No, it is not too late! M. de Winterset shall present me to Lady Mary Carlisle and you shall see it.

> [Winterset *enters*. Jolliffe *at the door announces* Lady Mary Carlisle *and* Captain Badger.]

Beaucaire. [*To* Molyneaux.] You see her and think one can go so easily!

Lady Mary. [*Looking at* Beaucaire.] Ah! 'Twas you, sir——

Winterset. Don't speak to him!

Lady Mary. But I dropped a rose on the Parade. This gentleman gave it back on his knees. It is not new that a gentleman stoops for a fallen rose—but, my faith! 'tis new that he gives it back. Should I not in turn——

Winterset. [*Half aside.*] A rose? To him? No! By the Lord!

Lady Mary. [*With cold amazement.*] My Lord of Winterset!

Winterset. [*To her.*] Madame, I am your slave. But I swear on my honor as a gentleman you shall thank me within the moment for this forbidding!

Beaucaire. At his bidding—and my heart witholds my rose.

Jolliffe. [*Announcing.*] The Master of the Ceremonies!

Molyneaux. [*Crossing to* Beaucaire *and speaking in a low voice.*] M. Beaucaire, go now!

Winterset. [*Seeing* Beaucaire *going, crosses to him, lifts his hand slowly toward* Beaucaire.] One moment, M. Beaucaire!

Molyneaux. Pass him; go straight by. Do not let him stop you. Go now!

> [Beaucaire *has advanced a step toward* Winterset *as the latter speaks, falls back for a*

second, immediately recovers himself. WIN-
TERSET *comes toward him.*]

WINTERSET. I must detain you for Mr. Nash!

FRANÇOIS. [*Stepping toward* BEAUCAIRE.] Monseigneur!

BEAUCAIRE. [*To* FRANÇOIS.] Silence!

> [LADY MARY *looks curiously at* BEAUCAIRE,
> *whose eyes are fixed upon her.* NASH *has
> entered. He bows and condescends to look
> upon* BEAUCAIRE. *He comes between* WIN-
> TERSET *and* BEAUCAIRE *and with pursed lips
> and waving a graceful but contemptuous ges-
> ture of command, says:*]

NASH. Ladies! Gentlemen! [*All make courtesy.*]
M. Beaucaire, I request your attention for a few moments.

BEAUCAIRE. I live but to carry out the wishes of Monsieur.

NASH. [*Very angry but showing his indignation only
in a ferocious courtesy and a sardonically quiet voice.*] I
thank you. [*To* LADY MARY *first, then to the others.*]
My Lady Mary, Ladies, and Gentlemen, I desire that you
will take a careful look at this person, if you will.

ALL. What!

LADY MARY. [*Slight pause.*] This is a somewhat
strange request, Mr. Nash.

NASH. Not so strange, My Lady.

LADY MARY. Is there an explanation or must we continue to stare the gentleman out of countenance?

NASH. [*Still looking at* BEAUCAIRE.] There is an explanation.

ALL. Yes! Yes!

LADY MARY. [*To* NASH.] It is——?

NASH. That I am here to expel this fellow from the
rooms publicly.

[*Every one is startled. They all say, "What"
—"What's he done?" "What's this mean?"
"Expel him!" etc.*]

LADY MARY. Oh!

[*She turns with a contemptuous air from both
    BEAUCAIRE and NASH and joins LUCY.
    BEAUCAIRE flinches.*]

BEAUCAIRE. [*In a very quiet voice to NASH.*] May
one interrupt this very be-au-ti-ful ceremony to ask the
stupid question—why, Monsieur?

NASH. [*With savage softness.*] Ah, one may inquire
why, and one may also be told why, and that very shortly.
[*Stops. His smile gives way to a harsh frown.*] You
come here and thrust yourself among people of fashion
and birth, by Gad, do you? What were you born that
you do this? Were you born a gentleman?

BEAUCAIRE. Why, how can one be?

NASH. [*Savagely striking his cane on the floor.*] I
ask you, were you born a gentleman?

BEAUCAIRE. No, M'sieur!

[LADY MARY *turns to* WINTERSET.]

ALL. Not a gentleman!

BEAUCAIRE. I was born a baby. In all my life I
nevaire have seen one baby that was a gentleman!

[*All laugh.*]

RAIKELL. [*Red-faced.*] Faith, Beau, what has the
man done?

NASH. [*Angrily.*] Sir, you shall know in good time!
[*Turning.*] Captain Badger, the esteemed friend of His
Grace, the Duke of Winterset, is present, I believe.

[BADGER *comes forward.*]

MOLYNEAUX. [*To* RAIKELL.] Esteemed friend!
Paid man!

RAIKELL. [*Chuckling.*] Not paid, owed man.

[*The company have been murmuring.*]

NASH. I beg your attention. Some of you may find the fellow at his tricks elsewhere.

BEAUCAIRE. [*Quietly.*] Where there is no Meestaire Nash!

NASH. [*Continuing.*] Society must be defended. Captain Badger!

BADGER. I happened to cross to Dover on the ship that brought the Marquis de Mirepoix, the French Ambassador. This man followed in his suite. I conversed with the sailors out of mere curiosity, asking information about the Marquis' passage.

> [NASH *stops him.* BADGER *shrugs his shoulders and steps back.*]

NASH. [*More and more possessed by his wrath, lifting his voice.*] I can tell you the rest. Captain Badger arrived in Bath last night and saw this fellow upon the Parade. He learned that he had the horrible insolence to mix with people of fashion, to approach persons of birth, to frequent the rooms, to thrust himself upon *us!* And do you know in what capacity he travelled with M. de Mirepoix—what was his position in his suite?

ALL. What?

NASH. I will tell you! [*In a voice breaking with a sense of outrage in enormity.*] It was as the Ambassador's hairdresser! This person is a barber!

ALL. A barber!

> [*All fall back. At the word "Hairdresser"* MOLYNEAUX *utters a slight exclamation and starts forward toward* BEAUCAIRE. *All the others cry and, except* FRANÇOIS, *fall away from* BEAUCAIRE.]

LADY MARY. Mr. Nash, I beg you will permit us to withdraw?

NASH. Your patience, My Lady, one moment, I beg. [*To* BEAUCAIRE.] You hear, sir! My advice to you is to leave Bath before night.

WINTERSET. [*Going to* BEAUCAIRE *and speaking harshly.*] If you dare ever to show your face here again, you'll be thrown into jail and lashed by your fellow grooms.

> [BEAUCAIRE *lifts his head, turns quickly to* WINTERSET *with a brilliant smile, and speaks in a clear voice.*]

BEAUCAIRE. Why not make the degradation perfect and say lashed by *you,* Monsieur?

WINTERSET. [*Outraged by his tone and gesture.*] Canaille!

FRANÇOIS. [*Hastily and in a low voice.*] Monseigneur! Monseigneur!

BEAUCAIRE. [*To* FRANÇOIS.] Mon fils! [*Then quietly.*] I will go, Messieurs! [*Stands with bowed head a moment, then bowing slightly.*] Adieu!

> [*He turns sharply on his heel and takes three steps when* WINTERSET *speaks.*]

WINTERSET. Remember! Leave Bath before night!

BEAUCAIRE. [*Whirls about sharply and stops, answering gaily in a loud clear voice.*] No, I shall not leave Bath.

ALL. What!

BEAUCAIRE. I cannot come here? Well, all gentlemen, they are welcome to my apartment, where I will play with them with the dice or the card, and al—ways fair, M'sieur —night or day, for any stake, for a shilling, a thousand pound, or ten thousand pound! With the card or dice — [*He turns suddenly upon the Duke.*] Or the small sword, M'sieur!

[*There is a snort of laughter from the company.*
BEAUCAIRE *is outraged.*]

TOWNBRAKE. [*At the same time.*] Fight a lackey!
Ha, ha, ha!

BANTISON. [*At the same time.*] Ho, ho! A cartel
from the barber!

RAIKELL. 'Twill kill them at White's.

TOWNBRAKE. Challenged His B'ged Grace, b'ged.

BEAUCAIRE. [*Humiliated.*] Mon Dieu—and she——
[*He looks at* LADY MARY, *whose face shows a
slight smile of scorn. He stands in suppressed
rage.*]

LADY MARY. Mr. Nash, are we to listen to the pitiful
business all day?

BEAUCAIRE. [*With a sharp intake of breath.*] Ah!
Mon Dieu! and—she—believe——
[*He turns with bent head and walks slowly toward the door.* MOLYNEAUX *turns and follows, overtakes him, stops him, speaks in a
short agitated voice.*]

MOLYNEAUX. The Duke of Orleans is in Bath!

WINTERSET. [*As* BEAUCAIRE *turns.*] Remember, if
you return here we'll have you flogged!

BEAUCAIRE. [*Upon the threshold turns upon the company with blazing eyes.*]. Night or day, gentlemen!
Night or day! At any time! For any stake and al—
ways fair, M'sieur! When you want to win money, come
to good M. Beaucaire. With the dice we play! [*He
raises his right hand, which holds his hat, with the level
of his shoulder.*] With the card we play! With the
sword we play! [*All lean forward looking at him.*] For
a shilling, for a thousand pound—for ten thousand pound
—or— [*As the curtain falls his uplifted hand descends*

outstretched to the level with the rose of WINTERSET'S
breast.]   Or jus' for that little red rose, M'sieur!

CURTAIN

ACT II

Act II opens a month later at BEAUCAIRE'S *lodgings in
    Bath.   The curtain opens to disclose a dark panelled
    room with a heavy mantel-piece at the left, and a
    small fire burning.   There is a wide, curtained en-
    trance in back at the left, a door halfway down at the
    right.   A window in the back, right centre, with cur-
    tains drawn back, admits the light of sunset.   The
    furniture is oak of Queen Anne style.   There are
    candles in sconces on each wall, unlit.   A table, left
    centre, completes the furnishings.*

Seated at the back of the table when the act begins are
    MR. RAIKELL, *right,* MR. BANTISON, *left, and* MON-
    SIEUR BEAUCAIRE.   *They are playing cards;* BAN-
    TISON *unable to conceal dismay; a great heap of gold
    and paper piled up before* BEAUCAIRE.   FRANÇOIS
    *stands at the door.   The gentlemen are dressed as in
    Act I, except* BEAUCAIRE, *who wears a purple dress-
    ing-gown, trimmed with dark fur to his heels and
    basket cuffs, like a modern grocer's, from wrist to
    elbow.*   RAIKELL *and* BANTISON *also wear these
    cuffs, and they have removed their coats.*   BANTISON
    and RAIKELL *both have cloaks on the back of chairs
    at the rise of the curtain.*

RAIKELL.   [*Shuffles top of table as the curtain rises.*]
Come tell us, Beaucaire, nay man, and why not?   Does
Winterset still come to play with you?

BANTISON.   Come, tell us!   I'll lay you five to one the

Duke comes here every night. [*Confidentially.*] Tell us, has he won?

BEAUCAIRE. [*Reproachfully.*] Ah, Monsieur! how you like that, now, if some ozzaire gentleman comes to me an' say: "Now please tell me, M. Beaucaire, does Monsieur Bantison come an' play with you?" Suppose then. I tell him yes: then all the company, all the pipple of fashion, all the lady, they know that you play cards with me. How you like that, Monsieur?

RAIKELL. [*Shuffles, laughing.*] Why, Egad! They *do* know it, I think. Never was such a comedy in Bath before. A farce! Ha, ha! Such a farce as I never knew. Nash excommunicates you, and then, ha, ha! Now, on your life, Beaucaire, on your life, doesn't the Beau come here to play himself? [*Strikes the table with his hand.*] I swear Nash does! Ha, ha, ha! I swear he does!

BANTISON. [*Angrily.*] Blood! *Play,* Harry!
        [*They cut.*]

BEAUCAIRE. Ah! The Ace, I am very sorry!

RAIKELL. [*Playing.*] Pay, you mean! He examines the cards, and then adds some coins and paper to Beaucaire's pile.

BEAUCAIRE. Merci, Monsieur.
        [*He shuffles.*]

RAIKELL. Come, Beaucaire. After all you've won from me you might at least own up to that. Winterset comes here to play. Why, man, we know he does, for this is the only place he can win thousands instead of hundreds. We know he would not play cards with *you,* unless he'd some very strong reason. Come, tell us, I say!

BEAUCAIRE. I am a—prison for secrets.

BANTISON. [*Playing his last card, striking the table with his fist.*] A prison for secrets, are you?

[*They cut.*]

BEAUCAIRE. Well now, the Ace again! Oh, I am so sorry. I am so sorry.

BANTISON. [*Shoves over a stack of gold to* BEAUCAIRE.] Put those in your keep. [*Taking notes from a wallet and throwing them upon the pile.*] And those—and those! Damme! I'll play no more.

RAIKELL. [*Rises laughing.*] Frederic's so rich that every little loss is the death of him.

BANTISON. Little? I play no more. [*He rises.*] I'll not play again.

[FRANÇOIS *brings* BANTISON'S *hat.*]

RAIKELL. [*Smiling.*] A noble resolution, Frederic. Well, I'll stand with you on that if you mean it.

BANTISON. Mean it! This is the last time. I come to Beaucaire's no more!

RAIKELL. Mine also! Here's a virtuous pair of us!

BEAUCAIRE. [*Clapping his hands lightly.*] I make my applause, messieurs. If you want to know why— [He *rises.*] Because after to-night there is no M. Beaucaire in this place.

RAIKELL. Leaving Bath!

BEAUCAIRE. [*Quietly.*] I have only one more thing to do. There is one other with whom I come to an understanding this evening. So you will find no M. Beaucaire in Bath to-morrow. [*Pauses.*] I bid you adieu, messieurs.

RAIKELL. [*Putting on cloak.*] Come, Frederic, I have an hour to spend with Flitch over my hairdressing before Lady Rellerton's Ball to-night, and I must have two bottles after that, so come along.

BANTISON. I'm waiting for you.

FRANÇOIS. [*At the door to* RAIKELL *and* BANTISON.] Pardon, m'sieur!

[He makes a sign to the two gentlemen.]

RAIKELL. *[Chuckling.]* Oh, the same farce!

> *[The two conceal their faces by lifting the high collars of their cloaks and pulling their hats down; they leave at the left.]*

FRANÇOIS. M'sieu!

> *[A man enters at the door just as* BANTISON *and* RAIKELL *are leaving. His face is muffled as* BANTISON'S *and* RAIKELL'S.]

BEAUCAIRE. *[Coming forward with both hands outstretched.]* My good frien'. My good frien'.

> *[The cloak drops from the newcomer's face and he takes off his hat; it is* MR. MOLYNEAUX.]

MOLYNEAUX. *[Coming forward and taking* BEAUCAIRE'S *hand.]* I come to serve you if I must—but first to remonstrate——

BEAUCAIRE. *[Quietly, gravely, lifting a protecting hand.]* Non!

MOLYNEAUX. To beg——

BEAUCAIRE. My frien', there is no use.

MOLYNEAUX. *[Turning away from him with impatience and sorrow.]* Ah! I tell you——

BEAUCAIRE. *[Smiling.]* My frien', 'tis all arranged. I make all my little plans.

MOLYNEAUX. You have only arranged to break your heart.

> *[He puts cloak and hat on chair.]*

BEAUCAIRE. You have not seen me as myself. You do not know how great change I——

MOLYNEAUX. If they recognize you, you will probably be killed before you declare yourself.

BEAUCAIRE. My frien', while I am alive that is one thing that I shall navre do—declare myself.

MOLYNEAUX. Do you know what Winterset will do

afterward if he falls into your trap? How do you *know* he will cheat?

[BEAUCAIRE *laughs and throws up his hands.*]

BEAUCAIRE. [*Smiling.*] You believe he gawn to be very angry? Me, I think that is true! But I am not soch a frighten one.

[MOLYNEAUX *comes over to table and sits down.*]

Oh! My frien', if you knew how great money I have paid that Groteux, my cousin's fencing-master! [*Moving toward* MOLYNEAUX, *he spreads his hands, palms out, toward him and speaks with confidential pathos.*] Shall I tell you something? Monsieur, in all my life—an' I am thirty-three years old, well, my frien', in that whole time I have navre had one fight. [*Over table.*] Jus' think of that, Monsieur. Of course, I don't wan' to *hurt* any pipple, an' have no bad feeling to any person in this whole world; but I don't think all that money I pay Groteux for his lessons ought to be jus' thrown away. My frien', you don't believe [*With naïve appeal.*] it is so bad in me to wan' jus' one li'l fight?

MOLYNEAUX. I think you will get your fight, Monseigneur.

[*Enter* FRANÇOIS *at the door. He comes to* BEAUCAIRE *and presents a card on a salver. He bows low and goes out left.*]

BEAUCAIRE. [*Reading note.*] He is here. I knew he would not fail.

MOLYNEUX. [*With despairing gesture.*] You draw the net about yourself.

BEAUCAIRE. [*Going toward the hearth.*] About *him!*

MOLYNEAUX. You throw your heart away upon— [*Vehemently.*] upon a coronet and a book of heraldry—

you think it is a woman with a heart. If Your Highness could see her as I do.

BEAUCAIRE. No "Highness," my frien'—if you please.

MOLYNEAUX. Lady Mary is a stone. They will discover you and denounce you as Beaucaire.

BEAUCAIRE. But they will not discover me.

MOLYNEAUX. She is a stone, I say! Stone to any but a Duke!

BEAUCAIRE. Well, I am gawn to be a Duke.

MOLYNEAUX. But when you are exposed, you swear you will not declare yourself for de Mirepoix's sake.

BEAUCAIRE. When that exposure come, I am gawn to show you the kindest lady in all the world.

MOLYNEAUX. [*Throwing up his hands hopelessly.*] Madness, madness!

> [*The rest of the room is very dark save for the last daylight on the window panes. From without a low plaintive chorus is heard, sung by* BEAUCAIRE'S *servants, the air of "Le Voyageur."*]

BEAUCAIRE. [*In a low voice as the chorus sounds.*] Listen, my frien'. It is my poor children who sing, those good lackeys who follow me from France. They are singing the song of the— [*He goes to window at the right.*] Voyageur, who die in the forest by Quebec. I love it. It have the forest in it. Yes, and the wind—and the stars—and all there is of lonely in a man's heart. [*Coming down to* MOLYNEAUX.] Listen, my frien'. You say I throw my heart away on a stone. You say they are gawn to discover M. Beaucaire in the new feathers I am gawn to put on this evening. Well, my Molyneaux, w'en that 'appen I am gawn show you a great heart. You say she is a coronet and book of heraldry, but I tell you she is a woman—and a woman is a heart. *This* woman, she is my heart! And I'm gawn to prove it. I set my life on it, you say? [*He crosses to the table and sits on it.*] Well, there is not a such great worth in this life left if the angels are not true. I am thirty-three, mon ami, and I tell you this being a great prince it is not the greates' entertainment in this worl'. I am tired of the toys they give you—of the words they set after your name— [*Rises.*] And, if I go to leave it all—why, then I can leave it— [*Gaily.*] Mon ami! But if I do find that the angel is true—and that is what I am *gawn* to find, my frien'—then there is one man who is happier than any gran' Seigneur ought to be. And *I* tell *you* she is pure gold. Pure gold.

FRANÇOIS. [*Entering left.*]   Monseigneur!

BEAUCAIRE.   He is here!

[*Exit* FRANÇOIS.]

Bien!

MOLYNEAUX. [*Rises and crosses to the left.*]   On your guard, Monseigneur, now and henceforth, as you love your life. And would to God I could stop you.

[*He leaves. Enter* FRANÇOIS *with* WINTERSET. WINTERSET *comes down, dropping his cloak from his face. Exit* FRANÇOIS.]

BEAUCAIRE.   Monsieur le Duc!

[*Bows.*]

WINTERSET.   Is this all the light we're going to have? Egad, I always come here half counting on being murdered as well as bled.

BEAUCAIRE.   Bled? Monsieur le Duc? [*A soft laugh.*] Milor', he bleed the poor Frenchman this las' two weeks. How much? Four thousan' pounds, eh? Five thousan'?

[*He tears the wrappings from one pack of cards*

*and places it on the table, at the left, evi-
dently carefully noting its position.*]

WINTERSET. [*Coming toward the table.*] What of
it? 'Tis not half that you took from me, a week ago, and
'tis scarce worth the trouble to sneak to this dirty thieves'
den.

BEAUCAIRE. [*Above table.*] Aha! Our thieves' den
is much honored this evening.   Monsieur is on his way to
Lady Rellerton's ball?

WINTERSET. Leave ladies' names out of the question, d'ye hear?   I'm in this place for one purpose, and
that is to play.   Are you ready?

BEAUCAIRE. Will Monsieur be seated?

> [*They are about to seat themselves at the table,
> when* FRANÇOIS *speaks from his station at the
> door.*]

FRANÇOIS. A gentleman for Monsieur Beaucaire.
Monsieur Jonsone.

WINTERSET. [*Rising in nervous haste.*] The devil
take you!   Who is it?

BEAUCAIRE. Ah, no one, Monsieur.   My lan'lord,
Monsieur Jonsone.   If Monsieur will excuse, to go to
him, in the entry below.   I return in a few minutes.
Monsieur will excuse?

WINTERSET. [*With a sudden significant glance at the
table and the cards.*]   A plague on you!   Yes!   Yes!

> [BEAUCAIRE *goes out at the left followed by*
> FRANÇOIS.   WINTERSET *looks at the cards on
> the table, then goes up to the door and comes
> down to the table.   With every elaboration of
> caution, he takes the cards from the pack on
> table, and hides them in the voluminous laces
> of his sleeves.   Hearing* BEAUCAIRE *return-
> ing, he hastily replaces the pack on the table,*

but on the right side.   As he is walking away,
BEAUCAIRE *appears in the doorway, notes the*
DUKE'S *position and that of the changed cards.*
FRANÇOIS *re-appears in the doorway, as*
BEAUCAIRE *moves down toward the table.*
BEAUCAIRE *makes a slight sign to him.   Exit*
FRANÇOIS.]

BEAUCAIRE.   [*Above table.*]   Is Monsieur the Duke
ready?

WINTERSET.   [*Crossing over to table.*]   'Tis my whim
we raise the stake to-night.

BEAUCAIRE.   Monsieur le Duc wan' to ruin the poor
Frenchman!

WINTERSET.   Bah!   I say three cuts of the cards and
triple the stakes.   Are you afraid?

[*They both sit.*]

BEAUCAIRE.   [*Starts shuffling.*]   There!   Afraid!   I
think I am always afraid, Monsieur.   I am afraid of *anything.*   I am afraid of the dark!   That is what makes the
fon, I think; life would be too dull, too flat, if one were
not a coward, but they have train' me never to show w'en
I am afraid.

[*Cuts again.*   BEAUCAIRE *loses and pays.   Then*
WINTERSET *shuffles.*]

I am afraid to play for such a high stake, Monsieur, and
because I *am* so afraid—well, that is what makes it in-
terestin'.

[*Cuts again.*   BEAUCAIRE *loses.*]

WINTERSET.   [*Taking over* BEAUCAIRE'S *stakes.*]
Well, what say you if we triple *these* stakes?

BEAUCAIRE.   [*Distinctly raising his voice.*]   But if I
lose?

[MOLYNEAUX *and* FRANÇOIS *noiselessly emerge*

*from a room at the right and stand against
the door.*]

WINTERSET. Ha! You *will* lose, Frenchman!

BEAUCAIRE. But to triple when we have already
tripled, Monsieur?

WINTERSET. You said being afraid made the "fon" of
life. Do you shirk?

BEAUCAIRE. Non—but——

WINTERSET. Then cut.

[BEAUCAIRE *fumbles in his wallet apparently
oblivious of everything but his search for the
notes.* WINTERSET, *observing him keenly,
with all the ease of a practised hand, exchanges
a card in his sleeve for one he has held.*]

The Ace! [*Reaching greedily for the stakes.*] Mine, by
God!

BEAUCAIRE. [*Seizes the Duke's left arm below the
elbow in a vice-like grip.*] At a price, Monsieur. [*With
his other hand, he lightly draws a card from* WINTERSET'S
*wrist ruffles. The other cards in his sleeve fall on the
table.* WINTERSET *staggers back.*] Ah! Merci, Monsieur.

WINTERSET. [*Rushes with intense rage toward* BEAU-
CAIRE.] Ah! Then this means the dirty work of silenc-
ing you with my bare hands.

[WINTERSET *raises his hand as if to strike* BEAU-
CAIRE. BEAUCAIRE *assumes an entire change
of tone and speaks with an authority so absolute that* WINTERSET *pauses involuntarily.*]

BEAUCAIRE. [*Drawing a dagger from a drawer in the
table.*] Just to make sure that he do nothing—foolish—
with his bare hands.

WINTERSET. It's to be murder—murder then, is it, you
carrion?

BEAUCAIRE. What words! Ah no! No—not murder; only—disgrace, Monsieur.

WINTERSET. You fiendish scullion! Do you dream that a soul in Bath will take your word, that I—that I——

BEAUCAIRE. That Monsieur de Winterset had a card up his sleeve!

WINTERSET. You pitiful stroller! Born in a stable——

BEAUCAIRE. Is it not honor to be born where Monsieur so evidently must have been bred?

WINTERSET. Fool! There are not five people in Bath who will speak with you. Every one knows that you come to England as the French Ambassador's barber! What man of fashion will listen to you? Who would believe you?

BEAUCAIRE. Will Monsieur not reseat himself?

[WINTERSET *sits.*]

So. We mus' not be too fatig' for Lady Rellerton's ball. François! [*Exit* FRANÇOIS.] So now we shall talk. I want Monsieur to listen very cool. I will be brief. It is well known that *I* am all entire hones' gamblist! Ah yes, but fair—always fair, every one say that. Is it not so? An'—is there never a whisper come to Monsieur le Duc, that not all people believe *him* to play always hones'? Did it not almos' be said to him, las' year, after he play with Monsieur Tappingford at the chocolate house——

WINTERSET. You dirty scandalmonger! I'll——

[*He rises.*]

BEAUCAIRE. Monsieur! Monsieur! It is poor valor to insult a helpless captor. Can he reply to his own victim? But it is for you to think of what I say! Will I not be believe?

WINTERSET. [*Rising.*]   Damn you! I'll chance it. Your sole word; and none but that lackey to witness it.

MOLYNEAUX. [*From the right.*]   One other, my Lord Winterset.

WINTERSET. [*Slows around and faces* MOLYNEAUX.] The devil! [*To* BEAUCAIRE.] How much is it to be? Your price—damnation—your price!

BEAUCAIRE.   Money! From Monsieur de Winterset? No—not money, but Monsieur le Duc, impoverish, something in bad odor, yet have the *entrée any*where.

WINTERSET.   You dare think to force *me*——

BEAUCAIRE.   Monsieur an' me goin' to Lady Rellerton's ball to-night, Monsieur le Duc an' me!

WINTERSET.   Curse your impudence!

BEAUCAIRE.   Oh, yes, we goin' together.

WINTERSET.   No!

BEAUCAIRE.   Yes, 'tis all arrange—I make all my little plan. We goin' to Lady Rellerton's ball; and you goin' to present me to Lady Mary Carlisle.

WINTERSET.   Lady Mary—present to her a man of no birth—a barber!

BEAUCAIRE.   'Tis all arrange; have no fear; nobody gawn to question Monsieur's guest.   So we goin' together.

WINTERSET. [*Thumping the table.*] No!

BEAUCAIRE.   Yes. [*Rises.*] An' after—then I have the *entrée.* Is it much I ask? Jus' this one night's introduction as the guest of Monsieur le Duc an' then my pledge that I never whisper a word of Monsieur's little misfortune.

> [*He walks around table, pretending to take imaginary cards out of sleeve.*]

WINTERSET.   The *entrée*—you! Go to a lackey's rout and dance with the kitchen maids.   If I would, I could not present you to Bath society.   I should have cartels from the fathers, brothers, and lovers of every woman in the place. You would be thrust from Lady Rellerton's door five minutes after you had entered it.

BEAUCAIRE. I do not think it, Monsieur.

WINTERSET. Half the gentlemen in Bath have been here to play. They would know you, wouldn't they? Fool! *You* to speak to Lady Mary Carlisle. S'death! *You!* She would know you, if you escaped the others. She stood within a yard of you, when Nash expelled you from the pump room.

BEAUCAIRE. Do you think I have forgotten that, Monsieur?

WINTERSET. And you think that because even Winterset introduces a lowborn fellow that he will be tolerated? That Bath will receive a barber?

BEAUCAIRE. I have the distinction to remind Monsieur—I have renounce that profession.

WINTERSET. Faugh!

BEAUCAIRE. And am now a man of fashion—a man of parts. Is it not so? Have you seen me gross, even—or —what shall I say? *Bourgeois?* Shall you be ashame for your guest's manner? So I goin' to be presented to Lady Mary Carlisle.

WINTERSET. Presented? As thus: "Lady Mary Carlisle, may I assume the honor of presenting the barber of the Marquis de Mirepoix?" So that's it—is it?

BEAUCAIRE. No, Monsieur—quite *not* so. You shall have nothing to worry you, nothing in the world. I'm going to assassinate my poor mustachio—the only murder I commit to-night, and then with my hair done à la mode, no one shall know me.

WINTERSET. Curse you! And do you think I am going to be saddled with you as long as you choose?

BEAUCAIRE. A mistake! All I require—all I beg of

Monsieur is this one evening—one night's introduction. After—I shall not need Monsieur.

WINTERSET.   Take heed to yourself, after! And you, sir. [*Approaching* MOLYNEAUX.] You pledge your rascally word that if to-night I lend myself to this fellow's damned scheme, your mouth is shut, whatever happens?

MOLYNEAUX.   This gentleman's price is mine. I take my leave. [*He crosses to* BEAUCAIRE *and says under his breath.*] Remember the after.

[*Exit* MOLYNEAUX.]

BEAUCAIRE.   Conquered! Conquered! [WINTERSET *crosses to fireplace.*] For this night! And I shall meet what you send—after. One cannot hope too much of your patience, eh? It were but natural, should you attempt a little revenge for the trap I was such a wicked fellow as to set for Monsieur, I shall meet some strange frien's of Monsieur—after—eh? Well, I mus' jus' try not to be too much frighten'. I shall be nobler from to-night. The barber's throat is cut with his own razor. Monsieur Beaucaire—is choke' with his own dice box. I choose my rank, eh? Shall I be a chevalier, marquis, viscomte? Non! Out of compliment to the rank of Monsieur, I too will be a Duke. I will be—shall we say the Duke de—de—de—Chateaurien? You see? You are my confrère!

WINTERSET.   [*Coming toward the table.*] And you fancy——

BEAUCAIRE.   [*Sitting on the table.*] I fancy, Monsieur, that I shall meet my dream. Pardon, you do not know what is my dream! Listen, I will tell you. It is to save a noble lady—a beautiful lady—the red rose of all this wide world's garden—from a slug, that would trail itself up to her dear beauty. Ah, what radiance! Haute

noblesse to her little finger tips—gold haired—an angel
of Heaven! A Diana of the chase! [*Over table.*] That
slug—it shall slip down to its slime again, before it have
touched one little leaf of that red rose! It is you and me,
Monsieur! And you are to lose, because you think such
ruin will be easy. How should you know? You have
not the fibre—the heart of a lady is a blank to you, is
sad for me—but I have almost cried out with rapture, at a
look I have seen her give another man, so beautiful it was
—so—mirthful and so tender! A look for another—*ah-
hi-me!* For many others! To-night, to-night, Monsieur,
I—even I—go to seek a rose.

WINTERSET. And after?

[*With a tense snarl.*]

BEAUCAIRE. And after! That is to-morrow's secret,
Monsieur the—slug. Ah, ah, ah!

CURTAIN

ACT III

Act III takes place at LADY RELLERTON'S. *The room is
in white and pale yellow, brilliantly lighted; sconces
on every wall; candelabra on tables near the walls;
wide curtained entrances left and right; a row of
slender columns across the back, beyond which a bank
of plants and flowers is set near the rear wall; from
this bank a stairway ascends. Musicians with fiddles,
flute, and clarionet are seated in a little balcony by
the door at the right. They play the gavotte of Act
I, and the rise of the curtain discloses the dance.*

NASH *is with* MISS PAITELOT; RAIKELL *with* MRS. MABS-
LEY; TOWNBRAKE *and* LADY RELLERTON; BANTI-
SON *and* MISS PRESBREY; LUCY *with* MOLY-

NEAUX. *The last two are nearest the front. On the landing of the stairway at the back* WINTER-SET *and* CAPTAIN BADGER *may be seen; they stand looking off left. The dance proceeds for a few minutes until it is noticed that all the ladies dance with their eyes and faces turned toward the left, in the direction in which* WINTERSET *and* CAPTAIN BADGER *are looking. No matter what the evolutions of the dance, all the ladies preserve their eager interest—sometimes stretching their necks to do so; the gentlemen, save* RAIKELL, *who is amused, and* MOLY-NEAUX, *who is preoccupied and anxious, note the behavior of their ladies with annoyance and call each other's attention to it with gestures.* MR. BANTISON *is particularly disturbed.* MISS PRESBREY, *in her anxiety to observe the object of her interest, several times misses her part of the figure, and* BANTISON *draws her attention to these slips each time by a "Madame" spoken with increasing choler. At last* MISS PRES-BREY, *dancing at the back, quite overcome by her curiosity, turns outside of the columns and stands looking off right. The others, except* BANTISON, *continue to dance. He stands, swelling with anger. Then* MRS. MABSLEY *leaves her place and rushes out to join* MISS PRESBREY. *At this,* BANTISON'S *anger breaks out.*

MISS PRESBREY.   Oh, there he is!

[*They go up to staircase.*]

BANTISON.   [*Coming down waving hand to musicians.*] Stop the music!

ALL.   [*Exclaiming.*]   Stop the dance!

[*The music ceases. All the ladies except* LUCY *join* MRS. MABSLEY *and* MISS PRESBREY.]

BANTISON.   Flesh and blood won't bear it!

TOWNBRAKE. Whoever saw such an exhibition! Look at the women!

LUCY. [*To* MOLYNEAUX.] What is it? What is the matter?

MOLYNEAUX. Hush!

>   [MOLYNEAUX *takes* LUCY *to door at left and lays finger on his lips.* RAIKELL *has been trying to stifle laughter. At the same time to* MAJOR MOLYNEAUX.]

RAIKELL. 'Twill be the death o' me. Pat me on the back, Major.

BANTISON. Ah! Look at 'em!

>   [*Enter* NASH.]

NASH. Why is the dance ended? [*With great wrath.*] Sirs, will some one explain?

BANTISON. Oh! 'Tis vile! Unheard of!

TOWNBRAKE. [*Plaintively.*] 'Tis b'gad hideous.

RAIKELL. [*Walking to* NASH *laughing.*] Explain! 'Tis simple, Beau! The women are all gone mad over the new French Duke, His Grace of Winterset's friend.

NASH. M. de Chateaurien? I thought he had left the house.

RAIKELL. Chateaurien is ensconced with Lady Mary at the end of the hall yonder. That's why— [*He is overcome with laughter for the moment, then proceeds.*] Bantison and Townbrake are in such a fury with the ladies; and why, the ladies are half mad with curiosity. The young French Duke has captured the Beauty.

NASH. I marked she seemed much taken with him the moment His Grace of Winterset presented him; and 'tis very fitting, sir; His Grace of Chateaurien is as proper a gentleman as ever I beheld, and a great noble as well, sir; a great noble.

RAIKELL. Marked it, did you? 'Twas the most mar-

vellous transformation ever known in England! The great
lady blushed like a little maid—and the young French
Duc carried her off in the face of all her suitors. Why,
'twas beautiful! And I'm for him! Damme! I'm for
him. [*Crossing and speaking to* MOLYNEAUX.] He's
young, noble, rich, and he drank seven bumpers with us in
the punch-room without a flush to his cheek! I'm for
him, I say!

BANTISON. Only seven!

RAIKELL. [*Moving forward again.*] He came to
Bath at five this afternoon.

[MOLYNEAUX *comes to* LUCY *seated at the left.*]
And now at twelve he leads the field. Bravo, the Duke of
Chateaurien!

[RAIKELL *goes up to staircase, then comes to
meet* MOLYNEAUX *and* LUCY. TOWNBRAKE
and BANTISON *fling themselves into chairs
against the wall and sit in gloomy solitude.*]

ALL. Bravo!

LUCY. [*Walking slowly with* MOLYNEAUX.] I have
been so happy. I could see how the Duke of Chateaurien
liked you as soon as you were introduced to him. Do you
know 'twas at his request that my cousin gave my hand to
you for the gavotte? Oh, has he *bewitched* cousin Mary?

[BADGER *talks aside to* WINTERSET.]

RAIKELL. [*Coming toward* MOLYNEAUX.] Isn't that
our friend Captain Badger talking to Winterset?

MOLYNEAUX. [*Still talking to* LUCY.] Ay, they seem
mightily concerned with the French Duke and not too
kindly either. 'Fore heaven, you're right. They mean
some mischief. Look at them!

[*They point to the* DUKE *and* BADGER, *whose attitude is sinister and threatening.*]

BADGER. [*Loudly, harshly, looking off right.*]   Who is the young popinjay with her ladyship yonder?

WINTERSET. [*Apparently horrified.*]   Hush! Captain! 'Tis a gentleman from Paris, whom I myself introduced—the Duke of Chateaurien.

BADGER.   Under your favor, I don't like Frenchmen.

BANTISON.   Lord!

BADGER.   A Frenchman once did me a scurvy turn. I'll make his acquaintance when he comes this way.

WINTERSET.   Hush! He's coming now!

> [*They descend from the landing. The ladies raise a slight buzz of voices and fall back to the left and right grouping with the gentlemen.* LADY MARY *and* BEAUCAIRE *come in sight.*]

LUCY. [*Looking at the* DUKE *and* BADGER.]   Oh, I hope nothing evil comes!

BANTISON. [*To* RAIKELL.]   Chateaurien's face baffles me.   It is as if—yet I can't name the face.

RAIKELL.   He's like and unlike some one.

BANTISON.   By Heaven! I have it.   It's like that poor devil of Beaucaire.

RAIKELL.   Damme, yes! Their looks are utterly different, but something in the expression—the voice——

MOLYNEAUX.   Absurd! It is the accent which deceives you.

LUCY.   Oh, he is splendid!

RAIKELL.   They are splendid. Faith, I don't believe they know there's a soul within miles!

BADGER. [*Speaking to* WINTERSET.]   Leave it to me!

LUCY. [*Sharply in a low voice.*]   Look! See Captain Badger's face!

> [*The people in the room are grouped toward the left and right.* BADGER *alone is in the centre.*

He coughs and shakes himself together, swaggeringly turns, then turns again toward WINTERSET.]

BADGER. I am sorry, Your Grace! And I admit all you say in this particular Frenchman's favor may be true —but I don't like Frenchmen, of any rank, and I don't care who knows it.

[*He turns slowly to* WINTERSET, *then walks toward the centre again.*]

MOLYNEAUX. [*Desperately to* RAIKELL *and* LUCY.] Cannot we stop him?

LUCY. Oh, can nothing be done?

MOLYNEAUX. [*Rapidly to* LUCY.] Beg your aunt take him to the supper-room.

[LUCY *instantly crosses to* LADY RELLERTON.]

RAIKELL. I'll do my share. [*He advances swiftly to* BADGER *and touches him on the shoulder.*] 'Pon my soul, Badger, I hadn't seen you before. Are you for punch?

[NASH *comes toward* WINTERSET.]

BADGER. Sir, I beg you not to detain me. I am going to make acquaintance with that Frenchman yonder. I don't like Frenchmen.

LUCY. [*In a clear voice coming from between them.*] Captain Badger, will you accept my hand for the supper-room? My aunt says we are all to go now.

BADGER. [*After staring at her dumfounded.*] Madame, I esteem the honor.

[*He bows and takes her hand. Music without plays a stately march.*]

NASH. Gentlemen, Lady Rellerton begs you to hand the ladies to supper.

[*The gentlemen bow before the different ladies and escort them out to the left of* BEAUCAIRE *and* LADY MARY, *who do not notice.* LUCY

and BADGER *go first.* *He starts up with her
so as to pass close by* BEAUCAIRE.]

LUCY. *This* way, Captain Badger.

[*They go out left.*]

LADY RELLERTON. [*Speaking to* LADY MARY *off-
stage.*] Bring M. de Chateaurien to the supper-room,
child.

LADY MARY. [*Turns slightly.*] Immediately, Aunt,
immediately.

[*All exit.* LUCY *and* CAPTAIN BADGER, MISS
PAITELOT *and* BICKSIT, MISS PRESBREY *and*
WINTERSET, MRS. MABSLEY *and* MOLYNEAUX,
LADY RELLERTON *and* NASH. *All have gone
but* RAIKELL, BANTISON, *and* TOWNBRAKE, *the
last two horribly dejected.* RAIKELL *goes to
the door at left, then turns and looks at them.*
BANTISON *and* TOWNBRAKE *go up to the staircase.* BICKSIT *also joins them.*]

TOWNBRAKE. Lady Mary, Lady Mary!

BANTISON. [*Pulling* TOWNBRAKE *away.*] Lady
Mary, Lady Mary!

TOWNBRAKE. De Chateaurien! We have no chance
with de Chateaurien.

BANTISON. Damn de Chateaurien!

[RAIKELL *goes gravely to* TOWNBRAKE. BICK-
SIT *goes to* BANTISON. *Then in burlesque
state they commence strolling back and forth.*]

RAIKELL. May I have the honor of your escort, Most
Noble? And did your Lordship enjoy the Italian Opera
Singers in town? [*Burlesquing the affected female voice.*]
You naughty gentlemen, I fear you spend all your time at
White's and the Coffee House.

BICKSIT. I hear you're vastly wicked, Mr. Bantison.

BANTISON. Oh, damn!

BICKSIT. Come, you must not say these things to me;
'tis too bad of you.

RAIKELL. And you, Mr. Townbrake, they say you're
in love!

TOWNBRAKE. Oh, damn!

RAIKELL. 'Twill never do to swear so. 'Tis a horrid
habit. Your Lordship, does love sit so hard on you?

TOWNBRAKE. [*Throws* RAIKELL *off*.] I vow, Harry,
you're a fool!

RAIKELL. [*Calling all to attention.*] Lady Mary is
bewitched! Sh! Now for a wager—ten thousand
guineas upon it. Lady Mary mistakes my voice for Lady
Rellerton's. [*He imitates* LADY RELLERTON'S *voice.*]
The supper-room, child. You must bring M. de Chateaurien.

LADY MARY. [*Wthout turning.*] Immediately, Aunt,
immediately.

> [BICKSIT, BANTISON, *and* TOWNBRAKE *double
> up with suppressed merriment.* RAIKELL
> *makes furious gestures and all rush off left.*]
> [*Pause.*]

LADY MARY. [*Tears a rose to pieces from her bou-
quet.*] No, M. de Chateaurien—no!

BEAUCAIRE. That rose I have beg for so long? Ah,
I do not deserve it, but——

LADY MARY. Never!

BEAUCAIRE. It is the greatness of my unworthiness
that alone can claim your charity; let your kin' heart give
this little red rose, this great alms, to this poor beggar.

LADY MARY. Never!

BEAUCAIRE. Madamoiselle, may I tell you something
—something just as it is in my heart?

LADY MARY. [*With raillery.*] Is there room for anything there, with all the pictures it must carry?

BEAUCAIRE. Pictures?

LADY MARY. Portraits.

BEAUCAIRE. Of whom?

LADY MARY. Of all those beautiful dark ladies of the French Court with whom you are in love.

BEAUCAIRE. Ah, you mock, Mademoiselle—but I—I say, not mocking, there is in my heart, till this night, but the picture of one woman.

LADY MARY. [*Startled and apprehensive.*] One woman?

BEAUCAIRE. One woman, Mademoiselle—the dear, dead woman who was my mother, Mademoiselle—may I tell you something more, something jus' as it is in my heart?

LADY MARY. [*With a change of manner—a little frightened, after a pause.*] Yes.

> [*He leads her to a chair. She turns from him slowly.*]

BEAUCAIRE. [*Smiling faintly.*] It is not so easy. [*Pauses.*] But it is—in part—this—that I hear, far, far, away of—of that wonderful lady they call the Beauty of the Bath.

LADY MARY. [*Softly.*] Heard of me? How?

> [*She sits.*]

BEAUCAIRE. In a strange way, Mademoiselle. In my service I have a poet, Berquin. This Berquin, he have a frien', a queer fellow—what shall we say?—an adventurer, a wild fellow, a gamblist, who cross to England and write a letter to Berquin, all about a beautiful lady he see in Bath. This poor gamblist—he have the impudence to fall in love with the beautiful lady, even without knowing her——

> [*She looks up.*]

He is a madman!

LADY MARY. Who was he?

BEAUCAIRE. Mademoiselle, I say he was a madman—
he had mad dreams; but so beautiful that w'en Berquin
give me those letters I make up my mind I see this lady
who make those dreams in him. For I may know her,
where that poor dreamer may not——

LADY MARY. Tell me his name?

BEAUCAIRE. Mademoiselle, his name was—Beaucaire!

LADY MARY. Beaucaire!

BEAUCAIRE. Monsieur Beaucaire.

LADY MARY. That impostor!

BEAUCAIRE. That great madman.

LADY MARY. Why, he was a servant, sir. He was one
of M. de Mirepoix's lackeys!

BEAUCAIRE. A heart beat in his breast.

LADY MARY. A heart? Aye, as all things with a body
may bear a heart.

BEAUCAIRE. [*Rises, then speaks.*] He loved you.

LADY MARY. [*Haughtily.*] Must I beg a greater respect from you, M. le Duc. [*Rises.*] If this—this
lackey—loved me, you might have spared me the knowledge of it!

BEAUCAIRE. [*Gaily.*] Pardon, Mademoiselle. Well,
I am not here to plead that poor mad fellow's forgiveness
from you. I am here to beg you again—again—for a
rose—one red rose.

LADY MARY. You shall have a rose, Monsieur.

BEAUCAIRE. [*Advancing.*] Ah!

LADY MARY. [*Touching the rose in her hair.*] A rose
from my—from my——

BEAUCAIRE. Ah!

LADY MARY. From my *garden,* in the morning, Monsieur.

[*She drops a courtesy.*]

BEAUCAIRE. You laugh at my prayers, Mademoiselle!

Ah, well, better the laughter of a goddess than the smile of a mere woman.

LADY MARY. It may be you prefer the laughter of a goddess—to—to—to——

BEAUCAIRE. Ah, Mademoiselle, to what?

LADY MARY. To a mere rose from the hand of a woman!

BEAUCAIRE. [*Going near her.*] Ah, mock me no more! A rose!

LADY MARY. If I give it you it will mean nothing.

BEAUCAIRE. Nothing to *you*. To me? Ah, a rose is a rose! Nothing to *you*. But to me—well, give it to me, and tell the King of England to send all his great army to get it back again and——

LADY MARY. Yes, what then?

BEAUCAIRE. And then—I run away! But they won't get li'l flower—the King's army! Will you give it to me?

[*There is laughter at the left.*]

LADY MARY. [*Faltering.*] M. de Chateaurien, I have been neglecting my aunt's guests for you. Now, I am going to imitate you—you will represent the armies of King George and—I—I— [*Imitating his accent.*] — shall run away!

BEAUCAIRE. [*Laughing, .protesting, .follows.*] Non, non, Mademoiselle! See, I turn pale that you should speak of leaving me. In my paleness—see, the King's army it raise the white flag. That is surrender. What can your captive do to serve you?

[*He kneels.*]

LADY MARY. If you would really serve me, Monsieur, help me to do my forgotten duty to my aunt's guests—once you have made me forget it.

BEAUCAIRE. Ah, nothing in the world!

[*He rises.*]

LADY MARY. Listen then. In the card-room above, [*Points to back up-stairs.*] is the Dowager Countess of Greenbury! A very old lady, the oldest woman of fashion in England. She is past ninety; she is overlooked by the young cavaliers. But will you—you—sir, seek her out and offer her your escort to the supper-room? [*He looks at her.*] The old Countess, Monsieur.

BEAUCAIRE. It would also vastly pleasure me! I am the humble servant of Madame de Greenburee.

> [*He bows. She courtesies. He reaches the columns at the centre of the room and turns to go. He bows again.*]

LADY MARY. M. de Chateaurien, my request was not instantly pressing. Any time within half an hour will do.

BEAUCAIRE. [*Coming radiantly.*] You give me half an hour.

LADY MARY. To escort Lady Greenbury!

> [*Both laugh.*]

BEAUCAIRE. Lady Greenbury, she shall be in the supper-room in half an hour. I pledge you on my word of honor, Mademoiselle.

LADY MARY. But for myself, I must leave you——

BEAUCAIRE. *Now?*

LADY MARY. At once.

> [*Going.*]

BEAUCAIRE. [*Coming down near her.*] And you will leave nothing behind you? Not one red rose?

LADY MARY. [*In a low voice.*] M. de Chateaurien, when I give you a rose——

BEAUCAIRE. Then you shall take an answering gift, Mademoiselle, all a man's soul! [*Their eyes meet.* WINTERSET *enters. He stands looking at them, himself unseen.*] The rose—now?

LADY MARY. [*Kisses rose breathlessly.*] Not yet.

[*She starts to run out.* BEAUCAIRE *follows her to the door, then returns.*]

WINTERSET. [*Coming close behind him.*] A rose lasts but till morning.

BEAUCAIRE. [*Turning gaily.*] Oh, you are there, my brother?

WINTERSET. Her rose is of an unlucky color, I think.

BEAUCAIRE. The color of a blush!

WINTERSET. [*Glooming upon him.*] Unlucky, damned unlucky.

BEAUCAIRE. You would say—the color of the veins of a Frenchman. Eh, bien! What price would be too high? A rose is a rose! I wish you dreams of roses, my brother le duc—beautiful red, red roses.

[*There is a commotion without. Enter* BADGER, *his face angry. He is followed by all of the gentlemen, except* NASH.]

WINTERSET. What is this? Where are the ladies?

BADGER. [*Harshly.*] We left them and came hither to settle a wager.

WINTERSET. What wager?

BADGER. Whether a Frenchman could be insulted.
[*He jostles* BEAUCAIRE *heavily in passing him. There is a muffled outcry from all.*]

BEAUCAIRE. Monsieur, I seem to be in your way. Permit the mos' homble apology.
[*He joins* MOLYNEAUX, *who tries to draw him away.*]

BADGER. [*Aside to* WINTERSET.] He won't fight.

WINTERSET. Try a sneer at the women of his country. Egad! How the Duke of Orleans refused to marry his cousin Henriette. Try that.

BADGER. 'Tis the very thing. [*Coming toward* BEAU-CAIRE.] Your Grace of Chateaurien?

MOLYNEAUX. [*To* BEAUCAIRE.] For God's sake, don't fall into this trap. Don't answer him!

BEAUCAIRE. [*Confronting* BADGER *courteously.*] I am at your service, Monsieur!

BADGER. I've wanted to meet a damn Frenchman for some time.

MOLYNEAUX. [*To* TOWNBRAKE.] This is beyond forbearance. Badger must be drunk. The man is forcing a quarrel.

BANTISON. [*At the same time.*] Hold your tongue, Philip.

BADGER. In the first place I don't like the French——

BEAUCAIRE. For that, my poor France is the mos' onfortunate of all nations.

BADGER. In the second place I wished to inquire from some Frenchman an explanation of the conduct of the French ladies.

BEAUCAIRE. Oh, that is simple, Monsieur. They are tutored by the angels.

BADGER. Devils, you mean. No, Frenchman. I refer to the easy conquests your women afford. They say a man has not even entertainment of the chase. For instance, take Henriette. [BEAUCAIRE *slowly takes off his left-hand glove.*] It is well-known that her cousin, the Duke of Orleans, has refused to marry her, preferring even a prison to a marriage with a woman whose gallantries are the talk of——

BEAUCAIRE. [*In a clear, low voice, interrupting.*] Monsieurs, there are no ladies near? [*He looks about, then at* BADGER.] It may have been clearly shown that the Duke of Orleans is a scurvy fellow, Monsieur le Capitaine, but not so scurvy that he may be discussed by such as thou, thou swine of the gutter!

[BEAUCAIRE *slaps* BADGER *on the mouth with his*

glove. BADGER *staggers back overpowered with pretended rage.*]

WINTERSET. What, what, gentlemen! This must be stopped! Captain Badger——

BADGER. [*Working to a half real fury.*] Spare me words, Your Grace, I've been struck.

BEAUCAIRE. My dear frien' Winterset, I entreat you will not interfere. [*Aside to him.*] Ah, naughty fellow, you work quickly, eh, ha, ha!

[*Nudging him with elbow.*]

BADGER. [*To* BEAUCAIRE.] You will meet me at once for this, not in the morning but *now*. Now, do you understand!

BEAUCAIRE. Then we must be quick, Monsieur. I have a commission for a lady to fulfil in half an hour.

BADGER. No, by God. You don't wait half an hour. You come now. The garden back of this house will do.

MOLYNEAUX. No, no! It's murder! You can't— This gentleman is——

[*He stands with folded hands.*]

BEAUCAIRE. [*Stopping him.*] Sh! Your word! [*To* BADGER.] Monsieur, I am at your service. But one thing, M. le Beau Nash allow no sword to be worn in Bath. We must send——

WINTERSET. I protest against this, and I warn my friend de Chateaurien that Captain Badger is supposed to be the best sword in the three kingdoms——

BEAUCAIRE. In three kingdoms?

MOLYNEAUX. Aye!

BEAUCAIRE. Maybe, but not in four. So generous ever! So honorable—His Grace of Winterset!

WINTERSET. But, as it seems the affair *must* go on, I happen to know there are a pair of blades which belong to the late Sir John Rellerton, in the next room, if Mr. Bantison will fetch them.

BANTISON. With pleasure.

[*Exit* BANTISON.]

MOLYNEAUX. [*To the men.*] This will have a black look, my friends.

RAIKELL. Ah, why this devil's own hurry? It should be stopped, I say!

MOLYNEAUX. By Heaven, it shan't go on.

BEAUCAIRE. Pardon, I think it mus' go on. Only keep the ladies from knowing.

BADGER. [*With* BICKSIT.] Why do we wait?

BEAUCAIRE. I will follow Monsieur if he will show the way.

MOLYNEAUX. No, no! You must——

BEAUCAIRE. We will fight without seconds, Monsieur, for if several gentlemen are sudden absent, the ladies might wonder. You let us have one witness, if you please.

BADGER. Choose him yourself.

WINTERSET. Monsieur!

BEAUCAIRE. My good friend Winterset mus' not be involved, an' these other messieurs I have no claim upon— but——

MOLYNEAUX. [*From the right of* BEAUCAIRE.] I should be proud to act for you, sir.

BEAUCAIRE. No, but——

[*He nods to* RAIKELL.]

RAIKELL. Gladly.

BEAUCAIRE. I thank you, Monsieur, and M. de le Capitaine agree?

BADGER. Agreed. [*To* BEAUCAIRE.] Now, sir— before we go, perhaps you will wish to appoint another person to execute that commission of yours—in case you do not return——

BEAUCAIRE.   It is very simple.   I shall take Mme. la Comtesse de Greenburee to the supper-room in half an hour.

BADGER.   You say: "I *shall*."

BEAUCAIRE.   Ah, Monsieur, there are only a few things one is sure of in this world.   And that I shall take Madame the Countess to supper in half an hour, this is one of those few things.   Monsieur le Capitaine!

[BEAUCAIRE *exits first, into the conservatory.*
BADGER *follows off right, stops.*]

BADGER.   Who is he?   Damn that look of his.

[*Exeunt* BEAUCAIRE, BADGER, *and* RAIKELL.]

MOLYNEAUX.   [*Starting to follow.*]   No, no.   [*To* WINTERSET *desperately.*]   Stop them, I say!   No man alive can stand against Badger, and he means to kill him. It is murder.   I tell you, cold-blooded murder.

TOWNBRAKE.   Murder, nonsense—it's not our business.

[*Sensation and commotion among the gentlemen.   Cries   of   protestation   and   wonder. "*MR. RAIKELL*" and "What does he mean?" —"Whom does he threaten?"*   NASH *and* MR. BICKSIT *come bustling in from the left.*]

NASH.   What!   What's the matter?

[WINTERSET *sits.*]

BICKSIT.   Gad, gentlemen, you've alarmed the ladies.

NASH.   What is it?   Why do——

BANTISON.   A bagatelle, Beau!   Badger and de Chateaurien have gone out to settle a difference.

NASH.   More of your infernal duels!   I tell you, sir——

TOWNBRAKE.   [*Crossing to the door at the left.*] Keep the ladies from knowing until it's over.   That's all.

BICKSIT.   Here they are.

NASH.   Gentlemen, the ladies!   On your guard!

Music, music, quickly, quickly, I say! [*He summons supposed musicians in the conservatory. The ladies all appear from the left exclaiming, "Oh, what is it?"—"What is the matter?" etc. Music starts. Continuing loudly.*] Matter, nothing is the matter, except that we complain bitterly that our fair partners keep us waiting too long for the gavotte! Music I say! [*Gavotte is played.*] Gentlemen, select your partners for the dance!

> [*They select partners and dance as before.*
> Lady Mary *with* Winterset.]

Lucy. [*During the dance.*] Where is M. de Chateaurien? [*Agitated.*] There is something wrong—I know it—I feel it. Tell me, tell me.

Miss Presbrey. [*To* Bantison, *as they dance.*] Was not Lady Mary kind? Each of us on leaving the supper-room received these roses. Her red roses as her favor.

> [Raikell *enters unobserved.*]

Townbrake. [*Crossing to* Bantison, *having suddenly seen* Raikell.] Raikell alone.

Several Gentlemen. Raikell alone!

Bantison. Both done for!

Molyneaux. Stop the dance!

> [*All murmur and clear from the centre of the stage.*]

All. What! Stop the music! Stop the dance!

Nash. Sir, have you no sense of manners?

Molyneaux. Manners! Are you all made of stone? Every one shall know that poor young Frenchman went out to fight Captain Badger.

All. Fight! Good Heavens!

Molyneaux. And you ask me to be silent when Raikell comes back to wait till the dance is over to ask where they have taken him? He had no chance. I knew he had no chance.

LADY MARY. He went to fight Captain Badger?

RAIKELL. [*Coming toward them.*] Aye, Madame, in the garden. The quarrel was forced upon M. de Chateaurien. We all saw that. It was well-known that the fellow Badger ran no danger in challenging any one in England. From the first second I could see that Captain Badger was determined to kill his opponent. The thing had a black look. He longed to kill.

[*Exclamations of horror from the ladies.*]

MOLYNEAUX. I knew the Frenchman had no chance. I said he had no chance.

RAIKELL. [*With rising excitement.*] No chance! No chance, say you, Major Molyneaux? By Heaven, I count my life worth living to have seen a sword like his in active play. No chance! I tell you the Frenchman *played* with Badger. Played with him, as a man plays with a spitting cat. He fought, laughing in Badger's face; and in twenty passes, not the Frenchman, but Badger lay upon the ground with a hole through his shoulder that will outwear the season.

ALL. [*Much excited, cry out.*] Beat Captain Badger! Badger defeated! The Frenchman! Bravo! Ran him through! Ran *Badger* through!

[*During this excitement* FRANÇOIS *enters.*]

RAIKELL. [*Observing* FRANÇOIS.] Here is a servant of Chateaurien's with a message for the Duke.

[RAIKELL *points out* WINTERSET. FRANÇOIS *goes to him. The Duke takes the note from* FRANÇOIS. FRANÇOIS *places a basket of roses near him and exits.*]

WINTERSET. [*Reads.*] Be under no fear, my brother.

I shall execute my commission, and to reassure your kind heart—I send you these red roses.

NASH. [*Taking note from* WINTERSET.] He reassures his friend of his safety. The act of a gentleman, damme!

ALL. Where is he? Where is he?

RAIKELL. There!

> [*All look to the stairway at the back.* BEAUCAIRE *is seen descending, smiling and attending devotedly upon a very old lady, who clings, fearful of the stairs, to his arm. She is very little and wizened and decrepit, though splendidly dressed, and is much pleased by his attention. As they reach the lower steps* RAIKELL *steps forward. He cries.*] Long live

M. de Chateaurien, the best swordsman in England!

ALL. Chateaurien! Chateaurien! Chateaurien!

> [*The crowd cries "Bravos" upon him as he comes down. The ladies begin to throw their roses at him.* RAIKELL *takes those from the great basket sent to the Duke and throws them about him so that as he reaches the centre he and Lady Greenbury stand in a storm of flying roses.* BEAUCAIRE *passes Lady Greenbury over to* LUCY. LADY MARY *steps toward him and throws all hers at his feet—then from her hair she takes one and gives it to Chateaurien, who takes it and kisses it.*]

CURTAIN

ACT IV

The action takes place at MR. BANTISON'S *near Bath.
The curtain opens on a well-ordered park, through
which a driveway runs from left to right. There are
trees, shrubbery, a marble Diana rising from a nook
at the right, and other statues in the distance. The
time is twilight, three weeks later.*

There is gay music in the distance. BICKSIT, NASH, MISS
PRESBREY, *and* MISS PAITELOT *are present.*

NASH.   Mr. Bantison is to be envied in his guests as
we are in our host.

BICKSIT.   Faith, yes! 'Tis not every man who has
an estate like this or can give such a fête.

NASH.   And then its adjacency to Bath! Once every
season for five years he has opened his doors to the fashion
of Bath in this way; but I never think with such splendor as to-day.

MISS PRESBREY.   [*Seated at a tree stump on the right.*]
Poor Mr. Bantison! I fear his efforts to dazzle the eyes
of beauty with his magnificence to-day will come to nothing. For indeed, I hear the young Duc's own do-
mains——

BICKSIT.   [*Rising.*]   Chateaurien? There never was
such a place in the world! I had the honor to visit it
under this young man's father and never have I been more
lavishly entertained! Poor Mr. Bantison! This is but
a sorry show, fine as it is—to what the fortunate Duchess
of Chateaurien will find at her command.

NASH.   Aye, poor Bantison. I fear he's done, and we
are to lose our English Beauty. Winterset is desperate;
he has the look of the bear of the pit; and as for Townbrake, he wears nothing nowadays but the deepest black.

BICKSIT.   Ten to one the French Duke proposes to-night.

MISS PRESBREY.   Do you think so?

BICKSIT.   There's a moon to-night—moonlight—young —opportunity—ten to one he does it to-night!

[MISSES PRESBREY *and* PAITELOT *rise.*]

MISS PRESBREY.   Fie, sir!   Bet on a lady's love affairs!

BICKSIT.   [*Chuckling.*]   You know you'll lose.   You know you'll lose!

NASH.   True!   He has it!   You'd lose!

MISS PAITELOT.   Aye, you should.

[*Exit laughing.* MOLYNEAUX *and* BEAUCAIRE
detach themselves from a group off left, MOLY-
NEAUX *drawing* BEAUCAIRE *away.* BEAU-
CAIRE *and* MOLYNEAUX *enter from the left.*]

BEAUCAIRE.   [*Strolling left and right.*]   Non, non, my frien', I am a happy man.   You cannot frighten me.

MOLYNEAUX.   Danger, I tell you, danger everywhere. The man is desperate.   He's a mad dog—and what is worse—a dog with *brains!*

BEAUCAIRE.   Danger!   Pouf!   None in the worl'. Now tell me, mon ami, what risk I run.

MOLYNEAUX.   Risk, great Heaven!   Every risk!

BEAUCAIRE.   None!   I am not a reckless man.   I am jus' the very greatest coward.   There is al—ways François.   'E followed me like I am a baby.   An' those other big li'l children of mine, the strange servants!   All from my regiment of the Guard, an' they think I am made of glass an' they won' let me out of their sight.   I scold them well; I say the bad word; what good that do?   François, 'e ride with me to-day; that look simple, one servant, but what you think, my frien'?   Be'hine me on the road I see a cloud of dust an' there is that army of mine.   They are now some place maybe jus' outside the park wall. François 'e is the general of my army. I think that is disgressful to be a baby—with an army!

[LUCY *approaches from the left.*]

LUCY. Your Grace— [*Courtesy.*] —you asked me but now if my cousin had returned to the house—I saw her a moment since on the East Terrace.

BEAUCAIRE. Ah, Mademoiselle Lucee! You 'ave such kindness to the poor stranger. All the pipple are gone back to the 'ouse. But you think maybe I better stay and company with you and my frien' Molyneaux? No? Well, then, if you are sure you don' think I ought to? [*Gravely.*] Then I will go an' fin'—you said it was the East Terrace?

[*Exit* BEAUCAIRE.]

MOLYNEAUX [*To* LUCY.] Sweetheart!

LUCY. I feel it my duty to say— [*Sitting in chair at the right.*] —I am displeased with you, sir.

MOLYNEAUX. [*Absently.*] I know.

LUCY. Ever since our great good fortune came with M. de Chateaurien, and my cousin changed her frown to a smile for you, because he made you his friend, when sir, I say the lady you professed to adore might look to see you a *little* happy—you have been—what? Dull—pre-occupied and gloomy!

MOLYNEAUX. I know, I know.

LUCY. Explain then, sir! He has made your fortune. Your fate runs with his.

MOLYNEAUX. Aye, it is bound up in his, for rise or fall.

LUCY. Fall!

MOLYNEAUX. Trust me yet a little! Ah, Lucy. If I have a secret, it is not my own.

[*Enter* JOLLIFFE *with a note which he hands to* MOLYNEAUX.]

You, Jolliffe?

JOLLIFFE. Yes sir, I'm in attendance here to-day. Sir, Hi jus' passed 'is Grace of Shaterann on the walk, hand 'e ast me to *deliver this* to you, sir.

[*He gives note to* MOLYNEAUX, *bows, and exits right.*]

MOLYNEAUX. Chateaurien? Strange, *he's only just* left me. [MOLYNEAUX *rises and opens note.* LUCY *rises and tries to look over his shoulder. He reads.*] "It is imperative that I return to Bath. I ride by the other gate, as the way is shorter. I implore you to call for your horse and follow me at once. I shall be at my apartment. Chateaurien!"

LUCY. [*Anxiously.*] Is it bad news?

MOLYNEAUX. Yes, yes.

LUCY. From whom?

MOLYNEAUX. Chateaurien. He has been summoned back to Bath, and begs that I follow at once.

LUCY. [*Angrily.*] You refuse!

MOLYNEAUX. [*Shakes his head.*] I cannot.

LUCY. Ah, I knew, I knew!

MOLYNEAUX. What *is* it, child?

LUCY. [*Crossing to* MOLYNEAUX.] Contemptuously. Are you familiar with the handwriting of M. de Chateaurien?

MOLYNEAUX. I see it here for the first time.

LUCY. Ah, I supposed it. [*She turns to him.*] Let me tell you, sir, I know the handwriting of Monsieur de Chateaurien. . . . I have seen it on missives addressed to my cousin many and many a time.

MOLYNEAUX. My love, what then? What then? I do not know your mood. I cannot stay to fathom it.

LUCY. [*Following* MOLYNEAUX, *who has started to walk away.*] You go to answer that note——

MOLYNEAUX. I must. I have no choice.

LUCY. Then sir, you can bid me good-by forever.

MOLYNEAUX. Lucy, I cannot, child.

LUCY. You will call me Mistress Rellerton.

MOLYNEAUX. Lucy!

LUCY. That letter you hold is not the handwriting of Monsieur de Chateaurien. I believe it's a woman's. I bid you good night.

[*Exit* LUCY.]

MOLYNEAUX. Why, nonsense! A woman's madness, child. I haven't time to explain now. I must find de Chateaurien at once!

[*Exit* MOLYNEAUX. *Enter from the right* BANTISON, TOWNBRAKE, BICKSIT, *and* RAIKELL.]

RAIKELL. A mighty mysterious message. Said he'd meet us here, did he?

BANTISON. Read it for yourself. It came from Bath an hour ago. I understand, for I had a conference with him at noon, but I leave the explanation to him, by his own wish.

RAIKELL. [*Reading a note which* BANTISON *gives him.*] "I shall be much delayed in attending your fête. Meet me at the Diana in your park at a quarter of an hour before nine. Bring Townbrake, Bicksit, Raikell, and no others. I have an act of reparation to make. Winterset." Faith, the Duke seems solemn enough.

[*Hands note to* BANTISON.]

BICKSIT. He is solemn enough. The man's changed beyond belief. He's something weighing on him.

BANTISON. [*Morosely.*] Well, and who wouldn't have?

TOWNBRAKE. [*Gloomily.*] These damned Frenchmen! B'ged!

RAIKELL. The hour is here.

BICKSIT. [*Looking off right.*] And so is the man.
His Grace is with us!

RAIKELL. [*Also looking in the direction of the approaching* WINTERSET.] I've seen livelier mutes at a
funeral.

> [WINTERSET *enters. He is in riding costume,
> booted and spurred. In his gauntleted hand he
> carries a huge whip, with three thongs, and a
> bundle of ropes. He salutes the others
> gravely. They are all standing.*]

WINTERSET. Gentlemen, your servant.

GENTLEMEN. Yours.

WINTERSET. You may have been puzzled, gentlemen,
by my note. I have an act of reparation to make. An
insult has been offered to the ladies of Bath.

ALL. What?

WINTERSET. There is a man within these gates for
whom I have brought *this*.

> [*Showing whip.*]

ALL. What!

WINTERSET. That man is to be beaten—beaten to
death, by lackeys.

> [RAIKELL, BICKSIT, *and* TOWNBRAKE *speak at
> the same time in their excitement.*]

RAIKELL. Who is it?

BICKSIT. Heaven save us!

TOWNBRAKE. Winterset!

WINTERSET. Gentlemen, do you recall the incident of
the barber, Beaucaire?

ALL. Yes, aye!

> [*They are excited and speak together as before.*]

WINTERSET. Have any of you forgotten the French lackey who tried to warn him that morning before his expulsion from the pump room?

ALL. No. Not I.

WINTERSET. Neither, it appears, did the head servant of the pump room, Jolliffe. I have borrowed Jolliffe for to-day.. [*He walks to the right, looks into the distance, and comes back.*] And the fellow is prompt. Yonder he comes with his companion. You are sure you all have a distinct recollection of the lackey who belonged to the barber?

ALL. Certainly.

WINTERSET. Then may I ask you to observe carefully the man who comes with Jolliffe. I shall retire for a moment. I would not bias you, gentlemen. Frame your own conclusion. [*To* BANTISON.] You do the talking, you understand.

BANTISON. Yes, your Grace!

> [WINTERSET *exits as* JOLLIFFE *enters with* FRANÇOIS. *The gentlemen whisper together and look at* FRANÇOIS *attentively. They stand in a group at the left.*]

FRANÇOIS. Mais, M'sieu Jeleef, my master, Monseigneur de Chateaurien; 'e not 'ere. You say 'e wan' me. Where is Monseigneur de Chateaurien?

BANTISON. What's wanted, Jolliffe?

JOLLIFFE. [*Coming toward* BANTISON.] The Duke de Shantoerenn sent me to find his servant for him. To meet him here, but it's like to have been a mistake. I don't see him; 'e said he was called to Bath and wanted his man to ride with him.

> [*Exit* JOLLIFFE.]

FRANÇOIS. To Bath? Alone? Mon Dieu! Monsieur Jolliffe, are you sure?

BANTISON.   Ah, you're my good friend de Chateaurien's lackey, are you?

FRANÇOIS.   Oui—yes, milor'.

[*Trying to go all the same.*]

BANTISON.   You are learning English.

FRANÇOIS.   [*With polite despair.*]   Ah, ver' slow, ver'
slow, milor'.

BANTISON.   Knew none when you landed?

FRANÇOIS.   Non, milor'.

BANTISON.   How long ago was that?

FRANÇOIS.   Long long time.   T'ree week.

BANTISON.   How long have you been in M. de Chateaurien's service?

FRANÇOIS.   All my life, milor'.

BANTISON.   You didn't wear that livery when you first
came to Bath, did you?

[*The gentlemen whisper together.*   RAIKELL
grabs FRANÇOIS *by the arm.*]

FRANÇOIS.   [*Uneasily.*]   If milor' pardon me, I mus'
hasten to Monseigneur.   'E sen' for me.   He mus' have
already gone an' Mon Dieu!   Alone!   Alone!

[*Exit* FRANÇOIS *hurriedly.*]

BICKSIT.   God save us!

TOWNBRAKE.   It is, by the Lord, it is!

RAIKELL.   It is that fellow!   The very man!   Damme!
The very man!

BANTISON.   He's gone in the wrong direction.   His
master is on the East Terrace.   Chateaurien is not riding
to Bath.

WINTERSET.   [*Enters from the right.   Violently.*]
Chateaurien!   Gentlemen, what if I told you that we have
all been duped, outwitted, laughed at, insulted by the
daily presence amongst us, as our equal—by God—the
vilest lackey above ground.   What if I had told you this

lackey made free not only with *us,* but had, through my stupidity, familiarly associated with our ladies.

[*Exclamations.*]

WINTERSET. When I discovered the truth this morning, gentlemen, I could have put a pistol to my head for my dulness in not having seen it before!

BANTISON. And I!! [*To others.*] But, I have received him so that he suspects nothing——

RAIKELL. [*Angrily.*] Now, no more beating about the bush. Out with it! Tell us the whole truth.

ALL. The truth!

WINTERSET. I wish one moment's conversation with Mr. Bantison. May I request you to precede us to the East Terrace and that there you will favor his features, height, and voice with the same attention which you have bestowed upon his lackey.

RAIKELL. [*Looks at* WINTERSET *strangely for a long moment, then speaks harshly.*] By God!

WINTERSET. You're with us?

ALL. With you? Ha, ha!

[*Exit* RAIKELL *followed by* BICKSIT *and* TOWN-BRAKE.]

WINTERSET. Will they be ready to help, think you, when they recognize him?

BANTISON. Help! They'll kill him!

WINTERSET. If that's done—it must be done with this —and before *her.*

[*He shows the whip.*]

BANTISON. Ah, the villain, the damned villain! What is our best plan? I have it. He shows her the Diana by moonlight.

[*He turns to* WINTERSET.]

WINTERSET. Then this is the very place to take him. We'll do it here, and let Jolliffe do the lashing.

[*Laughter.*]

BANTISON. Hark! My guests are leaving. We'll wait here just out of sight till the others return.

WINTERSET. Set your teeth for it!

[*Both exeunt. Enter* BEAUCAIRE *and* LADY MARY.]

BEAUCAIRE. That song I sing so badly, do you know it? It is the song of a poor wanderer in a strange country, who dreams—of home.

[*Music in the distance.*]

LADY MARY. [*Softly.*] What a night! Everything is so sweet—so sweet—one seems to smell the blossoms on all the hedge-rows in the world!

[*She sits on one of the chairs in the park.*]

BEAUCAIRE. Mademoiselle, I too am a wanderer in a strange land—but my dreams are not of France: No, Mademoiselle, it is of fairer country, a dream country— a land of gold and snow. Gold like a lady's hair, snow like her breast—and the blue sky above, like the Heaven of a lady's eyes.

LADY MARY. Gold and blue! I had thought—I had thought—the ladies of France were dark, sir.

BEAUCAIRE. Cruel! It is that she *will* not understand! Have I speak of the ladies of France? No, no, no! It is of the fairest country, yes, 'tis of a province of Heaven, mademoiselle, I speak, I am subjec'—no, content to be *slave*—in the lan' of the blue sky, the gold an' snow.

LADY MARY. 'Tis a vastly pretty figure, but—does it not hint you an adept in the making of such speeches?

BEAUCAIRE. Tormentress! No. It only proves the inspiration it is to one new at such words, to have the joy to say them to you.

LADY MARY. We English ladies hear often of the like,

sir; and we even grow wise enough to detect what lies beneath the courtesies of our own gallants.

BEAUCAIRE. [*Under his breath.*] Ma foi! I won't believe that!

LADY MARY. We believe that too great smoothness of speech betokens your artist rather than your—your true——

BEAUCAIRE. [*Huskily.*] Your—true—lover? [*Tremulously.*] Your name, in France, we say it, Marie—the English way, I think it so much sweeter—Ma-ry——

LADY MARY. [*Her hand to her heart.*] Ah!

BEAUCAIRE. Yes, that English way is better. They say—Mary——
　　　[*He stops.*]

LADY MARY. [*Rises with sudden brightness.*] M. de Chateaurien, the coach is near, and my poor cousin is waiting for us.

BEAUCAIRE. [*Suiting his gaiety to the change in her, as they go up to the coach, both laughing.*] Mon Dieu! Now isn't that soch a strange thing! I jus' forget that ol' coach clear out of my mind. I think these days I jus' forget everything.

LADY MARY. Lucy!

LUCY. Yes, cousin, I am here.
　　　[*She enters from the left.*]

LADY MARY. You are so patient, dear child! Have we lingered over much?

LUCY. Ah, no, not long. And is the Diana so beautiful in the moon?

BEAUCAIRE. Oh, I clean forgot that Diana, myself.

LADY MARY. [*Standing on the step.*] The Diana?

LUCY. Aye, the Diana? Well, you said it was to see the Diana, in the moonlight, you wished to come this longer way.

LADY MARY. To see—yes! It *was* to see the Diana!

BEAUCAIRE. [*Walking in front of the coach doors.*] Yes! It was to see the Diana—and as it is so close, will not you turn and look at it? It is not sisterly, Mademoiselle, that one goddess she pass another, an' no greeting.

LADY MARY. It is too late. Another time. I think we must be moving forward. Where is your horse, M. de Chateaurien?

BEAUCAIRE. I jus' forgot that ol' horse too.

LADY MARY. Your servant was to have him in waiting here?

BEAUCAIRE. [*Throwing up his hands.*] Merci! Well then—Isn't that soch a strange thing! That servant of mine was to meet me here—Yes, certainment! Where is the François, now?

[*Calling* FRANÇOIS! FRANÇOIS!]

LUCY. While you are waiting you may as well look at the Diana.

BEAUCAIRE. [*Pleading.*] Yes, an' since that is what we came for first, you won't refuse?

LADY MARY. Yes, since that is what we came for first, if you really think we ought?

BEAUCAIRE. Yes, if you think we *ought*.

LUCY. Oh, I can wait!

BEAUCAIRE. [*Catching* LUCY's *hand and kissing it. Aside.*] It is very strange about François—he *navre* fail. But for this good and wise failure he shall have fifty louis to-morrow! [*Aloud.*] There stand the other goddess!

LADY MARY. The Diana?

BEAUCAIRE. You ron away from me, jus' then, Mademoiselle.

LADY MARY. When?

BEAUCAIRE. When I try to say that beautiful English name of Mary.

LADY MARY. [*Turning away.*] You said it so well —so well—that——

    [*She sits.*]

BEAUCAIRE. Ah, Mademoiselle! I know what make you to doubt me. They have tol' you the French do nothing al—ways but make love, is it not so? Yes, an' you think *I*—am like that! You think I am like that *now?* [*He pauses and sighs deeply.*] That which is near Heaven, it is so high—it mus' ever wear the snow. But —but—I suppose I am unris'nable. I would have the snow not so cold for jus' me. [*He sits—pause.*] Turn to me——

    [*She gives no sign. A faint rustling is heard and crackling of branches from the shrubbery. In the darkness under the trees at the right, a figure is dimly disclosed, then another—two others are seen. Behind them are three others. They encircle* BEAUCAIRE *at a distance, keeping in the darkness of the shadows. One figure comes slowly half way into the moonlight and stands with sword drawn. It is* WINTERSET.]

—Turn to me! Turn to me! Ma-ry!

LADY MARY. I—I dare not!

BEAUCAIRE. An' why? Oh, perfect in loveliness, an' why?

    [*She tremulously puts her hand to her cheek— his is lifted to take it. Hers falls in his. She turns to him.*]

LADY MARY. Lest—lest you should see—that toward *you* all the chill has gone from the snow—long—long ago!

BEAUCAIRE. [*Whispering.*] My beautiful—my beautiful——

> [*Enter* LUCY. *Enter* WINTERSET. BEAUCAIRE *stops. He takes* LADY MARY *gently in his arms and lays his lips to hers. A silence.* LUCY *suddenly sees the motionless figure of* WINTERSET. *She makes a startled gesture, then peers at him earnestly under her hand. She sees the others.*]

LUCY. [*Shrilly, but not screaming.*] Who is *there?* What is *that?* Is that a man standing there? Who is it? [*She screams.*] Come back! Come back! Mary! Mary! *Ah!*

WINTERSET. [*Loudly.*] At him, lads! Take the dog.

> [RAIKELL *enters with the others, a little apart on the right. Servant and* BANTISON *enter from the right also.* WINTERSET, TOWNBRAKE, BICKSIT *come from the left.* JOLLIFFE *and two servants also enter. All rush from the shadows upon* BEAUCAIRE.]

ALL. Barber! Barber! Kill the barber!

> [WINTERSET *whirls* LADY MARY *out of the way. She screams and struggles.* LUCY *runs to* MARY.]

BEAUCAIRE. [*At the onset, drawing his sword swiftly.*] *A moi!* François. *A moi,* François! Louis! Berthier! *A moi!*

> [*They assail him.*]

WINTERSET. [*Struggling with* LADY MARY.] Quiet, Madame! Quiet! Can't you see we are your friends?

> [RAIKELL *stands between the ladies and the fight.*]

LADY MARY. Sir, let me pass!

RAIKELL.   Madame! Do not compel me.

BEAUCAIRE.   [*Getting his back to the Diana, cries out bitterly.*]   Canaille! To make this brawl in a lady's presence! To endanger a lady!

BANTISON.   Kill the barber!

BEAUCAIRE.   Feel how the barber—he use his steel!
[*He stabs* BANTISON *in the arm.*]

BANTISON.   [*Falling back with a groan.*]   He's got me! In the sword arm, the damned villain!
[*He limps away and sits upon the ground nursing himself.*]

BEAUCAIRE.   [*Laughing excitedly.*]   Ha! There! And there, my frien'! Ha!
[*He runs* TOWNBRAKE *through the shoulder.*]

TOWNBRAKE.   [*With a cry.*]   I'm pinked! These gad Frenchmen!
[*He drops his sword and goes to a seat by a tree.*]

BEAUCAIRE.   [*Gaily, running out through* JOLLIFFE *and* BICKSIT *into the open.*]   Oh, you are there, my frien'! A little in the rear, I think, a little in the background! Ah! 'Tis as one mus' expec', eh? Ha, Mr. Bicksit, you mus' keep out of the way, you are a li'l too ol' for this fon.   Join my frien' in the background.
[*He wounds* BICKSIT *in the leg.*]

WINTERSET.   Bind him!
[*He rushes behind* BEAUCAIRE *and seizes the latter's blade in his gauntlet, breaking the sword.* JOLLIFFE *binds* BEAUCAIRE.]

BEAUCAIRE.   *A moi!* François! *A moi!*
[LADY MARY *descends from the coach but is restrained from advancing by* RAIKELL.]

LADY MARY.   Cowards! Would you see the Duke murdered?

WINTERSET. "Duke." When the varlet has had his lashing, 'twill be explained, Madame, 'tis you we avenge upon him. Truss him up, lads! Lively, now!

> [*The servants raise* BEAUCAIRE *and begin to bind his arms.*]

LADY MARY. You would avenge *me*, sir? Me?

RAIKELL. By the lord, gentlemen, 'tis a shame! Does a *barber* bear himself like that?

> [*He indicates* BEAUCAIRE.]

WINTERSET. Madame, recall that morning in the pump room, when I warned you that you would thank me?

BEAUCAIRE. [*With a mighty effort breaks loose from the men that hold him. He strikes* WINTERSET *full across the mouth.*] Silence—slug!

> [*Hoofs are heard off left.* BEAUCAIRE *is instantly overpowered by the servants, who resume their binding of him.*]

WINTERSET. [*Furiously.*] You saw? If he dies under the whip—you saw? The villain struck me! Do your duty and be quick.

> [*The sound of galloping hoofs comes clearly nearer and nearer.*]

BANTISON. Horses!

WINTERSET. The devil!

BEAUCAIRE. François! *A moi*, François!

LADY MARY. Thank God! This way! This way!

> [*The horses stop with a wild clatter.* FRANÇOIS, MOLYNEAUX, *and the other servants seen in Act II rush on. They whirl* JOLLIFFE *and his men from* BEAUCAIRE, *flinging them down wounded.* BEAUCAIRE *steadies himself with an evident effort.*]

BEAUCAIRE. A sword, mon ami, give me a sword—I —I make ten thousand apology, to be the cause of such a *mêlée*, in Mademoiselle's presence! [*He faints into the arms of* FRANÇOIS *and whispers to him.*] A very little, mon enfant, and— [*He points to the whip which has fallen from the hand of one of the servants.*] You see, the whip!

FRANÇOIS. [*Kneeling. Thickly sobbing.*] Ah, non, Monseigneur! Non, non! Monseigneur! They—they did lie to me—they did—lie——

LADY MARY. [*Rushing to* BEAUCAIRE.] They haven't hurt you?

WINTERSET. Madame, do you know me?

LADY MARY. Know you— [*Turning to* BEAUCAIRE.] Ah, they didn't——

BEAUCAIRE. My beautiful, the time has come—Monsieur de Winterset has something to say to you.

LADY MARY. I will not listen.

WINTERSET. Madame!

BEAUCAIRE. It is my prayer. Listen to him.

LADY MARY. Be brief, then!

WINTERSET. Who is this?

LADY MARY. The Duke de Chateaurien!

WINTERSET. It's the barber Beaucaire. Look at him! Look! That's all I ask. You saw Beaucaire the day he was expelled. Look at this man and remember that! That's all I ask. Look at him!

ALL. Yes, look at him!

LADY MARY. Ah!

BEAUCAIRE. Look, Mademoiselle! Look at me and remember Monsieur Beaucaire.

LADY MARY. I am frightened! You mean what he says is a lie?

BEAUCAIRE. No, Mademoiselle.

LADY MARY. Not true. What he says is not true.

BEAUCAIRE. Yes, Mademoiselle!

LADY MARY. You say you are that——

BEAUCAIRE. I say it, Mademoiselle. I say it to speak what is true when you ask me. But is there nothing more to ask?

LADY MARY. Nothing from you, sir. My Lord, you heard.

MOLYNEAUX. Chateaurien—you're safe? Thank God.

WINTERSET. Ah, safe for the moment. But if one more day finds him in Bath——

BEAUCAIRE. One day, Milor' the Duke, and seven days——

ALL. What!

BEAUCAIRE. One li'l week from to-night, I have the honor to meet you in the Assembly Room, Gentlemen. An' w'en I am there, I think, My Lord of Winterset will again be found—in the background. Gentlemen—I——

> [*He leans dizzily against* MOLYNEAUX. *His handkerchief, which throughout he has kept pressed to his side, falls to the ground. It is drenched with crimson.*]

LADY MARY. [*Pointing in horror to his reddened shirt.*] What is that? Oh, what is that?

BEAUCAIRE. Don't be alarmed! Ma'm'selle! Do you not see? It is—it is—a—only a—red—rose——

> [*He falls into* MOLYNEAUX'S *arms as the curtain descends.*]

CURTAIN

ACT V

The scene is a large and elegant anteroom at the assembly. There are double doors both right and left. Candles are lit in sconces and on table. Also a tall gilt clock, and in the middle of the back a curtained alcove, curtains drawn. The time is night, a week later.

LUCY *is sitting in a chair at the right with elbows on table, her face in her hands.* MRS. MABSLEY *is near her.*

MRS. MABSLEY. [*Comforting.*] Come, child, look up. You must show a brave face to the world.

LUCY. [*Not moving.*] A brave face!

MRS. MABSLEY. And all the world will be here to-night. Mr. Nash has left nothing undone to greet the French Ambassador.

LUCY. The French Ambassador. He is here, then?

MRS. MABSLEY. Yes, the Marquis de Mirepoix. He arrived at noon and he is to visit the Assembly at nine. Come, child, you must look your best.

LUCY. [*Impatiently, turning.*] Ah, my best!
[*She covers her face again.*]

MRS. MABSLEY. Lucy! Lucy! You know now that Philip was not unfaithful to you. Winterset has admitted that that note from the Frenchman was a trick to get him out of the gentleman's way, from anxiety lest he might interfere.

LUCY. I know, I know. But this week's silence! Not a word from him—not to know where he is—disappeared——

MRS. MABSLEY. [*Gently.*] 'Tis said that he fled with the Frenchman.

LUCY. [*Passionately as she rises.*] But why—why? Why should he leave me for him, for an impostor? Why should he ruin us?

MRS. MABSLEY. Ruin you? Surely Lady Mary will forgive——

LUCY. Forgive? *Forgive!* I dare not so much as speak of it to her.

[*Laughter without.*]

MRS. MABSLEY. Calm yourself, child!

LUCY. No! No! Let me go to her.

> [*Exit* LUCY. *Enter* RAIKELL, MISS PRESBREY, *and* MISS PAITELOT. *They join* MRS. MABSLEY. *They are laughing.*]

RAIKELL. [*Bowing.*] Your servant, Madame. [*He looks at watch.*] I shall not need to begin running for yet five minutes.

MRS. MABSLEY. Run, sir, how so?

RAIKELL. Faith, from Monsieur Beaucaire. You have heard of his promise, have you not, Madame? He swore to attempt the entrance here to-night at nine o'clock, and faith, we know too much of him not to expect him. Do you wish to see the work of Monsieur Beaucaire? Behold our cripples.

> [*He points left where* TOWNBRAKE, BICKSIT, *and* BANTISON *enter.* BICKSIT *with a crutch and leaning on* TOWNBRAKE; BANTISON *with his left arm in a sling, and with long patches crossed over the bridge of his nose.* RAIKELL *laughs at the three standing close together very gloomily.*]

LADIES. Oh, dear!

RAIKELL. Winterset was in the most luck. He escaped with a cut on the head. When the Marquis de Mirepoix arrives we'll station them in a line before him in witness of what was done a week ago to-night by one French blade.

> [NASH *has entered during this speech.*]

NASH. [*Coming down.*] Nay, gentlemen, I trust no reference to this most miserable affair will be made in the presence of M. le Marquis de Mirepoix. It has been the most humiliating episode in the history of Bath.

BICKSIT. I knew him for an impostor. I knew him from the first.

RAIKELL. Then why didn't you expose him?

BICKSIT. I could not wish to humiliate my friend Winterset, who had introduced him.

NASH. Quite right.

MISS PAITELOT. But sir, sure I heard you describing the Frenchman's castle of Chateaurien! You said there never was such a place in the world.

BICKSIT. My exact words and they prove what I tell you, Madame. I said there never was such a place in the world, Madame, and there never was!

[All laugh.]

RAIKELL. [Laughing.] Bravo!

[All laugh.]

NASH. His Grace of Winterset comes out of the affair with great credit. Some men, having been so duped, would have shielded the scoundrel to shield themselves. I protest His Grace well deserves the reward for which he has waited so long, and which at last seems at hand.

MISS PAITELOT. [To MISS PRESBREY.] Reward? What does the Beau mean?

MISS PRESBREY. [Indicating TOWNBRAKE, BICKSIT, and BANTISON.] Don't you see how wretched these gentlemen are? 'Tis because they've only cleared the way for their rival. Lady Mary is seen now constantly with His Grace of Winterset. 'Tis sure he'll win her.

MISS PAITELOT. She'll wed him from a desperate pride then.

MISS PRESBREY. She *has* a desperate pride.

[Enter BADGER leaning on a stick.]

NASH. [Crossing to meet him.] Welcome, Captain

Badger. I trust you have fully recovered the injury received from that villain. As a protector of society, I offer you welcome! We greet you as a champion, sir.

RAIKELL. Stand over there, Captain Champion.

BADGER. [*Weakly.*] I thank you, but I am not yet myself. I am very far from being myself.

> [RAIKELL *takes* BADGER *alongside the other three wounded gentlemen.*]

NASH. [*To* RAIKELL.] That villain swore he'd attempt to enter here to-night, did he?

RAIKELL. He did. [TOWNBRAKE *goes to door.*] 'Tis a rash dog, sir, and I'm persuaded he'll do it. For my part, I've brought a ladder.

ALL. A ladder!

NASH. A ladder, and why?

RAIKELL. Because I'm in no mind to climb a tree.

NASH. [*Severely.*] Nothing is more sad than the misplaced levity of a harebrain. It would be easier for a camel to pass through the eye of a needle than for that impostor to enter this place to-night.

RAIKELL. Faith, I hope so.

TOWNBRAKE. 'Tis a rash begad dog, Nash, as I know.

NASH. Fourteen bailiffs wait without to drag him to jail. He could not get within gunshot, sir.

RAIKELL. Only fourteen. Why Nash is mad! Let us hope he has—provided fourteen undertakers to decently bury them!

> [*The cripples turn backs.* BANTISON *crosses to* BADGER. JOLLIFFE *flings open the door at the left.*]

JOLLIFFE. The Marquis de Mirepoix is approaching.

> [MRS. MABSLEY, MISS PAITELOT, *and* MISS PRESBREY *run toward the doors with little exclamations.*]

NASH. [*Severely.*] Ladies! [*They pause.*] The Ambassador of the French King comes amongst us to drink the waters. He will be received by the Master of Ceremonies.

> [*All bow.* NASH *proceeds to the door and passes out with a stately tread. As the three ladies follow,* RAIKELL *calls to* JOLLIFFE.]

LADIES. Oh, dear Mr. Nash.

RAIKELL. Jolliffe.

JOLLIFFE. Your Honor?

RAIKELL. Approach. Come hither! Join the invalid corps.

JOLLIFFE. Lord, sir! What next, Mr. Raikell?

> [*He walks seeming to nurse himself. Under his stocking bandages are seen. He adjusts them and rubs his calf painfully as* RAIKELL *forces him into the last place on the right, in the row of* BEAUCAIRE'S *victims.*]

RAIKELL. Through the calf of the leg, was it not, Jolliffe?

JOLLIFFE. Yes, sir, thank you, sir.

RAIKELL. Don't thank me, thank him. Now then, defenders of society, gentlemen of the guard—forward. [JOLLIFFE *steps back.*] You too, Jolliffe, you've won your spurs.

> [*They move in a sorry line.*]

Our sufferings attest our services, eh, gentlemen? Be proud, be happy! Ours was the victory; we conquered; therefore, let us wear the air of conquerors! Now, gentlemen, answer me. We won't run away, will we?

TOWNBRAKE. [*Pausing.*] 'Fore Heaven, Harry, I vow you're a fool—run!

BICKSIT. I can't run!

RAIKELL. [*Pointing.*]   There's a Frenchman yonder!
[*They run in confusion.*]

BANTISON. [*Angrily.*]   Faugh, Raikell, you're an ass.

BICKSIT.   A damned ass.

RAIKELL.   Then am I turned into a mirror as you face
me. But gentlemen, I implore you to let us not quarrel
with the Marquis! Faith, if the servant did this—what
would the master do?

BICKSIT.   Harry, of all the begad fools in Bath,
you——

TOWNBRAKE.   The worst——

RAIKELL.   On, heroes, on! I left my ladder in the
garden. If any of you care to climb, there are trees
enough for all.

[*All exit.   Enter* WINTERSET *and* LADY MARY.]

WINTERSET. [*Bowing.*]   Madame, the Ambassador
has arrived.

[*He offers his hand.*]

LADY MARY.   Sir, cannot I remain here? The
crowd——

WINTERSET.   Your pardon, Madame, but are there not
reasons?

LADY MARY. [*Desperately.*]   Oh, I am tired, tired!
I hate these faces—these eyes that stare so—that meet
me at every turn always watching, watching, watching!
And I must smile, forever smile—to show——

WINTERSET.   Appearances——

LADY MARY.   Oh, appearances—— We waste our souls
for appearances. We sell all our realities for appearances.
We make pictures for worms and butterflies and use our
heart's blood for the pigments! Appearances!

WINTERSET.   Madame, madame!

LADY MARY.   Oh, I am tired.

[*Slight pause.*]

WINTERSET. [*Going to* LADY MARY.] Madame, it may not become me to remind you that you owe me at least some little consideration, who——

LADY MARY. [*With a gesture of despair.*] Oh, oh! I know, I know! [*Collecting herself.*] I owe you all that gratitude can give, and I give it. You saved me from that impostor. I will not shrink from payment of the debt.

WINTERSET. Everything.
    [*Triumphantly.*]

LADY MARY. [*Brokenly.*] Aye, sir, everything——

WINTERSET. [*Kissing her hand repeatedly.*] Madame!

LUCY. [*Enters suddenly, crying out happily.*] Lady Mary!

LADY MARY. [*Going to* LUCY.] Not a word, child. My Lord of Winterset, you will present my cousin and myself to the Ambassador.

LADY MARY. Have your will, child. I dare not ask of you what I ask of myself. Await us here. [*Courtesy.*] Sir, I esteem the honor.

    [LADY MARY *walks to the door at the left.*
    WINTERSET *bows as she passes out with stately
        dignity. He follows her, closing the door.*
    LUCY *falls sobbing into an armchair, keeping
        her arm on the table and her face buried.*]

MOLYNEAUX. [*Entering from the alcove at the back and speaking from there.*] Lucy!

LUCY. [*Springs to her feet.*] Philip!

MOLYNEAUX. Lucy!

LUCY. Why have you ruined us, Philip?

MOLYNEAUX. Lucy, I told you my fate was bound up with Beaucaire. Every hope of my advancement lay in him——

LUCY. [*Bitterly.*] And he was our destruction.

MOLYNEAUX. He was my friend. I and his servants carried him to a farmstead near by, where he lay until to-day that he might recover from his wound——

[*Voices are heard in the distance.*]

LUCY. Is he mad enough to try to fulfil his oath? Have they arrested him?

[*Noise off left.*]

MOLYNEAUX. No. Hark! They are seeking him now. Wait here for me, Sweetheart.

[*They separate from each other and exit. A commotion without. Doors are flung open and* BANTISON, BICKSIT, RAIKELL, TOWN-BRAKE, JOLLIFFE, NASH, *and other gentlemen rush out.* NASH *closes the door.*]

BANTISON. The Park! Search the Park!

TOWNBRAKE. Aye, b'ged, he's hid in the Park!

NASH. Gentlemen! Gentlemen! Quietly, for Heaven's sake! No more scandal! This must at all hazards be kept from the Ambassador.

BANTISON. [*Hotly.*] Now you see, Beau, what comes of that damned rule of yours that keeps us from carrying swords in Bath. By Heavens, though, I have a cudgel to break his head with.

NASH. He wore no sword himself, or they wouldn't have let him pass.

RAIKELL. [*To* BICKSIT.] Gentlemen, let us unitedly thank Heaven for this especial mercy.

BANTISON. [*Rushing out.*] Lose no time! The Park! He's in the Park!

TOWNBRAKE. Beat every bush!

NASH. Nay, but gentlemen, quiet now! No scandal! No scandal!

RAIKELL. [*Following.*] Come, then. And mind I choose the pear tree—'tis easiest to climb.

[BANTISON, TOWNBRAKE, BICKSIT, NASH, RAIKELL, JOLLIFFE—*all rush out.*]

LUCY. [*Stealing back.*] Thank Heaven they're gone!

LADY MARY. [*Enters from the door at the left. She immediately closes the doors behind her and leans against them white, terrified, and trembling.*] Have they taken him?

LUCY. [*Running to her.*] Not yet. He's safe for the moment.

LADY MARY. Mr. Nash received word Beaucaire has long since entered—Major Molyneaux was with him.

LUCY. Oh!

[*Crosses to bolt door at the left.*]

LADY MARY. They are trying to keep it from the Ambassador. They decided that the two must be hiding in the garden; they would not have dared to join the throng in the rooms. Oh, to be taken like this— Oh, they are hiding like thieves, like hunted rats!

[*Voices in the garden.*]

LUCY. Mary, you speak of two gentlemen that do not hide!

LADY MARY. [*Vehemently.*] You say they do not hide! [*Voices.*] They skulk in the garden now. Hark! They beat up the bushes for them as if they were wild beasts.

[*Noise off right.*]

MOLYNEAUX. [*Throws open the curtains.*] Madame, he is here!

BEAUCAIRE. Pardon, Mademoiselle! Did I not say I should come! M. Molyneaux was so kind as to answer for me to the friends of M. de Winterset and Mistaire Nash!

LADY MARY. I desire to hear nothing from your companion, Major Molyneaux.

BEAUCAIRE. Mademoiselle, I could not tell you all on that night.

LADY MARY. You may inform your friend, Major Molyneaux, that I heard everything he had to say; that he had a chance to defend himself against accusation, that he said all——

> [BEAUCAIRE *beckons* LUCY *and* MOLYNEAUX.
> *They exit beyond the curtains.*]

BEAUCAIRE. That I did say all I could have strength to say. Mademoiselle, you did not see—as it was right—that I had been stung by a big wasp. It was nothing, a scratch; but, Mademoiselle, the sky went round and the moon danced on the earth. I could not wish that big wasp to see that he had stung me; so I must only say what I can have strength for, and stan' straight till he is gone. Besides there are other rizzons. Ah, you mus' belief! I would have tol' you everything long ago excep' because . . . well, for romance, the fun! So you do belief, Mademoiselle? Can there be no faith in—in——

LADY MARY. [*Indignantly.*] In an impostor——

BEAUCAIRE. If you had not belief me to be an impostor; if I had been jus' that Monsieur Beaucaire of the story they tol' you, but never with the heart of a lackey, a man, the man you knew, himself, could you—would you—would you have let me ride by your side in the Autumn moonlight? [LADY MARY *turns away.*] Mademoiselle? Mademoiselle, if you had known this Beaucaire was hones', though of peasant birth, would you— [*She shudders.* BEAUCAIRE *drops into chair with his head bent low, his arms outstretched on the table. His eyes fill slowly in spite of himself, and tears roll down the young man's cheeks.*] And live men are jus'—names!

LADY MARY. Oh, this is intolerable! You put *me* on *my* defense when it is you—you——

BEAUCAIRE. I, Mademoiselle!

LADY MARY. Names, names! What are they to me? I tell you I've lived for names all my life.

BEAUCAIRE. Names, they are shadows, Mademoiselle. They are not real.

LADY MARY. Do you need to tell me that? Oh! It is this week of intolerable anguish has taught me that names are toys, Monsieur. Do you suppose that I cared for you because I thought you were noble and rich?

BEAUCAIRE. [*Turns and faces her warningly.*] Mademoiselle!

LADY MARY. [*Vehemently.*] No! Hear me now. I was proud of it and cared not who read my heart——

BEAUCAIRE. [*Rises and faces her.*] Mademoiselle! Mademoiselle!

LADY MARY. I thought him an honorable gentleman —and it was to the honorable gentleman, not to the Duke, that I gave my heart!

BEAUCAIRE. [*Crossing to her with trembling but exultant voice.*] Mademoiselle, you remember when we stood there by the Diana in the white moonlight.

LADY MARY. [*Passionately.*] Ah! Do not speak of it—do not dare.

BEAUCAIRE. I had a secret and I was going to tell you then. [MOLYNEAUX *and* LUCY *go up into the alcove.* LADY MARY *sits.*] That secret you are going to hear to-night, Mademoiselle, I haf not lie to you, I haf——

LADY MARY. [*Bitterly.*] Not lied?

BEAUCAIRE. [*Eagerly.*] I can prove it, Mademoiselle. If that secret prove not dishonorable and me jus'— well jus' a poor young fellow who has been foolish but no more—nothing mean—nothing wicked—Mademoiselle—

There come a time in the life of every person, when he must chose between what is real and what is shadow. I am here, that most onworthy man to whom you say you give your heart. Look at me! Turn to me an' say you think I am a swindler, a pretender.

LADY MARY. [*Whispering.*] Stop!

BEAUCAIRE. Mademoiselle, listen! One day you drop a rose. I give that rose back to you. I am that man to whom you give your heart. I am not jus' names and shadows—I am I. [*He kneels beside her.*] I gave you back your rose, Mademoiselle, are you gawn to ask me that I give you back your heart? Mademoiselle, will you come back to France with me if I show you I have always been a man of honor? Never an impostor. [*Pause.*] Mademoiselle! Turn to me! Turn to me, Mademoiselle!

[*He kneels.*]

LADY MARY. [*Turning and looking into his eyes.*] Listen! All my life I have smothered every feeling Heaven ever sent me. And at last there comes one—one emotion that will not be smothered and kept down. I thought I could go on hating you. I think I should have had strength for anything if I had not seen you again— but I have seen you again—and I have seen your soul! An impostor you are not. I do not care what you have been. [*Going to him.*] I love you! Do you understand? I love you!

> [*Voices from the garden. They stand. There is commotion without the door at the right. The door is tried. There is knocking, growing louder and louder. Angry voices demand admittance.*]

LADY MARY. [*Speaks as the knocking begins, in a low, clear voice, intense with a rigidly controlled emotion. She*

stands at arm's length from him.] Oh! But I was forgetting—you're in danger. [*He follows her a few steps.*]
That locked door will keep them a moment. I will go out
by this. The door of the carriage will be open.

> [*She begins to leave.*]

BEAUCAIRE. [*Breathless, crossing to her.*] Oh,
Mademoiselle! Mademoiselle! You have reckoned all
the cost? You will go with me to France?

LADY MARY. I will go with you to France—I will go
where you will—I will go with you to the end of all the
earth.

BEAUCAIRE. Ma-ry! Ma-ry! Mother in Heaven,
do you hear this lady!

> [*He takes her hands and kisses them. Noise
> and voices without.* LADY MARY *goes out
> left.*]

BEAUCAIRE. [*In a loud voice.*] Mademoiselle Lucee!
Mademoiselle Lucee!

> [MOLYNEAUX *and* LUCY *come from the card
> room.*]

Follow her! Follow her! God is good to us, my frien's.
Go! Follow her to her carriage—hasten! Bring her
here in ten minutes. All will be well. [*Voices outside
loud and angry.*] Be careful of her; be careful of my
lady! My—my lady! Go! [*To* MOLYNEAUX.] Did
I not tell you she was pure gold?

> [*He hurries* LUCY *out.*]

WINTERSET. [*Without, his voice rising over the
knocking and other voices.*] Break it in! He's there!
I swear he is! Beat the door down!

BEAUCAIRE. [*Sits. To* MOLYNEAUX.] An' you, my
frien', open the door.

MOLYNEAUX. It will be a charge! You think we can
face it?

BEAUCAIRE. [*Smiling, yet with watchful eye on the door.*] I think, my frien'—it is only—six more large men.

> [MOLYNEAUX *opens the door and springs back.*
> *A babel of savage exclamations as* WINTERSET,
> BANTISON, RAIKELL, TOWNBRAKE, BICKSIT,
> NASH, *and* JOLLIFFE *rush in.*]

WINTERSET. By God! He's there!

BANTISON. There he is!

TOWNBRAKE. I knew it, damn him!

BICKSIT. [*At the same time.*] He was in the card room.

NASH. No scandal, gentlemen, no scandal, I beg.

WINTERSET. [*Suddenly checked in his rush on* BEAU-CAIRE, *falls back as do all the others.*] Od's blood! The dog hath murdered and robbed some royal Prince! Lay hands on him! Tear those orders from him!

> [*All make movement toward him.*]

MOLYNEAUX. [*Throwing himself between.*] One word! Gentlemen, hear me before you offer an outrage you will repent all your lives.

BEAUCAIRE. [*Laughing.*] Oh, let M. de Winterset come alone!

WINTERSET. Do you expect me to fight a cut-throat barber with bare hands?

BEAUCAIRE. I think one does not expec' Monsieur to fight anybody. Would I fight you, Monsieur, the slug? I would gladly fight almos' any one in all this worl' but I could not soil my hand with a——

WINTERSET. [*Furiously.*] Stop his lying mouth.

> [BADGER *raises a stick.* MOLYNEAUX *stops the*
> *others, and* BADGER, *finding himself alone,*
> *opposed to* BEAUCAIRE, *who lifts chair slightly,*
> *falls back with remarkable suddenness.*]

NASH. Stop! No scandal! Gentlemen! Gentlemen! Be prudent—be prudent!

RAIKELL. [*To* BADGER.] Captain, you'll find my ladder in the garden.

BEAUCAIRE. Of what are you afraid, M. de Winterset? I was not gawn to reveal that secret. You have not absolved me of my promise.

WINTERSET. Say what you like; tell all the wild lies you have time for. You have five minutes to make up your mind to get out quietly and without scandal.

BEAUCAIRE. [*Rises exultantly.*] You absolve me, then? Yes? Ah, now I am free—on the honor of a French gentleman?

BANTISON. [*Harshly.*] A French what?

TOWNBRAKE. Why, you villain barber, your master, the Marquis de Mirepoix, is in the next room.

MOLYNEAUX. [*With a gasp of relief.*] He is here! [*To* BEAUCAIRE.] Shall I——

BEAUCAIRE. Tell him to come here at once!

[MOLYNEAUX *goes.*]

TOWNBRAKE. Of all the damn impudence!

NASH. [*Following* MOLYNEAUX.] Are you raving mad?

MOLYNEAUX. No madness, sir. You heard. The Duke of Winterset gives us five minutes—'tis enough!

NASH. Stop him—Philip, for God's sake—the Ambassador! Oh! the scandal! Stop him I say.

[*He goes after* MOLYNEAUX.]

BANTISON. Molyneaux will pay for this.

WINTERSET. Were he ten times the Beau's best friend, he shall be expelled from the rooms—with no more compunction than in the case of the dog yonder.

[*Enter* LADY MARY. LUCY *follows swiftly.*]

LADY MARY. Why did you not come, Monsieur?

WINTERSET. [*Stepping toward her.*] Madame! This is no place for you. Let me——

LADY MARY. [*Checking him with a gesture.*] This is the place for me, sir, henceforth and always.

WINTERSET. [*Appalled.*] For God's sake, madame, do you remember who this man is?

BANTISON. A lackey who has had the infernal recklessness to send for his master. That will settle it.

BEAUCAIRE. Yes, Mademoiselle, now you gawn see Monsieur Beaucaire's master, M. le Mirepoix. My frien's, shall I tell you why I mus' be firs' the barber, the "Beaucaire," then "de Chateaurien" an' not myself?

TOWNBRAKE. To escape from the b'gad bailiffs for debts for razors and soaps.

BEAUCAIRE. Non, Monsieur. In France I have got a cousin who is a man with a very bad temper, an' he will never allow his relative to do what they wish——

BANTISON. [*Violently.*] Now damme, I'll hear no more! Your five minutes are gone! Will you go out to the bailiffs or——

BEAUCAIRE. Non, Monsieur.

WINTERSET. Then there's but one thing to do; ladies, I entreat you to retire.

LADY MARY. [*Haughtily.*] Not I!

LUCY. Not I!

WINTERSET. Gentlemen, are you ready?

RAIKELL. If Beaucaire is as good with a chair as with a sword, God help us. Come on!

[*All advance.* NASH *flings open the doors at the left.*]

NASH. [*In a loud voice.*] Gentlemen! [*They come to a dead stop.*] The Ambassador of His Most Christian Majesty King Louis of France, the Marquis de Mirepoix.

[*The* MARQUIS *enters through the door at the*

left. He is a stately personage, his breast covered with orders. MOLYNEAUX *precedes him and stands by* NASH, *bowing as* DE MIREPOIX *passes.*]

BEAUCAIRE. [*With emotion, yet in a ringing voice.*] Thou best of masters—my dear frien'!

DE MIREPOIX. [*Going straight to him.*] Monseigneur, mon Prince.

LADY MARY. [*Whispering and falling back a step.*] Monseigneur, mon Prince?

[LUCY *puts arm around her.*]

BEAUCAIRE. [*To* DE MIREPOIX.] No, no! My good master!

[*Takes both his hands.*]

RAIKELL. And my ladder can never hold them *all*.

DE MIREPOIX. Monseigneur, you need wear your incognito no more.

BEAUCAIRE. I know, Monsieur. I am forgiven again, but these gentlemen, they were jus' going to arrest me because I have been your hair-dresser.

DE MIREPOIX. [*Crying out.*] My honor, Gentlemen, I fought my best 'gainst His Highness' mad humor.

BEAUCAIRE. Gentlemen, there is one thing more. There is a man here who have forfeit his honor. He play cards with me and he cheat—then on condition I do not expose him, he introduce me as de Chateaurien at Lady Rellerton's ball. He introduce me at the cost of his honor and then betray me to redeem it. That liar—that card cheat—that coward, he stand there—Monsieur—le Duc de Winterset.

[*He points to* WINTERSET. *The gentlemen slowly withdraw from his neighborhood.*]

WINTERSET. I'll know the name of the man who dares bring such a charge.

DE MIREPOIX. Monsieur! [*A gesture from* BEAU-
CAIRE *checks him.*] Permit me to have the honor of pre-
senting you to His Royal Highness, Prince Louis Philippe
de Valois, Le Duc d'Orleans, Duke de Chartres, Duke de
Nemours, Duke de Montpensier, Count de Beaujolais,
First Prince of the Blood Royal, First Peer of France,
Lieutenant General of French Infantry, Governor of Dau-
phine, Knight of the Golden Fleece, Grand Master of the
Order of Notre Dame, of Mount Carmel, and of St. Laz-
arus in Jerusalem, and Cousin of His most Christian
Majesty, the King of France.

BEAUCAIRE. Mon Dieu! What a memory he has!

RAIKELL. [*To* BICKSIT *with a gasp.*] Where's my
ladder! My ladder!

BICKSIT. I knew him all the time.

[TOWNBRAKE *pulls him back.*]

WINTERSET. The Duke of Orleans will hear from me,
within the hour.

BEAUCAIRE. What gentleman will carry your message,
Monsieur? And whoever will shall receive a little beating from François. [WINTERSET *turns and sees the men
withdrawn and with averted faces.*] Mark, I promise
this, M. le Capitaine Badger.

[WINTERSET *goes slowly out with hanging head,
followed by* BADGER.]

LADY MARY. [*Trembling, steps to* BEAUCAIRE'S *side.*]
Monseigneur! [*He turns and looks at her.*] It is a terrible—mistake—I have made— [*She falters.*] Forgive——

BEAUCAIRE. Forgive—I? Ah, Mademoiselle, *forgive*
that you believed me that so much greater thing than
prince—an honorable gentleman?

NASH. [*At the doors, where* MRS. MABSLEY, MISS
PAITELOT, MISS PRESBREY, *and others are pressing in with*

wide eyes and a buzz of voices.] Your Excellency, the ladies of the Assembly have cared to hope for a presentation to His Royal Highness, the Duke of Orleans!

BEAUCAIRE. The honor is his, Monsieur! But first I want to introduce to all these good pipple that lady who is to be his Duchess.

[*He bows low and kisses* LADY MARY's *hand.*]

LADY MARY. Duchess! That is only a name, Monseigneur—and I am done with names—save one! Monseigneur, present me by that name.

BEAUCAIRE. The mos' beautiful name in all the worl' —only, only Mary.

CURTAIN

BIBLIOGRAPHICAL LISTS

NAMES AND ADDRESSES OF PUBLISH-
ERS REFERRED TO IN THE BIBLIO-
GRAPHICAL LISTS

FINDING LISTS OF PLAYS

BOOKS ON DRAMA AND THE THEATRE

VOLUMES OF ONE–ACT PLAYS

VOLUMES OF FULL–LENGTH PLAYS

BIBLIOGRAPHICAL LISTS

A. NAMES AND ADDRESSES OF PUBLISHERS REFERRED TO IN THE BIBLIOGRAPHICAL LISTS

(The address New York City is sufficient if no other is given.)

D. Appleton and Company.
Atlantic Monthly Press, Boston, Mass.
Richard Badger, Boston, Mass.
Walter Baker, 41 Winter Street, Boston, Mass.
Bobbs-Merrill, Indianapolis.
Boni & Liveright.
Brentano's.
T. Y. Crowell Company.
Dodd, Mead & Company.
George H. Doran Company.
Doubleday, Page & Company.
Duffield & Company.
E. P. Dutton & Company.
Samuel French, 25 West 45th Street, New York.
Harcourt, Brace and Company.
Harper & Brothers.
Henry Holt and Company.
Houghton Mifflin Company, Boston, Mass.
Alfred A. Knopf.
J. B. Lippincott & Company, Philadelphia.
Little, Brown and Company, Boston, Mass.
John Luce Company, Boston, Mass.
The Macmillan Company.
G. P. Putnam's Sons.
Charles Scribner's Sons.
Frank Shay, 14 Christopher Street, New York.
Small, Maynard & Company.
Viking Press.

B. FINDING LISTS OF PLAYS

Drama League of America. *Plays for Amateurs.* Arranged by Winifred Ward. Chicago, 1922.

Drummond, A. M. *Fifty One-Act Plays.* Quarterly Journal of Public Speaking. Volume I, 1915, p. 234 ff.

——. *One-Act Plays for Schools and Colleges.* Education. Volume IX, 1918, p. 372 ff.

Drury, Francis K. W. *Viewpoints in Modern Drama.* Chicago: American Library Association, 1925. (The most valuable of all the lists.)

Faxon, F. W. *Dramatic Index.* Annually since 1909. Boston: F. W. Faxon Co.

Johnson, Gertrude E. *Choosing a Play.* Century, 1920.

Kaplan, Samuel. *Actable One-Act Plays.* Chicago Public Library, 1916.

Koch, F. H., and Lay, E. A. *Plays for Amateurs.* North Carolina Record, January, 1920. (University of North Carolina, Chapel Hill).

Lewis, B. Roland. *The One-Act Play in Colleges and High Schools.* University of Utah Bulletin, Extension Series, No. 2, February, 1920.

Logasa, Hannah, and Ver Nooy, Winifred. *An Index to One-Act Plays.* Boston: F. W. Faxon Co., 1924.

National Council of Teachers of English. *Plays for High Schools and Colleges.* Chicago: National Council of Teachers of English, 1923.

New York Drama League. *Plays for Amateurs.* Wilson, 1923.

Pence, R. W. *Notes on the One-Act Play.* Urbana: Illinois English Bulletin, May, 1920.

Shay, Frank. *One Thousand and One Plays for the Little Theatre.* Appleton, 1923.

——. *A Guide to Longer Plays.* Appleton, 1925.

United States Copyright Office. *Dramatic Compositions Copyrighted in the United States 1870-1916.* Two volumes. Washington: Government Printing Office, 1918.

C. BOOKS ON DRAMA AND THE THEATRE

Andrews, Charlton. *The Changing Drama.* Holt, 1914.

——. *The Drama Today.* Lippincott, 1913.

——. *The Technique of Play Writing.* Home Correspondence School (Springfield, Mass.), 1915.

Andrews, Harry Lee, and Weirick, Bruce. *Acting and Play Production.* Longmans, 1925.

ARCHER, WILLIAM. *Old Drama and the New.* Small, 1923.
——. *Play-Making: A Manual of Craftmanship.* Small, 1912.
BAKER, GEORGE P. *Dramatic Technique.* Houghton, 1919.
BOYD, ERNEST A. *The Contemporary Drama of Ireland.* Little, 1917.
BRUNTIERE, FERDINAND. *The Law of the Drama.* Publications of the Dramatic Museum of Columbia University. New York, 1914.
BURLEIGH, LOUISE. *The Community Theatre.* Little, 1917.
BURTON, RICHARD. *How to See a Play.* Macmillan, 1914.
——. *The New American Drama.* Crowell, 1913.
CALVERT, LOUIS. *Problems of the Actor.* Holt, 1916.
CANNON, FANNIE. *Writing and Selling a Play.* Holt, 1915.
CARTER, HUNTLEY. *The New Spirit in Drama and Art.* Kennerley, 1914.
CHANDLER, F. W. *Aspects of Modern Drama.* Macmillan, 1914.
CHENEY, SHELDON. *The Art Theatre.* Knopf, 1917, 1925.
CLARK, BARRETT H. *The British and American Drama of To-day.* Appleton, 1915.
——. *Contemporary French Dramatists.* Appleton, 1915.
——. *The Continental Drama of Today.* Holt, 1914.
——. *European Theories of the Drama.* Appleton, 1919.
——. *How to Produce Amateur Plays.* Little, 1923.
——. *A Study of the Modern Drama.* Appleton, 1925.
CRAIG, GORDON. *The Theatre Advancing.* Little, 1919.
——. *Towards a New Theatre.* Dutton, 1913.
DEAN, ALEXANDER. *Little Theatre Organization and Management.* Appleton, 1926.
DICKINSON, THOMAS. *The Case of the American Drama.* Houghton, 1915.
——. *Contemporary Drama of England.* Little, 1917.
——. *The Insurgent Theatre.* Viking Press, 1917.
——. *Playwrights of the New American Theatre.* Macmillan, 1925.
——. *An Outline of Contemporary Drama.* Houghton, 1927.
DUKES, ASHLEY. *Modern Dramatists.* Small, 1912.
——. *Drama.* Holt, 1927.
GANNON, ROBERT. *The Technique of the One-Act Play.* Fordham University Press, 1925.
GOLDBERG, ISAAC. *The Drama in Transition.* Appleton, 1922.
HALE, EDWARD E. *Dramatists of Today.* Holt, 1911.
HAMILTON, CLAYTON. *Conversations on Contemporary Dramatists.* Macmillan, 1925.
——. *Problems of the Playwright.* Holt, 1917.
——. *Seen on the Stage.* Holt, 1920.

HAMILTON, CLAYTON. *Studies in Stagecraft.* Holt, 1914.

——. *The Theory of the Theatre.* Holt, 1911.

HENDERSON, ARCHIBALD. *The Changing Drama.* Appleton, 1919.

——. *European Dramatists.* Appleton, 1918.

HILLEBRAND, H. N. *Writing the One-Act Play.* Knopf, 1925.

HOPKINS, ARTHUR. *How's Your Second Act?* Knopf, 1918.

HORNBLOW, ARTHUR. *A History of the Theatre in America.* Two volumes. Lippincott, 1919.

HUNEKER, JAMES. *Iconoclasts: A Book of Dramatists.* Scribner, 1905.

HUNT, ELIZABETH. *The Play Today.* Dodd, 1914.

KROWS, A. E. *Play Production in America.* Holt, 1916.

LEWIS, B. ROLAND. *The Technique of the One-Act Play.* Luce, 1922.

LEWISOHN, LUDWIG. *The Drama and the Stage.* Harcourt, 1922.

MacCLINTOCK, LANDER. *The Contemporary Drama of Italy.* Little, 1920.

MacGOWAN, KENNETH. *The Art Theatre.* Liveright, 1922.

——. *The Theatre of Tomorrow.* Liveright, 1921.

MacGOWAN, KENNETH, and JONES, R. E. *Continental Stagecraft.* Harcourt, 1922.

MacKAY, CONSTANCE. *The Little Theatre in the United States.* Holt, 1917.

MANTLE, BURNS. *The Best Plays of 1919–1920, etc.* Dodd, 1920, etc.

MATTHEWS, BRANDER. *Playwrights on Playmaking.* Scribner, 1923.

——. *Rip Van Winkle Goes to the Play.* Scribner, 1926.

——. *A Study of the Drama.* Houghton, 1910.

MODERWELL, H. K. *The Theatre of Today.* Dodd, 1914.

MORGAN, A. E. *Tendencies of Modern English Drama.* Scribner, 1924.

MOSES, M. J. *The American Dramatist.* Little, 1925.

NATHAN, GEORGE JEAN. *The Critic and the Drama.* Knopf, 1922.

NICOLL, ALLARDYCE. *British Drama.* Crowell, 1925.

PHELPS, WILLIAM LYON. *Essays on Modern Dramatists.* Macmillan, 1921.

——. *The Twentieth Century Theatre.* Macmillan, 1918.

QUINN, ARTHUR. *A History of the American Drama from the Beginning to the Civil War.* Harper, 1923.

SAYLOR, O. M. *Our American Theatre.* Brentano, 1923.

SHAW, GEORGE BERNARD. *Dramatic Opinions and Essays.* Brentano, 1907.

SMITH, MILTON M. *The Book of Play Production.* Appleton, 1927.

STRATTON, CLARENCE. *Producing in Little Theatres.* Holt, 1921.

VERNON, FRANK. *The Twentieth Century Theatre*. Houghton, 1924.

WIENER, LEO. *The Contemporary Drama of Russia*. Little, 1924.

WILDE, PERCIVAL. *The Craftsmanship of the One-Act Play*. Little, 1923.

WISE, CLAUDE M. *Dramatics for Schools and Communities*. Appleton, 1925.

YOUNG, STARK. *The Flower in Drama*. Scribner, 1923.

——. *Glamour*. Scribner, 1925.

——. *Theatre Practice*. Scribner, 1926.

D. VOLUMES OF ONE-ACT PLAYS

ALDRICH, THOMAS BAILEY. *The Sister's Tragedy and Other Poems*. Houghton, 1876, etc. "Pauline Pavlovna."

Appleton Little Theatre Plays. Edited by Grace Adams. Appleton. Especially "The Ghost Story," by Booth Tarkington (1922); "A Fan and Two Candlesticks," by Mary MacMillan (1913); "The Trysting Place," by Booth Tarkington (1923); "Aria Da Capo," by Edna St. Vincent Millay (1920); "The Lamp and the Bell," by Edna St. Vincent Millay (1921).

Appleton Modern Plays. Edited by Frank Shay. Appleton. Especially "Hearts to Mend," by Harry A. Overstreet (1920); "Six Who Pass While the Lentils Boil," by Stuart Walker (1921); "The Emperor Jones," by Eugene O'Neill (1921); "Sweet and Twenty," by Floyd Dell (1921); "Two Slatterns and a King," by Edna St. Vincent Millay (1921); "Sir David Wears a Crown," by Stuart Walker (1922); "Thursday Evening," by Christopher Morley (1922); "Lithuania," by Rupert Brooke (1915); "The Fountain of Youth," by Serafin and Joaquin Alvarez-Quintero (1922); "The Giant's Stair," by Wilbur D. Steele (1924); "Words and Thoughts," by Don Marquis (1921).

Appleton Short Plays. Appleton. Especially "Exile," by A. Conan Doyle (1925); "The Managers," by Joseph Lincoln (1925); "The Eldest," by Edna Ferber (1925).

ARKELL, REGINALD. *Columbine*. London: Sidgwick & Jackson, 1911. Title play.

ASH, SHOLOM. See Goldberg, I. *Six Plays from the Yiddish Theatre*.

BAKER, GEORGE P. (Editor). *Harvard Plays: The 47 Workshop*. Brentano, 1918. "Three Pills in a Bottle," by Rachel L. Field.

——. *Harvard Plays: The Harvard Dramatic Club*. Brentano, 1918. "The Florist Shop," by W. Hawkridge; "The Bank Account," by H. Brock; "America Passes By," by K. Andrews.

——. *Harvard Plays: The Harvard Dramatic Club*. Second Series. Brentano, 1919.

——. *Harvard Plays: The 47 Workshop*. Second Series. Brentano, 1920.

——. *Harvard Plays: The 47 Workshop*. Third Series. Brentano, 1922. "The Crowsnest," by William F. Manley.

——. *Harvard Plays: The 47 Workshop*. Fourth Series. Brentano, 1925.

BANVILLE, THEODORE DE. *Charming Leander*. French, 1915.

BARKER, GRANVILLE. *Three Short Plays*. Little, 1918. "Vote by Ballot."

BARRIE, JAMES. *Echoes of the War*. Scribner, 1918. "The Old Lady Shows Her Medals," "Barbara's Wedding."

——. *Half-Hours*. Scribner, 1914. "The Twelve-Pound Look," "Rosalind," "The Will."

BEACH, LOUIS. *Four One-Act Plays*. Brentano, 1921.

BECHHOFER, C. E. (Editor). *Five Russian Plays*. Dutton, 1916. "A Merry Death," by Nicholas Evreinov.

BENNETT, ARNOLD. *Polite Farces*. Doran, 1912. "A good Woman," "A Question of Sex," "The Stepmother."

BRIGHOUSE, HAROLD. *Lonesomelike*. London: Gowans & Gray, 1914.

——. *The Price of Coal*. Gowans & Gray, 1911.

BRITISH DRAMA LEAGUE. *Double Demon and Other One-Act Plays*. Appleton, 1924. Title play by A. P. Herbert, and "Pan in Pimlico," by Helen Simpson.

BROOKE, RUPERT. *See* Appleton Modern Plays.

BROWN, ALICE. *One-Act Plays*. Macmillan, 1921. "Joint Owners in Spain."

BRUNNER, EMMA B. *Bits of Background*. Knopf, 1919. "Over Age," "The Spark of Life," "Strangers," "Making a Man."

BYNNER, WITTER. *Plays*. Knopf, 1922. "Tiger," "The Little King."

CAMERON, MARGARET. *Comedies in Miniature*. Doubleday, 1903.

CANNON, GILBERT. *Four Plays*. Brentano, 1913. "James and John," "Mary's Wedding."

CHEKHOV, ANTON. *The Boor*. French, 1915.

——. *A Marriage Proposal*. French, 1915.

CLEMENTS, COLIN CAMPBELL. *Plays for a Folding Theatre*. Appleton, 1923.

——. *Plays for Pagans*. Appleton, 1925.

——(Editor). *Sea Plays*. Small, 1925.

CLARK, BARRETT (Editor). *Four Plays of the Free Theatre*. Appleton, 1914. "The Fossil," by Françoise de Curel; "The Serenad," by Jean Julien; "Françoise's Luck," by Georges de Porto-Riche; "The Dupe," by Georges Ancey.

——(Editor). *Representative One-Act Plays by British and Irish Authors.* Little, 1921.

COHEN, HELEN LOUISE (Editor). *One-Act Plays by Modern Authors.* Harcourt, 1921.

COOK, GEORGE CRAM, and SHAY, FRANK (Editors). *Provincetown Plays.* Appleton, 1921.

CROCKER, BOSWORTH. *Humble Folks.* Appleton, 1923. "The Last Straw."

DAVIES, MARY CAROLYN. *See* Flying Stag Plays.

DELL, FLOYD. *King Arthur's Socks and Other Village Plays.* Knopf, 1922. "The Angel Intrudes."

——. *See* Appleton Modern Plays.

DICKINSON, THOMAS (Editor). *Wisconsin Plays.* Viking Press, 1914. "The Neighbors," by Zona Gale; "In Hospital," by T. Dickinson.

——. *Wisconsin Plays: Second Series.* Viking Press, 1918.

DIX, BEULAH M. *Allison's Lad and Other Martial Interludes.* Holt, 1910. "The Hundredth Trick," "The Captain of the Gate," "The Dark of the Dawn."

DOWN, OLIPHANT. *The Maker of Dreams.* London: Gowans and Gray.

DOWSON, ERNEST C. *The Pierrot of the Minute.* Baker, 1918.

DOYLE, A. CONAN. *See* Appleton Short Plays.

DREISER, THEODORE. *Plays of the Natural and Supernatural.* Dodd, 1916. "The Girl in the Coffin," "Laughing Gas."

DRINKWATER, JOHN. *Pawns: Four Poetic Plays.* Houghton, 1920. "The Storm," "The God of Quiet," "X Equal O," "Cophetua."

DUNSANY, LORD. *Five Plays.* Little, 1914. "The Gods of the Mountains" (three scenes), "The Golden Doom," "The Glittering Gate," "The Lost Silk Hat."

——. *Plays of Gods and Men.* Putnam, 1917. "The Night at an Inn."

EATON, WALTER PRICHARD (Editor). *One-Act Plays for Stage and Study: Second Series.* French, 1925.

ELIOT, SAMUEL (Editor). *Little Theatre Classics.* Little, v.d. Four volumes.

ELLIS, MRS. HAVELOCK. *Love in Danger.* Houghton, 1915. "The Subjection of Kezia."

ERVINE, ST. JOHN. *Four Irish Plays.* Macmillan, 1916. "The Magnanimous Lover," "The Orangeman."

EVRENOV, NICHOLAS. *See* Bechhofer, C. E., Five Russian Plays.

FENN, F., and PRYCE, RICHARD. "*'Op-o'-Me-Thumb.*" French, 1904.

FERBER, EDNA. *See* Appleton Short Plays.

FIELD, RACHEL L. *Six Plays.* Scribner, 1925. "Three Pills in a Bottle."

FILIPOPI, ROSINI. *Dialogues and Scenes from the Novels of Jane Austen.* London: Dent.

FITZMAURICE, GEORGE. *Five Plays.* Little, 1917. "The Pie-Dish."

FLYING STAG PLAYS. New York: Egmont Arens (Washington Square Book Shop). Especially "The Sandbar Queen" by George Cronyn (1918); "The Angel Intrudes," by Floyd Dell (1918); "Enter the Hero," by Theresa Helburn (1916); "The Slave with Two Faces," by Mary Carolyn Davies (1918).

FRANCE, ANATOLE. *The Man Who Married a Dumb Wife.* Two acts. Dodd, 1915.

GALSWORTHY, JOHN. *Six Short Plays.* Scribner, 1921. "The Little Man."

GERSTENBERG, ALICE. *Four Plays for Women.* Brentano, 1925.

——. *Ten One-Act Plays.* Brentano, 1921. "Fourteen," "Overtones."

GIACOSA, GIUSEPPE. *The Wager.* French, 1914.

GIBSON, W. W. *Collected Poems.* Macmillan, 1923. Contains many narratives in dramatic form.

GLASPELL, SUSAN. *Plays.* Small, 1920. "Trifles," "The People," "Close the Book," "Suppressed Desires" (with George Cram Cook).

GOLDBERG, ISAAC (Editor). *Six Plays from the Yiddish Theatre.* Luce, 1916. "Winter," by Sholom Ash, "Forgotten Souls," by David Pinski.

GOODMAN, KENNETH S. *Quick Curtains.* Chicago: Stage Guild, 1915. "Back of the Yards," "A Game of Chess."

GOODMAN, KENNETH S., and HECHT, BEN. *The Wonder-Hat and Other One-Act Plays.* Appleton, 1924.

GREGORY, LADY. *New Comedies.* Putnam, 1913. "Damer's Gold."

——. *Seven Short Plays.* Putnam, 1915. "Spreading the News," "The Travelling Man," "The Gaol Gate," "Hyacinth Halvey."

HALMAN, DORIS F. *Set the Stage for Eight.* Little, 1923. "Will o' the Wisp."

HANKIN, ST. JOHN. *The Constant Lover.* French.

HERVIEU, PAUL E. *Modesty.* French, 1913.

HOUGHTON, STANLEY. *Five One-Act Plays.* French, 1923. "The Dear Departed," "The Master of the House," "Phipps."

HOUSMAN, LAWRENCE. *Angels and Ministers: Four Plays of Victorian Shade.* Harcourt, 1922.

INDIANA PRIZE PLAYS. Bobbs, 1924.

JACOBS, W. W., and HUBBARD, P. E. *A Love Passage.* French, 1913.

JACOBS, W. W., and MILLS, HORACE. *Admiral Peters.* French, 1909.

JACOBS, W. W., and PARKER, L. N. *The Monkey's Paw.* French, 1910.

JACOBS, W. W., and ROCK, CHARLES. *The Ghost of Jerry Bundler*. French, 1908.

JACOBS, W. W., and SERGENT, H. *The Changeling*. French, 1908.

———. *The Boatswain's Mate*. French, 1907.

———. *In the Library*. French, 1912.

JENNINGS, GERTRUDE. *Between the Soup and the Savoury*. French, 1911.

JONES, HENRY ARTHUR. *The Theatre of Ideas*. Doran, 1915. "The Goal," "Her Tongue," "Grace Mary."

KELLY, GEORGE. *The Flattering Word and Other One-Act Plays*. Little, 1925.

KEMP, HARRY. *Boccaccio's Untold Tale*. Brentano, 1924. Title play and "Solomon's Song."

KENNEDY, CHARLES R. *The Terrible Meek*. Harper, 1912. Title play.

KOCH, FREDERICK (Editor). *Carolina Folk Plays*. Holt, 1922.

———. *Carolina Folk Plays: Second Series*. Holt, 1924.

KREYMBORG, ALFRED. *Six Plays for Poem-Mimes*. Others, 1918. "Lima Beans," "Manikin and Minikin."

———. *Puppet Plays*. Harcourt, 1923.

LANGNER, LAWRENCE. *Five One-Act Plays*. Appleton, 1922. "Matinata," "Another Way Out."

LEONARD, STERLING A. (Editor). *The Atlantic Book of Modern Plays*. Atlantic Press, 1922.

LEWIS, B. ROLAND. *Contemporary One-Act Plays*. Scribner, 1922.

LINCOLN, JOSEPH. *See* Appleton Short Plays.

McFADDEN, ELIZABETH A. *Why the Chimes Rang*. French, 1915.

MACKAY, CONSTANCE D. *The Beau of Bath and Other One-Act Plays*. Holt, 1915. Title play, "Gretna Green," "Counsel Retained," "The Prince of Court Painters."

———. *The Forest Princess and Other Masques*. Holt, 1916.

MACKAYE, PERCY. *Yankee Phantasies*. Duffield, 1912. "Chuck," "Sam Average."

McKINNEL, NORMAN. *The Bishop's Candlesticks*. French, 1908.

MacMILLAN, MARY. *Short Plays*. Appleton, 1913. "A Fan and Two Candlesticks," "Entr'Acte."

———. *More Short Plays*. Appleton, 1917. "His Second Girl," "The Dryad."

———. *Third Book of One-Act Plays*. Appleton, 1922.

MAETERLINCK, MAURICE. *The Miracle of St. Anthony and Five Other Plays*. Liveright, 1917. Title play.

MANNERS, J. HARTLEY. *God's Outcast*. Doran, 1920. Title play.

———. *Happiness and Other Plays*. Dodd, 1914. Title play.

MARKS, JEANNETTE. *The Merry, Merry Cuckoo, and Other Plays.* Appleton, 1927.

MARQUIS, DON. *See* Appleton Modern Plays.

MARTINEZ, SIERRA GREGORIO. *Plays, Volume One.* Dutton, 1923. "The Lover."

MASEFIELD, JOHN. *Collected Plays of.* Macmillan, 1919. "Campden Wonder," "Phillip the King," "Good Friday." "The Locked Chest."

MAYGORA, MARGARET G. (Editor). *Representative One-Act Plays by American Authors.* Little, 1919.

MAYNE, RUTHERFORD. *The Drone and Other Plays.* Dublin: Maunsel & Co. "Red Turf," "The Troth."

MEILHAC, HENRI, and HALEVY, LUDOVIC. *Indian Summer.* French, 1913.

MIDDLETON, GEORGE. *Embers and Other One-Act Plays.* Holt, 1911. Title play, "The Failures," "The Man Masterful."

——. *Masks.* Holt, 1920. Title play, "Jim's Beast," "Tides."

——. *Possession and Other One-Act Plays.* Holt, 1915. "The Groove," "The Black Tie," "Circles."

——. *Tradition and Other One-Act Plays.* Holt, 1913. Title play, "On Bail," "Mothers."

MILLAY, EDNA ST. VINCENT. *See* Appleton Little Theatre Plays.

MILNE, A. A. *First Plays.* Knopf, 1909. "Wurzel-Flummery."

MOELLER, PHILIP. *Five Somewhat Historical Plays.* Knopf, 1918. "Helena's Husband."

MORLEY, CHRISTOPHER. *One-Act Plays.* Doubleday, 1924. "Thursday Evening."

Morningside Plays. Frank Shay (New York), 1917. "Hattie," by Elva DePue; "Markhein," by Zellah MacDonald.

MOSES, M. J. (Editor). *Representative One-Act Plays by Continental Authors.* Little, 1922.

NICHOLSON, KENYON. *Garden Varieties.* Appleton, 1924.

——. *Revues.* Appleton, 1927.

O'BRIEN, SEUMAS. *Duty and Other Irish Comedies.* Little, 1916.

O'DEA, MARK. *Red Bud Women.* Appleton, 1922. "The Song of Solomon," "Miss Myrtle Says Yes."

OLIVER, M. S. *Six One-Act Plays.* Badger (Boston), 1914.

One-Act Plays from the Yiddish. Translated by Etta Block. Appleton, 1923.

O'NEILL, EUGENE. *Thirst and Other One-Act Plays.* Badger, 1914. Title play and "Fog."

——. *The Moon of the Caribbees.* Liveright, 1919. "Bound East for Cardiff," "In the Zone," "Ile."

——. *See* also Appleton Modern Plays.

OVERSTREET, H. A. *See* Appleton Modern Plays.

PARKER, LOUIS N. *The Man in the Street.* French, 1912.

PASTON, GEORGE. *Feed the Brute.* French, 1909.

PINERO, ARTHUR. *Playgoers.* French, 1913.

PINSKI, DAVID. *King David and His Wives.* Viking Press, 1923. "Michal."

——. *Ten Plays.* Viking Press, 1920. "Diplomacy," "A Dollar."

——. *See* also GOLDBERG, I. *Six Plays of the Yiddish Theatre.*

Provincetown Plays: First Series. Shay, 1916. "Bound East for Cardiff," by Eugene O'Neill.

——. *Second Series.* Shay, 1916. "Suppressed Desires," by George Cram Cook and Susan Glaspell.

——. *Third Series.* Shay, 1916. "Lima Beans," by Alfred Kreymborg; "Before Breakfast," by Eugene O'Neill.

——. *Fourth Series.* Shay, 1916.

——. *Fifth Series.* Shay, 1917.

——. *Sixth Series.* Shay, 1918. "The People," "Close the Book," by Susan Glaspell.

——. *See* also COOK, G. C. (Editor). *Provincetown Plays.*

RENARD, JULES. *Carrots.* French, 1904.

RILEY, ALICE C. D. *The Mandarin's Coat.* Brentano, 1925.

ROGERS, R. E. *Behind a Watteau Picture.* Baker, 1918.

ROSTAND, EDMUND. *The Romancers.* (Act one). French, 1915.

SAUNDERS, LOUISE. *Magic Lanterns.* Scribner, 1923.

SCHNITZLER, ARTHUR. *Anatol and Other Plays.* Liveright, 1917. "Episode," "The Farewell Supper," "The Lady with the Dagger," "Living Hours."

——. *Comedies of Words.* Appleton, 1917.

SHAW, GEORGE B. *Fanny's First Play.* Brentano, 1917. "The Dark Lady of the Sonnets."

——. *Heartbreakhouse, Great Catherine, and Playlets of the War.* Brentano, 1919.

SHAY, FRANK. (Editor). *Contemporary One-Act Plays: American.* Appleton, 1922.

——. *Fifty Contemporary One-Act Plays.* Appleton, 1920.

——. *A Treasury of Plays for Men.* Little, 1923.

——. *A Treasury of Plays for Women.* Little, 1922.

——. *Twenty-Five Short Plays.* Appleton, 1925.

SMITH, ALICE M. (Editor). *Short Plays by Representative Authors.* Macmillan, 1920.

STEELE, WILBUR D. *The Terrible Woman and Other One-Act Plays.* Appleton, 1925.

STRINDBERG, AUGUST. *Plays: Second Series.* Scribner, 1912. "The Stranger."

——. *Third Series.* Scribner, 1913. "Debit and Credit."

——. *Volume II.* Luce, 1912. "Facing Death."

SUDERMANN, HERMANN. *Morituri.* Scribner, 1910. "Fritzchen," "Teja."

——. *Roses.* Scribner, 1909. "The Faraway Princess."

SUTHERLAND, EVELYN G. *Po' White Trash and Other One-Act Plays.* Duffield, 1900. Title play and "The End of the Way."

SUTRO, ALFRED. *Five Little Plays.* Brentano, 1912. "The Man in the Stalls," "A Marriage Has Been Arranged," "The Bracelet."

SYNGE, JOHN M. *In the Shadow of the Glen.* Luce, 1914. Title play.

——. *Riders to the Sea.* Luce, 1911. Title play.

TARKINGTON, BOOTH. *See* Appleton Little Theatre Plays.

——. *Beauty and the Jacobin.* Harper, 1912.

THEURIET, ANDRE. *Jean Marie.* French, 1915.

THOMAS, AUGUSTUS (Editor). *One-Act Plays for Stage and Study.* French, 1925.

Three Modern Japanese Plays. Translated by Yozan T. Iwasaki and Glenn Hughes. Appleton, 1923.

TINSLEY, LILY. *Cinders.* French, 1899.

TORRENCE, RIDGLEY. *Plays for a Negro Theatre.* Macmillan, 1917. "Granny Maumee," "The Rider of Dreams," "Simon, the Cyrenian."

TRENT, J. J. *Owin' to Maggie.* Baker, 1904.

Vagabond Plays. Norman Remington (Baltimore), 1922.

WALKER, STUART. *Portmanteau Plays.* Appleton, 1917. "The Medicine Show," "The Six Who Pass While the Lentils Boil," "Nevertheless."

——. *More Portmanteau Plays.* Appleton, 1917. "The Lady of the Weeping-Willow Tree," "Jonathan Makes a Wish," "The Very Naked Boy."

——. *Portmanteau Adaptations.* Appleton, 1921. "Sir David Wears a Crown."

——. *See* also Appleton Modern Plays.

Washington Plays. University of Washington Press, 1921.

Washington Square Plays. Doubleday, 1916. "The Clod," by Lewis Beach; "Overtones," by Alice Gerstenberg; "Helena's Husband," by Philip Moeller.

WILCOX, CONSTANCE. *Told in a Chinese Garden.* Holt, 1920. Title play.

WILDE, PERCIVAL. *Dawn and Other One-Act Plays.* Little, 1915. Title play. "The Noble Lord," "The Traitor."

——. *A Question of Morality and Other One-Act Plays.* Little, 1916. Title play, "Confession," "The Beautiful Story."

——. *The Unseen Host.* Little, 1917. Title play, "Mothers of Men," "Pawns."

——. *Eight Comedies for Little Theatres.* Little, 1923.

WISCONSIN PLAYS. *See* Dickinson, T. (editor).

WOLFF, O. M. *Where but in America.* Baker, 1924.

YEATS, WILLIAM B. *The Hour-Glass and Other Plays.* Macmillan, 1904. Title play and "A Pot of Broth."

——. *The Unicorn from the Stars.* Macmillan, 1908. "Cathleen Ni Houlihan."

——. *Poetical Works.* Volume II. Macmillan, 1907. "The Land of Heart's Desire."

YOUNG, STARK. *Three One-Act Plays.* Appleton, 1921. "Addio."

E. VOLUMES OF FULL–LENGTH PLAYS

ADE, GEORGE. *The College Widow.* French, 1924.

——. *The County Chairman.* French, 1924.

AKINS, ZOE. *Déclassée and Other Plays.* Liveright, 1919. Title play.

ANDREYEV, LEONID. *He Who Gets Slapped.* Brentano, 1921.

ARCHER, WILLIAM. *The Green Goddess.* Knopf, 1921.

ASHTON, WINIFRED (DANE, CLEMENCE). *A Bill of Divorcement.* Macmillan, 1921.

AUSTIN, MARY. *The Arrowmaker.* Houghton, 1915.

BAKER, GEORGE PIERCE (Editor). *Modern American Plays.* Harcourt, 1920.

BARRIE, JAMES. *Alice-Sit-by-the-Fire.* Scribner, 1919.

——. *The Admirable Crichton.* Scribner, 1918.

——. *Dear Brutus.* Scribner, 1922.

——. *A Kiss for Cinderella.* Scribner, 1920.

——. *Quality Street.* Scribner, 1918.

——. *What Every Woman Knows.* Scribner, 1918.

——. *Mary Rose.* Scribner, 1924.

——. *Representative Plays.* Scribner, 1926.

BARRY, PHILIP. *You and I.* Brentano, 1923.

BEACH, LEWIS. *The Goose Hangs High.* Little, 1923.

BENAVENTE, JACINTO. *Plays.* (Fourth Series.) "The School of Princesses," "A Lady," "The Magic of an Hour," "The Field of Ermine." Scribner, 1917.

——. *Plays.* (Third Series.) "The Prince Who Learned Everything out of Books," "Saturday Night," "In the Clouds," "The Truth." Scribner, 1919.

——. *Plays.* (Second Series.) "No Smoking," "Princess Bébé," "Autumnal Roses," "The Governor's Wife." Scribner, 1923.

——. *Plays.* (First Series.) "His Widow's Husband," "La Malquerida," "The Evil Doers of Good," "The Bonds of Interest." Scribner, 1924.

BENNETT, ARNOLD. *The Great Adventure.* Doran, 1913.

——. *The Love Match.* Doran, 1922.

BENNETT, ARNOLD, and KNOBLOCK, EDWARD. *Milestones*. Doran, 1912.

BENRIMO, J. HARRY, and HAZELTON, GEORGE. *The Yellow Jacket*. Bobbs.

BERNSTEIN, H. *The Thief*. Doubleday, 1910

BRIEUX, EUGENE. *Three Plays*. Brentano, 1911.

BRIGHOUSE, HAROLD. *Hobson's Choice*. French, 1916.

BROADHURST, GEORGE. *Bought and Paid For*. French, 1910.

——. *What Happened to Jones*. French, 1897.

BROWN, ALICE. *Children of the Earth*. Macmillan, 1915.

CAPEK, KAREL. *R. U. R.* (Rossum's Universal Robots). Doubleday, 1923.

CHEKHOV, ANTON. *Plays: First Series*. Scribner, 1912. "The Sea-Gull."

——. *Second Series*. Scribner, 1916. "The Proposal," "The Bear," "The Cherry Orchard."

COHAN, GEORGE. *Seven Keys to Baldpate*. French, 1913.

COLTON, JOHN, and RANDOLPH, CLEMENCE. *Rain*. Liveright, 1922.

CONNELLY, MARC. *The Wisdom Tooth*. Doran, 1926.

——. *See* Kaufman, George.

CROTHERS, RACHEL. *Expressing Willie and Other Plays*. Brentano, 1924.

DAVIS, OWEN. *The Detour*. Little, 1922.

——. *Icebound*. Little, 1923.

DICKINSON, THOMAS (Editor). *Chief Contemporary Dramatists*. Houghton, 1915.

——. *Second Series*. Houghton, 1919.

DRINKWATER, JOHN. *Abraham Lincoln*, Houghton, 1918.

——. *Mary Stuart*. Houghton, 1921.

——. *Oliver Cromwell*. Houghton, 1921.

——. *Robert E. Lee*. Houghton, 1923.

DUNSANY, LORD. *Five Plays*. Little, 1917. "The Gods of the Mountains."

——. *Plays of Gods and Men*. Putnam, 1920. "A Night at an Inn."

EMERY, GILBERT. *Tarnish*. Brentano, 1923.

ERVINE, ST. JOHN G. *Jane Clegg*. Macmillan, 1914.

ESMOND, H. V. *When We Were Twenty-One*. French, 1903.

FITCH, CLYDE. *Works*. In four volumes. Little, 1915. "Nathan Hale," "Barbara Frietchie," "The Girl with the Green Eyes."

FLECKER, JAMES. *Hassan*. Knopf, 1923.

FORBES, JAMES. *The Famous Mrs. Fair and Other Plays*. Doran, 1920. Title play.

GALE, ZONA. *Miss Lulu Bett*. Macmillan, 1920.

GALSWORTHY, JOHN. *Plays: First Series.* Scribner, 1916.
"Strife."
——. *Second Series.* Scribner, 1913. "Justice."
——. *Third Series.* Scribner, 1914. "The Mob," "The Pigeon."
——. *Fourth Series.* Scribner, 1920. "A Bit o' Love," "The
Skin Game."
——. *Fifth Series.* Scribner, 1923. "Loyalties."
——. *Sixth Series.* Scribner, 1926. "Old English," "The
Show," "The Forest."
——. *Representative Plays.* Scribner, 1924.
GATES, ELEANOR. *See* MOORE, Mrs. ELEANOR GATES.
GILLETTE, WILLIAM. *Held by the Enemy.* French, 1898.
——. *Secret Service.* French, 1898.
HAUPTMANN, GERHARDT. *Dramatic Works, in Eight Volumes.*
Huebsch, 1912. "The Weavers" (Volume I), "The Sunken
Bell" (Volume IV).
HODGES, HORACE, and WIGNEY, PERCYVAL. *Grumpy.* French,
1914.
"HOPE, ANTHONY" (HAWKINS). *The Adventures of Lady Ur-
sula.* French, 1910.
HOUGHTON, STANLEY. *Works.* In three volumes. London:
Constable, 1914. "Hindle Wakes" (Volume II).
HOUSEMAN, LAWRENCE. *The Chinese Lantern.* French, 1908.
HOUSEMAN, LAWRENCE, and BARKER, GRANVILLE. *Prunella.*
Little, 1906.
HOWARD, SIDNEY. *They Knew What They Wanted.* Doubleday,
1925.
——. *Ned McCobb's Daughter.* Scribner, 1927.
——. *The Silver Cord.* Scribner, 1927.
HUGHES, HATCHER. *Hell-Bent for Heaven.* Harper, 1924.
IBSEN, HENDRIK. *Collected Works.* In twelve volumes. Scrib-
ner, 1906-8. "A Doll's House," "Ghosts" (Volume VII);
"Hedda Gabler," "The Master Builder" (Volume X).
JEROME, JEROME K. *The Passing of the Third Floor Back.* Dodd,
1921.
JONES, HENRY ARTHUR. *Representative Plays.* In four volumes.
Little, 1925. "The Liars," "Mrs. Dane's Defense" (Volume III);
"Mary Goes First" (Volume IV).
KAUFMAN, GEORGE S. *The Butter and Egg Man.* Liveright,
1926.
KAUFMAN, GEORGE S., and CONNELLY, MARC. *Beggar on Horse-
back.* Liveright, 1924.
——. *Dulcy.* Putnam, 1921.
——. *To the Ladies!* French, 1924.
KELLY, GEORGE E. *The Show-off.* Little, 1924.
——. *Craig's Wife.* Little, 1926.

KENNEDY, CHARLES. *The Servant in the House.* Harper, 1908.
KENYON, CHARLES. *Kindling.* Doubleday, 1914.
KLEIN, CHARLES. *The Lion and the Mouse.* French, 1917.
——. *The Third Degree.* French, 1917.
KNOBLOCK, EDWARD. *The Lullaby and Other Plays.* Putnam, 1924. Title play, "Marie Odelle," "Tiger, Tiger!"
——. *Kismet.* Doran, 1911.
——. *See* Bennett, Arnold.
McCARTHY, JUSTIN H. *If I Were King.* French, 1922.
MacHUGH, AUGUSTIN. *Officer 666.* French, 1912.
MacKAYE, PERCY. *The Scarecrow.* Macmillan, 1908.
MAETERLINCK, MAURICE. *The Blue Bird.* Dodd, 1909.
——. *Pelleas and Melisande.* Dodd, 1911.
MANNERS, J. HARTLEY. *Peg 'o my Heart.* French, 1918.
MANTLE, BURNS (Editor). *The Best Plays of 1919–1920.* Dodd, 1920.
——. *The Best Plays of 1920–1921.* Dodd, 1921.
——. *The Best Plays of 1921–1922.* Dodd, 1922.
——. *The Best Plays of 1922–1923.* Dodd, 1923.
——. *The Best Plays of 1923–1924.* Dodd, 1924.
——. *The Best Plays of 1924–1925.* Dodd, 1925.
——. *The Best Plays of 1925–1926.* Dodd, 1926.
MARKS, JOSEPHINE PRESTON PEABODY. *The Piper.* Houghton, 1909.
MASEFIELD, JOHN. *The Tragedy of Nan.* Macmillan, 1918.
MASON, A. E. W. *Green Stockings.* French, 1914.
MASSEY, E. EDWARD. *Plots and Playwrights.* Little, 1917.
MEGRUE, R. C. *Under Cover.* French, 1918.
MEGRUE, R. C., and HACKETT, WALTER. *It Pays to Advertise.* French, 1917.
MIDDLETON, GEORGE, and BOLTON, GUY. *Adam and Eva.* French, 1924.
MILLER, ALICE DUER, and MILTON, ROBERT. *The Charm School.* French, 1922.
MILNE, A. A. *Three Plays.* Putnam, 1922. "The Dover Road," "The Truth about Blayds."
——. *Mr. Pim Passes By.* French, 1921.
MOLNAR, FERENC. *Liliom.* Liveright, 1921.
——. *The Swan.* Liveright, 1922.
MOODY, WILLIAM VAUGHN. *Prose Plays.* Houghton, 1912. "The Great Divide," "The Faith Healer."
MOORE, ELEANOR GATES. *The Poor Little Rich Girl.* French, 1920.
MORTON, MARTHA. *A Bachelor's Romance.* French, 1912.
MOSES, M. J. (Editor). *Representative American Dramas.* Little, 1925.

O'NEILL, EUGENE. *Beyond the Horizon.* Liveright, 1919.
——. *The Emperor Jones; Diff'rent; The Straw.* Liveright, 1921.
——. *The Hairy Ape; Anna Christie; The First Man.* Liveright, 1922.
——. *Welded; All God's Chillun Got Wings.* Liveright, 1923.
——. *Desire under the Elms.* Liveright, 1924.
——. *The Great God Brown.* Liveright, 1926.
——. *Marco Millions.* Liveright, 1927.
PARKER, L. N. *Pomander Walk.* French, 1915.
PEABODY, JOSEPHINE P. *See* MRS. MARKS.
PEPLE, EDWARD. *The Prince Chap.* French, 1914.
PHILLIPS, STEPHEN. *Paola and Francesca.* Dodd, 1900.
PINERO, ARTHUR W. *Social Plays of.* In four volumes. Dutton, 1917. "The Second Mrs. Tanqueray" (Volume I); "Gay Lord Quex" (Volume II); "Mid-Channel" (Volume IV).
PINSKI, DAVID. *Three Plays.* Viking Press, 1918.
PIRANDELLO, LUIGI. *Three Plays.* "Six Characters in Search of an Author." Dutton, 1922.
POLLOCK, CHANNING. *The Fool.* Brentano, 1922.
——. *The Enemy.* Brentano, 1926.
QUINN, ARTHUR (Editor). *Representative American Plays.* Century, 1920, 1927.
——. *Contemporary American Plays.* Scribner, 1923.
RICE, ELMER L. *On Trial.* French, 1919.
——. *The Adding Machine.* Doubleday, 1923.
RICHMAN, ARTHUR. *Not so Long Ago.* French, 1924.
ROSTAND, EDMUND. *Chanticler.* Duffield, 1910.
——. *Cyrano de Bergerac.* Doubleday, 1908.
——. *The Romancers.* French, 1915.
RYLEY, MADELINE L. *An American Citizen.* French, 1895.
SHAW, GEORGE B. *Androcles and the Lion.* Brentano, 1913.
——. *Arms and the Man.* Brentano, 1913.
——. *Candida.* Brentano, 1913.
——. *Mrs. Warren's Profession.* Brentano, 1913.
——. *St. Joan.* Brentano, 1924.
SHELDON, EDWARD. *The Nigger.* Macmillan, 1910.
——. *Romance.* Macmillan, 1914.
SHERWOOD, ROBERT E. *The Road to Rome.* Scribner, 1927.
SMITH, HARRY J. *Mrs. Bumpstead-Leigh.* French, 1917.
SMITH, WINCHELL. *The Fortune Hunter.* French, 1909.
SMITH, WINCHELL, and HAZZARD, JOHN E. *Turn to the Right.* French.
STALLINGS LAWRENCE, and ANDERSON, MAXWELL. *What Price Glory?* Harcourt, 1925.

STRINDBERG, AUGUST. *Plays*. In five volumes. Scribner, 1912-20.

SUDERMANN, HERMANN. *The Fire of St. John*. Luce, 1904.

——. *John the Baptist*. Lane, 1909.

—— *Magda*. French, 1896.

SUTRO, ALFRED. *The Walls of Jericho*. French, 1906.

——. *The Perfect Lover*. French, 1905.

——. *The Walls of Jericho*. French, 1906.

——. *John Glayde's Honor*. French, 1907.

——. *The Builder of Bridges*. French, 1908.

——. *Far above Rubies*. French, 1924.

——. *A Man with a Heart*. French, 1925.

SYNGE, JOHN M. *The Playboy of the Western World*. Luce, 1907.

TARKINGTON, BOOTH. *Clarence*. French, 1921.

——. *The Intimate Strangers*. French, 1924.

——. *Penrod*. French, 1921.

——. *Seventeen*. French, 1925.

TARKINGTON, BOOTH, and WILSON, HARRY LEON. *The Man from Home*. Harper, 1908.

THOMAS, A. E. *Come out of the Kitchen*. French, 1921.

THOMAS, AUGUSTUS. *As a Man Thinks*. Duffield, 1911.

——. *The Copperhead*. French, 1921.

——. *The Witching Hour*. French, 1916.

VAN DRUTEN, JOHN. *Young Woodley*. Simon and Shuster.

VANE, SUTTON. *Outward Bound*. Liveright, 1921.

VARESI, GILDA, and BYRNE, DOLLY. *Enter Madame*. Putnam, 1921.

VEILLER, BAYARD. *The Thirteenth Chair*. French, 1922.

WALTER, EUGENE. *The Easiest Way*. Doubleday, 1917.

WILDE, OSCAR. *Plays*. Four volumes. Luce. "Lady Windemere's Fan," "A Woman of No Importance" (Volume I). 1907.

——. *Selected Plays*. "Modern Library," n.d.

WILLIAMS, JESSE LYNCH. *Why Marry?* Scribner, 1918.

——. *Why Not?* Scribner, 1918.

ZANGWILL, ISRAEL. *The Melting Pot*. Macmillan, 1914.

——. *Merely Mary Ann*. French, 1921.